W9-ADU-291

BREAKTHROUGHS
IN DIABETES

1,747 SCIENTIFICALLY PROVEN SECRETS THAT PREVENT, CONTROL AND CURE DIABETES

FROM THE EDITORS OF BOTTOM LINE HEALTH

BottomLineBooks

BottomLineInc.com

Breakthroughs in Diabetes

ISBN 0-88723-780-0

Recipes located on pages 109–135 are by Linda Gassenheimer, TV and radio personality and author of numerous American Diabetes Association books including *Fast and Flavorful* and the recently released *Simply Smoothies*. Her specialty is making delicious, healthy meals easily and quickly. She is the producer and host of the weekly segment, *Food News & Views*, on WLRN 91.3 FM National Public Radio and has appeared on a variety of radio and television programs. Her internationally syndicated *Miami Herald* column, "Dinner in Minutes," is read by more than six million people each week.

Bottom Line Books® is an imprint of Bottom Line Inc., publisher of print periodicals, e-letters and books. We are dedicated to bringing you the best information from the most knowledgeable sources in the world. Our goal is to help you gain greater wealth, better health, more wisdom, extra time and increased happiness.

Printed in the United States of America

Contents

3 • FOODS THAT FIGHT DIABETES

4 • DELICIOUS DIABETES-FRIENDLY RECIPES

10 • HEALTHY LIFE HABITS THAT KEEP DIABETES AWAY FOREVER

Preface

We are proud to bring to you *Bottom Line's Breakthroughs in Diabetes: 1,747 Scientifically Proven Secrets That Prevent, Control and Cure Diabetes*. This essential volume features trustworthy and actionable life-saving information from the best diabetes and general health experts in the world—information that will help you beat the condition that has become an epidemic in this country. In the following chapters you'll find the latest discoveries, best treatments and scientifically proven remedies to treat your prediabetes and keep your type 2 diabetes under control.

The editors of Bottom Line have worked with experts from the top diabetes clinics and research centers, such as Harvard's Joslin Diabetes Center and The Cleveland Clinic, to find out the information you need to know—whether it's effective prevention strategies, necessary tests, breakthrough treatments for type 1 and obesity, or solutions for the complications brought on by diabetes.

How do we find all these top-notch medical professionals? Over the past four decades, we have built a network of literally thousands of leading physicians in both alternative and conventional medicine. They are affiliated with the premier medical institutions and the best universities throughout the world. We read the important medical journals and follow the latest research that is reported at health conferences worldwide. And we regularly talk to our advisors in major teaching hospitals, private practices and government health agencies for their insider perspectives.

Breakthroughs in Diabetes is a result of our ongoing research and connection with these experts, and is a distillation of their latest findings and most important advice. We trust that you will glean new, helpful and affordable information about living a healthy, diabetes-free life.

As a reader of a Bottom Line book, please be assured that you are receiving well-researched information from a trusted source. But please use prudence in health matters. Always speak to your physician before taking vitamins, supplements or over-the-counter medication... stopping a prescribed medication...changing your diet...or beginning an exercise program. If you experience side effects from any regimen, contact your doctor immediately.

Be well,

The Editors, Bottom Line Inc.

Stamford, Connecticut

1

Risks and Prevention

The Dangers of Diabetes

More Americans than ever before have diabetes mellitus, a disorder characterized by elevated levels of blood sugar (glucose). About 29 million Americans (approximately 9.3% of the US population) are afflicted with the disease, according to the Centers for Disease Control and Prevention. More than eight million of these people don't even realize that they have it.

But that's not all. A staggering 86 million Americans show early signs of diabetes ("prediabetes") but don't know that they are at risk of developing the full-blown disease. This alarming trend is due, in part, to the ever-increasing number of Americans who are overweight, which sharply increases diabetes risk.

If you have been gaining weight, eating a lot of high-fat and high-sugar foods and/or not getting much exercise, I'm afraid that you're already in danger of getting diabetes.

Even though this is a frightening scenario, there is some good news. If you identify the warning signs early enough, you can prevent diabetes from developing. If you already have diabetes, proper monitoring and healthful eating can help you control your glucose levels and avoid many of the disease's serious complications, such as heart failure, stroke, kidney failure, eye disease, nerve damage and/or amputation.

WHAT IS DIABETES?

Whenever we eat or drink, the food or liquid we ingest is broken down into nutrients that our bodies need to function. Glucose (a simple sugar that acts as the main energy source for our bodies) is one of the key nutrients. When glucose is absorbed into the blood-

Mark A. Stengler, NMD, a naturopathic medical doctor and leading authority on the practice of alternative and integrated medicine. Dr. Stengler is author of the *Health Revelations* newsletter, author of *The Natural Physician's Healing Therapies*, founder and medical director of the Stengler Center for Integrative Medicine in Encinitas, California. MarkStengler.com

stream, it stimulates the pancreas to produce insulin. This hormone transports glucose into our body's cells, where it is then converted to energy for immediate or later use.

There are two main types of diabetes…

• **Type 1 (formerly known as juvenile-onset) diabetes affects only about 10% of people with diabetes.** Although the disorder usually develops in childhood or early adulthood (before age 30), an increasing number of adults are now being affected.

Researchers theorize that the increasing incidence of obesity in adults may accelerate the autoimmune destruction that characterizes type 1 diabetes—specifically, the body's immune system attacks and destroys the insulin-producing cells of the pancreas.

People with type 1 diabetes need frequent doses of insulin, which is typically delivered by injection with thin needles, a pen that contains an insulin-filled cartridge or a small special "pump" that delivers a continuous dose of insulin.

• **Type 2 (once known as adult-onset) diabetes affects 90% of people who suffer from the disease.** Most cases occur during adulthood, and risk increases with age. In recent years, many overweight children and teenagers have been diagnosed with type 2 diabetes.

In type 2 diabetes, the pancreas produces insulin (sometimes more than the usual amounts), but fat and tissue cells are "resistant," preventing the hormone from doing what it's supposed to do—which is to "unlock" cells so that blood glucose can enter.

Your risk of type 2 diabetes increases significantly if you eat a lot of foods that are high in simple carbohydrates (which are rapidly transformed into sugar) and foods that are low in dietary fiber (needed to slow the absorption of sugars from the food we eat and digest). Also, people who don't get much exercise are more likely to develop type 2 diabetes because of the insulin resistance that results from weight gain and an imbalance of stress hormones.

In addition to obesity, risk factors for type 2 diabetes include a family history of the disease (especially in parents or siblings)…apple-shaped body type…high blood pressure…high cholesterol…or, among women, a history of diabetes during pregnancy ("gestational diabetes," which usually disappears after delivery). People with type 2 diabetes who have difficulty controlling their glucose levels may require oral medication, such as *metformin* (Glucophage), and/or insulin injections.

HEADING OFF DIABETES

Prediabetes affects 35% of Americans between the ages of 40 and 74. In these people, blood glucose levels are elevated but not enough to be considered type 2 diabetes. Detecting the telltale signs of prediabetes—which show up in blood tests—helps you prevent the full-blown disease. Without these measures, there's a good chance that a person diagnosed with prediabetes will develop type 2 diabetes within 10 years.

I advise my patients (and readers) to get yearly blood tests to help identify many early-stage diseases, including diabetes. Diabetes-related tests should include…

Fasting blood glucose to determine whether you are showing signs of prediabetes. Before you go to your doctor's office for the test, you will need to fast for at least eight hours. Then blood is drawn and sent to a lab for a measurement of the glucose concentration, which is expressed in milligrams of glucose per deciliter (mg/dL). A fasting level of 100 mg/dL to 125 mg/dL is considered prediabetes. (For more on the diagnostic criteria for diabetes, see "Test for Diabetes" on page four.)

Too often, patients who have glucose levels of 100 mg/dL to 115 mg/dL are told by their doctors that they don't have a problem. In my view, a fasting blood glucose level in this range indicates prediabetes. I consider my patients to be free of any immediate risk only if their glucose levels are in the range of 70 mg/dL to 86 mg/dL. If a patient's glucose level is 87 mg/dL to 100 mg/dL, I recommend some of the same strategies that I prescribe for people with prediabetes.

Oral glucose tolerance test can be used to check for prediabetes. After fasting for eight to 12 hours, a blood sample is taken to determine your fasting blood glucose level. Then your doctor will ask you to drink a solution with a high sugar content. After one, two and three hours, your doctor draws a blood sample and checks your glucose reading. A level of 140 mg/dL to 199 mg/dL for any of the readings indicates prediabetes. A reading of 200 mg/dL or above indicates diabetes.

I recommend that doctors also check insulin levels with the blood sample used for the glucose tolerance test. If insulin levels are abnormally high (15 to 20 microunits per milliliter or higher), it's a sign that you are developing insulin resistance—which is often a step on the road to diabetes.

BETTER DIABETES MONITORING

If you have diabetes, proper monitoring of your condition literally can save your life. Blood sugar levels can change dramatically within a matter of minutes, causing confusion, dizziness, fatigue and, in serious cases, a life-threatening coma. People with diabetes can easily measure their blood sugar levels with a small portable device that analyzes a drop of blood obtained by pricking a fingertip with a lancet. I recommend self-monitoring at least twice daily (upon awakening and 30 to 60 minutes after dinner). In addition, people with diabetes should make regular visits to their primary care doctors, have annual physicals and get yearly eye exams from their ophthalmologists.

Other tests for people with diabetes...

• **Hemoglobin A1C.** This test measures the amount of glucose sticking to the hemoglobin in red blood cells. It can be used as a marker of average blood glucose level over the past two to three months. Studies show that for every percentage point drop in A1C blood levels, risks for circulatory disorders as well as eye, kidney and nerve diseases drop by 40%. Most doctors say that a hemoglobin A1C reading below 7% is acceptable. However, I believe that a reading below 6% is more desirable, because it shows better blood glucose control. People with an A1C reading of 7% or less should have this test twice a year. If your reading is above 8%, you should have it every three months.

• **Oxidative stress analysis.** This test measures the amount of tissue damage, or "oxidative stress," caused by free radicals (harmful, negatively charged molecules). Few medical

doctors know about oxidative stress testing, but I recommend it for patients with diabetes because they have high levels of oxidative stress, which accelerates the disease's progression. The markers of free radical activity can be measured by blood or urine tests. Elevated levels mean that the antioxidants that are normally produced in the body and ingested via foods and supplements are not effectively neutralizing the overabundance of free radicals.

Your doctor can use Genova Diagnostics (800-522-4762, *www.gdx.net*) for the test. It costs about $200, but most health insurers will cover it. People with diabetes should receive this test every six months until their values are normal.

• **Cardiovascular markers.** People with diabetes are more susceptible to heart disease (see Chapter 9). That's because elevated glucose levels accelerate the buildup of plaque in the arteries. For this reason, I recommend blood tests for homocysteine, C-reactive protein, fibrinogen, lipoprotein a, apolipoprotein a and b, and iron. Abnormal levels of these markers are linked to the development of heart disease. I recommend a baseline test and yearly follow-up testing for people who have abnormal readings for any of these markers. Most health insurers will cover the costs of these tests.

THE SUGAR CONNECTION

Everyone knows that people who have diabetes or who are at risk for it should pay close attention to their diet. However, I'm convinced that few people realize just how damaging certain foods can be.

For example, about 20% of the average American's energy intake comes from foods such as burgers, pizza, chips, pastries and soft drinks. A study published in the *American Journal of Clinical Nutrition* found that between 1980 and 1997, the average American's daily calorie consumption increased by 500 calories. Eighty percent of this increase was due to increases in carbohydrates, which include almost all sweet and starchy foods. During the same period, the prevalence of type 2 diabetes increased by 47% and the prevalence of obesity increased by 80%.

One of the worst culprits in the war on diabetes is the simple sugar fructose, which is naturally found in fruit and honey. Table sugar is half fructose (the other half is glucose, which is chemically the same as blood glucose). A type of fructose known as high-fructose corn syrup (HFCS) is especially harmful because it worsens insulin resistance. It has become the sweetener of choice for many soft drinks, ice creams, baked goods, candies/sweets, jams, yogurts and other sweetened products. My recommendation is to put a strict limit on your consumption of foods that contain HFCS. This can be done by reducing your intake of packaged, processed foods, avoiding drinks that are high in fructose and eating as many fresh foods as possible. (Natural sources of fructose, such as fruit and honey, can be safely consumed in moderation.)

There is one exception—some liquid nutritional supplements, such as liquid vitamin formulas, contain crystalline fructose, a natural sweetener that is far less processed than HFCS and is not believed to cause dramatic increases in insulin levels.

SYMPTOMS OF DIABETES

- Increased thirst
- Frequent urination (especially at night)
- Unexplained increase in appetite
- Fatigue
- Erection problems
- Blurred vision
- Tingling or numbness in the hands and/or feet

TEST FOR DIABETES

You have diabetes if any one of the following test results occurs on at least two different days...

- A fasting blood glucose level of 126 mg/dL or higher.
- A two-hour oral glucose tolerance test result of 200 mg/dL or higher.
- Symptoms of diabetes (see list above) combined with a random (nonfasting) blood glucose test of 200 mg/dL or higher.

Source: American Diabetes Association.

How America's Top Diabetes Doctor Avoids Diabetes

George L. King, MD, chief scientific officer at the Boston-based Joslin Diabetes Center, one of the country's leading diabetes clinical care and research centers. He is also a professor of medicine at Harvard Medical School and the author, with Royce Flippin, of *The Diabetes Reset*.

You might think that a diabetes researcher would never develop the disease that he's dedicated his life to studying. But I can't count on it.

My family's story: My father was diagnosed with diabetes at age 72 and was promptly placed on three medications to control his insulin levels.

What my father did next made all the difference: Even though he began taking diabetes medication, he simultaneously went into action—walking an hour a day and going on the diet described below. A year and a half later, he no longer needed the prescriptions. He still had diabetes, but diet and exercise kept it under control.

As a diabetes researcher and physician whose own diabetes risk is increased by his family history, I've got a lot at stake in finding the absolute best ways to avoid and fight this disease.

Here are the steps I take to prevent diabetes—all of which can benefit you whether you want to avoid this disease or have already been diagnosed with it and are trying to control or even reverse it...

Step 1: **Follow a rural Asian diet (RAD).** This diet includes the most healthful foods of a traditional Asian diet—it consists of 70% complex carbohydrates...15% fat...15% protein...and 15 g of fiber for every 1,000 calories. Don't worry too much about all these numbers—the diet is actually pretty simple to follow once you get the hang of it.

You might be surprised by "70% complex carbohydrates," since most doctors recommend lower daily intakes of carbohydrates. The difference is, I'm recommending high amounts of complex, unrefined (not processed) carbohydrates. This type of carb is highly desirable because it's found in foods—such as whole grains, legumes, vegetables and fruits—that are chock-full of fiber. If your goal is to reduce diabetes risk, fiber is the holy grail.

Why I do it: The RAD diet has been proven in research to promote weight loss…improve insulin sensitivity (a key factor in the development and treatment of diabetes) and glucose control…and decrease total cholesterol and LDL "bad" cholesterol levels.

To keep it simple, I advise patients to follow a 2-1-1 formula when creating meals—two portions of nonstarchy veggies (such as spinach, carrots or asparagus)…one portion of whole grains (such as brown rice or quinoa), legumes (such as lentils or chickpeas) or starchy veggies (such as sweet potatoes or winter squash)…and one portion of protein (such as salmon, lean beef, tofu or eggs). Have a piece of fruit (such as an apple or a pear) on the side. Portion size is also important. Portions fill a nine-inch-diameter plate, which is smaller than a typical 12-inch American dinner plate.

Helpful: I take my time when eating—I chew each bite at least 10 times before swallowing. Eating too quickly can cause glucose levels to peak higher than usual after a meal.

Step 2: **Fill up on dark green vegetables.** I include dark, leafy greens in my diet every day. These leafy greens are one of the two portions of nonstarchy veggies in the 2-1-1 formula.

Why I do it: Dark green vegetables contain antioxidants and compounds that help your body fight insulin resistance (a main driver of diabetes).

My secret "power veggie": A Chinese vegetable called bitter melon. It is a good source of fiber and has been shown to lower blood sugar. True to its name, bitter melon tastes a little bitter but is delicious when used in soups and stir-fries. It is available at Asian groceries. Eat bitter melon as one of the two portions of nonstarchy veggies in the 2-1-1 formula.

Step 3: **Adopt an every-other-day workout routine.** I try to not be sedentary and to walk as much as I can (by using a pedometer, I can tell whether I've reached my daily goal of 10,000 steps).

While this daily practice helps, it's not enough to significantly affect my diabetes risk. For that, I have an every-other-day workout routine that consists of 30 minutes of jogging on the treadmill (fast enough so that I'm breathing hard but can still carry on a conversation)…followed by 30 minutes of strength training (using handheld weights, resistance bands or weight machines).

Why I do it: Working out temporarily reduces your insulin resistance and activates enzymes and proteins that help your muscles use glucose instead of allowing the body to accumulate fat—a beneficial effect that lasts for 48 hours (the reason for my every-other-day routine). Strength training is crucial—your muscles are what really kick your body's glucose-burning into high gear. A weekly game of tennis helps shake up my routine.

Step 4: **Keep the temperature chilly.** At the courts where I play tennis, the temperature is naturally cool, but I wear a very thin T-shirt that leaves my neck exposed. This helps activate the "brown fat" in my body. Most people have this special type of body fat—mainly around the neck, collarbone and shoulders.

Why I do it: Brown fat burns calories at high rates when triggered by the cold. To help burn brown fat, exercise in temperatures of 64°F or lower…set your home's thermostat in the mid-60s…and dress as lightly as possible in cool weather. Walking for 50 to 60 minutes a day in cool weather also helps.

Step 5: **Get the "sleep cure."** I make a point to sleep at least six hours a night during the week and seven hours nightly on weekends.

Why I do it: Lack of sleep has been proven to dramatically harm the body's ability to properly metabolize glucose—a problem that sets the stage for diabetes. Research shows that seven to eight hours a night are ideal. However, because of my work schedule, I'm not always able to get that much sleep on weekdays. That's why I sleep a bit longer on weekends.

Research now shows that the body has some capacity to "catch up" on lost sleep and reverse some—but not all—of the damage that occurs to one's insulin sensitivity when you're sleep deprived.

The Best Way to Prevent Diabetes—No Drugs Needed

Nisa M. Maruthur, MD, assistant professor of medicine, The Johns Hopkins School of Medicine and the Welch Center for Prevention, Epidemiology, and Clinical Research, both in Baltimore. Her study was published in *Journal of General Internal Medicine*.

If your doctor ever tells you (or has already told you) that you have prediabetes, you'd be wise to consider it a serious red flag. It means that your blood sugar level is higher than normal—though not yet quite high enough to be classified as diabetes—because your pancreas isn't making enough insulin and/or your cells have become resistant to the action of insulin.

A whopping 35% of American adults now have prediabetes. Nearly one-third of them will go on to develop full-blown diabetes, with all its attendant risks for cardiovascular problems, kidney failure, nerve damage, blindness, amputation and death.

That's why researchers have been working hard to figure out the best way to keep prediabetes from progressing to diabetes. And according to an encouraging new study, one particular approach involving some fairly quick action has emerged as the winner—slashing prediabetic patients' risk for diabetes by an impressive 85%...without relying on drugs.

NEW LOOK AT THE NUMBERS

The new study draws on data from the national Diabetes Prevention Program, the largest diabetes prevention study in the US, which began back in 1996. The program included 3,041 adults who had prediabetes and were at least somewhat overweight.

Participants were randomly divided into three groups. One group was given a twice-daily oral placebo and general lifestyle modification recommendations about the importance of healthful eating, losing weight and exercising. A second group was given twice-daily oral *metformin* (a drug that prevents the liver from producing too much glucose) and those same lifestyle recommendations. The third group was enrolled in an intensive lifestyle-modification program, with the goal of losing at least 7% of their body weight and exercising at moderate intensity for at least 150 minutes each week.

The original analysis of the data, done after 3.2 years, showed that intensive lifestyle modification reduced diabetes risk by 58% and metformin use reduced diabetes risk by 31%, as compared with the placebo group.

Updated analysis: Researchers wanted to know whether those odds could be improved even further, so they did a new analysis, this time looking specifically at what happened in the first six months after prediabetes patients began treatment and then following up for 10 years. *What they found...*

• **At the six-month mark,** almost everyone (92%) in the intensive lifestyle-modification group had lost weight...while more than 25% in the metformin group (and nearly 50% in the placebo group) had gained weight. The average percentage of body weight lost in each group was 7.2% in the lifestyle group...2.4% in the metformin group...and 0.4% in the placebo group. Ten years later, most of those in the lifestyle group had maintained their substantial weight loss—quite an accomplishment, given how common it is for lost pounds to be regained.

• **In the intensive lifestyle-modification group,** those who lost 10% or more of their body weight in the first six months reduced their diabetes risk by an impressive 85%. But even those who fell short of the 7% weight-loss goal benefited. For instance, those who lost 5% to 6.9% of their body weight reduced their risk by 54%...and those who lost just 3% to 4.9% reduced their risk by 38%.

If you have prediabetes: Don't assume that diabetes is an inevitable part of your future...and don't assume that you necessarily have to take drugs. By taking action now, you can greatly reduce your risk of developing this deadly disease. So talk with your doctor about joining a program designed to help people with prediabetes adopt healthful dietary and exercise habits that will promote safe, speedy and permanent weight loss. Ask your doctor or health insurer for a referral...or to find a YMCA Diabetes Prevention Program near you, go to *www.ymca.net/diabetes-prevention*.

The Shocking Diabetes Trigger That Can Strike Anyone

Hyla Cass, MD, a board-certified psychiatrist and nationally recognized expert on integrative medicine based in Los Angeles. She is author of numerous books, including *8 Weeks to Vibrant Health* and *The Addicted Brain and How to Break Free*. CassMD.com

Everyone knows about high blood sugar and the devastating effects it can have on one's health and longevity. But low blood sugar (hypoglycemia) can be just as dangerous—and it does not get nearly the attention that it should.

Simply put, hypoglycemia occurs when the body does not have enough glucose to use as fuel. It most commonly affects people with type 2 diabetes who take medication that sometimes works too well, resulting in low blood sugar.

Who gets overlooked: In other people, hypoglycemia can be a precursor to diabetes that is often downplayed by doctors and/or missed by tests. Having low blood sugar might even make you think that you are far from having diabetes...when, in fact, the opposite is true.

Hypoglycemia can also be an underlying cause of anxiety that gets mistakenly treated with psychiatric drugs rather than the simple steps (see next page) that can stabilize blood sugar levels. That's why anyone who seems to be suffering from an anxiety disorder needs to be seen by a doctor who takes a complete medical history and orders blood tests. When a patient comes to me complaining of anxiety, hypoglycemia is one of the first things I test for.

What's the link between hypoglycemia and anxiety? A sudden drop in blood sugar deprives the brain of oxygen. This, in turn, causes the adrenal glands to release adrenaline, the "emergency" hormone, which may lead to agitation, or anxiety, as the body's fight-or-flight mechanism kicks in.

THE DANGERS OF HYPOGLYCEMIA

Hypoglycemia has sometimes been called carbohydrate intolerance, because the body's insulin-releasing mechanism is impaired in a manner similar to what occurs in diabetics. In people without diabetes, hypoglycemia is usually the result of eating too many simple carbohydrates (such as sugar and white flour). The pancreas then overreacts and releases too much insulin, thereby excessively lowering blood sugar.

The good news is that hypoglycemia—if it's identified—is not that difficult to control through diet and the use of specific supplements. Hypoglycemia should be considered a warning sign that you must adjust your carbohydrate intake or risk developing type 2 diabetes.

Caution: An episode of hypoglycemia in a person who already has diabetes can be life-threatening and requires prompt care, including the immediate intake of sugar—a glass of orange juice or even a sugar cube can be used.

Common symptoms of hypoglycemia include: Fatigue, dizziness, shakiness and faintness...irritability and depression...weakness or cramps in the feet and legs...numbness or tingling in the hands, feet or face...ringing in the ears...swollen feet or legs...tightness in the chest...heart palpitations...nightmares and panic attacks..."drenching" night sweats (not menopausal or perimenopausal hot flashes)...constant hunger...headaches and migraines...impaired memory and concentration...blurred vision...nasal congestion...abdominal cramps, loose stools and diarrhea.

A TRICKY DIAGNOSIS

Under-the-radar hypoglycemia (known as "subclinical hypoglycemia") is difficult to diagnose because symptoms may be subtle and irregular, and test results can be within normal ranges. Technically, if your blood sugar drops below 70 milligrams per deciliter (mg/dL), you are considered hypoglycemic. But people without diabetes do not check their blood sugar levels on their own, so it is important to be aware of hypoglycemia symptoms.

If you suspect that you may have hypoglycemia, talk to your physician. Ideally, you should arrange to have your blood glucose levels tested when you are experiencing symptoms. You will then be asked to eat food so that your blood glucose can be tested again. If this approach is impractical for you, however, talk to your doctor about other testing methods.

THE RIGHT TREATMENT

If you have been diagnosed with diabetes, hypoglycemia may indicate that your diabetes medication dose needs to be adjusted. The sugar treatment described earlier can work in an emergency but is not recommended as a long-term treatment for hypoglycemia. Left untreated, hypoglycemia in a person with diabetes can lead to loss of consciousness and even death.

In addition to getting their medication adjusted, people with diabetes—and those who are at risk for it due to hypoglycemia—can benefit from the following…

•**A high-protein diet and healthful fats.** To keep your blood sugar levels stabilized, consume slowly absorbed, unrefined carbohydrates, such as brown rice, quinoa, oatmeal and sweet potatoes. Also, get moderate amounts of healthful fats, such as those found in avocado, olive oil and fatty fish, including salmon…and protein, such as fish, meat, chicken, soy and eggs.

Recommended protein intake: 10% to 35% of daily calories. If you have kidney disease, get your doctor's advice on protein intake.

•**Eat several small meals daily.** Start with breakfast to give your body fuel for the day (if you don't, stored blood sugar will be released into your bloodstream) and then have a small "meal" every three to four waking hours.

•**Avoid tobacco and limit your use of alcohol and caffeine.** They cause an excessive release of neurotransmitters that, in turn, trigger the pancreas to deliver insulin inappropriately.

The supplements below also help stabilize blood sugar levels (and can be used in addition to a daily multivitamin)…*

•**Chromium and vitamin B-6.** Chromium helps release accumulated sugars in the liver, which can lead to a dangerous condition called fatty liver. Vitamin B-6 supports chromium's function and helps stabilize glucose levels.

Typical daily dose: 200 micrograms (mcg) of chromium with 100 milligrams (mg) of vitamin B-6.

•**Glutamine.** As the most common amino acid found in muscle tissue, glutamine plays a vital role in controlling blood sugar. Glutamine is easily converted to glucose when blood sugar is low.

Typical daily dose: Up to four 500-mg capsules daily…or add glutamine powder to a protein drink or a smoothie that does not contain added sugar—these drinks are good options for your morning routine. Glutamine is best taken 30 minutes before a meal to cut your appetite by balancing your blood sugar.

*Consult your doctor before trying any supplements, especially if you take prescription medication and/or have a chronic medical condition, including diabetes.

The Secret Invasion That Causes Diabetes

George L. King, MD, research director and chief scientific officer of Harvard's Joslin Diabetes Center, where he heads the vascular cell biology research section, and professor of medicine at Harvard Medical School in Boston. Dr. King is coauthor, with Royce Flippin, of *The Diabetes Reset: Avoid It, Control It, Even Reverse It—A Doctor's Scientific Program.*

It's easy to get the impression that diabetes is all about blood sugar. Most people with diabetes check their glucose levels at least once a day. Even people without diabetes are advised to have glucose tests every few years—just to make sure that the disease isn't creeping up on them.

But glucose is only part of the picture. Scientists now know that chronic inflammation increases the risk that you'll develop diabetes. If you already have insulin resistance (a precursor to diabetes) or full-blown diabetes, inflammation will make your glucose levels harder to manage.

A common mistake: Unfortunately, many doctors still don't test for inflammation even though it accompanies all of the main diabetes risk factors, including smoking, obesity and high-fat/sugar diets. *What you need to know about this important aspect of diabetes care...*

SILENT DAMAGE

You hear a lot about inflammation, but what exactly is it—and when is it a problem? Normal inflammation is protective. It comes on suddenly and lasts for just a few days or weeks—usually in response to an injury or infection. Inflammation kills or encapsulates microbes...assists in the formation of protective scar tissue...and helps regenerate damaged tissues.

But chronic inflammation—caused, for example, by infection or injuries that lead to continuously elevated levels of toxins—does not turn itself off. It persists for years or even decades, particularly in those who are obese, eat poor diets, don't get enough sleep or have chronic diseases, including seemingly minor conditions such as gum disease.

The diabetes link: Persistently high levels of inflammatory molecules interfere with the ability of insulin to regulate glucose—one cause of high blood sugar. Inflammation also appears to damage beta cells, the insulin-producing cells in the pancreas.

Studies have shown that when inflammation is aggressively lowered—with salsalate (an anti-inflammatory drug), for example—glucose levels can drop significantly. Inflammation is typically identified with a blood test that measures a marker known as CRP, or C-reactive protein (see the next page).

HOW TO FIGHT INFLAMMATION

Even though salsalate reduces inflammation, when taken in high doses, it causes too many side effects, such as stomach bleeding and ringing in the ears, to be used long term. *Safer ways to reduce inflammation and keep it down...*

•**Breathe clean air.** Smoke and smog threaten more than just your lungs. Recent research has shown that areas with the highest levels of airborne particulates that are small enough to penetrate deeply into the lungs have more than 20% higher rates of type 2 diabetes than areas with the lowest levels of these particulates.

Air pollution (including cigarette smoke) increases inflammation in fatty tissues and in the vascular system. In animal studies, exposure to air pollution increases both insulin resistance and the risk for full-fledged diabetes.

My advice: Most people—and especially those who live in polluted areas—could benefit from using an indoor HEPA filter or an electrostatic air filter.

Products such as the Honeywell QuietCare True HEPA Air Purifier (available at *www.amazon.com* for $124.19) will trap nearly 100% of harmful airborne particulates from indoor air.

If you live in a large metropolitan area, avoid outdoor exercise during high-traffic times of day.

•**Take care of your gums.** Even people who take good care of their teeth often neglect their gums. It's estimated that almost half of American adults have some degree of periodontal (gum) disease.

Why it matters: The immune system can't always eliminate infections that occur in gum pockets, the areas between the teeth and gums. A persistent gum infection causes equally persistent inflammation that contributes to other illnesses. For example, research shows that people with gum disease were twice as likely to develop diabetes as those without it.

My advice: After every meal (or at least twice a day), floss and brush, in that order.

And clean your gums—gently use a soft brush. Twice a day, also use an antiseptic mouthwash (such as Listerine).

It's particularly important to follow these steps before you go to bed to remove bacteria that otherwise will remain undisturbed until morning.

•**Get more exercise.** It's among the best ways to control chronic inflammation because it burns fat. When you have less fat, you'll also produce fewer inflammation-promoting cytokines.

Data from the Nurses' Health Study and the Health Professionals Follow-Up Study found that walking briskly for a half hour daily reduced the risk of developing diabetes by nearly one-third.

My advice: Take 10,000 steps per day. To do this, walk whenever possible for daily activities, such as shopping, and even walk inside your home if you don't want to go out. Wear a pedometer to make sure you reach your daily goal.

•**Enjoy cocoa.** Cocoa contains a type of antioxidant known as flavanols, which have anti-inflammatory properties. Known primarily for their cardiovascular benefits, flavanols are now being found to help regulate insulin levels.

My advice: For inflammation-fighting effects, have one square of dark chocolate (with at least 70% cocoa) daily.

•**Try rose hip tea.** Rose hips are among the richest sources of vitamin C, with five times as much per cup than what is found in one orange. A type of rose hip known as rosa canina is particularly potent because it may contain an additional anti-inflammatory compound known as glycoside of mono and diglycerol (GOPO). It inhibits the production of a number of inflammatory molecules, including chemokines and interleukins.

My advice: Drink several cups of tangy rose hip tea a day. It's available both in bags and as a loose-leaf tea. If you're not a tea drinker, you can take rose hip supplements. Follow the directions on the label.

•**Season with turmeric.** This spice contains curcumin, one of the most potent anti-inflammatory agents. It inhibits the action of eicosanoids, "signaling molecules" that are involved in the inflammatory response.

My advice: Eat more turmeric—it's a standard spice in curries and yellow (not Dijon) mustard. You will want something more potent if you already have diabetes and/or elevated CRP. I often recommend Curamin, a potent form of curcumin that's combined with boswellia, another anti-inflammatory herb.

Important: Be sure to talk to your doctor before trying rose hip or turmeric supplements if you take medication or have a chronic health condition.

CHECK YOUR CRP LEVEL

An inexpensive and accurate blood test that is often used to estimate heart attack risk is also recommended for people who have diabetes or are at increased risk for it. The blood test measures C-reactive protein (CRP), a marker for inflammation, which can lead to heart disease and impair the body's ability to regulate glucose.

Doctors may recommend the test for patients beginning in their 30s. It's wise to get it earlier if you have diabetes risk factors, such as obesity or a family history.

A high-sensitivity CRP (hsCRP) test typically costs about $20 and is usually covered by insurance. A reading of less than 1 mg/L is ideal. Levels above 3 mg/L indicate a high risk for insulin resistance and diabetes as well as for heart attack.

If the first test shows that your CRP level is elevated, you'll want to do everything you can to lower it—for example, through exercise, a healthful diet and weight loss. Repeat the test every four to six months to see how well your lifestyle improvements are working.

How Your ApoE Genes Lead to Diabetes or Heart Disease

Suzanne Steinbaum, DO, attending cardiologist and director of Women's Heart Health, Lenox Hill Hospital, New York City. SRSHeart.com

If you have a family history of diabetes or heart disease, you no doubt have been told to watch your diet—to consume whole grains, olive oil, lean protein, tons of produce and maybe some red wine. But could some of those supposedly heart-healthy foods actually be increasing your risk? Yes, depending on a particular gene that you may have…a gene that even many doctors don't know about.

Your family's ailments may be linked to a gene known as apolipoprotein E (ApoE), which determines how your body metabolizes certain foods. According to cardiologist Suzanne Steinbaum, DO, author of *Dr. Suzanne Steinbaum's Heart Book*, if your diet suits your ApoE type, you should be able to avoid following in your family's unfortunate medical footsteps. "The ApoE genotype is like a light switch—it is going to activate only if you turn it on by eating foods that are wrong for your type," she said.

There are three genotypes (gene subtypes) associated with the gene—ApoE-2, ApoE-3 and ApoE-4. A person inherits one of these from each parent.

About two-thirds of people have a "3/3" pairing, meaning they inherited ApoE-3 from their mother and Apo-E 3 from their father. These lucky folks don't need to adhere too closely to any particular type of diet in order to avoid heart disease and diabetes, provided they follow a reasonably healthful diet, control their weight, exercise regularly and don't smoke.

However…

• **People who inherited the ApoE-2 gene from one or both parents (a bit more than 10% of the population) have trouble metabolizing carbohydrates.** This makes them prone to diabetes.

• **People who inherited the ApoE-4 gene from one or both parents (just over 20% of the population) can't handle fat.** This increases their risk for coronary artery disease.

• **An unlucky minority (less than 2% of the population) have a "2/4" pairing**—meaning they inherited ApoE-2 from one parent and Apo-E 4 from the other parent—and thus are prone to both diabetes and coronary artery disease.

TELLING YOUR TYPE

A blood test can determine which genotype you have inherited. Dr. Steinbaum often recommends the test because she has found that patients generally comply better with dietary advice when there's a scientific indication that a particular diet will be especially protective for them. Some insurance policies cover the test (which costs about $150 or more, depending on the lab), so ask your insurance company.

If you choose not to get the blood test, you can get some idea—though not with certainty—of whether you carry the ApoE-2 and/or ApoE-4 genes.

People who inherited the ApoE-2 gene from one or both parents tend to have…

• **High triglycerides and blood sugar, and…**

• **A family history of diabetes and obesity.**

Diet recommendations: People with ApoE-2 often crave foods like cookies, jelly beans, bread and soda—but their bodies cannot metabolize sugars and simple carbohydrates, and they often wind up overweight or obese, Dr. Steinbaum said. Lean proteins and moderate amounts of complex carbohydrates (such as whole grains and legumes) are the keys to good health for these people.

Note: Even though a glass of red wine with dinner often is said to be heart-healthy, Dr. Steinbaum advises ApoE-2 carriers against drinking wine because it is loaded with sugars.

People who inherited the ApoE-4 gene from one or both parents tend to have…

• **High LDL cholesterol, and…**

• **A family history of coronary artery disease.**

Recommended: If this is your profile, you're likely to gravitate toward Buffalo wings, cheeseburgers, rich ice cream and other fatty foods—yet your body has a hard time breaking down and absorbing fats, and the receptors that are supposed to sweep up LDL cholesterol are suppressed. Dr. Steinbaum said, "For these people, I usually advise following an extremely low-fat diet, preferably a vegetarian or vegan diet, with less than 7% of calories coming from saturated fats." Even plant-based fats such as olive oil and nuts, which are considered heart-healthy for other people, should be consumed only in moderate amounts by people with the ApoE-4 gene. You also should be aware that cholesterol-lowering statin drugs are less effective in ApoE-4 individuals than in other people, so even if you take a statin, a low-fat diet is still very important for you.

People who inherited the ApoE-2 gene from one parent and the ApoE-4 gene from the other parent tend to have…

• **High triglycerides, high blood sugar and high LDL cholesterol, and…**

• **A family history of both diabetes and coronary artery disease.**

Recommended: If you have a "2/4" pairing, you're in the unfortunate minority of people who have trouble metabolizing not only sugars and simple carbohydrates but also fats. Your best choice is to be a vegetarian, Dr. Steinbaum said. Focus primarily on vegetables, legumes, whole grains and other complex carbohydrates…and avoid sweets, wine, white bread, white pasta and other simple carbs. You also need to keep your fat intake quite low, consuming only modest amounts of plant-based fats and little or no animal fat. Your healthiest food options are vegetables, legumes, whole grains and other complex carbohydrates.

Knowing your ApoE gene can be very empowering. "When you think of heart disease as being genetic, you might assume, 'Well, my dad got it, my aunts got it and my grandfather got it, so I'm going to get it, too.' But if your dad's whole family had eggs for breakfast,

chicken for lunch and beef for dinner most days, the real problem lies in the fact that everyone was eating the wrong way for their gene type," Dr. Steinbaum said. The same goes for a family legacy of diabetes when the family diet tended toward high-carb foods.

So remember—whether your genetic legacy leaves you vulnerable to heart disease, diabetes or both, committing to the right type of diet for you might well be enough to break that chain.

Could Antibiotics Give You Diabetes?

Yu-Xiao Yang, MD, associate professor of medicine, division of gastroenterology, department of medicine, department of epidemiology and biostatistics, Perelman School of Medicine at University of Pennsylvania, Philadelphia. His study was published in *European Journal of Endocrinology*.

Antibiotics can cure. They kill infectious bacteria and save lives. Type 2 diabetes is a chronic disease. It shortens lives.

Now there is disturbing evidence that the cure may be contributing to the disease—in other words, certain antibiotics may increase the risk of developing diabetes.

The connection is the ecosystem of bacteria in our gut that scientists call the microbiome. It affects digestion and immunity, and an unhealthy microbiome has been linked to diseases as diverse as obesity, certain cancers, inflammatory bowel disease, rheumatoid arthritis and…diabetes. Several studies have shown that type 2 diabetes, the kind that affects most people, is more common in people who have microbiomes with altered or low bacteria diversity. What we eat and drink changes the composition of the bacteria, and so can the medication we take…especially antibiotics.

Penicillin, the original wonder drug, saved soldiers from battlefield infections in World War II and later revolutionized medicine by curing once-fatal infections. But antibiotics by their very nature disturb the microbiome by killing bacteria...including beneficial bacteria in the gut.

Now, the newest research finds an association between the repeated use of certain antibiotics and the diabetes epidemic that affects 30 million Americans...and counting.

A STRONG ASSOCIATION IN A MILLION PEOPLE

In the latest study, researchers had access to nearly complete medical records of almost 10 million people living in the United Kingdom. The records included medical diagnoses, tests and procedures, prescription medications and lifestyle factors, including smoking and drinking history.

The research team identified 208,002 people who were diagnosed with diabetes (either type 1 or 2). Each case was matched with four controls...people of the same age and gender who did not have diabetes. In all, the study included more than one million men and women, with an average age of 60.

Looking deeper into the medical records of the participants, the researchers searched for prescriptions for several different antibiotics, including, yes, penicillin, still the most popular choice. They excluded antibiotics prescribed in the year before a diabetes diagnosis, since many of these patients may have had undiagnosed diabetes already. They adjusted statistically for many variables, including smoking, high cholesterol, obesity, heart disease, skin and respiratory infections, and previous blood sugar measurement. *The results...*

• **In most cases,** a single course of antibiotics was not associated with any increased risk for diabetes, compared with taking no antibiotics at all.

• **The exception was a class of antibiotics called cephalosporins,** broad-spectrum antibiotics often prescribed for strep throat and UTIs. Even taking a single course of these antibiotics was associated with a 9% increase in type 2 diabetes risk.

• **For the antibiotics linked with type 2 diabetes,** the more courses people took in any one year, the greater the risk. Taking two to five courses of penicillin in a single year was linked to an 8% increase in diabetes risk, for example, while taking more than five courses was linked to a raised risk of 23%. Similarly, taking two to five courses of quinolones, prescribed for skin and respiratory infections as well as UTIs, was linked to a 15% increase in diabetes risk, while taking more than five courses raised risk 37%.

• **Tetracyclines** were associated with a raised type 2 diabetes risk only in people who took them for five or more courses in a year.

• **Nitroimidazoles,** prescribed for vaginal infections as well as skin infections such as rosacea, were not associated with increased diabetes risk when taken at any frequency.

• **Neither antiviral nor antifungal medications were linked with diabetes risk.**

• **While there appeared to be an association between some antibiotics and type 1 diabetes,** an autoimmune condition, for some antibiotics, the results were inconclusive.

WITH ANTIBIOTICS, DO THE RIGHT THING

This study, while big and statistically powerful, doesn't tell us whether using antibiotics actually causes diabetes. That's because it's observational. It looks back and draws connections. A prospective study would assign one group of people to take antibiotics whether they need them or not, and deny them to another group, and follow them for years to see who gets diabetes. For practical and ethical reasons, of course, that's impossible.

So it's possible that people who would go on to develop diabetes even years later are more prone to infections, and so would need more antibiotics. On the other side, prospective animal studies have shown that antibiotics promote the growth of bacteria that promote diabetes. Because diabetes is so common and such a damaging disease, researchers are looking for other ways to tease out whether and how antibiotics contribute to diabetes.

You don't have to wait to do the right thing, though. These wonder drugs have been overused, both for human medicine and animal livestock, and many are losing their effectiveness due to rising antibiotic resistance, a scary prospect. Using antibiotics only when they are really needed not only protects your own health but helps keep these drugs effective when they are really needed.

By all means take an antibiotic if it's the right treatment. But there are already many good reasons to avoid antibiotics if possible, and the truth is, they are often prescribed for health conditions for which they can't possibly work. Antibiotics kill bacteria, so they won't help with, say, the common cold, which is caused by a virus. Most sinus infections, even those caused by bacterial infections, don't require antibiotics either.

In many cases, doctors prescribe antibiotics when they're not needed because a patient insists on it for almost any sort of infection or even suspected infection.

Don't be that patient!

These Drugs Can Raise Diabetes Risk

Armon B. Neel, Jr., PharmD, a certified geriatric pharmacist, adjunct instructor in clinical pharmacy at Mercer University College of Pharmacy and Health Sciences in Atlanta. Dr. Neel is also coauthor of *Are Your Prescriptions Killing You? How to Prevent Dangerous Interactions, Avoid Deadly Side Effects, and Be Healthier with Fewer Drugs.* MedicationXpert.com

When your doctor pulls out his/her prescription pad, you probably assume that your health problem will soon be improving. Sure, there may be a side effect or two—perhaps an occasional upset stomach or a mild headache. But overall you will be better off, right?

Not necessarily. While it's true that many drugs can help relieve symptoms and sometimes even cure certain medical conditions, a number of popular medications actually cause disease—not simply side effects—while treating the original problem.

Here's what happens: Your kidney and liver are the main organs that break down drugs and eliminate them from your body. But these organs weaken as you age. Starting as early as your 20s and 30s, you lose 1% of liver and kidney function every year. As a result, drugs can build up in your body (particularly if you take more than one), become toxic, damage crucial organs such as the heart and brain—and trigger disease, such as diabetes.

Older adults are at greatest risk for this problem because the body becomes increasingly less efficient at metabolizing drugs with age. But no one is exempt from the risk.

Many commonly prescribed drugs increase risk for type 2 diabetes. These medications include statins…beta-blockers…antidepressants…antipsychotics…steroids…and alpha-blockers prescribed for prostate problems and high blood pressure.

Safer alternatives to discuss with your doctor, consultant pharmacist or other health-care professional…

If you're prescribed a beta-blocker: Ask about using a calcium-channel blocker instead. *Diltiazem* (Tiazac) has the fewest side effects. The 24-hour sustained-release dose provides the best control.

If you're prescribed an antidepressant: Ask about *venlafaxine* (Effexor), a selective serotonin and norepinephrine reuptake inhibitor (SSNRI) antidepressant that treats depression and anxiety and has been shown to cause fewer problems for diabetic patients than any of the older selective serotonin reuptake inhibitor (SSRI) drugs.

If you're prescribed an alpha-blocker: For prostate problems, rather than taking the alpha-blocker *tamsulosin* (Flomax), ask about using *dutasteride* (Avodart) or *finasteride* (Proscar). For high blood pressure, ask about a calcium-channel blocker drug.

THE VERY BEST DRUG SELF-DEFENSE

If you're over age 60—especially if you take more than one medication or suffer drug side effects—it's a good idea to ask your physician to work with a consulting pharmacist who is skilled in medication management. A consulting pharmacist has been trained in drug therapy management and will work with your physician to develop a drug management plan that will avoid harmful drugs. These services are relatively new and may not be covered by insurance, so be sure to check with your provider.

To find a consulting pharmacist in your area, go to the website of the American Society of Consultant Pharmacists, *www.ascp.com*, and click on "Find a Senior Care Pharmacist."

Also helpful: Make sure that a drug you've been prescribed does not appear on the "Beers Criteria for Potentially Inappropriate Medication Use in Older Adults." Originally developed by the late Mark Beers, editor of *The Merck Manual of Medical Information*, the list has been recently updated by The American Geriatrics Society. To download the list for free, go to *www.geriatricscareonline.org* and click on "Clinical Guidelines & Recommendations."

Get More of This Mineral to Shield Against Diabetes

Ka He, MD, MPH, ScD, chair and professor of epidemiology and biostatistics, Indiana University, Bloomington.

Michael Wald, MD, physician and director of nutritional services at Integrated Nutrition of Mt. Kisco, New York. IntMedNY.com

Diabetes—the disease of chronically high levels of blood sugar—is an epidemic. Ten percent of American adults have it, including 40% of people 65 and older. In fact, the rate of diabetes is rising so fast, the Centers for Disease Control predicts the number of Americans with the disease will triple by 2050.

Key fact not widely reported: One reason so many of us get diabetes may be that so few of us get enough of the mineral magnesium in our diets.

In a recently completed 20-year study of nearly 4,500 Americans, researchers from the University of North Carolina at Chapel Hill found that those with the biggest intake of magnesium (200 milligrams [mg] per every 1,000 calories consumed) had a 47% lower risk of diabetes than those with the smallest intake (100 mg per every 1,000 calories consumed). The study also linked lower magne-

sium intake to higher levels of a biomarker of insulin resistance and three biomarkers of chronic inflammation (C-reactive protein, interleukin-6, fibrinogen).

What happens: Insulin is the hormone that ushers blood sugar (glucose) out of the bloodstream and into cells. In insulin resistance, cells don't respond to the hormone, and blood glucose levels stay high—often leading to diabetes. And inflammatory biochemicals trigger the manufacture of proteins that increase insulin resistance.

"Magnesium has an anti-inflammatory effect, and inflammation is one of the risk factors for diabetes," says Ka He, MD, the study leader. "Magnesium is also a co-factor in the production of many enzymes that are a must for balanced blood sugar levels."

COMPELLING SCIENTIFIC EVIDENCE

Other recent studies also link magnesium intake and diabetes...

• **Ten times more magnesium deficiency**—in people with diabetes. Compared with healthy people, people with newly diagnosed diabetes were 10 times more likely to have low blood levels of magnesium, and people with "known diabetes" were eight times more likely to have low levels, reported researchers from Cambridge University in the journal *Diabetes Research and Clinical Practice*.

• **Low magnesium, high blood sugar.** People with diabetes and low intake of magnesium had poorer blood sugar control than people with a higher intake of magnesium, reported Brazilian scientists. "Magnesium plays an important role in blood glucose control," they concluded in the journal *Clinical Nutrition*.

• **More nerve damage.** Nerve damage—diabetic neuropathy, with pain and burning in the feet and hands—is a common complication of diabetes. Indian researchers found that people with diabetic neuropathy had magnesium levels 23% lower than people without the problem.

• **Magnesium protects diabetic hearts.** High blood sugar damages the circulatory system, with diabetes doubling the risk of heart attack or stroke. In a study from Italian researchers, taking a magnesium supplement strengthened the arteries and veins of older people with diabetes. The results were in the journal *Magnesium Research*.

A magnesium supplement balances blood sugar—even if you're not diabetic. In a study of 52 overweight people with insulin resistance (but not diabetes), those who took a daily magnesium supplement of 365 milligrams had a greater drop in blood sugar levels and insulin resistance than those who took a placebo, reported German researchers in *Diabetes, Obesity and Metabolism*.

Bottom line: "Based on evidence from the study I led and other studies, increasing the intake of magnesium may be beneficial in diabetes," says Dr. He.

MORE MAGNESIUM

The recommended dietary allowance (RDA) for magnesium is 420 mg a day for men and 320 mg a day for women.

However: In a study conducted by the Centers for Disease Control, no group of US citizens tested—including Caucasian, African-American, Hispanic-American, men or women—consumed the RDA for magnesium. "Substantial numbers of US adults fail to consume adequate magnesium in their diets," concluded researchers in the journal *Nutrition*.

They also found that magnesium intake decreased as age increased—a troublesome finding, since diabetes is usually diagnosed in middle-aged and older people.

Healthful strategy: "I recommend increasing the intake of foods rich in magnesium, such as whole grains, nuts, legumes, vegetables and fruits," says Dr. He.

Best food sources of magnesium include...

- **Nuts and seeds** (almonds, cashews, pumpkin seeds, sunflower seeds, sesame seeds)

- **Leafy green and other vegetables** (spinach, Swiss chard, kale, collard greens, mustard greens, turnip greens, cabbage, broccoli, cauliflower, Brussels sprouts, green beans, asparagus, cucumber, celery, avocado, beets)

- **Whole grains** (whole-grain breakfast cereals, wheat bran, wheat germ, oats, brown rice, buckwheat)

- **Beans and legumes** (soybeans and soy products, lentils, black-eyed peas, kidney beans, black beans, navy beans)

- **Fruit** (banana, kiwi fruit, watermelon, raspberries)

- **Fish** (salmon, halibut).

CONSIDER A MAGNESIUM SUPPLEMENT

But magnesium-rich food may not be sufficient to protect you from diabetes, says Michael Wald, MD, director of nutritional services at Integrated Nutrition of Mt. Kisco clinic, New York. That's because many factors can deplete the body of magnesium or block its absorption. *They include...*

- **Overcooking greens and other magnesium-rich foods**

- **Eating too much sugar**

- **Emotional and mental stress**

- **Taking magnesium-draining medications,** such as diuretics for high blood pressure

- **Exposure to environmental toxins such as pesticides**

- **Bowel diseases and bowel surgery.**

"Low blood levels of magnesium are very common," says Dr. Wald. And conventional doctors rarely test magnesium levels.

Recommended: To help guarantee an adequate blood level of magnesium, Dr. Wald recommends taking Perque Mg (Magnesium) Plus Guard. For maximum absorption and effectiveness, this doctor-developed supplement contains four different forms of the mineral (magnesium glycinate, magnesium ascorbate, magnesium citrate, magnesium stearate). It also contains nutritional co-factors that help the mineral work in the body.

The supplement is available through many retail outlets, both online and in stores where supplements are sold. Follow the dosage recommendations on the label.

Supplement Safely with Magnesium

Dennis Goodman, MD, board-certified cardiologist, clinical associate professor of medicine at New York University School of Medicine. He is author of *Magnificent Magnesium: Your Essential Key to a Healthy Heart and More.* DennisGoodmanMD.com

If you feel that you are one of the majority of Americans who don't get enough magnesium from their diets, it may make sense to take a daily supplement, but always check with your doctor before taking any supplements.

If you decide to get your magnesium level checked, ask your doctor for a magnesium red blood cell (RBC-Mg) test. It measures the magnesium that is inside cells. It's a more accurate measure of magnesium than the standard serum magnesium test. An optimal RBC-Mg level is more than 5.5 mg/dL.

The test isn't essential. If you generally are healthy, you can't go wrong with extra magnesium. The Institute of Medicine advises women 31 years old and older to get 320 mg of magnesium daily. For men, the recommended amount is 420 mg. *These are conservative estimates based on your minimal needs. What I recommend…*

Multiply your weight in pounds by 3 mg to determine the optimal dose.

Example: A 140-pound woman would take 420 mg of magnesium. During times of stress, when your need for magnesium is higher, multiply your weight by five instead of three. Keep taking the higher dose until things calm down again. You will start to feel the benefits within a few days.

When you're shopping for supplements, look for products that end with "ate"—magnesium glycinate, taurate, malate, etc. These forms are readily absorbed into the bloodstream and less likely to cause diarrhea.

Splenda Raises Blood Sugar Levels and May Increase Diabetes Risk

M. Yanina Pepino, PhD, assistant professor of medicine, Internal Medicine and Nutritional Science, Washington University School of Medicine, St. Louis. Her study was published in *Diabetes Care.*

Are you watching your weight or just trying to reduce the amount of sugar you consume? Good for you! But what may not be so good is your habit of reaching for a yellow packet of Splenda to sweeten your coffee or tea…quenching your thirst with a diet soda…or having Splenda-sweetened cookies, ice cream or pudding when you want a sweet taste without the calories of sugar.

What's the problem? Even though this popular artificial sweetener doesn't have calories the way real sugar does, Splenda can mess with your blood sugar levels, a new study shows…and that might put you at increased risk for diabetes.

PUTTING A SWEET POWDER TO THE TEST

Researchers wanted to gauge the effects of sucralose (sold in the US as Splenda) on blood sugar and insulin levels. Study participants included 17 people who were obese but who were not diabetic and who had relatively normal insulin sensitivity (the ability of the body's cells to recognize and respond to insulin)…and who did not regularly consume any type of artificial sweetener.

All participants underwent glucose tolerance tests, the gold-standard measure of how the body handles sugar. The tests were done twice, about a week apart. One time, the participants drank plain water before the test… the other time, they drank water sweetened with about the same amount of sucralose as is in a 12-ounce diet soda.

Results: Compared with their glucose tolerance test results after drinking plain water, after drinking the sucralose beverage, the participants had four types of bad readings on the test. *These included…*

• **12% higher peak blood glucose levels.**

- **20% higher total insulin secretion.**
- **22% faster insulin-secretion rate.**
- **7% slower rate of clearing insulin from the blood.**

Why these results are troublesome: Higher blood levels of glucose and insulin increase the likelihood of developing insulin resistance, a condition in which the body's cells don't readily accept insulin. As the pancreas struggles to keep up with the increasing demand for insulin, the risk for diabetes rises.

It's also worth noting that the gastrointestinal tract has "sweet receptors" similar to the taste receptors that recognize sweetness on your tongue—which probably explains why consuming a non-nutritive sweetener such as sucralose could affect sugar metabolism despite having no calories.

A UNIQUE TWIST

One factor that made this study unique is that it excluded people who normally consumed any type of artificial sweetener, on the grounds that such a habit could have chronic effects that might skew the study results.

Here's why: Studies on animals show that regular sucralose consumption increases blood sugar after the glucose tolerance test. This probably means that, for people who habitually consume sucralose, the results on the control day (when they had plain water to drink and not sucralose-sweetened water) may already be higher—so the difference on the day that they had the sucralose solution would appear to be smaller.

Why this study matters so much: People who are overweight or obese are frequently advised to cut down on sugar to reduce their risk for diabetes and other health problems—and they often do so by substituting artificial sweeteners for the real thing. Though this study looked only at sucralose and not other types of artificial sweeteners, it does raise serious concerns about how blood sugar levels and diabetes risk are affected by "fake" sweeteners.

See the following article for more information.

Don't Let Artificial Sweeteners Sabotage Your Health

Study titled "Artificial sweeteners induce glucose intolerance by altering the gut microbiota," published in *Nature*.

We live in a crazy age in which some people who don't eat meat fill up on high-sodium soy products that pretend to be meat and in which some people who go sugar-free saturate themselves with artificial sweeteners. In one recent report, you were told that sucralose—the artificial sweetener marketed as Splenda—interferes with insulin secretion and glucose metabolism. That report knocked sucralose out of the water as a sweet alternative for people who need to keep their blood sugar in check. Now, a more recent study has found that the problem is much broader—it goes well beyond Splenda—and the study also got to the bottom of what exactly you're doing to your body when you opt for artificial sweeteners.

THE SUGAR-FREE TRUTH

After decades of thinking that artificial sweeteners were the answer to weight and sugar control, nutritionists and scientists are now realizing that it's not so. Sucralose isn't the only culprit—and glucose intolerance (a reduced ability to remove sugar from the blood) is not the only damage caused by artificial sweeteners. No-calorie artificial sweeteners in general have been linked to weight gain, as illogical as that sounds. And if you are thinking that folks who drink diet soda gain weight because they otherwise load up on other sugary foods, that's not so, says the research.

So, how do you get fat on sugar-free edibles? That part of the research equation wasn't clear until Israeli scientists discovered what artificial sweeteners do to the gut microbiome—the galaxy of bacteria that live in the gut, aid digestion and play a big role in whether someone is healthy.

The researchers conducted a series of experiments that began with mice. Some mice were fed water spiked with one of three different artificial sweeteners—saccharin, sucralose or aspartame. Then these mice were compared with mice fed either plain water or sugar water.

Result: Glucose intolerance developed within 11 weeks in the mice given each of the artificial sweeteners. Meanwhile, the mice given plain water—and even those given sugar water—were just fine.

Why that's bad: Glucose intolerance can lead to prediabetes.

When the researchers delved into whether the gut microbiome had something to do with these findings, they discovered that it sure did. Mice treated with antibiotics to wipe out their gut microbiomes didn't become glucose intolerant when fed artificial sweeteners because the artificial sweetener had nothing to react with once it hit the gut. But water-fed mice that lost their microbiomes became glucose intolerant when gut bacteria from mice fed artificial sweeteners was transplanted into them to repopulate their microbiomes.

Translation: The artificial sweeteners transformed the gut microbiomes to include a very unhealthful mixture of organisms.

Mice are mice, but what about people? Experiments in humans delivered the same results. The researchers already knew, from an earlier study they had done, that nondiabetic people who consumed artificial sweeteners were more likely than people who didn't use artificial sweeteners to gain weight and show signs of impaired glucose tolerance. They reconnected with a portion of those study participants to examine their microbiomes. Sure enough, just as in the mice, the microbiomes of people who consumed artificial sweeteners were altered compared with the microbiomes of people who didn't touch fake sugar.

SUGAR-FREE CHALLENGE

Going sugar-free but then consuming edibles that mimic or try to taste exactly like the food and drink you give up is the kind of trickery where the joke is on you. Not only are you *not* losing weight from substituting sugar with artificial sweeteners, you're training your body to be diabetic! There is a much better

way. You can retrain your taste buds to simply stop craving or expecting sugary flavors. Check out "Kick the Sugar Habit" on page 316. It provides information on how to detox from sugary-tasting foods and build a satisfying sugar-free, weight-conscious diet. That's true freedom from sugar.

Thin People Get Diabetes, Too

Mercedes Carnethon, PhD, associate professor of preventive medicine and epidemiology at Northwestern University Feinberg School of Medicine in Chicago, where she specializes in population studies of diabetes, obesity, cardiovascular disease and fitness.

It's widely known that type 2 diabetes tends to strike people who are overweight. In fact, about 85% of people with diabetes are carrying extra pounds. But what about those who aren't overweight?

A popular misconception: It's commonly believed—even by many doctors—that lean and normal-weight people don't have to worry about diabetes. The truth is, you can develop diabetes regardless of your weight.

An unexpected risk: For those who have this "hidden" form of diabetes, recent research is now showing that they are at even greater risk of dying than those who are overweight and have the disease.

What you need to know about diabetes—no matter what you weigh…

THE EXTRA DANGER NO ONE EXPECTED

No one knows exactly why some people who are not overweight develop diabetes. There's some speculation that certain people are genetically primed for their insulin to not function properly, leading to diabetes despite their weight.

Still, because diabetes is so closely linked to being overweight, even researchers were surprised by the results of a recent analysis of 2,600 people with type 2 diabetes who were tracked for up to 15 years.

Startling finding: Among these people with diabetes, those who were of normal weight at the time of diagnosis were twice as likely to die of non–heart-related causes, primarily cancer, during the study period as those who were overweight or obese.* The normal-weight people were also more likely to die of cardiovascular disease, but there weren't enough heart-related events to make that finding statistically significant.

Possible reasons for the higher death rates among normal-weight people with diabetes…

• **The so-called obesity paradox.** Even though overweight and obese people have a higher risk of developing diabetes, kidney disease and heart disease, they tend to weather these illnesses somewhat better, for unknown reasons, than lean or normal-weight people.

• **Visceral fat,** a type of fat that accumulates around the internal organs, isn't always apparent. Unlike the fat you can grab, which is largely inert, visceral fat causes metabolic disturbances that increase the risk for diabetes, heart disease and other conditions. You can have high levels of visceral fat even if you're otherwise lean. Visceral fat can truly be measured only by imaging techniques such as a CT scan (but the test is not commonly done for this reason). However, a simple waist measurement can help indicate whether you have visceral fat (see below).

• **Lack of good medical advice.** In normal-weight people who are screened and diagnosed with diabetes, their doctors might be less aggressive about pursuing treatments or giving lifestyle advice than they would be if treating someone who is visibly overweight.

HOW TO PROTECT YOURSELF

It's estimated that about 25% of the roughly 29 million Americans with diabetes haven't been diagnosed. *Whether you're heavy or lean…*

• **Get tested at least once every three years starting at age 45**—regardless of your weight. That's the advice of the American Dia-

*Normal weight is defined as a body mass index (BMI) of 18.5 to 24.9…overweight is 25 to 29.9…and obese, 30 or above. To calculate your BMI, go to *www.nhlbi.nih.gov* and search for "BMI Calculator."

betes Association (ADA). You may need even earlier testing and/or more frequent tests if you have risk factors, such as a family history of diabetes and/or a sedentary lifestyle. Talk to your doctor.

Remember: If your weight is normal, your doctor may have a lower clinical suspicion of diabetes—a fancy way of saying he/she wouldn't even wonder if you have the condition. As a result, the doctor might think it's OK to skip the test or simply forget to recommend it. Ask for diabetes testing—even if your doctor doesn't mention it.

A fasting glucose test, which measures blood sugar after you have gone without food for at least eight hours, is typically offered.

Alternative: The HbA1c blood test. It's recommended by the ADA because it shows your average blood glucose levels over the previous two to three months. Many people prefer the A1c test because it doesn't require fasting. Both types of tests are usually covered by insurance.

• **Pull out the tape measure.** Even if you aren't particularly heavy, a large waist circumference could indicate high levels of visceral fat. "Abdominal obesity" is defined as a waist circumference of more than 35 inches in women and more than 40 inches in men. Even if you are under these limits, any increase in your waist size could be a warning sign. Take steps such as diet and exercise to keep it from increasing.

To get an accurate measurement: Wrap a tape measure around your waist at the level of your navel. Make sure that the tape is straight and you're not pulling it too tight. And don't hold in your stomach!

• **Watch the sugar and calories.** The Harvard Nurses' Health Study found that women who drank just one daily soft drink (or fruit punch) had more than an 80% increased risk of developing diabetes.

Research has consistently linked sweetened beverages with diabetes. But it's not clear whether the culprits are the sweeteners (such as high-fructose corn syrup) or just the extra calories, which lead to weight gain. Either way, it's smart no matter what you weigh to eliminate soda and other supersweet beverages from your diet—or if you don't want to give them up, have no more than one soft drink a week, the amount that wasn't associated with weight gain in the study.

Remember: A single soft drink often contains hundreds of calories.

•**Get the right type of exercise.** People who want to lose weight often take up aerobic workouts, such as swimming or biking, which burn a lot of calories. But if you don't need to lose weight, strength training might be a better choice. When you add muscle, you significantly improve insulin sensitivity and enhance the body's ability to remove glucose from the blood.

Walking may not sound very sexy, but it's one of the best exercises going because it has both aerobic and muscle-building effects. In fact, walking briskly (at a pace that causes sweating and mild shortness of breath) for half an hour daily reduces the risk for diabetes by nearly one-third. That's pretty impressive!

Why Eating Too Quickly May Kill You

Lina Radzeviciene, MD, PhD, endocrinologist, Institute of Endocrinology, Lithuanian University of Health Sciences, Kaunas, Lithuania. Her study was published in *Clinical Nutrition.*

Jan Chozen Bays, MD, pediatrician and Zen teacher, Great Vow Zen Monastery, Clatskanie, Oregon. She is author of *Mindful Eating: A Guide to Rediscovering a Healthy and Joyful Relationship with Food.*

Think for a minute about how quickly you eat your breakfast, lunch and dinner.

Do you find yourself finishing your meals long before your family and friends finish theirs?

Do you ever put food into your mouth before you've finished chewing the previous bite?

Do you tend to squeeze in meals just before running off to an appointment or an event?

If any of the above sounds familiar, then you may be doing yourself tremendous harm by increasing your risk for type 2 diabetes, according to new research.

THE FAST-EATING DISEASE

Lithuanian researchers, including Lina Radzeviciene, MD, PhD, an endocrinologist and the lead author of the study, asked subjects to fill out a questionnaire about how quickly they ate compared with those around them (their choices were faster, the same and slower). And what they discovered is that participants who said that they ate "faster" were 2.5 times as likely to have type 2 diabetes as those who said that they ate "slower."

Now that's remarkable—it means that you can tell a lot about someone's risk for getting type 2 diabetes just by how quickly that person eats!

Why might this be? There are two potential reasons—and they both have to do with overeating, which is easy to do when you eat fast, because it takes your body about 20 minutes to register fullness. Overeating signals the pancreas to produce more insulin, and an overproduction of insulin can lead to type 2 diabetes, said Dr. Radzeviciene. Overeating also makes you more likely to become obese—another risk factor for type 2 diabetes.

Of course, it's possible that you've been eating quickly for your whole life and you have yet to overeat, become obese and/or develop type 2 diabetes. Congrats—you've been getting away with it! Fast eating doesn't guarantee that you'll overeat, become obese and/or develop type 2 diabetes. But it does raise your risk. That means that the more often you do it, the more likely you'll overeat and the more likely you'll develop these problems—especially as you age, when your metabolism slows and you're less apt to be very active and burn lots of calories. In other words, just because you haven't been negatively affected by fast eating yet doesn't mean that you'll be off the hook for life.

HOW TO SLOW DOWN

The news that fast eating is harmful was no surprise to Jan Chozen Bays, MD, a pediatrician, Zen teacher and author of *Mindful Eating: A Guide to Rediscovering a Healthy and Joyful Relationship with Food.* But she said that there

21

are simple ways to help yourself take your time while you eat. *Here are her tips…*

1. Have an appetizer. Instead of diving into an entrée on an empty stomach, tame your appetite first with a small, healthy appetizer, such as fresh celery slices with peanut butter or a spinach salad.

2. Control your portions. The more you love a food, the more critical it is to control your portions, because you're likely to crave more. Take one serving, put it on your plate and then put the food back in the refrigerator, freezer or pantry—or buy preportioned containers of the food.

3. Eat more real food and less processed food. This tip isn't just about nutrition—it's also, literally, about how long it takes to chew different foods. Real, whole foods such as whole grains, legumes, meats and vegetables take longer to eat because your teeth have to start "processing" them from their natural states. Think about how long it takes you to eat, say, a bean salad versus the way you might scarf down macaroni and cheese—you get the idea.

4. Don't multitask. Don't read the paper, watch TV, text, drive or answer e-mails while eating. When you're not paying attention to what's on your plate or in your mouth, it's much easier to gobble too much too quickly.

5. Take breaks. Put down your utensils (or your sandwich) between bites. As you chew your food slowly, savor the flavor. Then take a deep breath and count to 20. Next, take a sip of your beverage. Talk to the person next to you if you're eating with a group.

6. Eat as a guest. You would never invite someone to your home so he or she could stand over the kitchen sink eating leftovers out of a storage container. So why should you eat that way? Sit down at a table, set out some nice plates, play soothing music…and you'll be less likely to rush.

Acid-Producing Diet Increases Diabetes Risk

Study titled "Dietary acid load and risk of type 2 diabetes: the E3N-EPIC cohort study," published in *Diabetologia*.

When you sit down to a meal, you may think about how many calories it has…the amount of fat or carbs you're consuming…and which vitamins and minerals you're getting. You probably don't think about the meal's acid load. You should. Why? Because once they're inside you, certain foods lead to the production of a lot of acid—and that acid may increase your risk of developing diabetes, a recent study shows.

Shocker: Foods that you'd generally think of as acidic (oranges, tomatoes, lemons, etc.) are not the ones to worry about. Instead, the acid producers include some foods you probably consider healthful. *Here's what to watch out for…*

ACID SCORING

To understand the recent study, let's review a little chemistry. Remember that pH, ranging from zero to 14, is a measure of the acidity or alkalinity of a substance, which has to do with the concentration of hydrogen ions. A pH of 7.0 is neutral…numbers below 7.0 are more acid…numbers above 7.0 are more alkaline. The normal healthy pH range for human blood and tissues is slightly more alkaline than acid, with a pH of about 7.35 to 7.45.

Severe pH imbalances are known to be life-threatening, and moderate imbalances can compromise bone health and lead to kidney stones. Researchers decided to investigate how pH affects diabetes risk. They drew on data from more than 66,000 women who did not have diabetes at the start of the study. In 1993, these women completed questionnaires about how often and in what quantities they consumed 208 different foods. The researchers then did a nutritional analysis, calculating each woman's dietary acid load based on the potential renal acid load (PRAL) scores of the foods she ate. The PRAL score takes into account the intestinal absorption rates of protein, phosphorus, potassium, calcium and magnesium, all of which contribute to maintaining the acid-alkaline balance. Negative PRAL scores reflect alkaline-forming potential, while positive PRAL scores reflect acid-forming potential.

Based on their PRAL scores, participants were divided into four equal-sized groups. The lowest-scoring group had the most alkaline-forming diet...the highest-scoring group had the most acid-forming diet. Then, for the next 14 years, the researchers kept track of who developed diabetes—as almost 3,500 of the women did.

What the researchers found: Women with the lowest PRAL scores were the least likely to develop diabetes. Compared to that group, women with the highest scores (representing a high acid load) were 56% more likely to develop diabetes. This held even after researchers adjusted for other diabetes risk factors, such as body mass index (BMI), physical activity, smoking, high blood pressure, high cholesterol and family history of diabetes. Surprisingly, the association between a high acid load and diabetes risk was even more pronounced among women of normal weight (with a BMI of 25 or less) than among overweight women.

WHICH FOODS ARE ACID-FORMING?

In this study, the high-risk high-PRAL diets were characterized by higher consumption of fat and protein (mainly from animal protein—meat, poultry, fish) and also by consumption of bread and soft drinks, especially artificially sweetened drinks. In contrast, women who followed a low-risk low-PRAL diet tended to consume more fruits, vegetables, dairy products and coffee.

PRAL examples: A three-ounce chicken breast without the skin has a PRAL score of 9.43...whereas an orange scores -4.24 and a cup of broccoli scores -5.6.

What might be the metabolic mechanism behind these findings? Our lungs and kidneys are responsible for maintaining a healthy pH by eliminating excess amounts of acid or alkaline from the body. The lungs take care of carbon dioxide and the kidneys take care of all

other acids. But when the kidneys aren't able to keep up with the task, a condition called metabolic acidosis arises. According to the study researchers, a diet that creates a high acid load may contribute to chronic metabolic acidosis, which in turn leads to insulin resistance and metabolic syndrome—which are risk factors for diabetes.

Additional evidence: Animal studies have shown that metabolic acidosis decreases the ability of insulin to bind to insulin receptors... and human studies have shown that some markers of metabolic acidosis are associated with insulin resistance.

Bottom line: The study doesn't mean that you should shy away from fish, which has been shown to have cardiovascular health benefits. But it does give you one more excellent reason to make sure that your diet includes plenty of fruits and vegetables and a moderate amount of dairy.

Skipping Breakfast Raises Risk for Type 2 Diabetes by 21%

Skipping breakfast is associated with a 21% increase in type 2 diabetes risk. And the best breakfast is a combination of low-saturated-fat protein and low-glycemic-index carbohydrates.

Example: A western omelet with peppers, low-fat cheese and ham. Eating fruit is common at breakfast but not ideal—it contains too much sugar and may leave you hungry again within as little as an hour.

Other ways to avoid type 2 diabetes: Increase physical activity and intake of omega-3s and vitamin D.

The late Frederic J. Vagnini, MD, a cardiovascular surgeon at the Heart, Diabetes and Weight Loss Centers of New York, New Hyde Park.

High Triglycerides: This Heart Disease Threat Can Increase Your Diabetes Risk

Helene Glassberg, MD, physician, University of Pennsylvania Health System.

Mark A. Stengler, NMD, a naturopathic medical doctor and author of the *Health Revelations* newsletter, author of *The Natural Physician's Healing Therapies*, founder and medical director of the Stengler Center for Integrative Medicine in Encinitas, California, and former adjunct associate clinical professor at the National University of Natural Medicine in Portland, Oregon. MarkStengler.com

The medical mantra for people age 50 or over is to "know your numbers," which is to say, your cholesterol, blood pressure and blood sugar levels as they relate to cardiac risk, so that you can take action to address potential problems. While many people pay attention to this advice, and because there is enduring truth to this medical sound-bite, it is important to mention that there is one number that eludes even the savviest health consumers…it is tested right along with cholesterol and blood sugar and is becoming increasingly respected as a marker for cardiac risk—triglycerides.

Like cholesterol, triglycerides are a type of fat in the blood, but they are quite different from their more famous cousin. Triglycerides are produced by the body and ingested from food, as is cholesterol, but they serve a different purpose. If the body's energy needs are exceeded by food intake, the body converts the excess calories into triglycerides and stores them to provide extra energy when called for.

However, for a variety of reasons, triglyceride levels can rise to unhealthy levels in the blood, sometimes along with a rise in cholesterol, sometimes independently of that. Normal fasting levels of triglycerides are less than 150 mg/dL…and when triglycerides rise to a fasting level of 200 mg/dL or over it's considered high. Occasionally levels go to even 500 mg/dL or higher, though this is usually because of genetic disorders or an underlying disease.

A good deal of controversy exists about the exact role of high triglycerides and atherosclerosis, but there is definitely an association between high levels of them and heart disease. People who have triglycerides over 150 mg/dL and HDL cholesterol under 40 mg/dL have a higher risk for heart disease. And high triglycerides are associated with a number of other diseases as well, all of which make it important to pay attention.

According to cardiologist Helene Glassberg, MD, physician at the University of Pennsylvania Health System, high triglycerides are especially associated with insulin resistance—a prediabetic state—and diabetes, in particular when it is poorly controlled. In fact, high levels of triglycerides signal the need to check for the presence of diabetes. Other problems that are sometimes associated with high levels are hypothyroidism or kidney disease. Pancreatitis is also associated with high triglycerides, which Dr. Glassberg says can exacerbate or even cause this disease.

LOWERING YOUR TRIGLYCERIDES

The good news is that this is one problem that lifestyle can often turn around. *Dr. Glassberg recommends the following…*

- **Normalize your weight**—obesity is a risk factor for elevated levels, especially if you carry excess pounds in your abdomen.
- **Reduce or eliminate alcohol**—excessive drinking has been directly associated with elevated triglycerides… in some people even modest amounts of alcohol can affect the level.
- **Eat a nutritious diet**—pay special attention to getting plenty of omega-3s and eliminate excess carbohydrates, saturated fat and all trans fat.
- **Exercise at least 30 minutes each day**—push away from the table before dessert and go for a walk instead.
- **Avoid smoking.**

When lifestyle changes are not enough to lower levels sufficiently, Dr. Glassberg says that there are excellent medications patients can take that address the problem in addition to lifestyle changes. Of course pharmaceutical treatments often come with associated risks as well.

THE NATURAL APPROACH

For more natural ways to manage triglycerides, Mark Stengler, NMD, advises all individuals with high triglycerides to talk with a trained professional before trying any supplements. His favorites include aged garlic extract (AGE)—the most commonly available brand is Kyolic—with the caveat that people on blood-thinning medications clear it with their doctor first. And those on the muscle-relaxant drug *chlorzoxazone* or the antiplatelet drug *ticlopidine* must not take garlic supplements. Pantethine has also been shown to lower triglycerides.

Dr. Stengler adds his advice to Dr. Glassberg's in emphasizing how important it is to treat insulin resistance and diabetes, since triglycerides tend to be high in these people. In addition to a careful diet and regular exercise, Dr. Stengler suggests taking chromium picolinate, which research has shown may lower levels significantly. And to end on a tasty note, a recent study in Norway showed that eating two or three kiwi fruits each day lowered triglyceride levels by as much as 15%.

More Diabetes with Your Steak

Lawrence de Koning, PhD, clinical assistant professor of epidemiology, University of Calgary, Calgary, Canada.

Many health-conscious consumers adopt low-carb eating habits to lose weight and ward off heart disease and diabetes. But be careful—it can backfire. A low-carbohydrate, Atkins-style diet with lots of animal protein actually may increase your risk for type 2 diabetes.

Our study analyzed the medical records of 41,140 men (all free of heart disease, cancer and diabetes at the start) in the Health Professionals Follow-Up study. The participants completed questionnaires about their eating habits once every four years for more than 20 years, during which time 2,761 of the men developed type 2 diabetes.

After taking into account risk factors such as body mass index, physical activity, family history of diabetes, smoking, coffee and alcohol consumption and total caloric intake, we found that the men whose diets were lowest in carbohydrates (averaging 37% of calories) but high in animal protein (18% of calories) and animal fat (26% of calories) had a 41% higher risk for type 2 diabetes than men consuming a higher carbohydrate (57% of calories) diet where animal protein (10% of calories) and animal fat (12% of calories) were lower.

The findings are preliminary, based on an observational study, and further research is necessary.

WHAT TO EAT?

It isn't that low-carbohydrate, high-protein and high-fat diets are inherently harmful; it's the type of protein and fat you consume. The problem with animal sources of protein, especially red and processed meat, relates to their fat and iron content. Taking in lots of saturated fats (as found in these meats) can reduce insulin sensitivity. Additionally, iron can accumulate in body tissue, generating oxidative stress, insulin resistance and (if the iron accumulates in the pancreas) problems in secreting insulin.

Note: Iron is an important nutrient, and deficiency brings its own set of problems, so people who are anemic may be advised to eat meat. Red meat (beef, of course, but also lamb, pork and veal) is rich in heme iron, which is the most effective at reversing iron deficiency, since it is absorbed better than non heme. Moderation and balance are key.

A better way: The Nurses' Health Study (also from Harvard) found that eating greater quantities of vegetable proteins and vegetable fats as part of a low-carbohydrate diet was inversely associated with diabetes risk, said Dr. de Koning.

For most folks, the best high-protein, low-carb diet includes very little red or processed meat, a smattering of chicken and fish, and lots of vegetable proteins (including legumes and nuts) and vegetable fats. Good protein sources include tofu (10.3 grams of protein per one-half cup)...black beans (15.2 grams

25

of protein per cup)…roasted beets (3.9 grams of protein per one-half cup)…and almonds (6 grams of protein per quarter cup).

Eating a low-carb diet can be all-around healthy. It helps control your weight and, said Dr. de Koning, "may actually reduce your risk for chronic diseases if your sources of fat and protein (what you replace the carbs with) are chosen carefully." That means that red meat should be ordered rarely…rather than rare, medium or well-done.

For more information on what to eat to stop diabetes, see Chapter 3, "Foods That Fight Diabetes."

Certain Statins Are Linked to Diabetes…Is Yours?

Muhammad M. Mamdani, PharmD, MPH, professor, University of Toronto, director, Applied Heath Research Centre, St. Michael's Hospital, and senior adjunct scientist, Institute for Clinical Evaluative Sciences, all in Toronto, Canada. His study was published in *BMJ*.

Has your doctor put you on cholesterol-lowering statin medication or suggested that it's time to start? If so, you probably know that statins can have some very serious side effects, such as muscle aches, liver problems and perhaps impaired memory. But you may not have heard that the medication can increase your risk for developing a very common and potentially deadly disease—diabetes.

Now, thanks to a major recent study, we've learned that all statins are not created equal when it comes to diabetes risk. As it turns out, some are significantly riskier than others.

Which type are you taking?

STUDYING STATINS UP NORTH

Statin drugs reduce blood cholesterol levels by interfering with an enzyme that helps the liver make cholesterol. However, different types of statins work in slightly different ways and their effects on the body vary somewhat. Earlier studies suggested that statins in general made people more likely to get diabetes—but that one type, *pravastatin* (Pravachol), made people less likely to get diabetes.

So for the recent study, researchers set out to determine more specifically how the most commonly used types of statins affected the risk for diabetes relative to each other. With access to health and pharmacy records of 1.5 million older Canadians, researchers identified 471,250 people age 66 and up who did not have diabetes when they first started taking statins. Then they followed each statin user for up to five years to see which ones got diabetes. (Though this study took place in Canada, the same statin drugs are prescribed in the US.)

An earlier study suggested that patients taking pravastatin had a lower risk for diabetes compared with people taking a placebo. For that reason, in the new study, the researchers used pravastatin as the basis of comparison in gauging the diabetes risk associated with five other types of statins. After adjustments were made for various other diabetes risk factors (age, gender, health status, other medication use), here's how each drug fared relative to pravastatin…

- *Atorvastatin* (Lipitor), which accounted for more than half of all new statin prescriptions, was associated with a 22% increase in diabetes risk.

- *Rosuvastatin* (Crestor) was associated with an 18% increase in diabetes risk. However, the researchers noted that this risk may be dose-dependent, meaning present at higher dosages but not at lower dosages.

- *Simvastatin* (Zocor) was associated with a 10% increase in diabetes risk.

- Both *lovastatin* and *fluvastatin* (Lescol) were comparable to pravastatin.

THE STATIN/INSULIN CONNECTION

There are several possible explanations for why patients taking certain statins are more prone to develop diabetes. Some statins may cause damage to beta cells, which are responsible for storing and secreting insulin…and/or these statins may interfere with the process that transports glucose from the blood through the cell membrane and into the body's cells.

As for why pravastatin might reduce diabetes risk, animal studies have suggested that it improves cells' sensitivity to insulin. Lovastatin and fluvastatin may have similar beneficial effects on insulin sensitivity.

Bottom line: If you are taking or have been advised to take one of the statins associated with increased risk for diabetes (atorvastatin, rosuvastatin, simvastatin), talk with your doctor about the diet and lifestyle changes that could lower your cholesterol and perhaps reduce your need for the medication. Also, discuss whether it's appropriate to consider switching to pravastatin (or perhaps lovastatin or fluvastatin), particularly if you have other risk factors for type 2 diabetes, such as excess weight, high blood pressure, high triglycerides, a history of gestational diabetes or polycystic ovary syndrome, or a family history of diabetes.

What Women on Statins Need to Know About Diabetes

Yunsheng Ma, MD, PhD, MPH, an associate professor in the division of preventive and behavioral medicine at the University of Massachusetts Medical School in Worcester and coauthor of a meta-analysis published in *Archives of Internal Medicine.*

No doubt you're aware that cholesterol-lowering statin medications can have side effects, such as muscle pain, digestive problems and liver damage. What you may not realize is that statins also significantly increase the risk for diabetes, as a recent large-scale study showed.

Participants included 153,840 postmenopausal women ages 50 to 79, none of whom had diabetes at the start of the study. The women were tracked for an average of 7.6 years, during which time 10,242 or nearly 7% of them developed diabetes.

Finding: Even after researchers adjusted for other diabetes risk factors (such as age, race, diet, physical activity level, smoking, high blood pressure and a family history of diabetes), women who took statins were 48%

more likely to develop diabetes during the course of the study than those who did not take statins. All types of statins had this effect, regardless of the dosage, potency or how long the medication was used.

What this means for you: Remember that lifestyle changes—adopting a healthy diet, getting regular exercise, losing excess weight—are safe, effective, drug-free ways to reduce cholesterol and help guard against both heart disease and diabetes. If your doctor suggests that you start taking a statin, ask about the risks and benefits as well as possible cholesterol-lowering alternatives. If you already use a statin, do not simply stop taking it on your own, researchers cautioned. Instead, talk to your doctor about ways to reduce your need for the drug…discuss an appropriate schedule for screening for diabetes…and immediately alert your doctor if you develop any possible warning signs of diabetes, such as increased thirst, increased urination and/or blurred vision.

Don't Let Stress Raise Your Blood Sugar…and More

Irene Louise Dejak, MD, an internal medicine specialist who focuses on preventive health, including counseling patients on the dangers of chronic stress. She is a clinical assistant professor at the Cleveland Clinic Lerner College of Medicine of Case Western Reserve University in Cleveland and an associate staff member at the Cleveland Clinic Family Health Center in Strongsville, Ohio.

It's widely known that acute stress can damage the heart. For example, the risk for sudden cardiac death is, on average, twice as high on Mondays as on other days of the week, presumably because of the stress many people feel about going back to work after the weekend. People also experience more heart attacks in the morning because of increased levels of cortisol and other stress hormones.

Important recent research: In a study of almost 1,000 adult men, those who had three or more major stressful life events in a single year, such as the death of a spouse, had a 50% higher risk of dying over a 30-year period.

But even low-level, ongoing stress, such as that from a demanding job, marriage or other family conflicts, financial worries or chronic health problems, can increase inflammation in the arteries. This damages the inner lining of the blood vessels, promotes the accumulation of cholesterol and increases risk for clots, the cause of most heart attacks.

Among the recently discovered physical effects of stress...

•**Increased blood sugar.** The body releases blood sugar (glucose) during physical and emotional stress. It's a survival mechanism that, in the past, gave people a jolt of energy when they faced a life-threatening emergency.

However, the same response is dangerous when stress occurs daily. It subjects the body to constantly elevated glucose, which damages blood vessels and increases the risk for insulin resistance (a condition that precedes diabetes) as well as heart disease.

What helps: Get regular exercise, which decreases levels of stress hormones.

•**More pain.** Studies have shown that people who are stressed tend to be more sensitive to pain, regardless of its cause. In fact, imaging studies show what's known as stress-induced hyperalgesia, an increase in activity in areas of the brain associated with pain. Similarly, patients with depression seem to experience more pain—and pain that's more intense—than those who are mentally healthy.

What helps: To help curb physical pain, find a distraction. One study found that post-surgical patients who had rooms with views of trees needed less pain medication than those who had no views. On a practical level, you can listen to music. Read a lighthearted book. Paint. Knit. These steps will also help relieve any stress that may be exacerbating your pain.

Also helpful: If you have a lot of pain that isn't well-controlled with medication, ask your doctor if you might be suffering from anxiety or depression. If so, you may benefit from taking an antidepressant, such as *duloxetine* (Cymbalta) or *venlafaxine* (Effexor), which can help reduce pain along with depression.

•**Impaired memory.** After just a few weeks of stress, nerves in the part of the brain associated with memory shrink and lose connections with other nerve cells, according to laboratory studies.

Result: You might find that you're forgetting names or where you put things. These lapses are often due to distraction—people who are stressed and always busy find it difficult to store new information in the brain. This type of memory loss is rarely a sign of dementia unless it's getting progressively worse.

What helps: Use memory tools to make your life easier. When you meet someone, say that person's name out loud to embed it in your memory. Put your keys in the same place every day.

Also: Make a conscious effort to pay attention. It's the only way to ensure that new information is stored. Sometimes the guidance of a counselor is necessary to help you learn how to manage stress. Self-help materials, such as tapes and books, may also be good tools.

•**Weight gain.** The fast-paced American lifestyle may be part of the reason why two-thirds of adults in this country are overweight or obese. People who are stressed tend to eat more—and the "comfort" foods they choose often promote weight gain. Some people eat less during stressful times, but they're in the minority.

What helps: If you tend to snack or eat larger servings when you're anxious, stressed or depressed, talk to a therapist. People who binge on "stress calories" usually have done so for decades—it's difficult to stop without professional help.

Also helpful: Pay attention when you find yourself reaching for a high-calorie snack even though you're not really hungry.

Healthy zero-calorie snack: Ice chips.

Low-calorie options: Grapes, carrots and celery sticks. Once you start noticing the pattern, you can make a conscious effort to replace eating with nonfood activities—working on a hobby, taking a quick walk, etc.

STRESS-FIGHTING PLAN

There are a number of ways to determine whether you are chronically stressed—you may feel short-tempered, anxious most of the time, have heart palpitations or suffer from insomnia.

However, I've found that many of my patients don't even realize how much stress they have in their lives until a friend, family member, coworker or doctor points it out to them. Once they understand the degree to which stress is affecting their health, they can explore ways to unwind and relax.

In general, it helps to…

• **Get organized.** Much of the stress that we experience comes from feeling overwhelmed. You can overcome this by organizing your life.

Examples: Use a day calendar to keep your activities and responsibilities on-track, and put reminder notes on the refrigerator.

• **Ask for help.** You don't have to become overwhelmed. If you're struggling at work, ask a mentor for advice. Tell your partner/spouse that you need help with the shopping or housework.

Taking charge of your life is among the best ways to reduce stress—and asking for help is one of the smartest ways to do this.

• **Write about your worries.** The anxieties and stresses floating around in our heads often dissipate, or at least seem more manageable, once we write them down.

• **Sleep for eight hours.** No one who is sleep-deprived can cope with stress effectively.

If You Have Trouble Sleeping, You May Be at Risk

Women who take longer than 30 minutes to fall asleep have a higher risk for diabetes, heart disease and stroke.

Reason: These women tend to have higher levels of insulin…inflammatory proteins that are linked to heart disease…and fibrinogen, a protein that is associated with stroke and heart attack.

Best: If you often have difficulty sleeping, talk to your doctor about the risks and ways to fall asleep.

Edward Suarez, PhD, professor, department of psychiatry and behavioral sciences, Duke University Medical Center, Durham, North Carolina, and leader of a study of 210 people, published in *Brain, Behavior and Immunity.*

Up All Night? Watch Out for Diabetes

Frank B. Hu, MD, PhD, MPH, professor of nutrition and epidemiology at Harvard School of Public Health and a professor of medicine at Harvard Medical School, both in Boston. He also is coauthor of a study on shift work and diabetes published in *PLoS Medicine.*

Working a rotating shift that includes both nights and days is tough on many levels, as you've probably heard from sleep-deprived friends who do it. Now a new study reveals yet another concern with this increasingly common type of work schedule—an elevated risk of developing type 2 diabetes.

Researchers combed the data on 177,184 US women who participated in the Nurses' Health Study, analyzing age, weight, diet, exercise habits and work schedules…and tracking who got diabetes during the two-decade study period. For the study, a rotating night shift was defined as working three or more nights per month in addition to working some days and evenings in that same month.

Results: Compared with women who did not work rotating night shifts, those who worked such shifts for three to nine years were 20% more likely to develop diabetes. The risk for diabetes rose 40% when rotating night shifts were worked for 10 to 19 years…risk rose 58% with 20 or more years of such work.

Explanation: Rotating shift work disrupts the body's circadian rhythm, elevating blood

29

glucose and insulin levels as well as increasing blood pressure and reducing sleep efficiency.

Self-defense for rotating night-shift workers: Diabetes can be deadly, so be sure that your doctor is aware of your work schedule. Discuss an appropriate schedule for screening for diabetes. And immediately alert your doctor if you develop any possible warning signs of the disease (excessive thirst, increased urination, blurred vision). Also, remember that lifestyle changes—adopting a healthy diet, getting regular exercise, losing excess weight—go a long way in guarding against the development of diabetes.

Another Reason to Quit

Smoking increases risk for type 2 diabetes. Smoking can lead to insulin resistance, a precursor to type 2 diabetes.

Recent finding: Smokers have a 44% higher risk for developing diabetes than nonsmokers.

Self-defense: If you smoke, get help quitting from a health professional. Also, maintain a healthy diet and exercise regularly.

Carole Willi, MD, chief resident, department of community medicine and public health, University of Lausanne, Switzerland, and leader of a meta-analysis of 25 studies, published in *The Journal of the American Medical Association*.

Psoriasis Sufferers: Keep an Eye on Blood Sugar!

Joel M. Gelfand, MD, professor of dermatology at Perelman School of Medicine, University of Pennsylvania, Philadelphia. He was senior author of a study published in *Archives of Dermatology*.

If you have psoriasis—as millions of Americans do—the scaly, itchy patches of skin on your scalp and/or other body parts aren't the only health problems to be concerned about.

While there are the well-known increased risks, such as the risks for heart attack, stroke, arthritis and certain cancers, there's yet another disease to add to the already long list.

A recent study found that people with psoriasis are at increased risk for also developing type 2 diabetes—even if they don't have any of the risk factors that are common to both diseases, such as obesity. And the more severe the psoriasis, the greater the risk of type 2 diabetes.

How much extra risk do you have? In the study, people with mild psoriasis had an 11% greater risk of developing type 2 diabetes, compared with those who did not have psoriasis...and people with moderate-to-severe psoriasis had a 46% higher risk.

THE COMMON THREAD: INFLAMMATION

"Both diseases are caused by chronic inflammation," said senior study author Joel Gelfand, MD, "and we think that the same inflammation that causes psoriasis also prevents the body from responding to insulin as well as it should, which is what leads to type 2 diabetes."

A TWO-PART TO-DO LIST

So if you have psoriasis, what does this mean for you?

First of all: It's important to get regular blood sugar screenings to test for type 2 diabetes, since the earlier you find out that you have diabetes, the easier it is to keep it in check. "If you have psoriasis, I recommend beginning blood sugar screenings at age 18 and then getting checked at least every three years after that—depending on your particular health conditions and what your doctor advises," he said. For many people, blood sugar is checked as part of their annual physical.

"Think of your psoriasis as a window into what's happening in your body," he continued. "Those rashes on your skin aren't necessarily just exterior problems—they may be a sign of other metabolic issues that are happening in the interior of your bloodstream."

Second of all: In the meantime, do everything you can to help prevent (or at least delay) type 2 diabetes from developing. That means—you guessed it—following a healthy diet, exercising regularly and losing excess weight, Dr. Gelfand said.

He also stressed that these recommendations are especially important for people with psoriasis who are 40 or older because the risk of developing diabetes increases with age.

Does reducing psoriasis symptoms lower your risk of type 2 diabetes? "There is some evidence that it might help, so it's worth a shot, but scientists don't yet know," he said.

Natural Cures for Psoriasis

April Abernethy, ND, a naturopathic physician and former interim chief scientific and medical officer at the National Psoriasis Foundation in Portland, Oregon. She is also a member of the board of directors at International Dermatology Outcome Measures, an organization working to establish common measurements of treatment effectiveness and outcomes.

Living day in and day out with psoriasis—known for its silvery scales and itchy, painful red patches (plaques) on the skin—is hard enough for the more than 7.5 million Americans who have the disease.

But researchers are now finding that people with psoriasis also may be more likely to develop other inflammation-based conditions such as diabetes and cardiovascular disease. People with psoriasis should be screened for these conditions and talk to their doctors about ways to reduce other risk factors they may have for these diseases.

Problem: Even though drugs, such as *apremilast* (Otezla) and *adalimumab* (Humira), that inhibit parts of the immune system involved in psoriasis are now available, any therapy that suppresses immunity can increase the risk for infections, gastrointestinal upset and other conditions.

Solution: There's mounting evidence that natural therapies can be used to reduce overall inflammation and help support the immune system. These drug-free approaches can improve the effectiveness of psoriasis medication and sometimes even eliminate the need for it (with your doctor's approval). First, try the dietary approaches in this article—they

should result in improvements that increase over time. Supplements also can be used.

PUTTING YOUR DIET TO WORK

Eating the right foods (and using supplements when needed) can increase your ability to fight psoriasis on a systemic level by reducing inflammation and helping regulate your immune system—two key factors linked to psoriasis. *My advice…*

•**Go for anti-inflammatory foods.** Americans eat lots of processed foods—most of which promote inflammation in the body. Meanwhile, whole, nutrient-packed foods such as fresh fruits and vegetables help attack the inflammatory process that is increased in psoriasis.

Good choices: Beets, blueberries, kale or other leafy greens, salmon, garbanzo beans, quinoa, lentils, nuts and ginger. For other food choices, go to *www.psoriasis.org*, and search "anti-inflammatory diet."

•**Get more vitamin D.** People with psoriasis, like many Americans, are often deficient in vitamin D, which is known to help regulate immune function and inhibit inflammation. That's why it's important to consume foods that contain vitamin D, such as oysters, shrimp, salmon, sardines and any fortified milk. Vitamin D supplements also may be needed. If you have psoriasis, ask your doctor for a blood test to check your vitamin D level.

•**Spice things up.** Turmeric, which gives mustard its bright yellow color and curry its distinctive flavor, contains the medicinal compound curcumin.

A 2013 study published in the journal *Bio-Factors* showed that turmeric helps healthy, new skin cells form more quickly. If you don't like curry or mustard (you would need to eat 1 g to 3 g a day to get the therapeutic effect), you can try turmeric in supplement form—400 mg to 600 mg two to three times a day.

Talk to your doctor first if you take antacids, diabetes drugs or blood thinners, since turmeric may interfere with these medications—and if you have a history of gallstones (turmeric may cause stomach upset in these people).

•**Load up on omega-3s.** Get lots of anti-inflammatory omega-3 fatty acids. Daily amounts needed to fight psoriasis: Seven ounces of salmon...a small avocado...or two tablespoons of ground flaxseed (store in the refrigerator to prevent spoilage). If you don't like fish and other omega-3–rich foods, consider taking 2 g to 3 g daily of a fish oil supplement. Choose one that has more EPA than DHA, and check with your doctor first if you take a blood thinner or diabetes medication—fish oil could interact with them.

A 2014 study published in the *Journal of the American Academy of Dermatology* found that among many common supplements taken by people with psoriasis, fish oil—which may reduce tumor necrosis factor-alpha (TNF-alpha), a protein associated with systemic inflammation—demonstrated the greatest benefit.

FOR CRACKED SKIN AND PLAQUES

Among the more troubling symptoms of psoriasis are dry, cracked skin (that may even bleed) and the red, scaly, itchy plaques that can develop on the elbows, scalp, torso and other areas.

What works best...

• **Oregon grape root.** When used topically, this powerful, little-known antibacterial herb (also called Mahonia) helps reduce skin irritation and topical infections common to people with psoriasis.

A 2013 research review published in the *British Journal of Dermatology* showed that Oregon grape root reduced the development of red, raised psoriasis plaques and healed psoriasis-related cracked skin.

Oregon grape root is found in tincture form at health-food stores, and you can add two or three drops to your favorite skin cream. The herb also can be found in over-the-counter creams containing 10% Mahonia, which has been shown to help control mild-to-moderate psoriasis plaques.

FOR ITCHING AND FLAKING

Soaking in the high concentration of mineral salts found in the Dead Sea in Israel is a centuries-old remedy for the itching and flaking associated with psoriasis.

What helps: Adding one-quarter to one-half cup of Dead Sea (or Epsom) salts to a warm (not hot) bath has been shown to ease itching skin and remove dead, flaking skin cells. Dead Sea salts have a higher concentration of minerals than Epsom salts and are available online and at health-food stores and spas.

A substantial body of research, including a study published in the *Journal of Dermatological Treatment*, has shown that psoriasis patients who regularly take such baths report significant improvements in itch and irritation levels within three weeks.

For even greater benefits: Mix the salts with colloidal oatmeal, such as Aveeno. Take these baths two to three times a week.

Can Your Toiletries and Cosmetics Give You Diabetes?

Monica Lind, PhD, associate professor of occupational and environmental medicine, Uppsala University, Uppsala, Sweden. Her research was published in *Diabetes Care*.

We've known for years that chemicals called phthalates—types of plasticizers contained in many products, including furniture, toys, plastic bags and detergents, as well as in some cosmetics, including lotions, hair sprays and perfumes—can knock our endocrine systems out of whack, potentially raising our risk for obesity and hardening of the arteries.

What's worse—a recent study suggests that we can now add type 2 diabetes to the list of phthalate dangers.

The cosmetics part is especially creepy, since we do more than simply touch that stuff—we often massage lotions or makeup into our skin and spray perfume onto our necks, where we breathe it right in. And if you should kiss someone wearing phthalate-containing cosmetics or perfume—what's getting into your mouth?

The chemical and cosmetics industries dispute the latest research and tell us that we should be perfectly happy to smear and spray their phthalates onto our bodies. It might be that they turn out to be right and that the products are safe. But that's a long-term result that's not worth the risk to find out. We spoke with the researchers who found the diabetes link...and then learned how to find phthalate-free cosmetics and perfumes.

WHAT LURKS IN OUR COSMETICS

The phthalates are put into many types of cosmetics because they do have some benefits. In perfume, for example, they help the scent linger longer...in nail polish, the chemicals reduce cracking by making polishes less brittle...and in hair spray, phthalates allow the spray to form a flexible film on hair, avoiding stiffness. But phthalates in these products can be either absorbed through the skin or inhaled, which causes them to enter the bloodstream...and then, watch out!

In the study, the researchers from Uppsala University in Sweden drew fasting blood samples from more than 1,000 adults, looking for several toxins, including four substances specifically formed when the body breaks down phthalates. Even after adjusting for typical type 2 diabetes risk factors such as obesity, cholesterol levels, smoking and exercise habits, researchers found that participants whose phthalate levels were among the highest 20% of the group were twice as likely to have type 2 diabetes when compared with those whose phthalate levels fell into the lowest 20% of the group.

Study author Monica Lind, PhD, an associate professor of occupational and environmental medicine at the university, said that since she and her colleagues are among the first scientists to measure phthalate levels in blood, "high" and "low" are relative to this study—in other words, it's difficult to discern whether the levels of phthalates in this study were "high" on any kind of absolute scale. And researchers didn't track the amount of phthalate-containing products that participants used. But the study does suggest that the higher the levels of phthalates in the blood, the higher the risk of getting type 2 diabetes, and that might reflect a greater use of products that contain them.

CHECK THE LABELS

Phthalates may increase the risk for type 2 diabetes by disrupting insulin production and/or inducing insulin resistance, Dr. Lind said. But those ideas are disputed by the FDA, which states that "it's not clear what effect, if any, phthalates have on health."

In the US, the FDA does not require cosmetics or perfumes to be phthalate-free. It does require nonfragrance ingredients to be listed on cosmetic products, but the loophole is that any ingredients that are parts of a fragrance don't have to be listed—a manufacturer can simply put "fragrance" on the label. As a result, according to the nonprofit Campaign for Safe Cosmetics, most cosmetics and perfumes that contain phthalates don't list them on the label. In other words, if the word "fragrance" is listed, then you won't know for sure what's in the product, unfortunately.

If this is a concern for you, go through your makeup, perfumes and lotions. Search online for cosmetics that are "fragrance-free" using the nonprofit Environmental Working Group's Skin Deep cosmetics database at *www.ewg.org/skindeep* and then choose among the products that are also phthalate-free. For perfumes, specifically, search online using the phrase "phthalate-free perfumes," which should lead to many brands, such as Zorica of Malibu, Kai, Pacifica, Agape & Zoe Naturals, Rich Hippie, Honoré des Prés, Blissoma Blends, Red Flower Organic Perfumes, Tsi-La Organic Perfume and Ayala Moriel Parfums.

How to Keep the Toxic Chemical BPA Out of Your Food

Frederick S. vom Saal, PhD, curators' distinguished professor emeritus of biological sciences at the University of Missouri, Columbia. He is a leading researcher on the effects of BPA and has conducted dozens of studies on this topic.

BPA (bisphenol-A) is used in many plastic food and beverage containers, particularly those made of hard, clear polycarbonate plastic. BPA is also an additive in polyvinyl chloride (PVC) plastic, which is used in some plastic food wraps.

Surprising news: BPA is in the epoxy resins found in the lining of almost all cans used by the food industry (including baby formula cans!). In fact, canned food is the primary food source of BPA for adults.

The problem: BPA molecules that escape their chemical bonds can migrate into the foods and beverages they contact, especially if the container is heated or the food inside is acidic. We then ingest the BPA—thereby increasing our risk for numerous health problems. There's even BPA on the coated paper from cash registers—the toxin gets into our bodies when we touch the paper and then handle the food we're about to eat. BPA can also be absorbed through the skin.

Frederick S. vom Saal, PhD, curators' distinguished professor emeritus of biological sciences at the University of Missouri and a leading BPA researcher, explained that this chemical has estrogen-like effects on the body. It acts as an endocrine disruptor, interrupting our hormonal patterns —and actually reprogramming our genes. Roughly 1,000 published, peer-reviewed studies have linked BPA to negative health consequences. *These include…*

• **Breast cancer, ovarian cysts and uterine fibroids in females (and prostate cancer, sexual dysfunction and altered sperm in males).**

• **Type 2 diabetes and its precursor, insulin resistance.**

• **Heart disease and heart rhythm abnormalities.**

• **Liver disease.**

• **Thyroid dysfunction.**

• **Obesity and greater accumulation of fat in cells.**

Unborn babies, infants and children are especially susceptible to BPA's harmful effects because they are still growing. Exposure before birth and/or during childhood has been linked to…

• **Birth defects.**

• **Cognitive problems, including learning deficits.**

• **Behavioral problems, such as hyperactivity.**

• **Early puberty in females.**

• **Increased risk for cancer in adulthood.**

How much is too much? The EPA estimates that exposure of up to 50 micrograms (mcg) of BPA per kilogram (kg) of body weight per day is safe. However, recent studies suggest that even a tiny fraction of this amount—as little as 0.025 mcg/kg per day—may be dangerous.

Dr. vom Saal said, "No matter what you might hear from the plastics industry, which is trying to convince consumers that BPA is safe, hundreds of published papers show that BPA is a toxin with no safe levels."

Scary: When the CDC studied urine samples of more than 2,500 Americans age six and older, 93% of those tested had BPA in their urine.

BPA SELF-DEFENSE

Here are Dr. vom Saal's suggestions for minimizing your exposure to BPA…

• **Avoid canned foods as much as possible.**

Note: It does not help to store cans in the refrigerator or to use canned goods soon after you buy them. The harm is already done even before the cans reach the market because high heat must be used to sterilize the food during canning.

Exceptions: Several manufacturers—including Eco Fish, Eden Foods, Edward & Sons, Muir Glen, Oregon's Choice Gourmet Albacore and Wild Planet—have begun using BPA-free cans for some of their products. (See a manufacturer's website for information on its BPA-free canned products, or contact the company directly.)

• **Choose cardboard over metal.** Cardboard cartons (such as those used for juice or milk) and cardboard cylindrical "cans" (such as those used for raisins) generally are better options than metal cans—but they are not ideal because they may contain some recycled paper (which is loaded with BPA)…or they may be lined with a resin that contains BPA.

Best: Opt for foods that are fresh or frozen or that come in glass bottles or jars or in foil pouches.

• **Never give canned liquid formula to an infant.** Powdered is much safer.

• **When microwaving, never let plastic wrap come in contact with your food.** If a product has a plastic film covering that is supposed to be left in place during microwave cooking, remove the film and replace it with a glass or ceramic cover instead.

• **Transfer prepackaged food to a glass or ceramic container before cooking,** even if the instructions say to microwave the product in the plastic pouch it comes in.

• **Check the triangle-enclosed recycling numeral on plastic items that come in contact with foods or beverages**—storage containers, water pitchers, baby bottles, sippy cups, utensils and tableware. The numeral "7" indicates a plastic that may or may not contain BPA. To be safe, Dr. vom Saal said, "If you see a numeral '7' and it doesn't say BPA-free, assume there is BPA." The letters "PC" stamped near the recycling number are another indication that the plastic contains BPA.

• **Recheck what's in your cupboards.** Those new travel mugs? They might be made from number-seven plastic.

• **Plastics labeled number two or five, which also are often used for food containers, do not have BPA.** But they may contain other potentially harmful chemicals that can leach out, especially when heat breaks down the molecular bonds of plastic. To be safe, wash all plastic kitchenware in cold to room-temperature water with a mild cleanser, not in the dishwasher. Never microwave plastic containers—not even those labeled microwave-safe, such as frozen entrée trays. Instead use a glass or ceramic container. Before putting hot soup or gravy into plastic containers to freeze, first allow it to cool. Throw out any plastic kitchenware that is scratched, chipped or discolored—damaged plastic is most likely to leach chemicals.

• **Do not assume that plastics with no triangle-enclosed numeral are safe.** Dr. vom Saal cautioned, "Manufacturers know that consumers are looking for BPA, so they're taking identifying numbers off their products and packaging." Don't fall prey to such tricks.

More Ways to Avoid Toxic Plastics...

Patricia Hunt, PhD, a leading BPA researcher, reproductive biologist and geneticist and the Edward R. Meyer Distinguished Professor in the School of Molecular Biosciences at Washington State University in Pullman.

While you may not be able to avoid plastics altogether, you can minimize your risk. *Self-defense...*

• **Do not put plastics in the dishwasher or microwave.** High heat accelerates the migration of chemicals out of household plastics, such as food containers and spatulas. You know the plasticky smell that wafts from a plastic container that is fresh from the dishwasher or microwave? That is the odor of chemicals escaping.

Caution: Do not assume that products labeled "microwave safe" truly are safe—this label means only that the plastic won't melt in the microwave...it does not mean that it is chemical-free.

• **Don't let plastic wrap touch food.** Even at room temperature or in the refrigerator, Saran-type wraps potentially can release chemicals into the foods they touch. I recommend seeking alternatives to clear plastic wraps (such as foil or glass containers)...or using plastic wrap only to cover containers...or wrapping food in a paper towel or waxed paper before putting it into a plastic bag.

Note: A "wet" food is more likely to absorb toxic chemicals than a "dry" one.

• **Freeze safely.** Cold is less likely than heat to accelerate the migration of chemicals from containers into food. However, even very low levels of BPA can produce profound changes in the body. The longer a food is in contact with any BPA-containing plastic, the greater the risk of exposure, even when frozen.

Recommended: Freeze foods in wide-mouth, dual-purpose, glass jars made for freezing and canning.

- **Replace the plastic you use most often.** Once you realize how much plastic you have in the kitchen, it's tempting to give up on getting rid of it all—so a good first step is to find safer alternatives for the plastic things that you use regularly.

Examples: I replaced my plastic ice cube trays with metal trays, the old-fashioned kind with a lever to loosen the cubes. I use wood cutting boards instead of plastic. When I pack my lunch, I include a reusable bamboo spork, a spoon-and-fork combination.

- **Discard damaged containers.** We all have our favorite storage containers that are the perfect size and shape, and we tend to hang on to them even when the lids no longer fit right and the sides are warped. But damaged plastic is breaking down…and when this happens, chemicals are released. If you can't give up all your plastic, at least don't use damaged items.

Be wary of "BPA-free" plastics. Some companies have developed plastics that don't contain BPA. Unfortunately, other chemicals in plastics may be just as risky.

Example: Some BPA-free containers use plastics made from structurally related compounds, such as bisphenol-AF or bisphenol-S. Are they safer? We don't know—but recent studies suggest that bisphenol-AF actually may be more dangerous. Until we know more, I advise using food and drink containers made from glass or stainless steel.

- **Choose waxed paper bags.** We are so used to using plastic bags (for sandwiches, cut vegetables, leftover fruit, etc.) that we forget that these are fairly recent inventions. People used to use waxed paper bags, which are much safer. I use them when I pack my lunch—though I did have to check a few supermarkets before I found one that still carries them.

- **Buy from the butcher.** Supermarkets usually have the best prices on meats, but most of those meats are bedded on Styrofoam-like trays and then wrapped in plastic—so the meats are exposed to chemicals from above and below.

Better: Get your meats from a traditional butcher shop and ask to have them wrapped in old-fashioned butcher paper, not the new plastic-coated paper.

- **Opt for opaque.** The food industry prefers clear or translucent packaging because it looks "cleaner." But in many cases, clear plastics are more likely to contain BPA and/or other harmful compounds than opaque plastics.

- **Check recycling codes.** Some plastic containers are stamped with recycling codes that indicate the types of plastic used. Unfortunately, these codes don't tell very much about how safe a particular plastic is.

Helpful: Use the mnemonic, "5, 4, 1, 2—all the rest are bad for you." The "good" recycling codes may or may not contain harmful chemicals, but the "bad" ones almost certainly do.

- **Watch out for cans, too.** The vast majority of canned foods and beverages come in containers lined with a BPA-containing resin. I know that Eden Foods really works to ensure that its canned goods are safe (*www.edenfoods.com*). Other companies, such as H.J. Heinz, Conagra and Hain Celestial, use BPA-free linings in some of their cans. (See a manufacturer's website for information on its BPA-free canned products, or contact the company directly.)

- **Skip the receipt.** The thermal paper used for many supermarket receipts (and ATM and other receipts, too) often is coated with BPA to keep the ink from running. BPA is readily absorbed by the skin, particularly when you have cream or oil on your hands. Studies show that people who handle a lot of receipts tend to have higher-than-expected BPA levels. Unless you really need a receipt, don't take it. If you must handle it, wash your hands afterward—and whatever you do, don't hold that receipt in your mouth while fumbling for your car keys.

Toxic Tea Bags

Sonya Lunder, MPH, senior analyst, Environmental Working Group, Washington, DC. Lunder's research focuses on toxic chemicals in food, water, air and consumer products. EWG.org

Perhaps you wouldn't dream of microwaving plastic food containers, because you know that heating plastic can allow toxins to leach into your food. But you probably don't think twice before dunking your fancy mesh tea bag into boiling-hot water. Well, you may want to give that some thought right now.

Yes, those pyramid-shaped mesh sachets filled with pretty multi-hued leaves lend sophistication to your daily tea-drinking ritual.

But: Even though they're often called "silky," those bags aren't made from silk. Most are actually made from plastic, either *polyethylene terephthalate* (PET), *polylactic acid* (PLA, or "corn plastic") or food-grade nylon (indeed, nylon is a plastic).

PET, PLA and nylon are widely used for food packaging, and their safety as packaging materials has been tested. "However, when you subject plastics to stressors such as heat, the molecules begin to break down and they can leach—no matter whether it's a microwave oven or a cup of hot water that is warming the contents," said Sonya Lunder, MPH, a senior analyst at the Environmental Working Group, an environmental health research and advocacy organization. "So, is stuff leaching out of the plastic in the tea bag and getting into your beverage? The answer is yes."

Problems with plastics: No studies have looked specifically at leaching from plastic tea bags, so we don't yet know how much of any particular toxin might be getting into our tea. But past experience should teach us to be wary. After all, people used to think it was perfectly OK to microwave food in plastic containers—until we learned that certain plastics contain *bisphenol-A* (BPA), an endocrine disruptor that has estrogen-like effects on the body and that has been linked to breast cancer, prostate cancer, diabetes, obesity, heart disease, liver disease, thyroid dysfunction, in-fertility, early puberty, and cognitive and behavioral problems in children!

The plastics used for tea bags don't contain BPA. But PET plastics can contain phthalates (not because these chemicals are used as ingredients in the plastic, but rather because they may originate from recycled content)—and phthalates are another type of endocrine disruptor that has been linked to birth defects. There is also some concern that PET may leach antimony trioxide, a heavy metal. "We just don't know whether the amount of various substances in PET, PLA and/or food-grade nylon might someday prove to have negative health effects," Lunder said. "As yet, there is no scientific consensus about what is too much, who is at risk or what other health effects we may be seeing from plastic food packaging. But given the worrisome potential effects on our hormones, I advise that people avoid heating plastics at every opportunity."

It boils down to this: If you enjoy an occasional cup of tea made from a fancy "silky" tea bag, you probably don't need to worry too much—that once-in-a-while treat isn't likely to hurt your health. However, it's possible that your body may reach potentially harmful levels of various chemicals if you are drinking tea made from plastic tea bags multiple times each day—particularly if you try to be frugal by making a second cup from a single tea bag, given that repeated stress in the form of heat can make plastics leach even more.

What about good old paper tea bags? They might not be any better than plastic because many are treated with *epichlorohydrin*, a compound that has been linked to cancer, infertility and suppressed immune function.

Your best bet: Buy yourself a nice metal tea ball. They typically cost only a few dollars. When you want a cup of tea, fill the ball with your favorite organic loose-leaf tea and let it steep in the mug. When the drink is as strong as you like, remove the strainer and enjoy your tea—worry-free.

Can Drinking Water Lead to Diabetes?

Ana Navas-Acien, MD, PhD, associate professor, Johns Hopkins Bloomberg School of Public Health, Johns Hopkins University, Baltimore, Maryland.

W e've long considered most cases of diabetes a lifestyle disease, associated with poor diet and a lack of exercise, but now researchers have found that other factors beyond heredity may also play a role, specifically environmental ones. We spoke with one of the leading researchers in this area, Ana Navas-Acien, MD, PhD, associate professor and researcher at the Johns Hopkins Bloomberg School of Public Health at Johns Hopkins University, about how environmental toxins impact the development of diabetes and what we can do to protect ourselves.

IS IT SAFE TO DRINK THE WATER?

In one recent study, scientists found that arsenic, a naturally occurring element in the environment that results when minerals dissolve in rocks and soil, was related to the prevalence of type 2 diabetes. This is potentially very important, since an estimated 8% of public water supplies in the US have levels of inorganic arsenic higher than the safety standard established by the Environmental Protection Agency (EPA), which is 10 micrograms per liter. Previous research has linked exposure to this heavy metal with bladder, lung, kidney and skin cancer, as well as other health problems. To determine the relationship between arsenic and diabetes, Dr. Navas-Acien and her team of collaborators analyzed data from 788 adults age 20 and older whose urine was tested for traces of this toxin.

They found that...

• **Participants with type 2 diabetes had a 26% higher arsenic level than people who did not have the disease.**

• **Those with the highest levels of arsenic were more than three times as likely to have diabetes than those with the lowest levels.** Drinking water can be contaminated with arsenic in some mining areas and in areas with inappropriate arsenic waste disposal...also,

air pollution can be an additional source of arsenic exposure in certain areas.

The theory is that inorganic arsenic may contribute to diabetes by interfering with insulin sensitivity. When the body's cells are exposed to both insulin and arsenic, they absorb less blood glucose than when exposed to insulin alone and, of course, impaired ability to manage glucose is a hallmark of diabetes. Inorganic arsenic may also contribute to diabetes by encouraging inflammation. (*Note*: Inorganic arsenic is distinct from *arsenobetaine*, an organic arsenic compound often found in seafood that is not believed to pose health risks.)

These findings were published in *The Journal of the American Medical Association*. Further research is necessary to confirm the causal role of arsenic in diabetes development.

PESTICIDES AND DIABETES

Pesticides are also being implicated as a possible factor in increasing rates of diabetes, Dr. Navas-Acien said. Scientists at the US National Institutes of Health looked into the incidence of diabetes in workers who applied pesticides on farms and in other agricultural settings. They found that workers who used chlorinated pesticides for more than 100 days over the course of their lifetimes faced a significantly higher risk of diabetes. The associations between particular pesticides and diabetes ranged from a 20% to 200% jump in risk. Also, scientists at University of Cambridge in the UK have noted the need for more research on a possible link between persistent organic pollutants (POPs, a chemical group that includes many pesticides) and the risk of type 2 diabetes. Although POPs such as DDT have been banned, they persist in our environment, slowly biodegrading and entering the food supply. Other environmental chemicals, such as brominated flame retardants used in a range of consumer products, from electronic equipment to clothing, or bisphenol A, found in plastics, may be associated with the development of diabetes as well.

WHILE WE WAIT FOR MORE INFORMATION...

While researchers continue to study what role environmental toxins may play in susceptibility to type 2 diabetes, it is important to do what we can to limit exposure to those we know are potentially dangerous. *Reasonable steps to take to protect yourself and your family include…*

• **Ask your water utility company for a water quality report.** You can also review independent tests on bottled water brands at the National Resources Defense Council (NRDC) website, *www.nrdc.org/water/drinking/bw/appa.asp.*

• **Filter your tap water before drinking.** Reverse osmosis filters are effective at removing arsenic, but pitcher filters and water softeners are not.

• **Go green.** For example, instead of deadly pesticides, use pest-resistant grasses to manage your lawn. Read more about "integrated pest management" (IPM) at *http://www.epa.gov/pesticides/factsheets/ipm.htm…*replace chemical-laden cleaning products in your home with the common kitchen staples baking soda and white vinegar.

While the jury is still out on any direct causal relationship between environmental toxins and diabetes, there is a strong suggestion of such links. This just adds more to the already long list of health risks you may be able to avoid altogether by living life as naturally and healthfully as possible.

Want Diabetes?
Drink Soda

Frank Hu, MD, PhD, professor of nutrition and epidemiology at the Harvard School of Public Health.

Vasanti Malik, research scientist, department of nutrition, in the Harvard School of Public Health.

Lora Krulak, healthy foods chef and "nutritional muse" in Miami, Florida. LoraKrulak.com

Ann Lee, ND, LAc, naturopathic doctor and licensed acupuncturist in Lancaster, Pennsylvania. DoctorNaturalMedicine.com

---

To prevent diabetes, we're often told by health experts what not to eat, such as too many refined carbohydrates from breads, pasta and ice cream.

What not to drink may be just as important.

Latest finding: Researchers at the Harvard School of Public Health analyzed health data from 310,000 people who participated in 11 studies that explored the connection between sugar-sweetened beverages (SSBs) and diabetes.

Fact: SSBs include soda, fruit drinks (not 100% fruit juice), sweetened ice teas, energy drinks and vitamin water drinks. And in the last few decades, the average daily intake of calories from SSBs in the US has more than doubled, from 64 to 141. The beverages are now "the primary source of added sugars in the US diet," wrote the Harvard researchers in *Diabetes Care.*

The researchers found…

• **Drinking one to two 12-ounce servings of SSBs per day was linked to a 26% increased risk of type 2 diabetes,** compared with people who drink one or less SSB per month.

The increased risk for diabetes among those drinking SSBs was true even for people who weren't overweight, a common risk factor for diabetes. The researchers concluded that while SSBs are a risk factor for overweight, they're also a risk factor for diabetes whether you gain weight or not.

"The association that we observed between sodas and risk of diabetes is likely a cause-and-effect relationship," says Frank Hu, PhD, professor of nutrition and epidemiology at the Harvard School of Public Health.

Theory: A typical 12-ounce serving of soda delivers 10 teaspoons of sugar. That big dose of quickly absorbed sugar drives up blood sugar (glucose) levels…in turn driving up blood levels of insulin, the hormone that moves glucose out of the bloodstream and into cells…leading to insulin resistance, with cells no longer responding to the hormone and blood sugar levels staying high…eventually leading to diabetes.

SSBs also increase C-reactive protein, a biomarker of chronic, low-grade inflammation, which is also linked to a higher risk for diabetes.

• **"Cola-type beverages" also contain high levels of advanced glycation end products,** a type of compound linked to diabetes, say the researchers.

And many SSBs are loaded with fructose, a type of sugar that can cause extra abdominal fat, another risk factor for diabetes.

Bottom line: "People should limit how much sugar-sweetened beverages they drink and replace them with healthy alternatives, such as water, to reduce the risk of diabetes, as well as obesity, gout, tooth decay and cardiovascular disease," says Vasanti Malik, PhD, a study researcher.

GOOD-FOR-YOU BEVERAGES

"I help many of my clients break the habit of regularly drinking soda, sweetened ice tea and other sugary beverages," says Lora Krulak, a healthy foods chef and self-described "nutritional muse" in Miami, Florida. "I show them how to make other beverages that have natural sugar or are naturally sweetened, so they don't miss the sugary drinks."

One of her favorite thirst-quenching combinations:

2 to 3 liters of water (sparkling or non)
Juice of 2 lemons
Juice of 2 limes
Small bunch of mint
Pinch of salt
1 tablespoon of maple syrup, honey, or coconut sugar or stevia to taste (stevia is a natural, low-calorie sweetener)

Let the mixture steep for 30 minutes before drinking.

"It's good to make a lot of this drink, so it's in your refrigerator and you can grab it any time," says Krulak. When leaving home, put some in a water bottle and carry it with you.

CUT SUGAR CRAVINGS

"If one of my patients is craving sugary drinks, it means his or her blood sugar levels aren't under control," says Ann Lee, ND, LAc, a naturopathic doctor and licensed acupuncturist in Lancaster, Pennsylvania.

To balance blood sugar levels and control sugar cravings, she recommends eating every three to four hours, emphasizing high-protein foods (lean meats, chicken, fish, eggs, nuts and seeds), good fats (such as the monounsaturated fats found in avocados and olive oil)

and high-fiber foods (such as beans, whole grains and vegetables).

She also advises her clients to take nutritional supplements that strengthen the adrenal glands, which play a key role in regulating blood sugar levels.

Recommended: Daily B-complex supplement (B-50 or B-100) and vitamin C (2,000 to 5,000 milligrams daily, in three divided doses, with meals).

For healthy drinks, she recommends green tea sweetened with honey or stevia, or a combination of three parts seltzer and one part fruit juice.

What to Do at Noon to Help Prevent Diabetes

Rob M. Van Dam, PhD, adjunct associate professor in the Department of Nutrition at the Harvard School of Public Health, Boston.

Lori Barr, MD, physician in Austin, Texas, and author of *Think & Grow Well*. LoriBarr.com

Kenneth Davids, editor and principal writer of the web publication *www.coffeereview.com* and author of three books on coffee, including the bestselling *Coffee: A Guide to Buying, Brewing, and Enjoying*.

Lars Rydén, MD, professor of cardiology and diabetes specialist at the Karolinska Institute in Sweden.

Move over red wine, green tea and blueberry juice—black coffee may be the healthiest beverage of all...particularly if you want to prevent diabetes.

Standout scientific evidence: An international team of researchers from Australia, France, Holland, Scotland and the US analyzed data from 18 studies involving more than 500,000 people—and found a strong link between coffee consumption and the risk of diabetes. *Compared with people who didn't drink any coffee...*

• **Each daily cup of coffee consumed (caffeinated or decaffeinated) was linked to a 5% to 10% reduced risk**

• **Drinking 3 to 4 cups daily, to a 25% reduced risk**

• **Drinking 6 cups daily, to a 40% reduced risk.**

"It could be envisioned that we will advise our patients most at risk for diabetes to increase their consumption of coffee in addition to increasing their levels of physical activity and weight loss," wrote the researchers in the *Archives of Internal Medicine* (now *JAMA Internal Medicine*).

How safe? "There are sometimes claims that coffee may do harm by increasing the risk for cardiovascular disease, but there is no evidence for this," says Lars Rydén, MD, a professor of cardiology and diabetes specialist at the Karolinska Institute in Sweden. "People may drink coffee safely."

Why it works: There are many ways that the compounds in coffee might protect against diabetes, says Rob M. Van Dam, PhD, adjunct associate professor in the Department of Nutrition at the Harvard School of Public Health…

• **Magnesium** works with enzymes that are a must for glucose metabolism and insulin sensitivity.

• **Lignans** (a plant compound) are anti-inflammatory antioxidants.

• **Chlorogenic acids** (antioxidants) reduce chronic inflammation (linked to the development of diabetes)…help produce enzymes that cut glucose output by the liver…reduce the intestinal absorption of glucose and improve insulin sensitivity.

Recent finding: In a three-month study, 47 habitual coffee drinkers stopped drinking coffee for one month, consumed four cups a day for the second month, and eight cups a day for the third month.

Higher coffee intake increased blood levels of chlorogenic acid and decreased two biomarkers of chronic inflammation. "Coffee consumption appears to have beneficial effects on subclinical inflammation," concluded researchers from the German Diabetes Center in the *American Journal of Clinical Nutrition*.

IS TIMING EVERYTHING?

In another recent study on coffee and diabetes, Brazilian researchers analyzed 11 years of health data from nearly 70,000 women.

Results: Those who drank more than one cup of coffee a day had a 34% lower risk of developing diabetes compared with those who didn't drink any.

Surprising finding: But the link between coffee consumption and diabetes was true only in women who drank coffee at lunchtime!

"Our findings strongly suggest that only coffee taken with lunch may reduce diabetes risk," wrote the researchers in the *American Journal of Clinical Nutrition*.

A GOOD-FOR-YOU CUP OF COFFEE

Research links every kind of coffee to a reduced risk of diabetes—caffeinated or decaffeinated, filtered or instant, taken black or with cream and sugar. But it's healthier for a person who wants to prevent or control diabetes to avoid regular intake of the high-calorie, high-sugar, high-fat coffee concoctions so commonly served at today's coffee shops, says Lori Barr, MD, a physician and self-described "vibrant living expert" in Austin, Texas.

Maybe you don't like unsweetened coffee. What should you do if you want to enjoy its protective effect?

Unsweetened coffee may be more flavorful than you imagine—if you drink the right kind of coffee, says Kenneth Davids, editor and principal writer of the web publication *www.coffeereview.com* and author of *Coffee: A Guide to Buying, Brewing, and Enjoying*.

"The reason more people don't drink more black coffee is because they're not drinking good coffee," says Davids. "If you buy a good coffee, it has a natural balance of bitterness and sweetness that doesn't require sugar."

When Davids says good coffee, he means…

• **Fully ripened beans.** "The coffee bean is a fruit," he says. "If the bean is picked when it's ripe, sweet and juicy, and the green and overripe beans are separated out, the coffee will have natural sweetness to it, regardless of the variety or where it's grown."

• **Medium roast.** "Many people are into dark roasts, and dark roasts are typically served in coffee shops such as Starbucks," he says. "But a dark roast is bitter."

Bottom line: "I always encourage people to try a coffee with ripe beans, at medium roast, and discover whether they really need sugar—because a lot of people have never tasted coffee like that."

FINDING GOOD COFFEE

Davids provided this list of coffee companies that sell coffees that meet his criteria of ripeness and medium roast.

Large national roasters: Green Mountain Coffee Roasters (*www.keuriggreenmountain.com*; 866-901-2739)

Medium-sized roasters with some national presence: Intelligentsia Coffee Roasters, Chicago (*www.intelligentsiacoffee.com*; 888-945-9786); Stumptown Coffee Roasters, Portland (*www.stumptowncoffee.com*, 855-711-3385).

Small, elite roasters with the best possible coffees and good wholesale coffees on the Internet: Terroir Coffee, New England (*www.terroircoffee.com*, 866-444-5282); Café Grumpy, New York City (*www.cafegrumpy.com*, 212-255-5511, 718-499-4404, 718-349-7623); PT's Coffee, Topeka, Kansas (*www.ptscoffee.com*, 888-678-5282); Klatch Coffee, southern California (*www.klatchroasting.com*, 877-455-2824); Barefoot Coffee, northern California (*www.barefootcoffee.com*, 408-293-7200); Paradise Roasters, Minnesota (*www.paradiseroasters.com*, 763-433-0626); Temple Coffee, Sacramento (*www.templecoffee.com*, 916-454-1282).

Vitamin D May Lower Risk for Diabetes

Researchers in Germany have found that people with adequate blood levels of vitamin D had a lower risk for type 2 diabetes than those with low levels of vitamin D. Protection against diabetes, which is a chronic inflammatory condition, is believed to come from vitamin D's anti-inflammatory effect. People should have their vitamin D levels checked annually and ensure that they have blood levels of between 50 ng/ml and 80 ng/ml.

C. Herder, et al., "Effect of Serum 25-Hydroxy-vitamin D on Risk for Type 2 Diabetes May Be Partially Mediated by Subclinical Inflammation: Results from the MONICA/KORA Augsburg Study," *Diabetes Care* (2011).

The Real Truth About Testosterone

Peter J. Burrows, MD, a practicing urologist in Tucson and a clinical assistant professor of urology at The University of Arizona College of Medicine, also in Tucson, and an adjunct assistant professor in the department of urology at the University of Southern California Keck School of Medicine in Los Angeles. He is a member of the American Society of Andrology and the American Urological Association.

For many men, it's the holy grail: a treatment that promises to beef up their muscles...rev up their sex drive...improve their stamina and concentration...and perhaps even help prevent a heart attack.

So it's no surprise that prescriptions for testosterone shots, gels and patches have nearly quadrupled over the last decade. About 3% of American men over age 40 now use testosterone therapy.

But is it safe? The answer to this crucial question depends on many factors that aren't clearly spelled out in the slick advertising—and, in some cases, even by the doctors who prescribe testosterone therapy.

What every man needs to know about testosterone therapy...

HOW THE RESEARCH STACKS UP

Testosterone is manufactured by the body and plays a key role in a man's health. It helps maintain his bone density...builds his muscles...allows him to produce sperm...and fuels his libido.

A man's testosterone levels start to decline, however, after age 30—usually by about 1% a year. This is not an illness—it's a fact of aging. If a man's testosterone drops farther than normal, though, it can cause fatigue, reduced sex drive, an increase in fat and a decrease in muscle. Some research suggests that low testosterone may also increase a man's odds of having a heart attack, diabetes and other serious health problems.

No wonder so many men are turning to testosterone therapy, which drug companies are now marketing in successful "low T" ads. The problem is, however, that many doctors are growing increasingly concerned that men whose testosterone levels are simply declining are loading up on the hormone, perhaps to the detriment of their health. Adding to those worries is recent research raising new questions about the safety of testosterone therapy.

Troubling recent finding: In research published in *The Journal of the American Medical Association*, men using testosterone had nearly a one-third increase in the rate of heart attacks and stroke.

Of course, this research doesn't prove that testosterone increases cardiovascular risks. Other studies have shown the opposite—that men with higher testosterone may have fewer heart attacks. So what's going on? It's possible that the underlying low testosterone, rather than the treatment, was the cause of the increased heart attack risk. It's also possible that men who start testosterone feel so much better that they overextend themselves and get more exercise—and sex—than their hearts can handle.

For now, there is no clear explanation for the mixed research findings—that's why it's so important to use caution when considering testosterone therapy.

WHO CAN BENEFIT?

Even with these new safety questions, it's widely agreed that men who meet the clinical criteria for low testosterone need hormone replacement—the benefits outweigh the risks. But what about men whose testosterone levels are waning but do not meet that criteria? That's where it gets more complicated.

Researchers still argue over what testosterone level is "normal." When they test men of different ages, they find levels ranging from the low-300s to as high as 1,000 (expressed in nanograms per deciliter—ng/dL—of blood). The cutoff points between "healthy" and "de-ficient" are somewhat arbitrary. They're based on averages, not optimal levels.

For now, testosterone replacement is FDA-approved only for men with a clinical deficiency—currently defined as testosterone levels below 300 ng/dL. This condition (hypogonadism) is usually caused by problems in the testicles or the pituitary gland—both play a role in regulating a man's testosterone levels.

PLAY IT SAFE

For a reasoned approach to testosterone therapy, here's my advice…

• **Don't automatically blame testosterone.** The drop in testosterone in older men isn't caused only by their age. It can be due to chronic diseases, such as high blood pressure and kidney disease. Painkillers can cause it, too. (About three-quarters of men who take long-acting opioids, such as extended-release oxycodone, develop very low testosterone.) Stress is also a factor.

Bottom line: Consider using testosterone only after other health problems have been addressed—and corrected.

Obesity and a sedentary lifestyle are common causes of low testosterone. Overweight men who exercise and lose weight can increase testosterone naturally by up to 25%—in some cases preventing the need for hormone replacement.

• **Take the test.** If your doctor has ruled out any physical ailment that may be causing symptoms, get your testosterone level tested (both total and free levels). Low testosterone is easily diagnosed with a blood test. Have the test early in the day, when testosterone levels tend to be highest. If your level is low, ask your doctor to repeat the test on another day, since levels can vary.

• **Get your heart checked out.** If your testosterone level is low, don't start replacement therapy without getting your heart checked out with a stress test, complete blood count (CBC) and tests for cholesterol and high blood pressure. Any cardiac condition that shows up on these tests must be resolved before beginning testosterone therapy.

Even though the research is not yet definitive, there are enough studies linking testosterone use to heart attack and other cardiovascular problems—especially in men with risk factors for heart disease, including smoking and obesity—that it's not worth taking a chance on this.

• **Use the right dose.** Since a man's optimal testosterone level is still not clearly defined, I advise a conservative approach. When choosing a dose, I try to get patients' blood levels within the upper one-fourth of the range generally recommended by endocrinologists—say, about 750 ng/dL—but no higher.

Different forms of supplemental testosterone are equally effective. Injections are the cheapest, but they must be repeated every 10 to 14 days. Most men learn how to administer the shots themselves.

Patches are another option, although some men don't like them, since they can trigger a rash. Testosterone gels and creams are the easiest to use, but they're expensive—and the medication can transfer to other people through skin-to-skin contact. They're usually applied to the shoulders or upper arms.

• **Go for checkups.** For anyone on testosterone therapy, it's crucial to get regular checkups. I advise men to get their testosterone levels checked at three months, then every six months. After that, if they're doing well, they can come in once a year for testing of lipid levels and liver function (testosterone can affect both). I also order tests every six months to monitor a man's red blood cell (RBC) counts—testosterone increases RBC levels, which can boost his risk for blood clots.

Other tests you'll need: A prostate-specific antigen (PSA) test to check for prostate cancer every six months. Testosterone replacement doesn't cause prostate cancer, but it can cause tumors that are already present to grow more rapidly. Men with untreated prostate cancer should not take testosterone. However, testosterone can be given to those who have been successfully treated for prostate cancer. Studies show it does not trigger cancer recurrence.

In general, men who have low testosterone will feel better within a month after starting testosterone therapy. Optimal testosterone levels should help with weight loss and can boost natural production of the hormone—so many men find that they no longer need treatment.

Hidden GI Problems Can Cause Diabetes and More

Liz Lipski, PhD, CCN, a Duluth, Georgia–based nutritionist who is board-certified in clinical nutrition and holistic nutrition. She is author of several books, including *Digestive Wellness: Strengthen the Immune System and Prevent Disease Through Healthy Digestion.* InnovativeHealing.com

---

If you have a stomachache, nausea or some other digestive problem, you know that it stems from your gastrointestinal (GI) tract.

But very few people think of the GI system when they have a health problem such as arthritis, depression, diabetes, asthma or recurring infections.

Surprising: Tens of millions of Americans are believed to have digestive problems that may not even be recognizable but can cause or complicate many other medical conditions.

Latest development: There's now significant evidence showing just how crucial the digestive system is in maintaining your overall health. How could hidden GI problems be responsible for such a wide range of seemingly unrelated ills?

Here's how: If you can't digest and absorb food properly, your cells can't get the nourishment they need to function properly and you can fall prey to a wide variety of ailments.

Good news: A holistically trained clinician can advise you on natural remedies (available at health-food stores unless otherwise noted) and lifestyle changes that often can correct hidden digestive problems…*

*Consult your doctor before trying these remedies—especially if you have a chronic medical condition or take any medication.

LOW LEVELS OF STOMACH ACID

Stomach acid, which contains powerful, naturally occurring hydrochloric acid (HC1), can decrease due to age, stress and/or food sensitivities.

Adequate stomach acid is a must for killing bacteria, fungi and parasites and for the digestion of protein and minerals. Low levels can weaken immunity and, in turn, lead to problems that can cause or complicate many ailments, including diabetes, gallbladder disease, osteoporosis, rosacea, thyroid problems and autoimmune disorders.

If you suspect that you have low stomach acid: You can be tested by a physician—or simply try the following natural remedies (adding one at a time each week until symptoms improve)…

• **Use apple cider vinegar.** After meals, take one teaspoon in eight teaspoons of water.

• **Try bitters.** This traditional digestive remedy usually contains gentian and other herbs. Bitters, which also are used in mixed drinks, are believed to work by increasing saliva, HC1, pepsin, bile and digestive enzymes. Use as directed on the label in capsule or liquid form.

• **Eat umeboshi plums.** These salted, pickled plums relieve indigestion. Eat them whole as an appetizer or dessert or use umeboshi vinegar to replace vinegar in salad dressings.

• **Take betaine HC1 with pepsin with meals that contain protein.**

Typical dosage: 350 mg. You must be supervised by a health-care professional when using this supplement—it can damage the stomach if used inappropriately.

If you still have symptoms, ask your doctor about adding digestive enzymes such as bromelain and/or papain.

TOO MUCH BACTERIA

When HC1 levels are low, it makes us vulnerable to small intestinal bacterial overgrowth (SIBO). This condition occurs when microbes are introduced into our bodies via our food and cause a low-grade infection or when bacteria from the large intestine migrate into the small intestine, where they don't belong. Left untreated, this bacterial overgrowth can lead to symptoms, such as bloating, gas and changes in bowel movements, characteristic of irritable bowel syndrome (IBS). In fact, some research shows that 78% of people with IBS may actually have SIBO.

SIBO is also a frequent (and usually overlooked) cause of many other health problems, including Crohn's disease, scleroderma (an autoimmune disease of the connective tissue) and fibromyalgia.

SIBO can have a variety of causes, including low stomach acid, overuse of heartburn drugs called proton pump inhibitors (PPIs) and low levels of pancreatic enzymes. Adults over age 65, who often produce less stomach acid, are at greatest risk for SIBO.

Important scientific finding: A study recently conducted by researchers at Washington University School of Medicine found that, for unknown reasons, people with restless legs syndrome are six times more likely to have SIBO than healthy people.

To diagnose: The best test for SIBO is a hydrogen breath test—you drink a sugary fluid and breath samples are then collected. If hydrogen is overproduced, you may have SIBO. The test, often covered by insurance, is offered by gastroenterologists and labs that specialize in digestive tests. A home test is available at *www.breathtests.com*.

How to treat: The probiotic VSL 3, available at *vsl3.com*, can be tried. However, antibiotics are usually needed. *Rifaximin* (Xifaxan) is the antibiotic of choice because it works locally in the small intestine.

LEAKY GUT SYNDROME

The acids and churning action of the stomach blend food into a soupy liquid (chyme) that flows into the small intestine. There, the intestinal lining performs two crucial functions—absorbing nutrients and blocking unwanted substances from entering the bloodstream.

But many factors, such as chronic stress, poor diet, too much alcohol, lack of sleep, and use of antibiotics, prednisone and certain other medications, can inflame and weaken the lining of the small intestine. This allows organisms, such as bacteria, fungi and parasites, and toxic chemicals we encounter in our day-to-day activities, to enter the blood. The problem, called increased intestinal permeability, or leaky gut syndrome, is bad news for the rest of your body.

What happens: The immune system reacts to the organisms and substances as "foreign," triggering inflammation that contributes to or causes a wide range of problems, such as allergies, skin problems, muscle and joint pain, poor memory and concentration, and chronic fatigue syndrome.

To diagnose: A stool test that indicates the presence of parasites, yeast infections or bacterial infection is a sign of leaky gut. So are clinical signs, such as food intolerances and allergies. However, the best test for leaky gut checks for urinary levels of the water-soluble sugars lactulose and mannitol—large amounts indicate a leaky gut.

How to treat: If you and your doctor believe that you have leaky gut, consider taking as many of the following steps as possible…

• **Chew your food slowly and completely to enhance digestion.**

• **Emphasize foods and beverages that can help heal the small intestine,** including foods in the cabbage family, such as kale, vegetable broths, fresh vegetable juices (such as cabbage juice), aloe vera juice and slippery elm tea.

• **Take glutamine.** This amino acid is the main fuel for the small intestine—and a glutamine supplement is one of the best ways to repair a leaky gut. Start with 1 g to 3 g daily, and gradually increase the dosage by a gram or two per week to up to 14 g daily. Becoming constipated is a sign that you're using too much.

• **Try the probiotic L. plantarum.** A supplement of this gut-friendly bacteria, such as Transformation Enzyme's Plantadophilus, can help heal the small intestine.

• **Add quercetin.** This antioxidant helps repair a leaky gut. In my practice, I've found that the products Perque Pain Guard and Perque Repair Guard work better than other quercetin products.

Typical dosage: 1,000 mg daily.

• **Use digestive enzymes** with meals to help ensure your food is completely digested.

Good brands: Enzymedica, Thorne and Now.

Weight Loss: The Key to Diabetes Prevention

Anne Peters, MD, professor of clinical medicine, Keck School of Medicine of the University of Southern California in Los Angeles, and director of the USC Westside Center for Diabetes. She is author of *Conquering Diabetes: A Complete Program for Prevention and Treatment.*

Losing weight is the single most effective way to prevent diabetes.

Reason: Putting on even as little as 10 pounds—especially around your middle—automatically increases insulin resistance. Losing just 15 pounds reduces your risk of developing diabetes by more than half.

A simple, proven way to lose weight: Eat smaller portions. Use small (10-inch) plates at home—and therefore serve smaller portions—since studies show that people tend to finish whatever is on their plates. Also, avoid fruit juices and soft drinks as well as "white" foods (white bread, baked potatoes and French fries, pasta, white rice), all of which cause sharp rises in blood sugar. Finally, make sure that every meal contains a mix of high-fiber fruits and vegetables and high-quality protein (fish or lean meat).

Another key: Do an hour of exercise at least five times a week. A good program for most people is 45 minutes of aerobic exercise—such as walking, biking or swimming—and 15 minutes of light weight lifting.

Reason: Regular exercise encourages weight loss and increases your body's sensitivity to insulin. This effect only lasts a short time, however, which is why it's important to exercise often.

For many, these steps will be enough to prevent diabetes. If your body's ability to respond to insulin is 75% of normal and you can lower your insulin resistance by 25% through diet and exercise—a typical response—then your blood-sugar regulation will be brought back in balance.

Stand Up and Move

Exercise is not enough to take off the pounds if you spend a lot of time sitting. When people sit for long periods—doing desk jobs, using computers, playing video games, watching television or for other reasons—the enzymes that are responsible for burning fat shut down.

Result: People who sit too much have significantly greater risk for premature heart attack, diabetes and death.

Self-defense: In addition to exercising, it is important to stand up and move around as much as possible throughout the day—walk around the office, go up and down stairs, take a break from the computer and go outdoors, or do something else to get out of a seated position.

Marc Hamilton, PhD, former associate professor of biomedical sciences, University of Missouri-Columbia, and leader of a study of the physiological effects of sitting, published in *Diabetes*.

Too Much Sugar in Your Diet Carries More Risk Than Weight Gain

Richard J. Johnson, MD, professor and chief of the division of renal diseases and hypertension at the University of Colorado, Denver. He is author of *The Sugar Fix: The High-Fructose Fallout That Is Making You Fat and Sick*.

We all know that it's not good for our health to consume too much sugar. Excessive amounts of sugar in the diet are widely known to cause weight gain. But that's only part of the story.

Both table sugar and high-fructose corn syrup (HFCS) contain fructose, which recent research has shown can increase the risk for diabetes, fatty liver disease, high blood pressure and chronic kidney disease when consumed in excessive amounts. Currently, most Americans consume way too much added sugar in their daily diets, putting them at risk for all these diseases.

WHAT'S THE TROUBLE WITH FRUCTOSE?

Fructose is a simple sugar. It is found naturally in honey, fruits and some vegetables. But a typical fruit contains only about 8 g of fructose, compared to about 20 g in a sugary soda. Unlike soda, fruits and vegetables contain nutrients and antioxidants that are beneficial to health.

The two main sources of fructose in the American diet are table sugar (which is squeezed from beet and cane plants) and HFCS (which is processed using enzymes that turn corn starch into glucose and fructose). Table sugar and HFCS are almost identical in their chemical composition—and both, consumed in excess, can contribute to health problems.

But few Americans are aware of just how much added sugar they are getting in their diets. That's because many added sugars are often listed as ingredients that are not recognizable as sugar and are found in unexpected food sources (see next page for a list of these terms). For example, added sugar is found in not only obvious places like soft drinks and other sweet beverages, but also in great abundance in many salad dressings, condiments (such as ketchup), cereals, crackers and even bread.

EMERGING RESEARCH ON FRUCTOSE

While there are many studies being conducted on different types of added sugars, there is important research that now focuses on various forms of fructose. For example, recent research suggests that fructose is harmful because it increases levels of uric acid, a naturally occurring acid found in the urine. In crystalline form, uric acid can deposit in the joints and lead to gout.

Eating foods rich in a compound called purines (found in foods such as anchovies, beer, brewer's yeast supplements, clams, goose, gravy, herring, lobster, mackerel, meat extract, mincemeat, mussels, organ meats, oysters, sardines, scallops and shrimp) can also produce high levels of uric acid.

SMART WAYS TO LIMIT SUGAR

It's important to remove added sugar from your diet—with a special focus on fructose due to its unique potential risks that are now being discovered in new research.

To minimize the health risks associated with added sugars, try these steps…

• **Beware of "hidden" sugar.** When buying processed foods, remember that added sugars can appear on food labels in various ways. (See various names for sugar at the end of this article.)

• **Avoid any prepared or processed product that does not provide an ingredient list.**

• **Don't eat more than four fruits daily.** Even the naturally occurring fructose found in fruit counts toward your total daily intake of fructose. It's also important to limit your intake of fruit juice, which has been stripped of the nutritious fiber present in whole fruit and often contains added sugar.

• **Limit fructose intake to 25 g to 35 g per day.** Consuming more than that amount could trigger the physiological changes that may lead to disease.

To learn the fructose content of specific foods, go to the USDA Food Composition Database at *www.nal.usda.gov/fnic/foodcomp/search*.

• **Take nutritional supplements.** Limiting fruit in your diet may lower your levels of important nutrients. To replace them, take a multivitamin plus an additional 250 mg of vitamin C daily.

• **Be cautious when eating in restaurants.** Limit restaurant meals and takeout food to menu items for which you know the ingredients.

• **Be prepared for sugar withdrawal.** In rare cases, you may develop withdrawal symptoms from sugar and fructose, such as headache, fatigue and an intense craving for sweets.

To help ease these symptoms, be sure to drink plenty of water (five to eight cups daily).

SUGAR ALIASES

Take this list to the supermarket with you to help you identify the various terms for added sugars…

• **Beet sugar**
• **Brown sugar**
• **Cane sugar**
• **Corn sweetener**
• **Corn syrup**
• **Demerara sugar**
• **Fruit juice concentrate**
• **Granulated sugar**
• **High-fructose corn syrup**
• **Honey**
• **Invert sugar**
• **Maple syrup**
• **Molasses**
• **Muscovado sugar**
• **Raw sugar**
• **Sucrose**
• **Syrup**
• **Table sugar**
• **Tagatose**
• **Turbinado sugar**

How a Quick Massage Can Help You Beat Diabetes

Mark Tarnopolsky, MD, PhD, prfessor, division of neurology, department of pediatrics and medicine, McMaster University, Ontario, Canada.

No one wants to be overweight, have diabetes or grow old prematurely. Well, a new study shows that there's a simple strategy that may help prevent all three that is actually quite fun and relaxing.

A massage might do the trick!

We're not talking about an expensive, hour-long massage, either—recent research shows that an inexpensive massage lasting just 10 minutes can be beneficial.

STOP THE DAMAGE!

Mark Tarnopolsky, MD, PhD, a professor of medicine and head of neuromuscular and neurometabolic diseases at McMaster University in Canada, explained that the researchers in this specific massage study found two very interesting differences in muscles that had been massaged after exercise...

A gene pathway that causes muscle inflammation was "dialed down" in these muscles both immediately after the massage and 2.5 hours after the massage. (Specific genes can be present in our tissues but not always active.) Dr. Tarnopolsky said that this is helpful knowledge because muscle inflammation is a contributor to delayed-onset muscle soreness, so it confirms biologically what we've always believed through anecdotal observation—a post-exercise massage can help relieve muscle soreness.

Conversely, another sort of gene was "turned on" by the massage—this is a gene that increases the activity of mitochondria in muscle cells. Mitochondria are considered the "power packs" of our muscles for their role in creating usable energy. Better mitochondrial functioning has been shown by other studies to help decrease insulin resistance (a key risk factor for type 2 diabetes) and obesity and even to slow aging. When Dr. Tarnopolsky was asked about whether it's a stretch to link post-exercise massage to these benefits, he said that it's not unreasonable—there is a potential connection, and future research will need to be done to confirm it.

TREAT YOURSELF TO MASSAGE

The massage type that Dr. Tarnopolsky and his colleagues used was a standard combination of three techniques that are commonly used for post-exercise massage—effleurage (light stroking)...petrissage (firm compression and release)...and stripping (repeated longitudinal strokes). It's easy to find massage therapists in spas, salons, fitness centers and private practices who use these techniques. Or you could ask your spouse or a friend to try some of these moves on you (even if his or her technique isn't perfect) because there's a chance that it could provide the benefits, said Dr. Tarnopolsky—he just can't say for sure, since that wasn't studied.

Dr. Tarnopolsky studied massage only after exercise, so that's when he would recommend getting one, but it's possible that massaging any muscles at any time may have similar benefits—more research will need to be done to find out.

Remember, you don't have to break the bank on a prolonged 60-minute massage—a simple 10- or 20-minute rubdown (which usually costs $10 to $40) can do the trick.

2

Do You Have Diabetes? Symptoms and Tests

Do You Have Prediabetes? What You Must Know to Protect Yourself

As Americans continue to pack on the pounds, doctors are seeing a surge in weight-related health problems. An increasingly common condition that now affects about 40% of American adults is prediabetes, characterized by blood glucose (sugar) levels that are higher than normal but not yet at diabetic levels. People with prediabetes are five to 15 times more likely to develop full-blown diabetes than people without this condition.

These are alarming statistics. Diabetes has serious potential consequences, including blindness, kidney failure, erectile dysfunction, heart failure, stroke…as well as nerve damage and circulation problems that can necessitate amputation.

Good news: Diabetes and its devastating consequences often can be prevented—by reversing prediabetes.

HOW THE DISEASE PROGRESSES

There are two main types of diabetes. With type 1 diabetes, the body's immune system attacks the pancreas, impairing or destroying its ability to produce insulin, the hormone that helps cells absorb glucose and convert it to energy. Prediabetes and body weight generally are only minor contributors to type 1 diabetes.

In contrast, the development of type 2 diabetes—which accounts for about 90% of all diabetes cases—is greatly influenced by prediabetes and excess weight. An obese person

Mark A. Stengler, NMD, a naturopathic medical doctor and leading authority on the practice of alternative and integrated medicine. Dr. Stengler is author of the *Health Revelations* newsletter, author of *The Natural Physician's Healing Therapies*, founder and medical director of the Stengler Center for Integrative Medicine in Encinitas, California, and former adjunct associate clinical professor at the National University of Natural Medicine in Portland, Oregon. MarkStengler.com

51

is 80 times more likely to develop type 2 diabetes than a person of normal weight. With type 2 diabetes, the pancreas usually does produce insulin, but the body's cells cannot use it properly. A person generally passes through several stages on the way to developing type 2 diabetes. *What happens…*

• **When we eat, the amount of glucose in our blood rises, alerting the pancreas that it needs to produce insulin.** Excess fat, nutritional deficiencies and the stress hormone cortisol interfere with cells' ability to accept and use insulin, leaving excess glucose in the blood. When this happens, a person is said to have insulin resistance.

Sensing that the insulin is not doing its job, the pancreas churns out even more. But since the cells cannot accept the excess insulin, it remains in the blood, along with the excess glucose. When blood glucose levels reach a certain point (as measured with blood tests), the condition qualifies as prediabetes…and if levels climb higher still, it qualifies as diabetes.

High blood glucose levels cause many of the complications of diabetes, including damage to the kidneys, nerves and eyes. However, in the years during which prediabetes and diabetes are developing, a bigger problem is high blood insulin.

Reason: Insulin helps produce muscle—but when insulin levels get too high, the hormone instead promotes formation of visceral fat, which in turn makes insulin resistance even worse. Insulin elevations also increase production of triglycerides and cholesterol, which clog arteries…of C-reactive protein, which promotes damaging inflammation… and of cortisol, which contributes to various diseases.

WHAT THE TESTS SHOULD TELL US

Too many doctors use antiquated guidelines for interpreting test results, then tell patients all is well when, in fact, the patients are at risk. I urge you to ask your doctor for the specific results of your tests and compare them with my guidelines below, which I have based on the most recent evidence. You may spot a warning sign that your doctor missed.

• **Fasting glucose test.** Routinely given at annual checkups, this test involves fasting for at least eight hours (optimally 12 hours), then having blood drawn to measure glucose levels.

Do You Have Prediabetes?

If you are age 65 or older, you are at increased risk for prediabetes regardless of the characteristics described below. For this reason, you should ask your doctor about receiving a fasting glucose test.

If you are under age 65, answer the following questions. Speak to your doctor about receiving a fasting glucose test if you score 5 or higher.

Age	Points
20–27	0
28–35	1
36–44	2
45–64	4

Sex	
Male	3
Female	0

Family History of Diabetes	
No	0
Yes	1

Heart Rate (beats per minute)	Points
Less than 60	0
60–69	0
70–79	1
80–89	2
90–99	2
Greater than 100	4

To determine your heart rate, place the tips of the first two fingers lightly over one of the blood vessels in your neck or the pulse spot inside your wrist just below the base of your thumb. Count your pulse for 10 seconds and multiply that number by 6.

High Blood Pressure	
No	0
Yes	1

Body Mass Index (BMI)	
Less than 25	0
25–29.9	2
30 or greater	3

To determine your BMI, consult the National Heart, Lung and Blood Institute website, *www.nhlbi.nih.gov* (search BMI).

Source: Annals of Family Medicine

Problem: The range generally accepted as "normal"—from 65 milligrams per deciliter (mg/dL) to 99 mg/dL—is much too broad.

Evidence: A study published in *The New England Journal of Medicine* found that men with a fasting blood glucose level of 87 mg/dL had almost twice the risk of developing diabetes as did men whose level was 81 mg/dL or less. *My guidelines...*

- **Optimal**—76 mg/dL to 81 mg/dL
- **Normal**—82 mg/dL to 85 mg/dL
- **At risk**—86 mg/dL to 99 mg/dL
- **Prediabetic**—100 mg/dL to 125 mg/dL
- **Diabetic**—126 mg/dL and above

Though most doctors do not order it routinely, you can ask your doctor to have your insulin levels checked as part of your fasting glucose test. These results are not used to officially diagnose diabetes, but they do provide additional information about your risk. Although the generally accepted guidelines put the normal range for blood insulin levels at six micro-international units per milliliter (mcU/ml) to 35 mcU/ml, I think this range is far too wide to be meaningful. *My guidelines...*

- **Optimal**—7 mcU/ml or less
- **At risk**—8 mcU/ml to 10 mcU/ml
- **Prediabetic**—11 mcU/ml to 25 mcU/ml
- **Dangerous**—above 25 mcU/ml

- **Oral glucose tolerance test with glucose and insulin levels.** A more accurate way to measure blood insulin levels, this test requires fasting for 12 hours and having blood drawn...then drinking a glucose solution and having blood drawn again after one, two and up to three hours. Many medical doctors fail to order this test because they are unaware that it dramatically improves the ability to identify prediabetic patients. I often order this test for patients who are overweight, have a strong family history of diabetes or have a history of elevated fasting glucose levels—even if their most recent fasting glucose test results appeared normal. In this way, I have diagnosed type 2 diabetes in several patients whose fasting glucose results did not suggest any problems. My guidelines for blood drawn at the two-hour point...

- **Normal**—blood glucose below 140 mg/dL...or insulin levels at or below 55 mcU/ml.
- **Prediabetic**—blood glucose of 140 mg/dL to 159 mg/dL, or an increase in glucose of 50 mg/dL or more within one hour...or insulin levels at 56 mcU/ml to 90 mcU/ml.
- **Dangerous**—blood glucose of 160 mg/dL or higher...or insulin levels above 90 mcU/ml.

- **Hemoglobin A1C (HbA1c).** This blood test indicates damage to blood proteins caused when glucose binds to the oxygen-carrying hemoglobin in red blood cells, creating free radicals (harmful negatively charged molecules). Results are expressed as a percentage. A British study involving 10,232 adults indicated that HbA1c results accurately predict health problems, including heart attacks (for which prediabetes and diabetes are risk factors). For each 1% rise in HbA1c, study participants' heart attack risk increased by 20%. *My guidelines...*

- **Normal**—4.5% to 4.9%
- **At risk**—5.0% to 5.6%
- **Prediabetic**—5.7% to 6.9%
- **Diabetic**—7.0% or higher

STEPS TO TAKE TO PREEMPT PREDIABETES

Fortunately, there is a lot you can do to prevent prediabetes—or even to reverse it if you have it.

1. Lose excess weight. This is without question the most important step. To determine if you are at a healthful weight, calculate your body mass index (BMI), a ratio of your weight to the square of your height (for a free online BMI calculator, go to *www.nhlbi.nih.gov* and search "BMI calculator"). BMI of 30 or higher indicates obesity and a strong likelihood of developing prediabetes or diabetes... BMI between 25 and 29.9 puts you at risk for prediabetes. If necessary, a holistic doctor or nutritionist can help you devise a personal weight-loss plan.

2. Reduce body fat percentage. Apart from its effect on weight, excess body fat increases prediabetes risk. I measure a patient's body fat percentage with bioelectrical impedance, a painless test that involves placing electrodes on your hand and foot. For women, an ideal range is 21% to 24%…anything above 31% is risky. For men, ideal is 14% to 17%…above 25% is risky.

Self-defense: Build muscle and banish excess fat by doing 30 minutes of aerobic exercise, such as brisk walking, five days a week…plus 30 minutes of strength training twice weekly.

3. Eat right. Good dietary habits help to control weight…prevent spikes and drops in blood glucose levels…slow digestion, giving the pancreas time to produce insulin…boost energy, making it easier to exercise…and provide nutrients that optimize health.

•**Eat three meals a day at regular times, keeping portions moderate.** Never skip breakfast.

•**Keep snacks small.**

Options: Nuts, seeds, low-sugar protein drinks, vegetables or fruit.

•**Include a small portion of protein at every meal.**

Good choices: One or two eggs…1.5 ounces of nuts…or three ounces of fish, chicken, turkey or lean meat.

•**Eat at least one or two servings of whole grains daily.** For variety, try quinoa, couscous, and bread made with spelt or kamut flour.

•**Avoid sugary foods, processed foods, trans fats (found in some margarines, baked goods and crackers) and saturated fats (in meats, dairy foods and many vegetable oils).**

•**Have at least two servings of fruits and three or more servings of vegetables daily.**

4. Take appropriate supplements. Many manufacturers offer a "blood sugar control formula" that provides a combination of nutrients to help stabilize blood glucose and promote proper insulin function. Alternatively, you can follow the guidelines below.

If you are at risk for prediabetes, take…

•**Chromium, a mineral, at 500 micrograms (mcg) daily.**

•**Pycnogenol (maritime pine extract) at 200 mg daily.**

If you have been diagnosed with prediabetes, also take…

•**Biotin (vitamin B-7) at 500 mcg daily.**

•**Alpha lipoic acid, an antioxidant, at 300 mg daily.**

•**Magnesium at 400 mg daily.**

•**Vitamin D at 1,000 international units (IU) daily.**

If you use diabetes medication, check with your doctor before taking these supplements—your medication dosage may need to be adjusted. These supplements are sold in health-food stores, generally are safe, rarely cause side effects and can be taken indefinitely. Ideally, however, your improved diet and more healthful lifestyle will decrease your risk for prediabetes or reverse the condition, so the supplements eventually will no longer be necessary.

For a complete guide on prediabetes, I recommend *Stop Prediabetes Now,* by Jack Challem and Ron Hunninghake, MD, from which the following checklist has been adapted. Check off all the risk factors that apply to you. If you have five or more checks, see your doctor—you may be at high risk for prediabetes.

I have…

•**A brother, sister or parent with diabetes.**

•**A personal history of gestational diabetes (diabetes during pregnancy).**

•**A waist measurement of more than 35 inches (women) or 40 inches (men).**

I have been diagnosed with…

•**High blood sugar or insulin levels.**

•**High blood pressure.**

•**High cholesterol or high triglycerides (a type of fat in blood).**

•**Hypothyroidism (low thyroid hormone).**

•**Polycystic ovary syndrome.**

•**Carpal tunnel syndrome, Bell's palsy or gout (which may be linked to diabetes).**

I often…

•**Skip breakfast.**

- **Breakfast only on coffee and/or something starchy (bagel, muffin).**
- **Feel tired after meals, especially lunch.**
- **Nap during the day or early evening.**
- **Have trouble falling asleep at night.**
- **Have trouble getting up in the morning.**
- **Crave sweets.**
- **Crave starchy foods (pasta, pizza, bread).**
- **Snack late at night.**
- **Drink nondiet soft drinks daily.**
- **Have one or more sweet foods daily.**
- **Lack energy.**
- **Skip exercise.**
- **Feel thirsty.**
- **Urinate frequently.**
- **Have trouble maintaining an erection.**
- **Feel less interested in sex than I used to.**
- **Feel stressed, irritable or depressed.**

Hidden Diabetes—You Can Get a Clean Bill of Health and Still Be at Risk

Mark Hyman, MD, founder and medical director of The UltraWellness Center in Lenox, Massachusetts, DrHyman.com. A leading expert in whole-systems medicine that addresses the root causes of chronic illness, he is chairman of the Institute for Functional Medicine in Gig Harbor, Washington. Dr. Hyman also is author of several books, including *The Blood Sugar Solution: The UltraHealthy Program for Losing Weight, Preventing Disease, and Feeling Great Now!*

With all the devastating complications of type 2 diabetes, such as heart disease, stroke, dementia and blindness, you might assume that most doctors are doing everything possible to catch this disease in its earliest stages. Not so.

Problem: There are currently no national guidelines for screening and treating type 2 diabetes before it reaches a full-blown stage.

Research clearly shows that the damage caused by type 2 diabetes begins years—and sometimes decades—earlier, but standard medical practice has not yet caught up with the newest findings on this disease.

Fortunately, there are scientifically proven ways to identify and correct the root causes of diabetes so that you never develop the disease itself.

WHEN THE PROBLEM STARTS

Diabetes is diagnosed when fasting blood sugar (glucose) levels reach 126 mg/dL and above. "Prediabetes" is defined as blood sugar levels that are higher than normal but not high enough to indicate diabetes. Normal levels are less than 100 mg/dL.

What most people don't know: Although most doctors routinely test blood sugar to detect diabetes, it's quite common to have a normal level and still have "diabesity," a condition typically marked by obesity and other changes in the body that can lead to the same complications (such as heart disease, stroke and cancer) as full-fledged diabetes.

Important: Even if you're not diabetic, having "belly fat"—for example, a waist circumference of more than 35 inches in women and more than 40 inches in men—often has many of the same dangerous effects on the body as diabetes.

Important finding: In a landmark study in Europe, researchers looked at 22,000 people and found that those with fasting blood sugar levels of just 95 mg/dL—a level that's generally considered healthy—already had significant risks for heart disease and other complications.

AN EARLIER CLUE

Even though we've all been told that high blood sugar is the telltale sign of diabetes, insulin levels are, in fact, a more important hallmark that a person is in the early stages of the "diabetes continuum."

High blood sugar is typically blamed on a lack of insulin—or insulin that doesn't work efficiently. However, too much insulin is actually the best marker of the stages leading up to prediabetes and diabetes.

Why is high insulin so important? In most cases, it means that you have insulin resistance, a condition in which your body's cells aren't responding to insulin's effects. As a result, your body churns out more insulin than it normally would.

Once you have insulin resistance, you've set the stage to develop abdominal obesity, artery-damaging inflammation and other conditions that increasingly raise your risk for prediabetes and diabetes.

A BETTER APPROACH

Because doctors focus on prediabetes and diabetes—conditions detected with a blood sugar test—they tend to miss the earlier signs of diabesity. *A better approach...*

• **Test insulin as well.** The standard diabetes test is to measure blood sugar after fasting for eight or more hours. The problem with this method is that blood sugar is the last thing to rise. Insulin rises first when you have diabesity.

My advice: Ask your doctor for a two-hour glucose tolerance test. With this test, your glucose levels are measured before and after consuming a sugary drink—but ask your doctor to also measure your insulin levels before and after consuming the drink.

What to look for: Your fasting blood sugar should be less than 80 mg/dL...two hours later, it shouldn't be higher than 120 mg/dL. Your fasting insulin should be 2 IU/dL to 5 IU/dL—anything higher indicates that you might have diabesity. Two hours later, your insulin should be less than 30 IU/dL.

Cost: $50 to $100 (usually covered by insurance). I advise all patients to have this test every three to five years...and annually for a person who is trying to reverse diabetes.

STEPS TO BEAT DIABESITY

With the correct lifestyle changes, most people can naturally reduce insulin as well as risk for diabesity-related complications, such as heart disease.

Example: The well-respected Diabetes Prevention Program sponsored by the National Institutes of Health found that overweight people who improved their diets and walked just 20 to 30 minutes a day lost modest amounts of weight and were 58% less likely to develop diabetes. *You can reduce your risk even more by following these steps...*

• **Manage your glycemic load.** The glycemic index measures how quickly different foods elevate blood sugar and insulin. A high-glycemic slice of white bread, for example, triggers a very rapid insulin response, which in turn promotes abdominal weight gain and the risk for diabesity.

My advice: Look at your overall diet and try to balance higher-glycemic foods with lower-glycemic foods. In general, foods that are minimally processed—fresh vegetables, legumes, fish, etc.—are lower on the glycemic index. These foods are ideal because they cause only gradual rises in blood sugar and insulin.

• **Eat nonwheat grains.** Many people try to improve their diets by eating whole-wheat rather than processed white bread or pasta. It doesn't help.

Fact: Two slices of whole-wheat bread will raise blood sugar more than two tablespoons of white sugar. If you already have diabetes, two slices of white or whole-wheat bread will raise your blood sugar by 70 mg/dL to 120 mg/dL. Wheat also causes inflammation... stimulates the storage of abdominal fat...and increases the risk for liver damage.

These ill effects occur because the wheat that's produced today is different from the natural grain. With selective breeding and hybridization, today's wheat is high in amylopectin A, which is naturally fattening. It also contains an inflammatory form of gluten along with short forms of protein, known as exorphins, which are literally addictive.

Best: Instead of white or whole-wheat bread and pasta, switch to nonwheat grains such as brown or black rice, quinoa, buckwheat or amaranth. They're easy to cook, taste good—and they don't have any of the negative effects. Small red russet potatoes also are acceptable.

• **Give up liquid calories.** The average American gets 175 calories a day from sugar-sweetened beverages. Because these calories are in addition to calories from solid food, they can potentially cause weight gain of 18 pounds a year. The Harvard Nurses' Health

Study found that women who drank one sugar-sweetened soft drink a day had an 82% increased risk of developing diabetes within four years.

Moderation rarely works with soft drinks because sugar is addictive. It activates the same brain receptors that are stimulated by heroin.

My advice: Switch completely to water. A cup of unsweetened coffee or tea daily is acceptable, but water should be your main source of fluids.

Bonus: People who are trying to lose weight can lose 44% more in 12 weeks just by drinking a glass of water before meals.

Important: Diet soda isn't a good substitute for water—the artificial sweeteners that are used increase sugar cravings and slow metabolism. Studies have found a 67% increase in diabetes risk in people who use artificial sweeteners.

Surprising Symptoms of Prediabetes

The late Frederic J. Vagnini, MD, a cardiovascular surgeon and medical director of the Heart, Diabetes & Weight Loss Centers of New York in New Hyde Park. He was author of The Weight Loss Plan for Beating Diabetes.

One of the best ways to prevent diabetes is to spot blood sugar (glucose) problems before the full-blown disease develops. But most people don't realize that diabetes—and its precursor, prediabetes—can cause no symptoms at all or a wide range of symptoms that often are misinterpreted.

Common mistake: Because type 2 diabetes is strongly linked to excess body weight, many people who are a normal weight assume that they won't develop the disease. But that's not always true. About 15% of people who are diagnosed with diabetes are not overweight. And paradoxically, even weight loss can be a symptom of this complex disorder in people

(normal weight or overweight) who have uncontrolled high glucose levels.

Shocking recent finding: The Centers for Disease Control and Prevention now estimates that 37% of Americans 20 years and older have prediabetes, and half of adult Americans over age 65 have prediabetes or diabetes—most likely due to the increasing numbers of people who are overweight and inactive, both of which boost diabetes risk.

However, most primary care doctors aren't diagnosing and treating prediabetes early enough in their patients—often because they fail to order the necessary screening tests (see the next page). And because the symptoms of prediabetes can be subtle, especially in its early stages, most people are not reporting potential red flags to their doctors.

Fortunately, prediabetes can virtually always be prevented from progressing to diabetes if the condition is identified and treated in its early stages (by following a healthful diet, exercising regularly and taking nutritional supplements and medications, if necessary).

WHAT IS PREDIABETES?

Prediabetes occurs when the body's cells no longer respond correctly to insulin, a hormone that regulates blood sugar. With prediabetes, blood sugar levels are higher than normal but not high enough to warrant a diagnosis of diabetes.

Prediabetes affects about 86 million Americans—most of whom are unaware that they have the condition.

RED FLAGS FOR DIABETES

Being overweight (defined as having a body mass index, or BMI, of 25 or higher) is perhaps the best-known risk factor for type 2 diabetes.* The more excess body weight you have, the more resistant your cells become to the blood sugar–regulating effects of the hormone insulin, ultimately causing blood glucose levels to rise.

Greatest danger: Abdominal fat, in particular, further boosts diabetes risk. That's because belly (visceral) fat hinders the processing

*For a BMI calculator, go to the website of the National Heart, Lung and Blood Institute, *www.nhlbi.nih. gov* and search "BMI calculator."

of insulin. The single biggest risk factor for prediabetes is having a waistline of 40 inches or more if you're a man…or 35 inches or more if you're a woman. Lesser-known red flags for prediabetes (and diabetes)—if you have one of these symptoms, see your doctor…

• **Increased thirst and need to urinate.** Because excess blood glucose draws water from the body's tissues, people with elevated blood glucose levels feel thirsty much of the time. Even when they drink fluids, their thirst is rarely quenched. Therefore, they drink even more, causing them to urinate more often than is normal for them.

• **Unexplained weight loss.** While being overweight is a significant risk factor for prediabetes, the condition also can paradoxically lead to unexplained weight loss resulting from a lack of energy supply to the body's cells and a loss of glucose-related calories due to excessive urination.

• **Dry, itchy skin.** Excess blood glucose also draws moisture from the skin, leaving it dry and prone to itching and cracking—especially on the legs, feet and elbows.

• **Blurred vision.** Glucose can change the shape of the eye lens, making it difficult to focus properly.

• **Slow-healing cuts, sores or bruises and frequent infections.** For unknown reasons, excess blood glucose appears to interfere with the body's healing processes and its ability to fight off infection. In particular, women with prediabetes and diabetes are prone to urinary tract and vaginal infections.

• **Red, swollen and tender gums.** Because the body's ability to heal can be compromised by prediabetes, gum inflammation, involving red, swollen, tender and/or bleeding gums, may develop.

• **Persistent feelings of hunger.** When the body's cells don't get enough glucose due to prediabetes, the cells send signals to the brain that are interpreted as hunger, typically about one hour after consuming a meal.

• **Lack of energy.** Because their cells are starved of energy-boosting glucose, people with prediabetes tend to tire quickly after even mild physical effort. Dehydration due to excess blood glucose also can contribute to fatigue.

• **Falling asleep after eating.** An hour or so after eating, our digestive systems convert the food we've eaten into glucose. In people with prediabetes, the process is exaggerated—blood glucose levels spike, triggering a surge of insulin as the body attempts to stabilize high glucose levels. This insulin surge is ineffective in lowering blood glucose, causing the person to become drowsy. If you feel sleepy after meals, it can be a sign that your blood glucose levels are riding this prediabetic roller coaster.

• **Moodiness and irritability.** Lack of energy production in your cells, together with sharp rises and dips in blood glucose levels, can trigger feelings of restlessness, irritability and exaggerated emotional responses to stress.

• **Tingling or numbness in the hands and feet.** Excess blood glucose can damage small blood vessels feeding the body's peripheral nerves, often causing tingling, loss of sensation or burning pain in the hands, arms, legs or feet.

• **Loss of sex drive and erectile dysfunction in men.** Prediabetes is associated with low testosterone in men, which often reduces libido. In addition, glucose-related damage to the body's small blood vessels often impairs the ability of prediabetic men to have an erection.

THREE KEY DIABETES TESTS

If you suspect that you may have prediabetes, ask your doctor to order the following tests…

• **Fasting blood glucose.** This traditional blood test for diabetes is usually part of a standard physical. Until recently, a result over 125 mg/dL was considered a sign of diabetes, while 100 mg/dL to 125 mg/dL indicated prediabetes.

Standard guidelines established by the American Diabetes Association have not changed, but recent data suggest that a person who has a fasting blood glucose reading over 90 mg/dL should be evaluated by a physician.

• **Hemoglobin A1C.** This blood test, also included in many annual checkups, measures the average blood glucose level over a two- to three-month period. An A1C result of 4.5% to 5.9% is considered normal...6% to 6.5% indicates prediabetes...and two separate readings of 6.5% or above indicate diabetes.

Standard guidelines still use 6% as the lower end of the prediabetes range, but recent data suggest that results as low as 5.6% or 5.7% may signal prediabetes.

• **Oral glucose tolerance test.** Administered over two hours in your doctor's office, this test can spot problems with blood-sugar regulation that may not show up in the other tests. For the oral glucose tolerance test, blood levels of glucose are checked immediately before drinking a premixed glucose formula and two hours afterward.

A result of 140 mg/dL to 159 mg/dL is a sign of increased risk for diabetes...160 mg/dL to 200 mg/dL indicates high risk for diabetes... and over 200 mg/dL signals full-blown diabetes. Also ask your doctor to measure your insulin levels—insulin fluctuations can be an even earlier predictor of prediabetes than the tests described above.

Is It a Rash...Or Diabetes?

Cindy Owen, MD, an assistant clinical professor of dermatology and assistant program director at the University of Louisville School of Medicine, where she practices medical and inpatient dermatology with a focus on the skin signs of internal disease and drug reactions. She has published many articles in medical journals such as *JAMA Dermatology* and *Journal of Cutaneous Pathology*.

W e all know that we should keep an eye on moles and any other skin changes that might be a sign of skin cancer. But there's another reason to look closely at your skin: It can point to—or sometimes even predict—internal diseases that you might not be aware of.

Many internal diseases are accompanied by skin symptoms. The yellowish skin tint (jaundice) caused by hepatitis is a common one—but there are other serious health problems that most people don't associate with skin changes...

DIABETES

Skin symptoms: Rash or pimple-like eruptions (sometimes containing pus) under the breasts, between the buttocks or in other skinfolds.

Possible underlying cause: Candidiasis, a fungal infection that commonly affects people with diabetes. This infection also can lead to whitish spots on the tongue or inner cheeks.

Candidiasis of the skin or mucous membranes that is chronic or difficult to control can be a red flag for poor blood sugar control—and it can occur in patients who haven't yet been diagnosed with diabetes. People with poor blood sugar control often have impaired immunity, increasing their risk for infections such as Candidiasis.

Next step: Most Candidiasis infections are easily treated with topical antifungal preparations. People with persistent/severe cases may need an oral medication, such as over-the-counter (OTC) *clotrimazole* (Lotrimin) or prescription *fluconazole* (Diflucan).

Also: Dark patches of skin that feel velvety and thicker than normal (especially on the neck and under the arms) could be due to acanthosis nigricans, a sign of insulin resistance, a condition that often precedes diabetes. The skin may also smell bad or itch.

Acanthosis nigricans often will improve without treatment when you get your blood sugar under control, so get tested for insulin resistance and glucose tolerance.

What Is Type 1.5 Diabetes?

Anne Peters, MD, professor of clinical medicine, Keck School of Medicine, University of Southern California, Los Angeles, and director of the USC Westside Center for Diabetes. She is author of *Conquering Diabetes: A Complete Program for Prevention and Treatment*.

H ow does type 1.5 diabetes differ from other types of diabetes?

Type 1 diabetes is an autoimmune disorder in which the body's own immune system destroys the insulin-producing cells of the pancreas. As a result, the body does not produce enough of the hormone insulin to control blood sugar levels.

Type 2 diabetes is characterized by insulin resistance—the body responds to insulin inefficiently and fails to keep blood sugar at a normal level. The vast majority of people with diabetes have type 2.

A person who shows attributes of both type 1 and type 2 is said to have type 1.5 diabetes. What initially appeared to be type 2 diabetes is actually slowly evolving type 1 diabetes. Type 1.5 diabetes also is called slow-onset type 1 or latent autoimmune diabetes in adults (LADA). It is diagnosed through a blood test for antibodies. Diet, exercise and some oral medications may help keep the condition under control—but many type 1.5 patients require insulin within 10 years of diagnosis.

What's Going on with My Fingernails?

Jeffrey Benabio, MD, physician director of health-care transformation, Kaiser Permanente, San Diego. Benabio. com

Like wrinkles on your face, ridges and discoloration in fingernails are a normal sign of aging. One of my patients humorously refers to them as a "sign of maturity."

Fingernail ridges (which run from cuticle to nail tip) can appear as early as one's 30s but are most common after age 60.

Although fingernail ridges are usually on just one or two nails, they may eventually develop on all of your fingernails. Nails also become drier as you age and tend to split more easily.

In some people as they age, the lunula (the white half moon at the base of the fingernail) can even disappear.

Even though fingernails also can become yellowed or grayish over time, discoloration could indicate a fungal infection or even a health condition such as diabetes.

At your next checkup, be sure to show your doctor your fingernails so that he/she can examine them. You may need blood tests to check for diabetes or a scraping of the nail to determine whether you have a fungal infection.

Nothing can reverse age-related changes in the fingernails. But your fingernails will look and feel better if you moisturize frequently with hand cream. Also, since removing and reapplying nail polish dries the nails, try to do this no more than once a week.

This DIY Test for Diabetes Could Save Your Life

David L. Katz, MD, MPH, an internist and preventive medicine specialist. He is cofounder and director of the Yale-Griffin Prevention Research Center in Derby, Connecticut, and clinical instructor at the Yale School of Medicine in New Haven, Connecticut. Dr. Katz is also past president of the American College of Lifestyle Medicine and author of *Disease-Proof: Slash Your Risk of Heart Disease, Cancer, Diabetes and More—by 80 Percent.*

If you're conscientious about your health, you probably see your doctor for an annual physical…or perhaps even more often if you have a chronic condition or get sick.

But if you'd like to keep tabs on your health between your doctor visits, there's an easy, do-it-yourself test that can give you valuable information about your body.

Here's a self-test for diabetes—repeat it once every few months, and keep track of the results. *See your doctor if you don't "pass" this "Pencil Test"…*

Why this test? It checks the nerve function in your feet—if abnormal, this could indicate diabetes, certain types of infections or autoimmune disease.

The prop you'll need: A pencil that is freshly sharpened at one end with a flat eraser on the other end…and a friend to help.

*This self-test is not a substitute for a thorough physical exam from your doctor. Use it only as a way to identify potential problem areas to discuss with your physician.

What to do: Sit down so that all sides of your bare feet are accessible. Close your eyes, and keep them closed throughout the test.

Have your friend lightly touch your foot with either the sharp end or the eraser end of the pencil. With each touch, say which end of the pencil you think was used.

Ask your friend to repeat the test in at least three different locations on the tops and bottoms of both feet (12 locations total). Have your friend keep track of your right and wrong answers.

Watch out: Most people can easily tell the difference between "sharp" and "dull" sensations on their sensitive feet. If you give the wrong answer for more than two or three locations on your feet, have your doctor repeat the test to determine whether you have nerve damage (neuropathy).

Beware: Neuropathy is a common sign of diabetes…certain autoimmune disorders, including lupus and Sjögren's syndrome…infection, such as Lyme disease, shingles or hepatitis C…or excessive exposure to toxins, such as pesticides or heavy metals (mercury or lead).

What Your Urine Says About Your Health

Jonathan M. Vapnek, MD, a urologist and associate clinical professor of urology at Mount Sinai School of Medicine in New York City. A member of the American Urological Association, he was named by *New York Magazine* as one of New York City's best urologists. Dr. Vapnek has authored or coauthored more than 35 papers on urological topics.

You would be surprised by how much information can be gleaned from the urine that you produce each day (one to two quarts, on average). For example, the simple "dipstick" urine test that doctors often use to check for a urinary tract infection also can help them diagnose kidney disease, diabetes, cancer and other conditions. But there is more.

What you may not realize: If you know what to look for, you can tell a lot about your health just by being aware of the physical characteristics of your urine—such as color, smell and frequency. *What to watch out for…*

COLOR

When you're healthy and drinking enough water, your urine should be mainly clear or straw-colored with just a hint of yellow. The yellow color comes from urochrome, a pigment produced by the breakdown of a protein in red blood cells.

Urine is naturally darker in the morning because you don't drink water while you sleep. If a color change persists, however, it could be a problem. *For example…*

• **Brown or dark brown.** Pay attention if your urine is dark for more than a week.

What this usually means: Liver disease. The liver normally breaks down and excretes bilirubin, a pigment that's produced by the turnover of red blood cells. Patients with liver disease accumulate bilirubin. This initially will cause jaundice, a yellowing of the skin or the whites of the eyes. As more bilirubin accumulates, it can cause the urine to become brown. A combination of dark-colored urine and jaundice means that liver disease might be getting worse. See your doctor right away.

• **Dark-colored urine also can be a side effect of some antibiotics, laxatives and muscle relaxants.** Eating large amounts of fava beans, rhubarb or aloe can cause brown urine as well. In some cases, dark-colored urine can signal kidney failure.

• **Red or pink.** Urine that's tinged with red or pink could simply mean that you have been eating beets. (The medical term for beet-induced urine changes is beeturia). Or it could mean that you're urinating blood.

The amount of blood will affect the color. If the urine resembles cabernet wine, you're bleeding a lot…urine that's pinkish or just slightly red contains only traces of blood. A microscopic amount of blood won't be visible—it can be detected only with a laboratory test.

What this usually means: Blood in the urine is always a problem. Make an appointment to see your doctor. If you see blood and it also hurts when you urinate, you could have an infection—in the urethra, bladder or kidney or even a malignancy in the bladder, for example. Bleeding without pain also can indicate these conditions.

- **Green.** Though rare, a person's urine can turn a greenish color.

What this usually means: Green urine can appear when you've consumed a chemical dye—from food coloring, for example, or from taking medications such as *amitriptyline*, an antidepressant, or *indomethacin* (Indocin), a nonsteroidal anti-inflammatory drug. In some cases, urine with a greenish tint can signal a urinary tract infection with certain bacteria (such as pseudomonas) that affect the color.

If your urine is greenish, increase fluid intake to see if it clears. If it doesn't in two days, see your doctor or a urologist.

ODOR

If you're healthy, your urine should be highly diluted, consisting of about 95% water, with only small amounts of dissolved chemical compounds and metabolic by-products. It typically has no—or only a faint—odor.

Of course everyone is familiar with the effect that asparagus and some other foods, such as onions or fish, have on the smell of one's urine. This strong "rotten" smell is due to the chemical compounds in certain foods, particularly molecules that are not completely broken down by the body. The smell usually disappears within a day or so.

Some other less common urine smells include…

- **Ammonia-like.** If your urine is concentrated, with a larger-than-normal amount of urea (a chemical compound in urine), you might smell an aroma that resembles ammonia. Or you might just notice that it has a stronger smell than usual.

What this usually means: Dehydration. The less water you drink, the higher the concentration of urea and other substances—and the stronger the smell. You can diagnose this yourself by drinking, say, one extra glass of water an hour for several hours to add water to your urine. The strong urine smell will probably disappear within a few hours. If it does not, see your doctor.

- **Foul-smelling.** If your urine smells foul or unusual in any way for more than a few days, pay attention to the odor.

What this usually means: If it's not caused by a food that you've eaten, it could signal an infection in the bladder or kidneys. Less often, it's due to a metabolic disorder that reduces the body's ability to fully break down foods during digestion.

Uncontrolled diabetes can cause an abnormally sweet odor, and penicillin can cause a distinctive medicinal odor.

Even if you have no other symptoms, such as pain while urinating, but your urine continues to have an unusually strong smell for more than a couple of days, talk to your doctor.

FOAMY OR BUBBLY

It's natural to see foam in the toilet when you really have to go and have a heavy stream. But urine that's consistently foamy or bubbly could mean that you're losing protein.

What this usually means: Kidney disease. Large amounts of protein in the urine is one of the main signs of chronic kidney disease. See your doctor right away.

MUCUS OR CLOUDY

Mucus in urine could indicate inflammation in the urinary tract.

What this usually means: Urinary tract infection. See your doctor.

Cloudy urine also can be related to infection but often is just an indication that your urine is alkaline, which is harmless at low levels.

VOLUME AND FREQUENCY

The average adult typically urinates four to eight times in 24 hours. A change in the frequency of your urinary habits, including getting up more than twice a night to urinate, or an increase or decrease in the amount that you urinate, warrants attention.

What this usually means: An increase in the frequency of urination, along with an increase in volume, is one of the telltale signs of diabetes.

If the amount of urine seems the same but you're urinating more often, you could have a urinary tract infection. If this is the case, you'll probably have very strong urges to urinate even when just a small amount comes out.

Frequency of urination and/or urinary urgency in the absence of a urinary tract infection can indicate an overactive bladder.

In men, enlargement of the prostate gland can trigger urinary urgency. Patients with neurological conditions, such as multiple sclerosis, can also have this symptom.

Don't worry if there's been a decrease in the amount or frequency of urination. You probably just need to drink more water. If this doesn't help, see your doctor.

Get That Eye Exam

You may know that a good eye exam can reveal more than just your eye health. But did you know that it can detect signs of multiple sclerosis, diabetes, high blood pressure, rheumatoid arthritis, high cholesterol and Crohn's disease? In a study of insurance claims, 6% of these conditions were first detected by eye doctors.

Why: The eyes contain blood vessels, nerves and other structures that can be affected by chronic illness. If you're over age 40, get an eye exam at least every two years.

Linda Chous, OD, chief eye-care officer, UnitedHealthcare Vision, Minneapolis.

What a Good Physical Tells About Your Brain

Richard Carmona, MD, FACS, MPH, president of the Tucson, Arizona–based Canyon Ranch Institute and vice chairman of Canyon Ranch, a health resort, spa and wellness retreat. He served as US Surgeon General from 2002 to 2006 and is author of *Canyon Ranch's 30 Days to a Better Brain.*

Put yourself on a weight-loss diet, and you can measure your success with a bathroom scale. If fitness is your goal, you can track your improvement by charting how fast you can run or walk a mile.

But how can you tell if your brain is as fit as the rest of you?

If you're having memory problems, that's an obvious red flag. But even if you're basically healthy (or are being treated for a chronic condition such as high blood pressure), a routine medical exam can tell a lot about your brain health—if you know what the seemingly basic tests may mean, according to former US Surgeon General Richard Carmona, MD. *What a physical checkup reveals about your brain—and the additional tests you may need...*

LAY IT ALL OUT

Doctors aren't mind readers—they don't know what you're worried about unless you tell them. At your physical, tell your doctor about any changes in your health (even if you think they sound trivial).

Where most people get tripped up: There's always that routine question about medications you're taking. Don't assume that your doctor knows everything he/she has prescribed—include every medication and supplement you're taking.

Many common prescription or over-the-counter drugs—alone or in combination—can affect your brain. The following types of drugs are among the most commonly associated with dizziness, fuzzy thinking and/or memory problems. *All drugs within each class can addle a person's brain—not only the specific drug examples given...*

- **Allergy medications,** including antihistamines (such as Benadryl and Claritin).

- **Antianxiety medications** (such as Valium and Xanax).

- **Antibiotics** (such as Cipro and Levaquin).

- **Antidepressants** (such as Prozac and Lexapro).

- **Blood pressure medications** (such as Zestril and Procardia).

- **Sleep aids** (such as Ambien).

If you are taking one of these types of medications and are experiencing cognitive problems, ask your physician about switching to a different drug.

Fortunately, the fuzzy thinking and/or problems with memory usually go away when the drug is discontinued. And because everyone responds differently to individual medications, you may be able to safely take a different drug that's within the same class.

CLUES FROM YOUR PHYSICAL

Even if you're not having cognitive problems, your physical can give you a measure of key markers of brain health. For example, most people know that high blood pressure is linked to increased risk for certain types of dementia (normal blood pressure is 120/80 or below). But low blood pressure (lower than 90/60) may make you dizzy, fatigued and unable to think clearly. *Other important brain-health markers...*

• **Eyes.** When your doctor shines that bright light in your eyes, he is looking at the retina, the light-sensitive tissue at the back of the eye that is connected directly to the optic nerve leading to the brain. Blood vessels in the retina reflect vascular health in the whole body—including the brain.

• **Hearing, balance and coordination.** While many diseases can cause problems with hearing, balance or coordination, one possibility is dysfunction of the eighth cranial nerve, which connects directly to the brain. Ears have fluid-filled canals that relay information to the brain via the eighth cranial nerve and act as a kind of gyroscope, giving us our sense of orientation in space. When we change position, the fluid moves, and the brain adjusts our balance and coordination. With some inner-ear disorders, such as Ménière's disease or labyrinthitis, people are dizzy, lose hearing or fall frequently due to loss of balance and coordination.

• **Reflexes.** A tap on your knee with a tiny hammer sends an electrical impulse to the spinal cord, which then sends a signal back to the foot, triggering a kick. A weak or delayed response could indicate a problem with the nervous system or brain.

• **Sensation.** All of the senses are housed in the brain, including the sense of touch. Any change in sensation—tingling hands or feet... weak hands...and/or numbness anywhere in the body—could signal a problem in the brain.

DIGGING DEEPER

If your memory is failing or you're having other cognitive problems, such as difficulty making decisions or planning activities, your doctor may want to run tests for...

• **Inflammation.** A blood test for C-reactive protein (CRP) measures general levels of inflammation in the body. High levels of CRP (above 3.0 mg/L) could be due to a simple infection...cardiovascular disease that may also be putting your brain at risk...or an autoimmune disease, such as lupus or multiple sclerosis, which can cause problems with memory and thinking as well as physical symptoms.

• **Vitamin deficiencies.** A vitamin B-12 deficiency can lead to memory loss, fatigue and light-headedness. Other common nutrient deficiencies that can affect thinking include vitamin D and omega-3 fatty acids—there are tests for both.

• **Diabetes and glucose tolerance.** Left untreated, diabetes can dramatically increase one's risk for dementia. If your doctor suspects you have diabetes (or it runs in your family), get your blood glucose level tested (following an overnight fast).

Useful: An HbA1C test, which gives a broader picture of your glucose level over the previous six to 12 weeks. While most people, especially after age 45, should get glucose testing at least every three years, it's particularly important for those having cognitive symptoms.

• **Tick-borne illness.** Lyme disease and Rocky Mountain spotted fever can cause mental fuzziness.

Also helpful: Liver function tests, including new genomic tests, also may be ordered to assess your liver's ability to remove toxins. If the body doesn't clear toxins, this can alter brain metabolism, possibly leading to cognitive decline.

The Disease You Don't Know About

More than eight million Americans don't know they have diabetes. Three in 10 people with diabetes aren't diagnosed, even though they may have seen a doctor during the year.

Beware: Symptoms—fatigue, blurred vision, slow-healing cuts and scrapes, and more frequent urination—may be subtle and come on slowly.

Study by researchers at Emory University School of Medicine, Atlanta, published in *Annals of Internal Medicine*.

How Often Should You Get Screened for Diabetes?

Everyone over age 45 should be screened for type 2 diabetes and prediabetes every three years, according to the US Preventive Services Task Force. People who are found to have abnormal blood sugar—a precursor to diabetes—can then take aggressive measures to prevent the disease, such as eating healthier and exercising.

US Preventive Services Task Force, Rockville, Maryland.

Are You Getting the Most from Your Blood Tests? Even Doctors May Miss Signs of Health Problems

James B. LaValle, RPh, CCN, a clinical pharmacist, nutritionist and founder of Progressive Medical Center, Orange County, California. He is author of *Your Blood Never Lies: How to Read a Blood Test for a Longer, Healthier Life*. JimLaValle.com

Unless your doctor tells you there's a problem, you may not give much thought to the blood tests that you receive periodically.

But standard blood tests and certain other blood tests that you may request from your doctor can offer valuable—even lifesaving—clues about your health, including explanations for such vexing conditions as short-term memory loss and fatigue.

What you may not realize: If your doctor says that your test results are "normal," this is not the same as "optimal" or even "good."

For example, a total cholesterol reading of 200 mg/dL is considered normal, even though the risk of developing heart disease is sometimes higher at this level than it would be if your numbers were lower. Always ask your doctor what your target should be.

Blood test results that you should definitely make note of—and certain tests you may want to request...*

•**Low potassium.** Low potassium (hypokalemia) is worrisome because it can cause fatigue, constipation and general weakness, along with heart palpitations.

Causes: An imbalance of the hormone insulin often causes low potassium. It also can be due to problems with the adrenal glands or a loss of fluids from vomiting and/or diarrhea. A magnesium deficiency or a high-sodium diet can lead to low potassium, too. It is also a common side effect of certain medications, including diuretics, such as hydrochlorothiazide...laxatives...and some asthma drugs, such as albuterol.

Normal potassium: 3.6 mEq/L to 5.2 mEq/L.

Optimal potassium: 4.5 mEq/L to 5.2 mEq/L.

What to do: If your potassium is not optimal, your doctor will probably recommend that you eat more potassium-rich foods, such as fruits (bananas, oranges, cantaloupe)... vegetables (tomatoes, sweet potatoes)...and whole grains (quinoa, buckwheat). You'll also be advised to reduce your sodium intake to less than 2,300 mg daily—high sodium depletes potassium from the body. Additionally, you may be advised to take a magnesium and potassium supplement.

Also: Keep your stress level low. Chronic stress can lead to a high level of the hormone cortisol—this can overwhelm the adrenal glands and lead to low potassium.

*These blood tests typically are covered by health insurance.

• **"Normal" glucose.** Most people know that high fasting blood glucose (126 mg/dL or above) is a warning sign of diabetes. But you may not be aware that slight increases in blood sugar—even when it is still within the so-called normal range—also put you at greater risk.

Surprising: Among 46,000 people who were tracked for 10 years, for every one-point rise in fasting blood glucose over 84 mg/dL, the risk of developing diabetes increased by about 6%. Vascular and kidney damage may begin when glucose reaches 90 mg/dL—a level that's within the normal range.

Causes: High blood glucose usually occurs when the body's cells become resistant to the hormone insulin and/or when the pancreas doesn't produce enough insulin. Obesity and genetic factors are among the main causes.

Normal glucose: 65 mg/dL to 99 mg/dL.

Optimal glucose: 70 mg/dL to 84 mg/dL.

What to do: If your fasting glucose isn't optimal or if tests show that it's rising, try to get the numbers down with regular exercise, weight loss and a healthier diet.

Powerful spice: Add one-quarter teaspoon of cinnamon to your food each day. People who take this small dose can lower their blood glucose by 18% to 29%.

Alternative: A standardized cinnamon extract in capsule form (125 mg to 250 mg, two to three times daily).

• **High homocysteine.** Most doctors recommend a homocysteine test only for patients with existing heart problems. Everyone should get it. High homocysteine may damage arteries and increase the risk for heart disease and stroke.

Causes: Homocysteine rises if you don't get enough B-complex vitamins or if you're unable to properly metabolize methionine, an amino acid that's mainly found in meat, fish and dairy. Vegetarians tend to have higher homocysteine levels. Other causes include a lack of exercise, chronic stress, smoking and too much caffeine.

Normal homocysteine: Less than 15 umol/L.

Optimal homocysteine: 8 umol/L or below.

What to do: If your homocysteine level isn't optimal, take a daily B-complex vitamin supplement that has at least 50 mg of vitamin B-6.

Also helpful: A fish oil supplement to reduce inflammation and protect the arteries. Take 1,000 mg, two to three times daily.**

• **Low DHEA.** This is a hormone that's used by the body to manufacture both testosterone and estrogen. It's also an antioxidant that supports the immune system and increases insulin sensitivity and the body's ability to metabolize fats. DHEA is not usually measured in standard blood tests, but all adults should request that their levels be tested.

Low DHEA is a common cause of fatigue, weight gain, depression and decreased libido in men and women of all ages. Over time, it can damage the hippocampus, the "memory center" of the brain.

Causes: It's normal for DHEA to slightly decrease with age. Larger deficiencies can indicate an autoimmune disease (such as rheumatoid arthritis) or chronic stress.

Normal DHEA: Levels of this hormone peak in one's late 20s. Normal levels vary widely with age and gender.

Optimal DHEA: The high end of the normal range is optimal—it reflects a reserve of DHEA.

Examples: 200 mcg/dL to 270 mcg/dL for men…and 120 mcg/dL to 180 mcg/dL for women.

What to do: If your DHEA level isn't optimal, managing emotional stress is critical. Get at least eight hours of sleep every night…exercise aerobically for about 30 minutes, three to four times a week…and practice relaxation techniques, such as yoga and meditation.

Also helpful: A daily supplement (25 mg to 50 mg) of DHEA. If you take this supplement, do so only under a doctor's supervision—you'll need regular blood tests to ensure that your DHEA level doesn't get too high.

• **High LDL-P (LDL particle number).** Traditional cholesterol tests look only at triglyc-

---

**Check with your doctor before using fish oil, especially if you take a blood thinner—fish oil can interact with it and certain other medications.

erides and total LDL and HDL cholesterol. I advise patients to get a fractionated cholesterol test for a more detailed picture.

Important: Patients with a large number of small LDL particles have an elevated risk for a heart attack even if their overall LDL level is normal. The greater the number of these cholesterol particles, the more likely they are to lodge in the lining of blood vessels and eventually trigger a heart attack.

Causes: Genetics is partly responsible for high LDL and LDL-P. A poor reading can be due to metabolic syndrome, a group of factors that includes abdominal obesity, elevated triglycerides and high blood pressure. A diet high in animal fats and processed foods also can cause an increase in LDL-P.

Normal LDL-P: Less than 1,300 nmol/L.

Optimal LDL-P: Below 1,000 nmol/L on an NMR lipoprofile (this test is the most accurate).

What to do: If your LDL-P level is not optimal (and you have not had a heart attack or other coronary event), I recommend exercise… weight loss…blood pressure and blood sugar management…more antioxidant-rich foods such as vegetables, berries and legumes…and three to five cups of green tea daily—it's a potent antioxidant that minimizes the oxidation of cholesterol molecules, which is important for reducing heart attacks.

Also: Daily supplements of bergamot extract, which has been shown to change the size of cholesterol particles (Earl Grey tea, which is flavored with oil of bergamot, provides a less potent dose)…and aged garlic extract, which has a beneficial effect on multiple cardiovascular risk factors. If these steps do not sufficiently improve your LDL-P level, talk to your doctor about taking a statin and/or niacin.

3

Foods That Fight Diabetes

5 Surprising Foods to Help You Live Longer

Whether your blood sugar (glucose) levels are normal and you want to keep them that way… or you have diabetes and glucose control is your mantra…it is smart to eat a well-balanced diet to help keep your glucose readings healthy. In fact, maintaining healthy glucose levels may even help you live longer by avoiding diabetes— one of the leading causes of death in the US.

Most people already know that cinnamon is an excellent choice for blood sugar control. Consuming just one-half teaspoon to three teaspoons a day can reduce glucose levels by up to 24%. Cinnamon is great on cereals, vegetables, cottage cheese and snacks (think fresh apple slices sprinkled with cinnamon).

Other smart food choices…*

*If you take diabetes medication, consult your doctor before making significant changes to your diet— drug dosages may need to be adjusted.

GLUCOSE-CONTROLLING FOOD #1: BLACK BEANS

Beans, in general, are the most underrated food in the supermarket.

Beans are high in protein as well as soluble and insoluble fiber. Soluble fiber helps you feel fuller longer, and insoluble fiber helps prevent constipation. Beans also break down slowly during digestion, which means more stable blood sugar levels.

Black beans, however, are particularly healthful because of their especially high fiber content. For example, one cup of cooked black beans contains 15 g of fiber, while a cup of pink beans has just 9 g.

Bonus: Beans protect the heart by lowering cholesterol and reducing damage from free radicals. For example, one study showed that you can lower your total and LDL ("bad") cho-

Bonnie Taub-Dix, RD, a registered dietitian and owner of BTD Nutrition Consultants located in New York City. A nationally recognized nutrition expert and author of *Read It Before You Eat It*, she has advised patients on the best ways to control diabetes for more than three decades. BonnieTaubDix.com

69

lesterol by about 8% simply by eating one-half cup of cooked pinto beans every day.

Helpful: To shorten cooking times, use canned beans instead of dried beans. They are equally nutritious, and you can reduce the sodium in salted canned beans by about 40% by rinsing them.

Another healthful way to use beans: Hummus. In the Middle East, people eat this chickpea (garbanzo bean) spread as often as Americans eat bread. It is much healthier than bread because it contains both protein and olive oil—important for slowing the absorption of carbohydrate sugars and preventing blood sugar "spikes."

Hummus is a good weight-loss dish because it is high in fiber (about 15 g per cup) as well as protein (about 19 g). Ample amounts of protein and fiber allow you to satisfy your appetite with smaller portions of food.

Hummus is made with mashed chickpeas, tahini (a sesame seed paste), lemon juice, garlic, salt and a little olive oil. Stick to the serving size on the label, which is typically two to four tablespoons.

GLUCOSE-CONTROLLING FOOD #2:
COCOA

The flavanols in cocoa are potent antioxidants that not only fight heart disease but also help guard against diabetes. In recent studies, cocoa improved insulin sensitivity, the body's ability to transport sugar out of the bloodstream. It's wise for people with diabetes or high blood sugar to choose unsweetened cocoa and add a small amount of sugar or sugar substitute.

Cinnamon hot cocoa combines two glucose-controlling ingredients in one delicious recipe.

To prepare: Mix one-quarter cup of baking cocoa, one tablespoon of sugar (or Truvia to taste) and a pinch of salt. Gradually add one-quarter cup of boiling water and blend well. Add one cup of skim or 1% low-fat milk and a cinnamon stick. While stirring occasionally, heat on low for 10 minutes. Remove the cinnamon stick and enjoy!

GLUCOSE-CONTROLLING FOOD #3:
DATES

These little fruits are sweet enough to qualify as dessert but have more antioxidants per serving than oranges, grapes and even broccoli. The antioxidants can help prevent heart disease as well as neuropathy—nerve damage that frequently occurs in people who have diabetes.

A single serving (for example, seven deglet noor dates) has 4 g of fiber for better blood sugar management.

Be careful: Seven dates also have 140 calories and 32 g of sugar, so this must be added to your total daily carbohydrate intake, especially if you have diabetes. Dates, in general, have a low glycemic index, so they don't spike glucose levels. Medjool dates, however, are not an ideal choice. They have significantly more sugar and calories per serving than deglet noor dates.

GLUCOSE-CONTROLLING FOOD #4:
SARDINES

Many people know about the heart-healthy benefits of cold-water fish, such as salmon and mackerel. An analysis of studies involving hundreds of thousands of adults found that just one to two fish servings a week was linked to a reduced risk of dying from heart disease of more than one-third.

What's less well-known is that the high concentration of omega-3 fatty acids in cold-water fish also helps prevent a too-rapid rise in blood sugar. Besides being low on the glycemic index, fish contains protein, which blunts blood sugar levels.

Best for helping to prevent high blood sugar: In addition to salmon and mackerel, sardines are an excellent choice (when canned with bones, they also are a good source of calcium). Tuna, to a somewhat lesser extent, offers omega-3s (choose canned light—albacore white has higher levels of mercury). Also avoid large fish, such as king mackerel and swordfish, which have more mercury than smaller fish. Aim for a 3.5-ounce serving two or three times a week.

GLUCOSE-CONTROLLING FOOD #5: ALMONDS

High in fiber, protein and beneficial fats, nuts can significantly lower glucose levels. In fact, women who ate a one-ounce serving of nuts at least five times a week were nearly 30% less likely to develop diabetes than women who rarely or never ate nuts, according to one study.

The poly- and monounsaturated fats in nuts improve the body's ability to use insulin. Nuts also help with cholesterol control—important because diabetes increases risk for heart disease.

All nuts are beneficial, but almonds contain more fiber, calcium and protein than most nuts (and are best for blood sugar control). Walnuts are highest in antioxidants and omega-3 fatty acids. Avoid salted nuts—they have too much sodium.

Excellent way to add nuts to your diet: Nut butters. Almost everyone likes peanut butter, and it is healthier than you might think. Like butters made from almonds, cashews or other nuts, the fats it contains are mostly monounsaturated, which are good for the heart. The fiber in nut butters (about 1 g to 2 g per tablespoon, depending on the nut) can help lower blood sugar.

Good choice for blood sugar control: One serving (one to two tablespoons) of almond butter (rich in potassium, vitamin E and calcium) several times a week. Look for nut butters that have a short list of ingredients—they are the most nutritious.

A SIMPLE BLOOD SUGAR BUSTER

Taking two tablespoons of apple-cider vinegar in eight ounces of water with meals or before bedtime can slow the absorption of sugar into the blood—vinegar helps to block the digestive enzymes that change carbs to sugar.

For diabetes-friendly recipes and specific menu plans, see page 107.

One Food That People with Diabetes Really, Really, Really Need

David Jenkins, MD, PhD, DSc, professor, department of nutritional sciences, and Canada Research Chair in Nutrition and Metabolism, University of Toronto, Canada. He also is director of the Risk Factor Modification Centre, St. Michael's Hospital, Toronto, and lead author of a study on legumes and diabetes control published in *Archives of Internal Medicine*.

A humble everyday food is amazingly good at helping to control diabetes and prevent the complications of this deadly disease—yet many diabetes patients ban it from their diets.

I'm talking about legumes—beans, chickpeas, lentils—which truly are close to magical when it comes to their health effects, particularly for folks with type 2 diabetes.

So if you're among the crowd of "bean holdouts," you should try to give beans and other legumes a place of honor in your daily diet.

Your life could depend on it! *Here's why...*

BEANS AND YOUR BLOOD SUGAR

For diabetes patients, keeping blood sugar levels as close to normal as possible is crucial... but controlling those fluctuating levels can be a real challenge. Many patients take antihyperglycemic drugs for this purpose, yet diet remains a major factor in diabetes management.

A lot of people with diabetes focus on high-fiber foods such as whole grains to help avoid problems like heart disease. And fiber does help (though the exact mechanism is unknown). But now a recent Canadian study shows that beans and other legumes do the job even better.

The secret behind legumes' awesome power lies in their low glycemic index (GI) status. The GI is a scale from 0 to 100 that ranks foods based on their immediate effects on blood glucose levels. The lower its GI, the less of a blood sugar spike a particular food causes.

BEANS BEST THE COMPETITION

The study included 121 men and women with type 2 diabetes. Participants were divided into two groups and assigned to follow one of two healthful diets that were fairly equal in total calories, fat, protein and carbohydrates consumed.

As part of their diet, the first group was told to consume about 190 grams (two half-cup servings) of beans or other legumes each day. The second group's diet included an equal amount of whole grains, such as whole-wheat cereals and breads and brown rice. Each group also avoided the alternate food—in other words, the bean group avoided whole grains and the whole-grain group avoided beans.

After three months: The whole-grain group did benefit from their diet—but the bean-eaters benefited even more. *Specifically...*

• **Hemoglobin A1C values**—indicated by a blood test that measures average blood glucose levels for the previous three-month period—dropped significantly more in the legume group than in the whole-grain group.

Using an equation that calculates risk for coronary heart disease (CHD), researchers found that the legume group's CHD risk score fell from 10.7 to 9.6. This was largely the result of the legume eaters' decrease in systolic blood pressure (the top number of a blood pressure reading) from 122 to 118. In contrast, in the whole-grain group, neither the CHD risk score nor blood pressure decreased significantly.

Also: In the legume group, the average weight loss and waist-size reduction slightly exceeded those of the high-fiber group.

GIVE A HIGH-FIVE FOR LOW GI

The study's lead author, David Jenkins, MD, PhD, DSc, said that his team purposely chose study participants who already had reasonably good diets. "We wanted to see how people doing well could make further improvements," he explained.

And in fact, both the legume group and the high-fiber group did improve. On the hemoglobin A1C test, for instance, both groups got their levels down below 7.0—a benchmark that often allows patients to eventually decrease their diabetes medication.

Still, the legumes came out ahead for several reasons. Unlike whole grains, beans are a very good source of protein—and protein does not cause blood sugar to fluctuate the way carbs can. Beans also provide plentiful potassium, which may reduce blood pressure by counteracting the effects of sodium. But the primary factor in beans' favor, Dr. Jenkins said, is that they are among the lowest-GI foods because their complex carbohydrates are digested slowly.

WHO SHOULD GIVE A HILL OF BEANS

Legumes are particularly good for diabetes patients, but just about everyone can benefit from better blood sugar control. Are you hesitant because you don't care for the taste or texture? There are many types of beans and other legumes to choose from—so keep experimenting until you find some you enjoy!

It's easy to incorporate one cup of these potent orbs into your daily diet since they are so versatile.

Tasty suggestions: Add white beans to vegetable soups and meat stews...use black or kidney beans plus tofu as the basis for chili...top salads with edamame (boiled green soy beans)...serve lentils as a side dish or salad...enjoy the many varieties of hummus, made from chickpeas...or purée any type of bean to make dip, adding what tastes good to you—olive oil, pepper and/or other spices you love.

And don't worry about gas. Despite the "musical" reputation of beans, the study participants registered few complaints in this department. However, if you are concerned about bloating or flatulence, Dr. Jenkins advised starting with just one-half cup per day and increasing gradually over several weeks to give your digestive system time to adjust.

Amazing Food Cure: Help Diabetes with Chromium

Up to 90% of Americans are deficient in chromium, a mineral that makes the body's cells more responsive to insulin's effects.

What research shows: People with diabetes who eat more onions, which are high in chromium, typically have lower fasting blood glucose levels. They also have lower triglycerides and LDL cholesterol. High levels of triglycerides and LDL increase the risk for heart disease—a serious threat for diabetics.

How much: Aim for one to two servings of chromium-rich foods a day. In addition to onions, other high-chromium foods include brewer's yeast, sweet potatoes, oysters, beef and tomatoes.

Stephen Sinatra, MD, cardiologist and founder of Heart MD Institute, an educational platform that promotes complementary treatments for heart disease, Manchester, Connecticut. He published the monthly newsletter *Heart, Health & Nutrition* for more than 15 years and lectures worldwide about natural and nutritional remedies. DrSinatra.com

Control Blood Sugar and Keep Fit with Prebiotic Sunchokes

Tamara Duker Freuman, RD, CDN, a registered dietitian in private practice and a clinical preceptor for the Dietetic Internship Program at Columbia University's Teacher's College, both in New York City. TamaraDuker.com

The sunchoke looks like the love child of a potato and a piece of ginger. But this gnarled and knobby root vegetable has its own irresistible flavor…slightly nutty, crisp like jicama or water chestnut, with a hint of artichoke flavor that becomes more intense when cooked. If you're a veg-head, it's a fun addition to your daily menu.

Although nutritionists know that the sunchoke—a root vegetable also known as the Jerusalem artichoke—is great for glucose control, scientific studies to back up this idea have been few and far between. Now, a team of researchers from Japan has demonstrated that sunchokes may help prevent type 2 diabetes and fatty liver disease (a condition that often goes with diabetes and that can lead to life-threatening liver cirrhosis and hepatitis). But even if the researchers' claim is too ambitious, there are plenty of reasons to get familiar with sunchokes, their many health benefits and delicious recipes.

LESSONS FROM FAT RATS

The Japanese researchers fed rats a diet that was either 60% fructose (fruit sugar) or 60% fructose and 10% sunchoke powder to see whether sunchokes could prevent diabetes in the rodents. That is, they regularly fed the rats lots of sugar to get their blood sugar levels to spike (hyperglycemia) and their innate blood sugar controller—their insulin-producing pancreas—to malfunction. After four weeks of these diets, the blood and livers of the rats showed that, although signs of diabetes and fatty livers developed in all of them from all that fructose, the effects were milder in the rats that were also eating sunchokes. The sunchoke eaters did so much better, in fact, that the researchers suggested that at least 10% of the daily diet of people at risk for diabetes and fatty liver disease should consist of sunchokes.

A 10%-sunchoke-per-day diet seems a bit much. Tamara Duker Freuman, RD, CDN, registered dietitian and clinical preceptor for the Dietetic Internship Program at Columbia University's Teacher's College, agrees, noting that similar tests would need to be performed in humans to really know whether eating sunchokes could similarly lessen risk of diabetes in people, and if so, how much would be needed to cut diabetes off at the pass. Besides, rather than overloading your diet with sunchokes in quest of glucose control, it would be more reasonable to simply add them, in moderation, to the list of healthful nondrug food and remedies that you already know help prevent diabetes.

"Sunchokes have a low glycemic index, which is why they are considered to be a great food choice if you have diabetes—they don't cause blood sugar to spike. The new research from Japan, however, is suggesting that sunchokes work on a metabolic level to help prevent diabetes and fatty liver disease," Freuman explained. "That's an ambitious claim." Until human studies can confirm the findings of these Japanese researchers, Freuman offered these health-boosting reasons to enjoy the little tubers.

A PREBIOTIC POWER FOOD

Sunchokes are the tuberous root of a type of sunflower that's native to North America. They provide generous amounts of iron and potassium and help the body absorb certain minerals, such as calcium…and they are rich in fiber, which helps prevent certain types of cancer, such as colon cancer.

In fact, sunchokes are packed with an important type of fiber called inulin, which is a prebiotic. "Inulin is a carbohydrate, but because your body can't digest it, it doesn't affect your blood sugar," said Freuman. This characteristic gives the sunchoke its low glycemic effect. But even though you can't digest inulin, the healthful probiotic bacteria in your gut feast on it and, in fact, need it to provide their health benefits to you, explained Freuman.

But inulin does have one unfortunate downside—which also puts a crimp in the advice of the Japanese researchers to load your daily diet with sunchokes. Eating too much inulin—more than 10 grams a day—can make you gassy. Since one-half cup of sunchokes has 18 grams of inulin in it, Freuman suggests eating no more than one-quarter cup at a time if you are new to this root vegetable but want to add it to your diet. Within six to eight hours—the amount of time it takes for the sunchokes to travel from your mouth to your colon—you'll know whether your body tolerates the inulin well or not. As your body gets used to this new food, you may be able to increase how much you eat without the gassy side effect.

DELICIOUS WAYS TO EAT SUNCHOKES

Freuman also finds that cooking sunchokes, rather than eating them raw, lessens the inulin's gassy effect. So instead of chomping on your first chokes raw, try some of these ways to prepare them (no need to peel the sunchokes—just scrub them well)…

• **Roasted Sunchokes.** Roughly cut sunchokes into one-inch chunks, and toss them in olive oil and salt. Roast at 400°F for about 40 minutes until they are tender and golden brown.

• **Sunchoke Chips.** Slice the chokes thinly using a mandoline or sharp knife. Toss the slices in oil, salt, pepper and any of your favorite spices—these are especially yummy with garlic powder and thyme—and spread them in a single layer on a baking sheet. Bake at 400°F for 15 minutes, flip them over and bake for another 10 to 15 minutes or until crisp. These chips are addictive, so don't dive into a giant batch until you've made friends with inulin!

• **Sunchoke Mash.** Steam or boil sunchokes as you would potatoes, and season them with butter, salt and pepper. Or boil and mash them with potatoes to add a new taste sensation to an old standard.

• **Sunchoke Soup.** After roasting sunchokes, simmer them in a saucepan with onions and garlic sautéed in olive oil along with broth or water. Season with thyme or rosemary. Stir in one-quarter cup of milk, cream or yogurt. Then purée.

• **Sunchoke Salads and Snacks.** Slice or shave raw sunchokes, and add to salads (toss them in lemon juice or vinegar first, since the cut sides will discolor) or just eat out of hand.

So, certainly, if you are looking for new healthy foods to keep your blood sugar on an even keel as well as optimize the health of your friendly gut bacteria, look for sunchokes at farmers' markets and your grocery (they are in season from late fall to early spring).

Cinnamon—Cheap, Safe and Very Effective

Richard Anderson, PhD, lead researcher at the Beltsville Human Nutrition Research Center, US Department of Agriculture, Maryland.

Insulin is the hormone that controls blood sugar levels. Cinnamon is its twin.

"Cinnamon mimics the action of insulin," says Richard Anderson, PhD, a researcher at the Beltsville Human Nutrition Research Center in Maryland, and the coauthor of more than 20 scientific papers on cinnamon and diabetes. "Cinnamon stimulates insulin receptors on fat and muscle cells the same way insulin does, allowing excess sugar to move out of the blood and into the cells."

Several recent studies provide new proof of cinnamon's effectiveness in preventing and controlling diabetes…

NEWEST RESEARCH

•**Stopping diabetes before it starts.** In Britain, researchers studied healthy, young men, dividing them into two groups—one group received three grams of cinnamon a day and the other a placebo.

After two weeks, the men taking the cinnamon supplement had a much improved "glucose tolerance test"—the ability of the body to process and store glucose. They also had better "insulin sensitivity"—the ability of the insulin hormone to usher glucose out of the bloodstream and into cells.

•**Long-term management of diabetes.** The most accurate measurement of long-term blood sugar control is A1C, or glycated hemoglobin—the percentage of red blood cells that have been frosted by blood sugar. Seven percent or less means diabetes is under control—and a decrease of 0.5% to 1.0% is considered a significant improvement in the disease.

In a study by a doctor in Nevada, 109 people with type 2 diabetes were divided into two groups, with one receiving 1 gram of cinnamon a day and one receiving a placebo. After three months, those taking the cinnamon had a 0.83% decrease in A1C.

Those taking the placebo had a 0.37% decrease.

"We used standard, off-the-shelf cinnamon capsules that patients would find at their local stores or on the Internet," says Paul Crawford, MD, the study's author, in the *Journal of the American Board of Family Medicine*. And that cinnamon, he says, "gives diabetes care providers and diabetic patients an easily accessible, likely safe, and cheap alternative to help treat type 2 diabetes."

Important: He points out that the drop in A1C seen his study would decrease the risk of many diabetic complications—heart disease and stroke by 16%; eye problems (diabetic retinopathy) by 17% to 21%; and kidney disease (nephropathy) by 24% to 33%.

•**After a bad night's sleep, include cinnamon in your breakfast.** Several recent studies show that sleep deprivation—a nearly universal problem of modern life—increases the risk of diabetes.

Solution: Writing in the *Journal of Medicinal Food*, researchers in the Human Performance Laboratory at Baylor University recommend the use of cinnamon to reverse insulin resistance and glucose intolerance after sleep loss.

•**Oxidation under control.** Oxidation—a kind of biochemical rust—is one of the processes behind the development of diabetes. In a study by French researchers of 22 people with prediabetes, three months of supplementation with a cinnamon extract dramatically reduced oxidation—and the lower the level of oxidation, the better the blood sugar control.

"The inclusion of cinnamon compounds in the diet could reduce risk factors associated with diabetes," conclude the researcher, in the *Journal of the American College of Nutrition*.

Bottom line: Cinnamon works. In a review study of the best research on cinnamon and diabetes to date, researchers in England concluded the spice has the power to fight high blood sugar. Their findings were in *Diabetes, Obesity and Metabolism*.

ONE TEASPOON DAILY

"Try to get ¼ to 1 teaspoon of cinnamon daily," says Dr. Anderson. Sprinkle it in hot cereals, yogurt or applesauce. Use it to accent sweet potatoes, winter squash or yams. Try it with lamb, beef stew or chilies. It even goes great with grains such as couscous and barley, and legumes such as lentils and split peas.

Or you can use a cinnamon supplement.

Consider taking 1 to 3 grams per day, says Dr. Anderson, which is the dosage range used in many studies that show the herb's effectiveness.

Best: Cinnulin PF—a specially prepared water extract of cinnamon—is a supplement used in many studies showing the spice's effectiveness in supplement form. It is widely available in many brands, such as Swanson and Doctor's Best.

The dosage of Cinnulin PF used in studies is typically 250 mg, twice a day.

Eat Walnuts...Prevent Diabetes

Frank Hu, MD, PhD, professor of medicine, Harvard Medical School and Channing Division of Network Medicine, Brigham and Women's Hospital, and professor of nutrition and epidemiology, Harvard School of Public Health, all in Boston. His study was published in *Journal of Nutrition*.

We've been losing the fight against diabetes—the prevalence of this deadly disease has increased by more than 175% since 1980.

Good news: There's an easy and economical way to help guard against type 2 diabetes. Just eat a particular type of nut—the walnut.

The news comes from a huge Harvard study that looked at data on nearly 138,000 women.

Every two years, participants answered detailed questions about their health and lifestyle. Every four years, they completed lengthy questionnaires about their diets, indicating how often they consumed each of more than 130 foods, with answers ranging from "never or less than once per month" to "six or more times per day."

At the start of the study, none of the women had diabetes...by the end of the 10-year follow-up, nearly 6,000 had developed the disease.

The researchers performed a careful analysis that adjusted for age, body mass index, family history of diabetes, smoking, menopausal status and other factors that affect diabetes risk. They also adjusted for consumption of various unhealthful foods (such as sugar-sweetened drinks and processed meats) and healthful foods (whole grains, fish, fruits, vegetables and various types of nuts).

What they found: Women who ate two or more ounces of walnuts per week, on average, had a 24% lower risk for type 2 diabetes...those who ate just one ounce of walnuts per week had a 13% lower risk.

Other types of nuts conferred some benefits, but mainly through weight control, the researchers said. The walnut, however, has a number of properties that make it a winner in the fight against diabetes.

For one thing, of all the common tree nuts, walnuts are highest in polyunsaturated fats, containing 47% of these fats by weight—and there is good evidence that polyunsaturated fats have favorable effects on how the body uses insulin. Walnuts also are the richest of all nuts in a particular type of healthful polyunsaturated fat called alpha linolenic acid. What's more, walnuts are high in fiber and plant protein and have been shown to decrease total cholesterol and LDL "bad" cholesterol. These nuts also are loaded with vitamin E and polyphenols that have antioxidant properties.

Bonus: Even though walnuts (like other nuts) are high in calories, they don't seem to cause weight gain in a balanced diet—perhaps because they are so filling and satisfying.

Do men get similar protection against diabetes from eating walnuts? Research will have to prove it, but odds are good that they would.

Going nuts: The best part is that walnuts aren't some specialty product you have to go out of your way to buy, and you don't have to drown yourself in walnuts to get the benefits. Two ounces is only 28 walnut halves per week...that's just four halves per day.

Walnuts are a great snack to have on the road or at work because they don't need to be refrigerated (though if you're going to store them for a while, putting them in the fridge or freezer will keep them fresher longer). While this new study did not look at whether the participants ate their walnuts raw, roasted or otherwise cooked, you can certainly use them in cooking if you like because heat won't significantly affect their health benefits.

To increase your intake, try adding chopped walnuts to cereal, salad, rice or soup...stirring ground walnuts into a smoothie or yogurt... and spreading walnut butter on celery sticks or apple slices.

Onions—Big Flavor, Bigger Benefit

Mark A. Stengler, NMD, a naturopathic medical doctor and leading authority on the practice of alternative and integrated medicine. Dr. Stengler is author of the *Health Revelations* newsletter, author of *The Natural Physician's Healing Therapies*, founder and medical director of the Stengler Center for Integrative Medicine in Encinitas, California, and former adjunct associate clinical professor at the National University of Natural Medicine in Portland, Oregon. MarkStengler.com

Chances are you eat onions all the time without giving them a second thought. What you might not realize about this vegetable (yes, onions are vegetables) is that they offer much more than flavor. Onions are rich in antioxidants, which have anti-inflammatory properties. Even the onion's famous eye-watering effect is the result of volatile gases, many of which also are antioxidants. Raw onions provide slightly more health benefits than cooked onions, but cooked onions are nothing to sniff at. *Find out what onions can do for your health...*

• **Provide cancer protection.** An *American Journal of Clinical Nutrition* study found that people who eat a lot of onions (more than one cup of onions daily) have an 80% lower risk of developing prostate cancer than those who eat very few onions. Eating onions frequently also was found to provide protection against colorectal, laryngeal and ovarian cancers.

• **Reduce blood sugar.** Within four hours of eating three-quarters of a cup of chopped onion, study participants with diabetes had reduced blood sugar levels, according to a study by Sudanese researchers published in *Environmental Health Insights*.

• **Minimize scars and ease bug bite itch.** Onion extracts may reduce scar formation on the skin. In a study conducted by Korean researchers, the antioxidants in onions were found to reduce scarring by increasing the activity of an anti-inflammatory enzyme. Creams containing onion extract, such as Mederma (sold at most pharmacies), can reduce scarring. You also can slice an onion in half and rub it on a bug bite to relieve the itch.

IN THE KITCHEN

Add onions as an ingredient in omelets, salads and sauces—or let them take center stage, as in the delicious side dish described below. It features sumac, a Middle Eastern spice, available in the spice section of some grocery stores and online (*www.spicehouse.com*).

SAUTÉED ONION IN SUMAC

Chop two large red or sweet onions. Sauté in olive oil until soft. Sprinkle with sumac, a mild spice with a lemony flavor.

Why Go Nuts for Nuts?

Richard D. Mattes, PhD, MPH, RD, professor of foods and nutrition at Purdue University in West Lafayette, Indiana. He has published numerous studies on nuts and appetite.

If you've relegated nuts to the "occasional snack" category, it's time to get more creative. Substitute nuts for some or all of the meat in a stir-fry entrée...sprinkle sliced or chopped nuts over vegetables, rice, soup or cereal...add ground nuts to a smoothie or yogurt...dress salads with nut oils...spread nut butter on celery sticks or apple slices. From all corners of the nutrition world, wellness professionals are amazed by nuts' health benefits. *Recent research shows that eating a moderate amount of nuts on a regular basis may help...*

• **Control weight.** According to Richard D. Mattes, PhD, MPH, RD, a professor of foods and nutrition at Purdue University who has done extensive research on the topic, nut consumption increases your resting energy expenditure, which means that you burn more calories just sitting still than you otherwise would. Also, about 5% to 15% of the calories in nuts are excreted without being absorbed. And nuts' unique combination of protein, fiber, fatty acids and other characteristics quells hunger quickly and for prolonged periods.

• **Prevent heart disease.** Most of the fats in nuts are heart-healthy monounsaturated fats and omega-3 fatty acids that help lower LDL (bad) cholesterol and triglycerides…increase HDL (good) cholesterol…and prevent abnormal heart rhythms. Nuts also contain vitamin E, which inhibits arterial plaque buildup…and L-arginine, an amino acid that makes arteries more flexible and less vulnerable to clots.

•**Fight inflammation.** The soluble fiber in nuts appears to increase production of the anti-inflammatory protein interleukin-4. Antioxidant vitamin E also eases inflammation.

•**Reduce diabetes risk.** A Harvard study found that women who ate five or more ounces of nuts weekly were almost 30% less likely to get type 2 diabetes than women who rarely or never ate nuts.

Also: Spanish researchers found that nuts were even more effective than olive oil in combating metabolic syndrome, a condition that puts you at risk for diabetes and heart disease.

•**Combat cancer.** Some nuts (including Brazil nuts and walnuts) are high in selenium, a mineral associated with a decreased risk for colorectal, skin and lung cancers. In animal studies, walnuts appeared to inhibit breast tumors—perhaps due to their disease-fighting omega-3s and antioxidants.

•**Support brain function.** Evidence suggests that nuts' omega-3s may ease depression and boost thinking and memory by improving neurotransmitter function. Nuts also provide folate—and low levels of this B-vitamin are linked to depression and poor cognition.

NUT TYPES TO TRY

Per ounce, nuts typically have 160 to 200 calories and 13 to 22 grams of fat. Eating 1.5 ounces of nuts per day (a small handful) is enough to provide health-promoting benefits. Nuts naturally contain only a trace of sodium, so they won't wreak havoc with blood pressure, especially if you choose brands with no added salt.

"All types of nuts are good for you, so there's no such thing as a 'best' type of nut," Dr. Mattes emphasized. Still, each type does contain a different mix of nutrients—so for the widest range of benefits, eat a variety. Below are some excellent options and the nutrients that each is especially rich in. *Consider…*

•**Almonds for bone-building calcium…** and inflammation-fighting vitamin E.

•**Brazil nuts for cancer-fighting selenium.**

•**Cashews for magnesium,** which is linked to prevention of heart attacks and hypertension.

•**Hazelnuts for potassium,** which helps normalize blood pressure.

•**Peanuts for folate,** which lowers levels of the artery-damaging amino acid homocysteine.

•**Pecans for beta-sitosterol,** a plant compound that combats cholesterol.

•**Pistachios for gamma-tocopherol,** a form of vitamin E that may reduce lung cancer risk.

•**Walnuts** for the heart- and brain-enhancing omega-3 alpha-linolenic acid.

Vinegar for Weight Loss (and It Lowers Blood Sugar!)

Mark A. Stengler, NMD, a naturopathic medical doctor and leading authority on the practice of alternative and integrated medicine. Dr. Stengler is author of the *Health Revelations* newsletter, *The Natural Physician's Healing Therapies*, and *Bottom Line's Prescription for Natural Cures*. He is also the founder and medical director of the Stengler Center for Integrative Medicine in Encinitas, California, and former adjunct associate clinical professor at the National University of Natural Medicine in Portland, Oregon. MarkStengler.com

Carol S. Johnston, PhD, RD, associate director, nutrition program, Arizona State University, Mesa, and co-author of a study published in *Diabetes Care*.

We tend to think of vinegar mostly for salad dressing, but it actually has a long history as a folk medicine to ease such conditions as headaches and indigestion. Now several studies highlight vinegar's benefit for weight management and blood sugar control. Mark Stengler, NMD, a naturopathic medical doctor and founder and medical director of the Stengler Center for Integrative Medicine in Encinitas, California, tells why this common product is so uncommonly helpful—and how to use it for better health…

Researchers believe that it is the acetic acid in any type of vinegar (apple cider, balsamic, white or red wine) that produces the health effect, interfering with enzymes involved in the digestion of carbohydrates and those that alter glucose metabolism (so that insulin does not spike).

One study found that mice fed a high-fat diet—and given acetic acid—developed up to 10% less body fat than those not given acetic acid. Another study found that having small amounts of vinegar at bedtime seemed to reduce waking blood glucose levels in people.

Adding vinegar to a meal slows the glycemic response—the rate at which carbohydrates are absorbed into the bloodstream—by 20%.

Reason: Again, the acetic acid in vinegar seems to slow the emptying of the stomach, which reduces risk for hyperglycemia (high blood sugar), a risk factor for heart disease, and helps people with type 2 diabetes manage their condition.

Ways to add vinegar to meals: Use malt vinegar on thick-cut oven fries…marinate sliced tomatoes and onions in red-wine vinegar before adding the vegetables to a sandwich… mix two parts red wine vinegar with one part olive oil, and use two tablespoons on a green salad…mix a tablespoon or two with soy sauce, olive oil, garlic and herbs for a meat marinade.

For blood sugar balance (for those with diabetes or on diabetes medication) or for weight loss, dilute one to two tablespoons (some people start with teaspoons) in an equal amount of water—and drink it at the beginning of a meal.

Great "Whey" to Control Blood Sugar

Study titled "Incretin, insulinotropic and glucose-lowering effects of whey protein pre-load in type 2 diabetics: a randomized clinical trial," published in *Diabetologia.*

For people with type 2 diabetes, eating isn't the problem…it's what happens after eating that can be dangerous. Glucose accumulates in the bloodstream, where levels go way up after a meal. This phenomenon, called "spiking," irritates blood vessels and throws your metabolism out of whack, increasing risk for cardiovascular disease, eye and kidney damage, and possibly Alzheimer's disease and cancer, too.

A short, brisk exercise session before meals helps prevent post-meal blood glucose spiking. *Here's another, even easier (and surprising) trick for keeping your blood sugar where it should be—it involves using whey…*

WHEY TO GO!

It turns out that whey protein—yes, that stuff you see sold in giant tubs in the bodybuilder and sports section of health-food stores—is a great pre-meal tonic for glucose control. Whey protein products are powdered, concentrated milk protein—made from the watery stuff that accumulates and rises to the surface of containers of cottage cheese and yogurt that you probably drain off. Studies have shown that beginning a meal with a whey protein drink helps get post-meal insulin secretion into action, which, in turn, helps reduce glucose spiking.

This effect was recently confirmed in a small international study that also pinpointed how whey protein does its magic. The study took 15 people with type 2 diabetes, divided them into two groups, and fed them a sugary breakfast—with the difference being, one group drank 50 grams (about three-and-a-half tablespoons) of whey protein dissolved in water before eating breakfast…and the other group drank just plain water. Each group took a turn at drinking the whey protein on different days so that the effect could be gauged on every participant.

Results: When participants drank whey protein before breakfast, they accumulated an average 28% less blood glucose after the meal. And the whey had a strong and protective impact—insulin levels nearly doubled in whey drinkers within the first half-hour after eating and remained high. This happened because, in the whey drinkers, an insulin-stimulating hormone, called glucagon-like peptide-1 (GLP-1), didn't degrade as quickly as it normally would. The presence of additional GLP-1 gave insulin a better chance of doing its job.

Here's the kicker: The researchers pointed out that the effect of whey on glucose control and insulin secretion was better than what would be expected from using diabetes drugs such as *glipizide* (Glucotrol), *glyburide* (Glynase) and *nateglinide* (Starlix).

Whereas the side effects of diabetes drugs can include headaches, joint aches, nasal congestion, back pain and flu-like symptoms, whey protein is well-tolerated in doses of up to 50 grams per day.

WHEY FOR YOU

Although 50 grams per day taken before breakfast was looked at in the research study, how much daily whey protein do you need in an ordinary life setting to control blood sugar spiking? Naturopath Andrew L. Rubman, ND, founder and director of the Southbury Clinic for Traditional Medicines in Southbury, Connecticut, recommends using up to 800 milligrams per kilogram of body weight. That's a daily dosage of about 44 grams for a 120-pound person...54 grams for a 150-pound person...and 91 grams for a 250-pound person. These dosages refer to products that are whey isolate, not whey concentrate. Whey isolate provides more protein and significantly less lactose than whey concentrate, Dr. Rubman said.

The daily dosage should be adjusted so that you are taking the least amount you need to best control symptoms associated with blood sugar spiking—and this will differ from one person to another, said Dr. Rubman. People who have chronic kidney problems should seek medical supervision before supplementing their diets with any dose of whey protein.

Side effects of whey were not reported in the study, but high doses of more than 50 grams per day, particularly of whey concentrate, can cause digestive troubles such as increased bowel movements, nausea, thirst, bloating, cramps and lack of appetite, said Dr. Rubman. These effects are mostly caused by the lactose in whey products. Other possible side effects include tiredness and headache, low blood pressure and low blood sugar. So, everything

in moderation if you decide to include a whey protein supplement in your diet.

Also, people with allergies to milk should avoid whey (it is milk protein, after all). It can also interfere with certain drugs, such as *levodopa* for Parkinson's disease, *alendronate* (Fosamax) for osteoporosis, and quinolone antibiotics (such as Cipro) and tetracycline antibiotics such as *doxycycline*—so if you take any such drug, speak with your doctor or pharmacist for guidance on whether (and when) you can safely take whey protein and at what dosage.

A brand of whey isolate that Dr. Rubman recommends is NOW Foods Whey Protein Isolate.

How to Eat Fruit When You Have Diabetes

Mark A. Stengler, NMD, a naturopathic medical doctor and leading authority on the practice of alternative and integrated medicine. Dr. Stengler is author of the *Health Revelations* newsletter, author of *The Natural Physician's Healing Therapies*, founder and medical director of the Stengler Center for Integrative Medicine in Encinitas, California, and former adjunct associate clinical professor at the National University of Natural Medicine in Portland, Oregon. MarkStengler.com

---

Is it OK to snack on fruit if you have diabetes? Some fruits do, indeed, have a high sugar content, but that doesn't mean you have to give up this healthy habit. Fruits are low in fat and rich in phytonutrients, vitamins, minerals and fiber—and in moderation (two or three servings daily), they can be safely consumed by those with diabetes. One general way to choose fruits is using the glycemic index, which measures how slowly a food increases blood sugar (the lower the number, the more healthful). Choose low-to-mid-GI fruits such as cherries (22), plums (24), grapefruit (25) and bananas (47). A high-GI fruit is anything over 70.

Eating fruit with other foods also can prevent a spike in insulin. Combining fruit with low-GI foods, such as a slice of whole-grain bread, can prevent the insulin spike that comes with eating a high-GI fruit. To find the GI of specific fruits and other foods, go to *www.glycemicindex.com.*

Also helpful: Watch your serving size. One-half cup to one cup of most fruits counts as one serving. Some individuals have food sensitivities to certain fruits—and regardless of their GIs, these fruits (one example is grapefruit) can spike an individual's glucose level. Only by monitoring your diet and glucose levels closely will you truly know which fruits work best for you.

The "New" Superfood: Prunes...Yes, Prunes

Maria Stacewicz-Sapuntzakis, PhD, professor emerita, department of kinesiology and nutrition, University of Illinois at Chicago.

What comes to mind when you hear the word "prunes"? You probably think of one of two things—laxatives or senior citizens. That's why the prune industry is trying to change the name to "dried plums." But the fact is, prunes are amazingly good for us. They are nutrient-rich...inexpensive...they can satisfy a sweet tooth without the horrid effects of processed sugar...they can even help you get going with a healthy slimming diet. But there's a lot more to this simple, inexpensive superfood—yes, superfood—that could make you healthier and get you thinking about prunes in a whole new way...

A MAGIC INGREDIENT

"Prunes have a unique combination of nutrients that aren't found in other foods, not even other dried fruits," Maria Stacewicz-Sapuntzakis, PhD, said. She would know. She's been dedicated to research on the health benefits of prunes since year 2000 and has authored two scholarly reviews on research done on them. They're very high in a sugar alcohol called sorbitol, which is the key magic ingredient to the prune's health benefits, she said.

On its own, too much dietary sorbitol can cause gas and unwanted laxative effects, and 50 grams or more a day is considered excessive. In fact, the FDA makes companies add warning labels about the laxative effect of sorbitol to food products that contain it. But you'd have to eat more than a half a pound of prunes in one sitting to total 50 grams—and if you do try that at home, you sure will be "sitting." Dr. Stacewicz-Sapuntzakis went on to explain that five prunes contain a modest 7 grams of sorbitol and that the sorbitol in prunes combines with other nutrients in the fruit to pump up its nutritional and health-enhancing powers.

According to Dr. Stacewicz-Sapuntzakis, two daily servings of prunes (that's 10 to 12) can help your body...

• **Lose weight.** Despite the fact that they average 25 calories each, snacking on prunes can help you lose weight. Research recently reported at the European Congress on Obesity found that dieters who ate prunes lost more pounds and more inches and felt fuller longer than dieters who didn't eat them. The finding on satiety matched earlier research that found that eating prunes as a mid-morning snack can help you eat less at lunchtime.

• **Regulate blood sugar.** Although prunes are sweet, they rate relatively low on the glycemic index scale, which measures how fast and how much a certain food raises blood sugar levels. This makes prunes a good food choice for folks with hyperglycemia or diabetes. Sorbitol itself has a low glycemic value, which may explain why something that tastes so much like candy keeps blood sugar levels on an even keel instead of making them spike.

• **Strengthen bones.** Prunes contain several nutrients, including boron, copper, vitamin K and, as mentioned, potassium that help prevent bone loss. Plus, sorbitol—that secret ingredient—increases absorption of calcium from prunes and other foods.

• **Prevent or slow arteriosclerosis.** Studies in animals and humans suggest that compounds in prunes can lower blood levels of cholesterol and, thereby, prevent or slow the progression of arteriosclerosis—or hardening of the arteries—caused by buildup of cholesterol and other debris on artery walls.

• **Prevent colon cancer.** The fiber, phenolic compounds (which are antioxidant substances found in fruits) and sorbitol help prunes move waste through the colon quickly enough to keep bile acid by-products from injuring the lining of the colon, which can be cancer-causing.

THE BEST WAYS TO EAT PRUNES

Is drinking prune juice just as good as eating prunes? Dr. Stacewicz-Sapuntzakis recommends the latter. "If you eat the whole fruit, you get the benefits of all the great nutritional compounds in prunes. Some of these compounds become lost in prune juice," she said. But if you have never eaten prunes and now have an interest in adding them to your diet, start slow with four or five a day, Dr. Stacewicz-Sapuntzakis recommends. Once you're sure that your body can tolerate them without an unwanted laxative effect, work up to 10 to 12 each day. That racks up 240 calories, but you'll feel full longer than if you ate the same amount of calories in the form of, say, bread and cheese.

And prunes can be a lot more than wrinkled things you pluck from a box. *Consider these tasty ways to enjoy them...*

• **Homemade no-bake energy bars.** Place a handful of prunes in a food processor along with any combination of your favorite nuts and seeds, such as almonds, walnuts, and sesame, sunflower or pumpkin seeds. You can add some shredded coconut, too...maybe even sprinkle in some unsweetened cacao to sate a chocolate craving. Process the ingredients into a paste, and then press the mixture into a baking dish. Chill until firm and cut into squares for a perfect on-the-go energy boost and healthy sweet-tooth satisfier.

• **Prunes in a Blanket.** Wrap individual prunes in paper-thin slices of prosciutto—or do the same using turkey bacon if you prefer—then roast at 400°F until crisp on the outside, sweet and gooey inside. Bet you can't eat just one!

• **Spicy Moroccan-Style Stew.** Simmer prunes with lamb, beef or chicken and aromatic Moroccan spices, such as ginger, saffron, cinnamon and pepper, to serve up a traditional Moroccan stew called tagine.

Bon appétit and healthy eating with prunes!

More Healthful Fruit Picks...

Reduce risk for type 2 diabetes with blueberries, grapes and apples.

Recent finding: People who ate at least three servings of these fruits per week were up to 26% less likely to develop type 2 diabetes than people who ate less of these fruits. Eat the whole fruit, not just the juice. Fruit juice increases risk for diabetes.

Study of 187,382 health professionals by researchers from the US, UK and Singapore, published in *BMJ*.

The Fruit That Fights Hypoglycemia

David Grotto, RD, LDN, a registered dietitian and founder and president of Nutrition Housecall, LLC, a Chicago-based nutrition consulting firm that provides nutrition communications, lecturing and consulting services, along with personalized, at-home dietary services. He is author of *The Best Things You Can Eat*.

Hypoglycemia is a dangerous condition commonly associated with diabetes in which blood sugar levels fall below 70 mg/dL. It can happen periodically to some people with diabetes when the drugs used to treat the condition, such as insulin, work too well and cause an excessive drop in blood sugar.

Best food: Apricots. Seven to eight dried apricot halves provide 15 grams of a fast-acting carbohydrate when you have a crash in blood sugar. Fresh apricots also will help, but the carbohydrates (sugars) aren't as concentrated. And dried apricots are easy to store and take with you.

What to do: Eat seven or eight dried apricot halves as soon as you notice the symptoms of hypoglycemia, such as fatigue, dizziness, sweating and irritability.

Also helpful: Anything sugary, including a small amount of jelly beans. When your blood sugar is "crashing," you need sugar immediately. Toby Smithson, RD, LDN, a nutritionist who has had diabetes for 40 years, always carries jelly beans. They're even mentioned on the American Diabetes Association website.

Other sources of fast-acting sugars include honey and fruit juices.

How Full Fat Helps Diabetes

Dariush Mozaffarian, MD, DrPH, dean, Friedman School of Nutrition Science & Policy and the Jean Mayer Chair and professor of nutrition, Tufts University, Boston.

Surprise! According to a study from Harvard published in *Annals of Internal Medicine*, people with the highest circulating levels of a type of fatty acid that is found only in whole-fat dairy are one-third as likely to get diabetes as those with the lowest circulating levels. Higher levels of the fatty acid—called trans-palmitoleic acid—were also associated with lower body mass index (BMI)…smaller waist circumference…lower triglycerides (potentially harmful blood fats)…higher levels of HDL "good" cholesterol…less insulin resistance…and lower levels of C-reactive protein, a marker for general inflammation.

How the study was done: At the study's start, researchers began with baseline measurements of glucose, insulin, inflammatory markers, circulating fatty acids and blood lipids (such as triglycerides and cholesterol) from stored 1992 blood samples of 3,736 participants in the National Heart, Lung, and Blood Institute–funded Cardiovascular Health Study. Those data were compared with the same participants' dietary records and recorded health outcomes (including the incidence of diabetes) over the following 10 years. During this period, 304 new cases of diabetes were recorded. When the participants were grouped according to their circulating levels of trans-palmitoleic acid, the researchers discovered that those with higher levels had the lowest rates of diabetes.

HOW MUCH DAIRY?

While other studies have suggested a similar phenomenon with dairy consumption, this is the first to have used objective chemical markers in the blood to determine the relationship between this specific fatty acid and the onset of diabetes. The participants with the highest levels averaged about two servings of whole-fat dairy foods a day.

This is not a license to indulge yourself in a daily serving of strawberry shortcake with extra whipped cream or a giant ice cream from Cold Stone Creamery…but you might want to consider switching from skim milk to whole milk with your morning cereal and selecting full-fat yogurt over low-fat or nonfat. The difference in calories isn't great—and you may begetting some real metabolic and cardiovascular benefits.

Why Whole Milk May Be Better Than Skim

Mario Kratz, PhD, nutrition scientist, associate member, Public Health Sciences Division, Fred Hutchinson Cancer Research Center, and research associate professor, departments of epidemiology and medicine, University of Washington, both in Seattle. His study was published in *European Journal of Nutrition*.

Many health-conscious (and weight-conscious) consumers wouldn't touch whole milk or full-fat yogurt or cheese with a 10-foot pole. When it comes to dairy, they go low-fat or nonfat all the way…or maybe use a little whole milk in recipes when they are feeling decadent.

But: It's time to rethink this aversion to dairy fat—because it now seems quite likely that whole milk has gotten a bum rap for decades.

It started back in the 1950s, when saturated fat was linked to increased blood cholesterol levels. Because dairy fat is about 65% saturated, it was deemed harmful...and today the USDA still urges Americans to choose low-fat or no-fat dairy foods. However, there has never been strong evidence for the hypothesis that saturated fats cause disease, and now that myth seems to be dying for good. For instance, you could hardly have missed the headline-making news of a large study in *Annals of Internal Medicine* that found no link between increased cardiovascular disease risk and higher consumption of saturated fats.

PUTTING DAIRY FAT THROUGH ITS PACES

For decades now, people have judged the health effects of dairy fat mostly on its high saturated fat and cholesterol content, assuming that dairy fat is simply an unnecessary source of calories and fats that elevate LDL 'bad' cholesterol. However, they've been neglecting all the other fatty acids in there, some of which may be quite beneficial. We were overdue to look at the data and see whether dairy fat consumption is indeed associated with health risks, as has been assumed all these years—or whether it is not.

To that end, my colleagues and I carefully evaluated numerous studies on dairy fat and its effects on three important factors—obesity, metabolic health and cardiovascular disease. *Here's what we found regarding...*

•**Dairy Fat and Obesity.** Of the 16 studies that our team reviewed on this topic, 11 showed that people who ate more dairy fat or more high-fat dairy foods tended to be leaner and/or to gain less weight over time than people who ate less dairy fat. In studies that directly compared high-fat dairy to low-fat dairy, high-fat dairy was associated with better weight outcomes. None of the studies found a link between high-fat dairy and higher weight, nor between low-fat dairy and reduced risk for obesity.

Conclusion: The studies do not support the commonly held impression that dairy fat leads to weight gain. Rather, the evidence suggests that high-fat dairy foods, within the context of a normal healthy diet, may guard against weight gain.

•**Dairy Fat and Metabolic Health.** There were 11 observational studies that evaluated the association between dairy fat and the development of risk factors for diabetes, such as elevated blood sugar and insulin levels. Of these 11 studies, six showed that higher dairy fat consumption was associated with markers of better metabolic health...one was partially suggestive of such a beneficial relationship... and three found no association either way. Only a single study showed an association between higher dairy fat consumption and a marker of poorer metabolic health—and it was just one marker, the glycated hemoglobin value (an indicator of blood glucose concentration over time). As for the development of type 2 diabetes itself, of the eight studies that looked at this issue, three reported that high-fat dairy intake was associated with lower risk for diabetes...four found no association between full-fat dairy products and diabetes...and one had inconsistent evidence.

Upshot: The preponderance of evidence does not support the idea that high-fat dairy promotes metabolic disease. Instead, it appears that high-fat dairy may protect against metabolic disease and diabetes.

•**Dairy Fat and Cardiovascular Disease.** In the 15 studies that looked at a possible relationship between dairy fat and heart health, results were mixed, with some linking dairy fat to improved cardiovascular health...some showing no association...one finding different effects for men and women...and just one suggesting that dairy fat was bad for the heart.

What this means: Overall, the majority of the evidence indicates that dairy fat may be good rather than bad for cardiovascular health.

Alternative explanation? Could it be that lots of study participants who were already overweight or at risk for diabetes or heart disease might have chosen to avoid dairy fat in an effort to control their weight or reduce their risk...so that would be why lower consumption of dairy fat was associated with being heavier or having worse metabolic or cardiovascular health?

That is what's called reverse causation, and it could account for some of the favorable associations seen between full-fat dairy products and health outcomes. For most of the studies, however, this is unlikely to explain the results. For example, for the association between full-fat dairy products and obesity-related outcomes, the associations held even when investigators adjusted for baseline body weight. For studies focused on cardiovascular disease or diabetes, these were prospective studies, with no evidence of disease at baseline. And the main point still stands—that there is little in the literature to support the notion that full-fat dairy products promote obesity, diabetes or cardiovascular disease.

WHAT MUDDIES THE WATER

Why isn't the evidence for or against full-fat dairy foods more clear-cut? For one thing, geographic discrepancies muddy the water (or the milk, as the case may be). Dairy-fat studies conducted in the US often came to different or even opposite conclusions compared with studies conducted in Europe—in general, dairy fat came out looking safer in the European studies than in the US studies. *There are several possible reasons for that...*

• **The US has done a thorough job of publicizing the perceived risks of saturated fats**—so most Americans consider animal fats, including dairy fat, to be unhealthy. It makes sense, then, that people who habitually consume full-fat dairy foods despite their bad reputation might also have other habits that are considered unhealthful. Two studies confirmed that assumption, finding lower fiber intake, less exercise and more smoking among the people who consumed the greatest amounts of high-fat dairy. Thus, the higher risk for cardiovascular disease or diabetes in people in US studies who consumed the most full-fat dairy could really be due, at least in part, to other unhealthy lifestyle factors.

• **Sources of dairy fat in the US diet are different from those in Europe.** Here,

much of the dairy fat people eat comes from ice cream and prepared foods such as pizza. These products often contain lots of sugar, salt, preservatives and/or other unhealthful ingredients, making it hard to separate the health effects of the dairy fat from those of the other components. In contrast, the dairy fat in the typical European diet comes from whole-fat cheeses, butter and unsweetened yogurt—foods that do not mingle the dairy fat with so much unhealthy junk.

• **The quality of the dairy fat itself may differ.** In the US, dairy farming is highly industrialized. Our cows have little access to pasture, are fed corn- and soy-based concentrates, and receive a growth hormone that's banned in the European Union. However, European dairy production is far less industrialized, and in many regions the cows eat mainly grass. Grass-fed animals produce milk with higher amounts of many unique fatty acids that may have beneficial effects on health. It's important to note that, while we know that milk-fat composition is affected in a major way by what the dairy cows eat, we know very little about whether these differences between milk from grain-fed and pasture-fed cows affect the health of people who drink it.

Another reason why it's tough to make firm pronouncements for or against full-fat dairy has to do with research limitations. All of the studies included in our review were observational, not interventional—and there's a huge difference between the two. Observational studies simply watch what has happened with different groups of people over time, so they cannot show a cause-and-effect relationship. The best they can do is lead to hypotheses that must then be tested in interventional studies. However, interventional studies in nutrition are notoriously hard to carry out. It would be nearly impossible to control the diets of large groups of people for a long enough time to definitively determine whether one group develops more heart disease or diabetes, for example, than the other group.

BOTTOM LINE: WHAT TO BUY?

Here's what we do know—and it's different from what you've been taught: There is very little evidence to support the belief that low-fat or nonfat dairy foods are better for us than high-fat dairy foods. In fact, most of the evidence indicates that high-fat dairy foods are better. This is not to say that it's OK to eat premium ice cream by the gallon or to have prepackaged double-cheese pizza every night (there's too much other bad stuff in those products)…but it's fine to use whole milk in your cereal, soups, casseroles and coffee and to opt for cheese and yogurt made with whole milk. (If you're having trouble finding full-fat yogurt in your US supermarket these days, check for brands such as Stonyfield or Horizon.)

Do keep in mind that, like all fats, dairy fat is calorie-dense, so moderation is still important. But, if someone drinks a lot of milk, then I don't know of any reason to discourage him from having four or even five servings per day of whole milk. The one point I am adamant about is that it's OK as long as we consume the dairy fat in whole foods, as part of a normal, mixed dietary pattern. Adding sticks of butter to everything because now "dairy fat is healthy" is almost certainly not a great idea.

What about choosing organic? That's wise. According to a study from Washington State University that analyzed 384 samples of whole milk, organic milk had 62% more healthful omega-3 fatty acids than conventional milk. Yes, organic is more expensive…but hey, you're worth it.

How to Love Tofu…and Why You Should

Jackie Newgent, RDN, CDN, a registered dietitian, classically trained chef and author of *The With or Without Meat Cookbook* and *1,000 Low-Calorie Recipes.* Her blog, "Tasteovers by Jackie" (*JackieNewgent.com/recipe-blog*) features healthy makeovers of favorite indulgences.

Given the choice between a juicy steak, a nice piece of fish or a few cubes of tofu, which would you choose? Let's put it this way…for most Americans, it's not the tofu.

If you've told yourself that you don't like tofu—or can't figure out how to add it to your diet—you're missing out on an amazingly healthful, delicious and economical food. Don't believe it? *Consider this…**

Fact #1: **It's a protein powerhouse.** Tofu is one of the highest-protein plant foods on the planet. Made from soybeans, the highest-protein bean there is, tofu gives you 21 g of protein per cup. It's also one of the few nonanimal food sources that is considered a complete protein, meaning it offers all of the essential amino acids needed in your diet.

Tofu is also a great source of calcium with 300 mg to 450 mg per cup when it's made with calcium sulfate, which provides more calcium than the other commonly used coagulating agent magnesium chloride (known as "nigari").

Fact #2: **It tastes good…really.** Tofu's neutral taste has gotten a bad rap. But this is what makes tofu so versatile in recipes—it soaks up the flavors of whatever sauce or other ingredients you toss it with.

Fact #3: **Cost-wise, tofu is a cheaper calcium source than yogurt and a cheaper protein source than meat or fish.** It's also an excellent meal stretcher, meaning that you can mix it with more expensive proteins—think two parts beef to one part tofu for burgers—without affecting the taste. And if you're still not convinced that you should at least give tofu a try, take a look at the scientific evidence.

What the research says: Regular tofu consumption has been linked to a decreased risk for cardiovascular disease, type 2 diabetes, osteoporosis and other conditions, especially when this plant-based protein replaces part or all of the animal protein in a diet.

TOFU VARIETIES

When adding tofu to your diet, here are three main types, which vary mostly in water content…

*Avoid tofu if you are allergic to soy or have kidney stones. Talk to your doctor first if you take medication for a thyroid condition.

• **Soft** (or "silken") tofu has the highest water content and makes an excellent dairy replacement in smoothies, dips and creamy sauces such as hollandaise.

• **Firm** tofu comes in block form and keeps its shape in stir-fries and curries.

• **Extra-firm tofu,** with its low water content, can be marinated, then grilled, roasted or stir-fried.

Examples: Marinate large steaklike slices, then grill and serve alone or on a salad. Or marinate cubed tofu, then stir-fry with veggies.

Go for non-GMO: The vast majority of American soybean crops are genetically modified. But until more is known about the potentially harmful, long-term effects of genetic modification, I suggest you err on the side of caution and use non-GMO tofu whenever possible. Look for the "Non-GMO Project Verified" seal on packages...or simply buy organic—GMOs are not allowed in organic farming.

For extra convenience: You can now enjoy many tofu selections as is—no cooking required. More and more grocery stores now carry ready-to-eat baked tofu in bold flavors such as Italian or smoked...and a wide array of tofu-centric frozen entrées and breakfast burritos.

Good brands: SoyBoy, Wildwood SprouTofu and Twin Oaks. These companies all make organic, non-GMO, ready-to-eat tofu products. Check online for where to buy.

To start loving tofu, here's a delicious, super-easy recipe...

HOLLANDAISE-STYLE SAUCE

Try this recipe on eggs, poached salmon or roasted asparagus.**

4 ounces (about ½ cup) of silken tofu, drained

2 Tablespoons fresh lemon juice, ½ teaspoon lemon zest

2 Tablespoons plain unsweetened almond milk

1 Tablespoon tahini (sesame seed paste)

1 teaspoon Dijon mustard

½ teaspoon Worcestershire sauce

⅛ teaspoon sea salt

⅛ teaspoon ground turmeric

⅛ teaspoon ground cayenne

Puree all ingredients in a blender for one minute. In a small saucepan, simmer uncovered on medium-low heat. Stir occasionally until heated, then serve. *Servings:* Four.

**Reprinted with permission from *Tasteovers by Jackie* by Jackie Newgent, RDN, CDN.

If You Can't Eat Fish, Nuts, Soy, Dairy or Gluten— What to Eat for the Same Health Benefits

David Grotto, MS, RDN, founder and president of Nutrition Housecall, LLC, a Chicago-based nutrition consulting firm that provides nutrition communications, lecturing and consulting services and personalized, at-home dietary services. He is author of *The Best Things You Can Eat.*

You may know about all the health benefits of fish, nuts, soy, dairy and whole wheat. But what if you're allergic to those foods or for various other reasons cannot eat them? How can you get the same nutritional benefits?

Here, common food sensitivities—and the best substitutes...

FISH

Fish is among the healthiest foods you can eat. It is high in protein and healthful fats and rich in vitamin D, selenium and zinc.

It is the healthful fats—long-chain omega-3 fatty acids—that fish is best known for. People who eat as little as three to six ounces of fish a week can reduce their risk of dying from heart disease by more than one-third.

The problem: Many people are allergic to fish.

What to eat instead: There are plenty of choices if you can't eat fish. The alpha-linolenic acid (ALA) in plant foods is converted to healthful omega-3s in the body.

Examples: Walnuts, flaxseeds, pumpkin seeds and canola oil contain ALA. The catch is that ALA isn't efficiently converted to long-chain omega-3s. When you eat ALA-rich plant foods, you get only about 10% to 25% of the beneficial fats that you would get from fish.

My advice: Get these fats from as many different sources as you can. Snack on nuts during the day. Cook tofu in canola oil or soybean oil. Add some ground flaxseed to your morning cereal.

NUTS

A recent study found that people who ate nuts seven or more times a week were 20% less likely to die from any cause during the study period than those who didn't eat nuts. Nuts are high in zinc as well as phytosterols, compounds that reduce cholesterol and may protect against cancer. New research suggests that they also help relieve symptoms in men with enlarged prostate glands.

The problem: You potentially can be allergic to any one type of nut or to all of them. And peanuts—which technically are a legume, not a nut—are a serious (in some cases, life-threatening) allergen for some people.

What to eat instead: Pumpkin or sunflower seeds. You can eat them raw, roasted or salted. These seeds are just as healthful as nuts, and they have the crunch, rich flavor and grab-and-go convenience of nuts. *In my house, we enjoy this recipe for roasted pumpkin seeds...*

Take one cup of seeds, rinse them off and pat dry. Melt one tablespoon of butter (or no-trans-fat margarine spread) in a saucepan. Add one tablespoon of Worcestershire sauce. Toss the seeds and the butter sauce in a bowl. Spray a cookie sheet with nonstick cooking spray. Spread the seed mixture on the cookie sheet, and bake at 350°F for about 30 minutes, turning the seeds occasionally so that they brown on both sides.

DAIRY

There are plenty of reasons to enjoy milk, cheese and other dairy foods. The calcium is good for your bones. Dairy is high in protein. Even the fats seem to be beneficial. Studies have shown that people who eat dairy tend to lose more weight than people on low-dairy diets even when they get the same number of calories.

The problem: Millions of Americans don't produce enough lactase (an enzyme) to completely digest dairy. Others have a true allergy—they get symptoms such as a rash or hives when they consume one or more dairy proteins.

What to eat instead: You can buy milk and cheeses that are spiked with extra lactase. Also, research has shown that you can increase your natural supply of lactase. People who give up dairy for a few weeks and then slowly reintroduce it—say, by consuming an ounce a day for a week, then slowly adding to that amount over time—can boost their production of lactase.

It's tougher if you are allergic.

My advice: Give up cow's milk, and switch to soy milk or almond milk. These have many of the same nutrients that are found in cow's milk, and most people like the taste. Goat's milk is another possibility. People who are allergic to cow's milk usually can drink goat's milk without discomfort—but the musky taste isn't for everyone.

SOY

Tofu and other soy foods have long been the go-to protein source for people who don't eat meat. Soy also is rich in isoflavones, antioxidants that help balance hormones, increase bone strength and reduce the risk for some cancers.

The problem: Soy allergies are common, and they aren't limited to tofu. If you are allergic, you have to avoid a lot of different foods, including soy sauce, miso, soy milk, tamari, edamame, etc.

What to eat instead: Other beans, such as lentils, pinto beans, kidney beans and chickpeas. All of these legumes have healthful amounts of protein, fiber and antioxidants. If you're not sensitive to gluten, try seitan. It's a form of wheat gluten that's popular in Asia (and in some Asian restaurants) that mimics the texture—and the protein content—of meat. Just make sure that your seitan dish isn't made with soy sauce!

IF YOU CAN'T EAT GLUTEN...

Whole grains are high in fiber, B vitamins, vitamin E and other antioxidants. A diet that includes whole wheat and other whole grains can significantly reduce your risk for diabetes, cancer, heart disease and digestive problems.

The problem: About 5% to 6% of Americans are sensitive to gluten, a protein in wheat, barley and rye. A smaller percentage suffers from celiac disease, a serious autoimmune disease triggered by gluten.

What to eat instead: Gluten-free grains, such as rice, quinoa and amaranth, have similar nutritional benefits. I recommend teff, an African grain that has a mildly nutty flavor and about the same amount of fiber that you would get from wheat.

Unfortunately, gluten-free breads often are dry and crumbly—they lack the chewiness and mouth feel that comes from gluten. But manufacturers of gluten-free breads are getting better.

Example: The Udi's brand makes gluten-free bread that tastes (and feels) almost like traditional bread.

Caution: Oats don't contain gluten, but products such as oatmeal often are tainted when they are processed with the same machinery that is used for other grains or when oat crops are grown too close to wheat fields. Look for oats that are guaranteed to be gluten-free. It will be noted on the label.

Best Proteins for Diabetics

The number-one protein always is fish. If people have fish twice per week, it is more than enough. It is a very good source of good-quality fat—omega-3 fat—which reduces the triglycerides in blood. The second one is vegetable proteins—legumes, beans, peas, all those legumes. And then the third would be skinless chicken and turkey. Even for people who like to eat meat, just reduce the amount of fat and don't salt that much, it would be fine. But not every day.

Osama Hamdy, MD, PhD, medical director of the Joslin Diabetes Center's Obesity Clinical Program and an assistant professor of medicine at Harvard Medical School, both in Boston. He also is coauthor of *The Diabetes Breakthrough.*

Better Than Meat! Here Are Other Proteins You Should Try

Dawn Jackson Blatner, RD, a registered dietitian in private practice in Chicago. She is author of *The Flexitarian Diet: The Mostly Vegetarian Way to Lose Weight, Be Healthier, Prevent Disease, and Add Years to Your Life* and the nutrition consultant for the Chicago Cubs. As a flexitarian expert, she gets most of her protein from plants. DawnJacksonBlatner.com

When it comes to getting enough muscle-building protein, most people do just fine by having a juicy steak, a generous chicken breast or a tasty fish fillet a few times a week.

The problem is, most Americans need to get more protein from other foods and a little less from animals, since research suggests a more plant-based diet decreases risk for chronic health problems, such as heart disease, diabetes, cancer and obesity. Balancing animal protein (from meat, for example) with protein from plants and other foods is one of the simplest ways to improve your diet. Of course, you don't have to be a vegetarian or vegan to enjoy meat-free protein foods.* *My favorite options…*

FOR BREAKFAST

If you want protein in the morning, you may reach for some eggs and sausage. *But not so fast! Here are some other great ideas…*

•**Quinoa.** Often used as a dinner side dish, quinoa also can be eaten as a great nutty-tasting grain for breakfast. Technically a seed, quinoa wins points for being a high-protein whole grain with 8 g per cooked cup. It's also naturally gluten-free—a bonus for those who can't safely eat most oatmeal, since oats may be contaminated in the field or through processing with gluten-containing foods.

For a great protein-packed breakfast: Have a bowl of quinoa with chopped fruit and nuts…or top it with sautéed spinach and a poached egg. To make things easier, there's

*Adults over age 19 should consume 0.37 g of protein per pound of body weight, according to the Institute of Medicine (IOM). *Example*: If you weigh 150 pounds, you need about 55 g of protein daily.

nothing wrong with buying precooked, frozen quinoa—it is now sold at lots of markets.

•**Cottage cheese.** It is not a plant-based food, but it's an excellent source of protein. In fact, you may be surprised to find out that a half cup of 1% milkfat cottage cheese contains more than twice as much protein (14 g) as an egg.

Caution: Most cottage cheese is high in sodium, so be sure to stick to the low-sodium variety if you are on a low-sodium diet.

Not a fan of curds? Puree it. Make "whipped cottage cheese" in your blender and flavor it with cinnamon for a delicious spread to smear on apple slices or add chives and basil for a veggie dip.

FOR LUNCH OR DINNER

Want a quick and easy protein for lunch or dinner? Tofu or beans are excellent choices, but you may want to try something new. *Here's what I suggest…*

•**Split peas.** A bowl of delicious split pea soup will add some variety. Dried peas have four times more protein than brown rice—and four times more fiber. If you don't want to cook your own split pea soup, certain prepared varieties are worth trying.

Good choices: Fantastic Foods Split Pea Soup Mix and Tabatchnick Split Pea Soup.

•**Spinach.** Most people don't realize that cooked spinach—at 4 g per half cup—offers more protein than most other vegetables. Not only that, spinach is incredibly nutrient-dense—it contains antioxidant vitamins A, C and E and is a rich plant source of iron and calcium.

To get a lot of spinach, buy it frozen. Since frozen spinach is precooked, it's easier to eat more—toss it into soups, pasta sauce, bean burritos or lasagna—than if you are downing it raw in, say, a salad. Frozen spinach is picked at peak season before freezing, so it retains its nutrients for months. And it's a great value!

FOR SNACKS

You already know that nuts are excellent protein-rich snacks. *Some other options you may want to try…*

•**Edamame.** These young green soybeans are a versatile protein source. One-half cup of frozen edamame contains 6 g of protein…and a quarter cup of roasted soybeans has an impressive 15 g (roasting concentrates the protein by removing the water). Soy foods contain phytochemicals that may help slow or protect against certain cancers.

•**Hummus.** Here's a great way to spice up the hefty protein kick you get from beans.

What to do: Blend two 15.5-ounce cans of rinsed, drained garbanzo beans with one-quarter cup each tahini, lemon juice and water. Add one tablespoon each of olive oil and Frank's RedHot Cayenne Pepper Sauce (or any brand of pepper sauce you like). Cayenne pepper contains pain-relieving capsaicin. Then finish it off with one clove of minced garlic and one-half teaspoon of sea salt. Use it as hearty dip with whole-grain pita bread or veggies…and maybe some tabouli. It's scrumptious!

Beyond Broccoli: Healthy (Weird) Foods That Can Stop Diabetes and More

Tonia Reinhard, RD, a registered dietitian and codirector of clinical nutrition, Wayne State University, Detroit and author of *Superfoods: The Healthiest Foods on the Planet.*

Have you ever heard of bilberry? Enoki? What about noni or goji berry? When it comes to being loaded with nutrients and healthful phytochemicals, these unheard-of foods stand side-by-side with the likes of blueberries and broccoli. *Here's a list of seven unfamiliar foods that are worth knowing about…*

BILBERRY

Bilberries are high in phytochemicals, including a class of compounds known as anthocyanins. A 2010 laboratory study published in *Journal of Medicinal Foods* found that bilberry extract inhibited the growth of breast cancer cells. The berries also may improve blood glucose levels, helping to prevent diabetes. During World War II, British pilots who ate bilberries before evening bombing raids noticed improvements in their night vision. Some compounds in bilberries may help prevent macular degeneration, a common cause of blindness.

Helpful: You can substitute fresh bilberries for blueberries. Or look for bilberry juice. It won't provide the fiber that you would get from fresh berries, but it still has the phytochemicals. Bilberries are available online and in health-food stores.

TROUT

Salmon gets all the publicity, but like salmon, trout is a fatty fish with large amounts of omega-3 fatty acids. These "good fats" have been linked to a reduced risk for heart disease, rheumatoid arthritis, dementia and other chronic conditions. In 2009, scientists discovered that a peptide (short strands of amino acids) in trout reduced both cholesterol and triglycerides in rats. It may do the same in humans. Trout also is high in vitamins B-6 and B-12, selenium, thiamine and riboflavin.

Helpful: Trout is just as easy to prepare as salmon because the fat keeps it tender, making it less likely to suffer from overcooking than a leaner fish.

One delicious recipe: Combine the juice of three lemons (about six tablespoons of bottled lemon juice) with three tablespoons of olive oil, one-quarter cup of chopped parsley and ground pepper to taste. Dip trout fillets in the mixture…place them on a baking sheet…and bake at 400°F for about 15 minutes.

BITTER MELON

Also known as goya, bitter melon is a fruit that often is combined with pork or other meats and used in stir-fries in Asian restaurants. Many people love it, but its bitter taste takes some getting used to. The payoff is worth it. A report in *Nutrition Review* noted that a diet high in bitter melon (three or more servings per week) helps reduce insulin resistance, a condition that can progress to type 2 diabetes. Also, bitter melon is high in antiviral compounds, which can keep you healthier in cold-and-flu season. And bitter melon is among the best sources of vitamin C, with about 60 milligrams in a one-cup serving,

about the same amount as in one orange. It is available in Asian grocery stores.

Helpful: The bitterness can be tempered by adding sweetness to a recipe. For example, you could add dried cranberries or one tablespoon of apricot jam to a bitter melon stir-fry.

JICAMA

This crunchy, juicy vegetable (the "j" is pronounced like an "h") is as popular throughout Mexico and Central and South America as iceberg lettuce is in the US. In 2002, researchers in Thailand identified antiviral activity in jicama. It is rich in vitamin C and potassium and also high in fiber, with 5.9 grams supplying 24% of the recommended daily amount.

Helpful: Jicama usually is eaten raw—it's the best way to preserve the vitamin C content. You can add slices or cubes to a garden salad or serve it alone, drizzled with lime juice (and chili powder if you like), as a tangy counterpoint to richer dishes.

ENOKI

Unlike the standard white button mushrooms sold in every American supermarket, enoki mushrooms have long, threadlike stalks, each topped by a delicate white dome. A Singapore-based study found that enoki contains a protein that boosts immune function. It's also a powerful antioxidant that can suppress free radicals, important for reducing inflammation in arteries, joints and other parts of the body.

Helpful: The mushrooms have a mild, almost fruity taste. In Japan, they're added to miso soup. Or you can eat them raw, sprinkled on salads or in side dishes. They are available in Asian grocery and specialty stores.

NONI

This is not a fruit that you want to take a bite out of—in its unadulterated form, it has a singularly nasty taste. (Its nickname is "vomit fruit.") It's usually juiced and then combined with other fruit juices. After it's blended, it adds a sharp, but not unpleasant, taste, similar to the taste of unripened pomegranate. Noni is rich in many phytochemicals, including some with potent antioxidant effects. A 2010 animal study found that noni may help to lower blood pressure. It also appears to inhibit the growth of melanoma, a deadly form of skin cancer.

Helpful: In health-food stores, look for a product that is 100% pure noni juice. Then mix one to two ounces of noni juice with other fruit juices, such as apple or pear juice. Experiment to determine what tastes best to you.

GOJI BERRY

Dried goji berries are popular in Australia and Asia, where they are enjoyed as a slightly tangy-sweet snack. Goji also can be used to make juice or a fruity spread. Gojis are high in antioxidants. In a 2009 study published in *Nutrition Research*, participants who drank four ounces of goji juice daily for 30 days had significantly reduced free radical activity in the blood. The berries also are thought to help protect against diabetes and atherosclerosis. And they're high in fiber, with three grams in one-quarter cup. They are available online and in some health-food stores.

Helpful: Munch them as a snack, or add them to muffins or other baked goods.

Caution: If you're taking a blood-thinning medication such as *warfarin* (Coumadin), talk to your doctor before eating goji berries. They may change the drug's effects.

Unless otherwise noted, these foods are available at most supermarkets.

Calling All Carnivores: You Can Become a Veggie Lover

Susan Mitchell, PhD, RD, a registered dietitian and licensed nutritionist based in Winter Park, Florida. The coauthor of three books, including *Fat Is Not Your Fate*, she speaks nationally on nutrition, health and wellness issues. She also hosts the podcast *"Straight Talk About Eating Smart"* at GrowingBolder.com.

Let's say you are given the choice of a thick, juicy steak for dinner or a heaping plate of yellow squash, spinach and other brightly colored vegetables. What will it be?

If you're a hard-core meat eater, there's no contest. But if you don't like vegetables, the sad truth is that you are depriving yourself of proven health-promoting nutrients that help fight everything from heart disease to cancer.

Surprising: Even though nutritionists recommend that we eat three to five servings of vegetables each day, only 21% of men are meeting that goal. And the average woman isn't doing much better—just 31% consume that many veggies in their daily diets, and that's largely because women tend to eat more salads (mostly lettuce) than men do.

Why don't we eat more vegetables? Americans have traditionally been big meat eaters with vegetables thrown in only as side dishes. And some people just don't like the taste of vegetables. Fortunately, there's a way to conquer one's aversion to veggies—and gain the amazing nutritional benefits of these foods.

A TASTE EXPLOSION!

It's old news that boiling vegetables is not the way to go—too often, you end up with veggies that are limp, mushy and relatively tasteless.

What's a better choice? Steaming brings out the natural flavor of fresh vegetables and gives them the kind of crunch and texture that greatly increases their "mouth appeal."

But there's an even better alternative that gives vegetables the meaty texture that meat lovers crave. And by choosing ingredients carefully, you also can make the veggies more aromatic and flavorful. *To make veggies more appealing, try…*

• **Roasting or grilling.** If you roast or grill your veggies, their natural sugars will caramelize, which kicks up the flavor. For roasting, in particular, it helps to toss them in an aromatic oil such as pumpkin oil (this oil provides a hearty, full flavor that appeals to most meat lovers).

Good choices for roasting or grilling: Carrots…leeks…onions…butternut squash…potatoes (whole or wedged)…peppers (sweet and hot)…turnips and other root vegetables…tomatoes, eggplant and other vine-grown veggies.

What to do: Mix two cups of coarsely chopped veggie chunks with one tablespoon of cooking oil, such as pumpkin oil. You can place veggies on cookie sheets or racks lined with aluminum foil for easy cleanup. For root vegetables, roast at 400°F for about 40 to 45 minutes, stirring at the halfway point. For the last five to 10 minutes, you can add more fragile vegetables, such as thin asparagus or cherry tomatoes.

If grilling, use a veggie grill basket or wrap vegetables in foil packets. Start with four to five minutes of direct heat. Add another four to five minutes if needed.

SPICE IT UP!

Herbs (preferably fresh to provide maximum flavor) and spices are great ways to not only make vegetables taste delicious but also add even more disease-fighting nutrients.

Flavorful, health-promoting herbs: Rosemary...sage...tarragon...and basil.

Best spices to try: Cinnamon...cumin...and peppercorns.

For the die-hard meat lover, you also can add a saucy, bold flavor to your veggies by using condiments that are commonly associated with meat—for example, try some Worcestershire sauce on mushrooms such as baby portabellas.

Other good condiments: Horseradish, Pickapeppa sauce or any hot sauce of choice.

WHERE TO SHOP

One of the best ways to boost your veggie quota is to shop at local food co-ops, farmers' markets or "pick-your-own" farms for a wide selection of in-season locally grown vegetables and fruit.

Resource: To find a farmers' market near you, check the USDA's website at *www.usda localfooddirectories.com.*

IRRESISTIBLE QUESADILLAS

Black bean quesadillas are a great way to slip in veggies.

What to do: Spread refried black beans (or canned black beans that have been rinsed and drained) on a whole-wheat tortilla. Cover with corn (frozen, thawed and drained), chopped onion and/or green/red bell peppers...salsa... and shredded cheddar cheese, and top with another tortilla. Heat flat in a skillet until hot, turn over and heat again until the cheese has melted. Cut into wedges and serve with guacamole.

Helpful: Add a little chili powder or cumin to the beans to perk up the flavor!

Magnesium-Rich Foods Protect Against Type 2 Diabetes

Ka He, MD, chair and professor, epidemiology and biostatistics, Indiana University, Bloomington.
Environmental Nutrition. EnvironmentalNutrition.com

When researchers studied 4,497 healthy adults' diets for 20 years, those who consumed the most magnesium (about 200 mg per 1,000 calories) were 47% less likely to develop diabetes than those who consumed the least (about 100 mg per 1,000 calories).

Theory: Magnesium enhances enzymes that help the body process blood sugar.

Self-defense: Eat more magnesium-rich whole grains, nuts, legumes and green leafy vegetables to reach the recommended dietary allowance of 320 milligrams (mg) for women and 420 mg for men.

Examples: One-quarter cup of wheat bran contains 89 mg of magnesium...one ounce of dry-roasted almonds contains 80 mg...one-half cup of cooked frozen spinach, 78 mg...one ounce of dry-roasted cashews, 74 mg...three-quarters cup of bran flakes cereal, 64 mg...one cup of instant fortified oatmeal, prepared with water, 61 mg.

For more information about magnesium and diabetes, see page 15.

How to Juice for Healing Power

Michael T. Murray, ND, a naturopathic physician and leading authority on natural medicine. He is author of *The Complete Book of Juicing: Your Delicious Guide to Youthful Vitality.* DoctorMurray.com

Juice has gotten a bad rap. We're often advised to eat whole fruits and vegetables—for the fiber and because they are lower in calories than an "equal" amount of juice. But for the many Americans who don't eat the recommended three to five servings of vegetables and two to three servings of fruit daily, juice can be a lifesaver—literally. Juice is loaded with nutrients that protect against heart disease, cancer, diabetes, arthritis, Alzheimer's and other chronic conditions.

We can pack in a day's worth of fruits and vegetables in just 12 to 16 ounces of juice. *How to do it right…*

•**Opt for fresh juice, not packaged.** Packaged juices, whether in a can, bottle, carton or frozen, are lower in nutrients. And packaged juices have been pasteurized, which destroys health-giving compounds.

Example: Fresh apple juice contains ellagic acid, an anticancer nutrient that shields chromosomes from damage and blocks the tumor-causing action of many pollutants. In contrast, commercial apple juice contains almost no ellagic acid.

•**Use a quality juicer.** If you juice once or twice a week, try a high-speed centrifugal juicer. They're relatively inexpensive, starting at $100 or so. (*Examples:* Juice Fountain Duo or Juice Fountain Elite, both from Breville.)

•**If you juice more frequently,** consider investing in a "slow juicer" ($300 and up) that typically operates at 80 revolutions per minute (RPM), compared with the 1,000 to 24,000 RPM of a centrifugal model. (I use The Hurom Juicer.) A slow juicer expels significantly more juice and better preserves delicate nutrients. And because the damaged compounds produced by a centrifugal juicer taste a little bitter, a slow juicer provides better-tasting juice.

Follow this basic juice recipe: Use four unpeeled carrots and two unpeeled, cored apples cut into wedges as a base for creating other juice blends by adding such things as a handful of kale, spinach, radishes and/or beets. Ideally, use organic fruits and vegetables. If not, be sure to wash them thoroughly.

•**Keep blood sugar balanced.** Fruit and vegetable juices can deliver too much natural sugar, spiking blood sugar levels, a risk factor for diabetes.

What you need to know: The metabolic impact of the sugar in a particular food can be measured using the glycemic index (GI)—how quickly a carbohydrate turns into glucose (blood sugar). But a more accurate way to measure this impact is with the glycemic load (GL)—a relatively new calculation that uses the GI but also takes into account the amount of carbohydrate in a specific food. Beets, for example, have a high GI but a low GL. Charts providing the GI and the GL are available on the Internet. I like those at *www.mendosa.com.*

Bottom line: Limit the intake of higher-GL juices such as orange, cherry, pineapple and mango. You can use them to add flavor to lower-GL choices such as kale, spinach, celery and beets.

The Truth About Sugar and Artificial Sweeteners

Karen Collins, RD, a registered dietitian in private practice in Jamestown, New York, and nutrition adviser to the Washington, DC–based American Institute for Cancer Research, AICR.org.

We all know that getting too much added sugar carries a slew of health risks—from weight gain and heart disease to diabetes and obesity-linked cancers.

In fact, research shows that most Americans are getting so much sugar in their daily diets that they are increasing their heart attack risk by 20%. But with so many natural and artificial sweeteners to choose from—and new studies coming out all the time that raise questions about their safety—it's tough to know which claims are valid and which are not.

Facts you need to choose the best sweeteners for you…*

TRADITIONAL SWEETENERS

If you're not cutting calories and eat a healthful diet, it's OK to have up to two to three teaspoons of these sugars daily. But if your diet includes high-sugar snacks, cereals, drinks or other processed foods, limit these sugars to a few times a week.

•**Brown and white sugars.** You may think of brown sugar as a more wholesome choice than white sugar. But the fact is, they're both processed—white sugar is derived from sugarcane or sugar beets, while brown sugar is a combination of white sugar and molasses. These sugars also have roughly the same number of calories—16 calories per teaspoon for white sugar…and 17 for brown sugar.

How safe? When consumed in modest amounts, brown and white sugars are safe for most individuals. Brown sugar is really no more healthful than white sugar, but it does make baked goods moister and adds a hint of caramel flavor. Follow your taste preference.

•**Honey.** Even though honey contains trace amounts of minerals (mainly potassium, calcium and phosphorus), its nutritional value is not significantly different from that of white or brown sugar. Honey is about 25% to 50% sweeter by weight than sugar, so you can use less and still get a nice sweet taste.

How safe? Honey is safe for most adults when consumed in modest amounts. However, honey should never be given to babies under one year of age—it could contain bacterial spores that produce a toxin that causes infant botulism, a serious form of food poisoning. Honey's stickiness also may contribute to cavities in everyone else.

*People with diabetes can use any type of sweetener in their diets but must include it in their total daily carbohydrate limit recommended by their doctors or registered dietitians. Artificial sweeteners themselves have no carbohydrates, but the foods containing them usually do. To cook or bake with artificial sweeteners, check the labels for instructions.

•**Agave (ah-GAH-vay) nectar.** Made from the juice of the agave plant, this sweetener reminds some people of a sweeter, thinner version of honey. Agave and honey have about the same number of calories (21 calories per teaspoon).

How safe? Overall, agave is no more healthful than other types of added sugar. Compared with the same amount of white sugar, agave causes smaller increases in blood sugar, triggering fewer of the metabolic changes that can lead to diabetes and heart disease. However, agave is higher in fructose than other natural sugars, which may not be healthy in large amounts.

•**Molasses.** This syrupy liquid is created from the juice of sugarcane and beet sugar during the refining process. The type of molasses is determined by the degree of boiling that occurs—light molasses comes from the first boiling…dark molasses, which is darker and thicker than the light variety, comes from the second boiling…and blackstrap molasses, which is quite thick and dark, comes from the third boiling.

How safe? Molasses is safe for most people. Dark and blackstrap molasses provide health-protective polyphenol compounds. Blackstrap molasses is also a good source of iron. All types of molasses contain about 20 calories per teaspoon.

LOW- OR NO-CALORIE SWEETENERS

Many people believe almost as a matter of principle that all artificial sweeteners are harmful and should be avoided. But that view is simplistic. *Here is what the science shows about artificial sweetener safety…*

•**Aspartame.** Sold in a light blue packet as NutraSweet or Equal, this artificial sweetener has no calories and is about 200 times sweeter by weight than white or brown sugar. Aspartame is used in soft drinks, chewing gum, pudding and gelatins and hundreds of other products.

How safe? Some individuals get headaches and/or feel dizzy when they ingest too much aspartame. Despite animal studies that have linked aspartame to cancer, no such association has been found in humans. However, a recent study linked consumption of diet soft drinks containing aspartame to an increased risk for non-Hodgkin's lymphoma and multiple myeloma in men. The watchdog group Center for Science in the Public Interest (CSPI) advises against using aspartame. In addition, people with phenylketonuria should avoid aspartame completely—this genetic disorder makes it difficult to metabolize phenylalanine, one of the protein building blocks used to make the sweetener.

●**Saccharin.** Found in a pink packet and sold as Sweet'N Low, it is 300 to 500 times sweeter than sugar. Saccharin has less than four calories per packet.

How safe? Despite concerns about saccharin causing bladder cancer in male rats, many human studies have shown no link to cancer risk. Even so, CSPI believes the research is inconsistent and recommends against its use. There's some evidence that saccharin can cross the placenta, so some experts advise women to limit it during pregnancy.

●**Stevia.** A highly purified extract made from the leaves of a South American shrub, stevia (sold as stevia, rebiana and under the brand names Pure Via and Truvia) has zero calories and is about 250 times sweeter than sugar.

How safe? No health risks have been uncovered in a wide range of studies on stevia, but research is ongoing. Stevia may cause an allergic reaction in people who are allergic to ragweed and could interact with diabetes and blood pressure drugs.

●**Sucralose.** Known as Splenda and sold in a yellow packet, it has four calories per packet and tastes about 600 times sweeter than white or brown sugar. Sucralose is a processed sweetener derived from a molecule of sucrose (table sugar).

How safe? There's no evidence that sucralose harms humans when consumed in small amounts. One recent study suggested that it increases diabetes risk, but this was a small study of obese people looking at how sucralose affected their ability to metabolize a very large sugar load—about 19 teaspoons consumed all at once. More research is needed on how sucralose may affect metabolism with a more typical diet.

PROCESSED FOOD SWEETENERS

●**High fructose corn syrup (HFCS).** Derived from cornstarch, HFCS is found in a vast and sometimes surprising array of processed foods, ranging from many breads and yogurts to certain brands of applesauce and even macaroni and cheese. Beverages that contain HFCS include a wide variety of soft drinks, sports drinks and even tonic water.

How safe? Most experts have long insisted that there's no research showing that HFCS is any worse than other sweeteners—and, in fact, most HFCS contains only a little more fructose than regular table sugar. However, some studies have now linked HFCS-containing beverages (one or more servings a day) to greater risk for heart disease, diabetes, weight gain and obesity. But these associations may be due to increased calorie consumption from foods that contain HFCS, such as soda, rather than the HFCS itself.

Best: Avoid these beverages, and limit processed foods to substantially cut consumption of HFCS and calories.

●**Sugar alcohols.** Sorbitol, mannitol and erythritol are processed sweeteners that do not actually contain alcohol or sugar. They're about half as sweet as white sugar, with fewer calories. Sugar alcohols are slowly absorbed, so they don't raise blood sugar quickly. A serving of food with less than 5 g of these sweeteners generally will not affect blood sugar. Consuming more than 20 g at once can lead to gas, bloating and diarrhea.

5 Cups of Coffee a Day Can Be Good for You!

Frank B. Hu, MD, PhD, an epidemiologist, nutritional specialist and professor of medicine at Harvard Medical School and the Harvard School of Public Health, both in Boston. He is codirector of Harvard's Program in Obesity Epidemiology and Prevention.

Even coffee drinkers find it hard to believe that their favorite pick-me-up is healthful, but it seems to be true. People who drink coffee regularly are less likely to have a stroke or get diabetes or Parkinson's disease than those who don't drink it. There's even some evidence that coffee can help prevent cancer, although the link between coffee and various cancers is preliminary and still being investigated.

FOR LOWER DIABETES RISK

More than 20 studies have found that coffee drinkers are less likely to get diabetes than those who don't drink coffee. When we analyzed the data from nine previous studies, which included a total of more than 193,000 people, we found that those who drank more than six or seven cups of coffee daily were 35% less likely to have type 2 diabetes (the most common form) than those who drank two cups or less. Those who consumed four to six cups daily had a 28% lower risk for diabetes.

Some of the studies were conducted in Europe, where people who drink a lot of coffee—up to 10 cups daily—are the ones least likely to have diabetes.

Both decaf and regular coffee seem to be protective against diabetes. This suggests that the antioxidants in coffee—not the caffeine—are the active agents. It's possible that these compounds protect insulin-producing cells in the pancreas. The minerals in coffee, such as chromium and magnesium, have been shown to improve insulin sensitivity.

SKIN CANCER FIGHTER

It's not a substitute for sunscreen, but drinking coffee could protect you from the most common type of skin cancer.

In a new report presented at the American Association for Cancer Research meeting in Boston, researchers found that coffee drinkers were less likely to develop basal-cell carcinoma than noncoffee drinkers.

In the study, researchers followed more than 112,000 people for up to 24 years. During this time, they tracked the incidence of basal-cell carcinomas and other skin cancers. Men who drank the most coffee had a 13% lower risk for basal-cell carcinomas than those who drank the least…in women, the risk was 18% lower.

Decaffeinated coffee didn't provide the same protection, so it appears that caffeine is responsible—but the reason isn't known.

Coffee reduced the risk for only this one type of skin cancer. Other skin cancers, such as melanoma and squamous-cell carcinoma, weren't affected. Because this is the first large study to find this effect, it will have to be repeated—by different researchers and with different groups of people—to confirm that coffee does, in fact, protect the skin.

Caffeine may protect against other cancers as well.

Recent finding: Women who drink four or more cups a day of caffeinated coffee reduced their risk for endometrial cancer by 30%. And drinking two or more cups of decaffeinated coffee reduced risk by about 22%.

PROMISING, BUT NOT PROVED

It's important to remember that the majority of research about coffee is observational. Researchers interview large numbers of people…ask them about their coffee consumption and other habits…look at their health status…and then make conclusions about what caused what.

Unlike double-blind, randomized clinical trials, which are considered the gold standard of scientific research, observational studies cannot prove cause and effect, but they do offer evidence.

CAUTION

Some caveats about coffee…

•**Moderation matters.** Some people get the jitters or have insomnia when they drink coffee. In rare cases, the caffeine causes a dramatic rise in blood pressure. It's fine for most people to have three, four or five cups of coffee a day—or even more. But pay attention to how you feel. If you get jittery or anxious when you drink a certain amount, cut back. Or drink decaf some of the time.

•**Hold the milk and sugar.** Some of the coffee "beverages" at Starbucks and other coffee shops have more calories than a sweet dessert. Coffee may be good for you, but limit the add-ons.

•**Use a paper filter.** Boiled coffee, coffee made with a French press or coffee that drips through a metal filter has high levels of oils that can significantly raise levels of LDL, the dangerous form of cholesterol.

Better: A drip machine that uses a paper filter. It traps the oils and eliminates this risk.

Wine with a Meal

Drinking white wine with a high-carbohydrate meal reduces the postmeal rise in blood sugar levels. Although only white wine has been studied, the effect is expected to be similar for red wine. Wine lowers the meal's glycemic index by 37%, probably because its high acidity helps slow digestion—so sugar does not enter the bloodstream as quickly. Keeping blood sugar under control can help prevent diabetes and heart disease.

Jennie Brand-Miller, PhD, professor of human nutrition, University of Sydney, Australia, and leader of a study of alcohol consumption with meals, published in *American Journal of Clinical Nutrition*.

Raise a Glass…in Moderation

Anne Peters, MD, professor of medicine and director of the clinical diabetes programs, University of Southern California, Los Angeles. She is author of *Conquering Diabetes: A Complete Program for Prevention and Treatment.*

If you have diabetes and have always avoided liquor because of the sugar, you might want to reconsider your habits.

A study found that resveratrol, an antioxidant found in red wine, increases sensitivity to insulin in mice.

However: Resveratrol lasts only a short time in the body, so people with or without diabetes would have to consume huge amounts of resveratrol every day to see even a small benefit.

But according to the American Diabetes Association, people with type 2 diabetes can

probably drink wine or other alcoholic beverages as long as their blood sugar is under control and they don't have any complications affected by alcohol, such as hypertension.

Drinking alcohol in moderation—up to two alcoholic drinks a day for men and one for women—can help in other ways…

- **Reduce risk for cardiovascular disease.**
- **Relax and diminish stress.** Stress aggravates diabetes.
- **Interfere with the liver's manufacture of sugar and decrease blood sugar levels.**

Green Tea Fights Diabetes, Cancer, Stroke and More…

Patrick M. Fratellone, MD, executive medical director of Fratellone Medical Associates in New York City… attending physician at St. Luke's Hospital, Roosevelt Hospital and Beth Israel Hospital in New York City… former chief of medicine and director of cardiology at Atkins Center for Complementary Medicine… and coauthor of a comprehensive review article on the health benefits of green tea in *Explore.* FratelloneMedical.com

Green tea has remarkable powers to combat disease. I think we all should include green tea in our daily health regimen.

The leaves of the evergreen shrub *Camellia sinensis* are used to make green, black and oolong tea—but green tea contains the most *epigallocatechin* (EGCG). EGCG (a type of plant compound called a polyphenol, flavonoid or catechin) is a powerful anti-inflammatory and antioxidant. Research shows that chronic low-grade inflammation (produced by an immune system in overdrive) and oxidation (a kind of internal rust that damages cells) are the two processes that trigger and advance most chronic diseases. *Evidence shows that green tea can prevent and treat many of these diseases…*

TYPE 2 DIABETES

Type 2 diabetes is a major risk factor for cardiovascular disease and can lead to many other disastrous health problems, including kidney failure, blindness and lower-limb amputation.

In a study of 60 people with diabetes, those who took a daily supplement of green tea extract for two months significantly reduced hemoglobin A1C—a biomarker of blood sugar levels.

How it works: People with diabetes who drank green tea for 12 weeks boosted their levels of insulin (the hormone that helps move sugar out of the blood and into muscle cells)—and decreased their levels of A1C.

OVERWEIGHT

More than 65% of Americans are overweight. Those extra pounds are a risk factor in dozens of health problems, including cardiovascular disease, cancer, osteoarthritis and type 2 diabetes. Researchers from the Netherlands reviewed 49 studies on green tea and weight loss and analyzed the results of the 11 most scientifically rigorous. They found that drinking green tea "significantly decreased body weight" and "significantly maintained body weight after a period of weight loss."

Why it works: EGCG blocks the action of an enzyme that breaks down noradrenaline (NA). This hormone and neurotransmitter stimulates the sympathetic nervous system, which controls heart rate, muscle tension and the release of energy from fat. By preserving NA, EGCG triggers your metabolism to stay more active and burn more calories.

CANCER

Researchers have conducted more than 1,000 scientific studies on the ability of green tea and EGCG to prevent and reverse cancer, including…

Breast cancer: Researchers at Harvard School of Public Health found a 19% reduction in risk among women who drink more than three cups of green tea a day and a 27% reduction in risk for breast cancer recurrence.

Colon cancer: Japanese researchers studied 136 people with colorectal adenomas (benign tumors that often precede colon cancer). Half of the participants were given a green tea extract. A year later, only 15% of those receiving the extract had developed new adenomas, compared with 31% of those who didn't receive the extract.

Prostate cancer: In a study published in *American Journal of Epidemiology*, Japanese researchers found that men with prostate cancer who drank five or more cups of green tea a day had a 48% lower risk of developing advanced prostate cancer, compared with men who drank less than one cup a day.

Lung cancer: Chinese researchers found a 22% lower risk among those with the highest consumption of green tea, compared with those who did not consume green tea.

Why it works: EGCG interferes with cancer through various mechanisms, including stopping the production of factors that stimulate tumor growth and inhibiting movement of cancer cells.

HEART DISEASE AND STROKE

Researchers studied 14,000 people ages 65 to 84 for six years. They found that men who drank seven or more cups of green tea a day had a 30% lower risk of dying from heart disease or stroke, and women had an 18% lower risk, compared with those who drank less than one cup of green tea a day.

How it works: Green tea can…

• **Lower blood levels of "bad" LDL cholesterol** and reduce the oxidation of LDL, which generates the small, dense particles that can clog arteries and cause a heart attack or stroke.

• **Reduce the activity of platelets,** blood components that clump and form artery-plugging clots.

• **Prevent ventricular arrhythmia,** a rhythm problem in the heart's main pumping chamber that can trigger or worsen a heart attack.

• **Reduce high blood pressure,** a risk factor for stroke and heart attack.

• **Improve the flexibility of the endothelium (the lining of the arteries),** boosting blood flow to the heart and brain.

GUM DISEASE

Research links the chronic bacterial infection of gum (periodontal) disease to many health problems, including heart disease and diabetes. Japanese researchers studied nearly

1,000 men ages 49 to 59 and found that those who regularly drank green tea had fewer cases of, or less severe, periodontal disease. For every additional daily cup of tea the men drank, there was a significant decrease in the depth of periodontal pockets (the grooves around the teeth that deepen as gum disease advances), a decrease in the loss of attachment of the gum to the tooth and a decrease in bleeding.

How it works: The polyphenols in green tea may decrease the inflammatory response to oral bacteria.

THE RIGHT AMOUNT

To guarantee a sufficient intake of EGCG, I recommend one or more of the following strategies. You can safely do all three.

• **Drink green tea.** Five to 10 eight-ounce cups a day of regular or decaf.

Best: For maximum intake of EGCG, use whole-leaf loose tea rather than a teabag, using one teaspoon per cup. Steep the tea for at least five minutes.

• **Take a supplement of green tea extract.**

Minimum: 400 milligrams (mg) a day of a supplement standardized to 90% EGCG.

• **Add a drop of green tea liquid extract to green tea or another beverage.** Look for a product that is standardized to a high level (at least 50%) of EGCG, and follow the dosage recommendation on the label.

Example: HerbaGreen from HerbaSway, at 90% polyphenols, 50% from EGCG.

SAFE USE

Talk to your doctor if you use…

• **An antiplatelet drug (blood thinner),** such as *warfarin* (Coumadin), because green tea also thins the blood.

• **A bronchodilator for asthma or chronic obstructive pulmonary disease,** because green tea can increase its potency.

• **An antacid,** because green tea can decrease the effect.

Good News! Even More Health Benefits from Dark Chocolate

Bill Gottlieb, CHC, founder and president of Good For You Health Coaching. He is author of *Health-Defense: How to Stay Vibrantly Healthy in a Toxic World* and *The Every-Other-Day Diet: The Diet That Lets You Eat All You Want (Half the Time) and Keep the Weight Off*, with Krista Varady, PhD. BillGottliebHealth.com

About 29 million Americans, including one in four people over the age of 65, have diabetes, or chronically high blood sugar—a disease that raises the risk of dying from heart disease by 70%. Long-term complications can include kidney failure and blindness. Studies show that chocolate can prevent diabetes and help prevent complications in those who have the disease.

In a recent study of nearly 8,000 people published in *Clinical Nutrition*, those who ate one ounce of chocolate two to six times weekly had a 34% lower risk of being diagnosed with diabetes than people who ate chocolate less than once a month.

Prevention of diabetic complications: In a study of 93 postmenopausal women with type 2 diabetes published in *Diabetes Care*, those women who ate flavanol-rich chocolate every day for one year not only had better blood sugar control—they also had 11 times lower risk of developing heart disease, compared with women who ate low-flavanol chocolate.

More research: Cellular and animal studies show that cocoa flavanols can protect the insulin-producing beta cells of the pancreas (insulin is the hormone that ushers blood sugar out of the bloodstream and into cells)…the kidneys (diabetes is the cause of nearly half of all cases of kidney failure)…and the retina (nearly 30% of people with diabetes have diabetic retinopathy, a cause of vision loss and blindness).

WHICH CHOCOLATE IS BEST?

Nearly every client in my health-coaching practice gets a recommendation to consume a daily dose of about 400 milligrams (mg) of cocoa flavanols—the amount used in many of the studies that show a therapeutic effect.

Important: Higher doses don't produce better results.

And the healthiest way to get those flavanols is with unsweetened cocoa powder that delivers all the flavanols of dark chocolate without burdening your daily diet with extra calories and sugar. (Using cocoa powder also helps you control your intake—it's notoriously easy to consume an entire three-ounce bar of chocolate even though your optimal daily "dose" is only one ounce.)

Red flag: Do not use "Dutch" cocoa powder, which is treated with an alkalizing agent for a richer color and milder taste—a process that strips cocoa of 98% of its epicatechin.

My advice: Mix one tablespoon of unsweetened cocoa powder in an eight- to 12-ounce mug of hot water or milk (nondairy milks such as coconut, almond, soy and rice milk are delicious alternatives) and add a no-calorie natural sweetener, such as stevia.

Good products: I recommend CocoaVia, the powder developed by Mars, Incorporated. The Mars Center for Cocoa Health Science has conducted extensive scientific research on cocoa flavanols for two decades, and one "stick" of its powder reliably delivers 375 mg of cocoa flavanols, standardized for epicatechin. You can mix it with cold or warm milk, coffee drinks, smoothies, yogurt or oatmeal. Another high-quality cocoa powder is CocoaWell from Reserveage.

Dark chocolate bars don't reliably deliver a therapeutic dose of cocoa flavanols. But if you prefer to eat dark chocolate, look for a bar with 70% or more cocoa, and consume about one ounce (28 grams) per day. According to a report from *www.ConsumerLab.com*, dark chocolate brands with high levels of flavanols (about one-quarter to one-half the amount in the best brands of cocoa powder) include Endangered Species, Ghirardelli and Lindt.

Wild Kudzu Root May Help Metabolic Syndrome

J. Michael Wyss, PhD, professor of cell biology and medicine at the University of Alabama at Birmingham.

The kudzu root, a nuisance of a vine that grows wildly in the southern portion of the US, may soon be put to good use to help people who have metabolic syndrome, a constellation of symptoms, including hypertension, high cholesterol and abdominal obesity that increases risk for diabetes, heart disease and stroke. A recent study shows that kudzu root, an ancient Chinese herb historically used to treat menopausal symptoms, neck and eye pain, anginal pain and even the common cold, may actually help to remedy this modern-day epidemic.

Scientists have long suspected that controlling blood glucose levels might be the key to managing metabolic syndrome. To that end, researchers at the University of Alabama at Birmingham tested the effects of kudzu root on blood glucose, blood pressure and blood lipids (fats) in rats with high blood pressure and at risk for type 2 diabetes. For two months, half were fed a diet that contained a small (0.2%) amount of kudzu root extract. The others (the control group) were fed the same diet without the kudzu extract. At the end of the study, the kudzu-treated rats had lower blood pressure, blood lipids and blood glucose. Moreover, the kudzu-treated rats showed improved control of blood glucose. The study was published in the *Journal of Agricultural and Food Chemistry*.

HOW DOES IT HELP?

According to J. Michael Wyss, PhD, professor of cell biology and medicine at the University of Alabama at Birmingham, an isoflavone (an antioxidant found in plants) called puerarin might be the effective agent that reduces the symptoms of metabolic syndrome. "It appears that puerarin works by limiting the ability of glucose to cross from the gut into the blood, thereby buffering blood sugar so that it does not rise rapidly after a meal," he explained.

"This causes glucose in the blood to be taken up by muscle tissue. High levels would allow more to go into fat cells for storage."

Kudzu is available in health-food stores in pill and powder form. Dr. Wyss cautioned, however, that more testing is needed to determine safety and efficacy for metabolic syndrome, especially since it has the potential for drug interactions. He also warned that people with estrogen-sensitive cancers (such as breast, ovarian or prostate cancers) and those taking the drug *tamoxifen* should not take kudzu because the herb contains phytoestrogens, substances that mimic estrogen, and have the potential to interact with estrogen receptors. In fact, any use of kudzu should be considered only in consultation with a physician.

In the future, Dr. Wyss believes that kudzu most likely will be used as a complement to other treatment approaches to metabolic syndrome, which include lifestyle modifications (healthy eating habits, exercise and weight loss) and drugs to bring glucose, blood lipids and blood pressure to the recommended levels.

Grapes Protect Against Metabolic Syndrome

Metabolic syndrome is a cluster of symptoms that includes increased blood pressure, high blood sugar, excess body fat around the waist, low HDL and high blood triglycerides, all linked to inflammation. The syndrome raises the risk for heart disease, stroke and type 2 diabetes.

Study finding: Obesity-prone rats that were fed red, green and black grapes for 90 days had significantly lower inflammation markers, especially in liver and abdominal fat tissue.

Best: Eat 15 to 20 grapes per day.

E. Mitchell Seymour, PhD, a research investigator, department of cardiac surgery, University of Michigan.

Should We All Be Drinking Hydrogen-Rich Water?

Atsunori Nakao, MD, PhD, former research associate professor of surgery at the Thomas E. Starzl Transplantation Institute at the University of Pittsburgh. He specializes in gas therapy and has published numerous research studies on the medicinal uses of gases, including hydrogen.

The purported health benefits of hydrogen-rich water—which are said to stem primarily from protection against cell-damaging free radicals—merits further investigation. While at the University of Pittsburgh, Atsunori Nakao, MD, PhD, a research associate professor of surgery, conducted studies on the subject. He describes research that, while preliminary, is nonetheless intriguing.

How hydrogen works: You no doubt recall that a molecule of water, or H_2O, consists of one atom of oxygen bound to two atoms of hydrogen. In our bodies, hydrogen functions as an antioxidant, helping to prevent cell damage and inflammation, protect DNA and combat out-of-control cell growth.

The problem is that the hydrogen in water is not very accessible to the cells in our bodies. That's because "free" hydrogen (hydrogen molecules not bound to other molecules) is relatively rare and, being a light gas, evaporates quickly, Dr. Nakao said. The point of hydrogen-enriched water is to provide hydrogen that is easier for our cells to use. Hydrogen-rich water is created through a simple chemical reaction—when a ceramic stick containing metallic magnesium is placed in a bottle of plain water, the magnesium elicits a reaction that constantly generates hydrogen.

Research on the health benefits of hydrogen-rich water is limited and there is scant data on long-term effects. *However, pilot studies on humans suggest that consuming hydrogen-rich water may help...*

• **Prevent metabolic syndrome.** A disorder characterized by a constellation of symptoms (including obesity, insulin resistance, high cholesterol and hypertension), metabolic syndrome is associated with an increased risk for cardiovascular disease and type 2 diabetes. Dr. Nakao and colleagues conducted a study of 20 patients at risk for metabolic syndrome, instructing them to drink about two quarts of hydrogen-rich water per day for eight weeks. Blood tests were done at the start, middle and end of the study period.

Results: After eight weeks, participants showed, on average, a 39% increase in blood levels of antioxidant enzymes, 8% increase in blood levels of HDL "good" cholesterol and 13% decrease in total cholesterol—levels of improvement that significantly lowered their risk for metabolic syndrome.

• **Improve health for diabetes and prediabetes patients.** A Japanese study involved 36 patients with either type 2 diabetes or impaired glucose tolerance (a prediabetic condition in which blood glucose levels are higher than normal). Some patients drank about 30 ounces of hydrogen-rich water daily for eight weeks…the rest drank the same amount of plain water.

Results: Hydrogen-rich water consumption was associated with significant decreases in LDL "bad" cholesterol and urinary markers of oxidative stress as well as improved glucose metabolism…in two-thirds of prediabetes patients, oral glucose tolerance test results returned to normal. Among plain water drinkers, there were no significant changes.

• **Ease the negative side effects of radiation treatment for cancer.** In a 2011 study, Dr. Nakao's team looked at 49 liver cancer patients undergoing radiation, a treatment that often increases fatigue and negatively affects quality of life. Participants who drank about two quarts of hydrogen-rich water daily for six weeks showed lower blood levels of oxidative markers (by-products of cell injury caused by free radicals) and reported higher quality of life than participants who drank tap water. Hydrogen-rich water did not compromise radiation's therapeutic antitumor effects, Dr. Nakao noted.

In addition, animal studies show that consumption of hydrogen-rich water may help reduce the risk for atherosclerosis…prevent stress-induced declines in learning and memory…slow the progression of Parkinson's dis-

ease…prevent or ease colitis…reduce allergic reactions…improve kidney function in kidney transplant patients…and lessen kidney toxicity and other side effects of the chemotherapy drug *cisplatin.*

But is it safe? Some people who drink hydrogen-rich water report loose stools, mild heartburn and/or headaches. Because excess magnesium can be dangerous, are there any side effects associated with the increased intake of magnesium from the ceramic stick used to create the hydrogen-rich water? Dr. Nakao said that any effects would be negligible because the amount of magnesium in a normal daily diet is almost 800 times more than what's in hydrogen-rich water. (Like other over-the-counter magnesium products, magnesium water sticks do not require FDA approval.) "I have been drinking hydrogen-rich water myself for years," Dr. Nakao added. "It is not an overstatement to say that hydrogen's impact on therapeutic and preventive medicine could be enormous in the future."

If you are considering giving hydrogen-rich water a try: Talk to your doctor about this intriguing research. While Dr. Nakao declined to recommend any particular brand, he confirmed that the magnesium sticks used to create hydrogen-rich water are sold online for about $80 per stick at various sites. Resources include *www.livingwaterusa.com* and *www.hydrogenwater-stick.com.* How does hydrogen-rich water taste? Like regular water.

Spirulina Slows Aging and Prevents Chronic Disease

Jennifer Adler, MS, CN, a certified nutritionist, natural foods chef and adjunct faculty member at Bastyr University, Kenmore, Washington. She is the founder and owner of Passionate Nutrition, a nutrition practice with offices throughout the Northwest, and cofounder of the International Eating Disorders Institute. PassionateNutrition.com

W hen you think of a superfood, you probably think of salmon or blueberries—not the algae that floats on the surfaces of lakes, ponds and reservoirs.

But there's a type of blue-green algae that has been used for food and medicine in developing countries for centuries...that NASA has recommended as an ideal food for long-term space missions...that is loaded with health-giving nutrients...and that might be a key component in a diet aimed at staying healthy, reversing chronic disease and slowing the aging process.

THAT ALGAE IS SPIRULINA

Spirulina grows mainly in subtropical and tropical countries, where there is year-round heat and sunlight. It is high in protein (up to 70%), rich in antioxidants and loaded with vitamins and minerals, particularly iron and vitamin B-12. And it has no cellulose—the cell wall of green plants—so its nutrients are easy for the body to digest and absorb.

GREEN MEDICINE

Dried into a powder, spirulina can be added to food or taken as a tablet or capsule. And ingested regularly, spirulina can do you a lot of good. *Scientific research shows there are many health problems that spirulina might help prevent or treat...*

• **Anemia.** Researchers from the University of California at Davis studied 40 people age 50 and older who had been diagnosed with anemia (iron deficiency), giving them a spirulina supplement every day for three months. The study participants had a steady rise in levels of hemoglobin, the iron-carrying component of red blood cells, along with several other factors that indicated increased levels of iron.

• **Weakened immunity.** In the UC Davis study mentioned above, most of the participants ages 61 to 70 also had increases in infection-fighting white blood cells and in an enzyme that is a marker for increased immune activity—in effect, reversing immunosenescence, the age-related weakening of the immune system. Immunosenescence is linked not only to a higher risk for infectious diseases such as the flu but also to chronic diseases with an inflammatory component, such as heart disease, Alzheimer's and cancer.

• **Allergies.** Spirulina has anti-inflammatory properties and can prevent the release of histamine and other inflammatory factors that trigger and worsen allergic symptoms. Studies also show that spirulina can boost levels of IgA, an antibody that defends against allergic reactions. In one study, people with allergies who took spirulina had less nasal discharge, sneezing, nasal congestion and itching.

• **Cataracts and age-related macular degeneration.** Taking spirulina can double blood levels of zeaxanthin, an antioxidant linked to a reduced risk for cataracts and age-related macular degeneration, reported researchers in *The BMJ* (formerly *British Medical Journal*).

• **Diabetes.** In several studies, researchers found that adding spirulina to the diets of people with type 2 diabetes significantly decreased blood sugar levels.

Caution: Spirulina has not been approved by the FDA for treating diabetes, so consult your doctor before taking.

• **Lack of endurance.** In a small study, men who took spirulina for one month were able to run more than 30% longer on a treadmill before having to stop because of fatigue, reported Greek researchers in *Medicine & Science in Sports & Exercise.*

• **Heart disease.** Nearly a dozen studies have looked at the effect of spirulina intake on risk factors for heart disease, both in healthy people and people with heart disease. Most of the studies found significant decreases in negative factors (such as LDL cholesterol, total cholesterol, triglycerides, apolipoprotein B and blood pressure) and increases in positive factors (such as HDL cholesterol and apolipoprotein A1).

IDEAL DOSE

A preventive daily dose of spirulina is one teaspoon. A therapeutic dose, to control or reverse disease, is about one tablespoon.

Spirulina has been on the market for more than a decade, and it's among the substances listed by the FDA as "Generally Recognized as Safe" (GRAS).

Caution: If you have an autoimmune disease, such as multiple sclerosis, rheumatoid arthritis or lupus, talk to your doctor. Spirulina could stimulate the immune system, making the condition worse.

BEST PRODUCTS

Like many products, the quality of spirulina varies. *What to look for...*

• **Clean taste.** Top-quality spirulina tastes fresh. If spirulina tastes fishy or "swampy" or has a lingering aftertaste, it's probably not a good product.

• **Bright color.** Spirulina should have a vibrant, bright blue-green appearance (more green than blue). If spirulina is olive-green, it's probably inferior.

• **Cost.** You get what you pay for—and good spirulina can be somewhat pricey.

Example: Spirulina Pacifica, from Nutrex Hawaii—grown on the Kona coast of Hawaii since 1984 and regarded by many health experts as one of the most nutritious and purest spirulina products on the market—costs $50 for 360 1,000-mg tablets. Store it in the refrigerator.

• **Growing location.** The best spirulina is grown in clean water in a nonindustrialized setting, as far away as possible from an urban, polluted environment. If you can, find out the growing location of the product you're considering buying.

HOW TO ADD IT TO FOOD

There are many ways to include spirulina in your daily diet...

• **Put it in smoothies.** Add between one teaspoon and one tablespoon to any smoothie or shake.

• **Add to juice.** Add one teaspoon or tablespoon to an eight-ounce glass of juice or water, shake it up and drink it.

• **Sprinkle it on food.** Try spirulina popcorn, for instance—a great conversation starter at a potluck. To a bowl of popcorn, add one to two tablespoons of spirulina powder, three to four tablespoons of grated Parmesan cheese, two or three tablespoons of olive oil, one-half teaspoon of salt and one-eighth teaspoon of cayenne pepper.

• **Add it to condiments.** Put one-quarter teaspoon in a small jar of ketchup, barbecue sauce, mustard or salad dressing. This way you'll get a little each time you use these products.

4

Delicious Diabetes-Friendly Recipes

Eating diabetes-friendly meals does not mean you have to settle for bland food. The following recipes are packed with flavor, enough to delight the whole family. And they have been developed specifically according to the American Diabetes Association (ADA) guidelines to take the worry out of your meal planning.

One basic principle in a diabetes-friendly lifestyle is to eat portion-controlled, balanced meals. A quick way to size up portions is to divide your plate into sections. Draw a line down the center of a plate. Draw a line cutting one side in half. You will have three sections. Fill the largest section with non-starchy vegetables. Fill one of the small sections with whole grains such as brown rice or whole-wheat pasta. Fill the third section with a low-fat protein.

A meal should include a balance of complex carbohydrates, the right fats and lean protein. When you think of carbohydrates, think brown which means whole grains. Choose nutrient-rich sources rather than less-healthy sweets, refined grains and salty snacks.

As for fats, some are better for you than others. Monounsaturated fats, such as olive oil, are good fats, while saturated fats from animal products, such as butter and fatty meats, should be limited. Individuals with diabetes should try to keep consumption of saturated fats to less than 3.5 grams per meal. To complete the meal, choose a lean protein to limit the saturated fat level. Lean proteins include seafood, skinless chicken and meats such as grass-fed beef or pork tenderloin.

Use these recipes as a blueprint for understanding how much and what type of food you should include in your meal. This will depend on how active you are and what, if any, medicines you're taking. In general, think about 45–60 grams of carbohydrate per meal. ADA guidelines also recommend that you should consume less than 600 mg of sodium per meal.

—Linda Gassenheimer, cookbook author and recipe creator for the American Diabetes Association.

107

Sample Meal Plans

Here are a few suggested meals based on recipes in this chapter. Use these combinations as a guideline to put your own meals together. As with any meal plan, it's always best to create your menus according to your individual tastes and needs, taking into consideration daily exercise and medications. Your diabetes educator or doctor can help you decide your best food balance.

Hot and Spicy Stir-Fry Shrimp
Microwaveable Brown Rice

Mustard-Coated Grouper
Roasted Broccoli and Sweet Potatoes

Snapper Pizzaiola
Spinach Brown Rice

Lemon Peppered Chicken
Bulgur Wheat with Raisins and Pine Nuts
Sautéed Summer Vegetables

Crunchy Dijon Burger
Fresh Herb Salad

Southwestern Roast Pork
Roasted Baby Brussels Sprouts
Orange Barley

Middle Eastern Lamb
Kasha with Wild Mushrooms

Wasabi Swordfish
Thai Green Beans

Recipes

SNACKS AND APPETIZERS

Tomato-Basil Shooter

Serves 6.

Serve these shooters in shot glasses or a martini glass. It can be made a day ahead and stored in the refrigerator.

1½ pounds ripe tomatoes, quartered (about 4¼ cups)
¾ cup unsalted, fat-free chicken broth*
1 cup fresh basil leaves, plus extra leaves to garnish each glass
6 Tablespoons tomato paste
2 Tablespoons olive oil
2 medium garlic cloves, crushed
¼ teaspoon cayenne pepper
1 teaspoon unfiltered honey
⅛ teaspoon salt (8 turns of salt grinder)
¼ teaspoon freshly ground black pepper

Place tomatoes, chicken broth, basil, tomato paste, olive oil, and garlic in a blender or food processor. Process until smooth. Add cayenne pepper, honey and salt and pepper. Process to combine flavors. Pour into a pitcher and refrigerate until needed. Bring to room temperature and pour into shot glasses or into small martini glasses. Garnish with a basil leaf in each glass.

*Look for unsalted chicken broth with 20 calories and 150 mg sodium per cup.

Serving size: 5-ounce shooter
Per serving: 85 calories, 4.9 g fat, 0.7 g saturated fat, 3.3 g monounsaturated fat, 0 mg cholesterol, 2.6 g protein, 9.6 g carbohydrates, 2.4 g dietary fiber, 6.3 g sugars, 83 mg sodium, 520 mg potassium, 64 mg phosphorus

Black Bean Pâté

Serves 10.

For a colorful display, serve this pâté in a hollowed-out red cabbage or gourd. It can also be served in a dip bowl or ramekin. You can also serve a variety of vegetable sticks with the pâté.

1 can black beans (15 ounces), rinsed and drained (about 2 cups)
2 Tablespoons chopped red onion
2 Tablespoons balsamic vinegar
1 medium garlic clove, crushed
1 Tablespoon orange juice
⅛ teaspoon salt (8 turns of salt grinder)
¼ teaspoon freshly ground black pepper
¼ cup chopped parsley (optional)
60 whole-wheat crackers (about 2 inches diameter each)

Rinse and drain the black beans. Place in a blender or food processor with the onion, balsamic vinegar, garlic and orange juice. Blend until thick and smooth. Add salt and pepper. Place in a small bowl on a plate. Sprinkle chopped parsley on top (optional). Arrange crackers around the bowl.

Serving size: 2 ounces black bean mixture, 6 whole-wheat crackers

Per serving: 169 calories, 4.1 g fat, 0.6 g saturated fat, 0.9 g monounsaturated fat, 0 mg cholesterol, 6.0 g protein, 28.5 g carbohydrates, 6.3 g dietary fiber, 1.1 g sugars, 268 mg sodium, 167 mg potassium, 55 mg phosphorus

Honey Mustard Yogurt Dip

Serves 8.

This is a low-calorie dip that is creamy, tangy and sweet. It will keep in the refrigerator for several days.

½ cup low-fat plain Greek-style yogurt
4 Tablespoons Dijon mustard
2 Tablespoons unfiltered honey
2 cups carrot sticks
2 cups celery sticks
2 cups trimmed snow peas
2 cups red bell pepper cut into strips

Drain the yogurt. Place it in a colander lined with paper towels. Set the colander over a pan or bowl for about 2 to 3 hours in the refrigerator. Mix the mustard and honey together until smooth. Add the drained yogurt and mix well. Serve with vegetable sticks.

Serving size: 1 cup vegetables, 2 ounces yogurt dip

Per serving: 61 calories, 0.8 g fat, 0.2 g saturated fat, 0.2 g monounsaturated fat, 1 mg cholesterol, 2.9 g protein, 11.2 g carbohydrates, 2.3 g dietary fiber, 8.3 g sugars, 234 mg sodium, 267 mg potassium, 57 mg phosphorus

Salsa Guacamole

Serves 6.

To help an avocado ripen, keep it in a paper bag in a warm spot. Any type of vegetables can be used for dipping.

1 6-ounce Haas-style ripe avocado, cut into cubes (about 1½ cups)
½ cup tomato no-sugar-added salsa
2 cups celery sticks
2 cups jicama sticks
2 cups carrot sticks

Mix avocado and tomato salsa together. This can be done by hand or in a food processor. Place in a bowl on a tray and arrange the vegetables around it for dipping.

Serving size: 1 cup vegetables, ⅓ cup avocado dip

Per serving: 103 calories, 5.6 g fat, 0.8 g saturated fat, 3.6 g monounsaturated fat, 0 mg cholesterol, 1.9 g protein, 13.0 g carbohydrates, 7.1 g dietary fiber, 3.3 g sugars, 149 mg sodium, 440 mg potassium, 46 mg phosphorus

Soup is a welcoming start to any meal. These easy recipes are also satisfying enough to be the main attraction at lunch or at a light supper.

Savory Mushroom Soup

Serves 2.

Mushrooms, onions and a hint of nutmeg make a quick and tasty homemade soup.

1 Tablespoon olive oil
2 cups chopped onion
1 pound frozen or fresh sliced mushrooms
1 Tablespoon flour
4 cups fat-free, unsalted chicken broth*
$\frac{1}{16}$ teaspoon salt (4 turns of salt grinder)
$\frac{1}{8}$ teaspoon freshly ground black pepper
1 teaspoon ground nutmeg
2 Tablespoons parsley

Heat oil in a medium saucepan. Add onion and sauté 5 minutes or until starting to color. Add the mushrooms and flour. Stir. Add chicken broth. Bring to a boil, reduce heat and simmer for 10 minutes. Remove one cup of vegetables without broth and purée in a food processor or blender. Return to the soup. Add salt, pepper and nutmeg.

*Look for unsalted chicken broth with 20 calories and 150 mg sodium per cup.

Serving size: 4½ cups vegetables, 2 cups broth
Per serving: 236 calories, 8.2 g fat, 1.4 g saturated fat, 5.0 g monounsaturated fat, 0 mg cholesterol, 19.6 g protein, 28.4 g carbohydrates, 5.6 g dietary fiber, 11.8 g sugars, 394 mg sodium, 1598 mg potassium, 516 mg phosphorus

---

Greek Minestrone

Serves 2.

Keep some frozen vegetables on hand and you can have a soup ready in minutes.

10-ounce package frozen whole-leaf spinach
1 Tablespoon olive oil
2 cups frozen chopped onion
1 cup frozen cut green beans
1 cup frozen sliced carrots
2 teaspoons minced garlic
4 cups fat-free, unsalted chicken broth*
1 cup canned petite diced tomatoes with their juice
$\frac{1}{16}$ teaspoon salt (4 turns of salt grinder)
$\frac{1}{8}$ teaspoon freshly ground black pepper
2 Tablespoons crumbled feta cheese

Defrost spinach. Heat olive oil in a nonstick saucepan, and add onion. Cook until the onion starts to color. Add the cut green beans, carrots, the defrosted spinach and minced garlic. Sauté for a few minutes. Add the broth and bring to a boil. Reduce heat and simmer for 5 minutes. Add salt and pepper. Divide between two soup bowls and sprinkle crumbled feta cheese on top.

*Look for unsalted chicken broth with 20 calories and 150 mg sodium per cup.

Serving size: 5 cups vegetables, 2 cups broth, 1 tablespoon cheese

Per serving: 242 calories, 9.6 g fat, 2.5 g saturated fat, 5.4 g monounsaturated fat, 8 mg cholesterol, 17.1 g protein, 28.5 g carbohydrates, 8.1 g dietary fiber, 11.9 g sugars, 515 mg sodium, 1685 mg potassium, 425 mg phosphorus

Watercress and Zucchini Soup

Serves 2.

Using pureed vegetables, this becomes a thick, creamy soup without the addition of cream.

1 teaspoon olive oil
1½ cups sliced red onion
1½ cups sliced zucchini
2 cups fat-free, unsalted chicken broth*
¹⁄₁₆ teaspoon salt (4 turns of salt grinder)
⅛ teaspoon freshly ground black pepper
1 cup washed watercress leaves
2 Tablespoons snipped chives

Heat olive oil in a nonstick medium-sized saucepan over medium-high heat. Add onion and sauté for 3 minutes. Add zucchini and sauté for 3 additional minutes.

Pour in broth, and simmer for 10 minutes. Add salt and pepper. Remove from heat, add watercress and puree in a blender until smooth. Cool, slightly, store in the refrigerator and serve at room temperature. Sprinkle chives on top of soup before serving.

*Look for unsalted chicken broth with 20 calories and 150 mg sodium per cup.

Serving size: 2 cups vegetables, 1 cup broth

Per serving: 92 calories, 2.6 g fat, 0.4 g saturated fat, 1.7 g monounsaturated fat, 0 mg cholesterol, 7.5 g protein, 12.1 g carbohydrates, 2.6 g dietary fiber, 5.9 g sugars, 240 mg sodium, 652 mg potassium, 189 mg phosphorus

SEAFOOD

Basque-Style Tuna

Serves 2.

Caramelized onions flavored with brandy top fresh ahi tuna. Roasted red peppers finish the dish.

2 Tablespoons plus 2 teaspoons olive oil, divided use
2 cups sweet onion, thinly sliced
2 Tablespoons lemon juice
¾ pound yellow fin (ahi) tuna (or tilapia, cod or sea bass)
¼ cup brandy
1/16 teaspoon salt (4 turns of salt grinder)
⅛ teaspoon freshly ground black pepper
½ cup bottled roasted red peppers, drained and sliced

Heat 2 teaspoons olive oil in a skillet over medium heat. Add the onions, and gently sauté 15 to 20 minutes until golden. Do not let them turn black.

Meanwhile, place the remaining 2 tablespoons olive oil and lemon juice in a self-sealing plastic bag. Add tuna and marinate 10 minutes, turning once during that time.

When the onions are golden, add the brandy and cook for 2 to 3 minutes over high heat.

When ready to serve, remove the tuna from the marinade. Heat a heavy-bottomed (cast iron if possible) skillet over high heat. The skillet must be very hot. Add the tuna, and sear for 1 minute on each side for rare tuna. For medium-rare, remove the skillet from the heat and cover with a lid. Let sit for 1 minute or longer if desired. (If using other fish besides tuna, cook it using the rule of 8-minutes-per-inch.) Sprinkle with salt and pepper. Place the tuna on two plates, and spoon the onions on top. Arrange the roasted peppers over the onions.

*Look for unsalted chicken broth with 20 calories and 150 mg sodium per cup.

Serving size: 5 ounces tuna, ½ cup vegetables

Per serving: 390 calories, 7.8 g fat, 1.3 g saturated fat, 4.6 g monounsaturated fat, 78 mg cholesterol, 42.1 g protein, 18.5 g carbohydrates, 3.7 g dietary fiber, 8.5 g sugars, 146 mg sodium, 327 mg potassium, 56 mg phosphorus

---

Roasted Salmon with Dill Sauce

Serves 2.

Oven-roasted salmon, sprinkled with fresh dill and lemon juice, is served with a creamy dill sauce.

10 ounces wild-caught salmon fillet
1 Tablespoon olive oil
¼ cup snipped fresh dill (or 2 teaspoons dried dill)
1 Tablespoon fresh lemon juice
1/16 Tablespoon salt (4 turns of a salt mill)
⅛ teaspoon freshly ground black pepper

Preheat oven to 350 degrees. Line a baking sheet with foil, and brush a little olive oil on the foil. Place the salmon on the oil and brush remaining oil on it. Drizzle lemon juice on top and sprinkle half the dill over the salmon. Sprinkle with salt and pepper. Place in the oven for 15 minutes for a 1½-inch to 2-inch-thick fillet. Turn the oven to broil and place the salmon 6 inches from the heat. Broil the fillet for 2 minutes. Remove and sprinkle with remaining dill. Serve with dill sauce.*

*Dill Sauce

2 Tablespoons reduced-fat sour cream
2 Tablespoons fat-free plain yogurt
½ Tablespoon prepared horseradish
1 teaspoon lemon juice
2 Tablespoons snipped fresh dill (or 1 Tablespoon dried dill)
2 teaspoons drained capers

Mix ingredients together and serve with the salmon. *Serves 2.*

Serving size: 4 ounces salmon, 2 tablespoons sauce

Per serving: 293 calories, 17.7 g fat, 3.5 g saturated fat, 8.5 g monounsaturated fat, 86 mg cholesterol, 29.6 g protein, 3.3 g carbohydrates, 0.3 g dietary fiber, 0.6 g sugars, 254 mg sodium, 749 mg potassium, 303 mg phosphorus

Balsamic Mahi Mahi

Serves 2.

A sweet balsamic glaze coats this broiled fish. Mahi Mahi is also called dolphin fish. Any type of firm fish, such as grouper, catfish, haddock or cod, can be used.

¾ pound mahi mahi fillet
2 Tablespoons balsamic vinegar
¼ cup fresh cilantro
2 garlic cloves, crushed

Place fish in a self-sealing plastic bag with the balsamic vinegar, cilantro and garlic. Refrigerate 15 minutes to marinate. Line a baking sheet with foil.

Remove fish from marinade and strain (otherwise the garlic and cilantro will absorb the liquid) the marinade into a small saucepan. Place the fish on the baking sheet. Broil 6 inches from heat about 8 minutes for a 1-inch fillet. It will continue to cook once it is taken off the heat. While the fish broils, heat marinade for a minute. Spoon marinade over the cooked fish.

Serving size: 5 ounces mahi mahi, ¾ tablespoon sauce

Per serving: 159 calories, 1.2 g fat, 0.3 g saturated fat, 0.2 g monounsaturated fat, 126 mg cholesterol, 31.5 g protein, 2.8 g carbohydrates, 0 g dietary fiber, 2.4 g sugars, 154 mg sodium, 731 mg potassium, 250 mg phosphorus

Snapper Pizzaiola

Serves 2.

Sweet, fresh fish with a Neapolitan pizza-style sauce makes a quick and simple dinner.

¾ pound snapper fillet
1 cup canned, no-salt-added, peeled plum tomatoes, drained

¼ cup diced yellow onion

2 medium garlic cloves, crushed

2 teaspoons dried oregano

1 teaspoon balsamic vinegar

2 teaspoons olive oil

8 pitted black olives, cut in half

⅟₁₆ teaspoon salt (4 turns of salt grinder)

⅛ teaspoon freshly ground black pepper

2 Tablespoons freshly grated Parmesan cheese

Heat a nonstick skillet over medium-high heat. Brown fillet 2 minutes, turn, and brown second side 2 minutes. Lower heat and cook 3 to 4 minutes for 1-inch thick fillet. Remove to a plate and cover with foil or another plate to keep warm.

Lower heat to medium and add tomatoes, onion, garlic, and oregano to the skillet. Break up tomatoes with the edge of a cooking spoon. Cover and simmer 5 minutes. Stir sauce and add vinegar, oil and black olives. Add salt and pepper. Spoon sauce over fish. Sprinkle the top with grated Parmesan cheese.

Serving size: 5 ounces snapper, ¾ cup vegetables and sauce, 1 tablespoon cheese

Per serving: 286 calories, 10.3 g fat, 2.3 g saturated fat, 5.6 g monounsaturated fat, 64 mg cholesterol, 38.3 g protein, 9.7 g carbohydrates, 2.4 g dietary fiber, 4.0 g sugars, 399 mg sodium, 1090 mg potassium, 406 mg phosphorus

---

Wasabi Swordfish

Serves 2.

Spicy wasabi sauce gives the swordfish an Asian flavor. Wasabi is the Japanese version of horseradish. It is available in powdered form in the supermarket. It loses its flavor quickly. Make sure you have a fresh bottle.

2 Tablespoons reduced-fat no-sugar-added oil and vinegar dressing

2 teaspoons wasabi powder

1 teaspoon olive oil

¾ pound swordfish steaks

⅟₁₆ teaspoon salt (4 turns of salt grinder)

⅛ teaspoon freshly ground black pepper

Mix the oil and vinegar dressing with the wasabi powder and set aside. Heat oil in a large nonstick skillet over medium-high heat. Brown swordfish for 2 minutes on each side. Lower heat to medium and continue to cook 2 minutes or until fish is cooked. It will look opaque inside, not translucent. Sprinkle with salt and pepper. Remove from skillet, divide into 2 equal portions and spoon sauce over top.

Serving size: 5 ounces swordfish, 1 tablespoon sauce

Per serving: 245 calories, 10.1 g fat, 2.2 g saturated fat, 4.6 g monounsaturated fat, 67 mg cholesterol, 33.9 g protein, 1.8 g carbohydrates, 0.5 g dietary fiber, 0.7 g sugars, 233 mg sodium, 15 mg potassium, 2 mg phosphorus

---

Hot and Spicy Stir-Fry Shrimp

Serves 2.

Succulent shrimp is stir-fried with onion and bok choy for this quick Chinese dinner. Red pepper flakes give the dish a kick. A firm fish such as tilapia, grouper or mahi mahi, cut into 2-inch pieces, can be used instead of shrimp. Toss it carefully to avoid breaking up the fish.

1 Tablespoon low-sodium soy sauce
2 teaspoons cornstarch
1 Tablespoon chopped fresh ginger or 1 teaspoon ground ginger
¼ cup dry sherry (can substitute chicken broth)
⅛ teaspoon red pepper flakes
3 teaspoons toasted sesame oil, divided use
1 cup sliced red onion
2 cups washed, sliced bok choy
3 garlic cloves, crushed
¾ pound peeled and deveined shrimp

Mix together soy sauce, cornstarch, fresh ginger, sherry and red pepper flakes. Add 2 teaspoons sesame oil to wok and heat over high heat. When oil is smoking, add onion and stir-fry 2 minutes. Add bok choy and garlic and continue to stir-fry 2 minutes. Push vegetables to sides of wok and add shrimp. Toss with vegetables 1 minute. Push shrimp and vegetables to sides of wok and add sauce in the center. Toss the shrimp and vegetables with the sauce for 1 minute. Remove from heat and stir in the remaining sesame oil.

Serving size: 5 ounces shrimp, 1½ cups vegetables, 2 tablespoons sauce

Per serving: 304 calories, 7.9 g fat, 1.2 g saturated fat, 2.9 g monounsaturated fat, 276 mg cholesterol, 37.0 g protein, 15.3 g carbohydrates, 2.0 g dietary fiber, 3.7 g sugars, 513 mg sodium, 795 mg potassium, 433 mg phosphorus

---

Mustard-Coated Grouper

Serves 2.

A sweet and tangy sauce coats the fish as it bakes. Any type of white fish such as cod, halibut, flounder, sole or sea bass can be used in this recipe. Measure the thickness of the fish and allow about 8–10 minutes baking time per inch.

Olive oil spray
1 Tablespoon Dijon mustard
1 Tablespoon grainy mustard
2 teaspoons ground cumin
1 Tablespoon unfiltered honey
¾ pound grouper fillet

Preheat oven to 400 degrees. Line a baking tray with foil and lightly spray with olive oil spray. Mix two mustards, cumin and honey together. Spoon mustard coating on both sides of fish and place on prepared baking tray. For 1½-inch-thick fish, bake 15 minutes. Remove and place fish on individual plates and pour pan juices over the top.

Serving size: 5 ounces grouper, 1½ tablespoons sauce

Per serving: 227 calories, 5.0 g fat, 0.6 g saturated fat, 2.4 g monounsaturated fat, 60 mg cholesterol, 34.0 g protein, 11.0 g carbohydrates, 0.7 g dietary fiber, 8.8 g sugars, 472 mg sodium, 887 mg potassium, 303 mg phosphorus

---

Lemon-Peppered Chicken

Serves 2.

This 4-ingredient recipe can be made in minutes.

¾ pound boneless, skinless chicken breast
Juice of 2 lemons (about ¼ cup)
2 Tablespoons olive oil
1 Tablespoon cracked black pepper

Remove visible fat from chicken and pound flat with a heavy frying pan until meat is even (it doesn't need to be too thin). Place chicken, lemon juice, olive oil and cracked black pepper in a self-sealing plastic bag. Refrigerate and marinate 15 minutes. Remove chicken, discard the marinade and grill or broil about 3 to 4 minutes each side. A meat thermometer should read 165 degrees.

Serving size: 5 ounces chicken

Per serving: 210 calories, 4.9 g fat, 1.0 g saturated fat, 1.5 g monounsaturated fat, 126 mg cholesterol, 38.3 g protein, 0.4 g carbohydrates, 0.1 g dietary fiber, 0.1 g sugars, 78 mg sodium, 578 mg potassium, 361 mg phosphorus

Ginger-Crusted Chicken

Serves 2.

The secret to this recipe is baking in an oven that is very hot.

Olive oil spray
¾ pound boneless, skinless, chicken breast
¼ cup whole-wheat bread crumbs
¹⁄₁₆ teaspoon salt (4 twists of a salt mill)
⅛ teaspoon freshly ground black pepper
1 egg white
2 teaspoons ground ginger

Preheat oven to 450 degrees and line a baking sheet with foil. Spray with olive oil spray. Remove visible fat from chicken. Wrap loosely in plastic wrap and pound flat with a meat bat or the bottom of a heavy skillet to ½ inch thick. Mix bread crumbs with the salt and pepper. Break up egg white with a fork and dip chicken into the white. Sprinkle ginger on both sides of the chicken breasts. Roll chicken in bread crumbs, making sure chicken is completely coated. Place chicken on baking sheet and bake 10 minutes. A meat thermometer should read 165 degrees.

Serving size: 5 ounces chicken, ⅛ cup bread

Per serving: 275 calories, 7.2 g fat, 1.3 g saturated fat, 2.6 g monounsaturated fat, 126 mg cholesterol, 41.3 g protein, 8.1 g carbohydrates, 1.3 g dietary fiber, 0.9 g sugars, 214 mg sodium, 663 mg potassium, 400 mg phosphorus

Turkey Meat Loaf

Serves 2.

Meat loaf is one of America's great comfort foods. The secret to baking this one in a hurry is placing it in small loaves on a baking sheet. The heat will circulate around the loaf and bake faster than in a loaf pan.

Olive oil spray
½ cup thinly sliced onion
½ cup thinly sliced carrots
½ cup thinly sliced mushrooms
¼ cup whole-wheat bread crumbs
¾ pound ground white meat turkey
1 egg white
1/16 teaspoon salt (4 twists of salt mill)
⅛ teaspoon freshly ground black pepper

For topping:
½ cup low-sodium, no-sugar-added tomato sauce
2 Tablespoons diced onion
1 teaspoon minced garlic cloves

Preheat oven to 400 degrees. Line a baking sheet with foil and spray with olive oil spray. Heat a nonstick skillet over medium-high heat and spray with olive oil spray. Add onion, carrots and mushrooms. Sauté five minutes. Mix vegetables with bread crumbs, ground turkey and egg white. Add salt and pepper. Divide ground turkey in two, place on baking sheet and shape into two loaves about six inches by three inches. Bake for 15 minutes.

While meat loaf bakes, mix tomato sauce, onion and garlic in a microwave-safe bowl and heat in microwave on high 1 minute. Spoon over baked meat loaves.

Serving size: 6 ounces turkey breast vegetable mixture, ¼ cup sauce

Per serving: 307 calories, 5.5 g fat, 0.8 g saturated fat, 1.9 g monounsaturated fat, 96 mg cholesterol, 45.2 g protein, 18.2 g carbohydrates, 3.6 g dietary fiber, 6.6 g sugars, 358 mg sodium, 893 mg potassium, 434 mg phosphorus

---

Roast Garlic Chicken with Vegetables

Serves 4.

This is a one-pan meal that's great for Sunday supper. Whole garlic cloves are placed under the skin of the chicken while it roasts, giving the chicken a mild garlic flavor.

One 3½-pound whole chicken
6 whole garlic cloves, peeled
1 sprig fresh rosemary, leaves removed and stems reserved
1 sprig fresh oregano, leaves removed and stems reserved
¼ teaspoon freshly ground black pepper
2 whole carrots, peeled and halved vertically
2 ribs celery
1 medium onion, quartered
2 large russet potatoes (about 8 ounces each), skin washed, and cut into 16 pieces
2 parsnips (about 8 ounces), peeled and cut into ½-inch pieces

1 cup water
1 Tablespoon olive oil
¼ teaspoon salt
¼ teaspoon freshly ground black pepper

Preheat oven to 450 degrees. Remove visible fat from chicken neck and cavity. Carefully lift breast skin from the meat starting at the neck. Push garlic cloves under skin of the chicken, 3 on each breast. Push rosemary and oregano leaves under the skin of each breast; put herb stems in the cavity of the chicken. Rub skin with 1 tablespoon oil. Place carrots in a large roasting pan and top, crosswise, with celery ribs to form a bed for the chicken. Place the chicken over the carrots and celery. Surround the chicken with onions, potatoes, parsnips and water and roast 30 minutes. Reduce the oven to 375 degrees and roast until juices run clear, about 30 to 40 minutes more. A meat thermometer should read 160 degrees in the breast area and 170 degrees in the thigh meat. Remove from oven, and allow to rest 10 minutes.

Make the sauce: While the chicken rests, strain the juices from the roasting pan into a bowl and remove the fat. Or, use a fat separator measuring cup to remove fat. Place the onion from the roasting pan in a blender and add the strained juice. Blend to form a sauce.

Remove skin from chicken and sprinkle with salt and pepper. Cut the leg and thigh section from the chicken. Remove the breast and wings. Serve the chicken with the remaining vegetables and spoon the sauce on top.

Serving size: 5 ounces chicken, 1 cup vegetables, ½ cup potato

Per serving: 372 calories, 6.5 g fat, 1.6 g saturated fat, 2.2 g monounsaturated fat, 144 mg cholesterol, 40.5 g protein, 43.5 g carbohydrates, 6.6 g dietary fiber, 7.1 g sugars, 319 mg sodium, 1522 mg potassium, 483 mg phosphorus

LAMB, BEEF AND PORK

Middle-Eastern Lamb

Serves 2.

This delightful lamb dish features a Middle-Eastern yogurt sauce.

½ cup nonfat, plain yogurt
1 teaspoon minced garlic
1 teaspoon ground cumin
¼ cup peeled, diced cucumber
Olive oil spray
¾ pound lamb cubes, cut from the leg into ½-inch pieces
1/16 teaspoon salt (4 turns of salt grinder)
⅛ teaspoon freshly ground black pepper

Mix the yogurt, garlic, cumin and cucumber together, and set aside.

Heat a nonstick skillet over medium-high heat. Spray with olive oil spray. Add the lamb to the skillet. Sauté for 2 minutes, turning to brown on all sides. A meat thermometer should read 125 degrees for rare, 145 degrees for medium/rare and 160 degrees for medium. Sprinkle with salt and pepper. Remove the lamb to two dinner plates, and spoon sauce on top.

Serving size: 5 ounces lamb, 2 tablespoons vegetables, ¼ cup sauce

Per serving: 283 calories, 11.5 g fat, 3.4 g saturated fat, 5.1 g monounsaturated fat, 109 mg cholesterol, 37.0 g protein, 6.7 g carbohydrates, 0.3 g dietary fiber, 4.5 g sugars, 220 mg sodium, 640 mg potassium, 399 mg phosphorus

Crunchy Dijon Burgers

Serves 2.

Dijon mustard and a little oatmeal give these burgers added flavor and texture. If buffalo meat is not available, look for ground white meat chicken breast.

¾ pound ground buffalo meat
6 Tablespoons old-fashioned oatmeal
1 Tablespoon Dijon mustard
1/16 teaspoon salt (4 turns of salt grinder)
⅛ teaspoon freshly ground black pepper
Olive oil spray
2 whole-wheat hamburger rolls (1½ ounces each)
2 slices tomato
Several lettuce leaves (such as Romaine or Red Leaf)

Mix buffalo meat, oatmeal and mustard together. Add salt and pepper. Mix well. Press the mixture into 2 firm patties about 4 inches in diameter. Heat a nonstick skillet over medium-high heat and spray with olive oil spray. Add the burgers and cook 5 minutes per side or until a meat thermometer reads 160 degrees. Spray the hamburger rolls with olive oil spray and toast. Serve burgers on the toasted rolls with slices of tomato and a few lettuce leaves.

Serving size: 7 ounces buffalo meat mixture, 1 roll, ½ cup vegetables

Per serving: 424 calories, 12.7 g fat, 2.2 g saturated fat, 5.8 g monounsaturated fat, 108 mg cholesterol, 42.5 g protein, 32.0 g carbohydrates, 5.4 g dietary fiber, 3.0 g sugars, 459 mg sodium, 828 mg potassium, 441 mg phosphorus

Southwestern Roast Pork

Serves 2.

Spicy tomato salsa flavors pan-roasted pork tenderloin for this simple 4-ingredient dish. Chicken tenders can be used instead of pork tenderloin. Sauté them 3 minutes per side. Add the salsa and cook, covered, another minute. A meat thermometer should read 165 degrees.

¾ pound pork tenderloin
1 teaspoon ground cumin
Olive oil spray
½ cup tomato no-added-sugar salsa

Remove visible fat from the pork and butterfly it (cut it almost in half, lengthwise, and open it like a book). Cut the butterflied pork in half crosswise to form 2 pieces. Sprinkle the cumin on both sides of the pork. Heat a nonstick skillet over medium-high heat and spray with olive oil spray. Add the pork and sear for 5 minutes. Turn the pork over and cook another 5 minutes. Lower the heat to medium and spoon the salsa over the pork. Cover with a lid and cook 3 minutes. Check to see if the pork is cooked. A meat thermometer should read 145 degrees. It may need another 2 minutes.

Serving size: 5 ounces pork, ¼ cup sauce

Per serving: 234 calories, 6.2 g fat, 1.4 g saturated fat, 2.8 g monounsaturated fat, 108 mg cholesterol, 36.8 g protein, 5.6 g carbohydrates, 1.0 g dietary fiber, 2.0 g sugars, 373 mg sodium, 872 mg potassium, 444 mg phosphorus

VEGETABLES

These vegetable dishes, full of flavor, will enhance any type of meal. Several of these recipes use frozen vegetables—always have some on hand for a quick meal.

Pan-Roasted Vegetables

Serves 4.

Corn, broccoli and red bell pepper make this a colorful dish. Ginger adds extra flavor.

2 teaspoons olive oil
2 Tablespoons fresh ginger or 2 teaspoons ground ginger
3 cups frozen corn kernels
3 cups broccoli florets (½ pound)
1 cup sliced red bell pepper
¼ cup fresh basil
1/16 teaspoon salt (4 turns of salt mill)
⅛ teaspoon freshly ground black pepper

Heat oil in a nonstick skillet over medium-high heat. Add ginger, corn, broccoli and red pepper. Toss to coat vegetables with the oil, and cover with a lid. Cook 5 minutes. Stir vegetables and cook, covered, 5 minutes more. Sprinkle with basil leaves, salt and pepper.

Alternate microwave method: Place all the ingredients in a microwave-safe bowl, cover and microwave on high for 6 minutes. Remove and toss with basil leaves, salt and pepper.

Serving size: 1½ cups

Per serving: 136 calories, 3.4 g fat, 0.5 g saturated fat, 1.9 g monounsaturated fat, 0 mg cholesterol, 5.1 g protein, 26.1 g carbohydrates, 2.7 dietary fiber, 3.6 g sugars, 56 mg sodium, 469 mg potassium, 117 mg phosphorus

Lemon Swiss Chard

Serves 4.

Swiss Chard has crinkly green leaves and flat, celery-like stalks. Another, rarer variety has reddish stalks and stronger flavor. Look for baby chard. It is milder than the larger bunches.

1 pound Swiss chard (about 12 cups when sliced)
2 Tablespoons olive oil (divided use)
2 teaspoons lemon juice
1 Tablespoon unfiltered honey
⅛ teaspoon freshly ground black pepper

Carefully wash the Swiss chard. Cut the stems from the leaves and cut the stems and leaves into half-inch slices. Heat 1 tablespoon of the olive oil in a skillet over medium-high heat. Add sliced stems, cover with a lid and cook for 5 minutes. Add leaves, cover and cook 5 minutes more or until tender. Remove with a slotted spoon and stir in remaining 1 tablespoon oil, lemon juice and honey into the skillet. Return stems and leaves to the skillet and toss in sauce for about 30 seconds. Sprinkle with pepper.

Serving size: ¾ cup

Per serving: 99 calories, 7.0 g fat, 1.0 g saturated fat, 5.0 g monounsaturated fat, 0 mg cholesterol, 2.1g protein, 8.8 g carbohydrates, 1.9 g dietary fiber, 5.6 g sugars, 243 mg sodium, 435 mg potassium, 54 mg phosphorus

Broccoli Rabe Salad

Serves 2.

Also called rape or rapini, broccoli rabe resembles thin, sparsely budded broccoli and has a slightly bitter flavor. It makes a tasty salad.

1 Tablespoon balsamic vinegar
1½ Tablespoons olive oil
½ pound broccoli rabe (select a bunch with thin stems)
1 cup shredded carrots
¹⁄₁₆ teaspoon salt (4 turns of salt mill)
⅛ teaspoon freshly ground black pepper
2 Tablespoons chopped parsley

Mix vinegar and oil together in a bowl. Cut the stems, buds and leaves into bite-sized pieces. Bring a saucepan full of water to a boil. Add the stems, buds and leaves. Bring back to a boil. Cook for 3 minutes. Drain and add to the bowl. Add carrots and sprinkle with parsley, salt and pepper. Toss well. Serve warm or at room temperature.

Serving size: 2½ cups

Per serving: 146 calories, 10.8 g fat, 1.5 g saturated fat, 7.4 g monounsaturated fat, 0 mg cholesterol, 4.2 g protein, 10.2 g carbohydrates, 4.8 g dietary fiber, 4.3 g sugars, 151 mg sodium, 426 mg potassium, 104 mg phosphorus

Stir-Fried Bok Choy

Serves 2.

Bok choy has a mild flavor similar to celery. The most common variety has white stalks and dark green leaves. Toasted sesame oil has a rich sesame flavor, but regular sesame oil can be used.

5 cups thinly sliced bok choy (about 3 cups stems and 2 cups leaves)
1 Tablespoon toasted sesame oil, divided use
½ Tablespoon chopped fresh ginger
2 large crushed garlic cloves
¹⁄₁₆ teaspoon salt (4 turns of salt mill)
⅛ teaspoon freshly ground black pepper

Cut white part of stems from the leaves. Slice both stems and leaves separately. Heat ½ tablespoon oil in a wok or skillet over high heat. When the oil starts smoking, add the sliced white stems and stir-fry for 2 minutes. Add the ginger, garlic and sliced bok choy leaves and cook for 1 minute. Remove from heat and toss with remaining sesame oil and salt and pepper.

Serving size: 2 cups

Per serving: 88 calories, 7.1 g fat, 1.0 g saturated fat, 2.7 g monounsaturated fat, 0 mg cholesterol, 2.9 g protein, 5.2 g carbohydrates, 1.9 g dietary fiber, 2.1 g sugars, 189 mg sodium, 460 mg potassium, 71 mg phosphorus

Sautéed Summer Vegetables

Serves 2.

Brighten up your dinner with plentiful fresh summer produce.

Olive oil spray
1 small red pepper, cut into ½-inch squares (1 cup)
1 small green bell pepper, cut into ½-inch squares (1 cup)
1 small zucchini, cut into ½-inch cubes (1½ cups)
1 cup sliced red onion
1 tomato, cut into eighths
1 crushed garlic clove
1/16 teaspoon salt (4 turns of salt grinder)
1/8 teaspoon freshly ground black pepper
1 teaspoon olive oil
1 Tablespoon lemon juice
2 Tablespoons fresh oregano leaves

Heat a medium-sized skillet over medium-high heat and spray with olive oil spray. Add bell peppers, zucchini, onion, tomato and garlic. Sauté 20 minutes, stirring occasionally. The vegetables should be soft but still crunchy. Add salt and pepper. In a serving bowl, mix olive oil and lemon juice together. Add the sautéed vegetables and toss well. Sprinkle with oregano leaves.

Serving size: 1¾ cups

Per serving: 130 calories, 5.2 g fat, 0.6 g saturated fat, 3.0 g monounsaturated fat, 0 mg cholesterol, 3.6 g protein, 19.4 g carbohydrates, 5.3 g dietary fiber, 11.0 g sugars, 94 mg sodium, 842 mg potassium, 99 mg phosphorus

Mushroom Ragout

Serves 4.

These mushrooms taste great on their own or serve them over chicken or fish.

Olive oil spray
1 cup sliced red onion
2 cups sliced baby bello (crimini) mushrooms
2 cups sliced Shiitake mushrooms
2 Tablespoons tomato paste
½ cup red Vermouth
½ teaspoon dried thyme
½ teaspoon dried rosemary
2 teaspoons olive oil
1 Tablespoon grated Parmesan cheese
1/16 teaspoon salt (4 turns of salt grinder)
1/8 teaspoon freshly ground black pepper

Heat a medium-sized nonstick skillet over high heat and spray with olive oil spray. Add onions and sauté 2 minutes. Add mushrooms and continue to sauté 2 minutes. Mix the tomato paste and Vermouth together and add to the mushrooms. Sprinkle with the herbs, cover and reduce heat to medium. Cook 10 minutes. Sprinkle with Parmesan cheese and salt and pepper.

Serving size: 1 cup

Per serving: 102 calories, 4.1 g fat, 0.7 g saturated fat, 2.4 g monounsaturated fat, 1 mg cholesterol, 3.3 g protein, 9.8 g carbohydrates, 1.8 g dietary fiber, 3.6 g sugars, 31 mg sodium, 355 mg potassium, 84 mg phosphorus

Roasted Broccoli and Sweet Potatoes

Serves 4.

This colorful dish will dress up any plate.

1 Tablespoon olive oil
1⁄16 teaspoon salt (4 turns of salt mill)
1⁄8 teaspoon freshly ground black pepper
1¼ pounds sweet potatoes, skin scrubbed and cut into 1- to 2-inch pieces
½ pound broccoli florets
2 Tablespoons chopped fresh cilantro

Preheat oven to 400 degrees. Line a baking sheet with foil and add olive oil and salt and pepper. Place potatoes and broccoli on sheet, toss in the seasoned oil and spread out to one layer. Place in oven and roast 10 minutes, turn vegetables over and roast 10 more minutes. Sprinkle with cilantro.

Serving size: 1¾ cups vegetable potato mixture

Per serving: 169 calories, 3.7 g fat, 0.5 g saturated fat, 2.5 g monounsaturated fat, 0 mg cholesterol, 4.0 g protein, 31.7 g carbohydrates, 4.4 g dietary fiber, 6.0 g sugars, 130 mg sodium, 675 mg potassium, 106 mg phosphorus

Indian Spiced Carrots

Serves 4.

Frozen sliced or crinkle-cut carrots are available in most markets. Adding Indian spices adds zing. Spices lose their flavor and color over time. If yours are more than six months old, it's time for new bottles.

1 Tablespoon olive oil
2 teaspoons ground cumin
2 teaspoons ground coriander
2 teaspoons mild curry powder
4 cups sliced frozen carrots
1 Tablespoon grated fresh ginger
½ cup water
½ cup light coconut milk
1⁄8 teaspoon freshly ground black pepper
¼ cup chopped cilantro

Heat oil in a large, nonstick skillet over medium-high heat. Add the cumin, coriander and curry powder. Cook about 30 seconds. Add the carrots, ginger and water. Cover with a lid, and cook 5 minutes. Remove the lid. If any liquid remains, cook uncovered until it has evaporated.

Remove from the heat. Add the coconut milk and salt and pepper. Sprinkle the chopped cilantro on top.

Serving size: 1 cup

Per serving: 104 calories, 5.7 g fat, 2.1 g saturated fat, 2.7 g monounsaturated fat, 0 mg cholesterol, 1.9 g protein, 12.9 g carbohydrates, 4.0 g dietary fiber, 5.3 g sugars, 87 mg sodium, 424 mg potassium, 51 mg phosphorus

Thai Green Beans

Serves 4.

Look for thin, whole frozen green beans. Fresh green beans can be used. Toasted sesame oil has a rich sesame flavor, but regular sesame oil can be used.

- 1 Tablespoon crunchy no-sugar-added peanut butter
- 1 Tablespoon low-sodium soy sauce
- 1 Tablespoon toasted sesame oil, divided use
- 2 teaspoons grated fresh ginger
- 1 pound frozen whole green beans (about 4½ cups)
- ⅛ teaspoon freshly ground black pepper
- 2 Tablespoons roasted, unsalted peanuts, coarsely chopped

Mix the peanut butter, soy sauce, ½ tablespoon of the sesame oil and ginger together. Heat the remaining sesame oil in a large, nonstick skillet over medium-high heat. Add the green beans. Sauté for 5 minutes. Add the peanut butter mixture, and stir to combine with the beans. Add black pepper. Sprinkle peanuts on top.

Serving size: 1¼ cups

Per serving: 118 calories, 7.9 g fat, 1.1 g saturated fat, 3.4 g monounsaturated fat, 0 mg cholesterol, 4.5 g protein, 10.1 g carbohydrates, 3.8 dietary fiber, 4.2 sugars, 136 mg sodium, 315 mg potassium, 78 mg phosphorus

---

Roasted Baby Brussels Sprouts and Bacon

Serves 4.

Look for frozen baby Brussels sprouts. The roasted sprouts will be crisp on the outside and tender inside—and the bacon adds a delectable smoky taste. If you don't like bacon, you can sprinkle a little smoked paprika over them.

- 1 Tablespoon olive oil
- 1 pound frozen baby Brussels sprouts (about 4 cups)
- ⅛ teaspoon freshly ground black pepper
- 4 bacon slices, diced into ½-inch pieces

Preheat the oven to 400°F. Line a baking sheet with foil. Add the oil, and roll the Brussels sprouts in the oil, making sure all sides are covered. Sprinkle with salt and pepper, and toss well. Spread them in one layer on the sheet. Place the diced bacon over the Brussels sprouts. Roast 20 minutes. Remove from oven, and turn sprouts over. Roast another 10 minutes.

Serving size: 1 cup

Per serving: 111 calories, 7.0 g fat, 1.6 g saturated fat, 4.0 g monounsaturated fat, 9 mg cholesterol, 5.9 g protein, 8.0 g carbohydrates, 3.3 g dietary fiber, 1.9 g sugars, 104 mg sodium, 343 mg potassium, 61 mg phosphorus

---

Microwaveable Brown Rice

Serves 2.

Here's a basic recipe to use with many of the dishes in this chapter.

1 package microwaveable brown rice (for 1½ cups rice)

Microwave the rice according to package instructions. Measure 1½ cups cooked rice into a bowl to serve with any of the main entrees. Reserve the remaining rice for another meal.

Serving size: ¾ cup rice

Per serving: 162 calories, 1.3 g fat, 0.3 g saturated fat, 0.5 g monounsaturated fat, 0 mg cholesterol, 3.8 g protein, 33.6 g carbohydrates, 2.6 g dietary fiber, 0.5 g sugars, 8 mg sodium, 63 mg potassium, 122 mg phosphorus

Spinach Brown Rice

Serves 2.

Using microwaveable brown rice, you can make this dish in less than 5 minutes.

1 package microwaveable brown rice (for 1½ cups rice)
5 cups washed, ready-to-eat spinach
2 teaspoons olive oil
⅛ teaspoon freshly ground black pepper

Microwave the rice according to package instructions. Measure 1½ cups cooked rice into a bowl. Reserve the remaining rice for another meal. Add the spinach to the warm rice, and toss well. Add the olive oil and salt and pepper. Toss again.

Serving size: ¾ cup rice, 1½ cups vegetables

Per serving: 220 calories, 6.1 g fat, 0.9 g saturated fat, 3.8 g monounsaturated fat, 0 mg cholesterol, 5.9 g protein, 36.4 g carbohydrates, 4.4 g dietary fiber, 0.8 g sugars, 68 mg sodium, 482 mg potassium, 159 mg phosphorus

Rosemary Cannellini Beans

Serves 2.

Rosemary and garlic flavor these cannellini beans. This is another 5-minute dish.

1 cup rinsed and drained cannellini beans
3 Tablespoons fat-free, unsalted chicken broth*
2 medium garlic cloves, crushed
1 teaspoon dried rosemary

Place all ingredients in a saucepan over medium-high heat and bring to a simmer for 2 to 3 minutes to warm beans.

*Look for unsalted chicken broth with 20 calories and 150 mg sodium per cup.

Serving size: ½ cup cannellini beans, 1½ tablespoons broth

Per serving: 161 calories, 0.8 g fat, 0.3 g saturated fat, 0.1 g monounsaturated fat, 0 mg cholesterol, 10.4 g protein, 29.7 g carbohydrates, 7.2 g dietary fiber, 1.9 g sugars, 19 mg sodium, 516 mg potassium, 196 mg phosphorus

Kasha with Wild Mushrooms

Serves 4.

Kasha is toasted, hulled buckwheat groats. They are nutty and tender.

1 cup kasha (buckwheat groats)
1 cup fat-free, unsalted chicken broth*
1 Tablespoon olive oil
½ pound shiitake mushrooms, sliced
1 cup sliced onion
¹⁄₁₆ teaspoon salt (4 turns of salt mill)
⅛ teaspoon freshly ground black pepper
2 Tablespoons fresh thyme leaves

Place kasha in a nonstick saucepan. Heat over medium heat to toast them, 1 to 2 minutes. Remove to a bowl. Add broth to the saucepan and bring to a boil. Return kasha to saucepan. Lower heat, cover with a lid and boil, gently, for 12 to 15 minutes or until tender and water is absorbed. Heat olive oil in a nonstick skillet, add onion and mushrooms and sauté 5 minutes. When kasha is cooked, add onion and mushrooms and toss. Sprinkle with thyme, salt and pepper.

*Look for unsalted chicken broth with 20 calories and 150 mg sodium per cup.

Serving size: ¾ cup kasha, 1½ cups vegetables
Per serving: 206 calories, 4.7 g fat, 0.8 g saturated fat, 2.8 g monounsaturated fat, 0 mg cholesterol, 8.3 g protein, 36.8 g carbohydrates, 5.6 g dietary fiber, 2.9 g sugars, 83 mg sodium, 453 mg potassium, 225 mg phosphorus

---

Orange Barley

Serves 4.

Barley has a nutty flavor and chewy texture. Here, it's tossed with thyme, sage and orange juice for a simple side dish.

2 cups fat-free, unsalted chicken broth*
1 cup quick-cooking pearl barley
1 Tablespoon olive oil
1 cup sliced onion
½ teaspoon dried thyme
½ teaspoon dried sage
2 Tablespoons orange juice

Bring broth to a boil in a medium saucepan and add barley. Boil 10 minutes uncovered. Heat olive oil in a nonstick skillet and sauté onion 5 minutes. Drain barley and toss with onion. Add thyme, sage and orange juice.

*Look for unsalted chicken broth with 20 calories and 150 mg sodium per cup.

Serving size: ¾ cup barley, ½ cup vegetables, 1 tablespoon orange juice
Per serving: 232 calories, 4.0 g fat, 0.6 g saturated fat, 2.5 g monounsaturated fat, 0 mg cholesterol, 7.8 g protein, 43.0 g carbohydrates, 8.4 g dietary fiber, 2.3 sugars, 81 mg sodium, 346 mg potassium, 185 mg phosphorus

---

Bulgur Wheat with Raisins and Pine Nuts

Serves 4.

Raisins and pine nuts add a sweet flavor and crunchy texture to the bulgur wheat.

2 cups fat-free, unsalted chicken broth*
1 cup coarse bulgur wheat (cracked wheat)
1 Tablespoon olive oil
¼ cup raisins
¼ cup pine nuts
⅛ teaspoon salt (8 turns of salt grinder)
¼ teaspoon freshly ground black pepper

Bring broth to a boil in a medium saucepan and add bulgur. Lower heat, stir and cover with a lid. Gently simmer 10 minutes until liquid is absorbed. Remove from heat and let stand, covered, 10 minutes. Heat olive oil in a nonstick skillet over medium heat and add pine nuts and raisins. Sauté until pine nuts are golden, 1 minute. Toss with cooked bulgur. Add salt and pepper.

*Look for unsalted chicken broth with 20 calories and 150 mg sodium per cup.

Serving size: ¾ cup bulgur wheat, 1 tablespoon raisins, 1 tablespoon pine nuts

Per serving: 224 calories, 7.5 g fat, 1.1 g saturated fat, 3.9 g monounsaturated fat, 0 mg cholesterol, 7.8 g protein, 35.4 g carbohydrates, 7.4 g dietary fiber, 5.4 g sugars, 159 mg sodium, 253 mg potassium, 76 mg phosphorus

---

SALADS AND SANDWICHES

Spicy Salmon Salad

Serves 2.

Serve this spicy salad on a bed of Romaine lettuce leaves for lunch or a light supper. Cucumbers add a refreshing crunch to the salad. Wasabi is the Japanese version of horseradish. It is available in powdered form in the Asian foods section of your supermarket. You can substitute tuna for the salmon.

1 Tablespoon wasabi powder
3 Tablespoons reduced-fat mayonnaise
8 ounces drained canned salmon (visible bones removed)
¾ cup cucumbers, cut into ¼-inch cubes, drained
⅛ teaspoon freshly ground black pepper
2 Tablespoons chopped parsley

Mix the wasabi powder and mayonnaise together in a medium-sized bowl. Add the salmon, and break up the pieces with a fork. Add the cucumber cubes, and mix all the ingredients together. Add pepper. Sprinkle with the chopped parsley.

Serving size: 4 ounces salmon, ½ cup vegetables, 1½ tablespoons sauce

Per serving: 252 calories, 12.2 g fat, 1.9 g saturated fat, 2.8 g monounsaturated fat, 96 mg cholesterol, 28.7 g protein, 4.3 g carbohydrates, 1.2 g dietary fiber, 1.6 g sugars, 591 mg sodium, 466 mg potassium, 300 mg phosphorus

Tuna Pesto Salad

Serves 2.

Pesto is usually made by combining fresh basil, garlic, pine nuts, Parmesan cheese and olive oil. Here it adds pizzazz to canned tuna. A store-bought, low-fat version of pesto works well in this salad.

2 Tablespoons reduced-fat no-sugar-added vinaigrette dressing
2 Tablespoons reduced-fat pesto
10 ounces canned tuna packed in water, drained
6 pitted black olives, chopped
Several lettuce leaves (Romaine or Red Leaf lettuce) (about 2 cups)

Mix the dressing and pesto together in a medium-sized bowl. Add the tuna, and break up the pieces with a fork. Add the olives. Mix dressing, pesto, tuna and olives together. Serve on bed of whole leaves of lettuce.

Serving size: 5 ounces tuna mixture, 1 cup vegetables

Per serving: 212 calories, 8.1 g fat, 1.3 g saturated fat, 3.3 g monounsaturated fat, 54 mg cholesterol, 30.1 g protein, 5.2 g carbohydrates, 1.8 g dietary fiber, 2.7 g sugars, 579 mg sodium, 386 mg potassium, 211 mg phosphorus

Panzanella Salad

Serves 2.

This is a traditional Tuscan dish and a delicious way to use up leftover bread—and it is surprisingly simple to make.

4 slices day-old crusty whole-grain bread (1 ounce each)
Olive oil spray
1 garlic clove, peeled and cut in half
1½ Tablespoons olive oil
1 Tablespoon balsamic vinegar
1/16 teaspoon salt (4 turns of salt grinder)
⅛ teaspoon freshly ground black pepper
1½ cups ripe tomatoes, cubed
1½ cups yellow bell pepper, cubed
1½ cups red bell pepper, cubed
½ cup basil leaves, torn into pieces
8 pitted green olives

Spray the bread with olive oil spray. Rub the bread with the cut side of the garlic. Discard the garlic. Toast the bread in a toaster oven or under the broiler until golden. Mix olive oil and the balsamic vinegar together in a large bowl. Add salt and pepper. Add the tomatoes, peppers, basil and olives. Toss well. Cut the toasted bread into large cubes, and toss into the salad just before serving.

Serving size: 2½ cups vegetables, 1½ tablespoons dressing, 2 slices whole-grain bread
Per serving: 364 calories, 16.8 g fat, 2.3 g saturated fat, 10.4 g monounsaturated fat, 0 mg cholesterol, 9.9 g protein, 38.7 g carbohydrates, 8.8 g dietary fiber, 13.9 g sugars, 457 mg sodium, 765 mg potassium, 192 mg phosphorus

Grilled Asparagus, Chickpea and Quinoa Salad

Serves 4.

You can place asparagus directly on a grill grate and turn it with tongs. Or you can skewer several together crosswise—this keeps asparagus from falling through the grate. Place four spears together. Push a wooden skewer through all four near the top of the asparagus. Push a second skewer through near the bottom of the asparagus.

2 pounds fresh asparagus
Small disposable aluminum baking pan
2 Tablespoons olive oil
1 cup canned chickpeas, rinsed and drained
1 package short wooden skewers
1 cup quinoa
½ cup reduced-fat, no-sugar-added oil-and-vinegar dressing
¼ cup chopped fresh basil or parsley
1/16 teaspoon salt (4 turns of salt grinder)
⅛ teaspoon freshly ground black pepper

Snap off the stems of the asparagus at the point where they break easily, about 1 inch from the bottom. Pour olive oil onto the disposable baking pan, and roll the asparagus in the oil. Remove the asparagus. Add the chickpeas, and toss them in the oil. Heat the grill to medium.

Place the pan with the chickpeas on the grill grates. Skewer four asparagus at a time cross-wise. Place the asparagus on the grates. Grill, covered, 5 minutes. Turn the asparagus, and stir the chickpeas. Grill, covered, 3 minutes. If using thin asparagus, reduce grilling time to 2 minutes per side and remove from grill, leaving the chickpeas to grill about 5 to 10 minutes or until golden. Cut the asparagus into one-inch pieces.

While the vegetables are cooking, bring a large pot with about four quarts of water to a boil. Add the quinoa, and boil 15 to 20 minutes, or until soft. Drain.

Pour the dressing into a large bowl. Add the quinoa, asparagus and chickpeas. Sprinkle on the fresh herbs and salt and pepper. Toss again.

Serving size: 1¾ cups vegetables, 2 tablespoons dressing, ¾ cup quinoa

Per serving: 367 calories, 13.2 g fat, 1.6 g saturated fat, 6.6 g monounsaturated fat, 2 mg cholesterol, 15.4 g protein, 51.5 g carbohydrates, 11.5 g dietary fiber, 8.0 g sugars, 200 mg sodium, 347 mg potassium, 250 mg phosphorus

---

Fresh Herb Salad

Serves 2.

Make the dressing in advance and add the greens and pear just before serving to keep this salad fresh and crisp. This recipe is also delicious substituting a small apple for the pear.

1 Tablespoon olive oil
1 Tablespoon balsamic vinegar
½ cup diced white onion
¹⁄₁₆ teaspoon (4 turns of salt grinder)
⅛ teaspoon freshly ground black pepper
1 cup fresh basil leaves, torn into bite-size pieces
1 cup fresh mint, torn into bite-size pieces
2 cups washed, ready-to-eat fresh baby spinach leaves or mixed salad greens
1 small, ripe pear, cored and sliced (about 1 cup)

Place olive oil and vinegar in a salad bowl and mix with a whisk. Add onion, salt and pepper. Just before serving, add the basil, mint, spinach and pear. Toss well.

Serving size: 2¼ cups vegetables, ½ cup fruit, 1 tablespoon dressing

Per serving: 153 calories, 7.4 g fat, 1.1 g saturated fat, 5.0 g monounsaturated fat, 0 mg cholesterol, 3.5 g protein, 21.1 g carbohydrates, 6.9 g dietary fiber, 9.9 g sugars, 113 mg sodium, 561 mg potassium, 71 mg phosphorus

---

Strawberries with Greens

Serves 4.

Berries make delicious desserts and they also add a bright flavor to salads.

2 Tablespoons fresh chopped basil
1 Tablespoon grated Parmesan cheese
¼ cup reduced-fat, no-sugar-added vinaigrette dressing
4 cups washed, ready-to-eat greens
1 cup hulled, washed and quartered strawberries

Puree basil, Parmesan cheese and dressing in a blender. Toss dressing with the greens in a large bowl. Divide greens among 4 plates. Sprinkle strawberries on top.

Serving size: 1 vegetable, ¼ cup fruit, ¾ teaspoon cheese, 1 tablespoon dressing

Per serving: 38 calories, 1.6 g fat, 0.3 g saturated fat, 0.5 g monounsaturated fat, 2 mg cholesterol, 1.4 g protein, 5.5 g carbohydrates, 1.9 g dietary fiber, 3.3 g sugars, 27 mg sodium, 197 mg potassium, 35 mg phosphorus

Steak Pita Pocket

Serves 2.

These tasty pita sandwiches make a great lunch or simple supper. You can also serve this meal as a salad. Spoon the sauce onto a plate. Place the sliced steak on top and sprinkle the tomatoes over the steak. Serve warm pita bread on the side.

Olive oil spray
½ pound grass-fed strip steak
½ cup peeled, seeded (if desired) and coarsely chopped cucumber
¹⁄₁₆ teaspoon salt (4 turns of salt grinder)
⅛ teaspoon freshly ground black pepper
1 medium garlic clove, minced
1 Tablespoon chopped fresh dill or 1 teaspoon dried dill
2 Tablespoons chopped red onion
¼ cup plain, nonfat yogurt, drained
2 Tablespoons reduced-fat sour cream
2 6-inch whole-wheat pita breads
1 cup diced tomato

Heat a medium-sized skillet over medium-high heat. Spray with olive oil spray. Add steak and sear for 3 minutes. Turn over and cook 3 more minutes. A meat thermometer should read 125 degrees for rare or 145 degrees for medium rare. Sprinkle with salt and pepper. Remove to a cutting board and let sit while preparing remaining ingredients. Mix the cucumber, garlic, dill, onion, yogurt and sour cream together. Toast the pita breads in a toaster oven to warm slightly. Cut the pitas in half, open the pockets and spoon in half the yogurt mixture. Thinly slice the steak and add to the pockets along with the tomatoes. Finish with the remaining yogurt sauce.

Serving size: 3 ounces steak, ¾ cup vegetables, 1 bread, 3 tablespoons sauce

Per serving: 381 calories, 8.9 g fat, 2.8 g saturated fat, 3.3 g monounsaturated fat, 71 mg cholesterol, 35.2 g protein, 44.2 g carbohydrates, 6.3 g dietary fiber, 5.9 g sugars, 459 mg sodium, 845 mg potassium, 433 mg phosphorus

Barbecued Chicken and Portobello Sandwich

Serves 2.

Grill this inside on a stove-top grill or outside for a crusty sandwich.

4 crushed garlic cloves
½ cup balsamic vinegar
¾ pound boneless, skinless chicken breast

¼ pound whole Portobello mushrooms
4 slices Vidalia or other sweet onion
4 slices whole-grain bread (1 ounce each)
Olive oil spray
1/16 teaspoon salt (4 turns of salt grinder)
⅛ teaspoon freshly ground black pepper
1 cup arugula leaves

Mix garlic and balsamic vinegar in a self-sealing plastic bag. Add chicken and mushrooms. Marinate 15 minutes in the refrigerator, flipping the bag once during that time. Heat a stove-top grill or preheat a gas grill. (If using a stove-top grill, spray with olive oil spray.) Remove chicken and mushrooms from marinade. Discard marinade. Place on hot grill with onion slices and cook 5 minutes. Turn chicken, mushrooms and onion slices and cook 5 more minutes. While the chicken, mushrooms and onion cook, spray bread with olive oil spray and place on grill for 1 minute. Turn and grill 1 minute or until bread is golden. Slice chicken and mushrooms into thin strips on a carving board. Arrange on slices of bread and place onions on top. Pour chicken juices from the carving board over the top. Sprinkle with salt and pepper. Place arugula leaves on top. Cover with the remaining bread slices and cut sandwiches in half.

Serving size: 5 ounces chicken, 1¼ cups vegetables, 2 slices bread

Per serving: 368 calories, 9.1 g fat, 1.6 g saturated fat, 2.9 g monounsaturated fat, 126 mg cholesterol, 44.7 g protein, 30.8 g carbohydrates, 5.1 g dietary fiber, 6.3 g sugars, 220 mg sodium, 1007 mg potassium, 562 mg phosphorus

---

DESSERTS

You can enjoy fresh-fruit desserts without adding sugar or artificial sweeteners. All recipes make two servings.

Minty Strawberries and Pineapple

1 cup fresh, ripe strawberries, hulled, washed and dried
1 cup fresh pineapple cubes
⅛ teaspoon freshly ground black pepper
2 Tablespoons fresh mint, torn into small pieces

Thinly slice the strawberries lengthwise (hull to pointed end). This can be done using an egg slicer if you wish. Cut the pineapple cubes into thin slices. Arrange the fruit on two dessert plates. Sprinkle with black pepper and mint.

Serving size: 1 cup fruit

Per serving: 72 calories, 0.4 fat, 0 g saturated fat, 0 g monounsaturated fat, 0 mg cholesterol, 1.2 g protein, 17.8 g carbohydrates, 3.4 g dietary fiber, 12.2 g sugars, 3 mg sodium, 247 mg potassium, 29 mg phosphorus

Almond Fruit Cups

2 Tablespoons slivered almonds
1 kiwi, peeled and sliced
1 cup strawberries, hulled and sliced
1 teaspoon almond extract

Heat a small skillet over medium heat. Add the almonds, and toss until they are golden. *Caution*: They burn easily. Remove them from skillet. Place fruit in a bowl, and toss it with the almond extract. Spoon the fruit into two glasses. Sprinkle almonds on top.

Serving size: 1 cup fruit, 1 tablespoon almonds

Per serving: 106 calories, 4.9 g fat, 0.4 g saturated fat, 2.9 g monounsaturated fat, 0 mg cholesterol, 2.8 g protein, 13.6 g carbohydrates, 4.0 g dietary fiber, 7.8 g sugars, 1 mg sodium, 305 mg potassium, 73 mg phosphorus

Melon Twizzler

¾ cup ripe cantaloupe, cut into ½-inch cubes
¾ cup ripe honeydew, cut into ½-inch cubes
2 Tablespoons ouzo or Pernod liquor or 1 teaspoon coconut extract
¼ cup snipped fennel leaves

Divide melon between 2 dessert bowls. Drizzle 1 tablespoon ouzo over each serving. Snip the fennel leaves with scissors, and sprinkle over the melon.

Serving size: ¾ cup fruit, 1 tablespoon ouzo

Per serving: 99 calories, 0.2 g fat, 0.1 g saturated fat, 0 g monounsaturated fat, 0 mg cholesterol, 1.0 g protein, 17.2 g carbohydrates, 1.4 g dietary fiber, 15.6 g sugars, 27 mg sodium, 312 mg potassium, 16 mg phosphorus

5

Natural Treatments for Diabetes

Defeat Diabetes Without Drugs

Type 2 diabetes is one of the many chronic diseases that often can be managed entirely without medication, particularly when it is diagnosed at an early stage.

Among people with insulin resistance, a precursor to diabetes, nearly all can reverse it with the same changes. Even with longstanding diabetes, many patients can discontinue most of their insulin/oral drugs when they make significant dietary and other lifestyle changes.

CATCH IT EARLY

About 29 million Americans have type 2 diabetes (once known as adult-onset diabetes), and 86 million have prediabetes (according to the Centers for Disease Control and Prevention), an intermediate condition in which levels of fasting glucose (blood sugar) are between 100 milligrams per deciliter (mg/dL) and 125 mg/dL.

What they have in common: An inability to effectively utilize insulin, the hormone produced by the pancreas that allows glucose to move from the bloodstream into the body's cells.

Most people with diabetes are first diagnosed via a fasting blood sugar test. But by the time glucose levels are high, the disease already has progressed—and the cells that produce insulin may have suffered irreversible damage.

Better: The fasting serum insulin test.

Cost: About $50 (which may be covered by insurance). High levels of insulin indicate insulin resistance, a condition that precedes sharply elevated glucose.

Anyone with diabetes risk factors, including obesity, high blood pressure, elevated cholesterol or a waist circumference of more than 40

Stuart A. Seale, MD, former medical director of Lifestyle Center of America, a diabetes center in Sedona, Arizona. He is coauthor, with Franklin House, MD, and Ian Blake Newman, of *The 30-Day Diabetes Miracle.* FullPlateLiving.org inches in men or 35 inches in women, should have the fasting serum insulin test.

Those who have diabetes or are at risk for diabetes should consider making the following lifestyle changes. People sometimes complain about the "restrictive" nature of the changes needed to control diabetes. It does take some effort, but far less than dealing with the complications of the disease—which may include blindness, nerve damage and amputation.

NEAR-VEGETARIAN DIET

One study found that 21 of 23 patients were able to discontinue oral diabetes drugs after switching to a mainly meatless diet—of those on insulin, 13 out of 17 were able to quit taking the insulin.

A plant-based diet is high in fiber, which slows digestion and the rate of glucose absorption into the blood. This causes the pancreas to secrete less insulin, and it makes cells more sensitive to insulin's effects. People who consume little or no meat also tend to have lower cholesterol and blood pressure—important for minimizing the cardiovascular complications of diabetes.

The Diabetes Prevention Program study found that people at risk for developing type 2 diabetes who exercised regularly and ate a Mediterranean-style diet—mainly fruits, vegetables, legumes (beans, lentils) and whole grains, with only small amounts of meat a few times a month—decreased their risk of developing diabetes by 58%. In contrast, trying to prevent diabetes by using the popular medication metformin lowered the risk of developing diabetes by 31%.

CARBOHYDRATE COUNTING

Carbohydrate counting is among the most effective ways to control diabetes. *Main steps...*

• **Calculate net carbohydrate.** This is the amount of carbohydrate in a food minus fiber content. One cup of Kashi GoLean cereal, for example, has 30 grams (g) of total carbohydrates, but because this includes 10 g of fiber, the net carbohydrate is actually 20 g. You can find all of this information on food labels.

• **Identify carbohydrate choices.** One carbohydrate choice equals 15 g of net carbohydrates.

Example: A slice of whole-wheat bread is one carbohydrate choice (about 15 g of net carbs).

• **Eat 9 to 13 carbohydrate choices daily for optimal control.** Most people are advised to have three to five carb choices for breakfast.

Sample breakfast: One cup of old-fashioned oatmeal with milk or milk alternative, such as soy milk (two carbohydrate choices)...one cup of berries (one carb choice)...egg or tofu scramble with vegetables, such as mushrooms, bell peppers and onions (one carb choice)...one slice of toast with nut butter (one carb choice).

Have three to five carbohydrate choices at lunch and zero to three at supper. Eating lighter at night helps stabilize overnight and morning blood sugar levels.

Carbohydrate counting is confusing initially, but people quickly memorize the carbohydrate contents of the foods that they tend to eat most often.

Helpful: I advise patients to eat meals at the same time every day...and to eat about the same portion sizes to keep blood sugar levels stable.

GLYCEMIC INDEX

Some carbohydrates elevate blood glucose almost instantly—others much more slowly. The glycemic index (GI) is a measure of how quickly carbohydrates elevate glucose. A lower number indicates a slower glucose rise—and better glucose control.

Example: White bread has a GI of 73. It is transformed very quickly into glucose, which causes blood sugar levels to surge. A serving of carrots, on the other hand, has a GI of 32. The glucose conversion happens slowly, which causes steadier levels of blood glucose.

Recommended: Mainly consume foods with GIs of less than 55. Foods that are minimally processed, such as legumes and whole grains, generally have lower GI numbers. (See *www.glycemicindex.com* for a complete guide to the glycemic index.)

Helpful: Aboveground vegetables, such as grains and leafy greens, typically have lower

GIs than below-ground vegetables, such as potatoes and radishes. Fruit from the temperate climates, such as apples, pears and peaches, have lower GIs than tropical fruits, such as bananas.

Also, if you feel like eating a food with a high GI (such as white bread), combine it with a low-GI food, such as peanut butter, to reduce the glucose surge.

POSTMEAL EXERCISE

Exercise helps people lose weight, which improves insulin sensitivity and reduces cardiovascular risk factors.

Even without weight loss, exercise is very effective for managing diabetes, particularly when you exercise after meals. Exercise after meals makes it easier for muscle cells to absorb glucose from the blood. Patients who check their blood sugar two hours after eating, then test it again after a brisk 20-minute walk, typically see a drop of at least 30 points.

Strength training also is helpful. People who lift weights or engage in other forms of resistance exercise (such as push-ups) two or three times a week have an increase in muscle tissue, which increases metabolism and insulin sensitivity.

LOWER STRESS

In an emergency, the body releases cortisol, the "fight-or-flight" hormone that increases blood glucose to produce a quick surge of energy. Unfortunately, the same thing happens in people with daily stress. Their cortisol—and glucose—remains at chronically high levels, making diabetes more difficult to control.

Stress management is critical if you have diabetes. Most people find that a daily walk keeps them calmer. In addition, hobbies are a good way to defuse tension and stress. Others learn to meditate or practice yoga. Whatever you find relaxing, make time for it at least a few times a day.

Fight Diabetes Naturally— Three Proven Nondrug Remedies

Bill Gottlieb, CHC, a health coach certified by the American Association of Drugless Practitioners. He is author of several health books that have sold more than two million copies and former editor in chief of Rodale Books and *Prevention Magazine* Health Books. Based in northern California, he is author of *Defeat High Blood Sugar—Naturally! Super-Supplements and Super-Foods Selected by America's Best Alternative Doctors.* BillGottliebHealth.com

Scientific research and the experience of doctors and other health professionals show that supplements and superfoods can be even more effective than drugs when it comes to preventing and treating diabetes. I reviewed thousands of scientific studies and talked to more than 60 health professionals about these glucose-controlling natural remedies. One is magnesium. Studies show that magnesium significantly reduces the risk for diabetes. (*Note*: High doses of magnesium can cause diarrhea.)

Here are three more standout natural remedies…

Caution: If you are taking insulin or other medications to control diabetes, talk to your doctor before taking any supplement or changing your diet.

GYMNEMA

Gymnema has been the standard antidiabetes recommendation for the past 2,000 years from practitioners of Ayurveda, the ancient system of natural healing from India. Derived from a vinelike plant found in the tropical forests of southern and central India, the herb also is called gurmar, or "sugar destroyer"—if you chew on the leaf of the plant, you temporarily will lose your ability to taste sweets.

Modern science has figured out the molecular interactions underlying this strange phenomenon. The gymnemic acids in the herb have a structure similar to glucose molecules, filling up glucose receptor sites on the taste buds. They also fill up sugar receptors in the intestine, blocking the absorption of glucose.

And gymnemic acids stimulate (and even may regenerate) the cells of the pancreas that manufacture insulin, the hormone that ushers glucose out of the bloodstream and into cells.

Standout research: Studies published in *Journal of Ethnopharmacology* showed that three months of using a unique gymnema extract, formulated over several decades by two Indian scientists, reduced fasting blood glucose (a blood sample is taken after an overnight fast) by 23% in people with type 2 diabetes (defined as fasting blood sugar levels of 126 mg/dL or higher). People with prediabetes (defined as those with blood sugar levels of 100 mg/dL to 125 mg/dL) had a 30% reduction.

Important: The newest (and more powerful) version of this extract is called ProBeta, which is available at *www.pharmaterra.com*. A naturopathic physician who uses ProBeta with his patients told me that the supplement can lower fasting glucose in the 200s down to the 120s or 130s after five to six months of use.

Typical daily dose: ProBeta—two capsules, two to three times a day. Other types of gymnema—400 milligrams (mg), three times a day.

APPLE CIDER VINEGAR

Numerous studies have proved that apple cider vinegar works to control type 2 diabetes. Several of the studies were conducted by Carol Johnston, PhD, RD, a professor of nutrition at Arizona State University.

Standout scientific research: Dr. Johnston's studies showed that an intake of apple cider vinegar with a meal lowered insulin resistance (the inability of cells to use insulin) by an average of 64% in people with prediabetes and type 2 diabetes…improved insulin sensitivity (the ability of cells to use insulin) by up to 34%…and lowered postmeal spikes in blood sugar by an average of 20%. Research conducted in Greece, Sweden, Japan and the Middle East has confirmed many of Dr. Johnston's findings.

How it works: The acetic acid in vinegar—the compound that gives vinegar its tart flavor and pungent odor—blunts the activity of disaccharidase enzymes that help break down the type of carbohydrates found in starchy foods such as potatoes, rice, bread and pasta. As a result, those foods are digested and absorbed more slowly, lowering blood glucose and insulin levels.

Suggested daily intake: Two tablespoons right before or early in the meal. (More is not more effective.)

If you're using vinegar in a salad dressing, the ideal ratio for blood sugar control is two tablespoons of vinegar to one tablespoon of oil. Eat the salad early in the meal so that it disrupts the carb-digesting enzymes before they get a chance to work. Or dip premeal whole-grain bread in a vinaigrette dressing.

SOY FOODS

A recent 10-year study published in *Journal of the American Society of Nephrology* found that the mortality rate for people with diabetes and kidney disease was more than 31%. Statistically, that makes kidney disease the number-one risk factor for death in people with diabetes.

Fortunately, researchers have found that there is a simple way to counter kidney disease in diabetes—eat more soy foods.

Standout scientific research: Dozens of scientific studies show that soy is a nutritional ally for diabetes patients with kidney disease. But the best and most recent of these studies, published in *Diabetes Care*, shows that eating lots of soy can help reverse signs of kidney disease, reduce risk factors for heart disease—and reduce blood sugar, too.

The study involved 41 diabetes patients with kidney disease, divided into two groups. One group ate a diet with protein from 70% animal and 30% vegetable sources. The other group ate a diet with protein from 35% animal sources, 35% textured soy protein and 30% vegetable proteins. After four years, those eating the soy-rich diet had lower levels of several biomarkers for kidney disease. (In another, smaller experiment, the same researchers found that soy improved biomarkers for kidney disease in just seven weeks.) In fact, the health of the participants' kidneys actually improved, a finding that surprised the researchers, since diabetic nephropathy (diabetes-caused kidney disease) is considered to be a progressive, irreversible disease.

Those eating soy also had lower fasting blood sugar, lower LDL cholesterol, lower total cholesterol, lower triglycerides and lower C-reactive protein, a biomarker for chronic inflammation.

How it works: Substituting soy for animal protein may ease stress on the delicate filters of the kidneys. Soy itself also stops the over-production of cells in the kidney that clog the filters…boosts the production of nitric oxide, which improves blood flow in the kidneys… and normalizes the movement of minerals within the kidneys, thus improving filtration.

Suggested daily intake: The diabetes patients in the study ate 16 grams of soy protein daily. Examples: Four ounces of tofu provide 13 grams of soy protein…one soy burger, 13 grams…one-quarter cup of soy nuts, 11 grams…one-half cup of shelled edamame (edible soybeans in the pod), 11 grams…one cup of soy milk, 6 grams.

WHAT'S WRONG WITH DIABETES DRUGS?

Doctors typically try to control high blood sugar with a glucose-lowering medication such as *metformin* (Glucophage), a drug most experts consider safe. But other diabetes drugs may not be safe.

Example #1: Recent studies show that *sitagliptin* (Januvia) and *exenatide* (Byetta) double the risk for hospitalization for pancreatitis (inflamed pancreas) and triple the risk for pancreatic cancer.

Example #2: *Pioglitazone* (Actos) can triple the risk for eye problems and vision loss, double the risk for bone fractures in women and double the risk for bladder cancer.

Got Diabetes? Stop Blood Sugar from Spiking with Red Ginseng

Andrew L. Rubman, ND, founder and medical director, Southbury Clinic for Traditional Medicines, Southbury, Connecticut. SouthburyClinic.com

---

Adult-onset (type 2) diabetes is so common that it ultimately impacts a whopping one in four people age 65 and older. In this type of diabetes, blood sugar can go way up—or "spike"—after a meal. You'll know your blood sugar is spiking because instead of feeling energized and fit after nourishing yourself, you'll just crash. More than just wanting to take a nap—you won't be able to do anything but. That's right. You'll have to take a rest after eating a meal because you will feel sleepy…exhausted. Your eyes may even blur. If this happens often enough, hardening of the arteries can occur, which, as you know, can lead to a heart attack. But you can prevent this from happening naturally. Red ginseng extract may be just the thing to keep blood sugar on an even keel.

Why is it called "red" ginseng? Tonics, extracts and teas of Asian white ginseng (also called Chinese or Korean white panax ginseng) are natural powerhouses of health and vitality made from the raw dried root of the plant. They increase energy and stamina, reduce cholesterol and blood pressure and fight cancer and aging. But steaming the root before drying it starts a fermentation process that supports wellness even more. Once fermented, the ginseng is called red ginseng, and this is the kind that is especially good for people with diabetes and others who have problems with glucose control. Korean researchers have recently confirmed that red ginseng significantly reduces blood glucose levels and increases insulin levels after meals. That makes it especially helpful in preventing dangerous spikes in blood sugar that can happen after diabetics or borderline diabetics have a meal.

The researchers recruited 42 healthy men and women between the ages of 20 and 75 for their study. Nineteen of these participants had type 2 diabetes and the remaining 23 had prediabetes. Half of the group received capsules of fermented red ginseng extract, and half received capsules of a placebo. They were instructed to take one capsule three times a day for four weeks. The total daily dose of red ginseng for the treatment group was 2.7 grams (0.1 ounces).

The researchers found that red ginseng was able to regulate glucose and insulin after meals, thus preventing blood sugar spikes.

Compared with the placebo group, insulin increased and glucose decreased after meals. And no serious side effects were reported in the Korean study, although one person in the treatment group had to drop out because hypoglycemia (low blood sugar) developed.

NATURAL BUT POTENT
DIABETES CARE

"Red ginseng extract may be a good addition to a natural, broader approach to controlling, limiting or getting rid of type 2 diabetes," said Andrew Rubman, ND, a naturopathic physician and founder of the Southbury Clinic for Traditional Medicines in Southbury, Connecticut. In his opinion, however, alpha-lipoic acid, a powerful antioxidant that helps the body use glucose more efficiently, may be a better choice. Plus, it relieves pain, inflammation, burning, tingling and numbness in people who have peripheral neuropathy (nerve damage) caused by diabetes. But because it can reduce blood glucose levels (leading to hypoglycemia), it should not be used without the supervision of a health-care professional who can monitor your blood sugar levels.

Another readily available herbal supplement recommended by Dr. Rubman for type 2 diabetes is Gymnema extract, used in Ayurvedic medicine for centuries.

As for red ginseng, most people can use it daily with no side effects, according to Dr. Rubman. He cautioned that people who are taking several medications, especially antacids or statins, or who have liver or gastrointestinal diseases should hold off on taking ginseng extracts, since they can put an added burden on the liver. He also said that anyone who wants to try red ginseng for diabetes should do so under the supervision of a naturopathic doctor or clinically trained nutritionist—or at least let your doctor know that you are taking the extract so that he or she can monitor and interpret your physical exams and blood tests. Minor side effects include decreased energy, irregularity and/or intestinal gas.

Red ginseng is widely available online, in Asian-food stores and at large health-food and nutrition shops.

Say Good-Bye to Your Diabetes Medication

Mark A. Stengler, NMD, licensed naturopathic medical doctor in private practice, Stengler Center for Integrative Medicine, Encinitas, California...author of many books, including *The Natural Physician's Healing Therapies* and coauthor of *Prescription for Natural Cures*.

Some of my patients who have type 2 diabetes are able to keep the disease under control with diet, exercise and supplements. Lucky them! But for other diabetes patients, that's not enough and they must take pharmaceutical medications.

I'm happy to report that there is another natural treatment option for diabetes patients who currently take pharmaceutical medications. Research has found that a plant extract called berberine can control diabetes as well as, or better than, common medications such as *metformin* (Glucophage) and *rosiglitazone* (Avandia). And it does this with no side effects—and without damaging the liver, as some medications do. Here's how berberine can help people with diabetes...

A naturally occurring chemical compound, berberine is found in the roots and stems of several plants, including *Hydrastis canadensis* (goldenseal), *Coptis chinensis* (coptis or goldthread) and *Berberis aquifolium* (Oregon grape). Long used as a remedy in Chinese and Ayurvedic medicines, berberine is known for its antimicrobial properties and as a treatment for bacterial and fungal infections. Several decades ago, berberine was used to treat diarrhea in patients in China. That was when doctors noticed that the blood sugar levels of diabetes patients were lower after taking the herbal extract—and berberine began to be investigated for this purpose.

Over the past 20 years, there has been much research on berberine and its effectiveness in treating diabetes. In 2008, Chinese researchers published a study in *Metabolism* in which adults with newly diagnosed type 2 diabetes were given 500 milligrams (mg) of either berberine or the drug metformin three times a day for three months. Researchers found that berberine did as good a job as metformin at regulating glucose metabolism, as indicated by hemoglobin A1C (a measure of blood glucose over several weeks)…fasting blood glucose…blood sugar after eating…and level of insulin after eating. Berberine even reduced the amount of insulin needed to turn glucose into energy by 45%! In addition, those taking berberine had noticeably lower trigylceride and total cholesterol levels than those taking metformin.

In another 2008 study published in *Journal of Clinical Endocrinology and Metabolism*, researchers found that type 2 diabetes patients who were given berberine had significant reductions in fasting and postmeal blood glucose, hemoglobin A1C, triglycerides, total cholesterol and LDL (bad) cholesterol—and also lost an average of five pounds, to boot, during the three-month study period.

In a 2010 study in *Metabolism*, Chinese researchers compared people with type 2 diabetes who took either 1,000 mg daily of berberine or daily doses of metformin or rosiglitazone. After two months, berberine had lowered subjects' fasting blood glucose levels by an average of about 30%, an improvement over the rosiglitazone group and almost as much as people in the metformin group. Berberine also reduced subjects' hemoglobin A1C by 18%—equal to rosiglitazone and, again, almost as good as metformin. In addition, berberine lowered serum insulin levels by 28.2% (indicating increased insulin sensitivity)…lowered triglycerides by 17.5%…and actually improved liver enzyme levels. Pharmaceutical medications, on the other hand, have the potential to harm the liver.

These were remarkable findings. Here was a botanical that was holding up to scientific scrutiny—and performing as well as, or better than, some drugs that patients had been taking for diabetes for years.

HOW BERBERINE WORKS IN THE BODY

Berberine helps to lower blood glucose in several ways. One of its primary mechanisms involves stimulating the activity of the genes responsible for manufacturing and activating insulin receptors, which are critical for controlling blood glucose.

Berberine also has an effect on blood sugar regulation through activation of incretins, gastrointestinal hormones that affect the amount of insulin released by the body after eating.

HOW BERBERINE CAN HELP

I recommend berberine to my patients with newly diagnosed type 2 diabetes to reduce their blood sugar and prevent them from needing pharmaceutical drugs. When a diet, exercise and supplement program (including supplements such as chromium) is already helping a diabetes patient, I don't recommend that he/she switch to berberine.

Some patients are able to take berberine—and make dietary changes—and stop taking diabetes drugs altogether. People with severe diabetes can use berberine in conjunction with medication—and this combination treatment allows for fewer side effects and better blood sugar control. I don't recommend berberine for prediabetes unless diet and exercise are not effective. Berberine is sold in health-food stores and online in tablet and capsule form. The dosage I typically recommend for all diabetes patients is 500 mg twice daily.

For patients with diabetes who want to use berberine, I recommend talking to your doctor about taking this supplement. It's also important for every patient with diabetes to participate in a comprehensive diet and exercise program.

Note that berberine helps patients with type 2 diabetes, not type 1 diabetes (in which the body does not produce enough insulin).

Pycnogenol: Natural Anti-Inflammatory Few Know About

Mark Blumenthal, founder and executive director of the American Botanical Council and editor of *Herbal Gram*, Austin, Texas. HerbalGram.org

Growing abundantly in the South of France is the French maritime pine tree…source for Pycnogenol, a special patented, clinically studied pine bark extract. New clinical research finds it effective at lowering risk factors for heart disease and controlling blood sugar in people with type 2 diabetes.

PINE BARK EXTRACT IS POTENT MEDICINE

Pycnogenol, or pine bark, is a medicine with numerous benefits, notes Mark Blumenthal, founder and executive director of the nonprofit American Botanical Council. It's theorized that pine bark's high level of inflammation-fighting antioxidant bioflavonoids, known as procyanidins (these are the same potent compounds found in fresh fruits and vegetables), should get credit for these results. *In addition to these latest findings, Blumenthal says there are a number of benefits to Pycnogenol, including...*

• **Better diabetes control.** At the University of Arizona, researchers found that people with noninsulin-dependent type 2 diabetes who took Pycnogenol for three months experienced a 17% drop in blood glucose levels. The study also suggested that Pycnogenol may protect kidney function in people with diabetes.

• **Improved circulation, blood pressure and cardiovascular health.** Pycnogenol helps strengthen blood vessel walls, improve cholesterol levels and reduce the constriction of arteries, platelet stickiness and clotting that can lead to heart attack or stroke. In the University of Arizona trial, participants—who had mild high blood pressure as well as type 2 diabetes —were able to reduce their antihypertensive medication by 50%.

• **Less leg and ankle swelling on long flights.** In 2005, a study published in *Clinical and Applied Thrombosis/Hemostasis* demonstrated that Pycnogenol reduced edema (leg and ankle swelling) and the risk of deep vein thrombosis (DVT) on long-distance flights of seven to 12 hours. DVT—the formation of a blood clot, usually in the leg—is a dangerous condition, since if the clot breaks loose and travels to the lung, it can cause a potentially fatal pulmonary embolism.

• **Reduced joint pain.** In a study at Italy's Chieti-Pescara University, people with osteoarthritis of the knee took 100 mg of Pycnogenol daily for three months. Participants who took the pine bark extract experienced about a 50% decrease in osteoarthritis symptoms. They were able to lower their dosage of NSAIDs (nonsteroidal anti-inflammatory drugs, e.g., aspirin) by 58%.

• **Fewer menopausal symptoms.** Taiwanese researchers found that perimenopausal women who took Pycnogenol for several months experienced improvements in symptoms such as headaches, fatigue and vaginal dryness. With natural anti-inflammatory properties, this extract may also be helpful in controlling menstrual pain.

• **Other benefits.** More than 200 scientific studies have been conducted on French maritime pine extract—most of them on Pycnogenol—and research suggests that it may aid in the treatment of other disorders such as asthma, erectile dysfunction and other conditions.

DEMONSTRATED SAFETY AND EFFECTIVENESS

Pycnogenol is a well-researched botanical medicine with demonstrated safety and efficacy in study after study at the prescribed doses, says Blumenthal. Consult a physician trained in botanical medicine to determine what dosage best meets your specific medical needs. To prevent any minor stomach discomfort, it's best to take Pycnogenol with or after meals... and, as we always recommend, with doctor oversight.

Which Exercises Can Help Lower Your Blood Sugar?

John P. Porcari, PhD, program director of the Clinical Exercise Physiology (CEP) program at the University of Wisconsin–La Crosse. A past president of the American Association of Cardiovascular and Pulmonary Rehabilitation, he has authored or coauthored more than 350 abstracts and 150 papers on exercise physiology.

Everyone agrees that exercise is good for you. The goal for most people should be at least 150 minutes of moderate aerobic activity a week, plus strength training two days a week, according to the Centers for Disease Control and Prevention.

But what if you have a chronic condition, such as diabetes, that makes exercise difficult—or raises your concern about injury?

While exercise is helpful for most chronic health problems, some activities are likely to be easier, more beneficial and less risky than others.* *Best workout if you have diabetes…*

•**All aerobic exercises are beneficial, but those that use both your upper- and lower-body muscles are best** because they help deliver blood glucose to muscle cells throughout your body—try an elliptical machine, the Schwinn Airdyne (a stationary bike that adds arm movements) or NuStep (a recumbent stepper that incorporates arm movements). If you walk, use poles to involve your arms. Try to do some type of exercise every day—this helps ensure its blood sugar–lowering benefits.

Recent finding: Exercise can lower blood sugar almost as well as medication. Recent guidelines for people with diabetes recommend 150 minutes of moderate to strenuous aerobic exercise weekly, in addition to three strength-training sessions that work all the major muscle groups—increasing muscle mass is believed to be a particularly effective way of controlling blood sugar.

•**If you use insulin on a regular schedule**—exercise at the same time each day, if possible, to help maintain even, predictable blood sugar levels. Insulin should typically be used 60 to 90 minutes after your workout—check with your doctor or diabetes educator.

•**To prevent excessive drops in blood sugar**—eat something before or just after exercise and adjust your insulin dose on the days you work out. Talk to your doctor for specific advice.

*Always talk to your doctor before starting a new exercise program. If you have a chronic illness, it may be useful to consult a physical therapist for advice on exercise dos and don'ts for your particular situation.

How to Balance Antioxidants and Blood Sugar

Michael Ristow, MD, professor, Department for Human Nutrition, University of Jena, Germany.

Seth Baum, MD, medical director of Preventive Cardiology Inc. in Boca Raton, Florida, and author of *The Total Guide to a Healthy Heart.* VitalRemedyMD.com

Robin Jeep, chef, life coach and coauthor of *The Super Antioxidant Diet and Nutrition Guide.*

True to their name, antioxidants are nutrients that fight oxidation, the rustlike cellular injury that fuels the advance of many chronic diseases, including diabetes.

But recent studies show that taking a nutritional supplement containing antioxidants such as vitamins C, E and beta-carotene might actually harm people with diabetes. Or at least not help.

NEWEST RESEARCH

Blocking the benefits of exercise. Researchers from Germany studied 39 healthy young men, dividing them into two groups. All the men exercised 85 minutes, five days a week, for four weeks. During those four weeks, one group of men took a daily supplement with vitamin C (1,000 milligrams [mg]) and vitamin E (400 IU), and one group didn't.

After four weeks, the men who didn't take the antioxidant supplement had a beneficial increase in insulin sensitivity—the ability of the hormone insulin to move glucose out of the bloodstream and into muscle and fat cells. But the men who took the antioxidant supplement had a decrease in insulin sensitivity—and therefore a possibly higher risk of developing diabetes. The researchers theorize that exercise-caused bursts of oxidation are good for the body, improving insulin sensitivity. But antioxidant supplements block that beneficial effect of exercise, and "may harm glucose metabolism," says Michael Ristow, MD, the study leader.

No protection from diabetes. Researchers from the Harvard School of Public Health studied more than 8,000 women over age 40 with heart disease or risk factors for heart disease.

They divided the women into several groups. One group took a vitamin C supplement (500 mg a day), one took a vitamin E supplement (600 IU every other day) and one took a beta-carotene supplement (50 mg, every other day). Another three groups took placebos.

Overall, the study showed "no significant effects" of any of the three nutrients on the risk of developing diabetes, say the researchers in the *American Journal of Clinical Nutrition* (*AJCN*).

No protection from metabolic syndrome. In that same issue of *AJCN*, researchers from France reported another set of anti-antioxidant findings.

They studied more than 5,000 people, dividing them into two groups. One group took an antioxidant supplement (containing vitamins C, E and beta-carotene, and the minerals zinc and selenium). The other group didn't.

After seven years, the researchers found the supplements provided no protection against metabolic syndrome—the gang of risk factors for diabetes that includes insulin resistance, extra belly fat, low "good" HDL cholesterol, high triglycerides (a blood fat) and high blood pressure.

These results "are consistent with recent reports of a lack of efficacy of antioxidant supplements," say the researchers.

BALANCING ANTI- AND PRO-OXIDANTS

"There is a delicate balance in our bodies between antioxidants and pro-oxidants," says Seth Baum, MD, medical director of Preventive Cardiology Inc. in Boca Raton, Florida, and author of *The Total Guide to a Healthy Heart*. "On the one hand, pro-oxidants—the so-called free radicals we read so much about—are necessary to fight off infections and heal injuries. On the other hand, antioxidants are necessary to keep excessive pro-oxidant activity in check.

"An intricate biochemical network maintains this balance. But taking high doses of antioxidants in a nutritional supplement may destabilize that network.

"However, antioxidants are important in maintaining and improving health—every doctor and scientist knows that."

Here is the advice Dr. Baum gives his patients to help them get the right amount of antioxidants…

• **Don't take a high-dose antioxidant supplement.** Instead, take a multivitamin-mineral supplement that includes 100% of the Daily Value (DV) of antioxidants (vitamins C, E and beta-carotene and the minerals zinc and selenium).

• **For complete confidence, take an antioxidant test.** For patients who want the most accurate picture of their antioxidant status, Dr. Baum recommends the Spectrox antioxidant test. "It provides the most accurate picture of your antioxidant activity—not just your blood level of antioxidants. If your antioxidant activity is low, your physician can recommend an antioxidant supplement—because you actually need to take it," he says.

Your doctor can find out more about the Sprectrox test at *www.spectracell.com*.

• **Eat more antioxidant-rich food.** Dr. Baum counsels all his patients to increase their antioxidant intake from food. "The way to achieve a healthy level of antioxidants isn't by taking a pill," he says. "It's by increasing your daily intake of antioxidant-rich vegetables and fruits, which deliver a natural balance of these nutrients. Eat a wide range of vegetables and fruits, of many colors—for example, leafy greens, blueberries, yellow corn, oranges and red peppers."

"For the maximum daily intake of antioxidants, try to eat three to five cups of fresh salad, three cups of cooked vegetables and four to five servings of fruit," advises Robin Jeep, coauthor of *The Super Antioxidant Diet and Nutrition Guide*. Jeep points out that whole grains, legumes and nuts and seeds are also loaded with antioxidants.

"Eating an abundance of natural whole plant foods loaded with antioxidants gives you the ability to reclaim your health," she says.

Red flag: If you have prediabetes or diabetes, both Jeep and Dr. Baum caution against eating too many high-sugar fruits, such as bananas, watermelons, pineapples, kiwis and mangos.

"Snack" on This for High Blood Sugar Control

Monique Francois, doctoral candidate, exercise metabolism, nutrition and type 2 diabetes, The University of British Columbia, Canada. Ms. Francois was formerly a teaching fellow and research assistant at the School of Physical Education, Sport and Exercise Sciences, University of Otago, Dunedin, New Zealand, where this study was done as part of her master's degree. Her study was published in *Diabetologia*.

Remember when your mom would snap "No snacks!" before mealtime because it would "ruin" your appetite? It stands to reason that if you eat a rich snack before a meal, you either won't eat your meal, replacing nutritious meal calories with empty snack calories, or you will gobble down both the snack and the meal.

But what if the idea of "snack" were redefined? What if a snack right before meals could help you regulate your blood sugar and prevent cardiovascular disease? You'd stock up on that snack, wouldn't you? Well, such a snack actually exists, but it's not something you eat…it's something you do. It's a quick, easy, short burst of exercise right before meals, dubbed an "exercise snack."

If you're shaking your head, thinking, what kind of gimmick is this, clearly, it's a gimmick to get you to exercise. And it works! Although exercise and diet are proven to prevent type 2 diabetes and related heart disease, less than 10% of Americans get the exercise they need, often saying they do not have the time. How to get folks to make the time—and figuring out exactly how much time they need and whether shortcuts can do the trick—have been areas of study for researchers.

So a team from the School of Physical Education, Sport and Exercise Sciences at the University of Otago in New Zealand co-opted the catchy phrase "exercise snack" to refer to a much less catchy but more technically descriptive term…high-intensity interval training. That's a few brief minutes of intensive exercise, such as fitness walking, running or resistance training. "Exercise snack" was coined by Harvard cardiologist L. Howard Hartley, MD,

in 2007 in a column he wrote for *Newsweek* to define quick bursts of calorie-burning ordinary activity, such as pacing while talking on the phone or taking the stairs instead of the elevator. Studies have shown that exercise snacking in the form of high-intensity interval training is as effective as longer workouts for keeping fit and that it improves glucose control.

The researchers set off to see whether their idea of an exercise snack could help keep blood sugar from "spiking"—a problem among folks with diabetes and prediabetes whereby blood sugar goes way up after meals. Spiking is directly related to diabetes-associated cardiovascular disease, so prevention is a high priority.

The New Zealand study was small, including seven men and two women who had either prediabetes or newly diagnosed diabetes. The participants all practiced three different exercise regimens, each for five days with a break in between, to examine the impact of each regimen on blood sugar after meals.

One regimen, regarded as a traditional workout regimen, had participants do 30 minutes of moderate-intensity treadmill walking before their evening meals. Another regimen—referred to as an exercise snack—had participants do only six minutes of treadmill walking, alternating one minute at an intensive pace followed by one minute at a slow pace, a half hour before breakfast, lunch and dinner. The third exercise regimen, also a six-minute exercise snack done half an hour before each meal, involved alternating intensive one-minute walks with one-minute resistance exercises that worked the arms, back and core.

A QUICKIE IS BETTER!

The researchers found that a person doesn't have to huff and puff for 30 minutes a day to keep blood sugar in check—a few minutes of intensive exercise before meals was better in preventing blood sugar from spiking. Exercise snacking (either kind described above) before breakfast reduced postmeal blood sugar by an average 17%. Although exercise snacking before lunch didn't have much of an effect on blood sugar levels, exercise snacking before dinner reduced it by an average 13%. In comparison, the 30-minute daily workout had no effect on postmeal blood sugar.

"First and most important, exercise snacks are more time-efficient," said lead researcher and doctoral candidate Monique Francois. "Running an hour or two every day can help reduce blood sugar spikes after meals, but doing this is not feasible for most people. Short, intense exercise done right before a meal gives the same benefit."

HOW TO "EXERCISE SNACK"

You don't have to invest in a treadmill or buy any exercise gear to exercise snack, said Francois. If you want to do it as part of a regimen for blood sugar control, simply take a quick, brisk walk before mealtime. For blood sugar control or simply overall fitness, Francois echoed the advice that Dr. Hartley gave in his *Newsweek* article back in 2007: Rather than driving all the way to a destination, bike, jog or walk at a moderate to fast pace either part or all the way—and take the stairs instead of an elevator or escalator when you can. Francois cautioned, though, that people with health conditions such as diabetes should discuss exercise routines with their doctors before they start them to get guidance about doing them safely and effectively. This is one case in which, instead of doing strenuous, time-consuming exercise—which many people are likely to skip precisely because it seems so onerous—giving it all you've got for a few quick minutes brings better health results. So snack away!

Vitamin K Ko's Diabetes

Vitamin K protects men against diabetes by reducing insulin resistance—a major factor in the development of type 2 diabetes.

Recent finding: Men who took 500 micrograms (mcg) of vitamin K daily for 36 months were significantly less likely to develop insulin resistance. The effect was not found in women.

Good food sources of vitamin K: Cooked kale, with more than 1,000 mcg per cup… cooked spinach, 760 mcg per cup…cooked collard greens, about 700 mcg per cup.

Sarah L. Booth, PhD, associate director, Vitamin K Research Laboratory at Tufts University's Jean Mayer USDA Human Nutrition Research Center on Aging, Boston.

Omega-7: The New Omega Fat You Need

Jennifer Sygo, RD, dietitian, Cleveland Clinic Canada, Toronto. She also is the team dietitian for the Toronto Maple Leafs and Athletics Canada, and a nutrition columnist for the *Toronto Star*. JenniferSygo.com

Say omega and most people probably think of the healthful omega-3 fatty acids we generally need to get more of…or maybe the omega-6s, which we also need but tend to get way too much of. Yet lately another omega has researchers abuzz. It's omega-7—and it shows great potential for boosting health in several important ways. It even appears to help control appetite! So why hasn't it been on our radar until now? Because it's relatively uncommon in foods and scientists are just beginning to recognize its possible importance.

Jennifer Sygo, RD, a dietitian with the Cleveland Clinic Canada in Toronto, discussed the latest research on omega-7 and how we can use it to our advantage.

Omega-7s (like omega-3s and omega-6s) are fatty acids in the family of unsaturated fats. "Although much of the research has been conducted on animals, several recent human studies have shown promise," Sygo said. *For instance, omega-7 appears to…*

•**Improve insulin sensitivity, which can help protect against type 2 diabetes.**

•**Reduce inflammation in the body** (as measured through a common blood test for C-reactive protein).

• **Promote cardiovascular health** by reducing LDL "bad" cholesterol and triglycerides and smoothing artery walls.

• **Help control appetite.** A recent animal study found that, compared with rats who were fed a placebo, rats who were fed omega-7s ate significantly less—without showing any signs of ill effects. The researchers hypothesized that the omega-7s increased levels of hormones that enhance feelings of fullness and satiety.

FOOD VS. SUPPLEMENTS

The type of omega-7 that's of greatest interest when it comes to health benefits is called palmitoleic acid. While there aren't a lot of food sources, it is found in cold-water fatty fish (salmon, tuna, sardines, mackerel, trout)…macadamia nuts…and an orange-colored, grape-sized fruit called sea buckthorn berries.

What's tricky about palmitoleic acid is that, in foods, it's often found alongside a saturated fat called palmitic acid (aka palmitate or sodium palmitate). "Research suggests that palmitic acid, which is particularly abundant in palm oil but also exists in dairy foods and meats, promotes inflammation throughout the body and can ultimately contribute to heart disease, type 2 diabetes and cognitive decline over time," Sygo said.

Given that palmitic acid is not something you want to get a lot of, wouldn't it make sense to supplement with palmitoleic acid alone, rather than eat omega-7-rich foods and thus get both components? Perhaps someday—but for now, Sygo said, it's too soon to recommend omega-7 supplementation. For one thing, most of the omega-7 supplements currently on the market, such as those made from sea buckthorn berries, contain both palmitic acid and palmitoleic acid.

For another thing, unlike the isolated nutrients in supplements, foods provide a complex combination of components that may have as-yet-unappreciated benefits. For instance, sea buckthorn berries contain lots of antioxidants and 12 times as much vitamin C as oranges. Sygo added, "With foods that contain both palmitoleic acid and palmitic acid, the good effects appear to far outweigh the bad. For example, although macadamia nuts contain both acids, they've been shown to reduce cholesterol. Plus, food is always more complicated than just one or two nutrients. There are things we're only beginning to understand that exist in every food we eat, and omega-7s are a good example of that."

Researchers, including Sygo's colleagues at the Cleveland Clinic, are currently examining the effects on humans of supplements made with palmitoleic acid. So far the results are promising, but there are many questions still unanswered. Sygo explained, "We don't yet know what dosage you would need to see benefits, how much might be too much, or whether it makes a difference if you're male or female. We don't know whether omega-7 supplements would interact with certain medications or other supplements, or how people with heart disease or diabetes might respond."

Bottom line: For now, Sygo recommended, skip the omega-7 supplements and focus on boosting your intake of omega-7-rich foods. *For instance…*

• **You can add more low-mercury fish to your diet without hesitation.** The presence of omega-7s in fish may help explain something that has stymied researchers—why eating fish seems to yield more health benefits than taking omega-3 supplements. Sygo explained that, to make those supplements, manufacturers isolate the omega-3s—which means that they remove the omega-7s.

• **Have a small handful (about 10 to 12) of macadamia nuts each day.** Don't go overboard if you're watching your weight, because this size serving has about 200 calories.

• **Why not try sea buckthorn berries, too?** Various products are available online and in some health-food stores. They can be eaten in various ways—as dried berries, which have a citrusy, somewhat tropical taste…jelly…oil… or juice (if you find it tart, try blending with other juices).

Supplements That Help Manage Diabetes

Mark A. Stengler, NMD, a naturopathic medical doctor in private practice, Stengler Center for Integrative Medicine, Encinitas, California...author of many books, including *The Natural Physician's Healing Therapies* and coauthor of *Prescription for Natural Cures*.

Lifestyle change has always been the cornerstone treatment for people with type 2 diabetes. Beyond that, natural approaches are rarely discussed. Mark Stengler, NMD, author of several books on alternative health, recommends a number of plant-based remedies for those with diabetes, some of which date back hundreds, even thousands, of years...

According to Dr. Stengler, type 2 diabetes absolutely can be prevented and, in certain cases, even reversed with diet, exercise and appropriate dietary supplements. The following is some of his own "best practice" advice for prevention, maintenance and symptom management of this lifestyle-related disease.

To prevent diabetes...

•**Curb sugar cravings with gymnema sylvestre.** A staple of Ayurvedic medicine, this herb helps curb cravings for sugary foods that throw your blood glucose levels off balance. Scientists speculate that it works by positively influencing insulin-producing cells in the pancreas.

Dr. Stengler believes gymnema sylvestre works best when used in combination with other glucose-balancing herbs, such as bitter melon and fenugreek. Ask your doctor for advice on the best combination and dosage for you.

•**Chromium can normalize sugar levels.** Your body requires adequate levels of chromium to properly control blood glucose levels. This essential trace mineral aids in the uptake of blood sugar into the body's cells, where it can be used to generate energy more efficiently. It's also helpful in reducing sweet cravings.

Dr. Stengler advises up to 1,000 micrograms of chromium a day (under your physician's supervision). He adds that this is a good mineral to take with gymnema.

•**Regulate blood sugar with fiber and fiber supplements.** Soluble fiber helps prevent or control prediabetes and diabetes by slowing the rate at which intestines release glucose into the bloodstream, thus modulating fluctuations in blood sugar levels. Rich sources of soluble fiber include plant foods, such as legumes, oat bran, rye, barley, broccoli, carrots, artichokes, peas, prunes, berries and bananas. In a small study in Taiwan, scientists found that supplementation with glucomannan (a soluble dietary fiber made from konjac flour) lowered elevated levels of blood lipids, cholesterol and glucose in people with diabetes.

Most Americans eat too much junk food and too little fiber. For his patients who fall into that category, Dr. Stengler typically prescribes one glucomannan capsule 30 minutes before lunch and dinner, and another before bedtime with a large glass of water.

Managing symptoms and minimizing complications...

•**Boost antioxidant levels with alpha-lipoic acid.** This powerful antioxidant kills free radicals that damage cells and cause pain, inflammation, burning, tingling and numbness in people who have peripheral neuropathy (nerve damage) caused by diabetes. Studies also suggest that alpha-lipoic acid (ALA) enables the body to utilize glucose more efficiently.

Dr. Stengler says to take alpha-lipoic acid daily under a physician's supervision.

•**Decrease blood glucose levels with chamomile tea.** Drinking chamomile tea, a rich source of antioxidants, may help prevent diabetes complications, such as blindness, nerve damage and kidney problems, according to recent research by UK and Japanese scientists.

Drink chamomile tea along with antioxidant-rich black, white and green teas, says Dr. Stengler.

•**Take omega-3 fatty acids to reduce inflammation.** These healthy fats improve the body's ability to respond to insulin, reduce inflammation, lower blood lipids and prevent excessive blood clotting. Good dietary sources of omega-3 fatty acids include cold-water fish, such as salmon or cod (eat two or three times a week), olive or canola oil, flaxseed and English walnuts.

Dr. Stengler's advice: Unless you know you are getting sufficient omega-3 fatty acids in your diet, it's good to take a daily fish oil supplement that contains about 1,000 mg of the omega-3 fatty acid eicosapentaenoic acid (EPA) and about 500 mg of the omega-3 fatty acid docosahexaenoic acid (DHA).

Caution: Because many dietary supplements lower blood sugar, and fish oil supplements may alter the way anticoagulant therapy functions, it is critical to work closely with your doctor before and while taking any of the above supplements. He/she will prescribe the right doses for you and also may suggest that you alter other medications accordingly.

DON'T NEGLECT THE ABCS OF DIABETES SELF-CARE

When addressing a difficult disease such as diabetes, all the nutrients and vitamins in the world will do no good if you do not also follow the basics of diabetes self-care: Maintain a healthy weight…get 20 to 30 minutes of exercise most days of the week…follow a diet that emphasizes lean proteins and healthy fats and limits simple carbohydrates…monitor blood glucose levels…and take diabetes, blood pressure and cholesterol medicine as prescribed by your physician. Dr. Stengler adds that even as simple a measure as taking a 10-minute walk after each meal can keep blood sugar under control. Start today.

How to Supercharge Your Medications

Thomas Kruzel, ND, a naturopathic physician at the Rockwood Natural Medicine Clinic in Scottsdale, Arizona. He is author of *The Homeopathic Emergency Guide.* RockwoodNaturalMedicine.com

When you get a new prescription, most doctors don't talk about dietary supplements. If a conversation does take place, it probably focuses on the potentially dangerous interactions that can occur when people take a prescription medication and a supplement.*

The other side of the story: While some supplements can cause dangerous interactions with certain drugs, the reverse is also true—certain supplements can actually boost the effectiveness of a prescription drug and/or reduce its side effects. In some cases, this beneficial effect may allow you to take a lower dose of the drug…or even discontinue it at some point.

DRUG-BOOSTING SUPPLEMENTS

If you are interested in using a supplement as part of a medication regimen, always discuss this with your doctor. Medical supervision is necessary to ensure that you are using the combination safely.

Medication-supplement pairings that often work well…

•**Diabetes medication and alpha-lipoic acid.** Alpha-lipoic acid is an endogenous (made in the body) antioxidant that helps transform blood sugar (glucose) into energy. It is found in foods such as red meat and liver, though it is difficult to get enough from food to work effectively with your medication for type 2 diabetes.

When taken in the larger doses that are found in supplements, alpha-lipoic acid lowers blood sugar and may reduce pain, itching and other symptoms caused by diabetes-related nerve damage (neuropathy). For diabetic neuropathy, I typically recommend 400 milligrams (mg) to 500 mg of alpha-lipoic acid, twice daily. For general antioxidant benefit, 100 mg to 300 mg daily is usually sufficient.

If you're taking a diabetes medication that lowers blood sugar, such as *metformin* (Glucophage) or *glyburide* (DiaBeta), the addition of alpha-lipoic acid may allow you to use a smaller drug dose. If your glucose levels are stabilized through diet and regular exercise (without medication), you may want to take alpha-lipoic acid indefinitely.

Caution: Taking too much alpha-lipoic acid with a diabetes drug could lead to excessively low blood sugar, which can cause

*To see if a drug you have been prescribed may interact with a supplement you are taking, ask your doctor. You can also go to *www.medlineplus.gov* and click on "Drugs & Supplements."

anxiety, sweating, shakiness and/or confusion. Alpha-lipoic acid also may interact with chemotherapy drugs and thyroid medication such as *levothyroxine* (Synthroid). Talk to your doctor before taking alpha-lipoic acid with any prescription medication.

PGX Combats Diabetes and Weight Gain

Mark A. Stengler, NMD, naturopathic medical doctor, Encinitas, California...former adjunct associate clinical professor at the National University of Natural Medicine, Portland, Oregon...and author of many books, including *The Natural Physician's Healing Therapies*.

A fiber-blend supplement called PolyGly-copleX (PGX) not only prevents constipation, it also reduces diabetes risk and helps control appetite.

PGX is a trademarked blend of three natural sources of fiber—glucomannan from the root of the Asian konjac plant...sodium alginate from seaweed...and xanthan gum from a fermented sugar. Although each softgel capsule of PGX provides just 750 mg of fiber, its three viscous (sticky and gel-like) components work synergistically to bind hundreds of times their combined weight in water. In practical terms, one PGX softgel produces the same bulk as a bowl of oatmeal. *Here's what PGX can do for you...*

DIABETES PROTECTION AND MORE

PGX was developed by Vladimir Vuksan, PhD, and colleagues at the University of Toronto. Dr. Vuksan is a renowned expert on the role of diet in the development of diabetes and heart disease. He led the team that developed the glycemic index (GI)—a ranking system on a scale of 0 to 100 that indicates the effect specific foods have on blood glucose levels, with higher numbers representing more pronounced spikes (and consequent drops) in blood sugar.

After their GI breakthrough, these same researchers went looking for a way to blend fibers.

Their goal: To promote more stable—and therefore more healthful—blood glucose levels, as well as improved insulin sensitivity (ability of the body's cells to respond to the hormone insulin). Such a substance, they knew, would especially benefit people who had, or were at risk for, diabetes. PGX was the result. *Study findings...*

• **When subjects with metabolic syndrome (a prediabetic condition) took a standard dose of PGX for three weeks,** their average after-meal blood glucose levels fell by 23% and their blood insulin levels fell by 35%—indicating significantly better blood sugar control. A placebo group had no improvement. Also, among PGX users, body fat was reduced by 2.8% after three weeks, compared with a 1.4% reduction in the placebo group.

• **Adding PGX to a food or taking PGX before a meal can reduce the GI of that food or meal by 25% to 50%.** For example, study subjects had blood tests after eating white bread and again after eating white bread sprinkled with 5 g of PGX. The plain bread had a GI of 69—but the bread with PGX had a GI of 37.

PGX AND APPETITE SUPPRESSION

I interviewed Michael Murray, ND, director of product science and innovation at Natural Factors Nutritional Products, a supplement manufacturer in British Columbia. Working with Michael Lyon, MD, medical and research director of the Canadian Center for Functional Medicine, Dr. Murray turned PGX from a laboratory-produced mix into a viable commercial product.

Drs. Murray and Lyon had come across PGX while researching a book on how to prevent and treat diabetes with natural medicine. Experiment: The doctors monitored blood sugar levels for 24 hours in more than 100 overweight and/or diabetic people. Participants' blood sugar levels fluctuated greatly throughout the day—rising rapidly after high-GI foods were eaten, then falling rapidly and often leaving blood sugar levels too low. Such drops in blood sugar trigger feelings of hunger. When participants were given PGX, however, blood sugar levels stabilized, allowing them significantly more appetite control.

HOW TO USE PGX

Of course, people cannot indulge in a diet of french fries and hot fudge sundaes and think that PGX will protect them from the consequences. But for my patients who work hard to maintain a healthy weight and to prevent or control diabetes, PGX helps them achieve their goals.

PGX has been available for several years in the form of meal-replacement beverages, powder to mix with water and granules to sprinkle on food. At first, some users have problems with gas, bloating and constipation or diarrhea. When this happens, I advise reducing the dosage, then slowly increasing it as the body becomes accustomed to PGX.

Recommended: A form called PGX Daily, a softgel capsule with 750 mg of PGX in a base of coconut oil, causes few if any gastrointestinal problems. *I suggest that anyone over age 12 who seeks better control of weight and/or blood glucose levels do the following…*

• **Start by taking two capsules of PGX Daily,** 15 minutes before each of your three daily meals, with 10 ounces of water. Daily total: Six capsules.

• **Over one week, work up to three capsules before each meal.**

Daily total: Nine capsules.

• **For greater appetite control, work up to as many as six capsules before each meal.**

Daily total: Up to 18 capsules.

• **After achieving the desired weight loss and/or blood sugar stabilization,** take one or two capsules of PGX Daily per day before a meal, continuing indefinitely, to help maintain results.

Caution: Before using PGX, consult your doctor if you have congestive heart failure or kidney disease, because PGX could worsen fluid retention…a gastrointestinal disorder or difficulty swallowing, because in rare cases other fiber supplements have been linked to esophageal blockage…or if you are pregnant or breast-feeding, as a general precaution.

For more information on PGX: Read *Hunger Free Forever* by Drs. Murray and Lyon.

Move Over Blueberries… Olive Leaf Extract May Be the New Star

JoAnn Yanez, ND, Yanez Consulting, Sioux Falls, South Dakota. She is an expert in health policy and integrative medicine and former vice president of the New York Association of Naturopathic Physicians.

Olive leaf (*Olea europaea*) remedies are popular in countries ranging from Greece and Italy to Australia and New Zealand and in Africa. Leaves from olive trees contain flavonoid polyphenols such as *oleuropein* and *hydroxytyrosol*, which have antioxidant, antiviral, anti-inflammatory and antimicrobial effects. In fact, researchers have found that extract made from olive leaf has a greater antioxidant capacity even than other more highly touted sources, including pomegranate, blueberry, cranberry and even green tea. *Multiple studies have demonstrated olive leaf's potential in…*

• **Preventing or managing infection.** In lab and animal studies, scientists have discovered that olive leaf is effective against a wide range of bacteria, viruses, fungi and parasites—and without the worrisome side effects of antibiotics.

• **Lowering blood pressure.** In a South African study, olive leaf extract thwarted the development of severe hypertension in salt-sensitive, insulin-resistant rats.

• **Preventing heart disease.** Laboratory studies in Italy showed that olive leaf extract inhibits low-density lipoprotein (LDL) oxidation. An Australian study showed that liquid olive leaf extract (tested in vitro) has antiplatelet effects that may help prevent clots.

• **Controlling blood sugar.** Animal studies suggest that olive leaf improves sugar uptake, which may prove helpful in preventing or treating diabetes and metabolic syndrome.

THREE WAYS TO TRY IT

Olive leaf is readily available online and in health-food stores as an extract and in capsule form, as well as tea, though some find the taste bitter and unappealing.

Advice from Dr. Yanez: At the first sign of a cold or the flu, take three capsules three or four times a day…or, if you prefer the extract, drink it straight (follow the package directions for one serving) or diluted in water or juice three times a day…or drink two cups daily of olive leaf tea.

Olive leaf is generally considered safe, but as always when trying an herbal remedy, check with your doctor first. This is especially important if you have a chronic condition—olive leaf may interact with certain diabetes and blood pressure drugs, and some people are allergic to olive tree pollen and should be on the alert for hives or other signs of allergy to the extract.

Maca: The Super Food That Helps with Everything

Mark A. Stengler, NMD, naturopathic medical doctor, Encinitas, California…former adjunct associate clinical professor at the National University of Natural Medicine, Portland, Oregon…and author of many books, including *The Natural Physician's Healing Therapies.*

Super foods are foods and herbs considered to be especially healthful due to their hefty nutritional content. The list includes familiar favorites, such as blueberries, broccoli and beans. Now a more exotic super food you may never have heard of is generating excitement in the world of natural health—a Peruvian root vegetable called maca (*Lepidium meyenii* or *peruvianum*), pronounced MACK-ah.

The root of the maca is shaped like a large radish. It is a cousin to other cruciferous plants, such as cauliflower and brussels sprouts. Peruvians traditionally boil or roast the maca root or grind it into flour for baking. However, despite maca's popular description as a "super food," you won't see it in food form in this country. Instead, the root is dried and ground into a fine powder. It then is distributed primarily in capsules, although you also can buy the powder to blend into beverages or sprinkle on foods.

In addition to its healthful fiber, complex carbohydrates and protein, maca provides numerous minerals, including calcium, magnesium, phosphorous, potassium, sulfur, iron, zinc, iodine and copper…vitamins B-1, B-2, C and E…nearly 20 amino acids, including linoleic acid, palmitic acid and oleic acid…as well as various plant sterols, which are natural cholesterol-lowering agents. All of these nutrients have been shown to promote health in a multitude of ways.

Here is what this super food can do for you…

FIGHT STRESS AND DISEASE

Any kind of stress—from work, personal problems, illness, injury, toxins, hormonal imbalances or any other source—can negatively affect how our bodies function. Maca is what holistic doctors call an adaptogen, a plant or herb that boosts the body's ability to resist, deal with and recover from emotional and physical stress.

Practitioners of traditional medicine from China and India have known about and made use of adaptogens for centuries, though the term itself was not coined until the middle of the 20th century. Well-known adaptogens include the herbs ashwagandha, ginseng, rhodiola and licorice root, all of which I have prescribed to my patients with much success over the years.

How it works: To be classified as an adaptogen, a natural substance must meet specific criteria. It must be nontoxic…normalize levels of chemicals raised during periods of stress…and produce physical, chemical and/or biological responses that increase the body's resistance to stress.

Although all adaptogenic plants contain antioxidants, researchers do not believe that antioxidants alone account for adaptogens' normalizing powers. Rather, it is thought that a variety of phytochemicals helps balance the dozens of endocrine, digestive and neural hormones that operate throughout the body—including insulin (which regulates blood sugar levels) and dopamine (which enhances and stabilizes mood). Many adaptogens also stimulate immune system components, leading to better immune function.

MORE OF MACA'S SUPER POWERS

In addition to its documented beneficial effects on the human reproductive system, laboratory tests and animal studies suggest that maca may reduce the risk for...

• **Arthritis**—by promoting cartilage growth.

• **Blood toxicity**—by improving liver function.

• **Diabetes**—by allowing for better control over blood sugar levels and body weight.

• **Digestive health**—by combating ulcers.

• **Fatigue**—by increasing energy and endurance.

• **Heart disease**—by lowering levels of LDL "bad" cholesterol and triglycerides (a type of blood fat).

• **Infertility**—by stimulating production of estrogen and other hormones in women and boosting sperm count in men.

• **Memory and mood**—by enhancing certain brain chemicals.

• **Osteoporosis**—by increasing bone density.

• **Premenstrual syndrome (PMS)**—by regulating hormone levels.

• **Prostate problems**—by reducing prostate enlargement.

THE SAFEST WAY TO START

Maca generally appears to be safe, given its long history of use by Peruvians...but there are a few guidelines to bear in mind. Women who take estrogen to ease menopausal symptoms should talk to their doctors about using maca. They may be able to wean off hormone therapy or at least lower the estrogen dosage under a doctor's supervision.

Breast cancer patients taking tamoxifen or other estrogen blockers and women who have had breast cancer must not use maca, because it raises estrogen levels. Women in a family with a strong history of breast cancer should discuss maca use with their doctors first. People who take thyroid medication should be monitored by their doctors because maca may increase thyroid activity. Women who are pregnant or breast-feeding should not take maca, as a general precaution.

Since its long-term effects have not been scientifically studied, I recommend taking a break from maca now and then in order to give the body's cell receptors a break from any hormone stimulation. People who want to try maca to see if it is a "super food" for them should take supplements for three months (six months for women with severe menopausal symptoms), then stop using maca for one or two weeks. They may then continue this regimen as needed for symptom relief.

HOW MUCH TO TAKE

Maca is available in supplement and powder form. The average dose of maca supplements is 1,000 mg to 2,000 mg daily—which you can take with or without food at any time of day.

Or you can get your maca by adding powder to your favorite foods and drinks. It has a slightly nutty flavor, so you may enjoy mixing it with almond milk. *Other ways to incorporate maca into your diet...*

• **Sprinkle on cereal (hot or cold).**

• **Mix into your favorite smoothie or protein shake.**

• **Add to yogurt or applesauce, perhaps with a little cinnamon.**

• **Stir into tea**—especially chai blends, as the flavors complement each other.

• **Use in baking**—substitute maca powder for one-quarter of the flour in any recipe (no more, or it might affect texture or consistency).

Be aware: Maca powder has a high fiber content and may initially cause gassiness. I suggest beginning with one teaspoon a day, then gradually increasing your intake by one teaspoon every five days until you find your comfort zone. The optimum dosage is three to six teaspoons daily.

HOW TO GET YOUR MACA

I recommend organically grown maca products from Natural Health International, or NHI (888-668-3661, *www.naturalhi.com*, available online or through naturopathic doctors). The company sells a blend for women called Femenessence Macapause (the same blend used in the study of Polish women, who experienced significant improvement in their menopausal symptoms) and another for men, Revolution

Unfinished business

Macalibrium, formulated to enhance energy and vitality in men as they age.

Cost: $35 to $38 for 120 capsules of 500 mg each. The average dosage of maca supplements is 1,000 mg to 2,000 mg daily, which you can take anytime.

You can also sprinkle maca powder into your favorite foods and drinks. The powder costs about $17/pound and is available online from *www.superorganicfoods.com* and *www.iberb.com*.

Real Help from Hypnosis

Bruce N. Eimer, PhD, a clinical psychologist and hypnotherapist in private practice in Huntingdon Valley, Pennsylvania. He is a fellow and approved consultant of the American Society of Clinical Hypnosis. Dr. Eimer is also author of *Hypnotize Yourself Out of Pain Now!* and coauthor, with C. Roy Hunter, of *The Art of Hypnotic Regression Therapy.* BruceEimer.com

Hypnosis is best known for helping with weight loss and tobacco addiction. But research now shows that it also can be used for such conditions as irritable bowel syndrome (IBS), gastroesophageal reflux disease (GERD), high blood pressure and diabetes to help relieve symptoms and reduce one's need for medication.

WHAT IS HYPNOSIS?

The main idea behind hypnosis is that the mind and body work together and cannot be separated. Unconscious negative thought patterns and unresolved emotions can cause physical and mental illness…and the subconscious mind can be used to help resolve these issues.

During hypnosis, the doorway to the subconscious mind is opened. In this state, suggestibility heightens, mental absorption increases, senses become more acute and the imagination communicates with the subconscious to create change.

Hypnosis is not meant to replace standard medical treatment, but it can enhance the effectiveness of traditional treatment methods, including medication and surgery, for many conditions. In addition, it's simple, safe, effective and has no side effects.

RECENT DEVELOPMENTS

Research has demonstrated the effectiveness of hypnosis in reducing blood pressure in individuals with hypertension and blood sugar levels in people with diabetes. Recent research has also found that hypnosis is an effective treatment for hot flashes in postmenopausal women.

HOW HYPNOSIS WORKS

Unlike modern treatments, such as cognitive behavioral therapy, which require patients to consciously shift negative thought patterns, hypnosis bypasses the thinking mind and relies on the subconscious to relay messages.

The therapist induces a trance by having the patient focus on a single object such as a flickering candle…a sound such as a ticking clock…or a physical sensation such as breathing. The therapist then leads the patient into a peaceful, twilight state through relaxation and breathing exercises. This state awakens the imagination and produces heightened suggestibility. The therapist then can implant carefully selected suggestions in the patient's subconscious mind, which accepts these suggestions as already fact, and the new behavior becomes automatic.

Example: For a patient who suffers from panic attacks, a hypnotherapist would induce a trance state and suggest specific posthypnotic cues (actions, thoughts, words or images that will trigger a desired response after hypnosis). The patient can use these posthypnotic cues in his/her everyday, waking life to achieve a calm state on his own.

During the trance state, the hypnotherapist might say: "Whenever you feel anxious, you'll notice and feel the ring on your finger and take a slow, deep breath. This will make you feel grounded, safe and secure."

In general, people who can visualize, daydream or imagine can be hypnotized. The number of sessions needed depends on the person and his specific situation. Some people solve a problem after one session. For others, it takes longer. Patients typically have five sessions that last about 50 minutes to one hour each.

Each session with a licensed health professional trained in hypnotherapy related to the patient's specific problem costs about $150 to $300. Even though there is significant research-backed evidence supporting the use of hypnosis and hypnotherapy, they often are considered "alternative" or "complementary" therapies and are rarely covered by medical or mental health insurance. However, some hospital-based pain-management centers do provide insurance-covered hypnosis.

Caution: Anyone can call himself a "certified hypnotherapist" or "clinical hypnotist." Most states don't regulate the practice of hypnosis. Choose a licensed health professional—a psychologist, psychiatrist, medical doctor or clinical social worker—whom you trust and feel safe and comfortable with.

To find a qualified clinical hypnotherapist, contact the American Society of Clinical Hypnosis (ASCH) at 630-980-4740 or *www.asch. net.*

DO IT YOURSELF

After you have successfully entered a hypnotic state in a clinician's office, a qualified hypnotherapist can teach you self-hypnosis. Used regularly, self-hypnosis gives you the ability to relax at will, builds your capacity to control your mind and body and furthers the process of positive change.

How self-hypnosis works: First, choose one or two suggestions to repeat to yourself four or five times during self-hypnosis.

Examples: For high blood pressure, you might repeat, I stay relaxed as I complete my daily responsibilities...for pain you might say, I can manage discomfort.

The next step is to put yourself into a trance, which allows you to enter a state of heightened suggestibility. This can be done by focusing your complete attention on something (as described earlier). Then your focus can move to your breathing. Feel your belly expand on inhalation and contract on exhalation.

To relax more deeply, imagine slowly walking down a set of 20 stairs. Feel the soft carpet under your feet, the smooth, polished wood of the handrail. With each step, your relaxation deepens. At the bottom of the stairs, you find a door. You open it and enter a place where you feel happy, content, safe and comfortable. Maybe it's a balmy beach, cool meadow or favorite room. Notice the specific details of this "favorite place."

Once you master this deep relaxation, use positive suggestions and positive imagery to help change undesirable attitudes and behaviors and limiting beliefs. When you're ready to emerge from this hypnotic state, walk back up the stairs and into the present moment.

WHEN TO TRY HYPNOSIS...

Research shows hypnosis helps the following conditions and more...

- **Addictions**
- **Allergies and asthma**
- **Anxiety and stress**
- **Diabetes**
- **Gastrointestinal and other digestive disorders**
- **High blood pressure**
- **Hot flashes**
- **Insomnia**
- **Pain**
- **Phobias**
- **Skin conditions**
- **Weight gain**

6

Manage Your Diabetes

Stay-Well Secrets for People with Diabetes or Prediabetes

Many people downplay the seriousness of diabetes. That's a mistake. Because elevated glucose can damage blood vessels, nerves, the kidneys and eyes, people with diabetes are much more likely to die from heart disease and/or kidney disease than people without diabetes—and they are at increased risk for infections, including gum disease, as well as blindness and amputation. (Nerve damage and poor circulation can allow dangerous infections to go undetected.)

And diabetes can be sneaky—increased thirst, urination and/or hunger are the most common symptoms, but many people have no symptoms and are unaware that they are sick.

Despite these sobering facts, doctors rarely have time to give their patients all the information they need to cope with the complexities of diabetes. Fortunately, diabetes educators—health-care professionals, such as registered nurses, registered dietitians and medical social workers—can give patients practical advice on the best ways to control their condition.*

Good news: Most health insurers, including Medicare, cover the cost of diabetes patients' visits with a diabetes educator.

SAVVY EATING HABITS

Most doctors advise people with diabetes or prediabetes to cut back on refined carbohydrates, such as cakes and cookies, and eat more fruits, vegetables and whole grains. This maximizes nutrition and promotes a healthy body weight (being overweight greatly increases diabetes risk). *Other steps to take…*

*To find a diabetes educator near you, consult the American Association of Diabetes Educators, 800-338-3633, *www.diabeteseducator.org*.

Theresa Garnero, advanced practice registered nurse (APRN), certified diabetes educator (CDE) and former clinical nurse manager of the Center for Diabetes Services at the California Pacific Medical Center in San Francisco. She is author of *Your First Year with Diabetes: What to Do, Month by Month.*

• **Drink one extra glass of water each day.** The extra fluid will help prevent dehydration, which can raise glucose levels.

• **Never skip meals—especially breakfast.** Don't assume that bypassing a meal and fasting for more than five to six hours will help lower glucose levels. It actually triggers the liver to release glucose into the bloodstream.

Better strategy: Eat three small meals daily and have snacks in between. Start with breakfast, such as a cup of low-fat yogurt and whole-wheat toast with peanut butter or a small bowl of whole-grain cereal and a handful of nuts.

Good snack options: A small apple or three graham crackers. Each of these snacks contains about 15 g of carbohydrates.

• **Practice the "plate method."** Divide a nine-inch plate in half. Fill half with vegetables, then split the other half into quarters—one for protein, such as salmon, lean meat, beans or tofu…and the other for starches, such as one-third cup of pasta or one-half cup of peas or corn. Then have a small piece of fruit. This is an easy way to practice portion control—and get the nutrients you need.

Ask yourself if you are satisfied after you take each bite. If the answer is "yes," stop eating. This simple strategy helped one of my clients lose 50 pounds.

• **Be wary of "sugar-free" foods.** These products, including sugar-free cookies and diabetic candy, often are high in carbohydrates, which are the body's primary source of glucose. You may be better off eating the regular product, which is more satisfying. Compare the carbohydrate contents on product labels.

GET CREATIVE WITH EXERCISE

If you have diabetes or prediabetes, you've probably been told to get more exercise. Walking is especially helpful. For those with diabetes, walking for at least two hours a week has been shown to reduce the risk for death by 30% over an eight-year period. For those with prediabetes, walking for 30 minutes five days a week reduces by about 60% the risk that your condition will progress to diabetes. *But if you'd like some other options, consider…***

**Consult your doctor before starting a new exercise program.

• **Armchair workouts.** These exercises, which are performed while seated and are intended for people with physical limitations to standing, increase stamina, muscle tone, flexibility and coordination. For DVDs, go to *www.armchairfitness.com* or call 202-882-0974.

• **Strength training.** This type of exercise builds muscle, which burns more calories than fat even when you are not exercising.*** Use hand weights, exercise machines or the weight of your own body—for example, leg squats or bicep curls with no weights. Aim for two to three sessions of strength training weekly, on alternate days.

• **Stretching**—even while watching TV or talking on the phone. By building a stretching routine into your daily activities, you won't need to set aside a separate time to do it. If your body is flexible, it's easier to perform other kinds of physical activity. Stretching also promotes better circulation. Before stretching, do a brief warm-up, such as walking for five minutes and doing several arm windmills. Aim to do stretching exercises at least three times weekly, including before your other workouts.

CONTROL YOUR BLOOD GLUCOSE

If you are diagnosed with diabetes, blood glucose control is the immediate goal. Self-monitoring can be performed using newer devices that test blood glucose levels.

Good choices: LifeScan's OneTouch Ultra…, Bayer's Contour…or Abbott Laboratories' FreeStyle.

The hemoglobin A1C test, which is ordered by your doctor and typically is done two to four times a year, determines how well glucose levels have been controlled over the previous two to three months.

If you have prediabetes: Don't settle for a fasting glucose test, which measures blood glucose after you have fasted overnight. It misses two-thirds of all cases of diabetes. The oral glucose tolerance test (OGTT), which involves testing glucose immediately before drinking a premixed glass of glucose and repeating the test two hours later, is more reliable. If you

***If you have high blood pressure, be sure to check with your doctor before starting a strength-training program—this type of exercise can raise blood pressure.

can't get an OGTT, ask for an A1C test and fasting glucose test.

If you have diabetes or prediabetes, you should have your blood pressure and cholesterol checked at every doctor visit and schedule regular eye exams and dental appointments. *In addition, don't overlook…*

• **Proper kidney testing.** Doctors most commonly recommend annual microalbumin and creatinine urine tests to check for kidney disease. You also may want to ask for a glomerular filtration rate test, which measures kidney function.

• **Meticulous foot care.** High glucose levels can reduce sensation in your feet, making it hard to know when you have a cut, blister or injury. In addition to seeing a podiatrist at least once a year and inspecting your own feet daily, be wary of everyday activities that can be dangerous for people with diabetes.

Stepping into hot bath water, for example, can cause a blister or skin damage that can become infected. To protect yourself, check the water temperature on your wrist or elbow before you step in. The temperature should be warm to the touch—not hot.

STAY UP TO DATE ON MEDICATIONS

Once diabetes medication has been prescribed, people with diabetes should review their drug regimen with their doctors at every visit. *Insulin is the most commonly used diabetes drug, but you may want to also ask your doctor about these relatively new medications…*

• **DPP-4 inhibitors.** These drugs include *sitagliptin* (Januvia), which lowers glucose levels by increasing the amount of insulin secreted by the pancreas. DPP-4 inhibitors are used alone or with another type of diabetes medication.

• **Symlin.** Administered with an injectable pen, *pramlintide* (Symlin) helps control blood glucose and reduces appetite, which may help with weight loss. It is used in addition to insulin.

If you have prediabetes or diabetes: Always consult a pharmacist or doctor before taking any over-the-counter products. Cold medicines with a high sugar content may raise your blood glucose, for example, and wart removal products may cause skin ulcers. Pay close attention to drug label warnings.

Big Mistakes Most People with Diabetes Make…and the Right Ways to Stay Healthy

Richard K. Bernstein, MD, a diabetes specialist in private practice in Mamaroneck, New York. Dr. Bernstein is also author of several books on diabetes, including Dr. Bernstein's Diabetes Solution: A Complete Guide to Achieving Normal Blood Sugars. His free monthly teleseminars are available at AskDrBernstein. net.

If you have diabetes, you may think that you are taking all the right steps with your diet, medication and exercise habits.

But the truth is, virtually all people with this common disease make mistakes in managing their condition—and unknowingly increase their risk for diabetes complications, such as heart attack, stroke, kidney failure and blindness.

Small changes can give big results: Fortunately, you can correct these missteps if you understand some of the subtle aspects of diabetes that can easily derail one's care.

Guerrilla tactics that really work: Richard K. Bernstein, MD, an outspoken diabetes specialist, was diagnosed himself with type 1 diabetes at age 12, and remains vigorous and healthy at 80. He swears by the sometimes unconventional but highly effective approach that he has developed and adopted for himself and the thousands of patients with type 1 and type 2 diabetes he has treated.

Here's where Dr. Bernstein thinks people with diabetes—and many mainstream medical authorities—often get it wrong…

Mistake: **Not recognizing hidden causes of elevated blood sugar.** Acute stress—such as a fight with your boss or anxiety about a key presentation—can raise it. If your glucose

161

reading is higher than expected when you're stressed, an injection of rapid-acting insulin will bring it down if you have type 1 diabetes. If you have type 2, your own insulin secretions will likely lower blood sugar within 24 hours.

Infection raises blood sugar levels—and high blood sugar increases infection risk. Suspect infection if your glucose level is up and insulin isn't working as well as usual. Get prompt treatment so that your blood sugar will go down and the infection will heal. Beware of dental infections and gum disease.

What I do: I brush twice daily, floss after meals and get tartar and plaque scrapings from a periodontist every three months.

Mistake: **Using the wrong glucose meter.** Whether you inject insulin for type 1 diabetes or take oral drugs for type 2, or control your disease with diet and exercise alone, you must accurately track your blood sugar with home testing.

My advice: Test a meter you are considering buying in the store—take 10 readings in succession using the manufacturer's "normal" control solution. A pharmacy with glucose meters on display will usually let you test them—ask the pharmacist. Readings should be within 6 mg/dL of the midpoint of that normal range.

Important: Make sure that you can return the device if you find it to be inaccurate later. If your insurance company won't cover a meter you like, file an appeal.

My favorite glucose meter: Of the many glucose meters for home use that I have tried, the FreeStyle Freedom Lite by Abbott, available at most drugstores or online for about $20, has been the most accurate.

Mistake: **Pricking your finger the wrong way.** If you use a glucose meter, your doctor will probably tell you to wipe the site with alcohol before pricking it. I disagree.

First, it isn't necessary to wipe your finger with alcohol—this dries out the skin and can lead to calluses, which makes it difficult to get a blood sample. Neither my patients nor I have ever developed an infection from not using alcohol.

However, you should wash your hands before drawing blood. This is especially true if you've been handling food or glucose tablets or applied hand cream—all of which can cause false high readings.

Helpful: Rinse your finger with warm water to get the blood flowing, and prick the back of your finger between the joints—this area may produce more blood and cause less pain.

Mistake: **Overdoing vitamin C.** In excess, vitamin C raises blood sugar and inactivates the glucose-processing enzyme in the test strip, resulting in deceptively low glucose readings. You'll probably get all the vitamin C you need from vegetables (you shouldn't rely on fruit—it has too much natural sugar). If you must take supplements, 250 mg daily in a sustained-release form is tops. These formulations are less likely to cause blood sugar spikes.

Blood Sugar Tip: Eat This, Then That

Study titled "Food Order Has a Significant Impact on Postprandial Glucose and Insulin Levels" by researchers at Weill Cornell Medical College, New York City, published in *Diabetes Care.*

If your blood sugar sometimes runs a little high—and most definitely if you have prediabetes or diabetes—you'll get lots of advice about what to eat but rarely what to eat first in a meal. But the order of what you eat can make a big difference in your blood sugar response.

In a small pilot study of overweight people with type 2 diabetes, on days when they ate carbs at lunch first (ciabatta bread, orange juice), followed 15 minutes later by the foods rich in protein plus some fat (grilled chicken breast, salad with low-fat dressing, steamed broccoli with butter), their blood sugar levels were more than one-third higher 60 minutes later—compared with days on which they reversed the order and ate the protein-rich dish first. Insulin levels were higher, too.

It makes the common practice of munching from the bread basket before your main dish arrives particularly suspect! Instead, whether you're at home or eating out, try starting your meal with something that's high in protein, with some good fats, and perhaps even fiber-rich veggies—for example, veggies and hummus, peanut butter and celery or chilled shrimp with cocktail sauce—before you eat any carb-rich food. What you eat still matters, of course, but eating foods in the right order might help keep your blood sugar levels from spiking after a meal. It also helps if you're a little hungry before you eat.

How to Use Insulin the Right Way

Insulin injections are crucial for type 1 diabetes and often needed for type 2 diabetes. *To use effectively…*

•**Change with the seasons.** Most people need less insulin in summer than winter (or during a warm spell in colder months). Capillaries dilate when warm, and more blood containing insulin is delivered to peripheral tissues. Adjust your dose accordingly.

•**Prevent blood sugar spikes by correctly gauging how much insulin you need to cover each meal and when to inject it.** With Regular (a type of short-acting insulin), that's usually 30 to 45 minutes before the meal.

To determine your best timing: Inject an insulin dose, and check blood sugar after 25 minutes, then at five-minute intervals. When it has dropped by 5 mg/dL, it's time to eat. This may not work for people who have diabetic gastroparesis, which causes unpredictable stomach emptying.

Richard K. Bernstein, MD, a diabetes specialist in private practice in Mamaroneck, New York.

The All-Day, All-Night Guide to Controlling Your Diabetes

The late Stanley Mirsky, MD, associate clinical professor at Mount Sinai School of Medicine and founder of the Stanley Mirsky MD Diabetes Education Unit at the Mount Sinai Metabolism Institute, both in New York City. He is coauthor of *Diabetes Survival Guide*.

From the time you wake up until you go to bed, it is essential to keep your blood sugar as stable as possible if you have diabetes.

Reasons: Over time, uncontrolled elevated blood sugar harms the blood vessels, kidneys, eyes and nerves, increasing the risk for heart attack, stroke, kidney failure, blindness and tissue damage that can require limb amputation.

DIABETES ALSO IS LINKED TO DEMENTIA

Despite these dangers, scarcely half of the 21 million Americans who have been diagnosed with diabetes have their disease under control. If you're struggling, you can significantly improve your blood sugar control by eating the right foods and doing the right things at the right times of day.

THROUGHOUT THE DAY

It is key to eat foods that digest slowly, so blood sugar remains relatively stable…and avoid foods that are digested quickly, triggering rapid blood sugar spikes. This also helps control weight—an important factor because excess weight contributes to diabetes complications. *Guidelines…*

•**Have 40 grams (g) to 50 g of carbohydrates at each meal.** Stick with mostly complex carbs (whole grains, vegetables, nuts)…limit refined carbs (cakes, white pasta). Check labels!

•**Avoid foods with more than 10 g of sugar per serving.**

•**Have some lean protein every day—**chicken, fish, lean beef, low-fat dairy, eggs, tofu. Most people get enough protein, so you do not need protein with each meal unless your doctor recommends this.

•**Limit starches (corn, peas, potatoes, sweet potatoes) to one serving per meal.**

•**Limit fruit to two servings per day.** A serving equals one small handheld fruit (peach, plum)…half an apple or half a banana…12 grapes…one cup of strawberries…or one-half cup of blueberries, raspberries or diced fruit (such as melon). Avoid pineapples and dried fruits, which are high in sugar.

•**At wake-up time.** Test your blood sugar before breakfast. If it is high, you may have eaten too many carbohydrates too close to bedtime the night before. Or your levels may have fallen too low during the night, so your liver released more glucose (sugar), causing a blood sugar "rebound." Talk to your doctor—you may need to adjust your medication dosage and/or timing.

•**At breakfast.** The morning meal helps get your metabolism running efficiently, so don't skip it.

Ideal: One or two slices of whole-grain bread with a soft spread that contains cholesterol-lowering plant sterols, such as Smart Balance or Promise Activ…plus a two-egg vegetable omelet. It is fine to use whole eggs—but if you have high cholesterol, make your omelet with egg whites instead and limit egg yolks to two per week.

Another good choice: One cup of unsweetened or lightly sweetened whole-grain cereal that contains no more than 25 g of carbohydrates per cup, such as Cheerios or Product 19…plus one-half cup of blueberries and one cup of low-fat milk. Don't be fooled into thinking that high-fiber necessarily equals healthful—you still must check labels to see if the food is too high in carbs.

Your doctor may advise you to take a dose of diabetes medication right before breakfast.

Also: If you have diabetic nerve damage, take 100 micrograms of vitamin B-1 daily. If you take blood pressure medication, morning is the best time because blood pressure typically is higher during the day than at night. If you plan to drive, test your blood sugar before leaving home.

•**In midmorning.** A midmorning snack generally is not necessary unless your doctor advises you to have one (for instance, due to the type of insulin you are on). However, if you start to feel weak or dizzy, have a snack that provides no more than 10 g of carbohydrates—for instance, a small tangerine, half a banana or two graham cracker squares.

•**At lunch.** Good choices include a sandwich, such as turkey, lettuce and tomato on whole-wheat bread…or sushi with rice (preferably brown).

Common mistakes: Eating too much (especially at restaurants)…choosing a fruit plate (too much sugar and no protein)…overdoing it on chips or condiments (which can be high in fat or sugar).

•**In midafternoon.** Again, have a snack only if you feel weak or your doctor recommends it, and limit yourself to no more than 10 g of carbs.

Good choices: About 15 pistachios…10 almonds…or one-third of an ounce of whole-grain crackers.

•**At dinner.** Check your blood sugar before dinner. If you are on oral diabetes medication, take it just before your meal.

Dinner should include four ounces of lean protein…several generous servings of vegetables…and one serving of a starch. Have a green salad, but skip the high-carb, high-fat dressings. Instead, drizzle greens with lemon juice, balsamic vinegar, safflower oil and/or olive oil.

Limit: One alcoholic drink daily, consumed with a meal. Opt for five ounces of wine…12 ounces of a low-carb beer, such as Miller Lite…or one ounce of distilled liquor (Scotch, vodka). Avoid mixed drinks, which often are high in carbs.

Dessert options: A scoop of low-carb, no-sugar-added ice cream…berries…two Lorna Doone cookies…or three Social Tea Biscuits.

•**In the evening.** This is the best time to exercise to maximize muscle cells' absorption of glucose. Strength training and stretching are good, but aerobic exercise is most important because it increases insulin sensitivity (cells' ability to respond to insulin) for up to 14 hours. Each week, aim for two-and-a-half hours of moderate-intensity aerobic exercise, such as walking...or one-and-a-half hours of strenuous activity. For blood sugar control, 30-minute workouts generally are most effective. As part of your exercise regimen, consider tai chi. In one study, diabetes patients who did this martial art significantly lowered their blood sugar levels.

Caution: Ask your doctor before starting an exercise program. Test blood sugar before each workout. If it is below 100 milligrams per deciliter (mg/dL), have a snack before exercising. Do not work out when your blood sugar is higher than 250 mg/dL—when blood sugar is this high, exercise may elevate it even further. If you have retinopathy (damaged blood vessels in the retina), to protect vision, do not lift weights above eye level.

• **At bedtime.** If you are on long-acting insulin, a bedtime injection controls nighttime glucose levels. If you take cholesterol-lowering medication, do so now—it is most effective at night. Test your blood sugar at bedtime. If it is somewhat elevated (but not above 250 mg/dL), lower it with 10 minutes of moderate exercise.

Insomnia doesn't raise blood sugar, but the stress it creates can.

To promote sleep: Turn off the cell phone, TV and computer at least 30 minutes before bedtime so your mind can quiet down. Take a warm bath (checking your feet for wounds or signs of infection, because diabetes often damages nerves in the feet).

Have you been told that you snore? Diabetes patients are prone to sleep apnea (repeated halts in breathing during sleep), which contributes to poor blood sugar control. Do you frequently get up at night to urinate? It could be a sign that your medication needs adjusting. If you have either symptom, tell your doctor.

What Your Doctor May Not Tell You About Your Diabetes

The late Frederic J. Vagnini, MD, a cardiovascular surgeon and director of the Heart, Diabetes & Weight Loss Centers of New York in New Hyde Park. His clinical interests included heart disease, diabetes, weight loss and nutrition. He is author, with Lawrence D. Chilnick, of *The Weight Loss Plan for Beating Diabetes.*

For most of the 21 million Americans diagnosed with type 2 diabetes, the main goal of treatment is simply to control their glucose (blood sugar) levels with diet, exercise and sometimes medication.

But there's much more that should be done to help prevent serious complications, which can shorten the life expectancy of a person with diabetes—by about 7.5 years in men and 8.2 years in women.

Sobering statistics: About 80% of people with diabetes die from cardiovascular complications, such as a heart attack. About half the patients with poor glucose control will eventually suffer from nerve damage (neuropathy). Another 20% to 30% may experience retinopathy or other eye disorders.

Whether or not you're taking medication for diabetes, virtually all of these complications can be avoided—and, in some cases, reversed—with natural approaches.

Important: Be sure to speak to your doctor before following any of the steps in this article—some may affect diabetes drugs and other types of medication.

Best ways for people with diabetes to avoid complications...

CONTROLLING INFLAMMATION

People with diabetes typically have elevated levels of C-reactive protein, a blood protein that indicates chronic low-level inflammation, the underlying cause of most cardiovascular, eye and nerve disorders. Inflammation also exacerbates arthritis, which is more common in diabetics than in those without the disease. *Effective options...*

•**Stop eating wheat.** Many people with diabetes are allergic or sensitive to gluten, a protein found naturally in wheat, barley and rye—and sometimes in other grains, such as oats, because they become "cross-contaminated" during processing. Even trace amounts of gluten can stimulate the production of cytokines, substances that increase inflammation. (See self-test on the next page to determine whether you are sensitive to gluten.)

Besides increasing inflammation in these patients, exposure to gluten may lead to fatigue and joint problems. Gluten may also impair digestion in these people, making it harder to lose weight—a serious problem because excess body fat increases inflammation even more.

Important: Read food labels. Besides avoiding obvious sources of gluten such as wheat bread and wheat pasta, look for terms such as "amino peptide complex," "filler flour," "hydrolyzed protein" and "vegetable starch"—these indicate that gluten is or may be found in the product. Gluten is also present in unexpected sources, such as soy sauce, malt and graham flour, as well as thousands of nonfood products, including some medications. To determine if a medication contains gluten, call the drug manufacturer. For a list of foods and products that contain gluten, consult the Gluten Intolerance Group's website, *www.gluten.org*.

•**Give up dairy.** Oftentimes people who are sensitive to gluten also have problems digesting casein, a dairy protein.

To test for a gluten or dairy sensitivity: Eliminate each food type one at a time for several weeks. If you notice an improvement in energy, or a reduction in joint pain or digestion problems, you're probably sensitive to one or both. To make sure, reintroduce dairy and/or gluten foods one at a time to see if your symptoms return.

Important: Foods that are labeled "lactose-free" or "dairy-free" are not necessarily casein-free. Foods that are both gluten-free and casein-free can be found online at *www.trader joes.com* or *www.wholefoodsmarket.com*.

To keep it simple: Remember that all unprocessed meats, vegetables and fruits are gluten-free and dairy-free.

•**Supplement with omega-3 fatty acids.** The American Diabetes Association recommends a diet high in these fatty acids because of their ability to reduce inflammation and other diabetes complications. Unfortunately, many people find it difficult to eat enough omega-3–rich foods, such as salmon, mackerel and herring—two six-ounce servings a week are recommended—so supplements often are a good choice.

My advice: Take a daily supplement with at least 1,500 mg of eicosapentaenoic acid (EPA), the component in fish oil that helps reduce the inflammation that contributes to diabetes-related complications. If you're allergic to fish, you can use an omega-3 supplement derived from algae.

Omega-3 fatty acids, also found in flaxseed and walnuts, have the additional benefit of helping to lower triglycerides, blood fats that have been linked to atherosclerosis and cardiovascular disease.

FIGHT ARTERIAL CALCIFICATION

The Rotterdam Heart Study, which looked at the dietary histories of more than 4,800 patients, found that those with low blood levels of vitamin K2 were 57% more likely to develop heart disease, due in part to an increase in calcium in the arteries. Paradoxically, these patients had lower bone levels of calcium, which increases the risk for fractures.

Because diabetic patients have an extremely high risk for heart disease, I routinely recommend a daily supplement (45 mcg) of vitamin K2. You can also get more of this nutrient by eating such foods as liver, eggs and certain cheeses.

Caution: Because there are different forms of vitamin K—some of which interfere with the effects of *warfarin* (Coumadin) and other blood thinners—always speak to your doctor before taking any vitamin K supplement.

OVERCOME FATIGUE

Both inflammation and elevated blood sugar increase fatigue, making it one of the most common symptoms of diabetes. *Helpful…*

•**Coenzyme Q10** (CoQ10) increases the body's production of adenosine triphosphate (ATP), a molecule that enhances the performance of mitochondria, the energy-producing components of cells. CoQ10 is also an antioxidant that reduces inflammation. Typical dose: 100 mg to 200 mg, twice daily.

• **Magnesium** is involved in glucose and insulin reactions and is typically lower than normal in people with diabetes who experience fatigue. Patients who eat a healthy diet, including magnesium-rich foods such as nuts and oatmeal, and supplement with magnesium often report an increase in energy. They also show improvements in blood pressure and cardiac performance. Talk to your doctor about the appropriate dosage of a magnesium supplement—especially if you have kidney disease or heart disease, both of which can be worsened by too much magnesium.

All forms of supplemental magnesium can be used, but magnesium citrate causes diarrhea in some people. If this happens to you, take a different form, such as magnesium taurate or magnesium glycinate.

AVOID DIABETIC NEUROPATHY

Excess blood sugar can damage the tiny blood vessels that carry blood and nutrients to nerves in the fingers, legs and/or feet, causing neuropathy. Neuropathy can eventually lead to tissue damage that requires amputation. *What to try…*

• **Alpha-lipoic acid** makes the cells more sensitive to insulin and can relieve symptoms of diabetic neuropathy.

Typical dose: 600 mg to 1,200 mg daily for people with diabetes who have neuropathy. To help prevent neuropathy, 100 mg to 300 mg daily is the typical dose.

• **B-complex supplement** may help prevent neuropathy or reduce symptoms in patients who already have it.

Typical dose: Two B-100 complex supplements daily for people with diabetes who have neuropathy…one B-100 complex daily to help prevent neuropathy.

PREVENT EYE DAMAGE

High blood sugar can cause diabetic retinopathy, which can lead to blindness. It can also increase eye pressure and lead to glaucoma.

Self-defense: Eat more fresh fruits and vegetables. These foods contain antioxidants such as lutein, zeaxanthin and vitamin C, which strengthen eye capillaries, fight free radicals and reduce the risk for blindness. Frozen fruits and vegetables also can be used.

Best choice: Blueberries or bilberries—both contain anthocyanins, antioxidants that help prevent eye damage and appear to improve glucose levels.

Minor Missteps Can Make Your Diabetes Worse

Osama Hamdy, MD, PhD, medical director of the Joslin Diabetes Center's Obesity Clinical Program and an assistant professor of medicine at Harvard Medical School, both in Boston. He also is coauthor of *The Diabetes Breakthrough.*

Despite what you may have heard, type 2 diabetes doesn't have to be a lifelong condition. It can be controlled and even reversed in the early stages or stopped from progressing in the later stages—with none of the dire consequences of out-of-control blood sugar.

The problem is, even people who are following all the doctor's orders may still be sabotaging their efforts with seemingly minor missteps that can have big consequences. Among the most common mistakes that harm people with diabetes are oversights in the way they eat and exercise. For example…

Skimping on protein. The majority of people with type 2 diabetes are overweight or obese. These individuals know that they need to lose weight but sometimes fail despite their best efforts.

Here's what often happens: We have had it drummed into our heads that the best way to lose weight is to go on a low-fat diet. However, these diets tend to be low in protein—and you need more protein, not less, if you have type 2 diabetes and are cutting calories to lose weight.

What's so special about protein? You need protein to maintain muscle mass. The average adult starts losing lean muscle mass every year after about age 40. If you have diabetes, you'll probably lose more muscle mass than someone without it. And the loss will be even greater if your diabetes is not well controlled.

Muscle is important because it burns more calories than other tissues in your body. Also, people with a higher and more active muscle mass find it easier to maintain healthy blood-glucose levels, since active muscle doesn't require insulin to clear high glucose from the blood.

My advice: Protein should provide 20% to 30% of total daily calories. If you're on an 1,800-calorie diet (a reasonable amount for an average man who wants to lose weight), that's about 90 grams (g) to 135 g of protein a day. If you're on a 1,200- to 1,500-calorie diet (a sensible amount for an average woman who is dieting), that's about 60 g to 113 g of protein a day.

Examples: Good protein sources include fish, skinless poultry, nonfat or low-fat dairy, legumes and nuts and seeds. A three-ounce chicken breast has about 30 g of protein...a three-ounce piece of haddock, 17 g...one-half cup of low-fat cottage cheese, 14 g...and one-quarter cup of whole almonds, 7 g of protein.

Note: If you have kidney problems, you may need to limit your protein intake. Check with your doctor.

Not doing resistance training. It's widely known that aerobic exercise is good for weight loss and blood sugar control. What usually gets short shrift is resistance training, such as lifting weights and using stretch bands.

When you build muscle, you use more glucose, which helps reduce glucose levels in the blood. If you take insulin for your diabetes (see below), toned muscles will also make your body more sensitive to it.

An added benefit: People who do resistance training can often reduce their doses of insulin or other medications within a few months.

My advice: Do a combination of resistance, aerobic and flexibility exercises. Start with 20 minutes total, four days a week—splitting the time equally among the three types of exercise. Try to work up to 60 minutes total, six days a week. An exercise physiologist or personal trainer certified in resistance training can help choose the best workout for you.

IF YOU TAKE DIABETES MEDS...

Sometimes, diet and exercise aren't enough to tame out-of-control blood sugar. *Traps to avoid...*

• **Drug-induced weight gain.** Ironically, the drugs that are used to treat diabetes also can cause weight gain as a side effect. If you start taking insulin, you can expect to gain about 10 pounds within six months—with oral drugs, such as *glipizide* (Glucotrol), you'll probably gain from four to seven pounds.

My advice: Ask your doctor if you can switch to one of the newer, "weight-friendly" medications.

Examples: A form of insulin called Levemir causes less weight gain than Lantus, Humulin N or Novolin N. Newer oral drugs called DPP-4 inhibitors, such as Januvia, Onglyza and Nesina, don't have weight gain as a side effect.

Important: The newer drugs are more expensive and may not be covered by insurance. But if they don't cause you to gain weight, you might get by with a lower dose—and reduced cost.

• **Erratic testing.** You should test your blood sugar levels at least four to six times a day, particularly when you're making lifestyle changes that could affect the frequency and doses of medication. Your doctor has probably advised you to test before and after exercise—and before meals.

My advice: Be sure to also test after meals. This will help determine the effects of different types and amounts of foods.

Insulin May Not Be the Way to Go

Some diabetics may be better off not starting insulin, according to Sandeep Vijan, MD. For adults over age 50 who have type 2 diabetes but a low risk for complications because their glucose levels are under control

(A1C level of 8% to 8.5%), the side effects of taking a daily insulin shot or other diabetes medications may do more harm than good, a recent study reports. Common side effects such as low blood sugar may be worse than the small benefit of the medication. Diet and exercise may be better for these patients.

Caution: Do not stop taking insulin or other diabetes drugs without first consulting your doctor.

Sandeep Vijan, MD, professor of internal medicine, University of Michigan Medical School, Ann Arbor.

No Two Diabetes Patients Are the Same

Ildiko Lingvay, MD, MPH, an associate professor in the departments of internal medicine and clinical science and a practicing endocrinologist at The University of Texas Southwestern Medical Center in Dallas. Dr. Lingvay is an internationally recognized researcher who has authored several dozen articles related to type 2 diabetes, obesity and metabolic syndrome.

Chances are you know one or more people who have type 2 diabetes, or perhaps you have been diagnosed with the condition yourself.

The number of Americans with diabetes is truly staggering—a new case is diagnosed every 17 seconds. And, of course, the consequences of uncontrolled diabetes are dire, including increased risk for heart attack and other cardiovascular problems…blindness…leg amputation…kidney failure…and, ultimately, premature death.

To help meet this enormous challenge, medical research has been stepped up.

Now: American researchers have joined forces with their European counterparts to devise new strategies to diagnose and manage diabetes more effectively than ever before.

What you need to know…

EASIER DIAGNOSIS

In the US, 29 million people have diabetes. This includes roughly 21 million who have been diagnosed and an estimated eight million who are undiagnosed. Experts hope that a change in the diagnostic process will lead to more widespread testing and fewer undiagnosed cases.

Until recently, diabetes was typically diagnosed using one of two standard tests—a blood test that requires an overnight fast to measure blood glucose levels…and an oral glucose tolerance test, which involves drinking a high-sugar mixture and then having blood drawn 30 minutes, one hour and two hours later to show how long it takes blood glucose levels to return to normal.

The problem: Both of these tests are inconvenient for the patient, and they measure blood glucose levels only at the time of the test. Many people never get tested because they don't like the idea of having to fast overnight or wait hours to complete a test.

New approach: More widespread use of the A1C test. For decades, the A1C test, which provides a person's average blood glucose levels over a period of two to three months, has been used to monitor how well people with diabetes were controlling their disease. However, it wasn't deemed a reliable tool for diagnosis.

Now, after major improvements that have standardized the measurements from laboratory to laboratory, the A1C test is considered a practical and convenient diagnostic option.

The A1C requires no fasting or special preparation, so it's the perfect "no excuses" test. A1C tests analyzed by accredited labs (such as LabCorp and Quest Diagnostics) meet the latest standardization criteria.

UPDATED TREATMENT GUIDELINES

Recently, the American Diabetes Association and the European Association for the Study of Diabetes collaborated on recommendations for best treatment practices for type 2 diabetes. The most significant change in the recent guidelines is the concept of individualized treatment.

The problem: In the past, diabetes care was based on a one-size-fits-all strategy—with few exceptions, everyone with the condition got basically the same treatment.

New approach: The recently released guidelines acknowledge that there are multiple treatment options for each patient and that

169

the best treatment for one patient may be different from what another patient requires.

This is important because diabetes affects an enormously wide range of people. For example, diabetes can strike a thin 77-year-old woman or a 300-pound teenage boy, and their treatment needs and goals will be as different as their characteristics.

After reviewing a patient's medical history and individual lifestyle, the doctor and patient consider treatment options together and decide on the best fit. *Factors that are more explicitly spelled out in the new guidelines include...*

• **Other medical conditions and medications.** If diabetes treatments interact badly with a patient's current medications, it may cause one of the medications to become ineffective...amplify the effects of the drugs...or cause allergic reactions or serious, even life-threatening side effects. This is especially true for people being treated for kidney disease or heart problems, as many diabetes medications may exacerbate those health issues.

• **Lifestyle and daily schedule.** Diabetes management is easier for people who have predictable schedules. For example, a full-time worker who regularly wakes up at 7 am, eats breakfast, takes a lunch hour and is home for dinner will have simpler treatment needs than a college student who sleeps past noon, eats cold pizza for breakfast, then pulls an all-nighter.

If a physician gives standard insulin recommendations to someone who has an unusual eating and sleeping schedule, it is easy to have blood sugar drop too low—a dangerous condition called hypoglycemia. That's why it is important that patients share as many details of their lives as possible, even if the information seems irrelevant.

BETTER TREATMENT STRATEGIES

Until recently, diabetes has been treated with a stepwise approach—starting with conservative treatment, adding medication later only when needed. This sounds good, except that new treatments are incorporated only after previous treatments fail and blood glucose rises.

The problem: Depending on scheduled doctor visits, blood sugar may remain elevated for months or even years before anyone catches the change.

New approach: Research suggests that if physicians intervene more intensively at the beginning, they have the potential to stop the progression of diabetes. With this in mind, treatment aims to decrease the rate at which the body loses insulin-producing ability...and prevent diabetes complications by not allowing blood sugar to exceed safe levels.

Under this new scenario, doctors hit diabetes full force with the patient's individualized treatment plan (including lifestyle changes and medication), instead of with graduated, step-up treatments.

What the new guidelines mean for anyone diagnosed with diabetes: If your current diabetes treatment plan does not address the points described in this article, see your doctor. Your treatment may need to be more customized.

If You Have Diabetes... How to Fast Safely for a Medical Test

Paula Vetter, RN, MSN, a diabetes educator, holistic family nurse practitioner, personal wellness coach and former critical care nursing instructor at the Cleveland Clinic.

Recently, an employee at Bottom Line Publications was scheduled for a colonoscopy, the screening test for colon cancer. The medical test turned into medical mayhem.

The day before the test, the woman followed her doctor's orders to start ingesting a "clear liquid" diet, which includes soft drinks, Jell-O and other clear beverages and foods. But when she drank the "prep"—the bowel-cleaning solution that is consumed the evening before a colonoscopy (and sometimes also the morning of)—she vomited. Over and over. As a result, her colon wasn't sufficiently emptied to conduct the test, which had to be postponed.

What went wrong?

The woman has diabetes—and her glucose (blood sugar) levels had become unstable, triggering nausea and vomiting. Yet not one medical professional—not a doctor, not a nurse, not a medical technician—had warned her that people with diabetes need to take special precautions with food and diabetes medicine whenever they have any medical test that involves an extended period of little or no eating. Unfortunately, this lack of diabetes-customized instruction about medical tests is very common. *What you need to know…*

DO IT EARLY

If you're undergoing a test that requires only overnight fasting, which includes many types of CT scans, MRIs and X-rays, make sure that the test is scheduled for early in the morning—no later than 9 am. That way, you will be able to eat after the test by 10 am or 11 am, which will help to stabilize your blood sugar as much as possible.

Don't expect your blood sugar levels to be perfect after the test. The important thing is to keep them from getting too high or too low.

THE RIGHT CLEAR LIQUIDS

Conventional dietitians and doctors specify clear liquids and foods that reflect the conventional American diet, such as regular soda, sports drinks, Popsicles, Kool-Aid and Jell-O (no red or purple). But the pH of these products is highly acidic. And that could contribute to diabetic ketoacidosis, a potentially life-threatening condition where the body burns fat instead of glucose for fuel, producing ketones, substances toxic to the liver and brain.

When my clients with diabetes are on a clear-liquid diet before a test, I recommend that they consume liquids with essential nutrients and a more balanced pH, such as apple juice, white grape juice and clear, fat-free broth (vegetable, chicken or beef). A typical "dinner" could include up to three-quarters cup of juice (to limit sugar) and any amount of broth. A bedtime "snack" could include one-half cup of juice and any amount of broth. Plenty of good pure water between "meals" also is important to stay well-hydrated.

CHECK BLOOD SUGAR OFTEN

Many people with diabetes check their blood sugar a few times a day—typically right before a meal and again one to two hours afterward. But if you're on a clear-liquid diet or fasting before a medical test, you should check your glucose level every two to three hours. If it's too low, correct it with a fast-acting carbohydrate, such as four ounces of 100% fruit juice or a glucose gel (a squeezable, over-the-counter product).

Important: Take fruit juice or a glucose gel with you to the test—if the test is delayed for any reason, you can ingest the carb and keep your blood sugar on track.

STOP TAKING METFORMIN

Your doctor likely will recommend that you stop taking the diabetes medication metformin 24 hours before the test. *Metformin* (Glucophage) also can contribute to acidosis and typically is stopped 24 hours before and up to 72 hours after any test that requires a contrast agent (an injected dye often used in an X-ray, CT scan or MRI that helps create the image). Talk to your doctor about when to stop taking your medication and when to resume or about the possible need for an alternative diabetes drug during this period.

An unexpected threat: Metformin is a component of many multi-ingredient diabetes drugs—so you may not realize you're taking it and therefore may need to discontinue it. Drugs that include metformin are Actoplus Met and Actoplus Met XR…Glucovance…Janumet and Janumet XR…Jentadueto…Kazano…Kombiglyze XR…and PrandiMet. New drugs are being developed constantly, so check with your pharmacist to see if yours contains metformin.

Also important: Many X-rays, CT scans and MRIs utilize an injected dye or a contrast agent that can damage the kidneys in people with diabetes (contrast-induced nephropathy). Before restarting metformin, have a kidney function test (such as BUN, which requires a blood sample, and creatinine clearance, which requires a urine sample and a blood sample) that confirms that your kidneys are working normally. These tests are recommended 24 to

171

48 hours after your procedure is completed and usually are covered by insurance.

DECREASE INSULIN

Insulin is the hormone used by the body to regulate blood sugar—and many people with advanced diabetes give themselves shots of short- and/or long-acting insulin to keep glucose levels steady. But if you're consuming only clear liquids or fasting before a medical test, you likely will need to take less insulin.

Excellent guidelines for insulin use before a medical procedure have been created by the University of Michigan Comprehensive Diabetes Center. *In general, it recommends…*

• **Take one-half of your usual dose of long-acting insulin the evening before the procedure.**

• **Take one-half of your usual dose of long-acting insulin the morning of the test and no short-acting insulin the morning of the test.**

You can find the complete guidelines in downloadable PDF form at *www.med.umich. edu/1libr/mend/diabetes-outpatientprocedure. pdf.* Print them out, and discuss them with your doctor.

REDUCE ANXIETY

Anxiety triggers the release of the stress hormone cortisol, which in turn sparks the production of glucose. *To keep blood sugar balanced before a test, use these two methods to keep anxiety in check…*

• **Get all your questions answered.** Fear of the unknown is the greatest stress. Before your procedure, create a list of questions to ask your doctor or nurse practitioner. Examples: What is going to happen during the procedure? What is it going to feel like? What are the potential side effects from the test, and how can I best avoid them? When will I be informed of the test results? How will the test results affect future decision-making about my health?

• **Breathe deeply.** Deep breathing is the easiest and simplest way to reduce anxiety. *My recommendation, based on the approach of Andrew Weil, MD…*

Repeat this breathing exercise three times, and do it three times a day every day: Inhale for a count of four…hold for a count of seven…exhale for a count of eight. (Don't worry if you can't do the entire count— shorter counts also work.) Do this exercise when you get up in the morning, at midday and at bedtime. You can do it more often, but most people find three times simple and easy to integrate into their routines.

Also, you can use this breathing technique in any situation that you find anxiety-producing, such as before and during the test itself. Breathe deeply three times every 10 or 15 minutes, and be sure to keep the 4:7:8 ratio—inhale for four, hold for seven, exhale for eight.

Jewelry That Can Save Your Life

The late Richard O'Brien, MD, former spokesperson, American College of Emergency Physicians, and associate professor, The Commonwealth Medical College of Pennsylvania, Scranton.

Medical ID jewelry has evolved. Those simple and basic necklaces and ID bracelets that people used to wear to alert others to medical problems, such as a heart condition or a seizure disorder, have gone high-tech, offering an array of data-sharing options so emergency responders can gain instant access to your comprehensive medical information. The new generation of medical-emergency bracelets and tags uses portable computer memory devices (typically a USB drive) or an Internet component to store and share your medical information. *Here's a sampling of what's available…*

• **The CARE medical history bracelet is basically a USB drive you wear strapped to your wrist.** It holds software and forms. It alerts emergency personnel that you have a medical condition and, once plugged into a computer (it works on both PC and Mac), downloads a detailed medical history. The waterproof bracelet comes in five colors. (*http://medicalhistory bracelet.com*, 210-681-3840, $19.99)

• **Similar in appearance to a traditional dog tag, the American Medical ID is a USB**

drive that carries a summary of medical information. It is easy to use and update. The tag can be engraved with four lines summarizing your critical medical information, such as food or drug allergies or a seizure disorder. (*www.americanmedical-id.com*, 800-363-5985, $44.99)

• **ICEdot Invisible Bracelet,** a web-based service supported by the American Ambulance Association, assigns each wearer a personal identification number (PIN) that first responders use to trigger a text message detailing critical medical information, emergency contacts or whatever other data you choose to provide.

How it works: Your $20/year membership buys a sticker pack displaying the PIN (to be displayed in convenient places, for instance on your driver's license) that allows emergency responders to access your information. (*https://icedot.org*, 918-592-3722)

• **Road ID Interactive is an ID band, tag or pouch you can wear on your wrist, ankle or shoe.** It is engraved with two lines of personal information (name, address) and a toll-free phone number, web address and PIN that responders can use to get more details. (*www.roadid.com*, 800-345-6336, $19.99 to $39.99, including free online access for a year, then $9.99/year thereafter)

• **Medic Alert** is the classic line of jewelry, now in an updated variety of attractive styles (for instance, made with Swarovski "pearls" or sterling silver), including bracelets, necklaces, sports bands, shoe tags and even a watch. These pieces can be engraved with medical info and also provide phone access to a 24-hour emergency service that provides more detailed information. The service notifies anyone you designate that you've had an emergency and provides information on where you're being treated. (*www.medicalert.org*, 888-633-4298, $19.95 and up for the jewelry, plus a membership fee starting at $29.99/year)

HOW TO CHOOSE

Richard O'Brien, MD, a top emergency room physician said that only about 20% of patients come in with any sort of information at all. He's quite enthusiastic about these products and especially likes the flash drive devices, since they can provide comprehensive information very quickly.

This is especially helpful for patients with chronic conditions, but even healthy folks would be well-advised to take a few minutes to consider and make notes on their medical history in order to have important information at the ready in the event of an emergency. At minimum, write down your information on an index card, have it laminated (you can do this at many office-supply stores) and store it in your wallet, as EMTs know to look there.

Information that emergency physicians would like to get from every patient in order to deliver the best possible emergency care...

• **Name, date of birth, address(es).**

• **Your phone numbers,** contact for next of kin or significant other(s), identifying features—moles, tattoos, scars, etc.—that can positively distinguish you from others.

• **Contact information for your primary care physician and relevant specialists,** including name, phone number, location.

• **A list of all known allergies.**

• **An up-to-date list of medications and any supplements you take.**

• **Information on previous surgery or planned elective surgery** (such as an upcoming gallbladder surgery or a scheduled biopsy).

• **Current immunization information,** including flu and other vaccines, along with the date of your most recent tetanus shot and others as appropriate.

• **List of other medical problems such as diabetes, cancer, etc.**

List of any medical devices that you have or use: Pacemaker, prosthesis, cochlear implant, etc.

Whether it is recorded on a flash drive, a bracelet, an index card or elsewhere, putting this information together and keeping it with you can make all the difference—at the very least, by expediting treatment in the event of an emergency and quite possibly even saving your life.

Which Doctor Is Best for You...

Dennis Gottfried, MD, an associate professor of medicine at the University of Connecticut School of Medicine, Farmington, and an internist with a private practice in Torrington, Connecticut. He is author of *Too Much Medicine: A Doctor's Prescription for Better and More Affordable Health Care.*

You might assume that you will get better care when you spend extra time and extra money to see a medical specialist. But is that really true?

Not always. Generalists—such as internists, general practitioners and family physicians—have a broader, more holistic view of the patient's condition and provide integrated care, but they lack the in-depth knowledge that specialists have in their area of medicine. Specialists may provide more fragmented care and order unnecessary tests and more procedures that are risky, studies show.

So when does the benefit of a specialist's added expertise outweigh the problem of sometimes disjointed medical care and excessive testing, especially when you have a chronic condition such as diabetes?

Rule of thumb: Specialists are generally preferable when a single medical condition that requires expert knowledge dominates all other medical concerns, such as a cardiologist treating an acute heart attack or an oncologist prescribing chemotherapy. Generalists, however, are usually more suitable when multiple chronic conditions, such as hypertension, diabetes and high cholesterol, are present.

HOW TO GET THE BEST CARE FOR DIABETES

Where to start: A primary care physician. Type 2 diabetes is largely a lifestyle disease caused by obesity and inactivity. It is initially managed with diet, exercise and oral medications, although insulin may be required as the disease progresses. Cardiovascular risk factors, such as high blood pressure, as well as lifestyle factors and blood sugar levels need to be monitored. Because of the comprehensive care

that they require, people with type 2 diabetes should optimally be cared for by a generalist.

Diabetes specialists, or diabetologists, endocrinologists who specialize in diabetes, often take a narrow view. For example, they emphasize the importance of lowering blood sugar, frequently with insulin or oral medications.

Overall blood glucose control is monitored by the A1C blood test, which measures average blood sugar levels over the past two to three months. The major health risks for type 2 diabetics are heart disease and stroke, but lowering blood sugar too much (more than a full point in those at high risk) can actually increase risk for heart attack.

See a specialist when: Your A1C level is consistently above 8. (A normal level is below 6.3.) Elevated A1C increases the risk for some diabetes complications, including kidney disease. A specialist might be better able to lower consistently elevated A1C to healthier levels.

For type 1 diabetes: These patients should almost always see a diabetologist. Type 1 diabetes occurs more commonly in young adults and requires insulin shots from the onset. Also, the use of insulin and insulin pumps, which is recommended for type 1 diabetes patients, requires specialized knowledge.

Dangerous Overdiagnosis of Diabetes

H. Gilbert Welch, MD, MPH, professor of medicine at The Dartmouth Institute for Health Policy and Clinical Practice and general internist at the White River Junction VA in Vermont. He is author of *Overdiagnosed: Making People Sick in the Pursuit of Health* and *Should I Be Tested for Cancer? Maybe Not and Here's Why.*

There's a dangerous epidemic out there. It's called overdiagnosis—when you are diagnosed with a condition that will never hurt your health.

Overdiagnosis can lead to potentially harmful medical care, as you undergo invasive tests, take medications or have surgery—all for a condition that is harmless. Medical care also can be expensive, time-consuming and anxiety-producing. *Type 2 diabetes is a condition that is frequently overdiagnosed...*

More than 29 million Americans have type 2 diabetes, which can cause complications such as heart disease, kidney failure, blindness, nerve pain and leg infections that lead to amputation.

However: Like high blood pressure, type 2 diabetes has a range of abnormality, from the asymptomatic to the severe. Some people with diabetes will never develop complications.

That's even more likely nowadays because the medical definition of type 2 diabetes—and therefore, the criteria for who should and should not be treated—has changed. The definition of type 2 diabetes used to be a fasting blood sugar level higher than 140 mg/dL. Today, it is a fasting blood sugar level higher than 126 mg/dL—turning millions of people into diabetics. A newer test—hemoglobin A1C, a measurement of long-term blood sugar levels that detects the percentage of red blood cells coated with glucose (blood sugar)—defines diabetes as a level of 6.5% or higher.

My viewpoint: Physicians should use medication to reduce blood sugar in patients with an A1C of 9% or higher...discuss treatment with patients between 8% and 9%...and typically not treat patients under 8%.

In a randomized trial designed to test the effect of aggressive blood sugar reduction, more than 10,000 people with type 2 diabetes and A1C levels above 8% were divided into two groups. One group received intensive glucose-lowering therapy aimed at reducing A1C to less than 6%. The other group received standard therapy, targeting a level of 7% to 7.9%. After three years, the intensive-therapy group had about 25% increased risk for death, and because of that, the trial was stopped.

Don't Be One of the Millions of Americans Overtreated for Diabetes

Kasia Joanna Lipska, MD, MHS, assistant professor of medicine (endocrinology), department of internal medicine, Yale School of Medicine, New Haven, Connecticut. Her study was published in *JAMA Internal Medicine*.

Bringing blood sugar down with diabetes drugs might be too simple an approach and, worse, ineffective and even harmful for some of us, especially those of us who are 65 or older. What's more, the reason why so many Americans have diabetes might not be because their blood sugar levels are dangerously high but because the system that defines what constitutes diabetes is rigged. And even doctors might not realize it!

Here's how to really protect your health and protect yourself from overtreatment when a doctor tells you that your blood sugar is high...

FOLLOW THE MONEY

Diabetes management has become big business, amassing billions of dollars in annual sales. In 2014, sales of diabetes drugs alone reached $23 billion. For this we can thank, in part, the changing definition of what exactly diabetes is. Since 1997, the American Diabetes Association and other professional endocrinology groups have twice lowered blood sugar thresholds for type 2 diabetes and prediabetes. Each time they did this, millions more Americans were suddenly considered, by definition, diabetic or prediabetic.

But the doctors making these blood sugar threshold changes have strong incentives to do so that have nothing to do with your well-being, according to a recent exposé published by the medical news outlet *MedPage Today* and the *Milwaukee Journal Sentinel*. Many of these doctors receive speaking and consulting fees from diabetes-drug manufacturers. In one analysis, the authors of the exposé found that 13 of 19 members of a committee responsible for diabetes guidelines accumulated a combined sum of more than $2 million in speaking and consulting fees from companies that make diabetes drugs. Whether doctors responsible for diabetes guidelines are intentionally and systematically basing their decisions on their bank account balances isn't known, but the findings do reveal an obvious and material conflict of interest.

EFFECTIVENESS OF THERAPIES QUESTIONED

The authors of the exposé also pointed out that although they reduce blood sugar, none of the 30 diabetes drugs approved since 2004 has been definitively proven to reduce the risk of heart attack and stroke, blindness or any other diabetes-related complication. "In order to approve a new diabetes drug, the FDA requires evidence that the drug effectively reduces hemoglobin A1C levels—a measure of blood glucose—and that it doesn't result in an unacceptable increase in heart disease risk. The evidence that the drug reduces the risk of complications of diabetes, such as heart attacks and stroke, is not required," explained endocrinologist Kasia Lipska, MD, assistant professor of medicine at Yale School of Medicine. She is the leader of a recent, related study that showed that mature adults are being treated too aggressively for diabetes, sometimes with dangerous consequences. The study population of nearly 1,300 adults, selected from the National Health and Nutrition Examination Survey database, represents a cross section of senior Americans with diabetes.

Similar to a recent study showing that tight blood pressure control may not be beneficial in older adults, prior studies suggest that tight blood sugar control in people 65 and older who have serious health problems actually may do more harm than good. Tight blood sugar control is defined by the American Diabetes Association as a hemoglobin A1C level of less than 7%.

DANGEROUS SIDE EFFECTS

When it comes to drug treatment for diabetes, most doctors will turn to the older drug metformin first, said Dr. Lipska. It has been used in the United States since 1994 and has had a good safety record here and in Europe, where it has been used much longer. It is considered safe and effective. In addition, it does not cause low blood sugar reactions or weight gain. However, after metformin, there is no clear "winner" among the diabetes drugs, and the choice of drug depends on a number of trade-offs and risks, particularly for older adults, she said. Insulin and sulfonylurea drugs such as *glipizide* (Glucotrol), *glyburide* and *glimepiride* (Amaryl) have been associated with dangerously low blood sugar (hypoglycemia), and other drugs, such as *pioglitazone* (Actos), with risk of fluid retention and fractures. Some drugs, such as *saxagliptin* (Onglyza), may be associated with heart failure, while, for very new drugs, such as *canagliflozin* (Invokana), the risks are not yet known.

Although the American Diabetes Association and other professional groups have been lowering the threshold for what constitutes "diabetes" (and, thereby, driving the market for diabetes drugs, at least according to the Medpage exposé), the American Diabetes Association and the American Geriatrics Society discourage tight blood sugar control in older adults. They acknowledge that older adults whose blood sugar is too aggressively controlled are more vulnerable to the dangerous side effects mentioned above, said Dr. Lipska. She added that one treatment standard does not fit all in older adults, because their health and treatment preferences vary greatly. Tight control may be safe and appropriate for one person and not another.

AVOID OVERTREATMENT

Diabetes in older people should be generally managed through lifestyle modification first, including exercise, according to Dr. Lipska. Nevertheless, medications are often required to bring down blood sugar levels, she said. "For many older people with serious health problems or a history of hypoglycemia, tight blood sugar control may not be worth the risks involved. But for some relatively healthy people, tight blood sugar control may make sense. Treatment should be individualized, which requires a careful case-by-case approach," she said. Unfortunately, this is not always the case in practice. Her study found absolutely no difference in how people were treated based on their health. In other words, patients in poor health and at risk for hypoglycemia tended to be treated as aggressively as far healthier patients. What's more, 55% of older adults with diabetes who achieved tight blood sugar control were taking insulin or sulfonylureas—drugs that can lead to hypoglycemia—regardless of whether they were healthy, had complex health issues and/or were in poor health.

To avoid overtreatment for diabetes, Dr. Lipska recommends that you make the necessary lifestyle changes and work together with doctors and other health-care providers on a personalized approach to your specific health needs and safety. You need to be engaged and part of the plan. The plan should involve much more than simply prescribing a diabetes drug if your blood sugar is above the recommended threshold.

Glucose Monitor Updates

New apps share glucose levels. The FDA recently approved the first set of mobile medical apps that allow people with diabetes to automatically and securely share data from a continuous glucose monitor (CGM) with other people in real time using iPhones or other Apple devices.

How it works: With Dexcom Share Direct Secondary Displays, a sensor is implanted beneath the skin and glucose levels in the fluid around cells are tracked. An alert is sent when levels are dangerously high or low.

Helpful: CGM data can be shared with up to five people, such as family members, caregivers and doctors.

Eric Pahon, former spokesman, FDA, Silver Spring, Maryland.

Better Glucose Monitoring in the Hospital

The FDA recently approved the use of the Nova StatStrip Glucose Hospital Meter System—which quickly monitors blood sugar—for all hospitalized patients, including those who are critically ill. Accurate monitoring and blood glucose control are important for all hospital patients to reduce complications and length of stay and to speed recovery after surgery. The system was originally approved in 2006 for monitoring outpatients enrolled in hospital diabetes control programs.

Osama Hamdy, MD, PhD, medical director, Obesity Clinical Program, Joslin Diabetes Center, Boston.

Test Your Glucose Meter for Accuracy

Glucose meters that check blood sugar should be tested for accuracy every time users open a new pack of test strips, get a new meter or suspect a malfunction. A recent survey found that only 23% of patients with diabetes who use glucose meters said they followed these manufacturer recommendations.

Here's how to test a glucose meter: Use one drop of the control-solution liquid on the test strip (just like you would check your own blood sugar) to test the accuracy of both the meter and packages of test strips.

Katherine O'Neal, PharmD, assistant professor, The University of Oklahoma College of Pharmacy, Tulsa.

Can Bread Cause Diabetes?

Andrew L. Rubman, ND, medical director, Southbury Clinic for Traditional Medicines, Southbury, Connecticut. SouthburyClinic.com

We know that food—specifically too much of it and the resulting weight gain—can cause type 2 diabetes. But could what we eat be a cause of type 1 diabetes? Perhaps, says a new study that has linked wheat consumption to development of type

1 diabetes in young people (generally age 40 and younger), in a finding that has surprised many doctors and scientists. This is research that Andrew L. Rubman, ND, says is "quite amazing and hugely important."

Unlike the more common type 2, type 1 diabetes is a progressive autoimmune disorder that people develop early in life. Some cases have clear genetic roots, but scientists have believed that environmental factors could also play a role—including, possibly, something in the diet. This small study from the University of Ottawa demonstrates that one factor may be wheat consumption.

WHEAT AND DIABETES LINK

The study included 42 men and women, mostly young adults, with type 1 diabetes and a control group of 22 similar young people who did not have diabetes or any other known autoimmune disease. Researchers wanted to see how the immune systems in those with diabetes would respond to wheat.

What they learned: Twenty of the 42 diabetes patients were "high responders" to wheat, which was demonstrated by heightened immune system activity. According to the researchers, this response was found at a "significantly higher" rate than in the control group. Also, nearly all patients in this group carried a gene known to increase risk of diabetes.

WHEAT AND WHAT ELSE?

Wheat cannot be said to actually have caused the onset of diabetes in these patients, Dr. Rubman said, but the study does make a case that wheat consumption (specifically gluten found in wheat, rye and barley) could play a role in turning the genetic diabetes switch to "on" for those who carry the risk gene. Other factors may be involved too, he noted, while affirming that this study provides an early seed of knowledge that may someday help people avoid diabetes onset, or at the very least reduce the distress it causes. While there is more to learn, it is a healthy habit for all, especially children, to limit wheat consumption, rotating it with assorted other grains in order to minimize its impact on the body.

Dr. Rubman says that gluten avoidance might prove useful for people who already have type 1 diabetes because it may reduce the impact of the disease. If you have this type of diabetes, try a gluten-free diet for four to six months to see if symptom severity and blood sugar control improve. If the answer is yes, Dr. Rubman advises staying gluten-free for life.

Better Way to Eat

People with diabetes who ate the protein and vegetable portions of a meal 15 minutes before starting in on their carbs reduced their one-hour postmeal glucose levels by 37%, compared with their glucose on a day when they ate carbs first. Insulin levels were also lower when they ate protein and vegetables first.

Why: Carbs can cause glucose and insulin levels to spike, but protein appears to mitigate this effect.

Louis Aronne, MD, professor of metabolic research, Weill Cornell Medical College, New York City.

Diabetes Drug Caution

There's a diabetes medication risk for people with an underactive thyroid. *Metformin*, a drug often prescribed to regulate blood sugar levels, may lower thyroid-stimulating hormone (TSH) in patients who have an underactive thyroid. Low TSH increases risk for cardiovascular problems and broken bones. Talk to your doctor before beginning metformin therapy.

Laurent Azoulay, PhD, associate professor at McGill University, Montreal, and leader of a study of 74,300 patients over 25 years, published in *Canadian Medical Association Journal*.

Timing Is Everything... Especially with Your Medications

William J.M. Hrushesky, MD, former principal investigator at the Chronobiology and Oncology Research Laboratory at the Dorn Research Institute VA Medical Center in Columbia, South Carolina. He also is a retired adjunct professor of epidemiology and biostatistics at the University of South Carolina School of Medicine in Columbia and author of *Circadian Cancer Therapy*.

The time of day that you take your medication can make a big difference in how well you do.

Few doctors talk to their patients about the best time of day to take medication or undergo surgery, but it can make a big difference. *Examples...*

If you have high blood pressure, it's usually best to take slow-release medication at bedtime. For osteoarthritis, your pain reliever needs to work hardest in the afternoon. Why does the timing matter?

Virtually every bodily function—including blood pressure, heart rate and body temperature—is influenced by our circadian (24-hour) clocks. External factors, such as seasonal rhythms, also play a role in certain medical conditions.

For optimal results when treating your diabetes...

Physiological reactions that are more detrimental at night than in the morning are believed to play a role in both type 2 diabetes and metabolic syndrome—a constellation of conditions that includes insulin resistance (in which the body's cells don't use insulin properly), abdominal obesity, high blood pressure and elevated LDL "bad" cholesterol.

The body produces and uses insulin most effectively in the daytime hours and its metabolism is most active during the day. The liver, pancreas and muscles are better able to utilize blood sugar (glucose) and burn calories when metabolism is high. Because metabolism slows at night, someone who eats a lot of snack foods, for example, at night will be unable to efficiently remove the resulting glucose and fats from the blood. Over time, this can cause a chronic rise in insulin and cholesterol and may lead to metabolic syndrome.

For best results: People with metabolic syndrome or diabetes (or those who are at increased risk for either condition due to obesity or high blood pressure) should synchronize their meals with their metabolic rhythms. Consume most of your calories early in the day. Eat a relatively light supper—for example, a piece of fish, a green salad and vegetables—preferably at least a few hours before going to bed. Diabetes drugs, such as insulin, should be taken in anticipation of daytime calories and carbohydrates.

Measure Sugar Before Meals

Diabetics should measure blood sugar before meals to best establish their long-term blood sugar levels. Premeal sugar level is more closely aligned with long-term levels than standard blood sugar measurements taken two hours after a meal. Postmeal levels are still important to measure the effects of the meal on blood sugar.

Important: Those with diabetes should maintain a low-sugar and low-carbohydrate diet.

The late Stanley Mirsky, MD, associate clinical professor at Mount Sinai School of Medicine and founder of the Stanley Mirsky MD Diabetes Education Unit at the Mount Sinai Metabolism Institute, both in New York City. He is coauthor of *Diabetes Survival Guide*.

Are Two Large Meals Good for Diabetes?

A recent, highly publicized Czech study suggested that eating only breakfast and lunch is better for controlling blood sugar, weight and other factors than six smaller meals a day.

But the study was very small and went against years of diabetes research.

Best for people with diabetes: Patients who use insulin before meals to adjust blood sugar levels must wait at least five or six hours after a meal before adjusting blood sugar levels again and eating another meal. Patients who do not adjust blood sugar levels before meals may be able to control sugar levels with smaller, frequent meals.

Richard K. Bernstein, MD, a diabetes specialist in private practice in Mamaroneck, New York, and author of several books on diabetes, including *Dr. Bernstein's Diabetes Solution: A Complete Guide to Achieving Normal Blood Sugars.* His free monthly teleseminars are available at AskDrBernstein.net.

Chamomile Tea Protects Against Diabetes Damage

The late Stanley Mirsky, MD, coauthor of the *Diabetes Survival Guide.* Dr. Mirsky was a practicing internist and diabetologist, a past president of the American Diabetes Association of New York State and a board member of the Joslin Diabetes Center. He was named Endocrinologist of the Year for 2005 at the Mount Sinai School of Medicine.

Chamomile is one of the most popular herbal teas. Moms give it to their children to soothe tummy aches and may have a cup themselves to relieve stress or gastrointestinal discomfort. People turn to chamomile tea to calm themselves at bedtime or to reduce cold and flu symptoms...and now evidence has emerged that it may also be helpful in preventing complications of type 2 diabetes.

CHAMOMILE QUENCHES FREE RADICALS

According to Stanley Mirsky, MD, former associate clinical professor of medicine at the Mount Sinai School of Medicine in New York and coauthor of the *Diabetes Survival Guide,* chamomile is thought to be beneficial for people with diabetes because it is so rich in antioxidants, which quench free radicals in the body that contribute to disease by allowing inflammation to flourish. In Japan and the United Kingdom (same study, multiple international authors in different locations), researchers fed diabetic rats a chamomile extract prepared from the dried flowers of *Matricaria chamomilla* for 21 days. When compared with a similar group of rats who also had diabetes and were fed the same diet but without the chamomile, the chamomile-treated animals had a significant drop in blood sugar. There was also a decline in two enzymes that are associated with dangerous diabetic complications such as loss of vision, nerve damage and kidney damage.

Results of the study were published in the *Journal of Agricultural and Food Chemistry.* The researchers expressed hope that these preliminary findings might one day lead to a chamomile-based treatment for diabetes that would be cheaper and have less side effects than pharmaceutical treatments.

Even as this research continues, it may be helpful to add chamomile tea to your diet. For those who like it (and have no contraindications, as it is known to interact with certain medications), it may be a good substitute for sugary sodas or fruit juices, which can wreak havoc on blood sugar levels. Check with your doctor first.

Drinking Wine with Diabetes....

Is it safe to drink red wine—or even recommended—if you have diabetes?

Red wine in moderation usually is not harmful to people with diabetes and may benefit them by decreasing stress and lessening feelings of deprivation. *But talk to your doctor...*

If you take insulin: Alcohol lowers blood sugar, so you may need less insulin.

Also: Eat when you drink to buffer the alcohol's effect.

If you take the drug metformin (Glucophage)*:* The combination of metformin and alcohol can increase the risk for a serious condition called lactic acidosis.

Anne Peters, MD, professor of medicine, University of Southern California, and director of the USC Westside Center for Diabetes, both in Beverly Hills. She is author of *Conquering Diabetes.*

Is It Riskier to Be a Thin Diabetic?

Mercedes R. Carnethon, PhD, associate professor of preventive medicine, associate chair for faculty development and mentoring, department of preventive medicine, Feinberg School of Medicine, Northwestern University, Chicago. Her study was published in *The Journal of the American Medical Association*.

It's well-known that obesity raises the risk for type 2 diabetes, but roughly 11% of people with the disease have a "normal" body mass index between 18.5 and 24.9.

They are what you might call "thin people with diabetes."

If you're one of them, you might assume that you're at lower risk for serious complications from your diabetes—but a new study actually shows the opposite.

It has found that people with type 2 diabetes who are not overweight have a higher risk for death from any cause, compared with overweight or obese people with type 2 diabetes.

PUZZLING PARADOX

In the study, scientists analyzed data that followed a total of 2,625 people from the time of their type 2 diabetes diagnoses for anywhere from seven to 28 years (or their death).

It showed that people who were of normal weight at the time of diagnosis had more than twice the risk of dying from any cause as people who were overweight or obese at the time of diagnosis, and this held true even after adjusting for factors such as age, smoking and blood pressure.

That finding seems backward. Lead author Mercedes Carnethon, PhD, explains…

THE SKINNY ON RISK

Dr. Carnethon said that there are several possible explanations for why normal-weight people with diabetes might die sooner than overweight people with diabetes, including…

• **Loss of lean muscle.** As people age, some drop pounds because they lose muscle and bone—not fat. That's a problem, though, because fat isn't as sensitive to insulin as muscle is, so the higher your fat-to-muscle ratio, the less your body is able to use circulating glucose for energy. In other words, it's possible that a person with a "normal" weight who has a high fat-to-muscle ratio could have a higher risk for death than a person who is classified as "overweight" and has a lower fat-to-muscle ratio.

• **Other illnesses.** Diabetes is generally an obesity-related disorder, so having diabetes and a normal weight might reflect another underlying illness—and that underlying illness might be what raises the risk for death. The researchers did exclude participants who died within two years of developing diabetes, but they were not able to account for other diseases participants may have had, such as cancer.

• **Less aggressive treatment.** It's possible that leaner people with diabetes are screened less frequently and/or less carefully…or that they are undertreated once their diabetes is diagnosed, because doctors may mistakenly perceive them to be at lower risk for complications and death compared with overweight people with diabetes.

IT'S NOT AN EXCUSE TO EAT FRIED FOODS

So if you are of normal weight and have type 2 diabetes, what can you do to help prolong your life? Certainly, the results of this study do not suggest that you should just gobble food to gain weight. *But there are a few things that you can do, Dr. Carnethon said…*

1. Talk to your physician about it. Make sure that your doctor fully appreciates that even though you are not overweight or obese, your diabetes still represents a risk to your well-being and you should be evaluated and treated no less aggressively than your overweight counterparts. In fact, show him or her this article about death rates if you need to!

And ask: "Do we fully understand the reason I got diabetes…and are we doing everything possible to treat that underlying cause?"

2. Make yourself strong. Exercise of any kind will help improve your blood sugar control, but strength training, in particular, is a great way to lose fat and increase muscle.

By following these two simple tips, you'll have a better chance of living a long, healthy life!

Poor Sleep Might Worsen Diabetes

Kristen L. Knutson, PhD, assistant professor, medicine, University of Chicago.

Joel Zonszein, MD, director, Clinical Diabetes Center, Montefiore Medical Center, New York City.

Diabetes Care.

People with diabetes who sleep poorly have higher blood glucose levels and a more difficult time controlling their disease, a study shows.

Researchers compared 40 people with type 2 diabetes to 531 people without the blood sugar disease. The investigators looked at potential links between sleep quality, blood glucose levels and other measures of diabetes control.

"We found that in those with diabetes, there was an association between poor sleep quality and worse glucose measures," said study leader Kristen Knutson, PhD, an assistant professor of medicine at the University of Chicago.

"We did not see a relationship in people without diabetes," she said.

The study was published in the journal *Diabetes Care*.

EXAMINING A LINK

Previous research has found some linkage between diabetes and poor sleep. Dr. Knutson said it is just an association, not cause-and-effect. "It may be that people with diabetes are more vulnerable to the effects of impaired sleep," she said. "But it could go either way." Those who don't control their diabetes could have worse sleep than those who do, she said.

"We need to look more closely at the role of sleep in diabetes," she added.

STUDY DETAILS

For the study, Dr. Knutson monitored sleep by having people wear wrist activity monitors. "If you are moving your wrist a lot, you are probably awake," she said.

The participants also reported on their sleep quality.

The researchers found that those with diabetes who had trouble sleeping had a 23% higher fasting blood glucose level, a 48% higher fasting insulin level and an 82% higher insulin resistance than the normal sleepers with diabetes.

EXPERT REACTION

The findings tend to reflect what is seen in clinical practice, said Joel Zonszein, MD, director of the Clinical Diabetes Center at Montefiore Medical Center in New York City.

He, too, pointed out that the results beg the "chicken-egg" question. "They cannot tell us if the higher sugars were caused by the poor sleep or if the patients who have higher sugars don't sleep well or there are other factors causing that," Dr. Zonszein said.

Often, he noted, those with type 2 diabetes are overweight and that excess weight may impair sleep quality. Obesity is linked with sleep apnea, in which the patient often stops breathing during the night and is then awakened, for instance.

IMPROVING SLEEP IS KEY

The take-home message for those with diabetes is to pay attention to their sleep quality, agreed Drs. Zonszein and Knutson. "If no sleep studies have been done, they might want to ask their doctor [about doing some]," Dr. Zonszein said.

Reducing stress, which is easier said than done, should be another goal for those with diabetes and poor sleep, he added. "A lot of people are stressed, and they don't sleep well," Dr. Zonszein said.

"Don't wait for your doctor to ask you about sleep," said Dr. Knutson. "People with diabetes need to take their sleep seriously and talk to their doctor about it."

To learn more about how improving sleep habits can help you manage diabetes, visit the website of the Mayo Clinic, *www.mayoclinic. org*.

How People with Diabetes Should Exercise

Jane Yardley, PhD, assistant professor, social sciences, University of Alberta. She was formerly a postdoctoral fellow, Human and Environmental Physiology Research Unit, University of Ottawa, Ontario, Canada. Her study was published in *Diabetes Care*.

If you have type 1 diabetes (the kind where your body can't produce insulin), then you know that regular exercise is essential because it helps keep blood sugar under control and reduces the chance of complications such as high blood pressure and high cholesterol.

But when you exercise, which do you do first—cardio/aerobic...or strength training?

That may sound like a silly question, but a recent study suggests that the order in which you do your exercises can make a big difference in terms of how well you control your blood sugar.

USING THE PROPER FUEL

To understand the research, keep in mind that the human body can use either glucose or fats as fuel—and, of course, for people with diabetes, the level of glucose in the blood tends to be out of whack.

Now, in previous studies, it's been shown that in healthy people (who do not have diabetes), performing strength training immediately before aerobic exercise increases the body's use of fats—not glucose—as fuel. And insulin, which is key to the proper maintenance of blood glucose, plays a less important role when fats are being used as fuel. Therefore, researchers were curious to find out whether exercising in this particular order might better protect individuals with diabetes from hypoglycemia (low blood sugar).

LET'S GET MOVING

The research involved 12 men and women (average age 32) with type 1 diabetes who already lifted weights and ran at least three times a week. For the study, each participant completed two exercise sessions held at least five days apart. In one session, each subject ran on a treadmill for 45 minutes and then lifted weights for 45 minutes. In the other session, the sequence was reversed.

Both sessions were held at the same time of day and the participants ate the same foods the day before, the day of and the day after they exercised. Whenever a participant's glucose dropped too close to a hypoglycemic level during exercise, the exercise was interrupted and the participant was given a carbohydrate supplement to bring glucose back up. The participants were set up with continuous glucose monitoring starting the day before their exercise sessions and ending the following day.

Results: Those who performed strength training first were less likely to reach the hypoglycemic danger zone. In fact, 43% more glucose supplementation was needed when running came first.

Plus, the blood sugar benefits of strength training first lasted through the night. Researchers found that nighttime episodes of hypoglycemia were, on average, shorter (48 minutes rather than 105 minutes) and less severe following an exercise session that began with strength training.

LIFT BEFORE YOU RUN

Why might strength training first have such a positive effect on blood sugar? Jane Yardley, PhD, the study's lead author, said that more growth hormone is secreted during anaerobic exercise (such as strength training), and growth hormone might increase the use of fats as fuel, rather than glucose.

Another possibility: Performing strength training first can cause lactate to circulate in the blood. Some lactate could be converted to glucose, so blood sugar wouldn't drop as quickly.

So should all people with type 1 diabetes strength train before doing cardio? Dr. Yardley recommends it, though she did point out one limitation to the study, which is that the participants were fit, and fit people may use glucose differently than people who aren't in such good shape. But whether you're fit or unfit, it wouldn't hurt to strength train first, said Dr. Yardley. Even if you can't handle 45 minutes of each type of exercise, it's not the total time that matters—it's the order.

Dr. Yardley commented on whether this advice would also hold true for individuals with type 2 diabetes. She explained that most type 2 diabetics are not insulin-dependent, so hypoglycemia isn't as big a risk. Therefore, the order in which they do those exercises isn't likely as critical.

Control Diabetes with Qigong

Guan-Cheng Sun, PhD, assistant research scientist at Bastyr University, Kenmore, Washington, qigong teacher and executive director and founder of the Institute of Qigong & Integrative Medicine, Seattle.

Wouldn't it be great if you could just wave your arms to get better control over your blood sugar? A research scientist at Bastyr University in Washington has adapted the ancient Chinese practice of movement called qigong (pronounced chee-gong) to help people with type 2 diabetes achieve better blood sugar control…feel better…and even reduce their reliance on drugs.

Study author Guan-Cheng Sun, PhD, assistant research scientist at Bastyr, qigong teacher and executive director and founder of the Institute of Qigong & Integrative Medicine in Seattle, says there are many types of qigong. What makes his version unique is the way it explicitly incorporates a specific energy component.

Dr. Sun named his new system Yi Ren Qigong (Yi means "change" and Ren means "human") and says it works by teaching patients with diabetes to calm the chi, or "life energy" of the liver (to slow production of glucose) and to enhance the chi of the pancreas (exhausted by overproducing insulin). The goal of this practice is to "improve the harmony between these organs and increase energy overall," he said, noting that his patients have achieved significant results—reduced blood glucose levels, lower stress and less insulin resistance. Some were even able to cut back the dosages of their medications.

HOW DO THEY KNOW IT WORKED?

Dr. Sun's research team studied 32 patients, all on medication for their diabetes.

They were divided into three groups: One group practiced qigong on their own at home twice a week for 30 minutes and also attended a one-hour weekly session led by an instructor. The second group engaged in a prescribed program of gentle exercise that included movements similar to the qigong practice but without the energy component for an equivalent period of time. And the third group continued their regular medication and medical care but did not engage in structured exercise.

The results: After 12 weeks, the qigong patients had lowered their fasting blood glucose, their levels of self-reported stress and improved their insulin resistance. The gentle exercise group also brought down blood glucose levels, though somewhat less…and lowered stress. It was worse yet for the third group—blood glucose levels climbed and so did insulin resistance, while there was no reported change in their stress levels. The study was published in *Diabetes Care*.

While Yi Ren Qigong is not available anywhere beyond Bastyr, Dr. Sun is developing a training program for instructors who can then teach in their own communities.

The Martial Art That Defeats Diabetes

Beverly Roberts, PhD, RN, professor, University of Florida College of Nursing.
Paul Lam, MD, family physician, tai chi master, clinical teacher and lecturer, University of South Wales, Australia.
Daniel Caulfield, tai chi instructor at Flow Martial and Meditative Arts, in Keene, New Hampshire. FlowMMA.org

People with diabetes often assume that for exercise to be beneficial, you have to be huffing and puffing, sweating and red-faced afterward," says Beverly Roberts, PhD, RN, a professor at University of Florida College of Nursing. "However, we found that a gentle activity such as tai chi can be just as beneficial in improving the health of people with diabetes."

Dr. Roberts is talking about a recent study that she and her colleagues conducted showing that regular practice of tai chi—an ancient martial art from China consisting of deep breathing and gentle, flowing movements—can help you lower blood sugar, manage diabetes more effectively, improve mood and boost energy levels.

TAI CHI FOR GLUCOSE CONTROL

A team of researchers from Korea and the US studied 62 people with type 2 diabetes—31 practiced tai chi twice a week, and 31 didn't.

After six months, those practicing tai chi had a greater drop in fasting blood sugar (a test that measures blood sugar after you haven't eaten for eight hours)…a bigger decrease in A1C (a measurement of long-term blood sugar levels)…more participation in diabetic self-care activities, such as daily measuring of glucose levels…happier social interactions…better mood…and more energy.

"For those with type 2 diabetes, tai chi could be an alternative exercise to increase glucose control, diabetic self-care activities and quality of life," conclude the researchers, in the *Journal of Alternative and Complementary Medicine*.

"Tai chi has similar effects as other exercises on diabetic control," says Dr. Roberts. "The difference is that tai chi is a low-impact exercise, which means that it's less stressful on the bones, joints and muscles than more strenuous exercise.

"Tai chi provides a great alternative for people who want the benefits of exercise on diabetic control, but may be physically unable to complete strenuous activities because of age, health condition or injury."

HELPS IN SEVERAL WAYS

"These and other studies show that tai chi can have a significant effect on the management and treatment of diabetes," says Paul Lam, MD, of the University of South Wales School of Public Health, the author of five scientific studies on tai chi and diabetes.

"Tai chi can help with diabetes in several ways," he continues. "It can help you control blood sugar, reduce stress and minimize the complications of diabetes, such as high blood pressure, high cholesterol and the balance and mobility problems that accompany peripheral neuropathy."

Dr. Lam developed the tai chi program that was used in several studies on tai chi and diabetes—Tai Chi for Diabetes. It is available on DVD, and includes a complete tai chi routine, along with a warm-up, stretches, and qigong exercises (also from China) that increase the flow of chi (life force) in the parts of the body affected by diabetes.

Dr. Lam is also the coauthor of the book, *Tai Chi for Diabetes: Living Well with Diabetes*, which supplements the DVD.

Both the DVD and the book are available at *www.amazon.com*. You can also learn more about the Tai Chi for Diabetes program at Dr. Lam's website *www.taichifordiabetes.com*, where you can also order his DVD and book.

Also helpful: If you decide to take a tai chi class, look for an instructor who has practiced for at least three to four years, and who inspires you to the regular practice of tai chi, says Daniel Caulfield, a teacher of tai chi at Flow Martial and Meditative Arts, in Keene, New Hampshire. "The greatest benefit from tai chi comes from both taking a class with a qualified instructor and practicing at home at least 20 minutes a day."

Watch Out for Extreme Weather

Extreme heat is more dangerous for individuals with diabetes.

Recent finding: People who have type 1 or type 2 diabetes often have difficulty adjusting to rises in temperature. Also, due to nerve damage associated with diabetes, their sweat glands may not produce enough perspiration to cool them down. This may explain why people with diabetes have higher rates of hospitalization, dehydration and death in warmer months. Winter also can be a prob- lem for diabetics because poor circulation increases the likelihood of skin damage in the cold weather.

Jerrold S. Petrofsky, PhD, professor of physical therapy, School of Allied Health Professions, Loma Linda University, Loma Linda, California, and coauthor of a study published in *The Journal of Applied Research*.

7

Diabetes Treatment Breakthroughs

A Promising Treatment for Type 1 Diabetes

For people with type 1 diabetes, each day means carefully monitoring blood sugar, planning every bite of food and bit of physical activity, and injecting the insulin they need to stay alive. Many hope for a miracle that will free them from this relentless challenge. *Now that miracle may be at hand, thanks to breakthrough research from Israel...*

WHY IT'S SO HARD

Type 1 diabetes (formerly called juvenile diabetes) most often appears during childhood or adolescence—but it can develop at any age, so none of us are free from the threat.

An autoimmune disease, it occurs when the immune system mistakenly attacks the beta cells in the pancreas. Normally, beta cells detect the amount of sugar in the blood and release insulin, the hormone that converts sugar to energy for our cells. When the beta cells are destroyed, the body produces little or no insulin...so sugar builds up in the bloodstream, where it can cause life-threatening complications. To prevent these, type 1 diabetes patients must take insulin injections or use an insulin pump every day—but these carry the risk of triggering an injection-related plummet in blood sugar levels, or "insulin shock," which can be fatal.

What sets off the mistaken immune response is still a mystery, but research suggests that inflammation plays a key role. For instance, studies in mice that are genetically engineered to develop type 1 diabetes have shown that treatment with alpha-1 antitrypsin (AAT), an anti-inflammatory protein normally made by the liver and specialized white blood cells, can actually reverse type 1 diabetes...at least in mice.

Eli Lewis, PhD, director of the Clinical Islet Laboratory and senior lecturer in the department of clinical biochemistry and pharmacology, Ben-Gurion University of the Negev, Beer Sheva, Israel. This research was published in *Journal of Clinical Endocrinology and Metabolism*.

Of course, it's a huge leap to take a treatment from mice to humans—but that's what researchers from Israel, in collaboration with the University of Colorado Health Sciences Center, are trying to do. Eli Lewis, PhD, is director of the Clinical Islet Laboratory and senior lecturer in the department of clinical biochemistry and pharmacology at Ben-Gurion University of the Negev, one of the leaders of this promising research.

SAY GOODBYE TO INSULIN INJECTIONS?

Dr. Lewis and colleagues recently published an exciting Phase I study (phase I studies are typically the first studies done on people after preclinical animal studies are completed). For this study, 12 people with type 1 diabetes were given intravenous infusions of AAT once per week for eight weeks. Participants ranged in age from 12 to 39 years old, and all had been diagnosed within the previous four years. Blood samples were taken before treatment began and periodically afterward, ending 18 months after treatment initiation. All participants reportedly tolerated the 30-minute infusions comfortably (typically playing video games or otherwise amusing themselves during the treatment), and no one dropped out—an excellent outcome relating to safety and compliance.

Very encouraging results: Five of the 12 participants had a stunning response—they are no longer dependent on insulin injections!

Participants who were the most recently diagnosed tended to have the best response. This makes sense. Newly diagnosed patients are still experiencing an ongoing immune attack, and they still have some functioning beta cells left, just not enough to control glucose. The active immune system and residual beta cells provide the AAT with an optimal platform to work on.

Is AAT safe? The only adverse event reported was temporary hyperglycemia (high blood sugar)—not surprising because AAT already has a proven track record for safety. This FDA-approved drug has been on the market for more than two decades and is used to treat people with a rare genetic disorder that ren-

ders them incapable of producing enough of their own AAT. These patients receive injections of the AAT drug once each week for their entire lives, and most experience no side effects (though occasionally some patients have mild side effects, such as headache or light-headedness, associated with a too-rapid infusion). The dosage used in this study was the same as that used for people with this genetic disorder.

The lack of adverse effects is one of AAT's significant advantages. There are dozens of other clinical trials for diabetes treatments in the works, and some are very extreme, including chemotherapy and other immunosuppressive treatments. With AAT, however, the worst that happens is that it doesn't work in some individuals and they simply remain on insulin.

A PERMANENT SOLUTION?

It's too soon to say whether the diabetes patients who respond well to AAT therapy will remain in remission forever. However, in the study, none of the people who responded to AAT have yet experienced a relapse—and their treatment occurred more than two years ago. Also, some other type 1 diabetes patients for whom AAT was prescribed off-label as many as eight years ago are still free of the need for insulin injections, Dr. Lewis said.

Why it works: People with type 1 diabetes are not deficient in AAT, but the extra glucose in their blood ends up coating their own AAT molecules, making them unable to fight inflammation. In contrast, AAT molecules in the therapeutic infusion are "dry and clean," at least when they're first infused. After about a week, they do become coated with glucose and are too damaged to work...but before that happens, the AAT molecules stop inflammatory proteins from damaging the beta cells of the pancreas. Also, since the test-protocol treatment consists of weekly infusions, by the time one dose of molecules becomes coated with glucose, the next infusion arrives and provides a fresh supply of dry, clean molecules.

The dosage used in the study is very similar to the amount we naturally produce when our AAT production goes into high gear—for instance, when our bodies are in the midst of an inflammatory response due to the flu. Maintaining that level of AAT production for eight straight weeks was required in order to elicit a long-lasting response that sent type 1 diabetes into remission. We removed the inflammatory injury from the equation. This gave the beta cells a chance to survive and recover...and helped the immune system re-educate itself so it no longer sees the beta cells as targets for an immune attack. Unlike many other approaches, AAT treatment requires the presence of the immune system and does not attempt to get rid of it.

WHAT PATIENTS CAN DO NOW

Though this was a very small study, Dr. Lewis's team and collaborators have additional studies already under way, and so far the responses have been extremely encouraging. It will likely be a few years or so before AAT could receive FDA approval as an official ("on-label") treatment for type 1 diabetes.

In the meantime: The researchers are recruiting type 1 diabetes patients for additional trials. If you are interested in participating, check the National Institutes of Health clinical trial database (*http://clinicalstudies.info.nih. gov/*) (enter "type 1 diabetes" and "AAT" into the search box). Another option is to talk with your endocrinologist about using AAT off-label now. There's no guarantee of success... but for patients who do respond to AAT, the treatment may be truly life-altering. We have kids who are now leading totally normal lives, eating normally and feeling comfortable in school without having to see the school nurse four times a day.

Will the treatment ever work for people who were diagnosed years or even decades earlier? We still do not know. Our choice of adhering to recent-onset cases is to optimize the trial, but some success has also been evident in a few advanced patients. The closest AAT-related option for patients who appear too far down the road may be islet transplantation (transplantation of pancreas cells from a donor)—for this, we have evidence that AAT will provide profound protection with an extraordinary safety margin.

AAT is not cheap, costing several thousand dollars (depending on body weight) for the eight-session treatment. Because it is still experimental as a diabetes treatment, it is not covered by insurance. Still, compared to the price of a lifetime supply of insulin—plus the nonmonetary costs of needing to rely on an insulin pump or injections and constantly worrying about eating the wrong thing or injecting too much insulin—many patients may consider the cost of AAT to be a more-than-fair trade.

Stem Cell Success Raises Hopes of Type 1 Diabetes Cure

Douglas A. Melton, PhD, co-scientific director, department of stem cell and regenerative biology, Harvard Stem Cell Institute, Harvard University, Cambridge, Massachusetts.

Albert Hwa, PhD, operations director, cell-based therapy for diabetes, Joslin Diabetes Centrer Boston, former director, discovery research, JDRF.

Cell.

In what may be a step toward a cure for type 1 diabetes, researchers say they've developed a large-scale method for turning human embryonic stem cells into fully functioning beta cells capable of producing insulin.

Currently, people with type 1 diabetes need daily insulin injections to maintain blood sugar control. But "insulin injections don't cure the disease," said study coauthor Douglas Melton, of Harvard University. Patients are vulnerable to metabolic swings that can bring about serious complications, including blindness and limb loss, he said.

"We wanted to replace insulin injections using nature's own solution, being the pancreatic beta cell," Dr. Melton said. Now, "we are reporting the ability to make hundreds of millions of these cells," he added.

Dr. Melton ultimately envisions a credit card-sized package of beta cells that can be safely transplanted into a diabetes patient and left in place for a year or more, before needing to be replaced.

But between then and now, human trials must be launched, a venture Dr. Melton thinks could begin in about three years.

If that research pans out, the Harvard team's results may prove to be a benchmark in the multi-decade effort to deliver on the promise of stem cell research as a way to access new treatments for all sorts of diseases.

Dr. Melton, co-director of the Stem Cell Institute at Harvard, described his work as a "personal quest," given that he has two children with type 1 diabetes.

BACKGROUND ON STEM CELLS

Stem cells are essentially undifferentiated cells that can be induced into becoming specialized cells that are tissue- or organ-specific, according to the U.S. National Institutes of Health.

In some cases, such cells are sourced from embryonic tissue. Alternatively, it's possible to derive stem cells from prespecialized adult cells that are then reprogrammed to morph into an undifferentiated state. These are called induced pluripotent stem cells.

STUDY DETAILS

Because the current effort was launched before the innovation of induced pluripotent stem cells, Dr. Melton said his team conducted its work using embryonic stem cells. Nevertheless, he said the newfound ability to generate large supplies of beta cells will work using either type.

People without diabetes have an average of one billion beta cells, but only about 150 million are actually needed to do the job, Dr. Melton said. Producing that quantity is essentially no longer a problem, according to the researchers.

The induced beta cells have roughly the same genetic expression, structure and function as naturally produced human beta cells, the study authors explained. And ongoing animal testing suggests that when transplanted into mice they don't just control diabetes, they cure it.

"When provided to an immuno-compromised mouse, we can cure their diabetes right away, in less than 10 days," Dr. Melton said.

The trick going forward will be to replicate that scenario in animals whose immune system is healthy and on guard. It's possible that the launch of an automatic immune response could halt the cure in its tracks, the scientists said.

Work to solve this problem is already underway, however. So far, said Dr. Melton, "cells have lived for six months in animals. But that's still ongoing, so we don't know how long they will ultimately survive."

He and his colleagues outlined the recent results in the journal *Cell*.

EXPERT COMMENT

In addition, experts note that findings in animals often fail to be replicated in humans.

Albert Hwa, PhD, former director of discovery research at JDRF, formerly the Juvenile Diabetes Research Foundation, said the team's results to date are an "important milestone."

"We've always known the potential of stem cell research to produce this kind of result," he said. "One of the promises of stem cell research has been regenerative medicine to replace organs or tissue in order to cure disease. And this is an example of that promise. So this is very significant."

For diabetes, Dr. Hwa added, "the enabling of easy access to this kind of cell production will likely have a very, very high impact on treatment going forward."

Artificial Pancreas for Type 1 Diabetes

The first "artificial pancreas" was recently attached to an Australian boy. It is a small pump that senses a drop in glucose levels and automatically turns off the delivery of insulin, preventing a hypoglycemic attack.

JDRF, formerly the Juvenile Diabetes Research Foundation.

Diabetes Groups Issue New Guidelines on Blood Sugar

Vivian Fonseca, MD, past president, medicine and science, American Diabetes Association.

Joel Zonszein, MD, director, Clinical Diabetes Center, Montefiore Medical Center, New York.

Diabetes Care.

Type 2 diabetes is a complex metabolic disorder, and treating the disease often requires a personalized, multi-pronged approach, according to revised expert guidelines on treating high blood sugar levels issued recently.

The recommendations are a joint effort by the American Diabetes Association and the European Association for the Study of Diabetes.

"We're making a lot of progress in managing type 2 diabetes," said Vivian Fonseca, MD, past president of medicine and science for the American Diabetes Association. "The new guidelines are more patient-centered. The message is to choose an appropriate [blood sugar] goal based on the patient's current health status, motivation level, resources and complications.

"It is very possible to manage type 2 diabetes well and keep blood sugar under good control," he noted. "It's important that patients have a discussion with their doctor about what their [blood sugar] goals should be, and what is the best treatment or treatments to get them to that goal."

The guidelines were published in *Diabetes Care.*

Dr. Fonseca said the revised guidelines were necessary because the management of type 2 diabetes is becoming increasingly complex; there is a widening array of medications available to treat the disease, and new research studies are constantly being released highlighting both the benefits and the risks of current treatments.

The biggest change in the revised guidelines is an emphasis on a patient-centered approach to treatment. For example, the blood sugar goal for someone who's young, healthy and motivated to manage type 2 diabetes will be lower than it is for someone who's elderly and has additional health problems.

Blood sugar goals are usually expressed in terms of hemoglobin A1C levels (HbA1C). HbA1C, often just referred to as A1C, is a measure of long-term blood sugar control. It gives an estimate of what the average blood sugar level has been for the past two to three months. A1C is expressed as a%age, and in general, the goal for people with type 2 diabetes is to lower their A1C levels below 7%. Someone without diabetes generally has levels below 5.6%, according to the American Diabetes Association.

In the past, the below-7-percent goal was applied to most people with type 2 diabetes. But, the revised guidelines note that more stringent goals, such as keeping A1C between 6% and 6.5%, might be appropriate for someone who has a long life expectancy, no history of heart disease and who hasn't experienced significant low blood sugar levels (hypoglycemia). Low blood sugar levels can be a potentially dangerous side effect of many diabetes treatments.

The recent guidelines suggest that blood sugar targets should be looser (A1C between 7.5% and 8%) for people who are older than 65 or 70, because they're more at risk of having complications from hypoglycemia, as well as being more at risk of side effects from taking multiple medications.

Lifestyle changes remain an important part of any type 2 diabetes management plan in the revised guidelines. The recommendations are to lose 5% to 10% of body weight, and to participate in modest exercise for at least two-and-a-half hours each week.

The medication *metformin* is also recommended as a first-line treatment for people with type 2 diabetes. Metformin works by making the body more receptive to the hormone insulin. Metformin therapy should begin as soon as someone is diagnosed with type 2 diabetes, unless they have a near-normal A1C and are highly motivated to make lifestyle changes, according to the guidelines. In such a case, doctors may choose to follow up with the patient in three to six months to see if the lifestyle changes have been effective. If not, metformin should be started.

The guidelines also recommend adding another drug to metformin therapy if blood sugar levels aren't under control after three months on metformin alone. Again, this is an area where the patient needs to be considered and consulted. Each additional treatment option has its own risks and benefits. Talk to your doctor about which might be right for you.

"The new guidelines take a patient-centered view: Treat the patient and not the blood sugar. The type of medication should be tailored to the pathophysiology of the patient," explained Joel Zonszein, MD, director of the Clinical Diabetes Center at Montefiore Medical Center in New York City.

"I feel that we need to have combination therapy much earlier in the disease, but the issue is that we don't have research data on combination therapy, and we need studies to know what are the best combinations. But, I believe it's important to be aggressive early in the disease to prevent complications," Dr. Zonszein said.

And, he added, although the current guidelines only cover the treatment of high blood sugar, it's also important to remember to control cholesterol and high blood pressure in people with type 2 diabetes.

For more information: Learn more about the types of medications available to treat type 2 diabetes from the American Diabetes Association website *www.diabetes.org/living-with-diabetes/treatment-and-care/medication/*.

Type 1 Diabetes More Deadly for Women Than Men

Rachel Huxley, PhD, head, School of Public Health, Curtin University, Perth, Western Australia.
David Simmons, MD, professor of medicine, University of Western Sydney, Penrith, Australia.
The Lancet Diabetes & Endocrinology, online.

Women with type 1 diabetes have a nearly 40% greater risk of dying from any cause and more than double the risk of dying from heart disease than men with type 1 diabetes, Australian researchers report.

In an analysis of 26 studies that included more than 200,000 people, researchers found that women with type 1 diabetes had a 37% higher risk of dying from stroke compared to men with type 1 diabetes. The researchers also found that women with type 1 diabetes had a 44% greater risk of dying from kidney disease than men with type 1 diabetes.

"Type 1 diabetes increases the risk of premature death in both women and men, but type 1 diabetes is much more deadly for women than men with the condition," said lead researcher Rachel Huxley, PhD, head, School of Public Health, Curtin University, Perth, Western Australia.

The report was published in an online edition of *The Lancet Diabetes & Endocrinology*.

BACKGROUND ON TYPE 1 DIABETES

Type 1 diabetes an autoimmune disease that destroys insulin-producing cells in the pancreas. Insulin is a hormone needed to convert sugars, starches and other foods into energy. The worldwide incidence of type 1 diabetes in children 14 and younger has risen by 3% every year since 1989. In the United States, about 40,000 children and adults are diagnosed with type 1 diabetes each year, according to the researchers.

Because people with type 1 diabetes don't produce their own insulin, they must replace the hormone through multiple daily injections or with an insulin pump that has a tiny tube inserted underneath the skin to deliver the insulin.

However, insulin needs change constantly, depending on foods eaten, activity levels and even stress. This makes it difficult to get the dose just right. When too little insulin is given, blood sugar levels rise. Over time, this can cause dangerous complications, such as an increased risk of heart disease.

But, too much insulin can cause low blood sugar levels (hypoglycemia), which can quickly cause a number of uncomfortable symptoms, such as sweating, nausea, irritability and confusion. Left untreated, hypoglycemia can lead to unconsciousness and even death, according to JDRF (formerly the Juvenile Diabetes Research Foundation).

WHY WOMEN ARE HIT HARDER

Women may have a harder time controlling blood sugar levels due to a number of factors, such as changing hormone levels—particularly during puberty—that can affect the body's sensitivity to insulin and cause fluctuations in blood sugar levels, according to Dr. Huxley and her coauthors. The researchers also speculated that high levels of blood sugar might cause more damage to women's blood vessels than to men's.

"The findings suggest that young girls and women with type 1 diabetes may need additional monitoring, not only to ensure that they are keeping their blood sugar levels under control, but also to make sure that their levels for other major risk factors, such as blood pressure, are also closely monitored," she said.

"As soon as an individual is diagnosed with type 1 diabetes—irrespective of sex—they should receive greater support and assistance in managing their health and risk factor levels for heart disease and stroke," Dr. Huxley added.

EXPERT COMMENT

David Simmons, MD, a professor of medicine at the University of Western Sydney in Penrith, Australia, and author of an accompanying journal editorial, said, "Among people without diabetes, women live longer than men. This advantage is being lost among women with type 1 diabetes. Both women and men with type 1 diabetes are dying much younger than they should."

Dr. Simmons said he doesn't know why this disparity exists, but it appears that excess sugar may cause more harm to women's blood vessels than to men's. "There may be a need to treat women earlier with drugs to prevent heart disease and stroke," he said.

He doesn't think blood sugar control is worse in women than it is in men. However, everyone with type 1 diabetes needs better ways of controlling blood sugar to prevent episodes of hypoglycemia. Hypoglycemia can

be life-threatening and take a toll on overall health, he said.

"Much of the excess death among men and women is preventable with better access to methods of controlling blood sugar, such as insulin pumps," Dr. Simmons said. "But we still need to research why these early deaths are happening."

For more on type 1 diabetes, visit the American Diabetes Association at *www.diabetes.org*.

Vaccine May Stop Immune Attack in Type 1 Diabetes, Study Suggests

Lawrence Steinman, MD, professor, pediatrics, neurology and neurological sciences, Stanford University School of Medicine, California.

Richard Insel, MD, chief scientific officer, JDRF, New York City.

Joel Zonszein, MD, director, Clinical Diabetes Center, Montefiore Medical Center, New York City.

Science Translational Medicine.

A new type of vaccine may stop the autoimmune attack that occurs in people with type 1 diabetes, researchers report. Although an initial trial of the vaccine wasn't able to free anyone from their daily insulin injections, it did boost insulin production, which could help prevent some of type 1 diabetes' most devastating complications.

Instead of increasing the immune system's activity like the polio or influenza vaccine does, the new vaccine turns off a portion of the immune response, acting as a reverse vaccine. The researchers were able to isolate a part of the immune response that only seems to be involved with type 1 diabetes, according to the study. That means the vaccine likely wouldn't have the risks that medications that suppress the immune system do.

"We were able to destroy the rogue cells that are attacking the insulin-producing cells without destroying any other part of the immune system, and that's truly exciting," said senior study author Lawrence Steinman, MD, a professor of pediatrics and neurology and neurological sciences at Stanford University School of Medicine.

"Once the immune attack is stopped, I believe there's great potential for recovery in the beta cells," Dr. Steinman added.

BACKGROUND ON INSULIN

Beta cells in the pancreas produce the hormone insulin. In people with type 1 diabetes, it's believed that the immune system mistakenly destroys the healthy beta cells, leaving the person with no or too little insulin.

Insulin is a crucial hormone because it's involved in the metabolism of carbohydrates. It allows the glucose (sugar) from carbohydrates to fuel the cells in the body and brain. Without enough insulin, a person will die. That's why people with type 1 diabetes must take multiple daily injections of insulin, or deliver insulin through a catheter inserted under the skin that's attached to an insulin pump.

HOW THE VACCINE WAS DESIGNED

The vaccine was designed by changing a piece of immune-system DNA so that it would shut down the immune system's response to signals in the body that have previously triggered the mistaken destruction of beta cells. These signals come from fragments of a protein (peptides) called proinsulin, which is found on the surface of beta cells. Proinsulin is a precursor to insulin.

"We just wanted to throw the off switch for the one cell being attacked," Dr. Steinman explained.

STUDY DETAILS

The researchers recruited 80 volunteers diagnosed with type 1 diabetes during the past five years. They were randomly placed in one of five groups. Four groups received various doses of the vaccine, and the fifth group received placebo injections. Shots were given weekly for 12 weeks.

No one in the study was able to stop using insulin. "That's a possible goal, but it's too early to start saying cure," Dr. Steinman noted.

It's difficult to measure insulin levels, because they can vary rapidly and dramatically. Instead, researchers measured an increase of a substance called C-peptide, a part of proin-

sulin that stays in the body longer than insulin. C-peptide levels are used as measure of insulin production.

C-peptide levels improved at all doses of the vaccine compared to the placebo, according to the study. And, it's believed that higher levels of C-peptide may be related to a reduction in some of the serious complications associated with type 1 diabetes, such as eye disease, kidney problems and heart disease.

No serious adverse events occurred during the trial.

Dr. Steinman said it's too soon to know how the vaccine might work in the real world. It's not clear how often someone would need to be given the vaccine, and how well the body might recover its ability to produce insulin once the autoimmune attack has stopped. It's also not clear if the vaccine might be more effective in people who've recently developed the disease, or in people who have a high risk of developing type 1 diabetes.

Dr. Steinman said he hopes to have the next trial under way in a year or so.

The study appeared online in the journal *Science Translational Medicine*.

EXPERT RESPONSE

Richard Insel, MD, chief scientific officer at JDRF (formerly the Juvenile Diabetes Research Foundation), said, "The encouraging results from this initial trial...in established type 1 diabetes not only demonstrated safety, evidence during the vaccine dosing period showed preservation of beta cell function, a decrease in detectable immune cells [that likely attack the beta cells], and a relationship between the two."

He added that further clinical trials will be needed to figure out the optimal dose for vaccine efficacy and safety.

The study was funded by Bayhill Therapeutics, which helped to develop the vaccine. JDRF provided funding for the trial, as did the Iacocca Family Foundation.

Learn more about type 1 diabetes from the U.S. National Library of Medicine website at *http://www.ncbi.nlm.nih.gov/pubmedhealth/ PMH0001350/*.

People with Type 1 Diabetes May Still Have Insulin-Producing Cells

University of Exeter, news release.

Most people with type 1 diabetes still have active insulin-producing cells in their pancreas, a recent study shows. The finding suggests it may be possible one day to preserve or replenish these cells.

Type 1 diabetes occurs when the body's immune system destroys insulin-producing beta cells, and it was believed that all these cells were lost within a few years of developing the disease.

But British researchers used new technology that enabled them to detect far lower levels of insulin than was previously possible. They tested 74 people with type 1 diabetes, and found that 73% of them had working beta cells that produced low levels of insulin, regardless of how long they'd had the disease.

The study was published in the journal *Diabetologia.*

"It's extremely interesting that low levels of insulin are produced in most people with type 1 diabetes, even if they've had it for 50 years," study leader Dr. Richard Oram, of the University of Exeter Medical School in the United Kingdom, said in a university news release. "The fact that insulin levels go up after a meal indicates these remaining beta cells can respond to a meal in the normal way—it seems they are either immune to attack or they are regenerating."

Dr. Matthew Hobbs, head of research for Diabetes UK, added, "We know that preserving or restoring even relatively small levels of insulin secretion in type 1 diabetes can prevent hypoglycemia [low glucose levels] and reduce complications, and therefore much research has focused on ways to make new cells that can be transplanted into the body.

"This research shows that some of a person's own beta cells remain, and therefore it may be possible to regenerate these cells in the future," Dr. Hobbs said. "It is also possible that understanding why some people keep insulin production while others lose it may help answer key questions about the biology of type 1 diabetes and help advance us toward a cure for the disease."

Testosterone Therapy Helps Men with Diabetes

Sandeep Dhindsa, MD, endocrinologist and associate professor, State University of New York at Buffalo. His research was presented at the 2013 meeting of the American Association of Clinical Endocrinologists.

Diminished energy, reduced lean muscle mass, decreased libido, erectile dysfunction...these symptoms are common in men with low levels of the hormone testosterone. Men with type 2 diabetes are particularly prone to this hormonal deficiency—it affects about one-third of them—and it can make their blood sugar problems even worse.

Good news: Testosterone replacement therapy has multiple benefits for such men, a recent study shows.

Participants included 81 men with diabetes. Some had normal levels of free testosterone (the amount of the hormone in the bloodstream)...some had low levels of less than five nanograms per deciliter (ng/dL). At the start of the study, all the men were given a battery of tests and, as expected, men with low testosterone had a bunch of problems. They had more body fat, less lean muscle and more inflammation, and they were more insulin-resistant—meaning their bodies were less able to recognize and respond to insulin.

Next, the men with low testosterone were divided into two groups. One group received injections of testosterone every two weeks for 24 weeks...the other group received placebo injections.

What the testosterone did: In the placebo group, nothing improved. However, among the men who received testosterone injections, insulin resistance improved by nearly 30%—and that was enough of an improvement to essentially get rid of their insulin resistance. What's more, these men lost an average of 4.5 pounds of fat and gained 4.5 pounds of lean muscle…their inflammation decreased…and they reported significant improvement in libido and increased satisfaction with their erections.

Men with diabetes: Doctors generally do not screen diabetes patients for testosterone deficiency, so ask to be tested—it is a simple and inexpensive blood test. If your free testosterone level is below 5 ng/dL, talk to your doctor about bringing it back up to normal with testosterone replacement therapy. There are four forms of testosterone therapy—injections, topical gel, topical custom-compounded cream and surgically inserted pellets. The treatment could make it easier for you to manage your diabetes by lessening your insulin resistance…and it could boost your energy, strength and sex life, as well.

Testosterone therapy is safe for most men.

Exceptions: Testosterone boosts red blood cell production, which is good for anemia, but too many red blood cells can raise heart attack risk. Men with high hematocrit (a measure of red blood cell concentration) should use testosterone cautiously, if at all. Men with advanced kidney or liver disease should avoid testosterone therapy—it could cause fluid retention, which already is a problem for such men.

Note: Testosterone therapy may cause some decrease in testicle size.

Reassuring: For decades, it was believed that increasing testosterone made prostate tumors grow, but there is now strong evidence that raising testosterone levels in men who have testosterone deficiency does not increase prostate cancer risk.

New Weekly Diabetes Drug Gets FDA Nod

Recently approved by the FDA, *dulaglutide* (Trulicity) is a once-a-week injectable, single-dose pen that has been shown to safe-ly improve blood sugar levels in six separate trials of more than 3,300 people with type 2 diabetes. The medication, which requires no mixing (as do competing drugs), can be used alone or in combination with other diabetes medication, including *metformin* and mealtime insulin. Potential side effects include nausea, diarrhea and abdominal pain. People at risk for thyroid or endocrine gland tumors should not take dulaglutide.

Ralph A. DeFronzo, MD, deputy director, Texas Diabetes Institute, San Antonio.

Breakthrough Obesity Drug Now Available

Liraglutide (Saxenda) is a high-dose version of the diabetes drug Victoza to help control obesity. Like other weight-loss drugs, liraglutide curbs appetite—but it also acts like a natural hormone to slow stomach emptying. Gastrointestinal upsets are the most common side effect. Liraglutide, which is injected daily, is used with exercise and a weight-loss diet.

Whom it may help: Overweight people who have diabetes, prediabetes or another weight-related health condition.

Angela Fitch, MD, director of medical weight management and associate professor of medicine, University of Cincinnati College of Medicine.

One-Shot Glucose Control

In a laboratory study, animals with diabetes were given a single injection of growth factor (FGF1).

Result: Normal blood sugar that lasted for days—without any of the side effects of standard diabetes medications.

Nature.

Arthritis Drug May Help Diabetes

In a clinical trial, *salsalate*, used for arthritis pain, reduced hemoglobin A1c—a marker of overall blood sugar control—in patients with type 2 diabetes. Salsalate is an anti-inflammatory drug related to aspirin but is gentler to the stomach.

Allison B. Goldfine, MD, section head of clinical research, Joslin Diabetes Center, Boston, and co-principal investigator, TINSAL-T2D (Targeting Inflammation Using Salsalate in Type 2 Diabetes).

Program Your Genes to Fight Genetic Risks

The late Mitchell Gaynor, MD, founder of Gaynor Integrative Oncology and Gaynor Wellness, in New York City. He is author of *The Gene Therapy Plan: Taking Control of Your Genetic Destiny with Diet and Lifestyle.* GeneChanger.com

Your body is a war zone, especially in this day and age, with your immune system battling the effects of processed foods that are laced with refined sugar and dangerous fats...plus exposure to pesticide residues, heavy metals and other environmental pollutants. Mix these perils with your genetic makeup, and your risk of diabetes, cancer, cardiovascular disease or obesity can multiply.

But you don't have to think of your genes as time bombs waiting for the perfect storm of environmental factors to light their fuses. Instead, make your genes work for you—not against you.

According to the late Mitchell Gaynor, MD, founder of Gaynor Integrative Oncology in New York City, you can turn the genes that promote aging, cancer, heart disease, obesity and diabetes on or off through lifestyle choices—especially nutrition. He wrote the book *The Gene Therapy Plan: Taking Control of Your Genetic Destiny Through Diet and Lifestyle*, which teaches how to harness the power of ecogenetics—the science of how the environment affects our genes—and nutrigenetics, the science of how nutrients impact genetic disease.

"We're all born with the genes we received from our mother and father...that part is fixed," he said. "But what is not fixed is gene expression, which can change throughout your life for good or bad, depending on what you're putting into your body."

Generally speaking, gene expression is a process whereby genetic information is copied in a cell and used to create protein molecules that perform specific functions in the body. For example, gene expression can protect the body against cancer growth (via tumor suppressor genes) or cause it (via tumor promoter genes). Environmental pollutants or an unhealthy diet can rally less-than-favorable gene expression.

Another example: If you're consuming a lot of refined sugar and flour because your diet is heavy in fast foods and processed foods, you're turning on a lot of inflammatory genes. Dr. Gaynor explained, "Those inflammatory genes are making you gain weight, in part, by causing a hormone called leptin to go into overdrive. Leptin is responsible for regulation of appetite, food intake and metabolism. With leptin impaired, your cells' ability to properly respond to insulin also becomes impaired. In response, your body produces more insulin, your blood sugar drops and you feel hungry—and eat—all the time, setting yourself up for diabetes and heart disease."

The antidote is to apply nutrigenetics, according to Dr. Gaynor. "You have to strengthen your detoxifying genes through nutrition," he said. "We're talking about nutrients that literally turn on genes that code for detoxifying enzymes." But first, you need to know where your genetic vulnerabilities lie.

THE VALUE OF GENETIC TESTING

To learn about your genetic vulnerability, simply give thought to the health conditions your closest relatives are dealing with or have faced. Better, you may want to consider genetic testing, especially if you have a number of first-degree relatives (parents and siblings in particular, but grandparents, too) who have had breast, ovarian, uterine or colon cancer, said Dr. Gaynor. Most health insurers will pay for these tests if there is a strong family history.

Don't wait for your doctor to suggest genetic testing—actively open up a discussion with him or her. A recent survey of breast cancer patients showed that one-third expressed a strong desire for genetic testing. They were worried about being vulnerable to other cancers and worried for their relatives—but 43% of these women had not had a meaningful discussion about it with a health-care professional, either because they did not know how to address the topic or because their doctors never brought up the subject. "The more you know about your risk of specific diseases, the easier it is to design a lifestyle and diet regimen to counter your genetic vulnerabilities," said Dr. Gaynor.

BEAT DISEASE AT THE GENETIC LEVEL

To help avoid buildup of environmental toxins, Dr. Gaynor recommended eating organic foods and using nontoxic detergents, bath products and other household items as much as possible.

As for nutrigenetics, he worked with his patients on an individual basis to increase consumption of foods that will help promote good gene expression in them and provided general guidance through his book and website. For example, in patients concerned about cancer risk, he emphasized an antioxidant-rich diet that makes the most of olive oil, ginger, garlic, cruciferous vegetables (broccoli, cauliflower, Brussels sprouts, etc.), rosemary, beets, walnuts, carrots, cooked tomatoes and blueberries. For those concerned about heart disease risk, he emphasized a diet rich in watercress, goji berries, kale, cruciferous vegetables, pomegranate, almonds, apples, salmon, avocados, scallions and ginger.

Ecogenetics and nutrigenetics, as applied by Dr. Gaynor, are relatively new concepts not yet embraced by conventional Western medicine. But the number of hospitals and doctors embracing integrative medicine (combining alternative and standard Western medicine) to treat the individual rather than just the disease is rapidly on the rise. If you would like guidance

in working to optimize nutrition and well-being on the genetic level, Dr. Gaynor recommended working with a specialist in integrative medicine. You can find such a professional near you through the Academy of Integrative Health & Medicine, *www.aihm.org*.

Using Viruses to Cure Diabetes

M. William Lensch, PhD, executive director, Department of Stem Cell and Regenerative Biology, Harvard Medical School, Boston.

We're accustomed to thinking of viruses as "bad guys" that the world would be better without—but now that scientists have used a virus to transform a non-insulin-producing pancreatic cell into one that produced insulin, we may need to reconsider that position. Adding to the achievement is that the "programming" of the cell was done without use of sometimes controversial stem cells. This is a major breakthrough in the field of regenerative medicine, which aims to regrow or repair missing or damaged tissue.

In the study, which was published in the journal *Nature*, Douglas A. Melton, PhD, co-director of the Harvard Stem Cell Institute, and his fellow researchers used a modified virus to activate three key genes in non-insulin-producing pancreatic cells in mice. Within three days, the "infected" cells started producing insulin—far faster than the several weeks it's known to take to transform stem cells into specific organ tissues.

The findings are incredibly exciting for other researchers in the field of regenerative medicine as well. "This paper really got a lot of people's attention," says M. William Lensch, PhD, executive director, Department of Stem Cell and Regenerative Biology, at Harvard Medical School, who wasn't himself involved with Dr. Melton's research. "It expands the possible universe of where regenerated cells can come from and how to get there—that's exciting."

Though remarkable, it's important to note that this type of cell reprogramming is still a long way from becoming a viable mainstream treatment—it has yet to be tried in humans, and long-term safety is still to be determined. Nonetheless it deserves attention because of the thinking behind it—the idea that you can quickly, relatively easily and with no political debate, change a cell that's close to what's needed into exactly what's needed, perhaps to treat cancer, liver disease, cardiovascular disease and more.

Can Fecal Transplants Solve Obesity?

Andrew L. Rubman, ND, founder and director, Southbury Clinic for Traditional Medicines, Southbury, Connecticut. SouthburyClinic.com

An experimental new treatment for obesity involves nothing less than a fecal transplant—yes, you read that right! Scientists already know that heavy people have different bacteria in their guts than slim folks, so the researchers' theory is that altering the balance of intestinal flora with a transplant will improve insulin resistance and other obesity-related health problems.

Eyebrow raising? Yes…but scientifically speaking, not so surprising, observes naturopathic doctor Andrew L. Rubman, ND. Given all that we know about the importance of maintaining the right bacterial balance in the gut, the idea of using a fecal transplant to populate the gastrointestinal tract with more healthful bacteria sounds icky but makes scientific sense.

THE HISTORY OF FECAL TRANSPLANTS

The first medical reports of fecal transplants came in the 1950s when they were used as a treatment for *Clostridium difficile* cases that did not respond to other therapies such as antibiotics. It is estimated that about 100 fecal transplants have been done in the US for that purpose since then. Using donated stool (usually from a spouse, sibling or close relative), the transplants can be done from top to bottom (via nasogastric tube) or, more commonly, bottom to top (via colonoscopy or rectal enema). The goal is to introduce into the digestive system healthy colonies of bacteria that will prevail over the "bad" bacteria.

This new research on whether fecal transplants might help treat obesity and health problems associated with it was done at the Academic Medical Center in Amsterdam, the Netherlands. The study included 18 obese men between the ages of 21 and 65 with metabolic syndrome (a constellation of symptoms including high blood pressure, cholesterol and triglycerides that raises a person's risk for diabetes and heart disease). None of the men had taken medication for their condition or had been on any antibiotics (which also alter the bacterial colonies) in the previous three months. Prior to their transplants, all participants had their bowels therapeutically cleansed to remove most of their existing bacteria. They were then randomly assigned to receive either autologous transplants (their own feces) or fecal transplants from healthy, lean individuals. To verify that no other factors were affecting the outcome, all participants kept food and exercise diaries for the duration of the study.

There was limited success: After six weeks, researchers found no changes in the autologous group, while those whose transplants came from others showed improved insulin sensitivity—meaning better blood sugar control and lower levels of blood fats called triglycerides. The benefit was fleeting, though—after 12 weeks, both insulin sensitivity and triglycerides in these participants returned to pretransplant levels.

DID THEY LOSE WEIGHT?

Researchers had anticipated that the subjects would also lose weight, since animal experiments had shown this result, but these subjects did not get that benefit. However, Dr. Rubman said that he believes weight loss would come if the altered intestinal environment could be made to persist—he said that when insulin resistance is reduced, weight loss occurs quite naturally, but it takes time.

Researchers presented these results at a September 2010 conference of the European Association for the Study of Diabetes.

Potential concerns: The study was small, so further, larger-scale trials are necessary. Also, some fecal parasites cannot be detected through lab tests, so there is some concern that these transplants can introduce new problems—additional research will need to address this issue as well.

Weight-Loss Surgery May Help Obese Patients Beat Diabetes

Philip Schauer, MD, professor, surgery, director, Cleveland Clinic Bariatric and Metabolic Institute, Ohio

Joel Zonszein, MD, director, Clinical Diabetes Center, Montefiore Medical Center, New York City

Mitchell Roslin, MD, chief, obesity surgery, Lenox Hill Hospital, New York City

Samer Mattar, MD, spokesman, American Society for Metabolic and Bariatric Surgery, and professor, surgery, Oregon Health and Science University, Portland

New England Journal of Medicine.

There's more evidence that obese patients with type 2 diabetes can control the disease better with weight-loss surgery, compared to medication alone.

New research shows that five years after weight-loss surgery, known as bariatric surgery, those who had the procedure showed better improvements in quality of life and overall health, and some no longer needed insulin, compared with those who only took diabetes medications.

"About a third of the patients who had surgery were able to achieve a complete remission of their diabetes—their blood sugar returned to normal and they did not need medications," said lead researcher Philip Schauer, MD. He is director of the Cleveland Clinic Bariatric and Metabolic Institute in Ohio.

"Surgery has come as close as any treatment that we know of that can lead to long-term remission of type 2 diabetes, which is about as close to a cure as you can get," Dr. Schauer added.

Diabetes affects 29 million people in the United States, according to the U.S. Centers for Disease Control and Prevention. More than 70,000 people die each year from complications associated with the blood sugar disease, the American Diabetes Association reports.

According to Samer Mattar, MD, a spokesman for the American Society for Metabolic and Bariatric Surgery, "Bariatric surgery is the most effective and durable treatment we have for obese patients with type 2 diabetes. It goes way beyond weight loss and improves the health of many patients with chronic disease." Dr. Mattar is also a professor of surgery at Oregon Health and Science University in Portland.

STUDY DETAILS

For the study, Dr. Schauer and his colleagues followed 150 obese patients with type 2 diabetes who were randomly assigned to medication alone or to medication plus weight-loss surgery—either Roux-en-Y gastric bypass or sleeve gastrectomy.

In Roux-en-Y gastric bypass, the surgeon reduces the size of the stomach by creating a small pouch about the size of an egg that becomes the new stomach.

In sleeve gastrectomy, the size of the stomach is reduced by removing most of it and creating a new stomach about the size of a banana.

Five years later, the researchers looked for reductions in blood sugar and whether patients could stop taking their diabetes medications.

Among the patients who completed the study, two of the 28 patients assigned to medical treatment alone were able to stop their diabetes medications (5%). This compared with 14 of the 49 patients who had gastric bypass surgery (29%), and 11 of the 47 patients who underwent sleeve gastrectomy (23%), Schauer's team found.

In addition, patients who had weight-loss surgery also had lower blood sugar than patients treated with medication alone.

People who underwent surgery lost significantly more weight and had dramatically lower triglycerides and cholesterol (blood fats) than those who were treated with medication alone, the researchers found.

No major late surgical complications were reported, except for one reoperation, the study authors said.

EXPERT COMMENTARY

According to Joel Zonszein, MD, director of the Clinical Diabetes Center at Montefiore Medical Center in New York City, "This study shows that bariatric surgery is an option for management of patients with type 2 diabetes."

However, he added that treatment always needs to be "patient-centric, so that the different options are negotiated and the best option is available for each patient."

Another specialist, Mitchell Roslin, MD, chief of obesity surgery at Lenox Hill Hospital in New York City, said that obese patients should consider surgery to help them get their diabetes under control.

"All obese type 2 diabetics should look at these results and give greater consideration to surgery," Dr. Roslin said. "These data show that surgery should not be the last resort—it is the best treatment we have for type 2 diabetes."

Dr. Schauer noted that weight-loss surgery is a minimally invasive procedure, so the risks are dramatically reduced. The operation costs $20,000 to $25,000 and is usually covered by insurance, he said.

The report was published February 16, 2017, in the *New England Journal of Medicine*.

FDA Approves Breakthrough Device for Type 1 Diabetes

Medtronic MiniMed 670G monitors blood sugar in people with type 1 diabetes and automatically delivers insulin as needed. Patients still have to count and enter carbs to teach the device how much insulin they need for their intake. Also, the insulin delivery site dressings have to be replaced every three days, so patients must be capable of doing that. The device should be available mid-year 2017.

Robert A. Gabbay, MD, PhD, is chief medical officer at Joslin Diabetes Center and associate professor of medicine at Harvard Medical School, both in Boston.

About That Claim That Bariatric Surgery "Cures" Diabetes: Not So Fast...

Anna L. Marina, MD, former senior clinical research fellow, division of metabolism, endocrinology and nutrition, University of Washington, Seattle.

In addition to treating severe obesity, bariatric surgery now is touted by many hospitals as a "cure" for type 2 diabetes—but some physicians and researchers are skeptical. Although the procedure does in fact improve levels of hemoglobin-A1c (a marker of long-term blood sugar control) and fasting blood glucose, both markers of diabetes, continuous glucose monitoring shows that that isn't the whole story. It turns out that even after patients achieve weight loss as a result of having bariatric surgery, their blood sugar levels are still apt to spike after meals...which means that diabetes is not cured.

IMPROVEMENT, YES—CURE, NO

Bariatric surgery is weight-loss surgery that modifies your digestive system to limit how much food you can eat. There are various types. In Roux-en-Y gastric bypass (RYGB) surgery, the most frequently performed bariatric procedure, the surgeon staples the stomach to create a small pouch and a passage for food to bypass part of the small intestine. In a paper presented at an annual meeting of the American Association of Clinical Endocrinologists, Anna Marina, MD, a former senior clinical research fellow at the University of Washington (together with Dace L. Trence, MD) presented research raising important questions about the claim that the surgery banishes diabetes. Titled "Is Diabetes Mellitus Really Cured by Gastric Bypass Surgery?," the study presented the case of an obese 55-year-old man with diabetes who had RYGB surgery…

Immediately following surgery, his insulin requirement was reduced from 100 units a day to just 30.

Four months later, he had lost 100 pounds and his fasting blood glucose (FBG) and hemoglobin (A1C) measurements had become nearly normal, enabling him to stop taking insulin.

But there was a catch: Further testing of his after-meal (postprandial) glucose revealed blood sugar levels above 200 mg/dl—a level consistent with diabetes. The patient needed to take another drug—the oral glucose-lowering medication *repaglinide* (Prandin)—to bring his postmeal glucose to a safe level.

WHAT IT MEANS

According to Dr. Marina, this case suggests that while gastric bypass surgery can result in significant improvements in diabetes, even its remission, it cannot be considered a cure.

Further research is in order, but in the meantime Dr. Marina recommends that doctors begin to use a different measure (either postmeal glucose testing or continuous glucose monitoring, which requires implantation of a sensor) to more accurately track diabetes in people after gastric bypass surgery.

A BETTER BET: DIET AND EXERCISE

As with any major surgery, gastric bypass has serious—even life-threatening—risks. Dangers aside, do not make the mistake of believing gastric bypass gives you a free pass on diet and exercise. Indeed, success after surgery is contingent on making a lifelong commitment to changes in eating and exercise habits. It's not miracle surgery.

The Simple Supplement That May Prevent Killer Diseases

Joseph Maroon, MD, a professor of neurological surgery and Heindl Scholar in Neuroscience at the University of Pittsburgh School of Medicine and team neurosurgeon for the Pittsburgh Steelers. He is author of *The Longevity Factor: How Resveratrol and Red Wine Activate Genes for a Longer and Healthier Life*. JosephMaroon.com

When it comes to "hot" supplements, resveratrol is high on the list. Multiple studies conducted on laboratory animals have demonstrated the highly beneficial effects of this polyphenol (a class of plant chemicals), which is found most abundantly in the skins of grapes and in red wine—and now is available in supplement form.

Key animal findings: Resveratrol has been shown not only to enhance muscle strength and reduce fatigue, but also to help prevent heart disease, stroke, diabetes and cancer… clear away the toxic proteins that cause Alzheimer's disease…and even lengthen life span by 25%.

But can this substance do the same for humans?

AN IMPORTANT DISCOVERY

Resveratrol's emergence as an anti-aging and disease-fighting powerhouse began in the 1930s with a seemingly unrelated finding—that severe calorie restriction extended the lives of rodents by 40% to 50%.

It wasn't until the 1990s, however, that researchers at Harvard Medical School discovered the genetic basis for the beneficial effect of calorie restriction. Through various experiments in animal studies, calorie restriction was shown to trigger a kind of chain reaction that activates "survival genes" (sirtuins), which, in turn, energize an enzyme (SIR2) that stabilizes DNA. This process slows cellular aging. In further studies, researchers discovered that resveratrol is one of the most potent sources of the molecules that activate these survival genes.

CURRENT EVIDENCE

To further test resveratrol's benefits, researchers conducted other animal studies—this time without calorie restriction. Resveratrol and other polyphenols were found to increase the life span of fish by 60%...worms and flies by 30%...and mice by 25%—benefits attributed to improved cellular health.

Resveratrol-enhanced cells are believed to help fight...

•**Heart disease and stroke.** Resveratrol appears to decrease harmful inflammation, which contributes to cardiovascular disease.

Breakthrough research: A human study showed that drinking one-and-a-half glasses of red wine a day lowered, by 40%, levels of lipid peroxide, a by-product of inflammation that damages arteries. This and other health benefits are believed to be due to resveratrol and several other polyphenols in red wine.

Through various animal studies, resveratrol was shown to spark the production of the beneficial gas nitric oxide, which gives blood vessels more flexibility. Resveratrol also thins the blood, reducing the risk for an artery-clogging clot. In studies of animals with induced heart attacks, those given resveratrol had a significantly lower fatality rate. In similar studies on stroke, resveratrol prevented paralysis and limited brain injury in animals.

•**Cancer.** Eighteen different types of cancer—including lung, colon, skin, liver and pancreatic—have been markedly inhibited by resveratrol in laboratory studies using both animal and human cells.

•**Diabetes.** In animals, resveratrol helps normalize blood sugar (glucose) levels by moving glucose out of the bloodstream and into cells. Laboratory research also shows that resveratrol reduces diabetic neuropathy (nerve pain that often occurs in the legs and feet).

Recent finding: In a human study, a synthetic, resveratrol-like compound was shown to give people the same type of glucose control that resveratrol gives mice.

•**Alzheimer's disease.** In animal studies, resveratrol helps remove the amyloid-beta protein found in the brains of people with Alzheimer's disease.

Recent finding: In a study of 90 healthy people, researchers at Marywood University in Scranton found that a supplement containing resveratrol and other polyphenols improved memory and sped up reaction time.

RESVERATROL SOURCES

Even though the preliminary research is promising, there is a caveat. You would have to drink up to 1,150 bottles of red wine daily to get the amount of resveratrol used in most animal studies.

Since that's not feasible, I recommend a more practical approach that includes two things—a regular diet of resveratrol- and polyphenol-rich foods (the resveratrol is far lower than the doses used in animal studies, but these foods contain other beneficial compounds that may enhance absorption of resveratrol from food and/or supplements)...and the use of a mixed polyphenol supplement or a resveratrol supplement.

That strategy—along with regular exercise and a lifestyle that includes the health-promoting effects of close emotional ties with family and friends—is your best bet for fighting chronic disease and living longer. *My advice...*

•**Eat a polyphenol-rich diet.** Resveratrol is the superstar of polyphenols, but many scientists think that a combination of polyphenols—ingesting them together, as they are found in nature—is the best way to activate survival genes.

The foods richest in resveratrol and a variety of other polyphenols...

•**Red wine or red grape juice.** These are the top dietary sources of resveratrol.

Important: Wine grapes with the most resveratrol include pinot noir, merlot, grenache, cabernet sauvignon and tempranillo. (These wines also deliver up to about 500 different polyphenols along with resveratrol.)

Suggested daily intake: Four to 16 ounces of red grape juice daily (be mindful of the sugar content). Up to 12 ounces of red wine daily for men...and no more than six ounces daily for women (the potential health benefit of daily wine consumption by women must be weighed against a possible increase in breast cancer risk).

• **Pomegranate juice.** It is a good source of resveratrol and many other antioxidants.

Suggested daily intake: Three to five ounces.

• **Dark chocolate.** It is a rich source of concentrated flavonols, a potent type of polyphenol. Select unsweetened or semisweetened varieties with at least 70% cocoa.

Suggested daily intake: One bite-sized square.

• **Green tea.** Green tea contains resveratrol and is rich in epigallocatechin gallate (EGCG) and other polyphenols.

Suggested daily intake: Three eight-ounce cups. Decaffeinated green tea contains EGCG but relatively little resveratrol.

• **Blueberries.** They are rich in procyanidins and other polyphenols.

Suggested daily intake: At least one cup (fresh or frozen).

• **Take a mixed-polyphenol supplement.** I recommend the mixed polyphenol supplement Vindure 900, a product developed by Vinomis Laboratories based on Harvard University research. Vindure is available from Vinomis Laboratories (877-484-6664, *www.vinomis.com*).

Cost: $109.95 for 90 tablets. Follow the dosage recommendation on the label.

Because resveratrol absorption is thought to be enhanced when combined with other natural polyphenols, a mixed-polyphenol supplement is best.

However, an alternative is to…

• **Take a resveratrol supplement.** There are more than 300 resveratrol-containing products now available. The best products are made with trans-resveratrol (the active form of the substance shown by professional testing to activate the sirtuin "survival genes")…and produced by manufacturers who comply with "Good Manufacturing Practices" (GMP), which ensures that the product contains no major contaminants.

My favorite resveratrol products are manufactured by…

• **Longevinex,** *www.longevinex.com*, 866-405-4000…30 capsules for $32.95.

• **RevGenetics,** at *www.revgenetics.com*, 888-738-4363…30 capsules for $24.99.

Suggested intake for most resveratrol supplements: 250 mg to 500 mg daily.

8

Complications: What Diabetes Can Cause

The Diabetes Complication That Kills More People Than Most Cancers

A foot or leg amputation is one of the most dreaded complications of diabetes. In the US, more than 73,000 such amputations occur each year.

But the tragedy does not stop there. According to recent research, about half of all people who have a foot amputation die within five years of the surgery—a worse mortality rate than most cancers. That's partly because people with diabetes who have amputations often have poorer glycemic control and more complications such as kidney disease. Amputation also can lead to increased pressure on the remaining limb and the possibility of new ulcers and infections.

Latest development: To combat the increasingly widespread problem of foot infec-

tions and amputations, new guidelines for the diagnosis and treatment of diabetic foot infections have been created by the Infectious Diseases Society of America (IDSA).

What you need to know…

HOW FOOT INFECTIONS START

Diabetes can lead to foot infections in two main ways—peripheral neuropathy (nerve damage that can cause loss of sensation in the feet)…and ischemia (inadequate blood flow).

To understand why these conditions can be so dangerous, think back to the last time you had a pebble inside your shoe. How long did it take before the irritation became unbearable? Individuals with peripheral neuropathy and ischemia usually don't feel any pain in their feet. Without pain, the pebble will stay

James M. Horton, MD, chair of the Standards and Practice Guidelines Committee of the Infectious Diseases Society of America, *www.idsociety.org*. Dr. Horton is also chief of the department of infectious disease and attending faculty physician in the department of internal medicine, both at Carolinas Medical Center in Charlotte, North Carolina.

in the shoe and eventually cause a sore on the sole of the foot.

Similarly, people with diabetes will not feel the rub of an ill-fitting shoe or the pressure of standing on one foot too long, so they are at risk of developing pressure sores or blisters.

These small wounds can lead to big trouble. About 25% of people with diabetes will develop a foot ulcer—ranging from mild to severe—at some point in their lives. Any ulcer, blister, cut or irritation has the potential to become infected. If the infection becomes too severe to treat effectively with antibiotics, amputation of a foot or leg may be the only way to prevent the infection from spreading throughout the body and save the person's life.

A FAST-MOVING DANGER

Sores on the foot can progress rapidly. While some foot sores remain unchanged for months, it is possible for an irritation to lead to an open wound (ulcer), infection and amputation in as little as a few days. That is why experts recommend that people with diabetes seek medical care promptly for any open sore on the feet or any new area of redness or irritation that could possibly lead to an open wound.

Important: Fully half of diabetic foot ulcers are infected and require immediate medical treatment and sometimes hospitalization.

Don't try to diagnose yourself—diagnosis requires a trained medical expert. An ulcer that appears very small on the surface could have actually spread underneath the skin, so you very well could be seeing just a small portion of the infection.

WHAT YOUR DOCTOR WILL DO

The first step is to identify the bacteria causing the infection. To do this, physicians collect specimens from deep inside the wound. Once the bacteria have been identified, the proper antibiotics can be prescribed.

Physicians also need to know the magnitude of the infection—for example, whether there is bone infection, abscesses or other internal problems. Therefore, all diabetes patients who have new foot infections should have X-rays. If more detailed imaging is needed, an MRI or a bone scan may be ordered.

The doctor will then classify the wound and infection as mild, moderate or severe and create a treatment plan.

HOW TO GET THE BEST TREATMENT

Each person's wound is unique, so there are no cookie-cutter treatment plans. *However, most treatment plans should include...*

• **A diabetes foot-care team.** For moderate or severe infections, a team of experts should coordinate treatment. This will be done for you—by the hospital or your primary care physician. The number of specialists on the team depends on the patient's specific needs but may include experts in podiatry and vascular surgery. In rural or smaller communities, this may be done via online communication with experts from larger hospitals (telemedicine).

• **Antibiotic treatment.** Milder infections usually involve a single bacterium. Antibiotics will typically be needed for about one week. With more severe infections, multiple bacteria are likely involved, so you will require multiple antibiotics, and treatment will need to continue for a longer period—sometimes four weeks or more if bone is affected.

If the infection is severe...or even moderate but complicated by, say, poor blood circulation, hospitalization may be required for a few days to a few weeks, depending on the course of the recovery.

• **Wound care.** Many patients who have foot infections receive antibiotic therapy only, which is often insufficient. Proper wound care is also necessary. In addition to frequent wound cleansing and dressing changes, this may include surgical removal of dead tissue (debridement)...and the use of specially designed shoes or shoe inserts—provided by a podiatrist—to redistribute pressure off the wound (off-loading).

• **Surgery.** Surgery doesn't always mean amputation. It is sometimes used not only to remove dead or damaged tissue or bone but also to improve blood flow to the foot.

If an infection fails to improve: The first question physicians know to ask is: "Is the patient complying with wound care instructions?" Too many patients lose a leg because they don't take their antibiotics as prescribed or care for the injury as prescribed.

Never forget: Following your doctors' specific orders could literally mean the difference between having one leg or two.

More from Dr. Horton...

Foot Care Is Critical If You Have Diabetes

To protect yourself from foot injuries...

•**Never walk barefoot, even around the house.**

•**Don't wear sandals**—the straps can irritate the side of the foot.

•**Wear thick socks with soft leather shoes.** Leather is a good choice because it "breathes," molds to the feet and does not retain moisture. Laced-up shoes with cushioned soles provide the most support.

In addition, pharmacies carry special "diabetic socks" that protect and cushion your feet without cutting off circulation at the ankle. These socks usually have no seams that could chafe. They also wick moisture away from feet, which reduces risk for infection and foot ulcers.

•**See a podiatrist.** This physician can advise you on the proper care of common foot problems, such as blisters, corns and ingrown toenails. A podiatrist can also help you find appropriate footwear—even if you have foot deformities.

Ask your primary care physician or endocrinologist for a recommendation, or consult the American Podiatric Medical Association, *www.apma.org.*

Also: Inspect your feet every day. Otherwise, you may miss a developing infection. Look for areas of redness, blisters or open sores, particularly in the areas most prone to injury—the bottoms and bony inner and outer edges of the feet.

If you see any sign of a sore, seek prompt medical care. You should also see a doctor if you experience an infected or ingrown toenail, callus formation, bunions or other deformity, fissured (cracked) skin on your feet or you notice any change in sensation.

If You Have Diabetes, A Joint Replacement Or Arthritis...

The late George Cierny, MD, and the late Doreen DiPasquale, MD, physician-partners at REOrthopaedics in San Diego. Dr. Cierny was an international lecturer in orthopedic surgery who published more than 100 scientific papers and book chapters in the field of musculoskeletal pathology and infection. Dr. DiPasquale, an orthopedic surgeon, was residency program director at George Washington University in Washington, DC, and National Naval Medical Center in Bethesda, Maryland.

When most people think of bone problems, broken bones and osteoporosis (reduced bone density and strength) come to mind. But our bones also can be the site of infections that can sometimes go unrecognized for months or even years.

This is especially the case if the only symptoms of bone infection (a condition known as osteomyelitis) are ones that are commonly mistaken for common health problems, such as ordinary back pain or fatigue. *What you need to know...*

ARE YOU AT RISK?

Older adults (age 70 and older), people with diabetes or arthritis and anyone with a weakened immune system (due to chronic disease, such as cancer, for example) are among those at greatest risk for osteomyelitis.

Anyone who has an artificial joint (such as a total hip replacement or total knee replacement) or metal implants attached to a bone also is at increased risk for osteomyelitis and should discuss the use of antibiotics before any type of surgery, including routine dental and oral surgery. Bacteria in the mouth can enter the bloodstream and cause a bone infection.

TYPES OF BONE INFECTIONS

Before the advent of joint-replacement surgery, most bone infections were caused by injuries that expose the bone to bacteria in the environment (such as those caused by a car accident) or a broken bone...or an infection elsewhere in the body, such as pneumonia or a urinary tract infection, that spreads to the bone through the bloodstream.

Now: About half the cases of osteomyelitis are complications of surgery in which large metal implants are used to stabilize or replace bones and joints (such as in the hip or knee).

Osteomyelitis is divided into three main categories, depending on the origin of the infection...

• **Blood-borne osteomyelitis occurs when bacteria that originate elsewhere in the body migrate to and infect bone.** People with osteoarthritis or rheumatoid arthritis are prone to blood-borne infections in their affected joints due to injury to cells in the lining of the joints that normally prevent bacteria from entering the bloodstream.

• **Contiguous-focus osteomyelitis occurs when organisms**—usually bacteria, but sometimes fungi—infect bone tissue. These cases usually occur in people with diabetes, who often develop pressure sores on the soles of their feet or buttocks due to poor circulation and impaired immunity.

• **Post-traumatic osteomyelitis.** Trauma or surgery to a bone and/or surrounding tissue can open the area to bacteria and other microbes. The use of prosthetic joints, surgical screws, pins or plates also makes it easier for bacteria to enter and infect the bone.

Important: Any of the three types of bone infections described above can lead to chronic osteomyelitis, an initially low-grade infection that can persist for months or even years with few or no symptoms. Eventually it gets severe enough to literally destroy bone. Left untreated, the affected bone may have to be amputated.

DIFFICULT TO DIAGNOSE

When osteomyelitis first develops (acute osteomyelitis), the symptoms—such as pain, swelling and tenderness—are usually the same as those caused by other infections.

If the initial infection is subtle (low-grade) or doesn't resolve completely with treatment, it can result in chronic osteomyelitis. In this case, you may have no symptoms or symptoms that are nonspecific. For example, someone who has had surgery might blame discomfort on delayed recovery, not realizing that what they have is a bone infection.

Surprising finding: When we studied the histories of more than 2,000 osteomyelitis patients, we found that most of those with chronic infections had relatively little pain from the infection itself. About 28% of those who required surgery for infection had normal white blood cell counts—suggesting that, over time, the body adjusts to lingering infections.

If a doctor suspects that you may have osteomyelitis because of chronic pain...swelling... possibly fever...fatigue...or other symptoms, he/she will usually order special laboratory tests that detect the formation of antibodies. If the results indicate the presence of infection, he may then order an X-ray or magnetic resonance imaging (MRI) scan. These and other imaging tests can readily detect damaged bone tissue and reveal the presence of infection.

BEST TREATMENT OPTIONS

About 60% to 70% of people with acute osteomyelitis can be cured with antibiotics (or antifungal agents, if a fungal infection is present) if treatment begins early enough to prevent the infection from becoming chronic. In these cases, patients exhibit symptoms...test positive for infection...and readily respond to drug treatments. Most patients can be cured with a four- to six-week course of antibiotics. Fungal infections are more resistant to treatment—antifungal drugs may be needed for several months.

For chronic osteomyelitis, surgical debridement (the removal of damaged tissue and bone using such instruments as a scalpel or scissors) usually is necessary.

Reasons: Damaged bone can lose its blood supply and remain in the body as "dead bone"— without living cells or circulation. Such bone is invulnerable to the effects of antibiotics.

After debridement, the surgeon may insert a slow-release antibiotic depot, a small pouch that releases the antibiotic for up to a month. This approach can increase drug concentrations up to 100 times more than oral antibiotic therapy.

Even with these treatments, in people with chronic osteomyelitis who are otherwise healthy, up to 6% may require a second or even a third operation to cure the infection. In people with diabetes or other disorders, the percentage may be as high as 25%.

To improve your chances of a full recovery from chronic osteomyelitis: Eat well, maintain healthy blood sugar levels, stay active after treatment (to promote blood circulation, prevent blood clots and help maintain an appetite) and don't use tobacco products.

Natural Cures for Painful Neuropathy

Mark A. Stengler, NMD, a naturopathic medical doctor and leading authority on the practice of alternative and integrated medicine. Dr. Stengler is author of the *Health Revelations* newsletter, author of *The Natural Physician's Healing Therapies*, founder and medical director of the Stengler Center for Integrative Medicine in Encinitas, California, and former adjunct associate clinical professor at the National University of Natural Medicine in Portland, Oregon. MarkStengler.com

Peripheral neuropathy may be one of the most common conditions you've never heard of—and it is indeed common. Estimates are that it affects as many as two-thirds of people with diabetes, 10% to 20% of people with cancer and 8% of all people over age 55. One reason may be that neuropathy is not an isolated medical condition. Rather, it results from other medical problems including vitamin deficiencies, autoimmune disorders and heavy metal exposure, in addition to diabetes and cancer. Symptoms generally come on gradually over a period of weeks or even months, starting in the toes and sometimes the fingers. They include burning and tingling sensations, numbness, and occasional sharp, sudden pains similar to electrical shocks. Intensity of symptoms varies widely, from mild annoyance...to numbness severe enough to impair function...to debilitating pain.

MEDICAL TREATMENTS

Mainstream medical doctors often treat peripheral neuropathy with pharmaceutical drugs, but they all have serious side effects, including dizziness, sleepiness, dry mouth, blurred vision, weight gain, nausea, headache and in serious cases, allergic reaction and confusion, among others.

Given the problems with pharmaceuticals, it's good to be aware about natural approaches to the problem. The first step is to find the root cause and correct it as much as possible. For example, people with diabetes must control blood sugar levels to help slow further peripheral neuropathy development. People who suspect vitamin deficiencies should see a holistic physician for blood level tests and to help them establish a healthy diet and vitamin protocol. They must also avoid or greatly reduce alcohol consumption. Those having chemotherapy should alert the supervising doctor immediately if numbness or tingling starts in their feet or hands. The doctor may be able to alter the drugs somewhat to keep the neuropathy from escalating. However, when chemo-related peripheral neuropathy begins weeks or even months after completion of chemotherapy—as is often the case—the next step is to seek treatment to alleviate the discomfort and possibly help reduce or even heal it. This advice holds true for other causes of peripheral neuropathy as well, although you should check with your doctor to be sure it is appropriate for you.

NATURAL APPROACHES

The natural substance with the longest record for helping both diabetic peripheral neuropathy and chemotherapy-induced peripheral neuropathy is alpha-lipoic acid, a powerful antioxidant that scavenges many harmful free radicals. (*Note*: Alpha-lipoic acid can reduce blood sugar levels, so your doctor should monitor your medication and blood sugar for the duration.) It's not a quick solution however—you should wait eight to 12 weeks before assessing results. The other natural substance I recommend is acetyl-L-carnitine, which has a regenerative effect on the nerves. Again, stay on acetyl-L-carnitine therapy for eight to 12 weeks to assess its efficacy. To further reduce nerve irritation, I often prescribe a B complex including B-12, as well as vitamins E and C, selenium and pycnogenol, a plant-derived substance that has antioxidant, anti-inflammatory and other powerful properties. Injections or sublingual doses of vitamins B-12 and B-1, which you can get from your doctor, are also helpful.

ACUPUNCTURE

Acupuncture is an increasingly popular treatment for peripheral neuropathy, in particular that caused by chemotherapy. Yi Hung Chan, LAc, DPM, is a staff member at the Integrative Medicine Service of the Memorial Sloan Kettering Cancer Center in New York City. Dr. Chan treats many neuropathy patients, some of whom are still in chemo and others who develop peripheral neuropathy after chemo completion. To attain the greatest relief, he recommends starting acupuncture treatment at the first sign of symptoms—early intervention helps to avoid full-blown neuropathy and may reverse symptoms. In his clinical practice, Dr. Chan has found that about 80% of patients show substantial improvement after eight to 12 sessions of treatment.

Patients start acupuncture with one to two appointments per week. Those still in chemotherapy continue acupuncture sessions for about six weeks after completion of cancer treatment and taper off from there. When peripheral neuropathy begins post-chemo, Dr. Chan recommends one to two sessions per week for six or so months with occasional follow-up sessions after that. Although Dr. Chan's experience is mostly with chemo-related peripheral neuropathy, he notes that in a small study of seven individuals with diabetes, done at Harvard in 2007, acupuncture eased their neuropathy pain as well.

HEALTHY HABITS

All people with peripheral neuropathy should maintain a healthy lifestyle and keep their weight normal to lessen pressure on the feet. A regular practice of meditation, yoga or any other calming technique helps provide relaxation when neuropathy flares. Other ways to increase comfort are to keep the feet warm, wear soft-leather shoes with good support, and sleep with light blankets to avoid pressure on sensitive feet. Though some people are unable to obtain full relief from peripheral neuropathy, there is fortunately much you can do to make it bearable.

Blood Sugar Control Beats Neuropathy

Larry Deeb, MD, past president for medicine and science, American Diabetes Association, Tallahassee, Florida.

Up to 70% of diabetes patients have some form of neuropathy. The most common is peripheral neuropathy, in which nerves in the feet, legs, arms and/or hands are damaged. Symptoms include numbness that results in a reduced ability to feel pain. The first step in treating diabetic neuropathy is to bring blood glucose (sugar) levels within the normal range—high levels can injure nerve fibers throughout the body. Blood sugar levels should be 90 mg/dL to 130 mg/dL before meals and less than 180 mg/dL two hours after meals. Consistently keeping blood sugar within this target range can help delay progression of diabetic neuropathy and may improve existing symptoms. If you keep your blood sugar under control but continue to experience pain in your legs, feet, arms or hands, you may want to ask your doctor about taking *pregabalin* (Lyrica), an anticonvulsant drug that has been approved by the FDA to treat pain associated with diabetic neuropathy.

Vitamin B-12—Better Than a Drug for Diabetic Neuropathy

Anne L. Peters, MD, professor of medicine and director of the USC Westside Center for Diabetes and author of *Conquering Diabetes*.

Mariejane Braza, MD, former researcher, University of Texas Health Science Center and internist, East Texas Medical Center, Tyler, Texas.

Jacob Teitelbaum, MD, author of *Pain-Free 1-2-3* and *From Fatigued to Fantastic!*. EndFatigue.com

Twenty-five percent of people with diabetes develop diabetic neuropathy—glucose-caused damage to nerves throughout the body, particularly in the hands, arms, feet and legs (peripheral neuropathy).

You experience tingling and prickling. Numbness. And pain—from annoying, to burning, to stabbing, to excruciating. Drugs hardly help.

"Many studies have been conducted on drugs for diabetic neuropathy, and no drug is really effective," says Anne L. Peters, MD, professor of medicine and director of the USC (University of Southern California) Westside Center for Diabetes, and author of *Conquering Diabetes*.

But a new study says a vitamin can help…

LESS PAIN AND BURNING

Researchers in Iran studied 100 people with diabetic neuropathy, dividing them into two groups. One group received *nortriptyline* (Pamelor), an antidepressant medication that has been used to treat neuropathy. The other group received vitamin B-12, a nutrient known to nourish and protect nerves.

After several weeks of treatment, the B-12 group had…

• **78% greater reduction in pain,**

• **71% greater reduction in tingling and prickling and**

• **65% greater reduction in burning.**

"Vitamin B-12 is more effective than nortriptyline for the treatment of painful diabetic neuropathy," conclude the researchers, in the *International Journal of Food Sciences and Nutrition*.

Latest development: A few months after the Iranian doctors conducted their study, research in the US involving 76 people with diabetes showed that the widely prescribed diabetes drug *metformin* may cause vitamin B-12 deficiency—and that 77% of those with the deficiency also suffered from peripheral neuropathy!

Anyone already diagnosed with peripheral neuropathy who uses metformin should be tested for low blood levels of B-12, says Mariejane Braza, MD, who was a researcher at the University of Texas Health Science Center when she conducted the study. If B-12 levels are low, she recommends supplementing with the vitamin, to reduce the risk of nerve damage.

HEAL THE NERVES

"If you take metformin, definitely take at least 500 micrograms (mcg) a day of vitamin B-12, in either a multivitamin or B-complex supplement," advises Jacob Teitelbaum, MD, author of *Pain-Free 1-2-3*. "It's the single, most effective nutrient for helping prevent and reverse diabetic neuropathy.

"On a good day, the best that medications can do for neuropathy is mask the pain," he continues. "But vitamin B-12 gradually heals the nerves."

Best: If you already have neuropathy, Dr. Teitelbaum recommends finding a holistic physician and asking for 15 intramuscular injections of 3,000 to 5,000 mcg of methylcobalamin, the best form of B-12 to treat peripheral neuropathy. "Receive those shots daily to weekly—at whatever speed is convenient to quickly optimize levels of B-12," says Dr. Teitelbaum.

Resource: To find a holistic physician, Dr. Teitelbaum recommends visiting the website of the American Board of Integrative Holistic Medicine, *www.abihm.org*.

If you can't find a holistic physician near you, he suggests taking a daily sublingual (dissolving under the tongue) dose of 5,000 mcg for four weeks. (Daily, because you only absorb a small portion of the sublingual vitamin B-12, compared with intramuscular injections.)

At the same time that you take B-12, also take a high-dose B-complex supplement (B-50). "The body is happiest when it gets all the B-vitamins together," says Dr. Teitelbaum.

He points out that it can take three to 12 months for nerves to heal, but that the neuropathy should progressively improve during that time.

Also helpful: Other nutrients that Dr. Teitelbaum recommends to help ease peripheral neuropathy include…

• **Alpha-lipoic acid** (300 mg, twice a day)

• **Acetyl-l-carnitine** (500 mg, three times a day)

Diet to Ease Nerve Pain

Plant-based diet eases diabetic nerve pain, according to Anne Bunner, PhD. In a 20-week study of people with diabetic neuropathy (which often leads to pain and numbness in the legs and feet), half ate a low-fat vegan diet and took a vitamin B-12 supplement (diabetes patients are often deficient in B-12), and the other half took only the supplement.

Result: The group eating the plant-based diet had significantly greater pain relief and lost more weight than the other group.

Anne Bunner, PhD, associate director of clinical research, Physicians Committee for Responsible Medicine, Washington, DC.

High Triglycerides and Amputation—Yes, There Is a Connection

Kelli A. Sullivan, PhD, associate research professor, department of neurology, University of Michigan Medical School, Ann Arbor.

The feeling of being on "pins and needles" is wonderful—if it describes how children feel when looking forward to a birthday party or adults when anticipating a special vacation. But where diabetes patients are concerned, those words often are used to describe a painful chronic condition, called diabetic peripheral neuropathy, that results from damage to nerves (typically in the hands, arms, feet and legs) caused by elevated blood sugar. Affecting about 60% of people with type 1 and type 2 diabetes, neuropathy is the leading cause of diabetes-related hospital admissions and amputations, and it is not curable—so finding any information about how to prevent it or slow its progression is valuable.

Now a study from the University of Michigan has uncovered a crucial clue that helps identify patients most at risk for neuropathy progression. Researchers analyzed data from 427 people with diabetes and early-stage neuropathy using advanced technology to measure the amount of damage to patients' peripheral nerves at the beginning of the study and again one year later. The surprising finding was that those whose neuropathy got worse over the year were the same ones who also had elevated levels of triglycerides, a type of fat in the blood. In fact, having elevated triglycerides was a more accurate predictor of neuropathy progression than other factors such as blood sugar or high levels of cholesterol.

WHAT DOES THIS MEAN FOR YOUR HEALTH?

According to study coauthor Kelli A. Sullivan, PhD, associate research professor in neurology at University of Michigan Medical School, people with type 2 diabetes frequently have elevated triglycerides primarily because they are so often overweight, which is known to be associated with high triglycerides. The study's findings could be a crucial indicator to doctors that they should monitor triglyceride levels in overweight or obese diabetic patients as closely as they do blood sugar.

Fortunately, there are ways to bring elevated triglyceride levels down into a normal range. Lifestyle habits have a strong impact on normalizing triglycerides—this includes shedding excess pounds and having a healthy diet that limits fats and sugars…not smoking…and moderate alcohol consumption, especially red wine. Exercise is a must, says Dr. Sullivan, as demonstrated in a 2006 Italian study that showed regular long-term aerobic exercise improved neuropathy in early stages. And since having more muscle mass benefits nerve tissue as well, strength training is helpful too.

Help for Diabetic Foot Ulcers

Diabetic foot ulcers can be healed by acne medication.

Recent finding: In a study of 22 men with diabetes, more than 84% of ulcers treated with topical *tretinoin* (Retin-A), a popular acne medication, and antibacterial cadexomer iodine gel shrunk by at least half. In the group treated with a placebo solution and cadexomer iodine gel, 45.4% of ulcers shrunk by half.

Theory: Tretinoin stimulates blood vessel growth, which helps deliver oxygen to the wound site. Left untreated, diabetic ulcers may increase risk for amputation.

Wynnis Tom, MD, assistant clinical professor of medicine, University of California, San Diego.

Better Foot Care

Charcot foot (a condition in which bones in the foot weaken and break) is common in people with diabetes and/or peripheral neuropathy. They may have a loss of feeling in the feet due to nerve damage and are sometimes unaware that they have Charcot foot until it causes severe deformities.

If you have diabetes and/or peripheral neuropathy: See a podiatrist or orthopedic surgeon to be monitored for Charcot foot, which can be treated with surgery and/or specialized footwear. Warning signs include sudden swelling or pain of the foot and/or leg.

Valerie L. Schade, DPM, FACFAS, podiatric surgeon, Tacoma, Washington.

Toenail Fungus Trouble… and a Unique Cure

Mark A. Stengler, NMD, naturopathic physician in private practice, Encinitas, California…former adjunct associate clinical professor at the National University of Natural Medicine, Portland, Oregon…author of many books, including *The Natural Physician's Healing Therapies* and coauthor of *Prescription for Natural Cures.* MarkStengler.com

When is the last time you took a good look at your toenails? If it has been a while, you may be in for an unpleasant surprise—in fungal form. Toenail fungus,

also called onychomycosis, is a common condition that turns nails a yellow or brown color. In some cases, the nail thickens or splits and may fall off. Sufferers may experience pain around the nail and notice a foul smell. The infection is typically caused by any one of several types of fungi that feed on keratin, the protein surface of the nail. Occasionally, different yeasts and molds may cause the infection.

By age 70, almost half of Americans have had at least one affected toe. While the infection can occur in fingernails, it most often affects toenails—because feet are confined to the dark, warm environment of shoes, where fungi can thrive. The nails of the big toe and little toe are particularly susceptible, because friction from the sides of shoes can cause trauma to the nail surface, making it easier for fungi to penetrate. Nail fungus is not the same as athlete's foot—because athlete's foot affects the skin rather than the nail itself—but the two conditions may coexist and can be caused by the same type of fungus.

I find that athletes and others who commonly use gym locker rooms and showers are more likely to develop toenail fungus due to the damp floors and shared environment. Women who wear toenail polish are at increased risk because moisture can get trapped beneath the polish. Tight-fitting shoes and hosiery that rub the toenails also contribute to the problem. People with diabetes and other circulation problems that prevent infection-fighting white blood cells from adequately reaching the toes are particularly susceptible to the fungus, as are people with compromised immune systems, such as those with cancer or HIV.

Toenail fungus doesn't usually clear up on its own. In fact, it tends to get more severe over time—affecting a larger portion of the nail and spreading to adjacent toes and to the other foot. Therefore, I recommend starting treatment as early as possible.

CONVENTIONAL TREATMENTS

Medical doctors generally turn to topical and oral antifungal treatments. For mild cases that involve a small area of the nail, a medicated nail polish containing an antifungal agent, such as *ciclopirox* (Loprox), is often prescribed. For toenail fungus that covers a large portion of a nail or affects several nails, the typical medical approach is to prescribe oral antifungal medications, such as *itraconazole* (Sporanox) or *terbinafine* (Lamisil). These are quite powerful medications and may need to be taken for up to 12 weeks until the infection clears up. In 10% to 20% of cases, the fungus returns within several months.

The most worrisome side effect of oral antifungals is liver damage. To monitor the effect of these medications, liver enzyme tests should be performed before beginning treatment and every four to six weeks during treatment. An elevation in liver enzymes means that the drugs are irritating the liver and need to be discontinued. Several patients who were being treated by other doctors have come to see me after elevated liver enzymes forced them to stop this pharmaceutical treatment. As a last resort, the nail can be surgically removed—at which point the infection will clear up, and the nail will slowly grow back.

AN UNUSUAL CURE

The typical natural treatment for toenail fungus is to apply tea tree oil or oregano oil. Using a cotton swab, apply nightly to the affected area, continuing treatment for eight to 12 weeks. These oils work well to clear up mild toenail fungus, but they often are not strong enough for moderate to severe cases. There is an unusual, yet effective, therapy for severe toenail fungus developed by Mark Cooper, ND, an innovative naturopathic doctor. Years ago, Dr. Cooper treated an HIV-positive patient who commented on an article he had read stating that bleach killed HIV on surfaces (not in the body). Knowing that hospital bedsheets and floor surfaces are washed with bleach to kill all types of fungi, viruses and bacteria, Dr. Cooper theorized that bleach might also kill toenail fungus and clear up persistent cases of infection.

Dr. Cooper, who practices at Alpine Naturopathic Clinic in Colorado Springs, has treated hundreds of his patients with this topical bleach treatment. My patients have responded very well to it, too.

How it works: Mix one cup of household bleach with 10 cups of warm water. Soak the toes of the affected foot for three minutes, then thoroughly rinse off the bleach solution with water and dry the feet completely. Do this twice weekly, with three days between treatments. Most cases resolve in two to three months. Severe cases may take longer.

Boosting the strength of the bleach-and-water mixture beyond the one-to-10 ratio will not increase the effectiveness of the treatment—and it could irritate the skin. Nor is it wise to increase the frequency or duration of treatments. Dr. Cooper told me about a 74-year-old man who misunderstood the directions—instead of soaking his toes for three minutes, he tried to soak them for 30 minutes. The burning pain was so intense that he had to stop the soaking after 20 minutes. Obviously this treatment needs to be used with caution and should not be used when there is an open wound near the infection site.

Interesting: Bleach is composed of sodium hypochlorite (NaOCl). Household bleach usually contains 3% to 6% NaOCl, while industrial-strength bleach contains 10% to 12%. Near the end of the 19th century, after Louis Pasteur discovered its powerful effectiveness against disease-causing bacteria, bleach became popular as a disinfectant. It is still used today for household cleaning, removing laundry stains, treating waste water, sterilizing medical equipment and disinfecting hospital linens and surfaces.

FUNGUS-FIGHTING FOODS & SUPPLEMENTS

Dr. Cooper explains that the topical bleach treatment is even more effective when combined with an antifungal diet. Avoid simple sugars (white breads, pastas, cookies and soda) and alcohol—they suppress immune function and contribute to fungal growth. Eat raw or cooked onions, shallots and leeks, plus garlic (as a food or an extract) as often as possible for their antifungal action.

I also have found that severe cases of toenail fungus, especially in people with diabetes, clear up more quickly when natural antifungal supplements are taken orally. The most potent is oregano oil. It contains plant compounds, such as carvacrol and thymol, that have strong antifungal properties. I recommend taking three doses daily for four to eight weeks. Each dose equals one 500-mg capsule…or five to 15 drops of the liquid form mixed with two to four ounces of water. Some people may experience heartburn from oregano oil, so if you are prone to heartburn, you may need to reduce the dosage. Oregano oil should not be ingested by people with active stomach ulcers (since it can irritate the stomach lining) or by pregnant or nursing women (as a general precaution). It should be given to children only under the guidance of a doctor.

How will you know when the fungal infection is gone? When the discolored nail returns to its normal hue or when the damaged nail grows out and a new nail grows in normally.

FUNGUS PREVENTION STRATEGIES

• **Wash your feet every day using calendula soap.** Made from the marigold plant, it is gentle yet antiseptic. Find it in health-food stores.

• **Always dry feet thoroughly with a clean towel.** Do not share towels with other people.

• **Keep toenails clipped short to reduce the protein surface on which fungi feed.**

• **Avoid going barefoot in public places.** Wear plastic sandals in community showers and locker rooms and at poolside.

• **Choose socks made of breathable fabrics, such as cotton.** Change socks immediately after exercising and whenever feet perspire.

• **Be sure your shoes are not too tight.** If shoes get damp, change them promptly.

Free Yourself from Chronic Pain

Cecilia Norrbrink, RPT, PhD, department of neurobiology, care sciences and society, Karolinska Institute, Stockholm, Sweden.

Talk about piling on—many people who are chronically ill, for instance with diabetes or cancer or who have suffered a traumatic injury, ultimately end up with a condition called neuropathy, where their nervous systems turn against them, randomly sending out pain signals that can range from tingling that is merely uncomfortable to stabbing sensations so painful that they are debilitating. Opioids and antidepressants can help, but these drugs have side effects that can make them less-than-great choices. Acupuncture can be helpful, too, but generally speaking treatment is not all that effective.

So here's information from a recent study that's good news, even though the study was very small, did not include a control group and the treatment worked for only about one-third of the patients who tried it. New research evaluated the use of a therapy called transcutaneous electrical nerve stimulation (TENS) in people with neuropathy as the result of a spinal cord injury. This form of treatment involves placing electrodes (attached to a battery pack) on the skin along both sides of the spine at the level of and just above the spinal cord injury to deliver electrical current. The same technique has been used to treat other forms of chronic pain and muscle spasms.

SHOCKING BUT EFFECTIVE

Twenty-four patients were given TENS units and taught to self-administer the treatment three times a day for 30 to 40 minutes at a time. They did this for two weeks at high frequency and then for another two weeks at low frequency.

Results: About one-third of the patients reported pain was reduced at least somewhat—29% were helped by high-frequency stimulation and 38% by low-frequency stimulation. But what I thought was most notable about this study was that six patients—one-quarter of those who tried this therapy—asked if they could keep their TENS units so they could continue the treatments themselves at home. Clearly, they experienced some benefit.

To those who've never tried it, TENS may sound more like torture than treatment—after all, you'd think that stimulating nerves that have already gone haywire would simply cause more pain. According to Cecilia Norrbrink, RPT, PhD, from the department of neurobiology, care sciences and society, at the Karolinska Institute in Stockholm, Sweden, where the study was done, TENS is not painful and it does work well for some people. She said scientists believe that it works by using the body's own pain-inhibiting systems.

Here's her very simplified explanation: High-frequency TENS activates large nerve fibers, which are the ones carrying nonpainful signals such as touch. Stimulating these nerve fibers releases transmitter signals in the spinal cord that can inhibit the pain signals coming from small nerve fibers. Low-frequency TENS, on the other hand, seems to activate neurons in the brain stem (where inhibitory pathways start) by releasing pain-blocking endorphins.

Another option: There's a form of Japanese acupuncture that incorporates electrical stimulation through the needles, according to contributing medical editor Andrew L. Rubman, ND. It is called electro-acupuncture, and it might be a good option to explore with your acupuncturist or naturopathic doctor.

CAN YOU DO THIS AT HOME?

Side effects from the treatment are minimal—some patients experience muscle spasms and others find the electrodes irritating to their skin. But those are minor complaints compared with the pain relief the treatments sometimes deliver. If you're interested in exploring TENS treatment for neuropathic pain, discuss it with your doctor—there's a long list of medical cautions that are considered contraindications for its use. If you are among the lucky ones, this might provide welcome relief.

Say What? A Surprising Link to Hearing Loss for Women

Derek J. Handzo, DO, an otolaryngology resident, and Kathleen Yaremchuk, MD, the chair of the department of otolaryngology–head and neck surgery at Henry Ford Hospital in Detroit. They are coauthors of a study on diabetes and hearing loss presented at a recent Triological Society Combined Sections Meeting.

You might expect to lose your hearing a little bit as you age, but you may be shocked by a recent study that points to a risk factor that may make hearing loss even worse. Women with this specific condition need to listen up!

Needing to turn up the volume on the TV or radio yet again…straining to catch a dinner companion's words in a crowded restaurant… having trouble identifying background noises. It's normal to notice an increase in such experiences as we get older.

But: This recent study has highlighted an important and often overlooked risk factor that can make age-related hearing loss among women much worse than usual—diabetes that is not well controlled.

STUDY DETAILS

Researchers reviewed the medical charts of 990 women and men who, between 2000 and 2008, had had audiograms to test their ability to hear sounds at various frequencies…participants also were scored on speech recognition. Study participants were classified by age, gender and whether they had diabetes (and, if so, how well controlled their blood glucose levels were).

Results: Among women ages 60 to 75, those whose diabetes was well controlled were able to hear about equally as well as women who did not have diabetes—but those with poorly controlled diabetes had significantly worse hearing.

For men in this specific study, there was no significant difference in hearing ability between those with and without diabetes, no matter how well controlled the disease was, though this finding could have been influenced by the fact that men generally had worse hearing than women regardless of health status. But smaller studies have shown that diabetes can have an impact on hearing, no matter what your sex (see article that follows).

NOW HEAR THIS

Are you still not convinced this is a dangerous disease? Diabetes also increases the risk for heart disease, vision loss, kidney dysfunction, nerve problems and other serious ailments…so this recent study gives women with diabetes yet one more important motivation for keeping blood glucose levels well under control with diet, exercise and/or medication.

If you have not been diagnosed with diabetes: If your hearing seems to be worsening, ask your doctor to check for diabetes—particularly if you have other possible warning signs, such as frequent urination, unusual thirst, slow wound healing, blurred vision and/or numbness in the hands and feet.

Control Your Blood Sugar...Protect Your Hearing

Michael Seidman, MD, former director of the Otolaryngology Research Laboratory. He is director of the division of otologic/neurotologic surgery and chair of the Center for Integrative Medicine at the Henry Ford Health System in Detroit. Dr. Seidman is coauthor, with Marie Moneysmith, of *Save Your Hearing Now: The Revolutionary Program That Can Prevent and May Even Reverse Hearing Loss.* His formulations for preventing and treating hearing loss are available at BodyLanguage Vitamins.com.

If you're like most people, you probably assume that hearing loss is an inevitable part of growing older and that you can't do anything about it other than get a hearing aid. But that's not always true.

Most of the nearly 40 million Americans who don't hear as well as they used to have sensorineural hearing loss (SNHL)—damage to delicate, hairlike nerve endings (hair cells) in the inner ear. These tiny hair cells translate sound vibrations into electrical impulses that are sent to the brain.

While SNHL often does result from aging or loud noise (repeated exposure or a single exposure to a very loud noise, such as an explosion), it also can be due to unexpected causes such as certain health problems or even prescription or over-the-counter (OTC) drugs.

Latest development: Recent scientific research is revealing that there may be more opportunities to prevent or slow SNHL than once thought. *Surprising causes of SNHL and what you can do to prevent it...*

VIAGRA AND OTHER DRUGS

There are hundreds of "ototoxic" drugs that can damage hearing. For example, in a study published in *Laryngoscope*, researchers in the UK identified 47 cases in which men who took *sildenafil* (Viagra) or other drugs for erectile dysfunction experienced SNHL—and 67% of them developed it within 24 hours of starting the medication. *Other ototoxic drugs include...*

•**Nonsteroidal anti-inflammatory drugs (NSAIDs),** such as aspirin, *ibuprofen* (Motrin) and *naproxen* (Aleve).

•**Loop diuretics,** such as *furosemide* (Lasix), used for high blood pressure, congestive heart failure and kidney disease.

•**Antidepressants,** such as *fluoxetine* (Prozac), *clomipramine* (Anafranil) and *amitriptyline.*

•**Antianxiety medications,** such as *alprazolam* (Xanax).

•**Certain antibiotics,** including *erythromycin, gentamicin, neomycin* and *tetracycline.*

•**Chemotherapy drugs,** such as *cisplatin* and *carboplatin.*

•**Quinine-based antimalarial drugs,** such as Qualaquin.

Important: The hearing loss caused by these drugs may be temporary or permanent depending on factors such as dosage and the length of time the medication was taken.

Self-defense: If your doctor prescribes a new medication, ask whether it could cause hearing loss. You also can research drug side effects online at the Prescribers' Digital Reference website, *www.pdr.net.*

If the medication can affect hearing, ask your doctor if there are alternatives that are suitable for your particular condition. If not, an audiologist should conduct hearing tests before you begin taking the medication to obtain a baseline. These tests should be repeated several times during the course of treatment with the drug.

For the greatest protection: Normally, an audiologist checks hearing in the 250-Hertz (Hz) to 8,000-Hz range, but to monitor drug-related hearing loss, it is best to examine the high-frequency range (between 9,000 Hz and 20,000 Hz), where damage is likely to occur first.

If your hearing is affected, the prescribing physician should reconsider how best to treat the condition for which you were prescribed medication.

If you're already taking a drug that you suspect may be causing hearing loss, see an ear, nose and throat (ENT) specialist for advice. Also notify an ENT specialist if you develop a sense of fullness in one or both ears (which could signal hearing loss) or tinnitus (ringing, buzzing or other unwanted sounds with or without hearing loss).

BLOOD SUGAR PROBLEMS

Most physicians realize that diabetes slowly destroys blood vessels throughout the body, increasing risk for heart disease, stroke, Alzheimer's disease, chronic kidney disease, blindness and even amputation of circulation-starved limbs. Now, hearing loss has been identified as an underrecognized complication of diabetes.

Recent research: In a study of 46 people with type 2 diabetes and 47 with rheumatoid arthritis, those with diabetes had three times more cases of hearing loss than the study participants with arthritis.

Possible mechanism: Diabetes reduces circulation and causes nerve degeneration—two factors that can affect the viability of hair cells involved in hearing.

Another danger: Studies have linked obesity and high triglyceride levels—both of which often accompany diabetes—to SNHL.

To preserve your hearing: Take steps to prevent high blood sugar. Weight loss, regular exercise and a diet that limits processed foods and emphasizes unprocessed foods (such as vegetables, fruits, whole grains, legumes, fish, lean meat and poultry) are the best approaches to take.

RIDING IN A CONVERTIBLE AND LOUD NOISES

Most people know that loud noises such as jackhammers and explosions can damage hearing. But other causes now are being discovered. For example, researchers at the St. Louis University School of Medicine tested noise levels while riding in a convertible at 55 miles per hour or faster with the top down and windows open. Levels were found to be above 85 decibels (dB)—the point at which hearing damage begins.

Self-defense: Avoid regularly exposing your ears to any sounds above 85 dB. *To protect yourself…*

• **Use earplugs** when you operate noisy equipment of any kind, such as a lawn mower, power saw, chain saw, snowmobile—or even your vacuum cleaner.

Also helpful: If you are in an environment where you can't hear another person talking to you who is three feet away or closer, wear earplugs—or leave.

• **Lower the volume of your iPod** or other music player if you notice any signs of hearing damage, such as your ears feeling muffled or full, or ringing in your ears.

ANTIOXIDANTS = BETTER HEARING

In many cases, you may be able to prevent hearing loss that could require a hearing aid by consuming an abundance of certain antioxidants.* *For example…*

• **Coenzyme Q10 (CoQ10).** In people with SNHL, those who took the powerful antioxidant CoQ10 daily experienced improved hearing, according to recent research by Italian scientists.

• **Fish oil.** Several studies link diets high in omega-3 fatty acids from fish to preventing or delaying age-related SNHL.

Important: I recommend using molecularly distilled fish oil (check the label)—it is less likely to contain toxins such as mercury than other fish oil products.

Also helpful: Diets rich in vitamin C, vitamin E, the B-vitamin riboflavin, magnesium and the antioxidant lycopene were linked to better hearing, according to a recent study from researchers at Vanderbilt University in Nashville. Other nutrients that may help prevent hearing loss include resveratrol, lecithin,

*Consult your doctor before starting this or any other supplement regimen.

alpha lipoic acid, acetyl-L-carnitine and N-ace-tylcysteine.

Talk to an integrative physician for advice on the specific nutrients and dosages that would be best for you. To find an integrative physician, consult the Academy of Integrative Health & Medicine, *www.aihm.org.*

Alzheimer's: Is It "Type 3" Diabetes?

Isaac Eliaz, MD, LAc, an integrative physician and medical director of the Amitabha Medical Clinic & Healing Center in Santa Rosa, California, an integrative health center specializing in chronic conditions. Dr. Eliaz is a licensed acupuncturist and homeopath and an expert in mind/body medicine. He has coauthored dozens of peer-reviewed scientific papers on natural healing. DrEliaz.org

---

For years, scientists from around the world have investigated various causes of Alzheimer's disease. Cardiovascular disease factors, such as hypertension, stroke and heart failure...other neurological diseases, such as Parkinson's disease...accumulated toxins and heavy metals, such as aluminum, lead and mercury...nutrient deficiencies, including vitamins B and E...infections, such as the herpes virus and the stomach bacterium *H. pylori*...and head injuries each have been considered at one time or another to be a possible contributor to the development of this mind-robbing disease.

However, as researchers continue to piece together the results of literally thousands of studies, one particular theory is now emerging as perhaps the most plausible and convincing of them all in explaining why some people—and not others—develop Alzheimer's disease.

A PATTERN EMERGES

An estimated 5.5 million Americans are now living with Alzheimer's, and the number of cases is skyrocketing. Interestingly, so are the rates of obesity, diabetes and metabolic syndrome (a constellation of risk factors including elevated blood sugar, high blood pressure, abnormal cholesterol levels and abdominal fat).

What's the potential link? Doctors have long suspected that diabetes increases risk for Alzheimer's. The exact mechanism is not known, but many experts believe that people with diabetes are more likely to develop Alzheimer's because their bodies don't properly use blood sugar (glucose) and the blood sugar–regulating hormone insulin.

Now research shows increased dementia risk in people with high blood sugar—even if they do not have diabetes. A problem with insulin appears to be the cause. How does insulin dysfunction affect the brain? Neurons are starved of energy, and there's an increase in brain cell death, DNA damage, inflammation and the formation of plaques in the brain—a main characteristic of Alzheimer's disease.

AN ALZHEIMER'S-FIGHTING REGIMEN

Even though experimental treatments with antidiabetes drugs that improve insulin function have been shown to reduce symptoms of early Alzheimer's disease, it is my belief, as an integrative physician, that targeted nondrug therapies are preferable in preventing the brain degeneration that leads to Alzheimer's and fuels its progression. These approaches won't necessarily reverse Alzheimer's, but they may help protect your brain if you are not currently fighting this disease...or help slow the progression of early-stage Alzheimer's.

My advice includes...

•**Follow a low-glycemic (low sugar) diet.** This is essential for maintaining healthy glucose and insulin function as well as supporting brain and overall health. An effective way to maintain a low-sugar diet is to use the glycemic index (GI), a scale that ranks foods according to how quickly they raise blood sugar levels.

Here's what happens: High-GI foods (such as white rice, white potatoes and refined sugars) are rapidly digested and absorbed. As a result, these foods cause dangerous spikes in blood sugar levels.

Low-GI foods (such as green vegetables...fiber-rich foods including whole grains...and plant proteins including legumes, nuts and seeds) are digested slowly, so they gradually raise blood sugar and insulin levels. This is critical for maintaining glucose and insulin function and controlling inflammation.

Helpful: www.glycemicindex.com gives glucose ratings of common foods and recipes.

• **Consider trying brain-supporting nutrients and herbs.*** These supplements, which help promote insulin function, can be used alone or taken together for better results (dosages may be lower if supplements are combined due to the ingredients' synergistic effects)…

• **Alpha-lipoic acid (ALA)** is an antioxidant shown to support insulin sensitivity and protect neurons from inflammation-related damage.

Typical dosage: 500 mg to 1,000 mg per day.

• **Chromium** improves glucose regulation.

Typical dosage: 350 micrograms (mcg) to 700 mcg per day.

• **Alginates** from seaweed help reduce glucose spikes and crashes.

Typical dosage: 250 mg to 1,000 mg before meals.

• **L-Taurine,** an amino acid, helps maintain healthy glucose and lipid (blood fat) levels.

Typical dosage: 1,000 mg to 2,000 mg per day.

KICK UP YOUR HEELS!

Regular exercise, such as walking, swimming and tennis, is known to improve insulin function and support cognitive health by increasing circulation to the brain. Dancing, however, may be the ultimate brain-protective exercise. Why might dancing be better than other brain-body coordination exercises, such as tennis? Because dancing is mainly noncompetitive, there isn't the added stress of contending with an opponent, which increases risk for temporary cognitive impairment.

Best: Aerobic dances with a social component, such as Latin, swing or ballroom,

*Consult your doctor before trying these supplements, especially if you take any medications or have a chronic health condition, such as liver or kidney disease. If he/she is not well versed in the use of these therapies, consider seeing an integrative physician. To find one near you, consult The Institute for Functional Medicine, www.functionalmedicine.org.

performed at least three times weekly for 90 minutes each session. (Dancing for less time also provides some brain benefits.) If you don't like dancing, brisk walking for 30 minutes a day, five days a week, is also shown to help protect the brain against dementia.

Free courses: In addition to getting regular physical activity, it's helpful to learn challenging new material to "exercise" the brain. For 1,150 free online courses provided by professors at top universities such as Stanford and Johns Hopkins, go to *www.openculture.com/ freeonlinecourses*. Subjects include art history, geography, international relations and biology.

Blood Sugar Problems? Take Action Now to Protect Your Brain

Yutaka Kiyohara, MD, a professor in the department of environmental medicine in the Graduate School of Medical Sciences at Kyushu University in Fukuoka, Japan, and coauthor of a study on diabetes and dementia risk published in *Neurology*.

Knowledge is power—so even though the news from a recent study on dementia is not exactly welcome, the information is indeed beneficial if it inspires people to take steps that can help keep their brains healthy. The findings are particularly important for people with diabetes…and also, surprisingly, for those with prediabetes, a condition that now affects half of Americans ages 65 and older.

Study details: 1,017 seniors did oral glucose tolerance tests (in which blood sugar is measured after fasting and again after consuming a sweet drink) to determine whether they had normal blood sugar levels…impaired glucose tolerance, a prediabetic condition…or diabetes. Participants were then followed for 15 years to see who developed Alzheimer's disease, vascular dementia (caused by blood vessel damage) or some other form of dementia.

Findings: Compared with participants who had normal blood sugar levels, those with prediabetes were 35% more likely to develop some type of dementia and 60% more likely to develop Alzheimer's. People with diabetes fared even worse, having a 74% higher risk for dementia of any kind, an 82% higher risk for vascular dementia and more than double the risk for Alzheimer's.

The connection: Diabetes and prediabetes can damage blood vessels, causing inflammation and lack of blood flow to the brain, which in turn lead to brain cell death…and/or excess glucose carried through the blood vessels to the brain may allow accumulation of proteins that damage nerve cells.

Self-defense: More research is needed…but for now, maintaining good blood sugar control seems like a sensible way to reduce dementia risk. Ask your doctor about getting screened for prediabetes and diabetes, particularly if you are over age 45, are overweight, have high blood pressure, have a family history of diabetes and/or have a history of diabetes during pregnancy.

If you have prediabetes: According to the American Diabetes Association, you can reduce your odds of developing diabetes by more than half by doing moderate exercise (such as brisk walking) for 30 minutes five days per week and losing 7% of your body weight (about 14 pounds if you currently weigh 200 or about 10 pounds if you weigh 150).

If you have diabetes: Be conscientious about controlling blood sugar through diet, exercise and/or medication…and talk to your doctor about seeing a neurologist if you notice signs of cognitive problems, such as memory loss.

A Cup of Decaf May Prevent Memory Loss

Giulio M. Pasinetti, MD, PhD, professor of neurology and psychiatry, Mount Sinai School of Medicine, New York City, and lead researcher of a study reported in *Nutritional Neuroscience*.

When you need a boost, chances are you reach for a cup of caffeinated coffee.

And if you find that it's helping you to remember things more vividly and think more clearly while you're working on an important task, you probably chalk that up to the caffeine.

Well, the caffeine might help in the short term. But recent research conducted at Mount Sinai School of Medicine in New York City shows that coffee itself also may provide a long-term memory benefit—even when it's decaf!

In fact, the study showed that drinking a certain amount of decaf over the long term might reduce the odds of developing the neurological impairment that's associated with the early stages of Alzheimer's disease.

This is certainly promising news for those of us who are overly sensitive to caffeine but love the taste of coffee. And it's even more promising for people with type 2 diabetes, because they're often told by doctors to avoid caffeine to keep their blood sugar under control, and they're also at higher risk for Alzheimer's disease.

COFFEE'S SECRET WEAPON

To learn more, we contacted Giulio M. Pasinetti, MD, PhD, professor of neurology and psychiatry at Mount Sinai School of Medicine and the lead researcher in the study. Before the study, Dr. Pasinetti and his team had become interested in how chlorogenic acids—types of antioxidants found in coffee, as well as in grapes, cocoa and other foods—affect the brain. They were interested in seeing whether the positive health effects of chlorogenic acids could come from coffee without caffeine. And they wanted to analyze how decaf could affect people with type 2 diabetes, since, as mentioned earlier, people with that condition are usually advised by doctors to avoid caffeine.

Researchers used mice in the study because they could completely control what they ate. They gave the mice a high-fat diet that triggered the onset of type 2 diabetes. At the same time, they fed half of the mice a daily extract of decaffeinated coffee made from unroasted coffee beans.

221

WHAT THE DECAF DID

What they found? The decaf-drinking mice's brains used 25% more oxygen—meaning that these mice were less likely to experience neurological impairment. Researchers suspect that the chlorogenic acids in decaf are the reason for this result.

WILL IT TRANSLATE TO HUMANS?

Of course, just because decaf helps mouse brains doesn't necessarily mean that it helps human brains, but Dr. Pasinetti is hopeful because a great deal of previous medical research using mice has, in fact, been followed by similar results in humans. (That's a big reason mice are so often used in research.)

How much might humans consume to get a similar benefit? Dr. Pasinetti recommends asking your doctor about taking a daily supplement that contains 400-mg extract of decaf green (a.k.a. "unroasted") coffee. (Dr. Pasinetti used an extract called Svetol, which can be found at *www.swansonvitamins.com*. A month's supply costs $10.99) Or drink the equivalent (two cups of decaf per day), but Dr. Pasinetti said that roasting coffee beans sucks out some of the beneficial chlorogenic acids, so the benefit would not be as much as from the extract.

Another question is whether the results would be the same with regular (caffeinated) coffee. "Since we suspect that the benefits come from the chlorogenic acids in the coffee itself—and not the caffeine—caffeinated coffee is likely to prevent neurological impairment, too," said Dr. Pasinetti. "Other foods rich in chlorogenic acids, such as grapes and cocoa, are also likely to have similar benefits, but more research needs to examine that."

Statins Can Help Diabetes Complications

In addition to lowering risk for heart attack and stroke, statins lowered risk for diabetes complications, according to a recent finding. People with diabetes taking statins were 34%

less likely to be diagnosed with diabetes-related nerve damage (neuropathy)...40% less likely to develop diabetes-related damage to the retina...and 12% less likely to develop gangrene than diabetics not taking statins.

Børge G. Nordestgaard, MD, DMSc, chief physician at Copenhagen University Hospital, Herlev, Denmark, and leader of a study of 60,000 people, published in *The Lancet Diabetes & Endocrinology*.

Remedies for Edema: Swollen Feet, Swollen Ankles, Swollen Hands and the Rest of You

Study titled "Edema: Diagnosis and Management," published in *American Family Physician*.

If you are someone who puffs up with water retention in the warm weather, the prospect of cooler days might be a relief (although damp, heavy weather can make you swell up, too). Or you may be someone whose calves, ankles and feet are often a little "cushiony" with water retention despite the weather. They may be so cushiony that they dimple when you press into them. That kind of swelling can be painful, too—and it can be a sign of a serious health problem, even a medical emergency. But for most people who deal with limb swelling—men and women alike—it is simply a recurring nuisance that a doctor may or may not be able to diagnose. Here are some surefire remedies to soothe the swelling...and also advice for when limb swelling might be life-threatening...

WHY WE SWELL

Swelling caused by fluid buildup is called edema (pronounced "ih-dee-mah"). When it affects only your arms, legs, hands and feet, it is called peripheral edema. We retain water because blood vessels in our arms, legs, hands and feet expand, or dilate. This dilation can be caused by hot or humid weather or a number of other causes. The dilation makes it easier for fluid to leak out of blood vessels into surrounding tissue, causing the tissue to swell. Sitting or standing in one position for a long time without moving makes the swelling worse because gravity just pulls all that fluid down to pool in your hands, legs and feet.

RELIEF FOR SWOLLEN LIMBS

Besides weather-related effects on blood vessels, the reason why some people swell can't always be figured out, but common disease-related causes of swelling are kidney and cardiovascular disease. Whether a doctor can or cannot pinpoint the cause of peripheral edema, he or she too often prescribes a diuretic and suggests that you cut back on salt.

Although cutting back on salt may be great advice, taking a diuretic may not be unless the swelling is related to high blood pressure or high blood pressure medication. *But there are safe, natural ways to relieve swelling…*

• **Leg elevation.** Keep your legs elevated while sitting for prolonged periods. Yes, put a comfy, compact ottoman under your desk…or put your legs up and rest your feet on that extra chair. Also, prop your feet up on a few pillows while lying on the sofa or in bed. Don't just bear with swelling because, if it happens often, it can cause your skin and tissue to stretch and change. It can also lead to more serious and lasting edema.

• **Walking breaks.** If you really can't plop your feet up on a chair in a place where you regularly spend time—such as in an office or another "noncasual" setting—then make a point of getting up from the chair and taking five-minute walking breaks every hour or so. This increases circulation and gets your lymphatic system to pump out excess fluid.

• **Compression stockings.** If you need to stand for a long time during the day, wear support hose or compression knee-highs or stockings. These help blood circulation between your feet and your heart—with one benefit being more spring in your step. In fact, athletes often use compression stockings to enhance their performance.

Compression stockings come in many styles and colors, price ranges (from about $10 to $100), sizes and pressures. So, when buying compression stockings online, you will need to find sellers that provide guidance on sizing and compression needs. One source is Bright Life Direct (*www.brightlifedirect.com*). It carries all the major brands and has easy-to-follow guidance and FAQs to figure out what size and kind of compression stocking is right for you—and right for your budget.

• **Massage your hands.** Swollen hands? To enhance circulation and lymphatic drainage, apply lotion to your hands and massage one hand and then the other, starting with the fingertips and moving down the hand to the wrist. Also exercise the hands by holding them at chest level and clenching and unclenching them. To do this effectively, gently make a fist and then open your fist and spread your fingers. Massage and exercise your hands several times a day when edema is acting up.

WHEN EDEMA IS DANGEROUS

There are other factors that can cause edema…and they can be life-threatening. Besides cardiovascular and kidney disease, other causes, which were spelled out by the American Academy of Family Physicians in a recent article by and for doctors, include liver disease, sleep apnea, allergies, use of certain medications (such as nonsteroidal anti-inflammatory drugs, antihypertensives, corticosteroids, antidepressants, diabetes medications, hormone replacement therapy) and chemotherapy. Edema also can be caused by surgical removal or malfunction of the lymph nodes, which, as part of the lymphatic system, filter fluid and cleanse the body of bacteria, viruses and other debris.

What's the danger of unchecked edema? Besides the fact that you might have a serious underlying condition needing treatment, all that swelling and stretching of the skin can cause a flaky, eczema-like appearance and even skin ulcers. Ulcers, in turn, can lead to serious skin infections, such as cellulitis, where the infection bores through the skin and into underlying tissue. And you probably also know that chronic swollen legs and feet can put you at risk for blood clots that can lodge in a leg or travel up to the lungs, heart, brain or another part of your body. This is called thromboembolism (or stroke when it hits your brain)—and, just like a stroke, it can kill you.

If you are having symptoms such as shortness of breath, rapid heartbeat or pain and heat in a limb, be sure to get to a doctor or even an emergency room right away. You could be experiencing thromboembolism. The symptoms may be accompanied by chest pain, fever or intense anxiety (a feeling of doom). Once treated for a thromboembolic attack, you may be put on a medication to prevent blood clots and be instructed to wear compression stockings.

For all these reasons, if you have chronic edema—even if you can get relief from the self-treatments described above—it's a good idea to get it checked out by a doctor. *In addition to the suggestions listed above, additional steps a doctor might take if you have severe chronic edema include...*

●**Checking for clots.** Even if you are not having a thromboembolic emergency, your doctor may order an ultrasound of the swollen limb to see whether clots have formed. If so, he or she will likely put you on a blood-thinning drug to prevent a thromboembolic event.

●**Prescribing pneumatic compression.** If swelling is severe and related to surgical removal or malfunction of lymph nodes, you might be instructed in the use of a pneumatic compression device, an inflatable garment resembling a boot, sock or sleeve that does the work of a compression stocking but with greater intensity.

●**Recommended physiotherapy.** You also may be referred to a physiotherapist for massage and movement therapy and specialized compression techniques that involves use of bandage wrappings.

So do not endure swollen limbs simply because it's something that you've put up with for years. Keeping the swelling in check and getting a handle on the underlying cause, when possible, can save you from major health woes down the line.

How to Prevent Erectile Dysfunction

Sheldon Marks, MD, is the medical director for the International Center for Vasectomy Reversal (*DadsAgain.com*), directs the men's health and erectile dysfunction community at *WebMD.com* and is the integrative urologist for *DrWeil.com*. He has been associate clinical professor of urology at The University of Arizona College of Medicine, Tucson, and adjunct assistant professor of urology at Tufts University School of Medicine in Boston. Dr. Marks is also author of *Prostate & Cancer*.

Erectile dysfunction (ED) drugs have become so popular in the US—about 20% of American men over age 45 have used them—that the most obvious and safest solution to the problem is now being largely overlooked.

What works best for ED: Instead of taking a medication that can bring on side effects ranging from vision problems to headaches, it's much smarter to prevent the condition from developing.

Good news: Recent research shows that there are simple yet effective techniques to prevent ED. Men who already suffer from ED can improve their symptoms, too, by addressing these health issues.

THE NEW THINKING

While doctors have long known that ED can sometimes be caused by emotional factors, such as depression, there's now a growing body of evidence that shows how closely this problem is related to the same physical problems that can lead to heart disease, high blood pressure (hypertension) and stroke.

Example: The main artery in the penis is only about 0.02 inches in diameter. A man with atherosclerosis (plaques in the arteries) will often develop impotence years or even decades before he's diagnosed with cardiovascular disease.

What men need to know about the underlying causes of ED...

BELLY FAT

Men who are overweight or obese have a high risk of developing ED, particularly if they also have diabetes, hypertension or heart disease—all of which can damage the blood vessels and/or nerves that are needed for erections.

The risk is even higher in men who have excessive belly fat. That's because fat that accumulates in the abdomen, known as visceral fat, converts testosterone to estrogen. Men with a low testosterone-to-estrogen ratio frequently suffer from ED. Low energy is another warning sign.

What to do: Men who have excessive belly fat should lose weight. If weight loss does not eliminate the ED, it then makes sense to get a hormone test. Your doctor can check your testosterone-estrogen ratio with blood and/or saliva tests. Men with this hormone imbalance often improve when taking an aromatase inhibitor (such as Arimidex). This class of medications blocks the conversion of testosterone to estrogen.

Important: I don't recommend testosterone supplements because they could disrupt the balance between testosterone and estrogen, creating more visceral fat.

GUM DISEASE

Scientists have known for years that men with periodontal (gum) disease tend to have more cardiovascular disease, but gum problems also have recently been linked to an increased risk for ED.

It's possible that bacteria from infected gums can get into the bloodstream and cause inflammation in the arteries in the penis. Inflammation can, in turn, accelerate arterial obstructions that can lead to ED as well as heart disease.

What to do: Take better care of your gums with daily brushing and flossing.

Important: Dentists recommend brushing for at least two minutes twice daily—most people do not brush for nearly that long.

HEART DISEASE

There's now strong evidence showing that ED is often a marker for undiagnosed heart disease.

Here's what happens: When the narrow arteries in the penis become blocked by plaque (leading to ED), this is a good indicator that arteries in the heart also could be obstructed. It's crucial to recognize that arterial blockage in the heart can occur long before a man develops chest pain, shortness of breath or other cardiovascular symptoms.

What to do: I advise men with ED to see a cardiologist first. They should assume, until testing proves otherwise, that ED is an early sign of heart disease. You'll probably be given an echo stress test. With this test, you'll use a treadmill or bicycle while a technician monitors your heartbeat and uses ultrasound to show the heart's movements.

If you have early-stage heart disease, you can save your life—and your sex life—with a combination of lifestyle changes (such as regular exercise) and, if necessary, medication to lower cholesterol.

HIGH BLOOD PRESSURE

Both high blood pressure and the drugs used to treat it are among the most common causes of ED.

If you have high blood pressure, damage to the arteries from excessive blood pressure can interfere with erections. Unfortunately, the problem can get worse if you take blood pressure medication.

What to do: In addition to reducing high blood pressure—by lifestyle changes (such as getting more exercise, dropping some pounds if you're overweight and eating less salt) and taking medications, if needed—tell your doctor right away if you're suffering from ED. He/she might be able to switch you to a different antihypertensive medication that doesn't itself cause you to have ED. Every man responds to blood pressure drugs differently.

Also important: Prescription antidepressants are notorious for causing ED in some men. As with blood pressure drugs, switching to a different antidepressant is sometimes enough to solve the problem. Drugs for male pattern baldness, such as *finasteride* (Propecia), also may cause ED.

SLEEP APNEA

Sleep apnea is a condition in which breathing intermittently stops and starts during sleep. It causes a decrease in oxygen in the blood and an increase in carbon dioxide that can lead to hypertension, heart disease—and ED.

Obesity is among the main causes of sleep apnea. Apnea also can be caused, or increased, by excessive alcohol consumption, medications (such as sedatives) and smoking.

What to do: If you are a loud snorer or your partner reports that you frequently gasp or snort during sleep, you might have sleep apnea. Other symptoms include morning headaches and extreme daytime fatigue.

Ask your doctor if you should have a sleep test. If you're diagnosed with sleep apnea, you'll probably be advised to lose weight if you're overweight and perhaps be prescribed treatment such as a CPAP (continuous positive airway pressure) device. It delivers pressurized air to the nose and/or mouth while you sleep and can sometimes eliminate both apnea and ED.

A Cancer Risk Your Doctor May Not Know About

Lynne Eldridge, MD, medical manager of the Lung Cancer site for *About.com* and a former clinical preceptor at the University of Minnesota Medical School in Minneapolis. Dr. Eldridge practiced family medicine for 15 years and now devotes herself full time to researching and speaking on cancer prevention. She is author of *Avoiding Cancer One Day at a Time*.

If you don't have any of the well-known risk factors for cancer, including smoking, a family history of cancer or long-term exposure to a carcinogen such as asbestos, you may think that your risk for the disease is average or even less than average.

What you may not realize: Although most of the cancer predispositions (genetic, lifestyle and environmental factors that increase risk for the disease) are commonly known, there are several medical conditions that also can increase your risk, such as diabetes.

Unfortunately, many primary-care physicians do not link diabetes to cancer. As a result, they fail to prescribe the tests and treatments that could keep cancer at bay or reduce the condition's cancer-causing potential.

The high blood sugar levels that occur with type 2 diabetes predispose you to heart attack, stroke, nerve pain, blindness, kidney failure, a need for amputation—and cancer.

Recent research: For every 1% increase in HbA1c—a measurement of blood sugar levels over the previous three months—there is an 18% increase in the risk for cancer, according to a study published in *Current Diabetes Reports*.

Other current studies have linked type 2 diabetes to a 94% increased risk for pancreatic cancer...a 38% increased risk for colon cancer...a 15% to 20% higher risk for postmenopausal breast cancer...and a 20% higher risk for blood cancers such as non-Hodgkin's lymphoma and leukemia.

What to do: If you have type 2 diabetes, make sure your primary-care physician orders regular screening tests for cancer, such as colonoscopy and mammogram.

Screening for pancreatic cancer is not widely available, but some of the larger cancer centers (such as the H. Lee Moffitt Cancer Center & Research Institute in Tampa, Florida, and the Mayo Clinic in Rochester, Minnesota) offer it to high-risk individuals.

This typically includes people with long-standing diabetes (more than 20 years) and/or a family history of pancreatic cancer. The test involves an ultrasound of both the stomach and small intestine, where telltale signs of pancreatic cancer can be detected.

Also work with your doctor to minimize the cancer-promoting effects of diabetes. For example, control blood sugar levels through a diet that emphasizes slow-digesting foods that don't create spikes in blood sugar levels, such as vegetables and beans. Also, try to get regular exercise—for example, 30 minutes of walking five or six days a week. Studies have shown that regular exercise helps to control blood sugar. And consider medical interventions, such as use of the diabetes drug *metformin* (Glucophage).

Diabetics: The Body Part That's Aging Faster Than the Rest of You

Hongha Vu-James, MD, formerly clinical gastroenterology fellow, Washington University, St. Louis, and lead author of a study presented at a Digestive Disease Week conference in San Diego.

People with type 2 diabetes have a lot of balls to keep in the air, medically speaking.

They need to, of course, keep their blood sugar in check, get regular eye screenings and monitor their feet, which often can suffer from nerve damage.

Now recent research may add another item to that already-long checklist.

It suggests that people with type 2 diabetes should start getting colonoscopies earlier and, perhaps, get them more frequently.

Here's why...

TYPE 2 DIABETICS HAVE "OLDER" COLONS

Researchers from Washington University in St. Louis reviewed colonoscopy records of male and female patients over a six-year span, comparing the incidence of precancerous polyps in three groups—those ages 40 to 49 with type 2 diabetes...those ages 40 to 49 without type 2 diabetes...and those ages 50 to 59 without type 2 diabetes.

Their first finding was expected, since age increases the risk for precancerous polyps. Nondiabetics in their 50s had a much higher rate of precancerous polyps (32%) than nondiabetics in their 40s (14%).

But their second finding was alarming. Diabetics in their 40s had nearly the same rate of precancerous polyps (30%) as nondiabetics in their 50s (again, 32%). And this was after individual cancer risk factors—such as gender, race, obesity, smoking, high cholesterol and alcohol use—were taken into account.

"It's almost as if the colons of diabetics are 10 years older," study author Hongha Vu-James, MD, formerly clinical gastroenterology fellow at the university, said. It's believed that the culprit is a high level of insulin in type 2 diabetics, since insulin is thought to promote cell growth in the colon, she said.

SHOULD SCREENING GUIDELINES CHANGE?

Current guidelines from the American Cancer Society (ACS) suggest that colorectal cancer screenings should begin at age 50 for people at average risk for colon cancer. ACS advises those at high risk (anyone with inflammatory bowel disease, a personal history of colorectal cancer or a family history of colorectal cancer) to get screened even earlier (the age varies by risk factor). In addition, the site for the American College of Gastroenterology says, "Recent evidence suggests that African-Americans should begin screening earlier at the age of 45."

What about people with type 2 diabetes? The American Diabetes Association, while acknowledging that type 2 diabetes is linked with a higher risk for colorectal and other cancers, urges diabetics to reduce lifestyle-related cancer risk factors but doesn't deviate from the "begin screening at age 50" recommendation for those at average risk.

Dr. Vu-James, however, is hoping that her research —and future studies that replicate it— will change that. Her study suggests that people with type 2 diabetes should consider getting their first colorectal cancer screening earlier than age 50.

In her view, doctors should be open to discussing the idea of earlier colorectal cancer screenings with diabetic patients based on their overall risk factors, and it might help to bring a copy of this article with you if you want to broach the idea with your physician. Unfortunately, if you have type 2 diabetes and you want to get a colorectal cancer screening before the age of 50 but you're considered to be at "average risk," according to the current guidelines, it's unlikely that insurance will cover it, said Dr. Vu-James, and a colonoscopy can cost around $1,200 or more. If more research confirms Dr. Vu-James' findings and screening guidelines change, colonoscopies are more likely to be covered in the future.

If you have type 2 diabetes and are over the age of 50 and you've already started getting colorectal cancer screenings, Dr. Vu-James said that there is no data yet on whether or not more frequent screenings are necessary, but if you're concerned, talk to your doctor.

Also: This increased risk for colorectal cancer does not apply to people of any age with type 1 diabetes, said Dr. Vu-James, because type 1 is caused by a lack of insulin.

Diabetic Women at Risk for Colorectal Cancer

Jill E. Elwing, MD, is in private practice in St. Louis, Missouri.

There seems to be no end to the health risks associated with diabetes, a truly insidious disease that can lead to other serious health problems. Having diabetes increases risk for cardiovascular disease, kidney failure, hypertension, stroke and damage to the nerves and eyes. Recent research has also linked diabetes to a greater risk of certain cancers, including colorectal (colon or rectum) cancer. And now a study from Washington University in St. Louis concludes that diabetic women are at greater risk for developing colorectal adenomas—polyps that can turn into cancer. This is especially true for diabetic women who are also obese, defined in this study as having a body mass index of over 30.

The study compared the colonoscopy records of 100 women with type 2 diabetes with those of 500 non-diabetic women to evaluate the rate of adenomas in these women.

The results: Diabetic women had a significantly higher rate of adenomas compared with those who did not have the disease—37% versus 24%. Furthermore, women with type 2 diabetes were also more apt to have advanced adenomas—14% versus 6%. Apparently, at greatest risk of all are women who are obese and have diabetes. In fact, when compared with non-obese, non-diabetic women, these women faced nearly twice as high a risk of having any kind of adenoma and more than two times greater risk for having advanced adenoma.

We spoke with the study's lead author, Jill E. Elwing, MD, about these results. She explains that insulin is in itself a growth factor and that might be what is behind the link between diabetes and colorectal adenoma—the growth factor could produce a pro-cancerous effect. The immediate take-away from this study, she says, is that medical professionals and this group of vulnerable women should have greater awareness and pay more attention to regular screening. Women of any age who have type 2 diabetes should discuss a colorectal screening schedule with their doctors. And because being over age 50 is also considered a risk factor for colorectal cancer, diabetic women over that age should be particularly careful to follow their doctor's advice about regular screenings, she says.

Treating Diabetic Kidney Disease with a Supplement

Mahmood S. Mozaffari, PhD, DMD, professor of oral biology, Dental College of Georgia, Augusta.

Kidney disease is more common than you might guess—for instance, about 40% of people with diabetes will get kidney damage, or nephropathy, so news of a treatment that might ease the condition is certainly welcome. A recent study has found that the mineral supplement chromium picolinate may be helpful in staving off diabetic kidney disease, which is caused when high blood sugar destroys the small blood vessels of the kidneys. With 29 million Americans suffering from diabetes, this is welcome news.

First, a tiny bit of background on diabetic nephropathy. If it is left untreated, the kidneys won't filter waste from the blood efficiently, which will eventually lead to kidney failure and the need for dialysis. Conventional preventive advice for this condition focuses on regular exercise, known to improve insulin sensitivity…

228

keeping blood glucose levels down...controlling blood pressure, since high blood pressure can also damage the kidney's blood vessels... keeping cholesterol down...eating a low-fat diet...limiting salt and protein...and not smoking. But diabetic kidney disease continues to cause morbidity and mortality, thus indicating the need for other measures.

CAN CHROMIUM PICOLINATE HELP?

In research presented at an annual conference of the American Physiological Society, Mahmood Mozaffari, PhD, DMD, a professor at the Dental College of Georgia, and his colleague Babak Baban, PhD, tested the effectiveness and safety of the supplement chromium picolinate for people at risk for diabetic nephropathy. Chromium picolinate has been suggested to help enhance the action of insulin and control glucose levels in patients with diabetes, especially type 2.

The researchers compared three groups of mice—one healthy group and two groups that were genetically engineered for obesity and diabetes (two conditions that often coexist). For six months, the healthy mice and one group of diabetic mice were fed a regular rodent diet. The other group of diabetic mice was fed a diet enriched with chromium picolinate. The researchers measured blood glucose levels and urinary albumin, a marker for kidney damage. As expected, they found that the untreated diabetic mice excreted nearly 10 times more albumin (an indication of kidney disease) than the healthy mice... but, the diabetic mice eating the chromium picolinate-enriched diet excreted only about half as much albumin as the untreated diabetic mice. In addition, kidney tissue samples showed changes suggestive of less inflammation in the treated diabetic group than in the untreated group. However, chromium picolinate treatment resulted in only a mild improvement in glucose control. Thus the researchers believe that effects other than sugar control may underlie the impact of the chromium picolinate in reducing biomarkers of inflammation in the kidney.

Chromium picolinate supplements are sold at most pharmacies or online in doses from 200 mcg to 800 mcg.

SHOULD YOU TRY IT?

While you can get some of the chromium you need from foods—such as broccoli, beef, chicken, turkey, red wine, wheat germ, eggs, black pepper and molasses or the probiotic brewer's yeast—dietary chromium is poorly absorbed from the gut.

Dr. Mozaffari cautions that this promising animal study must be substantiated in other studies including human clinical trials, so he is not yet advocating that people with diabetes should take chromium picolinate to help reduce the impact of diabetic nephropathy. And you definitely shouldn't be taking supplemental chromium if you are on medication for your diabetes, including if you're taking insulin, *metformin* (Glucophage) or *glyburide* (Diabeta), as it will affect the way your body reacts to the drugs...or if you take NSAIDs and antacids.

A Walk Does Wonders for Chronic Kidney Disease

Che-Yi Chou, MD, PhD, Kidney Institute, division of nephrology, department of internal medicine, both at China Medical University Hospital, Taiwan. Dr. Chou's study appeared in the *Clinical Journal of the American Society of Nephrology*.

If you have chronic kidney disease (CKD), there is a stone simple way that you might save yourself from needing dialysis or a kidney transplant. CKD, a condition in which the kidneys struggle to filter waste from the blood, is a silent health threat that you can be completely unaware of until serious damage is done. One in three adults with diabetes and one in five with high blood pressure has CKD, and like so many illnesses, incidence increases after age 50. If left unchecked, end-stage renal disease—kidney failure—occurs. That's when you'll need to be hooked up to a dialysis machine to filter your blood or will require a kidney transplant to stay alive.

Although there is no cure once CKD sets in, it can often be kept from advancing, and now doctors have confirmed that a certain simple exercise can not only help you avoid dialysis or transplantation but also add years to your life. And that exercise is...walking! *Here's what to do...*

A PROVEN BENEFIT

We all know that exercise improves cardio-vascular fitness, and researchers had already confirmed that it improves fitness in people with CKD. But could walking actually help with the disease itself—and in a significant way? That question had never been tested by research...so a group of Taiwanese researchers decided to find out.

The study started out with 6,363 patients whose average age was 70. All had moderate to severe CKD, and 53% had CKD severe enough to need dialysis or a kidney transplant. The researchers recorded and monitored exercise activity and a range of other health and medical measurements in the group and identified 1,341 people who walked as their favorite form of exercise. These patients were compared with patients who did not walk nor exercise in any other way.

The results: Walkers were 33% less likely to die of kidney disease and 21% less likely to need dialysis or a kidney transplant than non-walkers/nonexercisers. And the more a person walked, the more likely he or she was not on dialysis or in need of a kidney transplant and still alive when the study ended. So, for example, someone who walked once or twice a week for an average 30 minutes to an hour had a 17% lower risk of death and a 19% lower risk of needing dialysis or a kidney transplant compared with someone who didn't walk or exercise. And someone who walked for an average 30 minutes to an hour seven or more times a week had a 59% lower risk of death and a 44% lower risk of needing dialysis or a kidney transplant.

Now, when researchers see this kind of dramatic result, they always should explore whether there was some reason other than the activity that was studied (in this case, walking) that could explain things. These are called confounding factors—for example, could it be that walkers walked because they were healthier, as opposed to being healthier

because they walked? But no confounding factors were found. The average age, average body size and degree of kidney disease was the same in the two groups, as was the prevalence of diabetes-associated coronary artery disease, cigarette smoking and use of medications for CKD.

The bottom line for people with CKD...walk! Walk everywhere! Walk often! Even a 30-minute walk once or twice a week can help. The more you walk, the greater the benefit.

ARE YOU AT RISK?

If you have diabetes or high blood pressure, your doctor should give you a simple blood test to see whether CKD is developing. *Otherwise, here are telltale signs to keep an eye out for—these may signal that you should be evaluated for CKD...*

- **Unexplained fatigue**
- **Trouble concentrating**
- **Poor appetite**
- **Trouble sleeping**
- **Nighttime muscle cramps**
- **Swollen feet and ankles**
- **Eye puffiness, especially in the morning**
- **Dry, itchy skin**
- **Frequent urination, especially at night**

Be sure to tell your doctor what medications you're on when you are examined for CKD. Because the kidneys also filter medications out of your body, meds can build up to toxic levels in your system if the kidneys aren't doing their job. If you have CKD, your doctor may take you off some medications and lower the dose of others.

While there's no cure for CKD once it sets in, it need not advance to severe and deadly stages that require dialysis or a kidney transplant. Besides exercising and keeping the underlying cause (whether it be diabetes, high blood pressure or something else) in check, mild CKD is managed by diet. *To do it right...*

- **Make walking a priority.**

- **Work with your doctor to manage the underlying cause,** and work with a dietitian to manage your nutrition requirements. A dietitian will plan a regimen that controls the amount of protein, salt, potassium and phosphorus you consume, all of which can build up to toxic levels in people with CKD. A dietitian will also balance your CKD diet needs with those related to glucose control or whatever condition may be associated with your CKD.

Metformin and Kidney Disease

For diabetes patients with kidney disease, the benefits of metformin may outweigh the risks. The drug *metformin* is very effective for type 2 diabetes, but an FDA label dating to 1994 restricts its use in patients with kidney problems. Recent evidence now shows that metformin is safe for patients with mild-to-moderate kidney disease.

James H. Flory, MD, MSCE, a fellow in medicine at Weill Cornell Medical College, New York City.

Nausea from Diabetes? Electrical "Acupressure" Eases Gastroparesis Symptoms

Jiande Chen, PhD, professor of medicine, Johns Hopkins University School of Medicine, Baltimore. He is former professor, division of gastroenterology and hepatology, University of Texas Medical Branch, Galveston. His study was presented at the American College of Gastroenterology's 77th Annual Scientific Meeting.

About 10% to 15% of diabetes patients develop a digestive complication called gastroparesis, in which food takes too long to leave the stomach—and the symptoms are nasty. But help may be on the horizon, a recent study shows. The secret weapon is a small electrical device that a patient simply straps onto his or her wrist or leg.

Background: Gastroparesis develops when high blood glucose levels cause chemical changes, damaging the vagus nerve. This nerve controls the muscles that move food through the digestive tract. Gastroparesis symptoms include nausea, vomiting, heartburn, bloating, abdominal pain, stomach spasms and an uncomfortable feeling of abdominal fullness. What's more, the condition can worsen diabetes by making blood sugar control more difficult. Medication often fails to relieve the problem. Some patients, unable to keep any food down, wind up needing feeding tubes that go straight to their intestines.

The recent study: Researchers developed a watch-sized microstimulator, a device that delivers a short, painless burst of electrical stimulation. Diabetes patients with gastroparesis were asked to wear the device on their wrists or legs for two hours after lunch and for two hours after dinner, continuing daily for eight weeks. For four of those weeks, the device was positioned to make contact with specific acupressure points associated with nausea relief. (The acupoints were PC6, on the inner wrist about two-and-a-half finger widths up from the wrist crease...and ST36, on the front of the leg about four finger widths below the kneecap, just outside the shinbone.) For the other four weeks, the device was positioned slightly differently so that it did not contact the acupoints, thus delivering a sham treatment.

Throughout the study, researchers monitored patients' symptoms and conducted electrogastrogram (EGG) tests, recording the electrical signals that control muscle contractions and nerve activity of the stomach.

Results: Electrical stimulation of the acupressure points, on average, reduced patients' nausea by 30%...vomiting by 40%...retching by 31%...bloating by 21%...and abdominal fullness by 21%. The treatment also improved muscle and nerve function in the stomach, as shown on the EGG. The sham treatment produced no improvement in symptoms or EGG results. No side effects from electrical stimulation were reported.

These are very promising results, especially since the treatment is noninvasive, risk-free and can be used at home—but there are some caveats. For one thing, this was a small study with just 26 participants, and though it was presented at a recent meeting of the American College of Gastroenterology, it has not yet been published in a peer-reviewed journal. Also, the device used in the study isn't available to the public yet. Though further studies are needed, researchers hope that the micro-stimulator treatment will be available by prescription within a year or two.

In the meantime: There is another approach that, in theory, might be helpful for patients with diabetes-induced gastroparesis. Talk to a licensed acupuncturist about having professional acupressure stimulation of the same acupoints used in the study...or consider electroacupuncture, which is similar to traditional acupuncture except that an electrical current makes the needle stimulation stronger and steadier. To find a licensed acupuncturist in your area, visit the American Association of Acupuncture and Oriental Medicine.

Dangers of a "Slow Stomach"

Gerard Mullin, MD, an associate professor of medicine at The Johns Hopkins University School of Medicine and director of the Celiac Disease Clinic, Integrative GI Nutrition Services and the Capsule Endoscopy Program at Johns Hopkins Hospital, all in Baltimore. He is author of *The Inside Tract*, editor of *Integrative Gastroenterology* and several other textbooks, and the author or coauthor of more than 50 scientific papers.

When you eat a meal, you probably don't think about the amount of time it takes your body to digest the food. But for many people, this is the key to uncovering a host of digestive ills—and even some seemingly unrelated concerns such as chronic fatigue.

WHEN FOOD MOVES TOO SLOWLY

In healthy adults, digestion time varies, but it generally takes about four hours for a meal to leave the stomach before passing on to the small intestine and colon.

What happens: When food enters the stomach, signals from hormones and nerve cells trigger stomach acid, digestive enzymes and wavelike peristaltic contractions of the muscles in the stomach wall. Together, they break down the meal into a soupy mixture called chyme, which peristalsis then pushes into the small intestine.

This process is known as gastric motility. And when gastric motility is impeded—when stomach emptying slows to a crawl, even though nothing is blocking the stomach outlet—it's called gastroparesis.

Surprising fact: An estimated one out of every 55 Americans suffers from gastroparesis—but the condition is diagnosed in only one out of every 90 people who have it.

When gastroparesis goes undetected: The symptoms of gastroparesis often are obvious—for example, nausea, vomiting, feeling full right after starting to eat a meal, bloating and abdominal pain. But the condition can cause other health problems such as unwanted weight loss and even malnutrition. It also can interfere with the absorption of medications and wear you down physically (one study found that 93% of people with gastroparesis were fatigued).

GETTING THE RIGHT DIAGNOSIS

If you're experiencing the symptoms of gastroparesis, see your primary care physician. He/she may refer you to a gastroenterologist. It's likely the specialist will order the "gold standard" for diagnosing gastroparesis, a test called gastric emptying scintigraphy.

Next step: At the test, you'll eat a meal that contains radioactive isotopes. (Radiolabeled Egg Beaters with jam, toast and water are typical.) A scan is taken at one, two and four hours after the meal with a scintigraph, or gamma camera. A one-hour scan after drinking liquid also is recommended. If images from any of the scans show that your stomach isn't emptying normally, you are diagnosed with gastroparesis.

Another approach: When I perform an endoscopy on a patient with gastroparesis-like symptoms (a thin, flexible tube with a light and camera on the end is inserted down the esophagus and into the stomach), if I see a significant amount of retained fluids or food despite an overnight fast, I make the diagnosis then and there, saving time and money.

FINDING THE CAUSE

Experts haven't discovered the exact mechanisms underlying gastroparesis. In fact, an estimated 40% of cases are idiopathic—the cause is unknown. Gastroparesis is a complication for about 30% of people with type 1 or type 2 diabetes.

What happens: Diabetes can damage the vagus nerve, which runs from the cranium to the abdomen and plays a key role in digestion.

Medication also can cause gastroparesis.

Examples: Narcotic pain relievers, such as *oxycodone* (OxyContin), and anticholinergics, a class of drugs that includes certain antihistamines and overactive bladder medications.

Small intestine bacterial overgrowth, in which abnormally large numbers of bacteria grow in the small intestine, also can lead to gastroparesis.

GETTING THE BEST MEDICAL CARE

I have found that an integrative approach that combines conventional and alternative medicine is the best way to control gastroparesis.

Conventional treatment typically includes medications that either speed stomach emptying or help control the symptoms of gastroparesis such as nausea and vomiting. *For example…*

• *Metoclopramide* **(Reglan).** This is currently the only FDA-approved medication for gastroparesis. Reglan works by blocking receptors of the neurotransmitter dopamine, which accelerates gastric motility.

Problem: The FDA has approved Reglan for no more than 12 weeks of use because long-term intake can cause *tardive dyskinesia*—involuntary, repetitive body movements, such as grimacing. Because of this risk, I rarely prescribe metoclopramide for my patients.

Another medication option: The drug *domperidone* has the same dopamine-suppressing action in the digestive tract as Reglan, but it does not cross the blood–brain barrier and, therefore, is much less likely to cause tardive

dyskinesia. Risks include breast tenderness and worsening of the heart condition Long QT Syndrome.

However, according to clinical guidelines for the management of gastroparesis published in *The American Journal of Gastroenterology*, domperidone "is generally as effective" as metoclopramide with "lower risk of adverse effects."

Domperidone is readily available in most countries, where it is a standard treatment for heartburn, but not in the US. However, your doctor can obtain it under the FDA's Investigational New Drug program.

• **Antinausea drugs.** *Prochlorperazine* and *ondansetron* (Zofran) are commonly prescribed for gastroparesis.

• **Botox.** Injections of botulinum toxin into the pylorus (the opening from the stomach into the small intestine) can help some patients for four to six months, after which the injection must be repeated.

New approaches: Physicians at Johns Hopkins are now using a new and effective procedure called through-the-scope transpyloric stent placement. With this procedure, an endoscope is used to place a stent (tube) that helps transfer stomach contents into the small intestine.

Another new approach, pioneered by John Clarke, MD, of Johns Hopkins, involves placing a stent across the pylorus to drain the stomach.

ALTERNATIVE THERAPIES

Certain alternative therapies may also help with stomach motility and/or with nausea and vomiting…*

• **Peppermint oil.** This can help gastroparesis, but it also can worsen heartburn in people with gastroesophageal reflux disease (GERD). If you have gastroparesis but not GERD, an enteric-coated softgel of peppermint oil may help you.

Recommended dose: 90 mg once a day.

• **Iberogast.** This pharmaceutical-grade, multi-herbal tincture can help with gastroparesis, studies have shown.

*Be sure to check with your doctor before trying these therapies, which are available online and at most health-food stores.

Recommended dose: 20 drops, two to three times a day, before meals. (Iberogast does contain alcohol.)

• **Ginger.** Gingerroot may help with nausea and improve gastric motility.

Recommended dose: 1,200 mg daily.

• **Acupuncture.** This treatment can help control the symptoms of gastroparesis. Acupuncture has been shown to be effective for nausea and vomiting and abdominal pain and bloating.

More from Dr. Mullin...

Diet/Lifestyle Tips

Many dietary and lifestyle habits can improve stomach motility...

• **Eat smaller, more frequent meals.** Eat smaller amounts of food every two, three or four hours.

• **Reduce dietary fiber and fat.** Both slow stomach emptying.

• **Chew food thoroughly.**

• **Chew sugarless gum.** Do so for about one hour after eating to stimulate peristalsis.

• **Take a leisurely five- or 10-minute (or longer) walk after every meal.**

The "Other" Bladder Problem

Michael B. Chancellor, MD, a urologist and director of neurourology at the Beaumont Health System in Royal Oak, Michigan. He is coauthor of *Atlas of Urodynamics* and a founding member of the Congress of Urologic Research and Education on Aging Underactive Bladder, which conducts research on novel therapies for treating UAB.

An overactive bladder usually gets all the attention in TV commercials. Incontinence is the big bathroom problem for aging bladders.

What few people realize: An estimated 20 million Americans are living with a different condition, which actually has the opposite effect on the bladder, but the problem is not getting diagnosed or treated by most doctors.

Known as underactive bladder (UAB), this disorder can make something as simple as going to the bathroom a chore...damage the kidneys...and even land a person in a nursing home.

RED FLAGS OF UAB

UAB occurs when the bladder loses its ability to contract and fully empty. Part of what makes this condition so vexing is that the symptoms can come and go, and they often mimic those of other diseases, such as prostate enlargement and urinary tract infections—both of which can cause frequent urination, another UAB symptom.

With UAB, sufferers have a hard time telling when their bladders are full. When they do have the urge to urinate, it may be painful, the urine may dribble or it may not come at all. In fact, it may take several minutes to start a stream of urine. They also may feel that there's urine left behind and end up heading to the bathroom again a short time later.

Of course, when the bladder does not completely empty, urine builds up. This can lead to embarrassing episodes of leakage from overflow incontinence...recurring urinary tract and kidney infections...and, in severe cases, kidney damage.

WHAT CAUSES UAB?

As we age, the muscles of the bladder lose some of their elasticity and ability to contract. However, UAB is not a normal part of aging.

When messages between the brain and the bladder are short-circuited in any way, your body doesn't register the normal urge to urinate when the bladder is full.

This breakdown in communication may be triggered by a stroke, Parkinson's disease, acute urinary tract infection, radiation therapy to the pelvic area, nerve damage after pelvic surgery or even a herniated disk. In people under age 40, multiple sclerosis is a common culprit, as is diabetes, which can damage peripheral nerves in the lower spinal cord that supply the bladder.

Even overactive bladder can be a trigger: In some cases, overactive bladder thickens the bladder wall in a way that interferes with the bladder's ability to contract during urination… leading to underactive bladder.

Certain medications can also lead to UAB: These may include antidepressants, antihistamines, blood pressure drugs and cholesterol-lowering statins.

DO YOU HAVE UAB?

If you're suffering from any of the symptoms of UAB, see your primary care doctor soon. He/she may refer you to a specialist—either a urologist or a uro-gynecologist, who treats urologic problems in women.

To find out whether you have UAB, the specialist will take your medical history…do a physical exam…and order blood and urine tests to see how well your bladder and kidneys are functioning. A cystoscopy, ultrasound or CT scan might also be ordered to determine whether your bladder muscles and nerves are working normally.

Helpful: Keeping a diary that lists how often and how much you urinate (using a measuring cup) can give your doctor valuable information. For a free online diary to track your bladder activity, go to *www.urodaily.com.*

HOW TO COPE WITH UAB

Doctors are still clearly defining UAB and working to understand what therapies are most effective. But if you've got this condition, you want help now! The research is ongoing, but here are some ways to cope with the condition—go ahead and bring up these approaches with your doctor. *Not all physicians are familiar with them…*

•**Double-voiding.** This technique gives you extra time to empty your bladder.

What to do: After urinating, stay at the toilet for a few additional minutes. After this short break, try to urinate again. If your bladder has not fully emptied, you will often be able to pass more urine.

•**Triggered-reflex voiding.** This involves the use of various stimulation techniques to trigger the brain signals that jump-start contractions of the bladder and the flow of urine. The technique may work for anyone with UAB but can be especially useful for a person with a spinal cord injury who still has some reflexes but may not be able to feel whether the bladder is full.

What to do: Rub the area just above the pubic bone…tug on your pubic hair…or gently squeeze the head of the penis. Test different trigger zones to see which one might work for you.

•**Medications.** Men with UAB may get relief from a drug often used for prostate enlargement, such as *doxazosin* (Cardura). It helps a man empty his bladder by relaxing the muscle of the urethra (the tube through which urine flows).

•**Catheterization.** This is another way to empty the bladder. With self-catheterization, you insert a catheter, a strawlike tube, into your urethra to drain urine from your bladder. For people who are unable to do this, an "indwelling" catheter can be inserted into the urethra by a health-care professional to automatically drain urine into a pouch for a set period of time. However, if the catheter is not changed every two to four weeks, it can injure the urethra and/or cause infection.

For people who can't tolerate an indwelling catheter, a suprapubic catheter may be used. It requires a surgical procedure to insert it through a small hole in the abdomen directly into the bladder.

•**Surgery.** When the therapies described above are not effective or practical, the only option is surgery—either to enlarge the bladder by using a small section of the stomach or bowel that helps the bladder to stretch more easily…or to insert a mesh stent that allows the bladder to empty into a pouch outside the body.

Promising new approach: Stem cell therapy is being studied as a possible treatment for UAB. Researchers theorize that transplanting stem cells to help the bladder regenerate new, fully functioning tissue could be an effective solution for UAB sufferers.

So Long, Syringoma: How to Get Rid of Bumps Under the Eyes

Neal B. Schultz, MD, assistant clinical professor of dermatology, Mount Sinai School of Medicine, and in private practice in New York City. Dr. Schultz also is author of *It's Not Just About Wrinkles*. NealSchultz MD.com

Got a smattering of hard white, yellowish or skin-colored bumps on the skin under your eyes? You may think that they're particularly persistent pimples—but they're probably syringomas, or benign tumors that form in the ducts of the sweat glands.

The bump you see is just the 'tip of the iceberg,' because at least half of the syringoma lies beneath the skin's surface. A syringoma forms when (for unknown reasons) there is an overgrowth of cells within a sweat gland duct. The duct becomes enlarged by and clogged with the extra cells, forming a hard round bump about one to three millimeters in diameter.

Syringomas can occur singly or in clusters. Though they most often appear below the eyes, they also can form elsewhere on the face, in the armpits, on the chest or lower abdomen, or on the male or female genitalia. Syringomas can affect just about anyone at any age, but they are more common in women than in men, and arise most frequently during adolescence and at midlife. People with diabetes or a family history of syringomas are at increased risk.

Though technically they are tumors, syringomas are harmless and painless...do not signal cancer or any underlying medical problem...and will not spread (like warts do). Thus they do not require treatment. However, many people consider the bumps unsightly—and want to get rid of them.

Unfortunately, there is no way to prevent syringomas from forming in the first place—and there's nothing you can do at home to banish the bumps once they appear. No squeezing, steaming, over-the-counter cream or other do-it-yourself treatment can make syringomas go away. All you'll accomplish is to irritate and perhaps scar the skin. Don't bother trying a wart remover on syringomas, either—this would just irritate the skin between the bumps without getting rid of the syringomas themselves. Makeup can mask their color, but the bumps will still be visible and may cast shadows under overhead light.

So what can you do? See your dermatologist. Once successfully treated, an individual syringoma will not regrow—however, with or without treatment, you may develop additional syringomas in nearby sweat ducts.

BUMP-BANISHING TREATMENT OPTIONS

Do not expect (or allow) the dermatologist to cut off the top of a syringoma with a scalpel or other tool—the growth would still be visible because its whitish-yellowish color is noticeably different from the surrounding skin. I don't advise having the entire syringoma scooped out under local anesthesia, because this could leave a pit that would be more unsightly than the bump. *Instead, talk to your dermatologist about...*

• **Bichloroacetic acid (BCA).** A dermatologist can apply this topical medication very precisely to the tip of each syringoma, causing a brief burning sensation. The bump crusts over. When the crust falls off, typically in a week to 10 days, it usually leaves excellent results—no bump, no hole, no permanent discoloration—after just a single treatment. For those reasons, BCA is his treatment of choice for his own patients.

• **Electrocautery.** With this treatment, after numbing the skin with a local anesthetic (such as Lidocaine), a small probe with an electric current running through it is used to burn away each syringoma. A single session can destroy the part of the syringoma that's above skin level. Usually, this does not leave you with mismatched skin color the way cutting off the top of the bump does. Or you can have multiple sessions spaced three to four weeks apart to remove the entire growth gradually enough that the area heals without leaving a hole. Be aware, though, that electrocautery may leave dark spots and even little holes if the syringomas are overtreated. That's why it should be used only when BCA doesn't work.

The cost of syringoma treatment varies depending on the doctor, your location, the technique used and the number of bumps being treated, but expect to pay several hundred dollars per session. Unfortunately, insurance does not cover the cost since syringoma treatment is considered strictly cosmetic—but people who want their bump-free complexions restored may consider the money well-spent.

How to Prevent Glaucoma Vision Loss Before It's Too Late

Harry A. Quigley, MD, A. Edward Maumenee Professor of Ophthalmology and director, Glaucoma Center of Excellence, Wilmer Eye Institute, Johns Hopkins University, Baltimore. Dr. Quigley's book is *Glaucoma: What Every Patient Should Know: A Guide from Dr. Harry Quigley.*

Imagine that, as you read on your computer screen, the many pixels on the screen begin to stop working, a few at a time…not right in the center, but in clusters all around the screen. It happens slowly, eventually wiping out all but a tiny central spot…which eventually drops out, too. The screen is blank then.

That's a pretty close analogy of what happens when glaucoma runs its course. You'll start losing your peripheral vision first, one eye at a time, and you likely won't even realize that it's happening until much of the damage has been done. The damage is irreversible, but the process can be stopped with early detection and treatment.

ARE YOU AT RISK?

Glaucoma is the second-leading cause of blindness in the world after cataracts, and it mostly affects people as they age past 60. The disease is characterized by dying ganglion nerve cells in the retina, the light-sensitive tissue at the back of the eye that catches the images we see. Once these cells die, they are never replaced, which makes early detection of glaucoma critical.

Among the many different types of glaucoma, the most common is open-angle glaucoma, caused by clogging of the eyes' drainage canals in people who have a wide angle between the iris and cornea. Besides older age, risk factors include genetic predisposition, nearsightedness, higher eye pressure, high and low blood pressure, diabetes and hypothyroidism.

DETECTION

The lack of symptoms is a major reason why glaucoma is often not detected early. And the idea that glaucoma always has something to do with high eye pressure is a prime reason why diagnosis is often missed by eye specialists during regular eye exams. Although high eye pressure is a hallmark of a condition called angle-closure glaucoma, it is not necessarily present in the more common open-angle glaucoma.

Annual eye exams are recommended for people who are over age 60 and anyone with a first-degree relative (parent, sibling or child) who has or had glaucoma. People younger than 60 should consider getting eye exams, including glaucoma screening, every two years.

To ensure that your exams are thorough enough to detect glaucoma, make sure that, besides having eye pressure measured, you receive a side vision test, which examines peripheral vision, or a visual field test, which examines both peripheral and central vision. The optic nerve head or optic disc (a part of the eye where ganglion cells enter the optic nerve) should also be examined by the eye specialist to evaluate the health of those ganglion cells.

TREATMENT

If glaucoma is detected, treatment can prevent further damage by restoring eye-fluid drainage and/or relieving eye pressure. This is accomplished by use of daily eye drops or a combination of eye drops and oral medication. Many different types of eye drops— some known as prostaglandin analogs (such as Xalatan, Lumigan and Travatan Z)…some alpha agonists (such as Alphagan P)…and some carbonic anhydrase inhibitors (such as Trusopt)—are prescribed, depending on glaucoma symptoms that need to be managed. Laser eye surgery or traditional types of eye surgery that relieve pressure and correct blocked drainage ducts are options for people who don't get adequate relief from eye drops or who experience allergy or severe side effects from medications—but these people still may need to continue using some form of medication after surgery until eye pressure and drainage aright themselves.

Side effects of eye drops can include change in color of the iris and eyelid skin, stinging and burning of the eye, blurred vision and related problems. But most people who become lax about eye drop use don't do so because of side effects. They do so because they forget to use them, sabotaging their fight against glaucoma symptoms.

In a study in which we electronically monitored people who were using eye drops for glaucoma management, we discovered that, under the best of circumstances, patients were taking their eye drops only 70% of the time. Of course, eye drops can't help relieve glaucoma unless they are consistently used.

Helpful: Set up a reminder system. For example, set your cell-phone alarm to alert you when to use the drops.

As for alternative treatments for prevention of open-angle glaucoma beyond early detection and management, scientific evidence shows no association between glaucoma and a person's personal habits, such as diet, use of vitamins and supplements, alcohol consumption and caffeine intake. Altering these behaviors, unfortunately, will not decrease your chances of getting glaucoma or prevent it from getting worse. However, aerobic exercise (20 minutes four times a week) can increase blood flow and reduce eye pressure, which can keep glaucoma from worsening.

WHERE TO GET TREATMENT

Optometrists can diagnose glaucoma and treat it with eye drops. Ophthalmologists can diagnose it and treat it with a wider range of therapies—eye drops as well as laser treatments and eye surgery. But whichever type of specialist you consult, make sure that he is up-to-date on how best to detect glaucoma during an eye exam. To find optometrists and ophthalmologists in your area who have specialized training in glaucoma diagnosis and treatment and have been given by glaucoma experts, visit the Glaucoma Research Foundation website at *www.glaucoma.org*.

Pycnogenol Helps Diabetic Retinopathy

Mark A. Stengler, NMD, a naturopathic medical doctor and leading authority on the practice of alternative and integrated medicine. He is founder and medical director of the Stengler Center for Integrative Medicine, Encinitas, California, and former adjunct associate clinical professor at the National University of Natural Medicine, Portland, Oregon. He is author of *The Natural Physician's Healing Therapies*. MarkStengler.com

Pycnogenol (pronounced pic-noj-en-all), an extract from the bark of the French maritime pine, is known to improve circulation, reduce swelling and ease asthma. Now Italian researchers have found another use for it—it helps patients with diabetes who are in the early stages of diabetic retinopathy, a complication of diabetes in which the retina becomes damaged, resulting in vision impairment, including blurred vision, seeing dark spots, impaired night vision, reduced color perception and even blindness.

All people with diabetes are at risk for diabetic retinopathy—and it's estimated that as many as 80% of people with diabetes for 10 years or more will have this complication.

Participants in the Italian study had been diagnosed with diabetes (the researchers did not specify whether the patients had type 1 or 2 diabetes) for four years, and their diabetes was well controlled by diet and oral medication. Study participants had early-stage retinopathy and moderately impaired vision. After two months of treatment, the patients given Pycnogenol had less retinal swelling as measured by ultrasound testing. Most important, their vision was significantly improved. This was especially noticeable because the vision of those in the control group did not improve.

My view: If you have type 1 or 2 diabetes, undergo a comprehensive eye exam at least once a year. If retinopathy is detected, it would be wise to supplement with Pycnogenol (150 milligrams daily). Because retinopathy among diabetes patients is so prevalent, I recommend this amount to all my patients with diabetes to protect their vision. Pycnogenol has a blood-thinning effect, so people who take blood-thinning medication, such as warfarin, should use it only while being monitored by a doctor.

FDA OKs Diabetic Retinopathy Treatment

The first treatment has been approved for diabetic retinopathy, reports Deeba Husain, MD. The FDA recently approved injections of the drug Lucentis—also used to treat macular degeneration in older adults—for diabetic retinopathy in patients with macular edema (swelling that occurs when fluid builds up in the eye). Diabetic retinopathy, which causes bleeding and/or abnormal blood-vessel growth in the retina, is the leading cause of blindness in Americans with diabetes.

Deeba Husain, MD, a retina specialist and associate professor of ophthalmology at Harvard Medical School, Boston.

How to See Better in the Dark

Marc Grossman, OD, LAc, holistic developmental/behavioral optometrist, licensed acupuncturist and medical director, Natural Eye Care, New Paltz, New York. He is coauthor of *Greater Vision* and *Natural Eye Care*. NaturalEyeCare.com

Aging often brings a reduction in the ability to see well in low light.

Reasons: Night vision has two elements. First, the pupils must dilate to let in as much light as possible. Normally this happens within seconds of entering a darkened environment—but as we age, the muscles that control pupil dilation weaken, slowing down and/or limiting dilation. Second, chemical changes must occur in the light-sensitive photoreceptors (called rods and cones) of the retina at the back of the eyeball. Some of these changes take several minutes and some take longer, so normally full night vision is not achieved for about 20 minutes. Even brief exposure to bright light (such as oncoming headlights) reverses these chemical changes, so the processes must start over. With age, these chemical changes occur more slowly…and some of our photoreceptors may be lost.

While we cannot restore the eyes' full youthful function, we can take steps to preserve and even improve our ability to see in low light. *Here's how…*

• **First, see your eye doctor to investigate possible underlying medical problems.** Various eye disorders can cause or contribute to reduced night vision, including cataracts (clouding of the eye's lens), retinitis pigmentosa (a disease that damages the retina's rods and cones) and macular degeneration (in which objects in the center of the field of vision cannot be seen). Night vision also can be compromised by liver cirrhosis or the digestive disorder celiac disease, which can lead to deficiencies of eye-protecting nutrients…or diabetes, which can damage eye nerves and blood vessels. Diagnosing any underlying disorder is vital because the sooner it is treated, the better the outcome is likely to be.

• **Adopt an eye-healthy diet.** Eat foods rich in the vision-supporting nutrients below…and ask your doctor whether supplementation is right for you. *Especially important…*

• Lutein, a yellow pigment and antioxidant found in corn, dark green leafy vegetables, egg yolks, kiwi fruit, oranges and yellow squash. *Typical supplement dosage:* 6 milligrams (mg) daily.

• Vitamin A, found in carrots, Chinese cabbage, dark green leafy vegetables, pumpkin, sweet potatoes and winter squash. *Typical supplement dosage:* 10,000 international units (IU) daily.

• Zeaxanthin, a yellow pigment and anti-oxidant found in corn, egg yolks, kiwi fruit, orange peppers and oranges. *Typical supplement dosage:* 300 micrograms daily.

• Zinc, found in beans, beef, crab, duck, lamb, oat bran, oysters, ricotta cheese, turkey and yogurt. *Typical supplement dosage:* 20 mg daily.

• Update prescription lenses. Many people just keep wearing the same old glasses even though vision tends to change over time, Dr. Grossman said—so new glasses with the correct prescription often can improve night vision.

• **Keep eyeglasses and contacts clean.** Smudges bend rays of light and distort what you see.

• **Wear sunglasses outdoors on sunny days, especially between noon and 3 pm.** This is particularly important for people with light-colored eyes, which are more vulnerable to the sun's damaging ultraviolet rays. Excessive sun exposure is a leading cause of eye disorders (such as cataracts) that can impair eyesight, including night vision. Amber or gray lenses are best for sunglasses, Dr. Grossman said, because they absorb light frequencies most evenly.

• **Do not use yellow-tinted lenses at night.** These often are marketed as "night driving" glasses, implying that they sharpen contrast and reduce glare in low light. However, Dr. Grossman cautioned that any tint only further impairs night vision.

Safest: If you wear prescription glasses, stick to untinted, clear lenses—but do ask your optometrist about adding an antireflective or antiglare coating.

• **Exercise your night vision.** This won't speed up the eyes' process of adjusting to the dark, but may encourage a mental focus that helps the brain and eyes work better together—thus improving your ability to perceive objects in a darkened environment.

What to do: For 20 minutes four times per week, go into a familiar room at night and turn off the lights. As your eyes are adjusting, look directly toward a specific object that you know is there...focus on it, trying to make out its shape and details and to distinguish it from surrounding shadows. With practice, your visual perception should improve. For an additional challenge, do the exercise outdoors at night...while looking at unfamiliar objects in a dark room...or while using peripheral vision rather than looking directly at an object.

• **When driving at night, avoid looking directly at oncoming headlights.** Shifting your gaze slightly to the right of center minimizes the eye changes that would temporarily impair your night vision, yet still allows you to see traffic.

Also: Use the night setting on rearview mirrors to reduce reflected glare.

• **Clean car windows and lights.** When was the last time you used glass cleaner on the inside of your windshield...or on rear and side windows...or on headlights and taillights? For the clearest possible view and minimal distortion from smudges, keep all windows and lights squeaky clean.

Beware of Eye Floaters—They Can Be a Telltale Sign of a Vision-Robbing Eye Condition

Adam Wenick, MD, PhD, assistant professor of ophthalmology in the Retina Division at the Wilmer Eye Institute at The Johns Hopkins School of Medicine in Baltimore. He is board-certified by the American Board of Ophthalmology, with special expertise in retinal tears and detachment as well as other diseases of the retina.

If you have ever noticed a few tiny dots, blobs, squiggly lines or cobweblike images drifting across your field of vision, you are not alone. These visual disturbances, called floaters, are common, and most people simply dismiss them as a normal part of growing older. But that's not always the case.

When it could be serious: In about 15% of cases, floaters are a symptom of a harmful condition known as a retinal tear, which can, in turn, lead to a vision-robbing retinal detachment in a matter of hours to days.

HOW DOES THIS HAPPEN?

The retina, which is an extremely thin, delicate membrane that lines the inside of the back of the eye, converts light into signals that your brain recognizes as images. However, with age, a jelly-like material called the vitreous that fills much of the eyeball commonly shrinks a bit and separates from the retina. If the shrinkage or some other injury exerts enough force, the retina can actually tear.

You might notice a sudden shower of new floaters or flashes of light that look like shooting stars or lightning bolts. What you're seeing when this occurs are actually shadows that are being cast on the retina by the tiny clumps of collagen fibers that comprise the floaters. The flashes of light are caused by the tugging of the vitreous on the retina, which stimulates the photoreceptors that sense light.

Why floaters and/or flashes are a red flag: The retina lacks nerves that signal pain, so these visual disturbances are the only way you will be alerted to a tear. Left untreated, fluid can leak through the retinal tear, and the retina can detach like wallpaper peeling off a wall. A retinal detachment is an emergency—if it's not treated promptly, it can lead to a complete loss of vision in the affected eye.

ARE YOU AT RISK?

Changes in the eye that increase risk for a retinal tear or detachment begin primarily in your 50s and 60s—and continue to increase as you grow older.

In addition to age, you can also be at increased risk for a retinal tear or detachment due to…

•**Nearsightedness.** People of any age with nearsightedness greater than six diopters (requiring eyeglasses or contact lenses with a vision correction of more than minus six) are five to six times more likely to develop a retinal tear or detachment. That's because nearsighted eyeballs are larger than normal. Therefore, the retina is spread thinner, making it more prone to tearing.

Important: If you're nearsighted, don't assume that corrective eyewear or LASIK surgery decreases your risk for a retinal tear or detachment. Neither does.

•**Cataract surgery.** This surgery alters the vitreous jelly, increasing the risk that the vitreous will pull away from the retina, possibly giving way to a retinal detachment.

Cataract surgery has been known to double one's detachment risk, but a new Australian study suggests that improvements in technology, such as phacoemulsification, which uses an ultrasonic device to break up and remove the cloudy lens, have cut the risk from one in 100 to one in 400.

•**Diabetes.** Because it impairs circulation to the retina over time, diabetes leads to a higher risk for a severe type of retinal detachment that is not associated with floaters and flashes and can be initially asymptomatic.

Individuals who have diabetes should be sure to have annual eye exams with dilation of the pupils to check for this and other ocular complications of diabetes. The Optomap test provides a wide view of the retina, but you also need pupil dilation for a thorough screening.

THE DANGER OF A RETINAL TEAR

Anyone who experiences a sudden burst of floaters or flashes, especially if they are large or appear in any way different from how they have in the past, should contact an ophthalmologist right away for advice.

If an eye exam confirms a retinal tear, it can be treated in an eye doctor's office, using either lasers or freezing equipment to "spot-weld" the area surrounding the tear. (Anesthetic eyedrops are used to numb the eye, but the procedure can still be uncomfortable.)

The resulting scar tissue will seal off the tear so the fluid doesn't leak behind the retina and pull it away. The good news is that both laser photocoagulation and freezing are more than 90% effective in preventing detachment. There is a small risk for tiny blind spots.

WHEN A DETACHMENT OCCURS

If you suffer a retinal tear but don't get treatment within a day or two, the fluid can seep through the tear, detaching the retina.

Red flag for detachment: A gradual shading in your vision, like a curtain being drawn on the sides or top or bottom of your eye, means that a retinal detachment may have occurred. If your central vision rapidly changes, this also may signal a retinal detachment or even a stroke.

Retinal detachment is an emergency! When your doctor examines you, he/she will be able to see whether the center of your retina is detached. When the center is involved, vision often cannot be fully restored.

If you have suffered a retinal detachment, your doctor will help you decide among the following treatments...

• **Vitrectomy.** This one- to three-hour surgery is performed in a hospital operating room, usually with sedation anesthesia plus localized numbing of the eye. The vitreous is removed, tears are treated with lasers or freezing, and a bubble (typically gas) is injected to replace the missing gel and hold the retina in place until the spot-welding treatment can take effect. (The bubble will gradually disappear.)

Important: It is necessary to keep your head in the same position for seven to 14 days in order to "keep the bubble on the trouble," as doctors say. Therefore, you will need a week or two of bed rest at home. You may have to keep your head facedown or on one side.

• **Scleral buckle.** With this procedure, a clear band of silicone is placed around the outside of the eyeball, where it acts like a belt, holding the retina against the wall of the eyeball.

Also performed in a hospital operating room, scleral buckle involves freezing the retina or treating it with a laser to create localized inflammation that forms a seal, securing the retina and keeping fluid out.

Scleral buckle takes from one to two hours and is sometimes combined with vitrectomy to improve the outcome. It is frequently used for younger patients and those who have not had cataract surgery.

• **Pneumatic retinopexy.** Depending on where the retinal detachment is located, a 20-minute, in-office procedure called a pneumatic retinopexy is an option for patients with smaller tears. With this procedure, a gas bubble is injected, and retinal tears are frozen or treated with a laser.

This is followed by up to two weeks of bed rest. Your head may need to be held in a certain position, such as upright at an angle, depending on the location of your tear.

With pneumatic retinopexy, the reattachment success rate is lower than that of scleral buckle or vitrectomy (70% versus 90%), but it is less invasive and no hospital visit is required. In addition, pneumatic retinopexy costs less than a hospital-based procedure, which could range from $5,000 to $10,000.

Even with a successful procedure, 40% of patients who suffer retinal detachments see 20/50 or worse afterward even when using glasses. The remainder have better vision.

Refreshing Solutions for Dry Mouth

Thomas Lackner, PharmD, professor of pharmacy, College of Pharmacy, University of Minnesota, Minneapolis.

Xerostomia (dry mouth) is a common condition with many possible causes, including regular consumption of caffeinated beverages (such as coffee and tea) and/or alcohol—all of which can have a dehydrating effect. Dry mouth also can be a side effect of over-the-counter pain/sleep medications (such as Tylenol PM and Advil PM) and antihistamines as well as certain prescription diuretics, antidepressants and medications for overactive bladder and Parkinson's disease. In addition, medical conditions such as diabetes and the autoimmune disorder Sjögrens syndrome can be to blame.

To alleviate dry mouth, drink more water (aim for at least 32 ounces daily) and limit or avoid alcohol, caffeinated soda, coffee and tea, salt and salty foods. During the winter, set your thermostat at the lowest comfortable temperature and use a humidifier. If you suspect that medication may be causing your dry mouth, ask your doctor if there are alternatives that you could take. Products such as Biotène mouthwash and toothpaste for dry mouth also can provide relief. If your dry mouth persists or worsens despite taking these steps, see your physician. If left untreated, dry mouth can reduce your sense of taste and raise your risk for gum disease, heartburn and other problems.

An Easier Way to Ease Dry Mouth

Ross Kerr, DDS, clinical professor in the Department of Oral and Maxillofacial Pathology, Radiology and Medicine at the New York University College of Dentistry in New York City.

Abraham J. Domb, PhD, Institute of Drug Research, School of Pharmacy, Faculty of Medicine, Hebrew University, Jerusalem.

Jonathan Bregman, DDS, a dental consultant and expert on the early detection of oral cancer. Bregman Consulting.com

---

Up to 30% of Americans experience dry mouth at some point. It sounds like little more than a nuisance. But it can desiccate your life.

As salivary glands stop working properly (producing less than half the normal amount of saliva), symptoms can include trouble swallowing…trouble speaking…bad breath…indigestion (from a lack of amylase, an enzyme in saliva that triggers starch digestion)…chronically dry lips, with cracks in the corners that are targets for yeast infections…and rampant tooth decay (as teeth-destroying bacteria are no longer flushed out of the mouth by lysozyme, another saliva enzyme).

"The decrease in the quality of life for someone with severe dry mouth can be devastating," says Ross Kerr, DDS, clinical associate professor at the New York University College of Dentistry.

There are many causes of dry mouth, including medications (the most common cause), menopause, diabetes, Parkinson's disease, depression, autoimmune diseases such as Sjögren's Syndrome, rheumatoid arthritis and cancer treatments such as radiation and chemotherapy.

Problem: "The mouth rinses, gels and sprays for easing dry mouth don't last very long, so the patient is dosing all the time," says Dr. Kerr.

Recent breakthrough: A new "mucoadhesive" patch for dry mouth sticks to the roof of the mouth for several hours, stimulating lubrication and providing long-term relief. And a recent study shows that it works.

PATCHING UP DRY MOUTH

Researchers in the Department of Oral Medicine at Hebrew University treated 20 people with dry mouth with either the patches (OraMoist) or the leading over-the-counter treatment for dry mouth (Biotene mouthwash).

The patches stimulated five times more saliva production than the mouthwash. Twice as many people using the patches said they felt more moisture in their mouths and reductions in the sensations of dry mouth. And 70% of those using the patches said they would use them again, compared with 30% of those using the mouthwash.

"OraMoist was superior to Biotene in improving xerostomia symptoms and in overall patient satisfaction," reported the researchers in the journal *Quintessence International*.

"Oral disorders such as dry mouth require sustained residence of the active remedy in the mouth for effective treatment," says Abraham J. Domb, PhD, a study researcher. "Mucoadhesive patches are made of safe ingredients that adhere to the oral mucosal tissue and slowly erode, while releasing active remedies for two to six hours, providing the desired residence time for effective therapy."

What kind: The mucoadhesive patch used in the study was OraMoist, from Quantum Health. *It includes several ingredients that help increase saliva flow…*

• **Tricaprin,** a patented fatty acid compound that makes the mouth feel lubricated

• **Xylitol,** a naturally occurring sugar substitute that reduces the amount of decay-causing bacteria and also stimulates saliva production

• **Citrus oil and natural lemon flavor,** both of which stimulate saliva production

• **Oral enzymes naturally found in saliva**

•**The patch itself,** which also stimulates saliva.

"People with dry mouth find the patches very easy to use and very effective," says Jonathan Bregman, DDS, a dental consultant and expert on the early detection of oral cancer. "I am also a believer in natural ways to heal, and this patch very much fits that model. I have recommended it to thousands of dentists and other health-care providers."

"Some of my patients now swear by the patches," adds Dr. Kerr. "They use them every single day."

OraMoist is widely available in drugstores and online. You can order it at *www.dentek. com*.

Diabetes Medication Linked to Bladder Cancer Risk

The Food and Drug Administration has found that people with type 2 diabetes who take *pioglitazone* (Actos) for one year or longer have a 40% increased risk for bladder cancer. The medication has other serious side effects including worsening congestive heart failure. If you are taking pioglitazone, speak to your doctor about whether changing medications is advisable...or work with a holistic doctor to treat diabetes naturally.

The FDA Safety Information and Adverse Event Reporting Program.

Diabetes Drug Causes Pancreas Problem

The FDA is recommending that the prescribing information for the diabetes drugs Januvia (*sitagliptin*) and Janumet (*sitagliptin/metformin*) include information about reported cases of acute pancreatitis among users. If you take either of these drugs, have your doctor monitor you for the development of pancreatitis, especially if you are just starting on this drug or if your dosage has increased recently.

Mark A. Stengler, NMD, a naturopathic medical doctor and leading authority on the practice of alternative and integrated medicine. He is founder and medical director of the Stengler Center for Integrative Medicine, Encinitas, California, and former adjunct associate clinical professor at the National University of Natural Medicine, Portland, Oregon. He is author of *The Natural Physician's Healing Therapies*. MarkStengler.com

9

Heart Disease and Diabetes

Natural Help for the Diabetic Heart

I f you have type 2 diabetes, you've already had a heart attack—whether you've had one or not!

"The guidelines for physicians from the American Heart Association are to treat a person with diabetes as if that individual has already had a heart attack," says cardiologist Seth Baum, MD, medical director of Preventive Cardiology in Boca Raton, Florida, and author of *The Total Guide to a Healthy Heart.*

HOW DOES DIABETES HURT YOUR HEART?

As excess sugar careens through the bloodstream, it roughs up the linings of the arteries.

Insulin resistance (the subpar performance of the hormone that moves glucose out of the bloodstream and into muscle and fat cells) raises blood pressure, damaging arteries.

Diabetes also injures tiny blood vessels called capillaries, which hurts your kidneys and nerves—damage that in turn stresses the heart.

The end result—an up to seven-fold increase in the risk of heart disease and stroke, the cardiovascular diseases (CVD) that kill four out of five people with diabetes.

But recent studies show there are several natural ways for people with diabetes to reverse the risk factors that cause heart disease...

RECENT RESEARCH

It's never too late to exercise—and a little goes a long way. Researchers at the University of British Columbia in Vancouver, Canada, studied 36 older people (average age 71) with type 2 diabetes, high blood pressure, and high cholesterol, dividing them into two groups.

Seth Baum, MD, medical director of Preventive Cardiology in Boca Raton, Florida, and author of *The Total Guide to a Healthy Heart.* VitalRemedyMD.com

Kenneth Madden, MD, associate professor of geriatric medicine at the University of British Columbia.

Robb Wolf, owner of NorCal Strength & Conditioning, Chico, California, and author of *The Paleo Solution.*

245

Breakthroughs in Diabetes

One group walked on a treadmill or cycled on a stationary bicycle for 40 minutes, three days a week. The other group didn't.

To find out if the exercise was helping with CVD, the researchers measured the elasticity of the arteries—a fundamental indicator of arterial youth and health, with arterial stiffness increasing the risk of dying from CVD.

Results: After three months, the exercisers had a decrease in arterial stiffness of 15% to 20%.

"Aerobic exercise should be the first-line treatment to reduce arterial stiffness in older adults with type 2 diabetes, even if the patient has advanced cardiovascular risk factors" such as high blood pressure and high cholesterol, conclude the researchers, in *Diabetes Care*.

WHAT TO DO

Kenneth Madden, MD, the study leader, and associate professor of geriatric medicine at the University of British Columbia, says, "You can improve every risk factor for diabetes and heart disease—and you can do it in a very short period of time."

Dr. Madden recommends that older people with diabetes and cardiovascular disease see a doctor for a checkup before starting an exercise program.

Once you get the okay from your physician, he says to purchase and use a heart monitor during exercise, so you're sure that you're exercising at the level used by the participants in his study—60% to 75% of maximum heart rate.

Example: An estimate of your maximum heart rate is 220, minus your age. If you're 60, that would be 220 − 60 = 160. Exercising at between 60% to 75% of your maximum heart rate means maintaining a heart rate of between 96 and 120 beats per minute.

Finally, Dr. Madden advises you exercise the amount proven to improve arterial elasticity—a minimum of three sessions of aerobic exercise a week, of 40 minutes each.

• **Maximize magnesium.** Researchers in Mexico studied 79 people with diabetes and high blood pressure, dividing them into two groups. One group received a daily 450 milligrams (mg) magnesium supplement; one didn't.

Results: After four months, those on magnesium had an average drop of 20 points systolic (the higher number in the blood pressure reading) and 9 points diastolic (the lower number). Those on the placebo had corresponding drops of 5 points and 1 point.

"Magnesium supplementation should be considered as an additional or alternative treatment for high blood pressure in people with diabetes," says Fernando Guerrero-Romero, MD, the study leader.

What to do: "Magnesium acts as a natural vasodilator, relaxing arteries and lowering blood pressure," says Dr. Baum. "People with diabetes should incorporate a magnesium supplement into their regimen."

He suggests a daily supplement of 400 mg, about the level used in the study.

"People with diabetes and high blood pressure should also be encouraged to increase their dietary intake of magnesium, through eating more whole grains, leafy green vegetables, legumes, nuts and fish," says Dr. Guerrero-Romero.

• **Eat like a Neanderthal.** Researchers in Sweden tested two diets in 13 people with type 2 diabetes—the diet recommended by the American Diabetes Association (ADA), a generally healthful diet limiting calories, fat and refined carbohydrates; and a "Paleolithic" diet, consisting of lean meat, fish, fruits, vegetables, root vegetables, eggs and nuts—and no dairy products, refined carbohydrates or highly processed foods, whatsoever.

In terms of lowering risk factors for heart disease, the Paleolithic diet clubbed the ADA diet.

Results: After three months, it had done a better job of decreasing…

• **High LDL "bad" cholesterol,**

• **High blood pressure,**

• **High triglycerides** (a blood fat linked to heart disease) and

• **Too-big waist size** (excess stomach fat is linked to heart disease).

The diet was also more effective at increasing HDL "good" cholesterol.

And it was superior in decreasing glycated hemoglobin (A1C), a measure of long-term blood sugar control.

"Foods that were regularly eaten during the Paleolithic, or Old Stone Age, may be optimal for prevention and treatment of type 2 diabetes, cardiovascular disease and insulin resistance," concludes Tommy Jönsson, MD, in *Cardiovascular Diabetology*.

What to do: "Eating a Paleolithic diet is far easier than most people think," says Robb Wolf, owner of NorCal Strength & Conditioning in Chico, California, and author of *The Paleo Solution*.

THE BASIC DIET

Eat more—lean meat, fish, shellfish, fruits, vegetables, eggs and nuts.

Eat less (or eliminate)—grains, dairy products, salt, refined fats and refined sugar.

Resource: You can order pre-packaged Paleolithic snacks and meals at *www.onestop paleoshop.com*.

• **Have a cup of hibiscus tea.** Researchers in Iran studied 53 people with type 2 diabetes, dividing them into two groups. One group drank a cup of hibiscus tea twice a day; the other drank two cups a day of black tea. (The hibiscus tea was made from Hibiscus sabdariffa, which is also known as red sorrel, Jamaican sorrel, Indian sorrel, roselle and Florida cranberry.)

Results: After one month, those drinking hibiscus had...

• **Higher HDL "good" cholesterol,**
• **Lower LDL "bad" cholesterol,**
• **Lower total cholesterol and**
• **Lower blood pressure.**

The black tea group didn't have any significant changes in blood fats or blood pressure.

The findings were in *The Journal of Alternative and Complementary Medicine* and the *Journal of Human Hypertension*.

What to do: Consider drinking a cup or two of hibiscus tea a day, says Hassan Mozaffari-Khosravi, PhD, an assistant professor of nutrition, Shahid Sadoughi University of Medical Sciences, Yazd, Iran, and the study leader.

Type 2 Diabetes Raises Risk for Stroke and Heart Attack...Especially For Younger Patients

Thomas Jeerakathil, MD, assistant professor of neurology, University of Alberta, Edmonton, Canada.

Diabetes gets a lot of press nowadays—which, fortunately, has prompted many patients to take greater care to control their blood sugar levels. Unfortunately, reducing blood sugar won't offer much in the way of protection against cardiovascular disease. This is a very real risk for people with diabetes...and one that few seem to grasp. A recent national survey reported that "a startling" 82% of people with type 2 diabetes are unaware of this connection—and that's of even greater concern given the findings of a study from the University of Alberta (Edmonton, Canada) that evaluated how diabetes impacts stroke risk in the first five years post-diagnosis. The study was published in the journal *Stroke*.

Thomas Jeerakathil, MD, assistant professor of neurology at the university, was the lead author of this first study examining the link between stroke risk and diabetes immediately after diagnosis and initiation of treatment—previous studies had evaluated longer-term impact, 10 to 15 years later. Since both stroke and heart attack stem from the same set of problems, Dr. Jeerakathil notes that although this study specifically concerned stroke, it is likely that the risk for heart attack is very similar. A total of 12,272 people recently diagnosed with type 2 diabetes were monitored for a period of five years, with the finding that diabetes doubles the risk of stroke within that time. That risk is even more dramatic for those aged 30 to 44—their relative risk is fivefold over those who don't have diabetes.

CONTROLLING BLOOD SUGAR DOESN'T FIGHT HEART DISEASE

Previous research suggests that a focus on blood sugar control alone does little to stem cardiovascular risks—so Dr. Jeerakathil stresses that people with diabetes should also make living a heart-healthy lifestyle a priority, right from the start. It's important to maintain an optimum blood pressure level, a healthy weight and waist-to-hip ratio, follow a low-fat diet and get plenty of exercise.

Dr. Jeerakathil believes statins (cholesterol-reducing medications) are in order for many people with diabetes, since the diagnosis itself puts them in the same CVD risk category as people who've had at least one heart attack. For those who have already had a stroke or heart attack, he strongly recommends statins. It is possible to balance cholesterol naturally, without risk of the side effects associated with statin use. A naturopathic physician can provide support and expertise in improving diet, lifestyle and using nutritional supplements to meet health goals... and work collaboratively with other members of your team—ideally a cardiologist to manage CVD risk and an endocrinologist to monitor your diabetes—to help make sure you live long and well.

Ask Your Doctor About Aspirin Therapy

Aspirin therapy may not prevent heart disease in diabetics. Diabetes increases the risk for heart attack and stroke, and daily aspirin use can help prevent these life-threatening events—so aspirin therapy would seem worthwhile for people with diabetes.

However: A recent study shows that aspirin has no protective effect in patients with diabetes who do not already have heart disease (but it seems to help diabetics who already have heart disease). Talk to your doctor.

Jill Belch, MD, head of the Cardiovascular and Lung Biology Centre, Ninewells Hospital, University of Dundee Medical School, Dundee, Scotland, and lead author of an eight-year study of 1,276 adults with diabetes, published in *The BMJ* (formerly *British Medical Journal*).

4 Must-Have Heart Tests

Joel K. Kahn, MD, a clinical professor of medicine at Wayne State University School of Medicine, Detroit, and director of Kahn Center for Cardiac Longevity, Bloomfield Township, Michigan. He is also a founding member of the International Society of Integrative, Metabolic and Functional Cardiovascular Medicine and author of *The Whole Heart Solution*.

Heart disease is tricky. Like other "silent" conditions, such as high blood pressure and kidney disease, you may not know that you have it until you're doubled over from a heart attack.

That's because traditional methods of assessing patients for heart disease, such as cholesterol tests and blood pressure measurements, along with questions about smoking and other lifestyle factors, don't always tell a patient's whole story.

Shocking finding: In a recent study, doctors followed nearly 6,000 men and women (ages 55 to 88) who had been deemed healthy by standard heart tests for three years and then gave them basic imaging tests.

Result: 60% were found to have atherosclerosis. These study participants were eight times more likely to suffer a heart attack or stroke, compared with subjects without this fatty buildup (plaque) in the arteries.

THE MUST-HAVE TESTS

Below are four simple tests that can catch arterial damage at the earliest possible stage—when it can still be reversed and before it has a chance to cause a heart attack or stroke.

My advice: Even though doctors don't routinely order these tests, everyone over age 50 should have them at least once—and sometimes more often, depending on the findings. Smokers and people with diabetes, very high cholesterol levels (more than 300 mg/dL) and/or a family history of heart disease should have these tests before age 50. *Having these tests can literally save your life...*

•**Coronary calcium computed tomography (CT) scan.** This imaging test checks for calcium deposits in the arteries—a telltale sign of atherosclerosis. People who have little or no calcium in the arteries (a score of zero) have less than a 5% risk of having a heart attack over the next three to five years. The risk is twice as high in people with a score of one to 10...and more than nine times higher in those with scores above 400.

While the American College of Cardiology recommends this test for people who haven't been diagnosed with heart disease but have known risk factors, such as high blood pressure and/or a family history of heart disease, I advise everyone to have this test at about age 50.* The test takes only 10 to 15 minutes and doesn't require the injection of a contrast agent.

Cost: $99 and up, which may be covered by insurance.

I use the calcium score as a one-time test. Unless they abandon their healthy habits, people who have a score of zero are unlikely to develop arterial calcification later in life. Those who do have deposits will know what they have to do—exercise, eat a more healthful diet, manage cholesterol and blood pressure, etc.

One drawback, however, is radiation exposure. Even though the dose is low (much less than you'd get during cardiac catheterization, for example), you should always limit your exposure.

My advice: Choose an imaging center with the fastest CT machine. A faster machine (a 256-slice CT, for example) gives less radiation exposure than, say, a 64-slice machine.

• **Carotid intima-media thickness (CIMT).** The intima and media are the innermost linings of blood vessels. Their combined thickness in the carotid arteries in the neck is affected by how much plaque is present. Thickening of these arteries can indicate increased risk for stroke and heart attack.

The beauty of this test is that it's performed with ultrasound. There's no radiation, it's fast (10 minutes) and it's painless. I often recommend it as a follow-up to the coronary calcium test or as an alternative for people who want to avoid the radiation of the coronary calcium CT.

* People already diagnosed with heart disease and/or who have had a stent or bypass surgery do not need the coronary calcium CT.

The good news is that you can reduce CIMT—with a more healthful diet, more exercise and the use of statin medications. Pomegranate—the whole fruit, juice or a supplement—can reduce carotid plaque, too. In addition, research has found Kyolic "aged" garlic (the product brand studied) and vitamin K-2 to also be effective.

Cost: $250 to $350. It may not be covered by insurance.

• **Advanced lipid test.** Traditional cholesterol tests are less helpful than experts once thought—particularly because more than 50% of heart attacks occur in patients with normal LDL "bad" cholesterol levels.

Experts have now identified a number of cholesterol subtypes that aren't measured by standard tests. The advanced lipid test (also known as an expanded test) still measures total cholesterol and LDL but also looks at the amounts and sizes of different types of cholesterol.

Suppose that you have a normal LDL reading of 100 mg/dL. You still might have an elevated risk for a heart attack if you happen to have a high number of small, dense LDL particles (found in an advanced LDL particle test), since they can more easily enter the arterial wall.

My advice: Get the advanced lipid test at least once after age 50. It usually costs $39 and up and may be covered by insurance.

If your readings look good, you can switch to a standard cholesterol test every few years. If the numbers are less than ideal, talk to your doctor about treatment options, which might include statins or niacin, along with lifestyle changes. Helpful supplements include omega-3 fatty acids, vitamin E and plant sterols.

• **High-sensitivity C-reactive protein (hs-CRP).** This simple blood test has been available for years, but it's not used as often as it should be. Elevated C-reactive protein indicates inflammation in the body, including in the blood vessels. Data from the Physicians' Health Study found that people with elevated CRP were about three times more likely to have a heart attack than those with normal levels.

If you test low (less than 1 mg/L) or average (1 mg/L to 3 mg/L), you can repeat the test every few years. If your CRP is high (above 3 mg/L), I recommend repeating the test at least once a year. It's a good way to measure any progress you may be making from taking medications (such as statins, which reduce inflammation), improving your diet and getting more exercise.

Cost: About $50. It's usually covered by insurance.

Artery Inflammation: Six Simple, Lifesaving Tests

Bradley Bale, MD, medical director, Grace Clinic Heart Health Program, Lubbock, Texas, and cofounder, Heart Attack & Stroke Prevention Center, Spokane. He is coauthor, with Amy Doneen, ARNP, and Lisa Collier Cool, of *Beat the Heart Attack Gene: The Revolutionary Plan to Prevent Heart Disease, Stroke and Diabetes.*

A fire could be smoldering inside your arteries…a type of fire that could erupt at any moment, triggering a heart attack or stroke. In fact, the fire could be building right this minute and you wouldn't even know it. That's because the usual things doctors look at when gauging cardiovascular risk—cholesterol, blood pressure, blood sugar, weight—can all appear to be fine even when your arteries are dangerously hot.

What does work to detect hot arteries? A set of six simple, inexpensive and readily available blood and urine tests.

Problem: Few doctors order these tests, and few patients know enough to ask for them. Without the warnings these tests provide, patients often have no way of knowing just how great their risk is for heart attack or stroke and whether or not their preventive treatments are working—until it's too late. *Here's how to protect yourself…*

THE BODY'S ARMY ON ATTACK

Hot arteries are not actually hot (as in very warm)—instead, in this case "hot" refers to the effects of chronic inflammation. Why call them hot, then? Chronic arterial inflammation can put you on the fast track to developing vascular disease by speeding up the aging of your arteries. It's so dangerous to the arterial lining that it's worse than having high LDL cholesterol. And if your arteries are already clogged with plaque—which acts as kindling for a heart attack or stroke—inflammation is what lights the match.

Inflammation in the body isn't always bad, of course. In fact, it's an important aspect of healing. When something in your body is under attack, the immune system sends in troops of white blood cells to repair and fight off the attacker, and temporary inflammation results. That's why when you cut yourself, for example, you'll see swelling at the site of the injury—it's a sign that your white blood cells are at work for your benefit.

But: When an attack against your body persists (for instance, as occurs when you have an ongoing infection of the gums), your white blood cells continue to drive inflammation. When it turns chronic, inflammation becomes highly damaging to many tissues, including the arteries.

Normally, the endothelium (lining of the arteries) serves as a protective barrier between blood and the deeper layers of the arterial wall. However, when that lining is inflamed, it can't function well and it gets sticky, almost like flypaper, trapping white blood cells on their way through the body. The inflamed endothelium becomes leaky, too, allowing LDL "bad" cholesterol to penetrate into the wall of the artery. The white blood cells then gobble up the cholesterol, forming fatty streaks that ultimately turn into plaque, a condition called atherosclerosis. Then when the plaque itself becomes inflamed, it can rupture, tearing through the endothelium into the channel of the artery where blood flows. This material triggers the formation of a blood clot—a clot that could end up blocking blood flow to the heart or brain.

THE 6-PART FIRE PANEL

Just as firefighters have ways of determining whether a blaze is hiding within the walls of a building, certain tests can reveal whether inflammation is lurking within the walls of your arteries. I use a set of six tests that I call the "fire panel." Each reveals different risk factors and, for several of the tests, too-high scores can have more than one cause—so it's important to get all six tests, not just one or two.

The fire panel can identify people at risk for developing atherosclerosis…reveal whether patients who already have atherosclerosis have dangerously hot arteries that could lead to a heart attack or stroke…and evaluate patients who have survived a heart attack or stroke to see whether their current treatments are working to reduce the inflammation that threatens their lives. Your individual test results will help determine your most appropriate course of treatment.

I recommend that all adults have this panel of tests done at least every 12 months—or every three to six months for patients at high risk for heart attack or stroke. All of these tests are readily available…are inexpensive and usually covered by insurance…and can be ordered by your regular doctor. *Here are the six tests*…

• **F2 Isoprostanes.** My nickname for this blood test is the "lifestyle lie detector" because it reveals whether or not patients are practicing heart-healthy habits. The test, which measures a biomarker of oxidative stress, helps determine how fast your body's cells are oxidizing, or breaking down. According to one study, people who have the highest levels of F2 isoprostanes are nine times more likely to have blockages in their coronary arteries than people with the lowest levels.

The score you want: A normal score is less than 0.86 ng/L…an optimal score is less than 0.25 ng/L.

• **Fibrinogen.** An abnormally high level of this sticky, fibrous protein in your blood can contribute to the formation of clots…it's also a marker of inflammation. One study divided people into four groups (quartiles) based on their fibrinogen levels and found that stroke risk rose by nearly 50% for each quartile. High fibrinogen is particularly dangerous for people who also have high blood pressure because both conditions damage the blood vessel lining and make it easier for plaque to burrow inside.

Normal range: 440 mg/dL or lower.

• **High-Sensitivity C-Reactive Protein (hs-CRP).** Your liver produces C-reactive protein, and the amount of it in your blood rises when there is inflammation in your body—so an elevated hs-CRP level generally is considered a precursor to cardiovascular disease. The large-scale Harvard Women's Health Study cited this test as being more accurate than cholesterol in predicting risk for cardiovascular disease…while another study of women found that those with high scores were up to four times more likely to have a heart attack or stroke than women with lower scores. A high hs-CRP score is especially worrisome for a person with a large waist. Excess belly fat often is a sign of insulin resistance (in which cells don't readily accept insulin), a condition that further magnifies heart attack and stroke risk.

The score you're aiming for: Under 1.0 mg/L is normal…0.5 mg/L is optimal.

• **Microalbumin/Creatinine Urine Ratio (MACR).** This test looks for albumin in the urine. Albumin is a large protein molecule that circulates in the blood and shouldn't spill from capillaries in the kidneys into the urine, so its presence suggests dysfunction of the endothelium. Though this test provides valuable information about arterial wall health, doctors rarely use it for this purpose.

Important: New evidence shows that MACR levels that have traditionally been considered "normal" can signal increased risk for cardiovascular events.

Optimal ratios, according to the latest research: 7.5 or lower for women and 4.0 or lower for men.

• **Lipoprotein-Associated Phospholipase A-2 (Lp-PLA2).** This enzyme in the blood is attached to LDL cholesterol and rises when artery walls become inflamed. Recent research suggests that it plays a key role in the atherosclerosis disease process, contributing to the formation of plaque as well as to the plaque's vulnerability to rupture. People with periodontal (gum) disease are especially likely to have elevated Lp-PLA2 scores—chronic inflam-

251

mation can start in unhealthy gums and, from there, spread to the arteries.

Normal range: Less than 200 ng/mL.

• **Myeloperoxidase (MPO).** This immune system enzyme normally is found at elevated levels only at the site of an infection. When it is elevated in the bloodstream, it must be assumed that it's due to significant inflammation in the artery walls and leaking through the endothelium. This is a very bad sign. MPO produces numerous oxidants that make all cholesterol compounds, including HDL "good" cholesterol, more inflammatory. If your blood levels of MPO are high, HDL goes rogue and joins the gang of inflammatory thugs. It also interacts with another substance in the bloodstream to produce an acid that can eat holes in blood vessel walls. Smokers are particularly prone to high MPO levels.

Normal range: Less than 420 pmol/L.

HOW TO PUT OUT THE FIRES

While the "fire panel" tests above may seem exotic, the solution to the hot artery problem, for most of us, is not. That's because the best way to combat chronic inflammation is simply to maintain a healthful lifestyle. You just have to do it! *Key factors include…*

• **Following a heart-healthy Mediterranean-style diet.**

• **Managing stress.**

• **Getting plenty of exercise.**

• **Guarding against insulin resistance.**

• **Taking good care of your teeth and gums.**

• **Not smoking.**

In some cases, lifestyle changes alone are enough to quell the flames of chronic inflammation and to put your arteries on the road to recovery. In other cases, patients also need medication such as statins and/or dietary supplements such as niacin and fish oil. Either way, the good news is that once you shut the inflammation off, the body has a chance to heal whatever disease and damage has occurred—so you're no longer on the fast track to a heart attack or stroke.

Hospitalized for Heart Attack? Make Sure They Check You for Diabetes

Suzanne V. Arnold, MD, MHA, cardiologist, Saint Luke's Mid America Heart Institute and research assistant professor, University of Missouri at Kansas City. Her study was presented at the 2014 annual meeting of the American Heart Association.

It's well-known among health-conscious people that heart disease and diabetes are linked, so it seems a shame to be hearing news from the American Heart Association that 10% of Americans who've had a heart attack probably have undiagnosed diabetes. What's worse, though, is news that doctors are missing opportunities to detect and treat diabetes in people even when they are hospitalized for a heart attack.

Are so many doctors this clueless?

Although it might be a great challenge for health-care professionals to identify everyone with diabetes before complications, such as heart attack, occur, a basic precaution can at least help those who do land in the hospital because of heart attack. So if you've had a heart attack or have cardiovascular disease—or you want to be prepared to give yourself the best odds if you ever have a heart attack in the future—here's what you need to insist that your medical-care team does for you, especially if you land in the hospital…

A SIMPLE OVERLOOKED TEST

It comes down to getting a simple blood test. Doctors who order a hemoglobin A1c test when a patient is being treated for heart attack are making the right move to ensure that diabetes won't be missed and the heart attack can be treated correctly, said Suzanne V. Arnold, MD, MHA, an assistant professor at the University of Missouri in Kansas City. She led a study on undiagnosed diabetes in heart attack patients that was reported at last year's American Heart Association meeting. The hemoglobin A1c test shows average blood sugar levels for the preceding three months and is widely used to diagnose both type 1 and type

2 diabetes and monitor how well blood sugar is being controlled after diagnosis.

In her study, Dr. Arnold and her team took 2,854 patients who were hospitalized for heart attacks but had never received a diabetes diagnosis and arranged for them to have the hemoglobin A1c test. Both the hospitalized patients and the doctors treating them were kept in the dark ("blinded" in scientific speak) about the test results, and doctors were left to their business-as-usual patient care. Diabetes was considered "recognized" by the researchers if a patient either received diabetes education while hospitalized and/or diabetes medication when sent home.

The study results were a real eye-opener. Sure, Dr. Arnold's team discovered that 10% of these patients had diabetes and didn't know it, but the far bigger issue that patients and their families need to know about was that doctors failed to recognize diabetes in 69% of these previously undiagnosed patients.

That's a major fail—especially when all it took for the treating doctors themselves to discover diabetes was to order the same simple, inexpensive A1c test that Dr. Arnold's team had already ordered for their study.

Six months down the road, the researchers checked in on the patients they themselves knew had diabetes. They found that 71% of the patients whose diabetes had also been discovered by a doctor during their hospital stays were getting diabetes care. As for the patients whose diabetes had not been discovered by doctors treating them in the hospital, only 7% were getting diabetes care, meaning that the likelihood was strong that no one, except Dr. Arnold's team, had yet checked these folks for diabetes. This left them at high risk for more cardiovascular complications, including additional heart attacks.

KNOWLEDGE THAT CAN ALSO GUIDE HEART ATTACK TREATMENT

Knowing that a heart attack patient has type 2 diabetes is important in the moment because it determines treatment decisions, explained Dr. Arnold. For example, patients with multivessel coronary artery disease and diabetes may do better with bypass surgery (rather than stents) and particular blood pressure medications, such as ACE inhibitors.

Dr. Arnold's advice for people who have heart attacks and survive...but don't know whether they have diabetes...is that they insist on having a hemoglobin A1c test during their hospitalization. She does not advocate routine hemoglobin A1c screening for everyone, though, calling it "impractical," although it's certainly something you can bring up with your doctor if you know you have heart disease. And although you may be in-the-know about diabetes and heart disease prevention, this seems like a good place to include a refresher for you or a loved one. You can assess your risks and the warning signs of diabetes with these checklists from the American Diabetes Association:

Your chances of diabetes increase if you...

- **Have a family history of type 2 diabetes**
- **Don't get much exercise** and are otherwise physically inactive
- **Are overweight**
- **Have high blood pressure**
- **Have low HDL cholesterol and high triglycerides**
- **Don't watch your diet** and feast on high-calorie, fatty, sugary and low-fiber foods
- **Smoke**
- **For women, had diabetes during pregnancy**

These are warning signs of diabetes...

- **Unquenchable thirst**
- **Excessive urination**
- **Increased appetite,** despite eating
- **Unexpected weight loss**
- **Tingling, pain and/or numbness in your hands and/or feet**
- **Blurred vision**
- **Cuts and bruises that take a long time to heal**
- **Extreme fatigue**

It's not very challenging for health-conscious people to avoid type 2 diabetes and heart disease, but keeping this bit of information on a simple blood test in mind can protect you or a loved one even more.

New Heart Attack Risk

In a recent finding, low blood sugar levels overnight may trigger prolonged slow heart rates during sleep in people with diabetes. This could lead to abnormal heart rhythms, which increase risk for heart attack.

If you have diabetes (especially if you also have cardiovascular disease): Talk to your doctor about ways to stabilize your blood sugar overnight, such as adjusting the timing, dose and/or type of medication you take.

Simon Heller, MD, professor of clinical diabetes, The University of Sheffield, UK.

Which Coronary Artery Surgery Is Best for People with Diabetes?

Study titled "Comparison of coronary artery bypass surgery and percutaneous coronary intervention in patients with diabetes: A meta-analysis of randomized controlled trials," published in *The Lancet Diabetes & Endocrinology*.

Heart doctors have been engaged in a hot debate about the best type of surgery for patients who have blocked coronary arteries and diabetes. Some strongly favor the major operation called a bypass, while others prefer the less invasive angioplasty—but no one really knew which procedure was safest and most effective for people with diabetes. Now a startling new study shows that one of these procedures carries a one-third lower risk of dying! *Here's the story…*

Background: Cardiovascular disease is the main cause of death and disability for people with diabetes. These patients frequently require a revascularization procedure to open up blocked coronary arteries. One option, coronary artery bypass, is a major operation that requires general anesthesia, a sizable incision and an artery graft—and that carries all the risks inherent in such an invasive procedure. The second option is a less invasive angioplas-ty procedure, percutaneous coronary intervention (PCI), done using local anesthesia. A catheter inserted into a blood vessel in the arm or groin is threaded through to the blocked area, then a small balloon and often a stent are used to open up the coronary artery.

Recent study: To figure out which option was best, researchers did a meta-analysis of eight studies that had randomly assigned adults with diabetes and coronary artery disease to either of the two treatments. In all, there were 3,612 people with diabetes included in the studies. Some of the studies also compared the type of stent—either bare metal or one coated with a drug—that was left to hold open the artery.

Startling result: The odds of dying within five years were 33% lower for diabetes patients who had the bypass operation rather than the angioplasty (no matter whether the angioplasty included a bare stent or a drug-coated stent). Those results held even after adjusting for other risk factors and the number of affected arteries.

Possible reason: People with diabetes tend to have more widespread and rapidly progressing coronary disease than people without diabetes. With a bypass, which grafts a healthy artery from elsewhere in the body to create a new path for blood to flow to the heart, the surgeon can literally "pass by" several dangerously narrowed and/or potentially vulnerable areas of the damaged original artery all at once—whereas a stent fixes only one spot.

It is worth noting that the bypass patients did have a somewhat higher risk for nonfatal strokes than the angioplasty patients did, though this may have been related to the fact that far fewer bypass patients used anticlotting medication after their procedures.

Important: If you have diabetes and are facing a revascularization procedure, be sure to discuss this recent study with your cardiologist. If he/she still favors angioplasty, it would be wise to get a second opinion. Note that the type of specialist you see may affect the recommendation you are given, because cardiologists can perform angioplasties, whereas bypasses must be performed by cardiac surgeons. Ideally, you would be under the care of a team of physicians that includes both types of specialists—so that they can work together to advise you on the most appropriate option for you.

See a Naturopathic Doctor for a Healthy Heart

Dugald Seely, ND, MSc, Fellow of the American Board of Naturopathic Oncologists (FABNO), director of research, Canadian College of Naturopathic Medicine, Toronto, Ontario, and executive director, Ottawa Integrative Cancer Centre, Ottawa, Ontario. His study was published in *CMAJ*.

Your MD frowns at your blood test results, weight or lifestyle and warns that you could be headed for heart trouble. What's a smart next move? Adding a naturopathic doctor (ND) to your health-care team could work wonders for your heart, a recent study shows.

Why an ND—and not automatically a cardiologist? Naturopathic medicine is a holistic medical system that emphasizes the importance of a healthful diet and lifestyle. Practitioners believe that the body has an innate ability to heal...that many common health problems can (and should!) be prevented...and that natural treatments, such as dietary supplements, can be preferable to drugs and/or invasive procedures. For the new study, researchers set out to examine the effects of adding naturopathic care to conventional medical care for people who were already at risk for cardiovascular disease based on their cholesterol levels and other modifiable risk factors.

Participants included 246 adults ages 25 to 65. At the start of the study, all participants received physical exams and blood tests to determine whether they had metabolic syndrome, a constellation of risk factors that increase a person's odds of developing cardiovascular disease and diabetes. Metabolic syndrome is defined as having at least three of five risk factors—abdominal obesity, elevated triglycerides (a type of blood fat), low HDL "good" cholesterol, high fasting blood sugar and high blood pressure.

In addition, the researchers used a risk score calculator from the large-scale Framingham Heart Study to estimate participants'

likelihood of experiencing a "cardiovascular event" (heart attack, stroke or heart-related death) during the subsequent 10 years.

For the following year, all participants remained under the usual care of their primary-care MDs...and half of the participants were randomly assigned to also see a naturopathic doctor seven times throughout the year for visits lasting 30 to 60 minutes. Though the NDs prescribed specific interventions based on each patient's individual needs, typical recommendations included dietary modification to reduce unhealthful fats and increase fish, fruit and vegetable consumption...weight loss...physical exercise...nutritional supplements such as fish oil, soluble fiber, plant sterols and/or coenzyme Q10...and/or stress-relieving breathing exercises.

Results: At the end of the year, all participants were examined and tested again. In the group that received conventional MD care only, the percentage of those who met the criteria for metabolic syndrome rose from 43% at the start of the study to 48% after one year. However, in the group that also received ND-care, the percentage of those who had metabolic syndrome dropped from 55% at the start of the study to 32% after one year.

That's a big (and healthful) drop!

As for the Framingham risk score, among participants who received conventional MD care only, the percentage of participants deemed likely to experience a cardiovascular event within 10 years increased from 6.9% at the start of the study to 10.8% after one year. In contrast, in the ND-care group, the percentage deemed at risk decreased from 8.1% at the start of the study to 7.7% after one year.

FINDING A NATUROPATHIC DOCTOR

Of course, if your MD recommends it or if you are concerned about your current heart health, it would be wise to see a cardiologist. But do keep in mind how much you could gain from adding a naturopathic doctor to your health-care team, too. If your MD dismisses the idea of consulting an ND, show this article to him or her and ask why the benefits seen in this study wouldn't apply just as much to you. Most recommendations that an ND would make are not difficult to follow through on, especially when you have the support of a knowledgeable and attentive physician.

Important distinction: A "naturopath" is not the same as a naturopathic doctor. Naturopaths (sometimes called "traditional naturopaths") aren't licensed…and their education may consist of correspondence courses or an apprenticeship, or they may be self-taught. In contrast, NDs must complete a four-year, graduate-level program that includes many of the same courses taught in conventional medical schools, with an added emphasis on nutrition, preventive care and natural treatments. In many states, NDs also must pass standardized board exams to earn licenses to practice.

There are six accredited naturopathic medical schools in the US and two in Canada—Bastyr University in Kenmore, Washington and San Diego, California…National University of Natural Medicine in Portland, Oregon…National University of Health Sciences in Chicago… Southwest College of Naturopathic Medicine in Tempe, Arizona…University of Bridgeport in Bridgeport, Connecticut…Boucher Institute of Naturopathic Medicine in Vancouver, British Columbia…and Canadian College of Naturopathic Medicine in Toronto, Ontario. To find a naturopathic doctor who graduated from one of these accredited programs, check the website of the American Association of Naturopathic Physicians, *www.naturopathic.org*, or the website of the Canadian Association of Naturopathic Doctors, *www.cand.ca.*

6 Secrets to Holistic Heart Care

Joel K. Kahn, MD, clinical professor of medicine at Wayne State University School of Medicine in Detroit and director of Kahn Center for Cardiac Longevity, Bloomfield Township, Michigan. He is a founding member of the International Society of Integrative, Metabolic and Functional Cardiovascular Medicine and author of *The Whole Heart Solution.* DrJoelKahn.com

You don't smoke, your cholesterol levels look good and your blood pressure is under control. This means that you're off the hook when it comes to having a heart attack or developing heart disease, right? Maybe not.

Surprising statistic: About 20% of people with heart disease do not have any of the classic risk factors, such as those described above.

The missing link: While most conventional medical doctors prescribe medications and other treatments to help patients control the "big" risk factors for heart disease, holistic cardiologists also suggest small lifestyle changes that over time make a significant difference in heart disease risk.* *My secrets for preventing heart disease…*

SECRET #1: Stand up! You may not think of standing as a form of exercise. However, it's more effective than most people realize.

Think about what you're doing when you're not standing. Unless you're asleep, you're probably sitting. While sitting, your body's metabolism slows…your insulin becomes less effective…and you're likely to experience a gradual drop in HDL "good" cholesterol.

A study that tracked the long-term health of more than 123,000 Americans found that those who sat for six hours or more a day had an overall death rate that was higher—18% higher for men and 37% for women—than those who sat for less than three hours.

What's so great about standing? When you're on your feet, you move more. You pace…fidget…move your arms…and walk from room to room. This type of activity improves metabolism and can easily burn hundreds of extra calories a day. Standing also increases your insulin sensitivity to help prevent diabetes. So stand up and move around when talking on the phone, checking e-mail and watching television.

SECRET #2: Count your breaths. Slow, deep breathing is an effective way to help prevent high blood pressure—one of the leading causes of heart disease. For people who

*To find a holistic cardiologist, go to the website of the American Board of Integrative Holistic Medicine, *www.abihm.org*, and search the database of certified integrative physicians.

already have high blood pressure, doing this technique a few times a day has been shown to lower blood pressure by five to 10 points within five minutes. And the pressure may stay lower for up to 24 hours.

During a breathing exercise, you want to slow your breathing down from the usual 12 to 16 breaths a minute that most people take to about three breaths. I use the "4-7-8 sequence" whenever I feel stressed.

What to do: Inhale through your nose for four seconds...hold the breath in for seven seconds...then exhale through the mouth for eight seconds.

Also helpful: A HeartMath software package, which you can load on your computer or smartphone, includes breathing exercises to help lower your heart rate and levels of stress hormones. Cost: $129 and up, at *HeartMath. com.* You can also sign up for some free tools on this website.

SECRET #3: **Practice "loving kindness."** This is an easy form of meditation that reduces stress, thus allowing you to keep your heart rate and blood pressure at healthy levels.

Research has shown that people who meditate regularly are 48% less likely to have a heart attack or stroke than those who don't meditate. "Loving kindness" meditation is particularly effective at promoting relaxation—it lowers levels of the stress hormones adrenaline and cortisol while raising levels of the healing hormone oxytocin.

What to do: Sit quietly, with your eyes closed. For a few minutes, focus on just your breathing. Then imagine one person in your life whom you find exceptionally easy to love. Imagine this person in front of you. Fill your heart with a warm, loving feeling...think about how you both want to be happy and avoid suffering...and imagine that a feeling of peace travels from your heart to that person's heart in the form of white light. Dwell on the image for a few minutes. This meditation will also help you practice small acts of kindness in your daily life—for example, giving a hand to someone who needs help crossing the street.

SECRET #4: **Don't neglect sex.** Men who have sex at least two times a week have a 50% lower risk for a heart attack than those who abstain. Similar research hasn't been done on women, but it's likely that they get a comparable benefit.

Why does sex help keep your heart healthy? It probably has more to do with intimacy than the physical activity itself. Couples who continue to have sex tend to be the ones with more intimacy in their marriages. Happy people who bond with others have fewer heart attacks—and recover more quickly if they've had one—than those without close relationships.

SECRET #5: **Be happy!** People who are happy and who feel a sense of purpose and connection with others tend to have lower blood pressure and live longer than those who are isolated. Research shows that two keys to happiness are to help others be happy—for example, by being a volunteer—and to reach out to friends and neighbors. Actually, any shared activity, such as going to church or doing group hobbies, can increase survival among heart patients by about 50%.

SECRET #6: **Try Waon (pronounced Wa-own) therapy.** With this Japanese form of "warmth therapy," you sit in an infrared (dry) sauna for 15 minutes then retreat to a resting area for half an hour, where you wrap yourself in towels and drink plenty of water. Studies show that vascular function improves after such therapy due to the extra release of nitric oxide, the master molecule in blood vessels that helps them relax.

Some health clubs offer Waon treatments, but the dry saunas at many gyms should offer similar benefits. I do not recommend steam rooms—moist heat places extra demands on the heart and can be dangerous for some people.

You Can Cure Heart Disease—With Plant-Based Nutrition

Caldwell B. Esselstyn, Jr., MD, surgeon, clinician and researcher at The Cleveland Clinic for more than 35 years. He is author of *Prevent and Reverse Heart Disease: The Revolutionary, Scientifically Proven, Nutrition-Based Cure.* DrEsselstyn.com
Centers for Disease Control and Prevention.

In the mid-1980s, 17 people with severe heart disease had just about given up hope. They had undergone every available treatment, including drugs and surgery—all had failed. The group had experienced 49 cardiovascular events, including four heart attacks, three strokes, 15 cases of increased angina and seven bypass surgeries. Five of the patients were expected to die within a year.

Twelve years later, every one of the 17 was alive. They had had no cardiovascular events. The progression of their heart disease had been stopped—and, in many cases, reversed. Their angina went away—for some, within three weeks. In fact, they became virtually heart-attack proof. And there are hundreds of other patients with heart disease who have achieved the same remarkable results. *What you need to know...*

HOW THE DAMAGE IS DONE

Every year, 370,000 Americans die of coronary artery disease (CAD). Double that number suffer heart attacks. Although considered a "man's disease," around the same number of men and women die each year of heart disease in the United States (CDC data).

Heart disease develops in the endothelium, the lining of the arteries. There, endothelial cells manufacture a compound called nitric oxide that accomplishes four tasks crucial for healthy circulation...

• **Keeps blood smoothly flowing,** rather than becoming sticky and clotted.

• **Allows arteries to widen when the heart needs more blood,** such as when you run up a flight of stairs.

• **Stops muscle cells in arteries from growing into plaque**—the fatty gunk that blocks blood vessels.

• **Decreases inflammation in the plaque**—the process that can trigger a rupture in the cap or surface of a plaque, starting the clot-forming, artery-clogging cascade that causes a heart attack.

The type and amount of fat in the typical Western diet—from animal products, dairy foods and concentrated oils—assaults endothelial cells, cutting their production of nitric oxide.

Study: A researcher at University of Maryland School of Medicine fed a 900-calorie fast-food breakfast containing 50 grams of fat (mostly from sausages and hash browns) to a group of students and then measured their endothelial function. For six hours, the students had severely compromised endothelial function and decreased nitric oxide production. Another group of students ate a 900-calorie, no-fat breakfast—and had no significant change in endothelial function.

If a single meal can do that kind of damage, imagine the damage done by three fatty meals a day, seven days a week, 52 weeks a year.

PLANT-BASED NUTRITION

You can prevent, stop or reverse heart disease with a plant-based diet. *Here's what you can't eat—and what you can...*

What you cannot eat...

• **No meat, poultry, fish or eggs.** You will get plenty of protein from plant-based sources.

• **No dairy products.** That means no butter, cheese, cream, ice cream, yogurt or milk—even skim milk, which, though lower in fat, still contains animal protein.

• **No oil of any kind—not a drop.** That includes all oils, even virgin olive oil and canola.

What you may not know: At least 14% of olive oil is saturated fat—every bit as aggressive in promoting heart disease as the saturated fat in roast beef. A diet that includes oils—including monounsaturated oils from olive oil and canola oil—may slow the progression of heart disease, but it will not stop or reverse the disease.

• **Generally, no nuts or avocados.** If you are eating a plant-based diet to prevent heart disease, you can have moderate amounts of nuts and avocados as long as your total cholesterol remains below 150 milligrams per deciliter (mg/dL). If you have heart disease and want to stop or reverse it, you should not eat these foods.

What you can eat...

• **All vegetables.**

• **Legumes**—beans, peas, lentils.

• **Whole grains and products that are made from them, such as bread and pasta**—as long as they do not contain added fats. Do not eat refined grains, which have been stripped of much of their fiber and nutrients. Avoid white rice and "enriched" flour products, which are found in many pastas, breads, bagels and baked goods.

• **Fruits**—but heart patients should limit consumption to three pieces a day and avoid drinking pure fruit juices. Too much fruit rapidly raises blood sugar, triggering a surge of insulin from the pancreas—which stimulates the liver to manufacture more cholesterol.

• **Certain beverages,** including water, seltzer water, oat milk, hazelnut milk, almond milk, no-fat soy milk, coffee and tea. Alcohol is fine in moderation (no more than two servings a day for men and one for women).

SUPPLEMENTS

For maximum health, take five supplements daily...

• **Multivitamin/mineral supplement.**

• **Vitamin B-12**—1,000 micrograms (mcg).

• **Calcium**—1,000 milligrams (mg) (1,200 mg if you're over 60).

• **Vitamin D-3**—1,000 international units (IU).

• **Flaxseed meal (ground flaxseed)**—one tablespoon for the omega-3 fatty acids it provides. Sprinkle it on cereal.

THE CHOLESTEROL CONNECTION

If you eat the typical, high-fat Western diet, even if you also take a cholesterol-lowering statin drug, you will not protect yourself from heart disease—because the fat in the diet will damage the endothelium cells that produce nitric oxide.

In a study in *The New England Journal of Medicine*, patients took huge doses of statin drugs to lower total cholesterol below 150 but didn't change their diets—and 25% experienced a new cardiovascular event or died within the next 30 months.

Recommended: Eat a plant-based diet, and ask your doctor if you should also take a cholesterol-lowering medication. Strive to maintain a total cholesterol of less than 150 and LDL ("bad" cholesterol) below 85.

MODERATION DOESN'T WORK

The most common objection physicians have to this diet is that their patients will not follow it. But many patients with heart disease who find out that they have a choice—between invasive surgery and nutritional changes that will stop and reverse the disease—willingly adopt the diet.

Why not eat a less demanding diet, such as the low-fat diet recommended by the American Heart Association or the Mediterranean Diet?

Surprising: Research shows that people who maintain a so-called low-fat diet of 29% of calories from fat have the same rate of heart attacks and strokes as people who don't.

Plant-based nutrition is the only diet that can effectively prevent, stop and reverse heart disease. It also offers protection against stroke...high blood pressure...osteoporosis... diabetes...senile mental impairment...erectile dysfunction...and cancers of the breast, prostate, colon, rectum, uterus and ovaries.

Diabetic Eye Disease May Predict Heart Failure

Diabetic eye disease may predict heart failure, says Tien Y. Wong, MD, PhD. According to a recent study, people who have diabetic retinopathy—diabetes-related damage to blood vessels in the retina—have more than double the risk for heart failure than diabetes patients with healthy retinas.

Self-defense: Everyone who has diabetes needs a comprehensive, dilated eye exam at least once a year. People in whom retinopathy is detected should have a complete cardiac exam—and regular follow-ups.

Tien Y. Wong, MD, PhD, professor of ophthalmology, National University of Singapore, and director, Singapore National Eye Centre, and senior author of a study of 1,021 adults with type 2 diabetes, published in *Journal of the American College of Cardiology.*

Diabetes Doubles Your Risk for Peripheral Artery Disease

Michael S. Conte, MD, a vascular surgeon and professor and chief of the division of vascular and endovascular surgery and codirector of the Heart and Vascular Center at the University of California, San Francisco. He is a former recipient of the Distinguished Achievement Award from the New York Weill Cornell Medical Center Alumni Council, and is on the editorial boards of *Vascular and Endovascular Surgery* and *Vascular Medicine.*

How serious is peripheral artery disease (PAD)? We all know that plaque in arteries near the heart can lead to heart attack and plaque in the arteries of the neck and brain can lead to stroke.

With PAD, plaque is typically found in arteries that supply blood to the legs—an indication that blood flow also may be inhibited throughout the body, which increases risk for heart attack and stroke, as well as severe disability or loss of a limb.

Doctors have long been aware of PAD, but the disease has received relatively little attention because patients either don't have symptoms or have only mild or moderate ones that are wrongly attributed to normal signs of aging.

What's new: The link between PAD and cardiovascular disease is now so strong that virtually all doctors agree that a diagnosis of PAD warrants a checkup and monitoring by a vascular specialist.

What you need to know to protect yourself or a loved one...

ARE YOU AT RISK?

PAD is surprisingly common. It affects up to 10 million Americans. Because PAD is associated with the same risk factors as heart attack and stroke, the risk for PAD is higher among adults who are over age 50 and/or people who have elevated cholesterol or high blood pressure.

Having diabetes doubles the risk of developing PAD. Prediabetes also increases risk. But the greatest risk comes from smoking. At least 80% of people with PAD are current or former smokers. Statistically, the worst combination is smoking and having diabetes—when combined, they increase the risk of developing PAD fivefold.

SYMPTOMS CAN BE TRICKY

PAD is dangerous because it can creep up on you without causing symptoms. In fact, up to half of people with PAD do not have symptoms.

When symptoms do occur, they start out mild and may be easy to dismiss. Because blood flow is compromised, activities that involve the use of the legs—walking, for example—can become more difficult and feel more tiring.

As plaque blockages become more severe, PAD causes intermittent claudication—legs become painful or achy or cramp up while walking.

At first, a person with PAD may experience symptoms of intermittent claudication only after walking long distances or up a hill or while climbing stairs. The discomfort usually goes away after sitting down and resting for a few minutes. If the condition is left untreated, even a short stroll will trigger the pain.

What most people don't know: In rare cases, PAD can occur in the hands and arms, leading to symptoms such as aching or cramping in the arms.

GETTING A PROPER DIAGNOSIS

Not all doctors agree on who should be screened for PAD. However, it's wise to be tested if any of the following risk factors developed by the American College of Cardiology and the American Heart Association apply to you...

Younger than age 50: If you have diabetes and one additional risk factor (such as smoking or high blood pressure).

Age 50 to 69: If you have a history of smoking or diabetes.

Age 70 and older—even if you have no known risk factors.

Many experts believe that screening also is warranted—regardless of your age—if you have…

• **Leg symptoms,** such as aches and cramping with exertion.

• **Diagnosis of atherosclerosis,** fatty build-up in the walls of the arteries, including those in the heart and neck.

• **Numbness,** tingling or loss of sensation in the feet or cold feet or areas of color change (bluish or dark color, for example) on your toes—an indication of compromised blood flow.

• **High blood levels of C-reactive protein (CRP),** an inflammation marker.

THE TESTS YOU NEED

If you meet one of the criteria described above, ask your doctor to test you for PAD. He/she will perform a measurement called an ankle-brachial index to get a sense of whether blood pumps equally through your arms and your legs. To perform this test, your doctor will measure your blood pressure in your ankle as well as in your arm and compare the two numbers.

BEST TREATMENT OPTIONS

There is no medication that will dissolve PAD plaque, so you should work with your doctor to manage your risk factors. If you're a smoker, stopping smoking is the most important step you can take to help control PAD.

Everyone with PAD should…

• **Get the right kind of exercise.** Surprising as it might sound, walking is the most beneficial form of exercise for PAD sufferers. It won't get rid of the plaque, but it can improve your stamina and make walking less painful.

What to do: Walk on flat ground every day—or try a treadmill if you prefer.

• **Use your level of leg pain to determine the amount of time you walk.** For example, walk until the leg pain reaches a moderate level…stop walking until the pain is relieved… then resume walking. This approach "trains"

the muscle to be more efficient in using its blood supply. Try to work your way up to 50 minutes of walking at least five days a week.

Be sure to consult your doctor before starting a walking program, especially if you have other conditions, such as heart disease, arthritis or spine disease. Supervised exercise, such as that offered at rehab centers, has been shown to be the most effective for PAD patients—perhaps because people are more likely to stick to a walking program in these settings.

• **Monitor other risk factors.** It is critically important to pay attention to all your other health-related risk factors. For example, if you have diabetes, monitor and keep glucose levels under control. If you have elevated cholesterol or high blood pressure, talk with your doctor about medication.

To reduce the risk for blood clots, which could lead to limb damage, heart attack or stroke, your doctor may suggest a daily aspirin (81 mg) or a medication that prevents clotting, such as *clopidogrel* (Plavix). A statin also may be prescribed. Statins not only lower cholesterol, but also lower levels of the inflammation marker CRP.

WHEN ADDITIONAL TREATMENT IS NEEDED

In about 30% of PAD patients, the condition causes severe pain that affects their quality of life or the amount of blockage significantly restricts blood flow. In these cases, your doctor may recommend a more invasive measure, such as angioplasty or bypass surgery, to improve blood flow in the affected artery.

With angioplasty, a tiny balloon and, possibly, stents are inserted via a catheter into the artery to widen the artery as much as possible. Bypass surgery involves creating a blood-flow "detour" around a blockage, allowing the blood to flow more freely.

Important: Treatment for PAD is highly individualized. If you've been diagnosed with the condition, you should see your doctor at least once or twice each year.

For more information on PAD, go to *www. nhlbi.nih.gov/health/educational/pad*. To find a vascular specialist near you, contact Vascular Cures at 650-368-6022, *www.vascular cures.org*.

Natural Treatments for Peripheral Artery Disease

Catherine Ulbricht, PharmD, cofounder of the Somerville, Massachusetts–based Natural Standard Research Collaboration, which collects data on natural therapies, and senior attending pharmacist at Massachusetts General Hospital in Boston. She is also author of *Natural Standard Herbal Pharmacotherapy* and *Natural Standard Medical Conditions Reference* and editor-in-chief of the *Journal of Dietary Supplements*.

You are walking or climbing up a set of stairs, and suddenly you notice a dull, cramping pain in your leg. Before you write off the pain as simply a sign of overexertion or just a normal part of growing older, consider this: You may have intermittent claudication, the most common symptom of peripheral artery disease (PAD).

PAD, also known as peripheral vascular disease, is a condition in which arteries and veins in your limbs, usually in the legs and feet, are blocked or narrowed by fatty deposits that reduce blood flow.

Intermittent claudication, leg discomfort (typically in the calf) that occurs during exertion or exercise and is relieved by rest, usually is the first symptom of PAD. But other possible symptoms may include leg sores that won't heal (chronic venous ulcers)...varicose veins (chronic venous insufficiency)...paleness (pallor) or discoloration (a blue tint) of the legs...or cold legs.

Why is "a little leg trouble" so significant?

If it's due to PAD, you have got a red flag that other arteries, including those in the heart and brain, may also be blocked. In fact, people with PAD have a two- to sixfold increased risk for heart attack or stroke.

Up to 10 million Americans—including up to one in five people age 60 or older—are believed to have PAD. While many individuals who have PAD experience the symptoms described earlier, some have no symptoms at all.

Those at greatest risk: Anyone who smokes or has elevated cholesterol, high blood pressure or diabetes is at increased risk for PAD.

What you need to know...

BETTER TREATMENT RESULTS

The standard treatment for PAD typically includes lifestyle changes (such as quitting smoking, getting regular exercise and eating a healthful diet). Medical treatment may include medication, such as one of the two drugs approved by the FDA for PAD—*pentoxifylline* and *cilostazol* (Pletal)—and, in severe cases, surgery.

For even better results: Strong scientific evidence now indicates that several natural therapies—used in conjunction with these treatments—may help slow the progression of PAD and improve a variety of symptoms more effectively than standard treatment alone can.

Important: Before trying any of the following therapies, talk to your doctor to determine which might work best for you, what the most effective dose is for you and what side effects and drug interactions may occur.

Do not take more than one of the following therapies at the same time—this will increase bleeding risk.

Among the most effective natural therapies for PAD...

• **Ginkgo biloba.** A standardized extract from the leaf of the ginkgo biloba tree, which is commonly taken to improve memory, is one of the top-selling herbs in the US. But the strongest scientific evidence for ginkgo biloba may well be in the treatment of PAD.

Scientific evidence: Numerous studies currently show that ginkgo biloba extract can decrease leg pain that occurs with exercise or at rest. The daily doses used in the studies ranged from 80 mg to 320 mg.

Warning: Because it thins the blood and may increase risk for bleeding, ginkgo biloba should be used with caution if you also take a blood thinner, such as *warfarin* (Coumadin) or aspirin. In addition, ginkgo biloba should not be taken within two weeks of undergoing surgery.

• **Grape seed extract.** Grapes, including the fruit, leaves and seeds, have been used medicinally since the time of the ancient Greeks. Grape seed extract is rich in oligomeric proanthocyanidins, antioxidants that integrative practitioners in Europe use to treat varicose veins, chronic leg ulcers and other symptoms of PAD.

Scientific evidence: In several recent studies, grape seed extract was found to reduce the symptoms of poor circulation in leg veins, which can include nighttime cramps, swelling, heaviness, itching, tingling, burning, numbness and nerve pain.

Caution: Don't use this supplement if you're allergic to grapes. It should be used with caution if you take a blood thinner.

• **Hesperidin.** This flavonoid is found in unripe citrus fruits, such as oranges, grapefruits, lemons and tangerines.

Scientific evidence: Research now shows that hesperidin may strengthen veins and tiny blood vessels called capillaries, easing the symptoms of venous insufficiency. Hesperidin also has been shown to reduce leg symptoms such as pain, cramps, heaviness and neuropathy (burning, tingling and numbness). Some hesperidin products also contain *diosmin* (Daflon), a prescription medication that is used to treat venous disease…vitamin C…or the herb butcher's broom—all of which strengthen the effects of hesperidin.

Caution: Many drugs can react with hesperidin. If you take a diabetes medication, antihypertensive, blood thinner, muscle relaxant, antacid or antinausea medication, be sure to use this supplement cautiously and promptly alert your doctor if you experience any new symptoms after starting to use hesperidin.

• **Horse chestnut seed extract.** The seeds, leaves, bark and flowers of this tree, which is native to Europe, have been used for centuries in herbal medicine.

Scientific evidence: Several studies now indicate that horse chestnut seed extract may be helpful for venous insufficiency, decreasing leg pain, fatigue, itchiness and swelling.

Caution: Horse chestnut may lower blood sugar and interfere with diabetes medication.

• **L-carnitine.** Also known as acetyl-L-carnitine, this amino acid may improve circulation and help with PAD symptoms.

Recent finding: Taking L-carnitine in addition to the PAD medication cilostazol increased walking distance in people with intermittent claudication up to 46% more than taking cilostazol alone, reported researchers from the University of Colorado School of Medicine in a recent issue of *Vascular Medicine*.

• **Inositol nicotinate.** This is a form of niacin (vitamin B-3) that is less likely to create the typical "flushing" (redness and heat) that is produced by high doses of niacin.

Several studies show that it is helpful in treating PAD. It is commonly used in the UK to treat intermittent claudication.

• **Policosanol.** This is a natural cholesterol-lowering compound made primarily from the wax of cane sugar. Comparative studies show that policosanol treats intermittent claudication as effectively as the prescription blood thinner *ticlopidine* and more effectively than the cholesterol-lowering statin *lovastatin*.

OTHER THERAPIES

You may read or hear that acupuncture, biofeedback, chelation therapy, garlic, omega-3 fatty acids and vitamin E can help with PAD.

However: The effectiveness of these particular therapies is uncertain at this time. For this reason, it is best to forgo these approaches until more scientific evidence becomes available.

The Big Statin Question— Here's How to Decide Whether You Need One…

Harlan M. Krumholz, MD, the Harold H. Hines Jr. professor of medicine (cardiology) and professor of investigative medicine and of public health (health policy) at the Yale School of Medicine in New Haven, Connecticut. Dr. Krumholz is also codirector of the Clinical Scholars Program and director of the Yale-New Haven Hospital Center for Outcomes Research and Evaluation.

With so many doctors now clashing over the recently released statin-drug guidelines (from the American College of Cardiology and the American Heart Association in 2014—additional guidance from the U.S. Preventive Services Task Force came out in 2016), it is no wonder that most Americans are left with lots of unanswered questions about their heart health.

Some medical experts say that the recent guidelines, which include a controversial online risk calculator, overestimate risk and recommend statin drugs for too many people. Other authorities argue that the recent guidelines represent a state-of-the-art upgrade.

What you need now are clear answers, not just claims and counterclaims from medical honchos. To provide some real perspective on the guidelines, we spoke to Harlan M. Krumholz, MD, one of the most respected cardiologists in the country and a leading "quality-of-care" researcher. He was not involved in the creation of the new statin guidelines. *Four steps that he uses to advise his patients on statins…*

Step 1: **Don't ignore cholesterol levels.** The most fundamental change in the new guidelines is that they now suggest the use of statin therapy for certain groups of people—for example, those with existing cardiovascular disease or diabetes—rather than focusing on very specific cholesterol targets when prescribing statins. However, even though targets have been largely abandoned, the guidelines do still indicate that everyone with very high LDL "bad" cholesterol levels should strongly consider taking a statin.

What this means for you: Knowing your cholesterol level is still vital in assessing your risk for cardiovascular disease and whether you would likely benefit from a statin. Therefore, a cholesterol test should be part of your initial evaluation. If you're not put on a statin, you can also retest every five years.

Step 2: **Forget about keeping score.** Until now, the generally accepted goal of cholesterol-lowering drug treatment was to bring LDL below a target level—100 mg/dL to 130 mg/dL for most people…and 70 mg/dL for those at very high risk for heart disease. If cholesterol failed to drop sufficiently, the statin dose was often increased or other drugs were added.

Why the targets? For years, doctors assumed that because higher LDL cholesterol means more risk for heart attack, reducing these levels with medication would mean fewer heart attacks. But research now shows that this isn't necessarily so.

What this means for you: If you start taking a statin, think of the medication not just as a cholesterol-lowering drug, but as a heart-protecting drug, since it will reduce risk regardless of your cholesterol level.

Once you're on a statin, there's no reason to measure your cholesterol levels. It would be useful only if you want to reconsider this decision, which might make sense if you're overweight but then lose weight, start exercising or make other lifestyle changes (see chapter 10, "Healthy Life Habits That Keep Diabetes Away Forever").

Step 3: **Start with nondrug approaches.** By shifting away from cholesterol targets, the new guidelines focus more on other factors affecting heart health.

What this means for you: Before you consider whether to use a statin, talk to your doctor about active steps you can take to reduce your risk with a healthier lifestyle…

- **If you smoke, stop!**

- **Improve your diet by curbing saturated fats…**and boosting "good" fats like those in olive oil and nuts.

- **Get regular exercise.**

- **Control your blood pressure.** If diet, weight loss, exercise and stress control do not bring your readings below 140/90 mmHg, talk to your doctor about blood pressure medication.

- **Lose weight if you need to.** Excess body weight not only raises your risk for heart disease but also makes you more vulnerable to diabetes—a major risk factor for heart attack and stroke in its own right.

Step 4: **Remember to think for yourself.** At best, guidelines can provide information about your risk of having a heart attack, stroke or dying and suggest strategies to modify it. But remember, the risk calculator provides no more than an estimate of your risk and should be used as only part of your assessment.

What's more, guidelines cannot say whether the benefit of taking medication is worth the risk to you. Statins can have side effects, including muscle damage and increased risk for diabetes.

Important: There's little convincing evidence that the newer cholesterol-lowering drugs, including the higher-priced option *ezetimibe* (Zetia), are as effective as statins. So don't take them unless you can't use statins because of side effects and until you have had a thorough discussion with your doctor.

Also, guidelines don't factor in your feelings about taking a drug simply on the chance—not with a guarantee—that it will make you healthier and perhaps live longer. Given the same facts, one person will choose treatment and another will not, and they can both be right based on their preferences and goals.

What it means for you: Use the guidelines as the starting point for a conversation with your doctor about treatment—not as the answer. Ultimately, the decision is yours.

More from Dr. Krumholz

Key Points of the New Statin Guidelines

According to recent guidelines issued by the American Heart Association and American College of Cardiology,* statins are recommended for people who have…

• **Cardiovascular disease.** This includes those with a history of heart attack, angina, stroke or transient ischemic attack or anyone who has undergone a procedure, such as angioplasty, to widen arteries.

• **Extremely high LDL "bad" cholesterol levels (190 mg/dL or above).**

• **Type 2 diabetes** and are ages 40 to 75.

• **An estimated 10-year risk for cardiovascular disease of 7.5% or higher,** based on the online calculator, and are ages 40 to 75.**

*The 2016 USPSTF report complies with these guidelines.

**To access the online risk calculator, go to the American Heart Association website, *www.heart.org*. Search for "Risk Calculator for Cardiovascular Disease."

The Great Big Statin Sham

David M. Diamond, PhD, professor, departments of psychology and molecular pharmacology and physiology and director of the USF Neuroscience Collaborative and the USF Center for Preclinical and Clinical Research Post-Traumatic Stress Disorder, University of South Florida, Tampa. His article appeared in *Expert Review of Clinical Pharmacology*.

Those so-called "wonder" drugs that help reduce cholesterol—the statins (Lipitor, Crestor and Zocor, to name a few)—aren't anywhere close to being all they're hyped up to be. Sure, they reduce cholesterol, but their use is fraught with questions. In fact, the hype on statins can be considered a statistical deception.

A review of several statin studies found that the results are often framed in ways that make them seem much more promising or beneficial than they really are. A major study called JUPITER, for example, shows how statistical data can be reported to overexaggerate benefit. JUPITER, stands for "Justification for the Use of Statins in Primary Prevention: An Intervention Trial Evaluating Rosuvastatin." The results of this study were used back in 2008 to get FDA approval to use *rosuvastatin* (Crestor) to help prevent heart disease in healthy people. Before that time, it was approved for use only in people who were known to be at high risk for heart attack and stroke.

The JUPITER trial compared Crestor to a placebo in 17,800 healthy people. The study results showed that, overall, a mere 0.76% of people taking the placebo had heart attacks, strokes or other major cardiovascular events compared with 0.35% of people taking Crestor—in both groups, less than 1% of participants. But in a press release about the study, the manufacturers of Crestor reported that the statin reduced the risk of heart attack "by more than half" because the percentage difference between 0.76 and 0.35 is 54 ("more than half"). Results were then framed in a similar way at a major medical meeting and published in the journal *Circulation*. Although the percentage of risk reduction was technically accurate, it alone completely failed to convey the fact that the absolute amount of risk even for the group that didn't take the drug was very small—less than 1%!

Other major studies engendered similar over-statements about the benefits of one or another statin. Take, for example, the study results that the manufacturer of Lipitor emblazoned on ads placed in medical journals—that Lipitor (known generically as *atorvastatin*) "reduces risk of heart attack by 36% in patients with multiple risk factors for heart disease." In the Lipitor study, which included 10,305 people who had high blood pressure and at least three other risk factors for heart disease, 3% of the people on placebo had heart attacks within three years versus 1.9% of the people on Lipitor, leading to a risk reduction rate of 36% using the same math as was used in the JUPITER study. A similar scenario was illustrated in a major study of *simvastatin*, marketed as Zocor.

THE CHOLESTEROL MYTH

Profit may be a driving force behind America's "high cholesterol" epidemic and drugs to keep it under control. Consider that more than 200 million statin prescriptions are written in the US each year—we're talking $26 billion in revenue for pharmaceutical companies. And if the updated clinical guidelines from the American College of Cardiology and American Heart Association are followed, 46 million more Americans may end up on statins. These guidelines recommend statin treatment for diabetics and almost all of the elderly. Not surprisingly, eight of the 15 panelists who created these guidelines have extensive ties to the pharmaceutical industry.

Doctors are pushing statins on us based on the fact that cholesterol is found in tissue that has become atherosclerotic, but there's no concrete evidence that cholesterol causes coronary heart disease. In older adults, atherosclerosis is found equally in those with high and low cholesterol. And you can have high levels of "bad" cholesterol (low-density lipoproteins) and not be at increased risk of heart disease and vice versa.

Lipoproteins (cholesterol and other blood fats called triglycerides) play a major role in our immune systems, and it's perhaps inaccurate to label them "good" or "bad." Low cholesterol levels have been linked to viral infection and cancer—there are several large and long-term studies showing associations between low cholesterol levels, use of statins as well as other cholesterol-lowering drugs and cancer risk. There are also several studies showing that low cholesterol is associated with neurological and mood disorders, including violent behavior, depression, suicide and dementia. In fact, there are two studies that showed that cognitive function improved in adults with memory problems or dementia when statin medication was stopped and returned when it was restarted.

THE ALTERNATIVE

You won't find good health in a pill. For the vast majority of people, the secret to longevity and to reducing the risk of heart disease is in weight and stress control, moderate exercise and maintaining a healthy diet. This means reducing the amount of sugar and fried foods you eat and, if you eat red meat or dairy, choosing natural sources of saturated fats that are free from antibiotics and hormones that can wreak havoc on your metabolism. These include grass-fed beef, eggs from free-range chickens, and butter and cheese from grass-fed cows.

Take This Test Before Starting a Statin

Before starting a statin, have a coronary artery calcium (CAC) test, advises Khurram Nasir, MD, MPH. The CAC test more accurately predicts cardiovascular risk than factors such as cholesterol, blood pressure, current smoking and diabetes. In 35% of people considered high risk according to those factors, a CAC test showed that risk was relatively low and could be managed by lifestyle modifications instead of medication. The test is widely available… takes about three minutes…and costs $75 to $100, which may be covered by insurance.

Khurram Nasir, MD, MPH, a cardiovascular disease specialist and director of Center for Prevention and Wellness at Baptist Health South Florida, Miami Beach. He is senior author of a study published in *European Heart Journal*.

Certain Statin Dangers Are Unique to Women: What You Need to Know

Beatrice A. Golomb, MD, PhD, a professor of medicine at the University of California, San Diego School of Medicine and lead author of a research letter published in *Archives of Internal Medicine* (now *JAMA Internal Medicine*). The findings in this study stem from a larger study that focused on statins' effects on thinking, mood and behavior.

Chances are that you or someone you love is taking a cholesterol-lowering statin medication. But these drugs can have numerous side effects, including muscle pain, liver damage, digestive problems, memory loss, even life-threatening muscle damage. Now a recent study adds two more side effects to that list…and, sorry to say, women are particularly likely to be affected.

The study involved 1,016 generally healthy adults who had moderately elevated levels of LDL (bad) cholesterol and no heart disease or diabetes. Participants were randomly assigned to take either a placebo…*simvastatin* (Zocor) at 20 mg…or *pravastatin* (Pravachol) at 40 mg. (These are standard, relatively modest statin dosages.) The capsules, taken daily for six months, looked identical, and neither the participants nor the researchers knew at the time which group was receiving which treatment. At the end of the study, participants reported how much energy they had, comparing how they felt after six months on the pills with how they had felt at the start of the study. They used a five-point scale ranging from "much less" to "much more" to rate their energy level and degree of exertional fatigue (such as fatigue during exercise).

Findings: Statin users were much more likely than placebo users to experience a decrease in energy…worsened exertional fatigue…or both. These side effects were somewhat worse with simvastatin than with pravastatin (though simvastatin was more effective at reducing cholesterol)…and were significantly more pronounced in women than in men. In fact, among female simvas-

tatin users, four out of 10 experienced one type of energy loss, while two out of 10 reported both types of energy loss.

Worrisome: Researchers noted that this side effect could signal some mechanism by which statins adversely affect cell health.

About 25% of Americans ages 45 and up take statins. *If you are among them and you feel that the drug is sapping your energy…*

• **Request that your doctor factor in your fatigue when gauging the drug's benefits versus its risks.** This is particularly important for patients for whom statins have not been shown to prolong life—groups that include women…people without heart disease…and seniors over age 70, even if they do have heart disease.

• **Discuss whether you can reduce your statin dosage** or switch to a different medication to see if your side effects lessen.

• **Ask your doctor about dietary and lifestyle changes** that may help lower your cholesterol to the point that statins would no longer be recommended.

Bonus: Such lifestyle changes should give you an energy boost, too.

Do Statins Really Raise Risk for Diabetes?

According to recent research, people taking high doses of the cholesterol-lowering drugs had a 12% higher risk for diabetes than those taking moderate statin doses. And users of high doses had a 20% higher risk for diabetes than people who do not take statins at all. But doctors say these statistics may be misleading. Statins increase blood sugar only a little, which may push a few patients over the threshold for diagnosis of diabetes. Most experts agree that the cardiovascular benefits of statin use far outweigh the increase in diabetes risk.

Steven E. Nissen, MD, chairman of cardiology, Cleveland Clinic.

If You Don't Want to Take a Statin…Here Are Natural Ways to Reduce Your Heart Attack Risk

Allan Magaziner, DO, an osteopathic physician and the founder and director of the Magaziner Center for Wellness in Cherry Hill, New Jersey. Dr. Magaziner is coauthor of *The All-Natural Cardio Cure: A Drug-Free Cholesterol and Cardiac Inflammation Reduction Program.* DrMagaziner.com

As the controversial new guidelines on statins begin to kick into use in doctors' offices around the country, the number of Americans for whom these drugs will be recommended is expected to double. But plenty of people don't like to take any type of prescription medication if they can avoid it.

Most integrative physicians, who prescribe natural therapies (and drugs when needed), agree that the majority of people who take statins—and most of those who will be recommended to do so under the new guidelines—could get many of the same benefits, such as lower cholesterol and inflammation levels, with fewer risks, by relying on targeted food choices (see examples on the next page) and supplements. Exercise—ideally, about 30 minutes at least five days a week—should also be part of a healthy-heart regimen.

The natural regimen that I've fine-tuned over the past 25 years for my patients…

THE BEST CHOLESTEROL-LOWERING SUPPLEMENTS

• **Fish oil (typical daily dose.** 1,000 mg total of EPA and DHA) fights inflammation, lowers LDL "bad" cholesterol and is part of most good heart-protective regimens.* In addition, I recommend using the first supplement below and adding the other three supplements if total cholesterol levels don't drop below 200 mg/dL…

• **Red yeast rice.** You have probably heard of this rice, which is fermented to produce

*Talk to your doctor before taking any of these supplements—they may interact with medications or affect certain chronic health conditions.

monacolins, chemical compounds with statin-like effects. It can lower LDL cholesterol by roughly 30%.

Red yeast rice can be a good alternative for people who can't tolerate statins due to side effects such as muscle aches and increased risk for diabetes. Red yeast rice also has other natural protective substances, such as isoflavones, fatty acids and sterols, not found in statins.

Typical dosage: 1.2 g to 2.4 g daily. I advise starting with 1.2 g daily. The dose can be increased as needed, based on your physician's advice.

What I tell my patients: Unfortunately, red yeast rice has gotten a bad rap because of the way some products were labeled. The supplements that I recommend are manufactured with high standards of quality control and contain therapeutic levels of active ingredients.

Good products: Choleast by Thorne Research, *www.thorne.com*…and High Performance Formulas' Cholestene, *www.hpfonline. com.*

When taking red yeast rice, some people have heartburn, gastrointestinal (GI) upset or mild headache—these effects usually are eliminated by taking the supplement with food.

• **Pantethine.** You may not be familiar with this supplement, a form of pantothenic acid (vitamin B-5). Recent studies show that it raises HDL cholesterol—and it prevents LDL from oxidizing, the process that causes it to cling to arteries.

Typical dosage: 900 mg, divided into two or three doses daily. Good pantethine products are made by Jarrow, *www.jarrow.com*… and NOW Foods, *www.nowfoods.com.*

What I tell my patients: Take pantethine with meals to reduce the risk for indigestion and to aid absorption.

• **Sterols and stanols.** These cholesterol-lowering plant compounds are found in small amounts in many fruits, vegetables and grains. But sterol and stanol supplements are much more powerful. In supplement form, the plant compounds reduce LDL by about 14% and cause no side effects.

Typical dosage: Take 3 g of a sterol/stanol supplement daily. Pure Encapsulations makes a good product, *www.pureencapsulations.com.*

Most integrative physicians are very knowledgeable about natural remedies. To find one in your area, consult the American College for Advancement in Medicine at *www.acam.org.*

YUMMY CHOLESTEROL FIGHTERS

For years, oat bran and oatmeal were touted as the best foods for high cholesterol. Rich in soluble fiber, these foods help prevent cholesterol from getting into the bloodstream. A daily serving of oats, for example, can lower LDL by 20%. Other good foods rich in soluble fiber include barley, beans, pears and prunes. But research has now gone beyond these old standby food choices. *Here are some other fiber-rich foods that have been found to give cholesterol the heave-ho…*

•**All nuts.** Walnuts and almonds are great cholesterol fighters, but so are pistachios, peanuts, pecans, hazelnuts and other nuts, according to recent research. Eat a handful (1.5 ounces) of nuts daily.

•**Popcorn actually contains more fiber per ounce than whole-wheat bread.** Just go easy on the salt and butter, and stay away from store-bought microwave popcorn (it can contain harmful chemicals).

Smart idea: Put one-quarter cup of organic plain popcorn in a lunch-size brown paper bag, and pop in the microwave. It's delicious—and there's no cleanup.

Make Cholesterol a Laughing Matter

Lee Berk, MPH, DrPH, associate professor of Allied Health and Pathology, Schools of Allied Health Professions and Medicine, Loma Linda University, Loma Linda, California.

Laughter is great medicine…it's not just a platitude. Nor should this come as a surprise, since previous studies regarding laughter have noted its impact on cardiovascular risk, blood pressure and stress. The latest finding is that it even can lower cholesterol.

In research presented at the 2009 meeting of The American Physiological Society, 20 high-risk diabetic patients who had both hypertension and high cholesterol were divided into two groups. One group received standard pharmaceutical treatments for diabetes (*metformin*, TZD and *glipizide*), hypertension (ACE inhibitors) and high cholesterol (statin drugs), while the second group received the same medication, but also were instructed to watch 30 minutes a day of humorous videos. Since different people find different things funny, participants were able to select their own.

LAUGHING ALL THE WAY TO GOOD HEALTH

By the end of the second month, the benefits were already evident. By the end of one year, the laughter group had increased their "good" cholesterol by 26% (compared with 3% for the control group) while also decreasing C-reactive protein, an inflammatory marker, by 66% (versus 26% in the control group). In addition, over the course of the year-long study, only one patient in the laughter group suffered a heart attack—compared with three in the control group.

"The benefits we see with laughter are very similar to what we see with moderate exercise," noted researchers Lee Berk, DrPH, of Loma Linda University and Stanley Tan, MD, PhD, of Oak Crest Research Institute. Dr. Berk has even coined a term—Laughercise—to describe the benefits of therapeutic laughter. This newest finding builds upon previous research by the same team in which laughter was found to boost blood flow to the heart. Dr. Berk said that further studies are planned to determine how long this positive effect will last.

HEALING POWER OF LAUGHTER

Dr. Berk said that "it's clear that the repetitive use of laughter produces physiological changes that lower stress hormones, increase endorphins, and—in our studies—lower risk factors for heart disease, including inflammation and cholesterol."

How Garlic Guards Against Heart Disease, Cancer and Infections

Ellen Tattelman, MD, director of the faculty development fellowship at the Residency Program in Social Medicine at Montefiore Medical Center in New York City. She is an assistant professor of family and social medicine at Albert Einstein College of Medicine of Yeshiva University, also in New York City, where she organizes the integrative medicine curriculum. Dr. Tattelman specializes in a variety of integrative modalities, including herbal therapy and nutrition.

Garlic is one of the most exhaustively researched herbs—the National Library of Medicine's website lists more than 3,700 studies addressing garlic's effect on everything from elevated cholesterol and various types of cancer to fungal infections.

So why is there still so much confusion about the health benefits of garlic?

Even though garlic has been used medicinally by some cultures for thousands of years, much of the contemporary research on garlic is mixed—some studies show that it has positive effects, while others indicate no significant benefits.

Here's what the research shows…

HEART HEALTH

Over the years, scientists have investigated garlic's ability to reduce cholesterol levels and blood pressure and act as an anticlotting agent to prevent blood platelets from being too sticky—a main cause of heart attack.

Key scientific finding: A recent meta-analysis in China looked at 26 randomized, double-blind, placebo-controlled trials—the "gold standard" in scientific research. In that meta-analysis, researchers concluded that garlic reduces total cholesterol by 5.4% and triglyceride levels by 6.5% compared with a placebo. Garlic powder and aged garlic extract were found to be the most effective at lowering total cholesterol, while garlic oil had a greater effect on lowering triglyceride levels.

When it comes to high blood pressure, some credible research shows that garlic can help lower it.

Important scientific findings: Two meta-analyses showed that garlic reduced systolic (top number) blood pressure by 8 mmHg to 16 mmHg and diastolic (bottom number) blood pressure by 7 mmHg to 9 mmHg in people with high blood pressure.

As for garlic's antiplatelet effect—that is, its ability to make blood less sticky and therefore less prone to clotting—a meta-analysis of 10 trials showed a modest, but significant, decrease in platelet clumping with garlic treatment when compared with placebos in most of the studies.

Bottom line: Garlic does help reduce risk for cardiovascular disease, with positive effects on both total cholesterol and blood pressure. It also has enough of an effect on clotting that I recommend patients discontinue garlic supplements seven to 10 days before surgery because it may prolong bleeding.

My advice: If you have a personal or family history of heart disease, ask your doctor about using garlic (in food or supplements) as part of a heart-healthy lifestyle. Be sure to consult your doctor first if you take a blood pressure or statin drug.

CANCER

Large population studies have shown that people who live in countries where a lot of garlic is eaten—as well as onions and chives—are at lower risk for certain cancers.

Key scientific findings: In China, high intake of garlic and other alliums, including onions, was associated with a reduced risk for esophageal and stomach cancers. Specifically, the study found that people who ate alliums at least once a week had lower incidence of both forms of cancer than people who ate these foods less than once a month.

Meanwhile, the European Prospective Investigation into Cancer and Nutrition, which involves 10 different countries, found that higher intakes of garlic and onions lowered the risk for intestinal cancer.

My advice: If you are concerned about cancer—especially if you have a family history or other risk factors for stomach or esophageal cancer—include one to two cloves of garlic in your diet each day.

INFECTIONS

Historically, garlic has received attention as a potent antibacterial agent. In 1858, Louis Pasteur touted garlic as an antibiotic. Garlic was later used in World War I and World War II as an antiseptic to prevent gangrene.

Bottom line: There have been few contemporary studies looking at the use of garlic to treat infections. However, preliminary research suggests that it may reduce the frequency and duration of colds when taken for prevention and may speed the healing of a fungal infection or wart.

My advice: For most people, garlic is worth trying as a preventive/treatment for these infections (see options described below).

SHOULD YOU USE GARLIC?

It's wise to make garlic part of a healthful diet that includes plenty of fruits, vegetables, whole grains and fiber.

Caution: Consuming large quantities of garlic—either in the diet or as a supplement—may cause body odor and/or bad breath. Chewing a sprig of fresh green parsley, mint or cardamom can work as a breath freshener. Hot tea also can help by rinsing away garlic oil still in your mouth. Drinking a glass of milk—full-fat or fat-free—may be effective as well. Garlic, especially on an empty stomach, can cause gastrointestinal upset and flatulence.

Because garlic may also interact with certain prescription drugs, such as *warfarin* (Coumadin), consult your doctor before significantly increasing your intake of the herb if you take any medication or have a chronic medical condition.

Options to consider…

•**Raw garlic.** If you prefer raw garlic, try eating one or two cloves a day. You can chew and swallow it or use it in pesto, guacamole or a salad dressing. Cooked garlic is less powerful medicinally—heat inactivates the enzyme that breaks down alliin, the chemical precursor to allicin.

•**Aged garlic extract (AGE).** If you prefer liquid, AGE is available in this form, which is popular in Europe. Follow label instructions.

•**Powdered garlic supplements.** These are typically sold as capsules or tablets and standardized to contain 1.3% alliin. They usually contain 300 mg.

Typical dose: Two or three capsules or tablets a day.

FACTS ABOUT GARLIC

Garlic has been used since ancient times as a medicinal remedy. It is a member of the allium family of plants, which also includes onions, chives and leeks. Garlic's medicinal powers are attributed to its sulfur compounds, including a substance called allicin, which is formed when garlic is crushed or chopped. Besides fresh cloves, garlic is available in supplement form made from fresh, dried or freeze-dried garlic, garlic oil and aged garlic extracts.

Surgery Better for Some Patients

For diabetes patients with severe heart disease, bypass surgery is more effective than medication.

Recent finding: Only 22.4% of diabetes patients with severe coronary disease who had immediate bypass surgery died or had a heart attack or stroke within the next five years, versus 30.5% who elected to take medication instead.

Study of 2,368 people by researchers at University of Pittsburgh Graduate School of Public Health, presented at a recent meeting of the American Diabetes Association.

Certain Diabetes Drugs Can Raise Heart Disease Risk

Overall, thiazolidinediones (TZDs), such as *rosiglitazone* (Avandia) and *pioglitazone* (Actos), raise heart-failure risk by 42%. Overall, dipeptidyl peptidase-4 (DPP-4) inhibitors, including *saxagliptin* and *alogliptin*, raise heart-failure risk by about 25%.

Good news: If you are overweight, losing weight to control blood sugar reduces the risk.

Jacob A. Udell, MD, MPH, a cardiologist at Women's College Hospital, Peter Munk Cardiac Centre, Toronto General Hospital and University of Toronto, all in Toronto, Canada. He was principal investigator in a study published in *The Lancet Diabetes & Endocrinology*.

Apples Reduce Cardiovascular Deaths Nearly as Well as Statins Do—Without Dangerous Side Effects

Adam D.M. Briggs, MD, academic clinical fellow, British Heart Foundation Health Promotion Research Group, Nuffield Department of Population Health, University of Oxford, Oxford, UK. His study was published in *BMJ*.

A raging controversy was ignited when new statin drug guidelines were released here in the US in 2013. Many experts, critical of the new guidelines, argued that far too many people would be pushed onto statins needlessly—people who did not have heart disease or high cholesterol and whose risk for heart attack or stroke was small. The critics said that the benefits of cholesterol-lowering drugs were vastly overstated…the drugs' potential risks, including severe muscle damage and diabetes, were understated…and that short shrift was given to the dietary and lifestyle changes that safely reduce cardiovascular risk.

A newer study from across the Atlantic makes a creative and compelling argument supporting the dietary approach rather than the sweeping use of statins. Researchers figured out a way to compare the potential effects on cardiovascular death rates of widespread statin use with the widespread adoption of one very simple and delicious habit—eating an extra apple a day.

BRITISH MATH MODEL

For the new study, researchers developed mathematical models using data from previously published scientific studies. First they considered how many deaths from cardiovascular causes (stroke, heart attack, heart failure, abdominal aortic aneurysm) might be prevented if statins were prescribed to everyone in the UK age 50 or older, not just to those with high cholesterol or other cardiovascular risk factors. Based on general compliance rates found in other studies, they estimated that 70% of people would comply with the statin recommendation…and that this widespread statin use would prevent 9,400 deaths per year.

Next they considered how many annual cardiovascular deaths would be avoided if everyone in the UK age 50 or older added one apple to his/her daily diet, eliminating something else with the same number of calories (about 50 calories for a small, 100-gram apple). It was presumed that people who were currently taking statins would continue on the medication while also adding the daily apple to their diets, not that current statin users would switch from the drug to the fruit. Again assuming that just 70% of the population complied with the "apple prescription," the researchers calculated that those daily apples would prevent 8,500 cardiovascular deaths per year in the UK—which is pretty close to the benefit estimated for widespread use of statins. (You don't fancy apples? That's OK—surprisingly, the researchers noted that the same number of deaths prevented would also apply to other fruits.)

Apple advantage: Yes, the statins came out slightly ahead in raw numbers, topping apples by 900 lives saved. However, the researchers did not calculate the degree to which that 900-person difference might diminish if the side effects of statins were factored in. But they did estimate that, as a side effect of having 70% of people age 50 and up on statins, an additional 1,200 people in the UK would develop myopathy…200 would develop rhabdomyolysis (serious muscle damage that can lead to kidney failure…and another 12,300 would develop type 2 diabetes, which itself can be fatal. Apples, in contrast, do not cause any side effects…except perhaps, the researchers quipped, the distress caused by a bruised apple or the theoretical risk of identifying half a worm inside!

From the UK to the US: Comparing UK residents to US residents is a little like comparing, well, apples to oranges, given that the two populations have a different baseline cardiovascular risk status, age distribution and diet. However, we can say that the number of deaths averted if Americans added an apple a day to their diets could be about five times higher than the number of UK deaths averted, since the age 50-plus population of the US is about five times that of the UK.

This is not to say that all statin users should drop the drugs and switch to apples. For certain people at significant risk for heart attack or stroke, statins can be hugely beneficial—so the decision about whether to take the drugs is one that must be made by each individual in consultation with his/her doctor. But this study does add an interesting insight to the controversy about very widespread use of statins versus healthful lifestyle changes.

How apples may help: Apples (and other fruits) contain heart-healthy antioxidants and anti-inflammatory compounds. Apples also are rich in pectin, a dietary fiber that reduces cholesterol. If drug companies could patent apples and corner the market on them, you bet they would try! Luckily they can't, and we can all eat heart-healthy foods—including an apple a day—to help keep the heart doctor away.

Small Drops in Blood Pressure Can Save Individuals with Type 2 Diabetes—Reduce Risk of Dying by One-Fifth

Anne Peters, MD, director, University of Southern California (USC) Westside Center for Diabetes, Beverly Hills, California.

Type 2 diabetes is now considered a global pandemic, which is alarming since many people who have this disease will eventually be disabled by or even die from complications of it. That's the bad news. The good news is that you can reduce your risk of heart attack, stroke and kidney disease—three common complications, often fatal—by bringing your blood pressure (BP) down, even by just a little. About 73% of adults with diabetes have high blood pressure (defined in this case as greater than or equal to 130/80 mm Hg) or use prescription medications for hypertension. Research demonstrates that treatment with blood pressure drugs can reduce the risk of dying by one-fifth, generally with few side effects.

LOWER BLOOD PRESSURE = BETTER OUTCOMES

People with diabetes are extra-sensitive to changes in blood pressure, explains Anne Peters, MD, director of the University of Southern California (USC) Westside Center for Diabetes in Beverly Hills. The ADVANCE (Action in Diabetes and Vascular Disease) trial, involving more than 11,000 people with type 2 diabetes from 20 countries, clearly demonstrated that lowering blood pressure significantly improved certain outcomes. It should be noted that the trial was funded by Servier, the manufacturer of Preterax, and the National Health and Medical Research Council of Australia.

Participants were randomly given the blood pressure drug Preterax—a combination of the ACE inhibitor *perindopril* and the diuretic *indapamide*—or a placebo, and were followed for more than four years. Researchers found that treatment with Preterax significantly reduced the risk of serious complications of diabetes. Specifically, those who took Preterax…

• **Reduced their risk of death from cardiovascular disease by 18%.**

• **Cut their risk of kidney-related events by 21%.**

• **Lowered their risk of death from any cause by 14%.**

The findings were published online in the September 2, 2007, issue of *The Lancet.*

MORE AGGRESSIVE TREATMENT REQUIRED IN PEOPLE WITH DIABETES

Commenting on the study, Dr. Peters said that in her view, the improvements were small and actually less than she would have expected. She said that physicians treat blood pressure more aggressively in people with diabetes, typically prescribing medications for those whose pressure is above 130/80. Participants in the ADVANCE trial had a far higher mean starting BP of 145/81, and were only treated to an average of 135/75—an improvement, to be sure, but one that doesn't go far enough to reach target levels for people with diabetes.

That said, Dr. Peters notes that the study does add to the literature that even small reductions in blood pressure are beneficial. Also, she said, ace inhibitors and diuretics have long track records for safety and effectiveness in people with diabetes, as well as those who don't have the disease. Generic versions of these blood pressure–lowering drugs are also available.

We asked naturopathic doctor Andrew Rubman, ND, whether these results could be achieved without pharmaceutical drugs. He believes they could and suggests beginning with dietary and lifestyle modifications. "Specifically, calcium and magnesium are important for both hypertension and adult-onset diabetes," he says, but notes that managing blood pressure to target levels for a person with diabetes is complicated and requires specialized care. "Just as you'd not take heart medications without oversight from a cardiologist, you can't treat a medical condition with supplements without specialist oversight."

---

5 Foods That Fight High Blood Pressure (You Might Not Even Need Medication)

Janet Bond Brill, PhD, RD, a nationally recognized nutrition, health and fitness expert who specializes in cardiovascular disease prevention. She has authored several books on the topic, including *Blood Pressure DOWN, Prevent a Second Heart Attack* and *Cholesterol DOWN*. DrJanet.com

---

I s your blood pressure on the high side? Your doctor might write a prescription when it creeps above 140/90—but you may be able to forgo medication. Lifestyle changes still are considered the best starting treatment for mild hypertension. These include not smoking, regular exercise and a healthy diet. *In addition to eating less salt, you want to include potent pressure-lowering foods, including...*

RAISINS

Raisins are basically dehydrated grapes, but they provide a much more concentrated dose of nutrients and fiber. They are high in potassium, with 220 milligrams (mg) in a small box (1.5 ounces). Potassium helps counteract the blood pressure–raising effects of salt. The more potassium we consume, the more sodium our bodies excrete. Researchers also speculate that the fiber and antioxidants in raisins change the biochemistry of blood vessels, making them more pliable—important for healthy blood pressure. Opt for dark raisins over light-colored ones because dark raisins have more catechins, a powerful type of antioxidant that can increase blood flow.

Researchers at Louisville Metabolic and Atherosclerosis Research Center compared people who snacked on raisins with those who ate other packaged snacks. Those in the raisin group had drops in systolic pressure (the top number) ranging from 4.8 points (after four weeks) to 10.2 points (after 12 weeks). Blood pressure barely budged in the no-raisin group. Some people worry about the sugar in raisins, but it is natural sugar (not added sugar) and will not adversely affect your health (though people with diabetes need to be cautious with portion sizes).

My advice: Aim to consume a few ounces of raisins every day. Prunes are an alternative.

BEETS

Beets, too, are high in potassium, with about 519 mg per cup. They're delicious, easy to cook (see the tasty recipe on page 276) and very effective for lowering blood pressure.

A study at The London Medical School found that people who drank about eight ounces of beet juice averaged a 10-point drop in blood pressure during the next 24 hours. The blood pressure–lowering effect was most pronounced at three to six hours past drinking but remained lower for the entire 24 hours.

Eating whole beets might be even better because you will get extra fiber.

Along with fiber and potassium, beets also are high in nitrate. The nitrate is converted first to nitrite in the blood, then to nitric oxide. Nitric oxide is a gas that relaxes blood vessel walls and lowers blood pressure.

My advice: Eat beets several times a week. Look for beets that are dark red. They contain more protective phytochemicals than the gold or white beets. Cooked spinach and kale are alternatives.

DAIRY

In research involving nearly 45,000 people, researchers found that those who consumed low-fat "fluid" dairy foods, such as yogurt and low-fat milk, were 16% less likely to develop high blood pressure. Higher-fat forms of dairy, such as cheese and ice cream, had no blood pressure benefits. The study was published in *Journal of Human Hypertension*.

In another study, published in *The New England Journal of Medicine*, researchers found that people who included low-fat or fat-free dairy in a diet high in fruits and vegetables had double the blood pressure–lowering benefits of those who just ate the fruits and veggies.

Low-fat dairy is high in calcium, another blood pressure–lowering mineral that should be included in your diet. When you don't have enough calcium in your diet, a "calcium leak" occurs in your kidneys. This means that the kidneys excrete more calcium in the urine, disturbing the balance of mineral metabolism involved in blood pressure regulation.

My advice: Aim for at least one serving of low-fat or nonfat milk or yogurt every day. If you don't care for cow's milk or can't drink it, switch to fortified soy milk. It has just as much calcium and protein and also contains phytoestrogens, compounds that are good for the heart.

FLAXSEED

Flaxseed contains alpha-linolenic acid (ALA), an omega-3 fatty acid that helps prevent heart and vascular disease. Flaxseed also contains magnesium. A shortage of magnesium in our diet throws off the balance of sodium, potassium and calcium, which causes the blood vessels to constrict.

Flaxseed also is high in flavonoids, the same antioxidants that have boosted the popularity of dark chocolate, kale and red wine. Flavonoids are bioactive chemicals that reduce inflammation throughout the body, including in the arteries. Arterial inflammation is thought to be the "trigger" that leads to high blood pressure, blood clots and heart attacks.

In a large-scale observational study linking dietary magnesium intake with better heart health and longevity, nearly 59,000 healthy Japanese people were followed for 15 years. The scientists found that the people with the highest dietary intake of magnesium had a 50% reduced risk for death from heart disease (heart attack and stroke). According to the researchers, magnesium's heart-healthy benefit is linked to its ability to improve blood pressure, suppress irregular heartbeats and inhibit inflammation.

My advice: Add one or two tablespoons of ground flaxseed to breakfast cereals. You also can sprinkle flaxseed on yogurt or whip it into a breakfast smoothie. Or try chia seeds.

WALNUTS

Yale researchers found that people who ate two ounces of walnuts a day had improved blood flow and drops in blood pressure (a 3.5-point drop in systolic blood pressure and a 2.8-point drop in diastolic blood pressure). The mechanisms through which walnuts elicit a blood pressure–lowering response are believed to involve their high content of monounsaturated fatty acids, omega-3 ALA, magnesium and fiber, and their low levels of sodium and saturated fatty acids.

Bonus: Despite the reputation of nuts as a "fat snack," the people who ate them didn't gain weight.

The magnesium in walnuts is particularly important. It limits the amount of calcium that enters muscle cells inside artery walls. Ingesting the right amount of calcium (not too much and not too little) on a daily basis is essential for optimal blood pressure regulation. Magnesium regulates calcium's movement across the membranes of the smooth muscle cells, deep within the artery walls.

If your body doesn't have enough magnesium, too much calcium will enter the smooth muscle cells, which causes the arterial muscles to tighten, putting a squeeze on the arteries and raising blood pressure. Magnesium works like the popular calcium channel blockers, drugs that block entry of calcium into arterial walls, lowering blood pressure.

My advice: Eat two ounces of walnuts every day. Or choose other nuts such as almonds and pecans.

DR. JANET'S ROASTED RED BEETS WITH LEMON VINAIGRETTE

Beets are a delicious side dish when roasted, peeled and topped with a lemony vinaigrette and fresh parsley. This recipe is from my book *Prevent a Second Heart Attack*.

6 medium-sized beets, washed and trimmed of greens and roots

2 Tablespoons extra-virgin olive oil

2 teaspoons fresh lemon juice

1 garlic clove, peeled and minced

1 teaspoon Dijon mustard

¼ teaspoon kosher salt

¼ teaspoon freshly ground black pepper

¼ cup chopped fresh flat-leaf Italian parsley

Preheat the oven to 400°F. Spray a baking dish with nonstick cooking spray. Place the beets in the dish, and cover tightly with foil. Bake the beets for about one hour or until they are tender when pierced with a fork or thin knife. Remove from the oven, and allow to cool to the touch.

Meanwhile, in a small bowl, whisk together the olive oil, lemon juice, garlic, mustard, salt and pepper for the dressing. When the beets are cool enough to handle, peel and slice the beets, arranging the slices on a platter. Drizzle with vinaigrette, and garnish with parsley. Serves six.

Soy Lowers Blood Pressure Naturally

Safiya Richardson, MD, physician, Northwell Health, Great Neck, New York. The study was performed while she was a medical student at Columbia University's College of Physicians and Surgeons in New York City.

Trying to keep your blood pressure in check?

Eating soy-based foods, such as tofu, soybeans, soy milk and soybean chips, may help, according to a recent study from Columbia University's College of Physicians and Surgeons. The isoflavones that are found in large quantities in most soy products (and in smaller quantities in a few other foods, such as split peas, peanuts and kidney beans) help relax the blood vessels.

But loading up on soy isn't without its own risks—soy is estrogenic, meaning it mimics the effect of the hormone estrogen in the body. And the concern is that consuming it in excess might raise the risk for estrogen-sensitive diseases such as certain types of breast cancer and prostate cancer.

So exactly how little soy can you consume and still get help with your blood pressure?

YOU DON'T HAVE TO EAT MUCH

We spoke with Safiya Richardson, MD, the lead researcher and a physician at Northwell Health in Great Neck, New York. She and her colleagues compared a teeny-tiny intake of isoflavones (less than 0.33 milligrams per day or about one-fifth of a tablespoon of soy milk) to relatively larger intakes of isoflavones.

The results? The more isoflavones that people ate, the lower their systolic blood pressure was.

Those who ate the most (2.5 mg or more per day) had, on average, 5.5 points lower systolic pressure, compared with those who ate the least (less than 0.33 mg per day). Even those who ate between 0.33 mg and 2.5 mg per day had blood pressure that was, on average, 2 to 3.5 points lower, compared with those who ate the least.

So this study suggests that if you're trying to keep your blood pressure under control but you're concerned about eating large amounts of soy to get large amounts of isoflavones, even eating as little as just 0.33 mg of isoflavones per day may help (but, of course, this study showed only an association—not cause and effect).

EASY TO SNEAK IN

Lots of different foods made from soy contain isoflavones (although soybean oil and soy sauce do not—the isoflavones get processed out). If you want to consume more isoflavones, keep reading for a list of isoflavone-packed soy foods.

What about overdoing it? "Soy has estrogenic properties, but I don't know of any studies that have proven that eating soy has harmful effects," said Dr. Richardson. She doesn't see a reason to hold back, but the issue is controversial. Some doctors advise certain people to either limit soy intake or avoid soy altogether—these people include those who have been diagnosed with (or are at high risk for) hormone-sensitive conditions, such as breast, ovarian, prostate or uterine cancer or endometriosis…women who are on hormone therapy…pregnant women…and people with thyroid or kidney problems. If you fall into one of those categories…if eating soy causes any side effects (such as stomach problems or migraines)…or if you're simply worried about consuming too much, consult your doctor before changing your diet.

If you take blood pressure medication and you add some soy to your diet, you might be able to reduce your need for the medication, said Dr. Richardson, so ask your doctor. As for isoflavone supplements, hold off. Dr. Richardson doesn't know what their effect on blood pressure would be.

One challenge to eating more foods that contain isoflavones is that isoflavone content is not listed on packaging, but here are some estimates from the USDA of the isoflavone content in particular soy products. As you'll see, eating just one serving of each of the following foods each day will provide your body with plenty of isoflavones—so if you are concerned about overdoing it on soy and are focused on eating the minimum amount of isoflavones (just 0.33 mg per day), you need to eat only a tiny fraction of a portion of any of the following foods…

- **100 grams (3.5 ounces) of soy flour, defatted = 151 mg isoflavones**
- **3.5 ounces (about ⅓ cup) of soybeans = 49 mg (raw), 18 mg (boiled)**
- **3.5 ounces (about seven pieces) of fried tofu = 35 mg isoflavones**
- **One 8-ounce glass of soy milk = 25 mg isoflavones**
- **One 1.3-ounce bag of soybean chips = 20 mg isoflavones**

It's also possible to consume extremely tiny amounts of isoflavones from nonsoy foods, such as split peas, peanuts and kidney beans. But to consume at least 0.33 mg or more isoflavones per day, stick with soy foods.

Eat Celery to Lower Blood Pressure

Jamey Wallace, ND, a naturopathic physician and chief medical officer at Bastyr Center for Natural Health, the teaching clinic of Bastyr University, in Kenmore, Washington.

If you've got high blood pressure or want to prevent it, you may want to stock up on celery. Why? Celery contains phthalides, chemicals that dilate the blood vessels and act as a diuretic, actions found in certain blood pressure–lowering drugs.

Some risks of high blood pressure are widely known (such as increased risk for heart attack and stroke). But high blood pressure also makes you more likely to develop dementia, kidney disease, eye disease, sleep apnea and sexual dysfunction. Normal blood pressure is less than 120/80.

What to do: For a consistent blood pressure–lowering effect, eat four medium-sized celery stalks per day. One easy way is to cut them into snack-sized pieces to munch on throughout the day—at midmorning, midafternoon and bedtime. (Talk to your doctor, though, if you have sun sensitivity—celery can increase skin reactions.)

Even better: Liven up your celery with other blood pressure–lowering foods—for example, hummus or nut butter (such as almond). People who eat these foods have lower blood pressure—possibly due to the foods' fiber and protein content.

Important: Four stalks of celery a day won't completely control high blood pressure. Use this remedy as part of an overall plan that includes increasing your intake of vegetables and fruits...exercising regularly...controlling your weight...reducing stress...and taking blood pressure medication, if necessary.

Also: Consult a physician familiar with natural therapies, if possible. Or talk with your regular doctor before you try this remedy—celery can interact with some medications.

The Sweet Snack That Does Wonders for Blood Pressure

Harold Bays, MD, medical director and president of the Louisville Metabolic and Atherosclerosis Research Center in Louisville, Kentucky, and principal investigator of a study on the effects of raisins on blood pressure, presented at the American College of Cardiology's 61st Annual Scientific Session.

It's good news when a health study produces scientific evidence in support of advice that seems sensible but previously lacked proof. And it's particularly nice when that advice deals with something sweet and yummy. In this case, the elusive scientific evidence supports the idea that raisins can reduce blood pressure.

Why is this important? Blood pressure that is even slightly elevated—a condition called prehypertension—increases the risk for heart attack, stroke and kidney disease. Prehypertension is defined as a systolic pressure (the top number in a blood pressure reading, as measured in "millimeters of mercury" or mmHg) of 120 to 139...or a diastolic pressure (the bottom number) of 80 to 89.

For the recent study, researchers randomly assigned 46 prehypertension patients, average age 61, to eat a snack three times a day for 12 weeks. For one group, each snack consisted of a one-ounce package of raisins. The other group ate prepackaged processed commercial snack foods, such as crackers or cookies, that did not contain raisins, other fruit or vegetables. The raisins and the other snacks each contained about 90 to 100 calories per serving. Participants' blood pressure was measured at the start of the study and after four, eight and 12 weeks.

Results: Blood pressure did not change significantly among participants in the commercial snacks group. In comparison, in the raisin group, systolic pressure decreased significantly, with reductions ranging from 5 mmHg to 7 mmHg—an amount that has cardiovascular benefits, clinical trial evidence suggests. Raisin eaters' diastolic pressure also dropped, though not as much.

Explanation: Raisins are high in potassium, a mineral that reduces blood pressure by promoting the proper balance of electrolytes and fluids in the body...helping offset the adverse effects of dietary sodium...and increasing the amount of sodium excreted via the urine. Raisins also have antioxidants and other components that may make blood vessels less stiff.

Best: If your blood pressure is elevated—or if your blood pressure is fine and you want to keep it that way—consider forgoing processed snack foods in favor of a handful of natural raisins. Not fond of raisins or crave more variety? Other potassium-rich snack options include bananas, cantaloupe, carrots, honeydew melon, papayas and yogurt.

The Mysterious Link Between Popcorn and Blood Pressure

In a recent study, researchers who reviewed health and nutrition data for 31,684 men found that those who consumed the most whole grains (about 52 g daily) were 19% less likely to develop high blood pressure than those who consumed the least whole grains (about 3 g daily).

Best sources: Oatmeal (instant or cooked)— one cup, 30 g to 35 g…popcorn—one cup, 10 g to 12 g…whole-wheat bread—one slice, about 15 g…and bran cereal—one cup, 5 g to 10 g.

Alan Flint, MD, DrPH, research scientist, department of nutrition, Harvard School of Public Health, Boston.

The Red Wine That Does the Most for Your Health

Ramon Estruch, MD, PhD, senior consultant, associate professor, department of internal medicine, University of Barcelona, Spain, and coauthor of a study published in *Circulation Research*.

Raising a glass of red wine and drinking to your health may give you a sense of satisfaction because you've heard that a bit of wine can be good for your heart.

But: There are downsides, too—alcohol increases the risk for certain cancers, and too much of it can harm the liver and increase blood pressure.

So you'll want to toast a new Spanish study that reveals how people who enjoy the taste of red wine can indulge in the beverage and get the health benefits—without the health risks.

The secret: Opt for red wine that contains no alcohol.

RAISE A GLASS!

The study participants included men ages 55 to 75 who were at high risk for heart prob-lems because they had diabetes or various cardiovascular disease risk factors. First, after a two-week period of abstinence from alcohol, each participant's baseline blood pressure was measured and certain blood tests were done.

Then, during one four-week period, each participant drank 9.2 ounces (about two glass-es) of regular red wine with dinner each day. During a second four-week period, each man drank 9.2 ounces of nonalcoholic red wine with his evening meal. And during a third four-week period, each drank 3.4 ounces (about two shots) of gin daily with dinner. (The men knew what they were drinking, but this knowledge wouldn't affect results.) Par-ticipants all followed a similar diet and drank no other alcohol during the study. At the end of each four-week period, participants' blood pressure readings were compared with their baseline readings.

Results: After drinking regular red wine, the men's blood pressure dropped insignifi-cantly…and after they drank gin, their blood pressure didn't change at all. However, after consuming the alcohol-free red wine, the men's blood pressure dropped, on average, nearly six points for systolic pressure (the top number of a blood pressure reading) and more than two points for diastolic pressure (the bottom number). This represents a signif-icant decrease—perhaps more than enough to reduce heart disease risk by 14% and stroke risk by 20%!

THE REAL POWER IN WINE

Polyphenols—healthful antioxidants found in fruits, vegetables and wine—in nonalcohol-ic wine had more potent effects than those in regular wine, probably because alcohol inter-feres with antioxidant activity. Gin contains no polyphenols and thus does not have antioxi-dant benefits. While white wine and plain old grape juice do contain polyphenols, red wine contains more, which is why the researchers focused on it.

When participants were drinking alcohol-free wine, their blood levels of nitric oxide were four times higher than when they were drinking regular red wine. This is an im-portant change—because nitric oxide helps blood vessels relax, thus reducing blood pressure and allowing more blood to reach the heart and other organs. Again, polyphenols get the credit for the improvement in nitric oxide levels.

The researchers suspect that women experience the same effects from drinking nonalcoholic red wine, and are planning to do an all-female study to find out.

IS IT REALLY WINE?

Unlike grape juice, nonalcoholic wine is fermented just like regular wine—in fact, it is regular wine—but then the alcohol is removed. Though the process does not affect polyphenol levels, true wine aficionados may recognize that taking out the alcohol leaves the wine lighter and less robust (and also leaves you without the buzz, of course). Many people find the nuanced taste of alcohol-free wine quite appealing—and perhaps all the more in light of this new evidence for the beverage's health benefits.

Important: It is impossible to remove all alcohol from wine, though the amount left in is small at less than one-half of 1%. Still, if you are avoiding alcohol completely, nonalcoholic wine may not be appropriate for you. Also, if you have diabetes, keep in mind that alcohol-free wines do contain some sugar, so it is best to check with your doctor to see whether it is OK for you to consume nonalcoholic wine.

There are many types of nonalcoholic wine, including various reds and whites as well. Cabernet sauvignon, petit syrah and pinot noir have the highest levels of polyphenols—and a general guideline is, the drier the wine, the higher the polyphenol content. These days, alcohol-free wines are sold just about anywhere that regular wine is sold—even in many fine wine stores—and you can find them at many supermarkets and health-food stores. They're sold online too (for instance, at *www.ariel vineyards.com*) and typically cost less than $10 per bottle.

Lower Blood Pressure with This Vitamin

Stephen Juraschek, MD, lead investigator, department of epidemiology, Johns Hopkins University, Baltimore.

Andrew Rubman, ND, medical director, Southbury Clinic for Traditional Medicines, Southbury, Connecticut.

The study was published in the *American Journal of Clinical Nutrition*.

Many of us swallow a daily multivitamin and assume that we're getting all the vitamin C that we need.

After all, most multivitamins provide 100% of the USDA's recommended Dietary Reference Intake (DRI) per day for vitamin C—75 to 90 milligrams (mg).

So we're all set, right?

Well, a recent analysis from Johns Hopkins University in Baltimore shows that getting even more than the DRI each day might go a long way in terms of reducing blood pressure or maintaining healthy blood pressure.

But how much is enough?

"C" IS FOR CONTROLLING PRESSURE

Scouring 45 years of medical literature, lead investigator Stephen Juraschek, MD, and his colleagues looked at 29 clinical trials comparing blood pressure measurements among participants taking vitamin C supplements with those taking placebos. The range of supplementation taken was 60 mg per day to 4,000 mg per day—the median amount was 500 mg per day—so most subjects were taking far more than the USDA's recommended amount. Subjects took the supplements for, on average, eight weeks. Some had high blood pressure and some didn't.

Results: Participants with normal blood pressure who took vitamin C had 3.8 points lower systolic blood pressure (the top number of the reading), on average, than the placebo group and 1.5 points lower diastolic blood pressure (the bottom number of the reading), on average…and those with high blood pressure who took vitamin C had 4.9 points lower systolic, on average, and 1.7 points lower diastolic, on average.

These reductions may not be as significant as the results you might get from blood pressure medications, but if your blood pressure is only slightly high, the vitamin might help keep your pressure in a healthy range or help you take less or no medication.

Dr. Juraschek said that the dips in blood pressure are thought to result from vitamin C's action as a diuretic—it prompts the kidneys to excrete more salt and water from the body, which can relax blood vessels.

MAY HELP, WON'T HARM

Again, this research was a meta-analysis of many studies, and each study was conducted slightly differently, so Dr. Juraschek can't tell us exactly how much vitamin C is the ideal amount to take.

But since the people in the study were taking more than the USDA's recommended amount of vitamin C and their blood pressure was lowered, then should we all be taking more than 75 mg to 90 mg per day?

There's mixed advice from experts on the topic.

Dr. Juraschek takes a very cautious approach, saying that more research is needed before people increase how much vitamin C they take. He warned that doses larger than the USDA's recommendation could lead to diarrhea or kidney stones in some people, such as those prone to those problems.

But we're talking about vitamin C here! A vitamin that's good for you that is naturally in many healthy foods. Is so much caution necessary, given that vitamin C is, generally speaking, quite benign?

Excess vitamin C is excreted in urine, so how dangerous could it really be for most people? We spoke to naturopathic doctor Andrew Rubman, ND, medical director of the Southbury Clinic for Traditional Medicines in Southbury, Connecticut, to find out the answers.

Dr. Rubman said that people who are prone to diarrhea or kidney stones might have problems consuming extra vitamin C, so those people, in particular, may want to be cautious. "But that's not most of us," he said. "Chances are that most people—especially those who are prehypertensive (blood pressure between 120/80 and 139/89) or hypertensive (blood pressure of 140/90 or higher)—would benefit from taking more than 75 mg to 90 mg per day."

If you're interested in taking more vitamin C than you already do as a way of controlling blood pressure, discuss it with your doctor…especially if you have diabetes or another chronic condition.

Fish Oil's Omega-3s Lower Blood Pressure

Study titled "Long-Chain Omega-3 Fatty Acids Eicosapentaenoic Acid and Docosahexaenoic Acid and Blood Pressure: A Meta-Analysis of Randomized Controlled Trials," published in *American Journal of Hypertension*.

Eat less salt, get more exercise, drink less alcohol. Yeah, yeah, yeah. You've heard this advice a hundred times, but you don't always do it…even though you know it could help lower your blood pressure. Or maybe you do do it quite conscientiously… but it's not enough to get your blood pressure down where it ought to be.

Well, listen to this. There's a drug-free way to reduce blood pressure that can work as well as or even better than these lifestyle modifications, according to a huge new study. It's easy to do, and it's inexpensive—and it can make a significant enough difference that some people wind up not even needing the medication they would otherwise have to take.

The key: Fish and fish oil.

THE 70-STUDY MEGA-INVESTIGATION

High blood pressure (hypertension) is a huge problem in this country. Nearly one-third of Americans have the dangerous condition already…fewer than half of them have it under control…and 20% of them don't even know they've got it. Another 30% have prehypertension, meaning blood pressure that's higher than normal but not yet in the hypertension range. All are at increased risk for heart attack and stroke. Medications can help lower blood pressure, but they have risks, too—so safe, natural alternatives are of keen interest.

Numerous studies have looked at whether the omega-3 fatty acids *eicosapentaenoic acid* (EPA) and *docosahexaenoic acid* (DHA), found primarily in fish oil, can help reduce blood pressure. But the study designs have been all over the map and results have been inconsistent. To remedy that, researchers conducted a meta-analysis, combining the results of 70 high-quality randomized, placebo-controlled clinical trials—the gold standard in studies—that examined the effects of EPA/DHA on blood pressure in adults.

The average length of the studies was 69 days. The average dose of EPA/DHA was 3.8 grams (g) per day…and sources included different types of seafood, omega-3-fortified foods and various omega-3 supplements, such as fish oil, algae oil and purified ethyl esters. The placebos were mostly vegetable oils, especially olive oil.

What the researchers found: People who consumed EPA/DHA had lower average numbers for both systolic blood pressure (the top number of a blood pressure reading, which indicates the force during the heart's contraction) and diastolic blood pressure (the bottom number, which indicates the force in between the contractions). For instance, compared with placebo users…

• **Overall, participants who consumed EPA/DHA** had a 1.52-point lower systolic reading…and a 0.99-point lower diastolic reading.

• **Among people who had documented high blood pressure** and who were not taking medication to reduce it, results were most impressive—EPA/DHA consumers had a 4.51-point lower systolic reading…and a 3.05-point lower diastolic reading.

Comparison: The improvement in the systolic number with EPA/DHA is on par with or even beats the average systolic blood pressure reductions seen with lifestyle modifications—3.6 points for reducing sodium intake…4.6 points for increasing physical activity…and 3.8 points for reducing alcohol consumption.

• **People with normal blood pressure benefited, too**—EPA/DHA consumers had a 1.25-point lower systolic reading…and a 0.62-point lower diastolic reading.

• **When evaluating only those studies in which participants took fish oil supplements,** the EPA/DHA consumers had a 1.75-point lower systolic reading…and 1.11-point lower diastolic reading.

• **As for dosage,** the most benefit overall was seen with daily doses of 2.0 to 4.0 g of EPA/DHA per day.

GAINING PERSPECTIVE

The blood pressure reductions seen in this meta-analysis may not seem huge to you—but they are clinically meaningful.

Consider this: In adults, systolic blood pressure normally rises by 0.6 points each year—so the 1.25-point reduction seen among participants who did not have high blood pressure would be enough to delay a person's progression from prehypertension to hypertension by two years. And the 4.51-point reduction seen among unmedicated hypertension patients could be enough to allow such a person to avoid having to start taking blood pressure drugs. EPA and DHA probably help blood pressure by improving the function of the endothelium (inner lining of the blood vessels), thus reducing vascular resistance.

Disclosure: This study was funded by Global Organization for EPA and DHA Omega-3s (GOED), an association of manufacturers, marketers and supporters of omega-3 fatty acids. However, GOED had no role in the study design or management of the data collected…and because this study was a meta-analysis, the data came from other published studies that were not funded by GOED.

Getting your omega-3s: Fish oil supplements are a convenient way to boost EPA/DHA intake—but the pills can increase bleeding risk, so it is important to get your doctor's OK and discuss dosage before taking them, especially if you are on blood-thinning medication or are anticipating any surgery. Eating fatty fish such as salmon, mackerel and sardines also is a great way to get your omega-3s—but as the researchers pointed out, some people don't like fish.

Stress Busters That Help Beat High Blood Pressure

The late C. Tissa Kappagoda, MBBS, PhD, professor of medicine in the Preventive Cardiology Program at the University of California, Davis. Dr. Kappagoda published more than 200 medical journal articles on matters relating to cardiology and cardiovascular health.

We don't mean to cause undue alarm—especially since the point of this article is to reduce stress, not add to it—but a disturbing set of facts need to be brought to light. It's the reality that high blood pressure is becoming an increasingly significant problem for women. *Consider...*

A recent study in the journal *Circulation* found this alarming trend—that rates of uncontrolled hypertension are increasing among women even as rates among men are decreasing.

The Centers for Disease Control and Prevention reports that more than one-third of women age 45 to 54 now have high blood pressure...while among women age 75 and older, 80% do!

A more recent report from the National Center for Health Statistics states that, in the past decade, there has been a 62% increase in the number of visits to the doctor due to high blood pressure.

How much the lousy economy might be contributing to the problem (though studies have shown that worries about job stability increase a person's risk for high blood pressure) is up for debate—other research has shown that chronic stress is a significant contributor to hypertension. As C. Tissa Kappagoda, MBBS, PhD, a professor in the preventive cardiology program at the University of California, Davis, explained, "Chronic stress raises blood pressure by increasing levels of adrenaline and cortisol, hormones that promote artery spasm and salt retention. It also increases vascular resistance, the resistance to flow that must be overcome to move blood through the blood vessels, which is a primary cause of hypertension." Stress also can impede basic self-care, such as eating healthfully and exercising—which probably explains why stress is such a "massive multiplier of the effects of conventional risk factors," Dr. Kappagoda added.

Though high blood pressure doesn't cause pain or other obvious symptoms, it does damage arteries—increasing the risk for heart attack, diabetes, stroke and kidney problems. How high is too high? Hypertension is diagnosed when blood pressure hits 140/90 mmHg or higher...but doctors now realize that prehypertension (blood pressure between 120/80 and 139/89) also is risky.

Of course, it's important to follow your doctor's advice regarding blood pressure–lowering lifestyle changes, such as limiting salt and alcohol and losing excess weight. But stress reduction should be a priority, too, Dr. Kappagoda said—and may reduce the need for hypertension medication. That's good, because these drugs can have side effects, such as dizziness, chronic cough and muscle cramps, and often are taken for the rest of a person's life.

Research shows that the following stress-lowering techniques help reduce blood pressure. *If you have hypertension or prehypertension, consider...*

• **Breathing control.** When you're relaxed, your breathing naturally slows...and if you slow down your breathing, your body naturally relaxes. This encourages constricted blood vessels to dilate, improving blood flow.

Target: Practice slow breathing for 15 minutes twice daily, aiming to take six breaths per minute.

If you find it difficult (or even stressful!) to count and time your breaths, consider using a biofeedback device instead. One example designed for home use is Resperate (800-220-1925, *www.resperate.com*, from $299.95), which looks like a portable CD player with headphones and uses musical tones to guide you to an optimal breathing pattern. Typically, it's used for 15 minutes three or four times per week, and results are seen within several weeks. In studies, users experienced significant reductions in systolic pressure (the top number of a blood pressure reading) and diastolic pressure (bottom number). There are many similar and effective devices, said Dr. Kappagoda, so ask your doctor about the options. Biofeedback devices are safe and have no side effects.

• **Meditation.** A recent analysis of nine clinical trials, published in *American Journal of Hypertension*, found that regular practice of transcendental meditation reduced blood pressure, on average, by 4.7 mmHg systolic and 3.2 mmHg diastolic. Though these results are for transcendental meditation specifically, many experts believe that any type of meditation works.

Goal: Meditate for 20 minutes daily.

• **Exercise.** Regular physical activity reduces blood pressure not only by alleviating stress, but also by promoting weight loss and improving heart and blood vessel health. Research shows that becoming more active can reduce systolic pressure by 5 mmHg to 10 mmHg, on average. An excellent all-around exercise is walking, Dr. Kappagoda said—so with your doctor's OK, take a 30-minute walk at least three times weekly.

Caution: Weight training can trigger a temporary increase in blood pressure during the exercise, especially when heavy weights are used. To minimize this blood pressure spike, use lighter weights to do more repetitions…and don't hold your breath during the exertion.

Reduce High Blood Pressure by Tapping Your Toes

Ann Marie Chiasson, MD, family practitioner and codirector of the Fellowship at the Arizona Center for Integrative Medicine, University of Tucson. She is author of *Energy Healing: The Essentials of Self-Care*. Her video *Energy Healing for Beginners: Ten Essential Practices for Self-Care* includes a tapping demo. AnnMarieChiassonMD.com

There's a killer running rampant amongst us—and its name is high blood pressure. Overly dramatic? Not really.

High blood pressure increases your risk not only for heart attack, heart failure and stroke, but also for grave maladies that you may never have considered, such as kidney failure, dementia, aneurysm, blindness and osteoporosis.

Yes, medications help reduce blood pressure…but their nasty side effects can include joint pain, headache, weakness, dizziness, heart palpitations, coughing, asthma, constipation, diarrhea, insomnia, depression and erectile dysfunction!

But there's a promising alternative therapy that's completely risk-free—and costs nothing.

We're talking about tapping, which is based on the principles of Chinese medicine. *Here's how it works…*

SOMETHING OLD, SOMETHING NEW

The tapping method was described by Ann Marie Chiasson, MD, of the Arizona Center for Integrative Medicine. For her own patients with high blood pressure, Dr. Chiasson has adapted a tapping technique that is part of the ancient Chinese practice called qigong.

Qigong involves simple movements, including tapping on the body's meridians, or "highways" of energy movement. These meridians are the same as those used during acupuncture and acupressure treatments. According to a review of nine studies published in *The Journal of Alternative and Complementary Medicine*, qigong reduced systolic blood pressure (the top number) by an average of 17 points and diastolic blood pressure (the bottom number) by an average of 10 points. Those are big reductions! In fact, they are comparable to the reductions achieved with drugs—but the qigong had no unwanted side effects.

Though Dr. Chiasson has not conducted a clinical trial on her tapping protocol, she has observed reductions in blood pressure among her patients who practice tapping. The technique she recommends also could conceivably benefit people who do not have high blood pressure if it reduces stress and thus helps lower the risk of developing high blood pressure.

TAP AWAY

Some tapping routines are complicated, involving tapping the top of the head, around the eyes, side of the hand and under the nose, chin and/or arms. But Dr. Chiasson's technique is a simpler toe-and-torso method that is quite easy to learn. It is safe and can be done in the privacy of your own home—so if it might help you, why not give it a try?

First, you may want to get a blood pressure reading so you can do a comparison later on. If the tapping technique is helpful, you eventually may be able to reduce or even discontinue your high blood pressure drugs (of course, for safety's sake, you should not stop taking any drugs without first talking to your doctor about it).

Dr. Chiasson's plan: Each day, do five minutes of toe tapping (instructions below)…five minutes of belly tapping…and five minutes of chest tapping. You may experience tingling or a sensation of warmth in the part of the body being tapped and/or in your hands, which is normal. You can listen to rhythmic music during your tapping if you like. As you tap, try to think as little as possible, Dr. Chiasson said—just focus on your body, tapping and breath.

Rate: For each tapping location, aim for a rate of about one to two taps per second.

• **Toe tapping.** Lie flat on your back on the bed or floor. Keeping your whole body relaxed, quickly rotate your legs inward and outward from the hips (like windshield wipers), tapping the sides of your big toes together with each inward rotation. Tap as softly or as vigorously as you like.

• **Belly tapping.** Stand with your feet a little wider than shoulder-width apart. Staying relaxed, gently bounce up and down by slightly bending your knees. At the same time, tap softly with gently closed fists on the area below your belly button and above your pubic bone. Try to synchronize your movements to give one tap per knee bend.

• **Chest tapping.** Sit or stand comfortably. Using your fingertips, open hands or gently closed fists, tap all over your chest area, including the armpits. Tap as softly or as vigorously as you like without pushing past your comfort level.

Cautions: If you are recovering from hip or knee surgery, skip the toe tapping (which might strain your joint) and do only the belly tapping and chest tapping. If you are preg-

nant, stick with just the chest tapping—lying on your back during toe tapping could reduce blood flow to the fetus…and tapping on your belly may not feel comfortable and could stimulate the acupressure points used to induce labor, Dr. Chiasson said.

Follow-up: Continue your tapping routine for eight weeks, then get another blood pressure reading to see whether your numbers have improved. If they have—or if you simply enjoy the relaxing effects of the tapping—you might want to continue indefinitely.

Fish Oil Is Good for Your Heart

Fish oil can help your heart despite a report to the contrary, says Michael D. Ozner, MD. A recent study found that taking fish oil pills, which are rich in omega-3 fatty acids, didn't appear to prevent heart attacks or stroke. But the study (which was a review of previous studies) actually demonstrated that fish oil was beneficial in preventing death from heart disease.

Bottom line: Fish oil reduces inflammation, a factor in heart disease…is FDA-approved to lower harmful triglycerides…and has a very low risk for side effects.

Michael D. Ozner, MD, medical director, Center for Prevention and Wellness, Baptist Health South Florida, Miami, and author of *Heart Attack Proof.*

Alpha-Lipoic Acid Helps Reduce Diabetes and Heart Disease Risk

Alpha-lipoic acid, which is found in foods such as red meat and liver, works as an antioxidant, so it fights disease all over the body. It also regenerates other antioxidants, such as vitamins A and E, and improves insulin sensitivity, so it reduces your risk for cardiovascular disease and diabetes, and it may help reduce blood sugar levels. Dr. Horowitz typically prescribes 300 mg to 600 mg per day in pill form…while those patients with diabetes and/or cardiovascular risk factors will often be prescribed up to 1200 mg per day.

Richard Horowitz, MD, Hudson Valley Healing Arts Center, Hyde Park, New York.

Diet Soda Danger

If you're hoping to keep your waist trim by drinking diet soda, watch out! According to a nine-year study of nearly 500 adults ages 65 and older, daily diet soda drinkers had more than a threefold increase in waist circumference compared with people who did not drink diet soda. Diet soda is linked to an increase in belly fat, which raises the risk for diabetes, heart disease and stroke.

Possible reason: Artificial sweeteners may interfere with glucose metabolism.

Sharon Fowler, MPH, obesity researcher, The University of Texas Health Science Center at San Antonio.

The Truth About Vitamin D

Michael F. Holick, PhD, MD, director of the Vitamin D, Skin and Bone Research Laboratory at Boston University Medical Center and author of *The Vitamin D Solution*.

Low blood levels of vitamin D have been linked to many diseases including osteoporosis, heart disease, cancer, type 2 diabetes, Alzheimer's and autoimmune diseases.

But what about recent headlines declaring that high blood levels of vitamin D can cause heart disease? They were based on a study published in *The Journal of Clinical Endocrinology & Metabolism*, which showed that people with high levels of vitamin D (25-hydroxy-vitamin D) were 30% more likely to die of a heart attack, heart failure or stroke.

As I wrote in a recent paper in the journal *Nutrients*, citing 49 studies that involved millions of people, vitamin D toxicity is rare. Yes, high levels increase calcium and phosphate, which can damage kidneys and clog arteries. But research shows that daily doses as high as 20,000 international units (IU) of vitamin D-3 (much higher than levels found in most vitamin D-3 supplements, which typically supply 400 IU to 2,000 IU) do not raise blood levels above 100 ng/mL, the level traditionally considered a sign of possible toxicity.

The reality is that many Americans have either an insufficient blood level of vitamin D (21 ng/mL to 29 ng/mL) or an outright deficiency (less than 20 ng/mL). An analysis of 73 studies on vitamin D, involving nearly 900,000 people, shows that low levels raise the risk of dying from heart disease (or any cause) by 35%.

My advice: Blood levels of vitamin D should be at least 30 ng/mL (the preferred range is 40 ng/mL to 60 ng/mL).

To achieve that level, the Endocrine Society recommends that adults take 1,500 IU to 2,000 IU of vitamin D-3 daily, even in the summer when sun exposure gives us more natural vitamin D.

Stroke: You Can Do Much More to Protect Yourself

Ralph L. Sacco, MD, chairman of neurology, the Olemberg Family Chair in Neurological Disorders and the Miller Professor of Neurology, Epidemiology and Public Health, Human Genetics and Neurosurgery at the Miller School of Medicine at the University of Miami, where he is the executive director of the Evelyn McKnight Brain Institute. He is also the chief of the Neurology Service at Jackson Memorial Hospital and the 2014 recipient of the American Heart Association's Cor Vitae Stroke Award.

No one likes to think about having a stroke. But maybe you should. The grim reality: Stroke strikes about 800,000 Americans each year and is the leading cause of disability.

Now for the remarkable part: About 80% of strokes can be prevented. You may think that you've heard it all when it comes to preventing strokes—it's about controlling your blood pressure, eating a good diet and getting some exercise, right? Actually, that's only part of what you can be doing to protect yourself. *Surprising recent findings on stroke—and the latest advice on how to avoid it…*

• **Even "low" high blood pressure is a red flag. High blood pressure**—a reading of 140/90 mmHg or higher—is widely known to increase one's odds of having a stroke. But even slight elevations in blood pressure may also be a problem.

An important recent study that looked at data from more than half a million patients found that those with blood pressure readings that were just slightly higher than a normal reading of 120/80 mmHg were more likely to have a stroke.

Any increase in blood pressure is worrisome. In fact, the risk for a stroke or heart attack doubles for each 20-point rise in systolic (the top number) pressure above 115/75 mmHg—and for each 10-point rise in diastolic (the bottom number) pressure.

My advice: Don't wait for your doctor to recommend treatment if your blood pressure is even a few points higher than normal. Tell him/her that you are concerned. Lifestyle changes—such as getting adequate exercise, avoiding excess alcohol and maintaining a healthful diet—often reverse slightly elevated blood pressure. Blood pressure consistently above 140/90 mmHg generally requires medication.

• **Sleep can be dangerous.** People who are sleep deprived—generally defined as getting less than six hours of sleep per night—are at increased risk for stroke.

What most people don't realize is that getting too much sleep is also a problem. When researchers at the University of Cambridge tracked the sleep habits of nearly 10,000 people over a 10-year period, they found that those who slept more than eight hours a night were 46% more likely to have a stroke than those who slept six to eight hours.

It is possible that people who spend less/more time sleeping have other, unrecognized conditions that affect both sleep and stroke risk.

Example: Sleep apnea, a breathing disorder that interferes with sleep, causes an increase in blood pressure that can lead to stroke. Meanwhile, sleeping too much can be a symptom of depression—another stroke risk factor.

My advice: See a doctor if you tend to wake up unrefreshed…are a loud snorer…or often snort or thrash while you sleep. You may have sleep apnea. (For more on this condition, see page 351.) If you sleep too much, also talk to your doctor to see if you are suffering from depression or some other condition that may increase your stroke risk.

What's the sweet spot for nightly shut-eye? When it comes to stroke risk, it's six to eight hours per night.

• **What you drink matters, too.** A Mediterranean-style diet—plenty of whole grains, legumes, nuts, fish, produce and olive oil—is perhaps the best diet going when it comes to minimizing stroke risk. A recent study concluded that about 30% of strokes could be prevented if people simply switched to this diet.

But there's more you can do. Research has found that people who drank six cups of green or black tea a day were 42% less likely to have strokes than people who did not drink tea. With three daily cups, risk dropped by 21%. The antioxidant epigallocatechin gallate or the amino acid L-theanine may be responsible.

• **Emotional stress shouldn't be pooh-poohed.** If you're prone to angry outbursts, don't assume it's no big deal. Emotional stress triggers the release of cortisol, adrenaline and other so-called stress hormones that can increase blood pressure and heart rate, leading to stroke.

In one study, about 30% of stroke patients had heightened negative emotions (such as anger) in the two hours preceding the stroke.

My advice: Don't ignore your mental health—especially anger (it's often a sign of depression, a potent stroke risk factor). If you're suffering from "negative" emotions, exercise regularly, try relaxation strategies (such as meditation) and don't hesitate to get professional help.

• **Be alert for subtle signs of stroke.** The acronym "FAST" helps people identify signs of stroke. "F" stands for facial drooping—does one side of the face droop or is it numb? Is the person's smile uneven? "A" stands for arm weakness—ask the person to raise both arms. Does one arm drift downward? "S" stands for speech difficulty—is speech slurred? Is the person unable to speak or hard to understand? Can he/she repeat a simple sentence such as, "The sky is blue" correctly? "T" stands for time—if a person shows any of these symptoms (even if they go away), call 911 immediately. Note the time so that you know when symptoms first appeared.

But stroke can also cause one symptom that isn't widely known—a loss of touch sensation. This can occur if a stroke causes injury to the parts of the brain that detect touch. If you suddenly can't "feel" your fingers or toes—or have trouble with simple tasks such as buttoning a shirt—you could be having a stroke. You might notice that you can't feel temperatures or that you can't feel it when your feet touch the floor.

It's never normal to lose your sense of touch for an unknown reason—or to have unexpected difficulty seeing, hearing and/or speaking. Get to an emergency room!

Also important: If you think you're having a stroke, don't waste time calling your regular doctor. Call an ambulance, and ask to be taken to the nearest hospital with a primary stroke center. You'll get much better care than you would at a regular hospital emergency room.

A meta-analysis found that there were 21% fewer deaths among patients treated at stroke centers, and the surviving patients had faster recoveries and fewer stroke-related complications.

My advice: If you have any stroke risk factors, including high blood pressure, diabetes or elevated cholesterol, find out now which hospitals in your area have stroke centers. To find one near you, go to *heart. org/myhealthcare.*

10

Healthy Life Habits That Keep Diabetes Away Forever

The Neighborhood Where No One Has Diabetes

Imagine a utopia for glucose—a neighborhood where normal, balanced blood sugar is a way of life, a neighborhood where…

- **There are many opportunities to be physically active**
- **Local sports clubs and other facilities offer many opportunities to get exercise,**
- **It is pleasant to walk**
- **It is easy to walk**
- **You often see other people walking**
- **You often see other people exercising—** jogging, bicycling or playing sports
- **There is a large selection of fresh fruits and vegetables available**
- **The fresh fruits and vegetables are of high quality**
- **A large selection of low-fat food products are available.**

Well, scientists conducted a survey asking thousands of people if they lived in just such a neighborhood. Their answers—published in the *Archives of Internal Medicine* (now *JAMA Internal Medicine*)—have produced new insights into the causes of diabetes…

REDUCING RISK BY 38%

Researchers from the School of Public Health at Drexel University in Philadelphia analyzed the survey responses of 2,285 people, aged 45 to 84, who checked "yes" next to any of the above nine descriptions that fit their neighborhood, and checked "no" next to any of those that didn't fit.

In the five years after taking the survey, those who lived in healthy neighborhoods—neighborhoods where opportunities to exercise are abundant and fresh, low-fat food is available—were 38% less likely to develop diabetes.

Amy Auchincloss, PhD, MPH, associate professor and researcher, department of epidemiology and biostatistics, Drexel University School of Public Health, Philadelphia.

Christopher Ervin, MD, public health specialist and former director of programs for the Georgia Diabetes Coalition.

WALK AND EAT WELL

Even if you live in a healthy neighborhood, you might not do what is best for your health, says Amy Auchincloss, PhD, the study leader. *She recommends…*

• **Personal action.** "Choose routine activities that involve physical exertion—activities that will help you be physically active, even when you don't feel like it," she says. "Walk rather than use a car if the traveling distance is less than two miles. Take the stairs instead of the elevator or escalator."

She also says to minimize your purchase of processed, prepared foods, opting instead for fresh.

"To prevent diabetes, eat more 'anti-diabetes' foods, which include whole grains, fruits and fresh vegetables—particularly dark green leafy vegetables," agrees Christopher Ervin, MD, a specialist in public health and former director of programs for the Georgia Diabetes Coalition. "And walk as often as possible—starting with 15 minutes a day, and gradually working your way up to one hour a day."

• **Social action.** "There are community groups and planning organizations that you can join to help advocate for making your city or town healthier," says Dr. Auchincloss.

"Many cities, for example, have public transportation advocacy organizations that also advocate for improving infrastructure for safe walking and bicycling." *Examples…*

• **Transportation Alternatives.** 111 John Street, Suite 260, New York, NY 10038. 212-629-8080, *www.transalt.org.*

• **Smart Growth Network.** Maryland Department of Planning, 410-767-7179, *www.smartgrowth.org.*

Similarly, says Dr. Auchincloss, many organizations advocate for more fresh food in urban areas. Two such organizations…

• **The Food Trust.** One Penn Center, Suite 900, 1617 John F. Kennedy Blvd., Philadelphia, PA 19103. 215-575-0444, *www.thefoodtrust.org.*

• **The Prevention Institute.** 221 Oak Street, Oakland, CA 94607. 510-444-7738, *www.preventioninstitute.org.*

Gourmet Cooking Secrets for People with Diabetes

Chris Smith, The Diabetic Chef, is an executive chef working in the healthcare field. Author of two cookbooks, *Cooking With the Diabetic Chef* and *The Diabetic Chef's Year-Round Cookbook,* he lectures widely about cooking for people with diabetes.

Can people with diabetes eat healthfully and enjoy their meals at the same time? The answer is a resounding "yes," says Chris Smith, author of *The Diabetic Chef's Year-Round Cookbook.* Smith uses fresh, seasonal ingredients to create healthy, interesting meals full of flavor for individuals with diabetes and everyone else at the table, while reducing the salt, sugar and fat that many have come to rely upon to add taste.

HEALTHY EATING…WITH DIABETES

Just like the rest of us, people with diabetes should eat nutritious meals that are low in fat (especially saturated and trans fat), moderate in salt and very sparing in sugar, while emphasizing whole grains, vegetables and fruit. However, because people with diabetes are at a greater risk for life-threatening complications such as hypertension, heart disease and stroke, it's particularly important that they keep blood glucose control while maintaining normal levels of blood pressure and blood lipids (cholesterol). It can be challenging to do all that while still preparing flavorful and appealing food. Here The Diabetic Chef shares his secrets for preparing foods that are appropriate for people with diabetes and delicious enough for everyone.

HERBS AND SPICES ARE ESSENTIAL

Liven up your meals with garden-fresh herbs, many of which are available year-round. Fresh herbs are densely packed with flavor. You can use herbs in a variety of ways throughout the seasons.

• **Fine herbs, such as thyme, oregano, dill, basil and chives, are usually available in the spring and summer.** These should be added as a finish (at the end of the cooking process) to release their delicate flavors and aromatic qualities. "Use fresh basil with summer tomatoes and olive oil for pasta, or as a finish to a tomato sauce," said Smith. "Use chives as a delicate finish to soups, salads and sauces."

• **Hearty herbs (rosemary, sage), available year-round,** can be added earlier on in the cooking process. Use them with stews, soups and Crock-Pot dishes. They can withstand the heat of cooking without losing flavor and, in fact, the longer they're cooked, the more mellow and flavorful they are, says Smith.

• **Dried herbs must be rehydrated,** so use at the beginning of the cooking process (adding as you sauté onions for a sauce, for example). Your homemade tomato sauce with dried oregano and basil tastes better the next day as the flavor of the dried herbs fully blooms and combines with the other ingredients.

Herb typically describes the leaves of a plant, while spices are derived from any other part—including the root, seeds, bark or buds. Spices can be used to create a medley of flavors and can be evocative of different types of ethnic cuisines. "Spices bring great diversity to food," Smith says.

OTHER TIPS FOR HEALTHFUL EATING

Overall, Smith points out that healthful eating is a matter of practicing what he calls "Nutritional MVP," which stands for moderation, variety and portion control.

From his cookbook, another suggestion is to learn how to do template cooking. Template cooking is taking one recipe and adapting it in different ways by using the same cooking method but substituting different ingredients, says Smith. "It gives you the freedom to be creative, which is the essence of good cooking." It also brings much-needed diversity to meals, so you are not forever serving the same old thing. One example of a template recipe is the Simple Chicken Breast (see the next page). "There are only seven ingredients in this recipe but you can vary it with fresh, seasonal ingredients," says Smith. "For instance, in springtime you can exchange the olive oil for sesame oil and use lemon grass rather than garlic to create an Asian flavor. In summer, substitute fresh cilantro for the rosemary."

Try different cooking techniques to bring out the essence of foods.

• **Grill, broil, roast, sauté or steam food to enhance flavor without added fat or salt.** Slow-roast vegetables with a drizzle of olive oil in a 400-degree oven to bring out their true flavors. Many develop a natural sweetness when roasted. Season with garlic or add herbs to vary the taste. Rather than sautéing garlic or onions with butter or oil before adding them to soups or stews, try roasting in the oven.

• **Marinate foods in a few ingredients.** "The herbs, lemon and spice in the Simple Chicken Breast recipe create a vibrant flavor, and the extra-virgin olive oil allows the herbs and spices to reach their full bouquet," said Smith.

• **Sear meat (brown on both sides in a pan for a few minutes before placing it in the oven)** to enhance flavor without adding extra fat or salt. "Any kind and cut of meat can be seared," said Smith.

• **Pair dishes with colorful sides.** Instead of a plate full of brown items such as chicken and rice, liven up your plate with deeply colored fruits and vegetables that add variety and important phytonutrients (components of fruits and vegetables that are thought to promote health) to your diet.

• **Keep the pantry stocked with these healthy ingredients.**

Oils: extra-virgin olive oil, sesame oil and grapeseed oil.

Vinegars: balsamic, champagne, rice and aged sherry vinegar.

Essential spices: cayenne pepper, chili powder, cinnamon, mustard, nutmeg, paprika and pepper.

Essential dry herbs: bay leaves, dill, basil, oregano, rosemary, thyme and sage.

Other essential products: chicken, vegetable and beef broth, dried beans, whole gluten-free grains such as quinoa and amaranth.

Essential fresh ingredients: lemons, limes, oranges, garlic, onions, shallots, carrots, tomatoes, potatoes, mushrooms, butter (salt free), sour cream (fat free), eggs, hard cheeses (Parmesan and Romano), mustard (grain, Dijon), capers and olives.

Template Recipe: Simple Chicken Breast

Serves 4

4 chicken breast halves
1 tablespoon extra-virgin olive oil
1 tablespoon dried rosemary
1 tablespoon poultry seasoning
1 teaspoon salt-free lemon pepper
1 tablespoon minced garlic
½ teaspoon red pepper flakes
Cooking spray

1. In medium bowl, combine all ingredients and place chicken breasts in it. Cover and refrigerate 1 hour.

2. Preheat oven to 375°F.

3. Preheat sauté pan to medium-high heat. Spray pan with cooking spray. Add chicken breast to pan and sear to desired color, about 10 seconds, then turn over and sear other side.

4. When both sides are seared, remove chicken from pan and place in a baking dish or cookie sheet. Do not cover. Place in oven. Cook meat until internal temperature reads 165°F. When chicken is done, remove from oven and let rest for two to four minutes.

For more tips from Chef Smith go to: *www.thediabeticchef.com.*

Delicious Ways to Cut Back on Carbs

Sandra Woodruff, RD, LD/N, a registered dietitian and nutritionist based in Tallahassee, Florida. She is a past president of the Florida Dietetic Association and author of several books, including *Secrets of Good-Carb/Low-Carb Living*.

To lose weight and help control elevated blood sugar, many people resort to ultra-low-carb diets—only to find them boring and hard to sustain for the long term.

Good news: A reduced-carb diet—done right—can be satisfying and delicious while providing many of the benefits of low-carb plans.

TASTY REDUCED-CARB EATING

If you're reducing carbs by simply avoiding refined and processed carbs, such as sugar and white flour, that's a huge accomplishment. But there may be more that you can do.

For example, many carb reducers still tend to overdo portions of starchy foods (such as bread, cereal and rice) and starchy vegetables (such as potatoes and corn).

Even though it's a good rule of thumb to limit starchy foods to no more than one-fourth of your plate, you don't have to feel deprived of all higher-carb foods. Just choose them carefully, and you'll be amazed at how tasty your meals can be.

What to do: When you do eat higher-carb foods, it's wise to opt for those with a low glycemic index (GI). Low-GI carbs are absorbed into the bloodstream slower than those with a high GI, which helps prevent spikes in blood glucose. Pasta, oatmeal, barley, bulgur wheat, dried beans, sweet potatoes, berries, apples, milk and yogurt are examples of low-GI foods.

Good news: Within a week or two of reducing your carb intake, many people find that their cravings subside—and that big bagel or ultra-sugary cookie is a lot less appetizing.

Best ways to eat a variety of delicious meals while also reducing your carb intake…

BREAKFAST

What to avoid: Cereal, toast and juice—a common but very high-carb breakfast.

Good choice: A yogurt parfait. Layer Greek-style yogurt (which is lower in carbs and higher in protein than regular yogurt) with fresh berries and a sprinkling of walnuts. Or use cottage cheese instead of yogurt.

Tea or coffee without sugar are fine. If you like, add a bit of low-calorie sweetener such as stevia or a splash of milk.

LUNCH

What to avoid: A sandwich on "big" bread (such as a large bagel or sub roll), chips and sweet tea.

Good choice: A sandwich made with bagel thins or a reduced-carb wrap (such as Flatout

Flatbread or a Toufayan multigrain wrap) instead of regular bread.

Add a lean protein filling, such as tuna, turkey or chicken, and pile on vegetable toppings. Pair your sandwich with a cup of vegetable soup, garden salad or fruit cup.

Best bets for beverages: Have some iced tea flavored with mint or lemon instead of sugar. Sparkling mineral water with lemon or lime is another good choice.

Milk is also relatively low-carb (12 g per glass), and it has a low GI—be sure to choose low-fat to save calories. Nondairy options such as plain soy milk and almond milk are fine as well.

DINNER

What to avoid: Pasta and bread. Although pasta is low-GI, many people overdo portions and make matters worse with extra carbs in the bread.

Good choice: Try a reduced-carb personal pizza. Top a round of whole-grain pita bread with marinara sauce, part-skim mozzarella cheese and your favorite toppings (I like turkey "pepperoni," olives, mushrooms, onions, roasted red bell peppers, cooked spinach and/or artichoke hearts). Bake at 400° F for eight to 10 minutes. Add a big side salad topped with lots of colorful vegetables.

DESSERT

What to avoid: High-sugar, flour-based desserts, such as cake and cookies.

Good choices: Fruit pies with low-sugar fillings and whole-grain crust (see next column)…fruit crisps made with oatmeal and nut toppings. Try replacing half or more of the sugar in fruit pie and fruit crisp recipes with stevia or sucralose. A reduced-carb pumpkin pie is also delicious.

Pumpkin Pie

1 Flaky Oat Piecrust (see recipe at right)
1½ cups canned or cooked mashed pumpkin
¼ cup honey
Sugar substitute equal to ½ cup sugar (check the label)
2 to 2½ teaspoons pumpkin pie spice
⅛ teaspoon sea salt
1½ teaspoons vanilla extract
1¼ cups evaporated nonfat or low-fat milk
½ cup fat-free egg substitute or two large eggs, beaten

1. Preheat the oven to 400° F. Prick several holes in the crust with a fork, and bake for five minutes. Remove from the oven, and set aside.

2. Place the pumpkin, honey, sugar substitute, pumpkin pie spice, salt and vanilla in a large bowl, and stir with a wire whisk to mix well. Whisk in the evaporated milk and then the egg substitute or eggs.

3. Pour filling into the crust, and bake for 15 minutes. Reduce heat to 350° F, and bake for about 35 minutes more or until a sharp knife inserted near the center of the pie comes out clean. Cool to room temperature and refrigerate until ready to serve.

Flaky Oat Piecrust

¾ cup whole-wheat pastry flour
½ cup quick-cooking (one-minute) oats
⅛ teaspoon baking powder
⅛ teaspoon sea salt
¼ cup coconut oil
2 tablespoons nonfat or low-fat milk

1. Place the flour, oats, baking powder and salt in a medium bowl, and stir to mix well. Add the oil and milk, and stir until the mixture is moist and crumbly and holds together when pinched. Add a little more milk, if needed. Set aside.

2. Place a 12-inch square of waxed paper on a flat surface. Shape the dough into a ball, and then pat into a seven-inch circle. Top with another 12-inch square of waxed paper, and use a rolling pin to roll the dough into a roughly 10-inch circle.

3. Coat a nine-inch pie pan with cooking spray. Carefully peel off the top sheet of waxed paper, and place the other sheet, crust side down, over the pie pan. Peel away the waxed paper, and press the crust into the pan.

Nutrition facts: 209 calories and 29 g of carbohydrates per serving. Yields eight servings.

The Perfect 10 Diet

Michael Aziz, MD, founder and director of Midtown Integrative Medicine, which blends traditional and complementary therapies, and past president of the American Academy of Anti-Aging Medicine. He is an internist and attending physician at Lennox Hill Hospital in New York City, where he also maintains a private practice. He is author of *The Perfect 10 Diet*. Perfect10Diet.com

Like most physicians, I used to advise overweight patients to follow the American Heart Association's low-fat guidelines, but most of these patients continued to gain. After years of research, I discovered that most diets fail because they don't take into account the hormones that regulate appetite and control weight.

The body contains more than 100 hormones, substances that regulate bodily functions. People who maintain an optimal hormonal balance are more likely to maintain a healthy weight than those who count calories.

Overall, I have found that the diet that is best for hormone optimization has 40% carbohydrates (vegetables, fruits, legumes and whole grains)...40% fat (saturated fats from dairy products, coconut and palm oils, and monounsaturated fats in olive oil, avocados and nuts)... and 20% protein (eggs, fish, shellfish and poultry, plus red meat in moderation).

Many people are surprised that I recommend eating saturated fats. Probably the single greatest nutritional myth of past decades has been that saturated fat is unhealthful. Eating foods rich in saturated fat boosts the production of anti-aging hormones, including estrogen, progesterone and testosterone.

The important hormones* for weight control and how to regulate them...

INSULIN

Up to 75% of American adults produce too much insulin. This increases appetite and leads to obesity as well as diabetes.

What happens: A low-fat diet with excess carbohydrates causes the pancreas to overproduce insulin. Excess insulin increases fat storage and makes it extremely difficult to lose weight.

Solution: A diet high in natural foods (whole grains, vegetables, fish, etc.) with a minimum of processed carbohydrates. Also helpful: One to two tablespoons of brewer's yeast daily. It's high in chromium, a trace mineral that reduces blood sugar and improves glucose tolerance. Better glucose tolerance reduces the amount of insulin that is produced by the pancreas.

GLUCAGON

Levels of glucagon (glu-ca-gon) rise when insulin is low. Unlike insulin, which transports the sugar in blood into the body's cells, glucagon pulls sugars out of storage to provide energy. It melts away fat in the process.

What happens: Glucagon and insulin can't be present in large amounts simultaneously, because they have opposing actions. If your insulin levels are high, your levels of glucagon will always be low.

Solution: Limit yourself to three meals a day. It was once thought that "grazing" (having frequent small meals) would help people lose weight. This style of eating promotes weight gain because it elevates insulin and depresses glucagon.

LEPTIN

The hormone leptin is secreted by fat cells and is the main hormone that controls satiety, the feeling of fullness after eating.

What happens: People who produce too little leptin—or, paradoxically, too much—tend to gain weight because they're hungry all the time. A diet high in processed foods, particularly those that contain trans fatty acids or high-fructose corn syrup, causes the body to burn fewer calories and store fat even in the presence of leptin.

Solution: A diet high in natural fats, such as the omega-3 fatty acids in fish, along with whole grains, vegetables and fruits.

THYROID

About 25 million Americans suffer from hypothyroidism, an underactive thyroid gland. This lowers the body's metabolism and can

---

*Few physicians routinely test all of these hormones in overweight patients. To find a specialist in your area who uses this approach, go to the website of the American Academy of Anti-Aging Medicine at *www.worldhealth.net.*

lead to obesity even in people who don't eat very much.

Hypothyroidism is an autoimmune disease that requires medical care, but it can be exacerbated by a poor diet.

What happens: People who follow a low-fat or low-carbohydrate diet often develop low thyroid hormone levels. So do people who eat mainly processed foods. Iodine from excess salt blocks enzymes that produce thyroid hormones.

Solution: Use sea salt instead of regular salt. It contains less iodine. Eat sea vegetables (such as wakame and nori) at least twice a week. They contain just enough iodine to help you maintain optimal thyroid function. Eat plenty of fruits and vegetables—they enhance the body's production of thyroxine, the active form of thyroid hormone.

HUMAN GROWTH HORMONE (HGH)

HGH is produced by the pituitary gland to promote the growth and repair of muscle tissue.

What happens: People who don't produce enough HGH tend to have less muscle and more body fat. Excess body fat further depresses HGH.

Solution: As with glucagon, HGH rises when people eat less frequently. Eat just three meals a day. Also helpful: Eat eggs, poultry or fish most days. These foods increase HGH. Get a good night's sleep. Most of the body's HGH is produced during sleep.

CORTISOL

Cortisol is a stress hormone because it rises during times of stress. In our high-stress society, virtually everyone has elevated levels of cortisol.

What happens: It promotes the storage of fat, particularly the dangerous visceral (belly) fat.

Solution: Maintain your emotional equilibrium with activities such as yoga and meditation. Also, people who eat natural foods and avoid processed foods tend to have healthier cortisol levels.

SEX HORMONES

Men start producing less testosterone at about age 20, while women have a sharp drop in estrogen and progesterone as they approach menopause. It's not a coincidence that most people start to gain weight when levels of these hormones decline.

What happens: Declines in sex hormones are a natural, age-related phenomenon. But excessive drops in these hormones usually are caused by too much sugar in the diet and lack of natural fats, such as butter, along with lifestyle factors, such as smoking and alcohol consumption.

Solutions: Men and women can improve their hormonal profiles by exercising regularly...not smoking...and drinking alcohol only in moderation (no more than two drinks daily for men and one for women). Also important: Drink less coffee. Caffeine lowers testosterone.

Women can maintain a healthier estrogen/progesterone balance by eating high-quality proteins and fats (from eggs, butter, whole milk and poultry) at least once a day. The same foods will help increase testosterone in men.

DHEA

DHEA is the "precursor" hormone produced by the adrenal gland that the body uses to manufacture other hormones, including estrogen and testosterone.

What happens: People who drink too much coffee or eat margarine or other foods that contain trans fats tend to have lower levels of DHEA. Processed carbohydrates, including white bread, also can cause DHEA to decline.

Solution: Avoid processed foods, and eat some saturated fat most days of the week. This will help increase the body's production of DHEA.

10 STEPS TO THE PERFECT 10

To optimize your hormones and lose weight...

40% carbohydrates: Vegetables, fruits, legumes and whole grains

40% fat: Saturated fats from dairy products, coconut and palm oils and monounsaturated fats in olive oil, avocados and nuts

20% protein: Eggs, fish, shellfish, poultry and red meat, in moderation

Also...

• **Limit yourself to three meals a day** (avoid snacking).

• **Have one to two tablespoons of brewer's yeast daily.**

• **If you have low thyroid,** eat sea vegetables twice a week and choose sea salt over regular iodized salt.

• **Reduce stress with yoga and meditation.**

• **Get regular exercise.**

• **Limit alcohol and caffeine, and don't smoke.**

• **Get a good night's sleep.**

The Eat-What-You-Want Diet

Krista Varady, PhD, associate professor of kinesiology and nutrition at the University of Illinois at Chicago, the author or coauthor of more than 45 scientific papers that have been published in *Obesity, The American Journal of Clinical Nutrition* and many other leading medical journals. She is also coauthor of *The Every-Other-Day Die*t.

Some people fast to "rest" the digestive tract, while others do so as part of a religious tradition. The last time you fasted may have been before a medical test, such as a colonoscopy.

But as a weight-loss technique, fasting has always been controversial. Its detractors claim that it shifts the body into a starvation mode that makes unwanted pounds even harder to drop.

What's gaining favor: More and more scientists are now studying fasting as a method for losing extra pounds and fighting disease. But does it work?

As one of the few scientists worldwide who has studied fasting in humans, I consider it to be the most effective—and healthful—method for most people to lose weight.* *How it works...*

THE SIMPLE FORMULA

With intermittent fasting, you eat a reduced number of calories every other day. Scientifically, this is called alternate-day modified fasting.

The principle is simple: Most people find it easier to stay on a diet in which they can eat whatever they want half of the time. In the eight clinical studies I have conducted involving about 600 people (including an ongoing three-year study funded by the National Institutes of Health), intermittent fasters typically have lost 1.5 to 3 pounds per week, depending on how much weight they had to lose.

People lose weight by eating just 500 calories one day ("fast day") and all they want and anything they want the next day ("feast day")—alternating fast days with feast days until their weight-loss goal is reached. Goal weight is maintained by increasing calories on fast days to 1,000 three days a week and enjoying feast days the rest of the time.

WHY IT WORKS

Key points about using this method to lose weight...

• **Why 500 calories?** Animal studies showed that consuming 25% of the normal calorie intake on fast days produced the best results in preventing and reversing disease.

Translating this finding to people, I calculated 25% of daily recommended calories, which resulted in a general recommendation of 500 calories on fast day using foods with optimal nutrients.

Those 500 calories are consumed with one 400-calorie meal and a 100-calorie snack, since people tend to overeat if calories are broken up throughout the day. Lunch or dinner works best for the meal—if you eat your 400-calorie meal for breakfast, you'll be too hungry later in the day.

Example of a lunchtime meal: A turkey and avocado sandwich (two slices of turkey, one slice of Swiss cheese and one-quarter of an avocado on one slice of multigrain bread) and fruit (such as one-half cup of strawberries) for dessert.

Before or after your meal, you can have a snack such as a smoothie.

Tasty option: In a blender, mix one cup of unsweetened chocolate almond milk with one-half cup of unsweetened frozen cherries and one cup of ice.

• **Hunger disappears.** After two weeks of alternate-day modified fasting, hunger on fast day disappears for most people. During those two weeks, ease your fast-day hunger by drinking eight to 10 eight-ounce glasses of water and other no-cal beverages such as coffee and tea and chewing sugar-free gum. Some people reported mild constipation, weakness and irritability, which subsided after two weeks.

• **You won't overeat on feast day.** My studies show that people almost never overeat on feast day—on average, they consume 110% of their normal caloric intake. Over the two-day fast/feast cycle, that's an average of 67.5% of normal caloric intake—a perfect formula for safe, steady weight loss but without the nonstop deprivation of every-day dieting.

• **Add exercise—and lose twice as much weight.** Every-other-day fasters can exercise on fast day without feeling weak or lightheaded. Exercising before the fast-day meal is best because you'll feel hungry afterward—and can eat.

Good news: People who go on an intermittent fast and exercise (45 minutes of brisk aerobic exercise, three times a week) lose twice as much weight, on average, as people who only fast. You can exercise on both fast and feast days.

• **You won't lose muscle.** Five out of six conventional dieters who lose weight gain it all back. That's probably because the typical dieter loses 75% fat and 25% muscle—and never regains that calorie-burning muscle mass after the diet is over.

But people who lose weight using alternate-day modified fasting lose only about 1% muscle—a unique and remarkable result. And my one-year maintenance studies show that these alternate-day fasters maintain their weight. Longer-term studies are also needed.

AS A DISEASE-FIGHTER...

People who have followed alternate-day modified fasting not only lose weight but also improve their overall health. *In weight-loss studies of 600 people that lasted up to one year, average reductions in risk occurred for...*

• **Heart disease.** Total cholesterol dropped 21%...and LDL "bad" cholesterol dropped 20 points. Triglycerides fell from 125 mg/dL (considered "normal") to 88 mg/dL (defined as "optimal").

• **Type 2 diabetes.** Glucose (blood sugar) levels dropped by up to 10% after eight weeks on the diet.

Animal studies have shown that intermittent fasting may help prevent...

• **Cancer.** The diet may also slow the growth of existing malignancies.

• **Cognitive decline.** Intermittent fasting helped protect the brains of mice genetically programmed to develop Alzheimer's...stopped the early development of nervous system problems in mice programmed to develop Parkinson's...and helped animals recover from stroke.

*Check with your doctor before trying this diet—especially if you have diabetes. Fasting is not recommended for pregnant women.

Drink Vegetable Juice to Lose Weight

Researchers at Baylor School of Medicine studied overweight adults who had metabolic syndrome, a constellation of risk factors for heart disease and diabetes (such as high blood sugar, high blood pressure and high triglycerides). One group of participants drank at least eight ounces of low-sodium vegetable juice daily for 12 weeks as part of a calorie-restricted diet... a second group followed the same diet but did not drink the juice.

Results: Participants assigned to the vegetable juice group lost four pounds, on average—compared with a loss of only one pound, on average, for the no-juice group.

More research is needed…but in the meantime, drinking vegetable juice on a regular basis can't hurt and may help you meet the goal of increasing vegetable intake while reducing your appetite.

Carl L. Keen, PhD, a professor of nutrition and internal medicine at the University of California, Davis, and coinvestigator of a study of 81 people.

The Easiest Diet Ever

Marla Heller, RD, a Los Angeles–based registered dietitian who developed plans to bring the DASH diet from the research phase to patients. She is author of *The DASH Diet Action Plan: Proven to Lower Blood Pressure and Cholesterol Without Medication, The DASH Diet Weight Loss Solution* and *The Everyday DASH Diet Cookbook.* DashDiet.org

Following a healthful diet is undoubtedly one of the best things we can do to protect ourselves from chronic disease. So why is it such a struggle?

Unfortunately, many diets just aren't practical over the long haul. Sure, you may be able to white-knuckle it for the first few days or weeks. But what happens when you can no longer withstand the unhealthful temptations at parties, restaurants and just about anywhere else? *The solution…*

A POWERHOUSE DIET

Many people are surprised to learn that one of the most widely studied diets is also perhaps the easiest to follow on a long-term basis because it provides enough food choices to be truly appealing—even enjoyable—to virtually anyone.

Perhaps you've heard of the DASH diet. It is commonly known as the "blood pressure diet." Short for Dietary Approaches to Stop Hypertension, the DASH plan has long been known to effectively lower blood pressure—sometimes in just 14 days, according to research.

Now: After years of scientific scrutiny, this "sleeper" of a diet, with its wide range of foods—vegetables, fruits, low-fat and nonfat dairy, whole grains, lean poultry and fish, and nuts, beans and seeds—is winning more proponents because of its other health benefits.

In addition to being linked to a lower risk for heart disease and stroke, this diet has also been shown to cut risk for kidney stones by 45% and risk for colon cancer by 20%. If that's not enough, the DASH diet also prevents (and sometimes even reverses) diabetes by controlling blood sugar spikes. And it makes you feel younger and lighter, because the low-sodium component helps you to retain less fluid.

The "Best" Diet: Because of its many health benefits, nutritional completeness and the ease with which it can be followed, the DASH diet was named "Best Overall Diet" in 2013 by *US News & World Report,* based on analyses by experts in nutrition and various chronic diseases. The DASH eating plan beat other better-known diets, such as the Mediterranean Diet and Weight Watchers.

WHY DASH WORKS

The DASH diet might seem like nothing more than a commonsense eating plan, but very few Americans actually eat according to its basic principles. Not only are most of us sorely lacking in vegetables and fruits, but we take in an average of 3,500 mg of blood pressure–raising sodium per day—far more than the amount that's recommended for healthy adults (up to 2,300 mg daily) or the amount for people with high blood pressure (up to 1,500 mg).

The magic behind DASH lies in its high amounts of potassium, calcium and magnesium. Potassium, found in fruits and vegetables, naturally lowers blood pressure by ridding the body of excess sodium. Calcium from dairy and other sources, including broccoli and fish with bones, such as sardines, works in the same way—plus it relaxes your blood vessels, making it easier for blood to pass through. Magnesium, found in whole grains, nuts and seeds, also promotes healthy blood vessels.

MAKING IT EASY

When first considering the DASH daily eating plan, you may think that you'd never be able to eat such a seemingly large amount and wide variety of food, but that's not true.

The standard 2,000-calorie plan includes…*

• **Fruits**—Four to five servings per day (one serving equals one medium-sized whole fruit or one cup diced raw fruit).

• **Vegetables**—Four to five servings per day (one serving equals one-half cup cooked vegetables or one cup leafy greens).

• **Low-fat/nonfat dairy**—Three daily servings (one serving equals one-half cup fat-free or low-fat cottage cheese or eight ounces skim or low-fat milk or low-fat or fat-free yogurt).

• **Whole grains**—Three daily servings (one serving equals one slice of bread, one-half cup cooked brown rice or one ounce dry cereal).

• **Refined grains**—A few servings a week (one serving equals one-half cup pasta or one cookie as a treat).

• **Healthy fats (such as olive oil and avocado)**—Two to three daily servings (one serving equals one teaspoon olive oil or one-eighth of a small avocado).

• **Lean meat, poultry or fish**—Seven ounces daily.

• **Beans and nuts**—Four to five servings per week (one serving equals one-quarter cup beans or nuts).

Why so much food and so many different choices? The diet delivers all the disease-fighting benefits that can be derived from good nutrition. Plus, the emphasis on low-calorie, high-volume produce and hunger-fighting protein means that you'll feel satisfied and less likely to give in to cravings for unhealthful foods that cause weight gain.

If five daily servings of veggies sounds daunting, think of it this way: A dinner including one cup sautéed broccoli (two servings)…a small side salad (one serving)…and one cup roasted potatoes (two servings) equals five full servings of veggies.

Other ways to meet DASH goals…

Fruits: Try one small banana at breakfast, one plum at lunch, one cup berries as a midafternoon snack, one-half cup sliced Bartlett pears for dessert.

*2,000 calories daily is appropriate for men age 51 and older. Women age 51 and older usually need 1,600 calories daily. Younger adults can have more calories. Weight loss requires less calories and fewer servings.

Low-fat/nonfat dairy: Try eight ounces nonfat milk on cereal (pour it on, then drink the rest), one ounce light Swiss cheese added to a sandwich for lunch, one cup light yogurt as an afternoon snack.

Whole grains: Try three-quarters cup whole-wheat cereal or oatmeal, two slices thin-sliced whole-wheat bread at lunch, one small whole-wheat dinner roll.

Healthy fats: Try one tablespoon salad dressing and a few avocado slices.

Lean meat, poultry or fish: Try three ounces of turkey slices at lunch and four ounces of salmon at dinner.

Beans and nuts: Try a small handful of nuts for a snack.

If you are eating out, try these DASH-friendly items…

• **A Grande Starbucks Caffé Latte with nonfat milk, or any 16-ounce coffee drink with eight ounces milk.**

• **A slice of thin-crust veggie pizza plus a salad.**

• **A Subway double-meat six-inch roasted chicken sandwich** topped with all of your favorite veggies, minus the top half of the bread.

For a tasty DASH snack at home, try celery dipped in hummus.

For a free copy of the complete DASH diet, go to *www.nhlbi.nih.gov/health/public/heart/hbp/dash/new_dash.pdf.*

The New Nordic Diet

Anja Olsen, PhD, researcher, Institute of Cancer Epidemiology, Danish Cancer Society, Copenhagen, Denmark.

Have you heard about the "new" Nordic diet? It turns out that Scandinavians who follow their countrymen's traditional way of eating seem to live longer. But, sorry to tell you, the key is not Danish pastries and Swedish meatballs…they eat a lot of whole-grain rye bread—real rye bread, not the mushy "rye" found alongside white bread in supermarkets—and cabbage. *But there's more to the Nordic diet than that…*

LIVE LIKE A VIKING

Anja Olsen, PhD, a researcher at the Danish Cancer Society, and a team of researchers collected information about the diets and lifestyles of approximately 57,000 Danes ages 50 to 64. Over the 12-year study period, 4,126 died. After accounting for lifestyle differences (such as exercise, weight, smoking, alcohol use and education), the researchers found a strong correlation between eating traditional Nordic foods and length of life. For instance, men who followed the traditional Nordic diet most closely had a nearly 36% lower risk of dying during the 12 years of follow-up. And women who ate the most Nordic staples reduced their risk for death by 25%.

These results appeared in the *Journal of Nutrition*.

Whole-grain rye bread, which most study participants ate daily (the median amount was two-and-a-half slices) appeared to have the strongest protective effect, especially in men. This is not the prepackaged rye bread with additives and sugars found in most supermarkets. (See next column.)

Adding further to the chance of living longer, both whole-grain rye and cabbage help in the battle against obesity. And cabbage has been related to a decreased risk for both cancer and heart disease.

However, as in other Western countries, many Nordic folk today eat too much processed and/or fatty food, including pasta, french fries, pizza and sugary desserts, and, as a result may suffer from high rates of heart disease, diabetes and cancer.

DANISH MODERN…NOT?

To encourage better health, Dr. Olsen recommends that we focus on old-style dietary habits as they've long existed in most traditional cultures, be they Nordic or from other countries. They tend to emphasize natural, whole and often wild foods—in contrast to our modern approach of eating highly refined foods.

Luckily, you don't have to be a Dane, Swede or Norwegian to eat like one. *Here are some ways you can enjoy the benefits of the healthy Nordic diet…*

• **Eat real rye bread.** Whole grains such as rye, barley and oats abound in dietary fiber, minerals and antioxidants that protect against heart disease, type 2 diabetes and cancer. In this study, whole-grain rye had the most positive impact on health—but it's important to realize that this is not the rye bread we grew up with in the US.

Instead, in this country, you'll most easily find this European-style rye by looking for German whole-grain rye, such as the Mestemacher brand, usually found in the deli section of grocery stores, and also in health-food stores, health-oriented markets such as Whole Foods and even online from *www.amazon.com*.

• **Cut up some cabbage.** Cabbage is packed with fiber and isothiocyanates (the sulphur-containing compounds found in cruciferous vegetables). Enjoy both red and green cabbage shredded raw in salads and slaws or lightly steamed.

• **Root for root vegetables.** Root vegetables, especially carrots, are rich in phytochemicals such as carotenes, which neutralize free radicals that damage cells in your body and may cause cancer. Parsnips and turnips also are good choices.

• **Enjoy apples, pears and wild berries.** Wild berries, which are easily available in Scandinavia, are especially rich sources of substances such as omega-3 fatty acids, essential to normal growth and development, as well as antioxidants and phytoestrogens such as lignans, which help lower cancer risk. But even though wild berries contain many more of these healthful components, the berries you find in US grocery stores—i.e., cultivated ones—are still a good source of these important nutrients.

Can't Keep the Weight Off? You Could Have a Food Addiction

Joel Fuhrman, MD, family physician who specializes in natural and nutritional medicine, Flemington, New Jersey, and author of the two-book series *Eat for Health: Lose Weight, Keep It Off, Look Younger, Live Longer*. DrFuhrman.com

Most diets are guaranteed to fail. Popular diets focus on limiting calories, fat and/or carbohydrates. They don't address addiction, which is the underlying cause of both weight gain and repeated failures to lose weight.

Like other addictions, an addiction to food causes intense cravings, particularly during times of stress. People also experience withdrawal when they go without food for even a short time. The discomfort of cravings and withdrawal is so intense that people find themselves unable to reduce portion sizes, eat less often or avoid fattening foods. It hurts too much when they try.

TOXIC HUNGER

The American diet is loaded with fried foods, sugar-laden baked goods, soft drinks and other foods that stimulate the production of free radicals and other toxins. After eating, the body goes through a detoxification phase in order to break down and remove these toxins.

●**Detox is painful.** People who eat a lot of unhealthy foods invariably experience both physical and emotional discomfort, including feelings of anxiety, irritability and fatigue, in the hours between meals. In an effort to stop the discomfort, they eat again…and again. As long as the digestive tract is working, detoxification is delayed. Without knowing why, people find themselves eating all the time just to forestall these uncomfortable feelings.

I call these feelings "toxic hunger" because they're produced by a toxin-producing (and fattening) diet—and because people often confuse the sensations of withdrawal with the sensation of hunger.

●**Detox takes a few weeks.** You may feel strange the first week, but during week two, the sensations will start to change and soon you will not be driven to overeat.

To break the cycle…

EAT HIGH-ANTIOXIDANT FOODS

These include beans, fresh vegetables, nuts, seeds and berries. The body experiences high levels of oxidative stress when it's detoxifying between meals. This is largely what fuels the symptoms of toxic hunger. People can reduce this discomfort by consuming foods high in disease-fighting antioxidants. These foods also make it easier for the liver to eliminate metabolites (chemical by-products that are produced during digestion and that intensify discomfort between meals).

RECOGNIZE TRUE HUNGER

Most people who struggle to lose weight complain that they're always hungry. What they're really experiencing is the discomfort of detoxification, which includes symptoms such as a growling stomach and irritability. They eat to feel better, not because they need to.

People should eat only when they feel true hunger, the body's call for nutrients. True hunger feels different from toxic hunger. *What to notice…*

●**A hard-to-describe sensation in your throat that only occurs when you're genuinely hungry.** It's like an itch that's relieved by eating.

●**A slight increase in salivation.**

●**A dramatically heightened taste sensation, in which anything you eat tastes wonderful.** If you notice that you're craving a specific food, you're not experiencing true hunger, because everything should taste wonderful at this point.

I often advise patients to delay or skip meals so that they learn to distinguish true hunger from toxic hunger. The first step is to eat a high-antioxidant diet for two weeks. Then try eating a light breakfast and postponing lunch for perhaps six hours until you are sure that you feel hungry. This simple experiment can be revelatory for those who rarely go more than a few hours without eating. They discover that even ordinary foods taste great (and extraordinary foods taste amazing).

EAT MORE, NOT LESS

Food volume is critical for controlling hunger. Feelings of satiety are largely controlled by stomach stretch receptors. Eating large amounts of healthy, low-calorie foods activates these receptors and "turns off" hunger sensations to a degree that's not possible with snacks or high-fat or fried foods—unless you eat way too many calories.

Example: Imagine two different stomachs, each containing 400 calories of a single kind of food. The stomach with 400 calories of protein (such as beef) would be mainly empty space—all of the calories come from a small volume of food. A stomach filled with 400 calories of vegetables and legumes, on the other hand, would be filled to capacity, prompting the stomach to send "I'm full" signals to the brain.

This is why people who eat two to three servings of vegetables, fruits, legumes, whole grains or other wholesome foods at every meal are more likely to lose weight—and experience less discomfort—than those who diet.

CHOOSE NUTS AND SEEDS

Even though these foods are high in fat, people who eat nuts and seeds regularly are more likely to lose weight than people who don't eat them. Nuts and seeds are high in plant sterols, which promote feelings of fullness and contain substances that suppress appetite.

Bonus: Clinical trials have shown that diets that include nuts can lower cholesterol and reduce the risk for diabetes. On average, people who eat one or more servings of nuts a day have a 59% lower risk of developing fatal heart disease than those who don't eat nuts.

Recommended: One ounce daily of unsalted nuts (all nuts are good) and/or seeds, such as pumpkin seeds and sunflower seeds.

SOCIALIZE MORE

Many people who are overweight use food for emotional comfort just as other addicts use drugs or alcohol. Eating temporarily increases dopamine, a brain chemical that elicits feelings of well-being, temporarily suppressing feelings of unworthiness or depression. This naturally encourages people to eat more.

Better: An active social life. People who engage in pleasurable activities with other people experience the same dopamine surge that they would otherwise get from eating. They also tend to have higher self-esteem and are more motivated to take care of themselves and improve their health.

DON'T OVERLOAD ON CAFFEINE

People who are trying to lose weight often use caffeinated beverages, such as coffee, tea and diet colas, in place of food to forestall between-meal discomfort. It doesn't work. People feel even worse when caffeine levels drop. At that point, they're even more tempted to "self-medicate" with food.

I usually advise patients to give up caffeine initially because it will help them get through the detox phase more quickly. Once they've reached a satisfactory weight, they can start drinking caffeine again.

How Food Preservatives Make You Fat

Study titled "Dietary emulsifiers impact the mouse gut microbiota promoting colitis and metabolic syndrome," from researchers in the department of biology, Center for Inflammation, Immunity and Infection, Institute for Biomedical Sciences at Georgia State University in Atlanta, published in *Nature*.

It's no secret that we've become a heavy population. Changes to our food supply—with our heavy reliance on packaged and processed foods—may have something to do with it. If you were never a stickler about reading food labels, you will be after reading what two common food stabilizers do to your gut and your body. The additives in question are emulsifiers—a type of food additive that helps maintain food texture.

THE FATE OF EMULSIFIED MICE— IS IT YOURS?

Researchers have suspected that emulsifiers damage the gut, allowing bacteria to cross the delicate epithelium the porous lining of the intestine off a chain reaction that can lead to weight gain, metabolic syndrome (the triad of high cholesterol, high blood pressure and diabetes) and/or inflammatory bowel disease. So researchers used mice in a series of experiments to learn more about what two of the most commonly used food emulsifiers do to the intestinal tract. Their names may be quite familiar to you from reading food labels—carboxymethylcellulose (also known as cellulose gum) and polysorbate-80.

For 12 weeks, mice were either given drinking water that was mixed with one of the two emulsifiers at concentrations similar to real-world human consumption…or plain water.

The results: Bacteria in mice that drank emulsifier-spiked water could be found clinging to the intestinal epithelium. The mucus barrier was much thinner in most of the mice consuming emulsifiers compared with mice that drank plain water…and they also had a different mix of bacteria than the mice that drank plain water. Carboxymethylcellulose and polysorbate-80 each caused the same type and degree of change to the gut epithelium, mucous membrane and gut microbiome.

Why this matters: Mice that drank emulsifiers ate more and so gained more weight. They also become glucose intolerant, setting them up for diabetes and metabolic syndrome. And the altered mix of bacteria in their gut promoted intestinal inflammation.

The researchers then toyed with the amount of emulsifiers given to the mice to see just how little it takes for the microbiome to react. Just one half of the equivalent amount of carboxymethylcellulose permitted by the FDA for humans led to low-grade inflammation and increased fat. Just one tenth of the amount permitted by the FDA led to weight gain and glucose intolerance. And when the research team switched the experiment by adding emulsifiers to food instead of water, the results were the same.

This study doesn't defy the notion that eating and drinking too much is responsible for weight gain and metabolic syndrome. What it does show is that food additives may be contributing to obesity and intestinal inflammation and the range of problems that come with these conditions.

Surefire Way to Stop Overeating: The Five-Point Hunger Scale

Osama Hamdy, MD, PhD, medical director, Obesity Clinical Program, Joslin Diabetes Center, and assistant professor of medicine, Harvard Medical School, both in Boston. He is a coauthor of *The Diabetes Breakthrough: Based on a Scientifically Proven Plan to Reverse Diabetes Through Weight Loss*. TheDiabetesBreak through.com

It happened again. You sat down to a meal or started to snack and, despite your intention not to overindulge, somehow kept eating until you were stuffed. Curses! Perhaps you've tried that "mindful eating" business in the past—paying attention to the physical and emotional sensations during every moment with food—because you've heard that it helps people avoid overeating. Problem is, that "every moment" aspect is tough to pull off. After all, sometimes you want to converse with your meal companions or look at the newspaper or just gaze out the window while you eat, rather than focusing fully on every single bite.

Well, there's an easier way to achieve the same kind of control that mindful eating provides. It's called the five-point hunger scale. *The idea is to simply rate your hunger on the following scale…*

1 – Starved
2 – Hungry
3 – Comfortable
4 – Full
5 – Stuffed

The beautiful simplicity of the five-point scale is that, rather than thinking about it constantly while you eat, you need only to give it a moment's focus three times—before, midway through and after any given meal or snack. *Here's what to do…*

When you're tempted to eat, before you begin: Rate your hunger, asking yourself.…

•**Are you feeling ravenous, spacey or light-headed?** Do you feel like almost any kind of food would satisfy you? You're at point one, starving, and you must eat—in fact, you have waited too long. When you're feeling starved, self-control becomes extremely difficult and you're likely to end up overeating... after which you'll feel guilty, so you'll starve yourself again. In essence, you bounce back and forth from starving to stuffed all day, without ever feeling truly comfortable and satisfied.

Best: Don't let your hunger reach point one.

•**Is your stomach growling, letting you know that your body needs fuel?** Has the feeling come on gradually? You're at point two, hungry. Hunger is a slow sensation. It doesn't jump into your brain all of a sudden... and it usually occurs around the same time that you're used to having breakfast, lunch or supper.

Remember: Point two is the perfect point at which to eat.

•**Are you physically comfortable but still feel like eating—with a specific type of food in mind?** You're at point three, and you're facing a craving, not true hunger. A craving is a psychological issue rather than a physical one...a spark sensation that comes on suddenly.

What to do: Don't jump right into eating. Instead, consider what emotion is driving your urge to eat.

Then try to satisfy that need with a food-free activity to see whether the craving goes away. Feeling lonely? Pick up the phone. Bored? Tackle a crossword puzzle, or clear some clutter out of your garage or closet. Stressed? Soak in the tub, or take a hike. If you still desire that particular food afterward, go ahead and indulge in moderation, eating only as much as you need to satisfy the craving.

Halfway through your meal: After you've been eating for five to 10 minutes, put down your fork and rate your hunger again...

•**Have your physical sensations of hunger lessened but still linger?** You're just past point two, on your way to three. Some people stop here, especially when they want to lose weight. But this backfires because it usually triggers a second eating period not much later.

Better: Keep eating!

•**Do you feel pleasantly sated?** You're at point three, comfortable—which is ideal, especially if you're trying to lose weight. If you stop now, you should have enough energy to last until your next scheduled meal. But if you're enjoying your food, you don't have to stop yet...it's OK to keep eating slowly for a few more minutes.

•**Are you on your way to discomfort?** Is your waistband starting to feel snug? You're at point four, full—and you should definitely stop eating now. Remember, it takes 15 to 20 minutes for your stomach to send the signal to your brain that it is full. If you eat until your stomach feels full, you will be beyond full—in fact, you'll be painfully stuffed, point five—by the time your brain gets that signal.

Twenty minutes after your meal: Rate your hunger level one last time...

•**Is your belly a bit distended but not painful?** Congratulations—you're at point four, full. You stopped eating in time.

•**Do you feel the urge to groan or lie down?** Are you so full that you couldn't put another bite into your mouth? You're at point five, stuffed...and you definitely went too far. Your body would have been satisfied if you had stopped several hundred calories sooner, and you would have avoided the discomfort and weight gain that come with overeating.

Helpful: Don't starve yourself for the rest of the day...but at your next meal, do pay closer attention to your mid-meal hunger rating, and stop when you're at point three.

For the first few weeks: While you're learning to recognize how your body feels at each point, keep a written log of your hunger scale scores before, midway through and after each meal. If you need a reminder, set a timer or program your cell phone to beep. Keep it up, and you'll soon become adept at waiting to reach point two before you start eating (without delaying too long and hitting point one)... and at stopping when you reach point three or four (without ever hitting point five). Once that happens, you're on your way to a life-time of sensible, pleasurable eating and easy weight control.

Foods That Rev Up Your Metabolism

Ridha Arem, MD, an endocrinologist, director of the Texas Thyroid Institute, an endocrinologist practice at Texas Medical Center in Houston. He is a former chief of endocrinology and metabolism at Houston's Ben Taub General Hospital and is author of *The Thyroid Solution Diet.* AremWellness.com

---

Forget about calories! Most people who are trying to lose weight worry too much about calories and not enough about the actual cause of those extra pounds.

The real culprit: Out-of-balance hormones.

Best approach for controlling weight: A diet that rebalances the body's hormones. Carefully chosen foods and food combinations rebalance levels and/or efficiency of metabolism-regulating hormones, such as ghrelin, leptin and thyroid hormone. You'll burn more calories, and your body will be less likely to store calories as fat. *Here's how…*

TWEAKING THE BEST DIETS

Hands down, the Mediterranean diet is one of the healthiest diets out there. With its emphasis on plant-based foods (such as vegetables, fruits, grains and nuts) and healthful fats (from fatty fish and olive oil), it is good for your heart and helps control blood sugar levels.

But for more efficient weight loss, you need to go a step further. That's where the Protein-Rich Oriental Diet, developed by Korean researchers, enters the picture. With its heavy focus on high-protein foods, this diet has been found to provide twice the weight loss offered by calorie restriction alone.

To achieve and maintain an optimal body weight: The diet I designed includes elements of both these diets—as well as some important additional tweaks such as timing your meals (see the next page) and consuming a mix of proteins in order to get the full comple-ment of amino acids, which is essential for increasing metabolism and controlling hunger. On my diet, you will eat a combination of at least two proteins, good fats and vegetables at each meal. *For example…*

• **Fish, turkey and chicken contain all of the essential amino acids that are in red meat,** but with fewer calories and less saturated fat. They're particularly rich in arginine, an amino acid that increases the speed at which your body burns calories.

My advice: Aim for six to eight ounces of these foods as the primary protein for dinner. You also can include these foods at breakfast and lunch as one of your protein choices. (If you're not a fish lover, see "fish oil supplements," next page.)

• **Reduced-fat cottage cheese, ricotta, yogurt and goat cheese.** Certain forms of dairy are high in branched-chain amino acids, which suppress appetite and increase the ability of mitochondria (the energy-producing components of cells) to burn fat.

My advice: Each day, eat about a half-cup of low-fat or nonfat dairy as a protein.

• **High-protein beans, lentils and grains,** such as black beans, kidney beans, quinoa and brown rice. Eat one of these protein sources (three-fourths cup to one cup) at lunch—usually combined with a small serving of fish or lean meat. In addition to packing plenty of protein and fiber, these foods provide large amounts of amino acids that will help you get fitter and have more energy.

• **Egg whites contain all of the amino acids that you need for efficient weight loss,** and they are my favorite choice as a protein for breakfast. An egg-white omelet with onions, mushrooms and other vegetables can be prepared in just a few minutes. Limit your intake of egg yolks due to their cholesterol.

LOW-GLYCEMIC CARBS

Carbohydrates that are digested quickly—mainly refined and processed foods such as juices, white rice and French fries—increase insulin and fat storage. Carbohydrates with a lower glycemic score are absorbed more slowly and don't cause unhealthy changes in insulin or fat storage.

Good choices: Whole oats, chickpeas and fruit (see below) at breakfast and lunch, and vegetables at each meal.

MORE FIBER

The fiber in such foods as beans and vegetables reduces appetite and slows digestion, important for preventing insulin "spikes." Research shows that people of normal weight tend to eat significantly more fiber than those who are overweight or obese.

For efficient weight loss: Get 35 g of fiber daily.

• **Fruit is also a good source of fiber.** Just be sure that you choose fresh fruit that's low in natural sugar (fructose).

Good choices: Raspberries, strawberries, papayas, apples and cranberries. Avoid fruit at dinner to make it the lowest glycemic meal.

GREEN TEA

Green tea is high in epigallocatechin gallate (EGCG), a substance that can decrease the accumulation of body fat. It also increases insulin sensitivity and improves an obesity-related condition known as metabolic syndrome. Drink a few cups every day. Do not sweeten the tea with honey or other sweeteners—they are among the main causes of high insulin and weight gain.

FISH OIL SUPPLEMENTS

The omega-3 fatty acids in fish increase the rate at which calories are burned. However, even if you eat fish every day, it doesn't contain enough omega-3s for long-term weight control.

Solution: Take a daily supplement with 600 mg of EPA and 400 mg of DHA—the main types of omega-3s. Check first with your doctor if you take blood thinners or diabetes medication, since fish oil may interact with these drugs.

NOT JUST FOR WEIGHT LOSS

A hormone-balancing eating plan can rev up your metabolism even if you don't need to lose weight, giving you more energy and mental focus. If you aren't overweight and you follow this eating plan, you may lose a pound or two, but mostly you'll just feel better.

More from Dr. Arem…

Timing Matters!

When you eat is almost as important as what you eat…

• **Plan on eating four or five daily meals—** breakfast between 6 am and 8 am…an optional (and light) late-morning snack…lunch between 11 am and 12:30 pm…a mid-afternoon snack…and supper between 5 pm and 7 pm.

• **Plan your meals so that you get more protein at supper.** It will stimulate the release of growth hormone, which burns fat while you sleep.

• **Avoid all food three hours before bedtime.** Eating late in the evening causes increases in blood sugar and insulin that can lead to weight gain—even if you consume a lower-calorie diet (1,200 to 1,500 calories a day).

The Right Way to Take Your Vitamins

Jacob Teitelbaum, MD, board-certified internist, holistic physician and nationally known expert in the fields of chronic fatigue syndrome, fibromyalgia, sleep and pain. Based in Hawaii, he is author of numerous books, including *The Fatigue and Fibromyalgia Solution*…*Pain Free 1-2-3*…and *Real Cause, Real Cure*, as well as the popular free iPhone and Android application *Cures A–Z*. Vitality101.com

---

Many of us take vitamins and other nutritional supplements. In fact, researchers from Harvard analyzed data from nearly 125,000 middle-aged and older people and found that an astounding 88% of women and 81% of men took supplements.

Unfortunately, a lot of us take nutritional supplements wrong.*

We don't take high-enough doses…or we take them at the wrong time of day…or we combine them with other supplements, foods or drugs that can block absorption.

*Be sure to check supplement dosage amounts with your doctor, especially if you have diabetes or another chronic condition.

Good news: I've counseled thousands of patients on the best ways to take vitamins, and I can assure you that taking them correctly can be simple and straightforward.

What you might be doing wrong—and how to quickly fix the problem...

Vitamin mistake #1: **You take a dose that's too low.** There are many nutrient-nutrient interactions that can reduce the absorption of individual nutrients by 5% to 10%. Example: Iron cuts the absorption of zinc—the more iron in a supplement, the less zinc you're likely to absorb.

My advice: Don't take a multivitamin that supplies 100% of the "Daily Value" of nutrients, a level intended only to prevent deficiency diseases. Instead, take a multivitamin that supplies an optimal amount of nutrients—an amount that will easily overcome every absorption issue caused by nutrient-nutrient interactions.

For simplicity, use the B-vitamins as your reference point. Look for a product that supplies about 40 milligrams (mg) each of thiamin, riboflavin, niacin and vitamin B-6 (*pyridoxine*), and 200 micrograms (mcg) of vitamin B-12. These levels are safe and therapeutic, improving energy and mental clarity. When a product contains the above levels of these nutrients, it usually will have optimal levels of other nutrients as well.

Vitamin mistake #2: **You take a dose that's too high.** It can be detrimental to your health to take high doses of vitamin A and vitamin E. *Reasons:* Taking more than 3,000 international units (IU) of vitamin A (retinol) daily can increase your risk for osteoporosis, the bone-eroding disease. Vitamin E actually is a family of eight compounds called tocopherols and tocotrienols. Alpha-tocopherol—the compound commonly found in multivitamins—can be toxic in doses higher than 100 IU daily.

My advice: Take a multivitamin that contains no more than 3,000 IU of vitamin A total, with approximately one-half from retinol and one-half from beta-carotene (which turns into vitamin A in the body and does not cause osteoporosis).

Choose a multivitamin with no more than 100 IU of vitamin E. If you take the nutrient as a separate supplement for a specific condition, such as for breast tenderness, take it in the form of mixed tocopherols and tocotrienols.

Vitamin mistake #3: **You try to take vitamins two or three times a day.** Taking vitamins in divided doses—two or even three times a day—is ideal because the body sustains higher blood levels of the nutrients. But very few people can stick with this type of regimen.

My advice: Take vitamins first thing in the morning, with breakfast. (The fat in the meal will help you absorb vitamins A, D and E, which are fat-soluble.) Yes, there's a tiny trade-off of effectiveness for convenience, but it's worth it.

Exception: If you take magnesium as a separate supplement, you might want to take it at bedtime for deeper sleep. Avoid magnesium oxide and magnesium hydroxide, both of which are poorly absorbed. Magnesium glycinate or magnesium malate is preferred.

Vitamin mistake #4: **You take a second-rate formulation.** Vitamins come in a range of forms—tablets, caplets, capsules, chewables, softgels, liquids, powders—and some are better than others.

Vitamin tablets, for example, are a poor choice. They may not dissolve completely—and you can't absorb any nutrients from a pill that doesn't dissolve. Tablets (and some of the other forms listed above) also may contain binders, fillers and other additives. These supposedly "inert" compounds may have all kinds of unknown effects on the body.

My advice: I recommend powders, which are highly absorbable. Just add water and stir. My favorite is the Energy Revitalization System, from Enzymatic Therapy, which I formulated. (So that I can't be accused of profiting from my recommendation, I donate 100% of my royalties from sales to charity.) I recommend one scoop each morning combined with 5 grams of ribose (a naturally occurring sugar) to optimize energy.

Don't like drinks? Try a combination of My Favorite Multiple Take One by Natrol plus two tablets of Jigsaw Sustained Release Magnesium plus two chewable ribose tablets (2 grams to 3 grams each).

***Vitamin mistake #5*: You take calcium.** One-third of people who take supplements take calcium—and I think just about every one of those people is making a mistake. The scientific evidence shows that taking a calcium supplement provides little or no protection against bone fractures, and research now links calcium supplements to increased risk for heart attacks and strokes.

My advice: I strongly recommend that you get your calcium from food, eating one or two servings of dairy a day. Almonds, broccoli and green leafy vegetables such as kale also are good calcium sources. Unlike supplemental calcium, calcium from food is safe. If you decide to take a calcium supplement for stronger bones, take no more than 100 mg to 200 mg daily, and always combine it with other bone-supporting nutrients, such as vitamin D, magnesium and vitamin K. Take these at night to help sleep.

***Vitamin mistake #6*: You don't realize that your medication can cause a nutrient deficiency.** Some medications block the absorption of specific nutrients. *In my clinical experience, the two worst offenders are…*

• The diabetes drug *metformin*, which can cause a B-12 deficiency.

What to do: Metformin is an excellent medication, but be sure to take a multivitamin containing at least 200 mcg of B-12 daily.

• Proton pump inhibitors such as Nexium (*esomeprazole*), which block the production of stomach acid and are prescribed for heartburn, ulcers and other gastrointestinal problems. Long-term use can cause deficiencies of magnesium and B-12.

What to do: Take a multivitamin with 200 mcg of B-12 and additional magnesium (200 mg daily)—and talk to your doctor about getting off the drug. (A gradual decrease in dosage is safest.) Proton pump inhibitors are toxic when used long term and addictive, causing rebound acid hyper-secretion when stopped. The solution? Improve digestion using plant-based digestive enzymes, deglycyrrhizinated

licorice (DGL), marshmallow root and other stomach-healing supplements. Follow directions on the labels.

Say Yay for Whey and Lose Weight

Chris D'Adamo, PhD, a nutritional research scientist, is an assistant professor in the department of family and community medicine and the department of epidemiology and public health and assistant director for medical education at the Center for Integrative Medicine, all at the University of Maryland School of Medicine in Baltimore. He also is a certified sports nutrition consultant and certified personal trainer with a Baltimore-based private practice.

A recent study published in *The Journal of Nutrition* provides proof that whey protein supplementation helped overweight and obese people drop unwanted pounds and trim belly girth.

What's more, whey can help you keep weight off for good. That's because protein is one of the keys to sustainable weight loss and weight management, according to Chris D'Adamo, PhD, a nutritional research scientist at the University of Maryland School of Medicine in Baltimore.

The pluses of protein: Consuming sufficient protein is an important weight-control strategy. For one thing, protein increases satiety—you feel less hungry after eating protein than after eating carbohydrates or fats, so you're less likely to feel deprived and blow your diet. Also, protein is more thermogenic than carbs and fats, meaning that your body tends to burn it off rather than store it as fat. Protein promotes lean muscle mass, too, which improves metabolism—so you use up more calories without doing anything extra. And there's no need for women to worry about winding up with bulging muscles or a bulked-up appearance, Dr. D'Adamo said. Instead, protein simply promotes a higher muscle-to-fat ratio that results in a healthier body composition and easier weight management.

Why whey? Whey protein is a derivative of milk and contains all of the essential amino acids that your body cannot produce on its own. Compared to other protein supplements that have been studied, such as soy and casein (another milk protein), whey is a clear winner for weight control and for overall good health. *That's because whey…*

• **Increases levels of satiety-boosting hormones,** such as leptin and cholecystokinin, more than other proteins do. "It's tough to lose weight when you're starving yourself and you're hungry all the time. Whey helps prevent that situation of persistent hunger," Dr. D'Adamo said.

• **Has the highest bioavailable value among proteins,** which means that our bodies can easily absorb and use it.

• **Improves insulin sensitivity,** thus lowering the risk for metabolic syndrome, diabetes, coronary artery disease and stroke.

• **Stimulates production of glutathione,** an antioxidant that improves liver efficiency, allowing the body to clear toxins and make better use of nutrients.

• **Contains 10% to 15% immunoglobulins,** which are known to enhance immune system activity.

• **Is easy to digest.** Even people who have problems with lactose (a sugar found in milk) usually can tolerate whey protein. Whey also contains little or no casein, a milk protein that also can cause digestive upset. However, Dr. D'Adamo noted that people with lactose or casein intolerance should initially consume small amounts of whey to test their tolerability.

Patients with liver or kidney problems who have been told to monitor their protein intake should check with their doctors before taking any protein supplement. Except for people with a milk allergy, who should avoid whey altogether, whey protein generally is safe.

Yummy ways to add whey to your diet: Whey protein powder is sold at health-food stores, drugstores and online. Options include whey concentrate, which is more economical…and whey isolate, which goes through an extra filtering step to remove more fat and carbs (in the form of lactose) and thus may be preferable for people with lactose or casein intolerances who are using whey as a weight-loss aid.

One or two servings of whey protein per day should be an appropriate amount for the average woman who wants to lose weight, Dr. D'Adamo said. A one-tablespoon serving contains about 40 calories. Breakfast is a great time to consume your whey because it helps suppress hunger for hours afterward. You also can have some whey about an hour before exercising—it will provide an extra energy burst and help maximize the body-composition benefits of your workout.

Combine your whey powder with the cold or hot liquid of your choice, following label directions. *Easy recipe ideas…*

• **Mix whey powder with plain water for the lowest-calorie protein drink and a neutral taste.** For a tastier beverage, add your favorite drink-flavoring product—for instance, Mio Liquid Water Enhancer or Crystal Light lemonade powder.

• **For a smoothie,** blend whey powder with milk or juice…berries, bananas or other fruit…and ice.

• **Stir whey powder into hot cereal before cooking…**or add to soups or stews before serving.

---

10 Hydrophilic Foods That Satisfy Hunger and Help You Lose Weight

Keren Gilbert, MS, RD, nutritionist and the founder and president of Decision Nutrition, a nutrition consulting firm in Great Neck, New York, and author of *The HD Diet: Achieve Lifelong Weight Loss with Chia Seeds and Other Water-Absorbent Foods.*

What if you could swallow a pill right before dining that would make your stomach swell like a balloon so you would feel artificially full? Well, such a pill is in the works, but there's a much better solution for you—hydrophilic foods. They attract and absorb water, which makes them swell in size—in a natural process—so you naturally feel satisfied and automatically consume fewer calories. Plus, unlike a weird new diet pill or other diet gimmicks, they are full of nutrients that your body needs. And besides helping you lose or maintain weight, hydrophilic foods—because they contain digestible soluble fiber—also help control blood sugar and cholesterol.

And it's all real food. What more could you want?

THE TOP 10 HYDROPHILIC FOODS

• **Chia seeds.** Chia seeds are the perfect example of a hydrophilic food. They start out as tiny, crunchy, nutty-tasting seeds (just a little bigger than poppy seeds), but each seed can absorb up to 12 times its weight in water, so they form a gel that's filling and extremely nutrient-rich—each seed is supercharged with omega-3s and packed with antioxidants, fiber, iron, magnesium, calcium and potassium! So sprinkle a tablespoon into your smoothie for breakfast, add some to soups and porridges or even use them in place of breadcrumbs to bind meatballs. You can even make a simple and nutritious pudding by combining two tablespoons of chia seeds per cup of almond milk or other liquid, sweetening to taste and refrigerating overnight—no cooking needed.

• **Okra.** OK, okra might be a turnoff for some people because it gets sappy—or downright slimy—when cooked, but that texture speaks volumes about its soluble fiber, which, along with a host of vitamins and minerals, turns okra into a dietary powerhouse. Add sliced okra to soups and stews, where the consistency doesn't stand out so much and, in fact, the okra acts as a natural thickener. Also consider cooking okra at high heat (in a wok, for example), or slicing it lengthwise and grilling it—both cooking styles will reduce the vegetable's slipperiness. To use it raw, slice and toss into salads or dress with oil and vinegar all on its own. It's tasty, with a good crunch, and its slight sappiness enhances the texture of the dressing.

• **Oatmeal.** Oatmeal is a hydrophilic food you might already be filling up on since it's well-known for its cholesterol-controlling abilities. Just picture the way raw oats absorb water while they cook, and you'll understand why they make my top-10 list of hydrophilic foods. Don't like oatmeal? Maybe it's because the only kind you know is rolled oats—the kind that look flattened and may have even been partially cooked before you buy them. Rolled oats can cook up mushy and without much natural flavor. Try steel-cut oats. They cook up into a hearty, pleasantly toothsome and nutty-tasting dish.

• **Pears.** Pears are naturally full of pectin, a type of soluble fiber found in the walls of plant cells. If you've ever made jam, you've probably added pectin powder to thicken it. In addition to helping you feel full, pectin acts as a detoxifier, a gastrointestinal tract regulator and an immune system stimulant. Grab a pear for a juicy snack, or try these delicious ways to use them—add thin slices to sandwiches...toss into salads...or cut them in half, core them and either grill or roast them. To grill, simply place them, cut side down, on a lightly oiled stovetop grill until they are seared. To roast, place them, cut side down, in a baking pan, warm up a half cup of apple juice and a tablespoon or two of honey, pour the apple juice over the pears, and bake at 400°F for 30 minutes.

• **Barley.** Like oats, barley absorbs a substantial amount of water as it cooks—and like oats, it also expands further in your stomach, providing heart-healthy nutrition and natural fullness. Americans aren't very familiar with barley and don't use it very much in their kitchens—which is ironic since it was one of the original foods grown by the Pilgrims and may have been eaten at the first Thanksgiving. Beyond the standard beef-barley stew (which, by the way, can be a very healthful meal!), it's actually very easy to use and enjoy barley. Just follow cooking instructions on the package, and then use barley as the base in your favorite whole-grain salad recipe (instead of wheat berries, for example)...use it instead of small pastas in soups (it lends an earthier tone than pasta)...sauté it with some butter and sliced mushrooms, salt and pepper. You can even cook barley like risotto—barley's soluble fiber creates the right kind of creaminess for risotto-like dishes.

•**Brussels sprouts.** Serving for serving, Brussels sprouts are among the vegetables highest in soluble fiber. For a taste revelation, try tossing fresh Brussels sprouts with olive oil and salt, then roasting in the oven at 400°F for 30 to 40 minutes or until they are softened and caramelized...or shred them raw and use in slaw. You can also make an easy, delicious boiled Brussels sprouts dish. Cut the sprouts in half, then boil them with a variety of herbs such as garlic, basil, thyme, and rosemary in one part wine vinegar and one part water until they are tender. Drain, dress with balsamic vinegar and olive oil, salt, pepper and more herbs to taste. Let cool and serve at room temperature.

•**Kidney beans.** Like all beans, kidney beans soak up water as they cook and keep doing it after you eat them. I especially favor kidney beans because their red color indicates a high level of disease-fighting antioxidants—the darker red, the better. Of course, they are a great addition to chilies, salads and soups such as minestrone. You might also like to partly mash a cup and a half of cooked kidney beans and mix them with olive oil, a dash of balsamic vinegar, salt, garlic and other spices to taste for a delicious bean spread served with crostini or Italian bread.

•**Chickpeas.** Also called garbanzo beans, these might be the single most easy and versatile food on this top-10 list. You know you can toss them onto any salad—but you don't even need the salad. You can simply open a can of chickpeas, drain, add any salad dressing and start eating—and if you like this idea, don't miss trying them in Caesar dressing with Parmesan cheese sprinkled on top. If you have a little more time, purée chickpeas with garlic, cumin, tahini, olive oil and lemon juice for a healthy, homemade hummus. For a portable snack, toss chickpeas with a bit of olive oil and your favorite spice blend, then roast until irresistibly crunchy. Or make pasta e fagiole—the Italian version of "rice and beans"—by adding cooked chickpeas and small pasta to a saucy sauté of diced onions, carrots, celery or fennel, zucchini and stewed tomatoes and their juice.

•**Oranges.** That an orange easily fits in a purse or jacket pocket makes it one of my favorite snacks. Besides the famous vitamin C content, oranges are packed with soluble fiber. To get the most nutritional (and weight-loss) benefit, don't peel off all the pith—the white substance beneath the peel. It's got loads of pectin and almost as much vitamin C as the juicy fruit it covers.

•**Agar.** Unless you are really into baking or fancy cooking, agar (also called agar-agar) is the hydrophilic food you're least likely to have in your pantry, but you might want to consider stocking it. It's a gelling agent made from seaweed that has a whopping 80% soluble fiber with no fat and virtually no calories, carbs or sugar. If you want a homemade sweet, agar is the perfect ingredient for making custards, puddings and fruit gels. And it couldn't be easier to use—just substitute it for gelatin in recipes.

Bon appétit to your health and waistline!

Suicide by Sugar

Nancy Appleton, PhD, a clinical nutritionist in San Diego. She is author, with G.N. Jacobs, of *Suicide by Sugar: A Startling Look at Our #1 National Addiction*.

The phrase "addictive white powder" probably makes you think of illegal drugs. Add sugar to that addictive group. Americans consume vast quantities—and suffer withdrawal symptoms when they don't get it. In fact, animal studies indicate that sugar is more addictive than cocaine.

Excess sugar has been linked to obesity, cancer, diabetes and dementia. *What to do…*

SUGAR, SUGAR EVERYWHERE

In the US, the average person consumes about 142 pounds of sugar each year, the equivalent of 48 teaspoons a day. Of that amount, 74 pounds is "added" sugar—about 23 teaspoons every day. Added sugars are defined as those sugars added to foods and beverages during processing or home preparation as opposed to sugars that occur naturally.

People who want to cut back on sweeteners usually start with the sugar bowl. They spoon less sugar on their breakfast cereal, for example, or use a sugar substitute in their coffee.

This doesn't help very much. The vast majority of added sugar in the diet comes from packaged foods, including foods that we think are healthful.

For example, eight ounces of one brand of sweetened apple yogurt contains 44 grams of sugar, according to the nutrition facts label. Four grams equals one teaspoon, so that's 11 teaspoons of sugar. (You cannot tell from the label how much sugar is from the yogurt, how much is from the apples and how much is added sugar.)

Most of the added sugar that we consume comes from regular soft drinks (there are about 10 teaspoons of sugar in 12 ounces of nondiet soda), candy, pies, cookies, cakes, fruit drinks and milk-based desserts and products (ice cream, sweetened yogurt).

If you look carefully at ingredients labels, which list ingredients in order of quantity, you will see that the first two or three ingredients often are forms of sugar, but many have innocuous-sounding names, such as barley malt, galactose and agave nectar. Other forms of sugar include honey, maple syrup, corn syrup, corn sweetener, dextrine, rice syrup, glucose, sucrose and dextrose.

DANGEROUS IMBALANCE

The difference between sickness and health lies in the body's ability to maintain homeostasis, the proper balance and performance of all of the internal functions. Excess sugar disturbs this balance by impairing immunity, disrupting the production and release of hormones and creating an acidic internal environment.

It's not healthy to maintain a highly acidic state. The body tries to offset this by making itself more alkaline. It does this, in part, by removing calcium and other minerals from the bones.

Result: People who eat too much sugar experience disruptions in insulin and other hormones. They have an elevated risk for osteoporosis due to calcium depletion. They also tend to have elevated levels of cholesterol and triglycerides (blood fats), which increase the risk for heart disease.

BREAK THE CYCLE

Sugar, like drugs and alcohol, is addictive because it briefly elevates levels of serotonin, a neurotransmitter that produces positive feelings. When a sugar addict doesn't eat sugar, serotonin declines to low levels. This makes the person feel worse than before. He/she then eats more sugar to try to feel better—and the vicious cycle goes on.

For the best chance of breaking a sugar addiction, you need to ease out of it. This usually is more effective than going cold turkey. Once you've given up sugar entirely and the addiction is past, you'll be able to enjoy small amounts of sugar if you choose, although some people find that they lose their taste for it. *How to break the habit…*

•**Divide sugar from all sources in half.** Do this for one week.

Examples: If you've been drinking two soft drinks a day, cut back to one. Eat half as much dessert. Eat a breakfast cereal that has only half as much sugar as your usual brand, or mix a low-sugar brand in with your higher-sugar brand.

•**Limit yourself to one sweet bite.** The second week, allow yourself to have only one taste of only one very sweet food daily. This might be ice cream, sweetened cereal or a breakfast muffin. That small "hit" of sugar will prevent serotonin from dropping too low, too fast.

After about two weeks with little or no sugar, your internal chemistry, including levels of serotonin and other neurotransmitters, will stabilize at a healthier level.

•**Eat fresh fruits and vegetables.** These foods help restore the body's natural acid-alkaline balance. This will help reduce sugar cravings and promote better digestion. Be sure to substitute fresh fruits for juices. Whole fruit is better because the fiber slows the absorption of sugars into the bloodstream. The fiber also is filling, which is why few people will sit down and eat four oranges—the number you would need to squeeze to get one eight-ounce glass of juice.

Helpful: All fruits are healthful, but melons and berries have less sugar than other fruits.

Meet the Real Villain of High Blood Pressure—Sugar

James J. DiNicolantonio, PharmD, cardiovascular research scientist, department of preventive cardiology, Saint Luke's Mid America Heart Institute, Kansas City, Missouri...Sean Lucan, MD, MPH, Montefiore Medical Center, Bronx, New York. Their article appeared in *Open Heart*.

When it comes to high blood pressure, Public Enemy #1 has always been salt. For years, our doctors, governments, dietary guidelines, health institutes (such as the American Heart Association) and the media have bombarded us with warnings to reduce our sodium intake or face a higher risk of hypertension, cardiovascular disease and death. We listened...and most of us did what we thought was right and cut back on salt. But some researchers are suggesting that this has all been one more big, long-standing jag of health misinformation. They provide evidence that salt isn't all that bad and has a minimal effect on blood pressure and that another ubiquitous food flavoring—sugar—is the real culprit behind the explosive rate of high blood pressure and cardiovascular disease in America. Could sugar be affecting your blood pressure?

THE "ADDED SUGAR" EFFECT

Sugar, mainly in the form of fructose added to processed foods, is the more aggressive villain behind the explosion of hypertension rates and cardiovascular disease. Americans consume an average of 24 to 47 teaspoons of sugar a day in the form of processed foods loaded with fructose. Neither the American Heart Association nor the World Health Organization provides a recommendation about daily limits of fructose consumption, but animal and human studies have shown that a diet high in fructose affects blood pressure by increasing blood levels of insulin and sabotaging how the body metabolizes it. Insulin excess, in turn, overstimulates the sympathetic nervous system (the part responsible for the fight-or-flight response), which then can result in high blood pressure.

Numerous studies showing strong associations between insulin resistance and high blood pressure, including one showing that, whereas insulin resistance affects approximately 25% of the general population, it affects up to 80% of people with high blood pressure. Two other studies cited by them showed that although only 10% of people with normal blood pressure have abnormally high blood levels of insulin, 50% of people with high blood pressure do.

Meanwhile, people strictly following the American Heart Association's guidelines on sodium intake (about half a teaspoon of salt per day) may be putting their health at risk by not getting the amount of sodium they need. There was a study of more than 100,000 people showing that consuming three to six grams of sodium a day was associated with a lower risk of death, heart attack and stroke compared with consuming any other amount. Three to six grams of sodium equals about one-and-a-half to three teaspoons of salt (salt itself is composed of 40% sodium and 60% chloride)—and this is about the average amount Americans ingest each day despite what the American Heart Association recommends.

Also, on average, sodium reduction has a minimal effect on reducing blood pressure, with studies showing blood pressure reductions of up to 4.8 mm Hg systolic and 2.5 mm Hg diastolic at best. Additionally, when salt intake is restricted, heart rate can increase (a harmful effect that is generally not mentioned by doctors and others who advocate salt restriction).

READ LABELS AND EAT "CLEAN"

Sugars in their natural form found in fruits and other complex carbohydrates aren't the ones you should be worried about. We all know that a diet rich in fruits, legumes and

313

leafy vegetables is good for heart health. It's the added sugar you want to avoid. Consider that those of us who consume 10% to 25% of our daily calories from added sugar have a 30% increased risk of death from cardiovascular disease compared with those who get less than 10% of their calories from added sugar. Beyond that 25% mark, the risk of death increases three-fold, the team said.

So if you're not on board already, strongly consider avoiding foods with added sugar, whether that sugar is listed as simply "sugar" or one of sugar's many other identities, including high-fructose corn syrup, fructose, corn sweetener, corn syrup, syrup, invert sugar, malt sugar, and even honey, molasses and fruit juice concentrate…and avoid the "ose" additives such as dextrose, glucose, lactose, maltose, and sucrose—those are also sugars (although the sugars containing fructose seem to have greater metabolic harms versus other sugars).

Don't Drink That!

Nancy Appleton, PhD, nutritional consultant based in San Diego. She created an advanced curriculum for the National Institute for Nutritional Education and is author, with G.N. Jacobs, of *Killer Colas: The Hard Truth About Soft Drinks.*

No one thinks soda is good for you, but you might not realize just how bad it is for you. And fruit juice is almost as bad.

The American Heart Association has concluded that the safe upper limit of daily added sugar—which includes all of the sugar that isn't naturally present in foods—is six teaspoons for women and nine teaspoons for men. A 12-ounce can of Pepsi has about 10 teaspoons of sugar. Most soft drinks have a similar amount. And bottled teas and sports drinks contain about the same amount of sugar per ounce as colas.

In addition to sugar, these beverages may contain phosphoric acid (which disrupts mineral balance), high-fructose corn syrup (a form of sugar that may increase the risk for metabolic syndrome) and caffeine (which can cause heart palpitations and insomnia). None of it is good for you.

Even real fruit juice—including fresh apple, grape and orange juice—contains about 10 teaspoons of sugar in every 12-ounce glass. Yes, it is naturally occurring sugar, but it upsets your body chemistry in the same way that added sugar does.

HIGH CONSUMPTION, SERIOUS RISKS

The average American drinks about 11.5 gallons of fruit juice and fruit beverages and more than 50 gallons of soft drinks a year. This works out to about 600 12-ounce cans of soda and 125 12-ounce servings of juice.

Our bodies aren't designed to process this much sweetness. Excess sugar breaks down the process of homeostasis, the body's ability to maintain a healthy chemical balance. *What this can lead to…*

•**Calcium depletion.** Sugar acidifies the blood. The body attempts to restore a normal state of alkalinity by removing calcium from the bones. This increases blood levels of calcium while decreasing bone levels. Results: A higher risk for bone fractures and osteoporosis, along with an increased risk for cardiovascular disease from arterial calcification.

•**Autoimmune diseases.** The mineral imbalances caused by excess sugar and phosphoric acid impair the normal functions of enzymes, including digestive enzymes. When the digestive enzymes can't function, protein molecules from incompletely digested foods can pass through the intestine and into the bloodstream. These "foreign" molecules then are attacked by the immune system.

This condition, known as leaky gut syndrome, could increase the risk for and/or severity of lupus, rheumatoid arthritis and other autoimmune diseases.

•**Pancreatic cancer.** Swedish researchers sent food questionnaires to nearly 80,000 men and women. They found that those who consumed the most sugar, particularly from soft drinks, were significantly more likely to get this deadly cancer than those who consumed less. Other studies have reported similar results.

- **Hypertension, heartburn, asthma, more.** The consumption of soft drinks has been linked to an increased risk for high blood pressure, gout, heartburn and even asthma.

DIET SODAS, BAD TOO

A presentation at the International Stroke Conference in Los Angeles looked at information from more than 2,500 participants. Researchers found that those who drank diet soda daily were 61% more likely to suffer a cardiovascular event, such as a heart attack or stroke, than those who didn't drink these beverages.

Although the reason for this isn't known, there is enough information about sugar substitutes (such as aspartame and saccharin) to make them a good guess. The phosphoric acid could be a likely cause, too.

Whatever the cause, I do not recommend diet soft drinks.

HARD TO QUIT

When French researchers gave cocaine-addicted rats a choice between more cocaine or an artificial sweetener, the animals consistently chose the artificial sweetener.

Like cocaine, sweeteners elevate dopamine, a neurotransmitter that makes us feel good. However, the sugar "high" doesn't last very long. In the absence of more sugar, dopamine declines precipitously, which causes classic symptoms of withdrawal—mood changes, fatigue and irritability.

To relieve these symptoms, soda drinkers unconsciously "self-medicate" with more soft drinks.

HEALTHIER CHOICES

Manufacturers have promoted sports drinks (such as Gatorade), bottled teas and fruit juices as being healthier than carbonated beverages such as 7UP, Coca-Cola and Pepsi. They're not. A 16-ounce bottle of lemon tea has 10.5 teaspoons of sugar. A 20-ounce bottle of Gatorade Original Lemon-Lime contains about six teaspoons.

You can enjoy the occasional soft drink, just as you might enjoy the occasional rich dessert. But people with health challenges should not drink any soft drinks, sugar or no sugar, caffeine or no caffeine.

The challenge for those who are accustomed to sugary beverages and have developed a chemical dependence is cutting back. They'll invariably experience intense cravings.

You can quit cold turkey or do it gradually. *If you want to do it gradually, try the following strategies…*

- **Water it down.** You don't need full-strength fruit juice to get the satisfying taste. Add about three-quarters cup of water to one-quarter cup of juice. You'll get a little sweetness and fruit flavor, without the excess sugar.

- **Add bubbles.** Many people like the carbonation in soft drinks as much as the sugar. You can make your own carbonated beverage by adding about one-half cup of soda water to one-half cup of fruit juice or iced tea.

- **Add lemon.** Many restaurants routinely add lemon slices to glasses of water. You also can add a little puréed fruit, such as melon or peaches, for flavor.

- **Try commercial substitutes.** A few companies make tasty beverages with little or no added sugar. Brands such as Metromint and Hint use purified water that is lightly flavored with peppermint, lemon mint, raspberry-lime, etc.

GOOD, WITHIN LIMITS

The following are additional ways that soda and juice drinkers can cut back on sugar as long as they're used in moderation…

- **Coconut water.** It's the base ingredient in several commercial beverages, such as those made by Nature Factor Organic Young Coconut Water and ZICO. Although these drinks are lower in sugar than most soft drinks, they're not sugar-free. I advise drinking no more than about four to six ounces a day.

- **Stevia.** This plant-based, noncaloric sweetener is hundreds of times sweeter than sugar. You can use a little to sweeten tea or other beverages. It's also the sweetener that's used in some commercial diet beverages, such as Zevia Natural Diet Soda.

Caution: Stevia appears to be healthier than artificial sweeteners, but still use it in moderation. The sweetness can keep you "hooked" on sweetness and make it harder to reduce or eliminate excess sugar from your diet.

Kick the Sugar Habit: 4-Week Plan

Patricia Farris, MD, FAAD, clinical associate professor at Tulane University, New Orleans, and member of the board of directors for the American Academy of Dermatology. She is coauthor, with Brooke Alpert, MS, RD, CDN, of *The Sugar Detox: Lose the Sugar, Lose the Weight—Look and Feel Great.*

The average American consumes 32 teaspoons of added sugar per day. That's right—32 teaspoons a day.

We all know that sugar can lead to weight gain, but that's just the beginning. People who eat a lot of sugar have nearly double the risk for heart disease as those who eat less, according to data from the Harvard Nurses' Health Study. They're more likely to develop insulin resistance and diabetes. They also tend to look older because sugar triggers the production of advanced glycation endproducts (AGEs), chemical compounds that accelerate skin aging.

If you want to avoid these problems, it's not enough to merely cut back on sugar. In my experience, patients need to eliminate it from their diets—at least at the beginning—just like addicts have to eliminate drugs from their lives. In fact, a study showed that sugar cravings actually are more intense than the cravings for cocaine.

You don't have to give up sugar indefinitely. Once the cravings are gone, you can enjoy sweet foods again—although you probably will be happy consuming far less than before. After a sugar-free "washing out" period, you'll be more sensitive to sweet tastes. You won't want as much.

Bonus: Some people who have completed the four-week diet and stayed on the maintenance program for four or five months lost 35 pounds or more.

FIRST STEP:
3-DAY SUGAR FIX

For sugar lovers, three days without sweet stuff can seem like forever. But it's an essential part of the sugar detox diet because when you go three days without any sugar, your palate readjusts. When you eat an apple after the three-day period, you'll think it's the sweetest thing you've ever tasted. You'll even notice the natural sweetness in a glass of whole or 2% milk (which contains about three teaspoons of naturally occurring sugar).

You may experience withdrawal symptoms during the first three days. These can include fatigue, headache, fogginess and irritability, but soon you'll feel better than you have in years.

Caution: If you have any type of blood sugar problem, including hypoglycemia, insulin resistance or diabetes, you must consult your physician before starting any type of diet, including the sugar detox diet. In addition, if you are on insulin or an oral medication to control blood sugar, it is likely that your dosage will need to be adjusted if you lower your daily sugar intake.

During the three days...

• **No foods or drinks with added sugar.** No candy, cookies, cake, doughnuts, etc.— not even a teaspoon of sugar in your morning coffee.

• **No artificial sweeteners of any kind, including diet soft drinks.** Artificial sweeteners contribute to the sweetness overload that diminishes our ability to taste sugar.

• **No starches.** This includes pasta, cereal, crackers, bread, potatoes and rice.

• **No fruit, except a little lemon or lime for cooking or to flavor a glass of water or tea.** I hesitate to discourage people from eating fruit because it's such a healthy food, but it provides too much sugar when you're detoxing.

• **No dairy.** No milk, cream, yogurt or cheese. You can have a little (one to two teaspoons) butter for cooking.

• **Plenty of protein,** including lean red meat, chicken, fish, tofu and eggs.

• **Most vegetables,** such as asparagus, broccoli, cauliflower, celery, peppers, kale, lettuce and more—but no corn, potatoes, sweet potatoes, winter squash, beets or other starchy vegetables.

• **Nuts—two one-ounce servings a day.** Almonds, walnuts, cashews and other nuts are high in protein and fat, both of which will help you feel full. Nuts also will keep your hands (and mouth) busy when you're craving a sugary snack.

• **Lots of water, but no alcohol.** It's a carbohydrate that contains more sugar than you might think. You can drink alcohol later (see below).

NEXT STEP:
A FOUR-WEEK PLAN

This is the fun part. During the three-day sugar "fix," you focused on not eating certain foods. Now you'll spend a month adding tasty but nutritious foods back into your diet. You'll continue to avoid overly sweet foods—and you'll use no added sugar—but you can begin eating whole grains, dairy and fresh fruits.

Week 1: **Wine and cheese.** You'll continue to eat healthy foods, but you now can add one apple a day and one daily serving of dairy, in addition to having a splash of milk or cream in your coffee or tea if you like. A serving of dairy could consist of one ounce of cheese… five ounces of plain yogurt…or one-half cup of cottage cheese. You also can have one serving a day of high-fiber crackers, such as Finn Crisp Hi-Fibre or Triscuit Whole Grain Crackers.

You also can start drinking red wine if you wish—up to three four-ounce servings during the first week. Other alcoholic beverages such as white wine, beer and liquor should be avoided. Red wine is allowed because it is high in resveratrol and other antioxidants.

Week 2: **More dairy, plus fruit.** This is when you really start adding natural sugar back into your diet. You can have two servings of dairy daily if you wish and one serving of fruit in addition to an apple a day. You can have one-half cup of blackberries, blueberries, cantaloupe, raspberries or strawberries each day. Or you can have a grapefruit half. You'll be surprised how sweet fruit really is. You also are allowed one small sweet potato or yam (one-half cup cubed) daily.

Weeks 3 and 4: **Whole grains and more.** The third and fourth weeks are very satisfying because you can start eating grains again. But make sure it's whole grain. Carbohydrates such as white bread, white pasta and white rice are stripped of their fiber during processing, so they are easily broken down into sugar. Whole grains are high in fiber and nutrients and won't give the sugar kick that you would get from processed grains.

Examples: A daily serving of barley, buckwheat, oatmeal (not instant), quinoa, whole-grain pasta, whole-wheat bread or brown rice.

You might find yourself craving something that's deliciously sweet. Indulge yourself with a small daily serving (one ounce) of dark chocolate.

Deadly Diet Drinks

Drinking two or more diet sodas or diet fruit drinks a day resulted in a 30% greater risk for heart attack or stroke than rarely or never consuming these diet drinks, an eight-year observational study of nearly 60,000 women (average age 62) has found.

Theory: Diet sodas and diet fruit drinks (as well as the nondiet versions) have been linked to weight gain and metabolic syndrome, which raise risk for heart disease.

Ankur Vyas, MD, cardiovascular diseases fellow, University of Iowa Health Care, Iowa City.

---

5 Ways to Get Rid of Stubborn Belly Fat

Timothy McCall, MD, an internist and medical editor of *Yoga Journal*. He is author of *Yoga As Medicine: The Yogic Prescription for Health and Healing*, in which he reports on the connection between stress and weight gain. DrMcCall.com

---

Don't count on the latest diet to shrink an expanding waistline. Belly fat is stubborn. Unlike fat in the thighs, buttocks and hips, which visibly diminishes when you cut calories, belly fat tends to stick around. Even strenuous exercise might not make a dent.

The persistence of a belly bulge isn't merely cosmetic. Beneath the subcutaneous fat that you can pinch with your fingers, fat deep in the abdomen is metabolically different from "normal" fat. Known as visceral fat, it secretes inflammatory substances that increase the risk for heart attack, type 2 diabetes and some cancers. Even if you're not overweight, a larger-than-average waistline increases health risks.

Surprisingly, even thin people can have a high percentage of visceral fat. It might not be visible, but the risks are the same.

Weight-loss diets can certainly help you drop pounds—and some of that weight will come from the deep abdominal area. But unless you take a broader approach than the standard diet and exercise advice, it's very difficult to maintain visceral fat reductions over the long haul. *Here are better approaches to shrink your belly…*

• **Don't stress over losing weight.** Everyone knows about "stress eating." After a fight with your spouse or a hard day at work, food can be a welcome distraction. What people don't realize is that the struggle to lose weight may itself be highly stressful and that it can cause your belly fat to stick around.

How this happens: Cortisol, one of the main stress-related hormones, increases appetite and makes you less mindful of what you eat. It causes the body to store more fat, particularly visceral fat. People who worry a lot about their weight actually may find themselves eating more.

Take action to reduce stress by practicing yoga (see page 345), meditation or tai chi (see page 341) for even just a few minutes a day. One study found that there was little or no obesity among more than 200 women over age 45 who had practiced yoga for many years. The key is regular practice—it's better to do 10 minutes of yoga a day than a 90-minute class once a week.

Also helpful: Belly breathing. Sit up straight in a chair or lie down on your back, close your eyes, and tune into your breathing. Breathe in and out through your nose slowly and deeply but without straining. You'll feel your belly gently moving out as you inhale and then in as you exhale.

This type of breathing is an effective form of stress control. Try it for one to five minutes once or twice a day…or anytime you're feeling stressed.

• **Cultivate mindfulness in your everyday life.** According to yoga and Ayurvedic medicine (a system of healing that originated in India), an overly busy mind can play as big a role in weight gain as diet or exercise. We all need to step back from the chaos of life and give our nervous system a chance to unwind. Take it one step at a time. Do less multitasking. Try to move a little more slowly and deliberately. Spend less time on the Internet and watching television—especially when you're eating. Although these activities may seem relaxing, they can stimulate the mind and the nervous system and lead to overeating.

Bonus: When you eat mindfully, you'll enjoy your food more and need less to feel satisfied.

• **Exercise, but don't go crazy.** Exercise, particularly aerobic exercise, can obviously be good for weight loss. But for many people, the intensity at which they exercise becomes yet another source of stress.

Example: One of my medical colleagues described a "Type A" patient who was an exercise fanatic. Despite her strenuous fitness program, she had a stubborn 10 pounds that she couldn't get rid of. He suggested that she might have more luck if she'd simply relax a bit. She ignored his advice—until she broke a leg and had to take a break. The 10 pounds melted away.

My advice: Get plenty of exercise, but enjoy it. Don't let it be stressful—make it a soothing part of your day. Go for a bike ride…swim in a lake…take a hike in nature. Exercise that is relaxing may burn just as many calories as a do-or-die gym workout but without the stress-related rise in cortisol.

Tip: If you've practiced belly breathing (see previous page), try to bring that kind of breath focus to your exercise. It's even possible to slowly train yourself to breathe through your nose while you exercise, potentially lowering cortisol levels and the rebound hunger that is so common after a workout.

• **Eat more fresh, unprocessed food.** What really matters for health and healthy weight is the quality of your food. Many diets that have been shown to be effective—such as the low-fat vegetarian Ornish program…the Mediterranean diet…and some high-protein plans—disagree with one another, but they all emphasize old-fashioned unprocessed food.

My advice: Worry less about micronutrients such as specific vitamins, minerals and types of fat or your protein/carbohydrate balance, and instead focus on eating more fresh vegetables, legumes, whole grains, fruit, nuts and seeds. If you eat animal foods, choose free-range and pasture-raised meat and dairy products, organic if possible.

• **Cut back on refined sugar.** If you follow the advice above and avoid processed foods, you'll naturally consume less sugar, refined grains (such as white bread) and other "simple" carbohydrates. This will help prevent insulin surges that can lead to more visceral fat.

As always, balance is important. I don't advise anyone to give up all sources of sugar or all carbohydrates. After all, a plum is loaded with the sugar fructose—and fruits are good for you! It's the added sugar in junk and fast food that's the problem. Just be aware that any processed food—including many snacks that are marketed as healthier alternatives—will make it harder to control your weight.

Gastric Band Hypnosis: "Virtual" Alternative to Weight-Loss Surgery

Jennie J. Kramer, MSW, LCSW, founder and executive director, Metro Behavioral Health Associates Eating Disorder Treatment Centers, New York City and Scarsdale, New York. She is coauthor, with Marjorie Nolan Cohn, of *Overcoming Binge Eating for Dummies.* MBHANY.com

There's a new option for people who have considered stomach-shrinking bariatric surgery as a solution to their weight problem but are put off by the serious risks of the operation. It's a "virtual" surgery that uses the power of hypnosis to convince people that their stomach size has been surgically reduced. Even though no actual surgery is done, hunger abates dramatically…and the pounds start dropping off.

It's risk-free, effective and relatively economical. And unlike real bariatric surgery, which is only for people who are severely obese, this virtual surgery is an option for people who are merely overweight as well as for those who are obese. *Here's how it works…*

NEW WAY TO "THINK THIN"

Real bariatric surgery involves stapling off or removing part of the stomach…or cinching a plastic gastric band around the stomach. Either way, the amount of food that can be consumed is drastically reduced and rapid weight loss typically occurs. However, surgery carries significant risks, including the possibility of cardiac problems, pneumonia, bowel obstructions, bleeding, infection and even death. Also, certain foods must be permanently avoided after surgery because they would cause serious cramping, diarrhea or other upsets.

Safer alternative: The "virtual surgery" called gastric band hypnosis (GBH) carries none of those risks, according to Jennie J. Kramer, MSW, LCSW, founder and executive director of Metro Behavioral Associates Eating Disorder Treatment Centers in New York City and Scarsdale, New York, whose center provides GBH in conjunction with psychotherapy and nutritional counseling. With GBH, surgery takes place only within the "theater of the mind," not in an actual operating room, Kramer said. In essence, during hypnosis, the person's brain is retrained to believe that the stomach has undergone surgery to make it smaller—so that afterward, he feels satisfied with much smaller amounts of food and thus loses weight. "And since there is no cutting, there is no anesthesia, no pain, no scarring, no recovery time and no risk," Kramer said.

The GBH experience: After an initial consultation, the GBH protocol typically consists of four weekly hypnosis sessions, each lasting 60 to 75 minutes. The virtual "surgery" is done during the first session. The patient reclines comfortably and is hypnotized so that he is in a fully conscious yet deeply relaxed state.

Then the practitioner mentally guides the patient by describing each phase of the procedure...donning a hospital gown, signing a consent form, being wheeled into the surgical prep area, receiving anesthesia, having the gastric band applied around the stomach, closing the incision and being wheeled into the recovery room. To make the experience seem more real, the patient listens to hospital sounds (doctors and nurses talking, monitors beeping, etc.) through headphones. Some practitioners also may arrange for the patient to smell an appropriate aroma (such as an antiseptic) and/or feel a scratch on the back of the hand when "anesthesia" is administered. When the virtual procedure is finished, the patient is brought back out of the hypnotic state.

Why might this work? "The subconscious mind, which is where hypnosis takes effect, is very susceptible to positive suggestions and does not really differentiate between fantasy and reality," Kramer said. "So if your subconscious mind believes that you have had actual gastric banding surgery, your body—including your appetite and satiety cues—responds as if you'd really had the surgery."

EFFECTIVE, BUT NOT MAGIC

The patient's work doesn't end when the hypnosis component of the therapy is finished—because he still has to make permanent changes in his diet. "Let me be clear that GBH is no more a miracle than bariatric sur-

gery. GBH can fail in exactly the same way that surgery can fail if the proper supports are not in place and the underlying causes of food addiction are not addressed," Kramer said. "You have to look at the patterns in your life to find out how your relationship to food got so distorted, then develop a healthier and sustainable relationship with food. That way, GBH can be a kick-start that sets you on the road to losing weight and keeping it off."

To that end, Kramer said, a complete GBH program includes not only the virtual surgery element, but also additional hypnotherapy and counseling during which patients explore the issues that underlie their weight problems and that trigger their overeating.

During the second, third and fourth hypnosis sessions, which take place a week apart, the hypnotherapist addresses the emotional aspects of overeating. For example, Kramer said, the patient might be asked to recall past incidents related to eating...or to summon up an image of himself as a child, then have a kind and gentle conversation about food with that child. Another exercise might involve imagining a beautiful, safe, comfortable place—one to which he can return, in his own mind, whenever he needs help coping with cravings, anxiety or stress. The patient also works on these emotional issues at home every day, guided by CDs and workbooks provided by the hypnotherapist.

Following that, patients participate in six monthly sessions of individual and/or group therapy that reinforce positive lifestyle changes as the excess weight is being lost. Kramer also recommends participating in a relevant 12-step group such as Overeaters Anonymous and receiving nutritional counseling as further insurance against going back to old unhealthy eating patterns after GBH.

PRACTICAL MATTERS

How effective is GBH? Numerous studies have shown that hypnosis is an effective means of bringing about weight loss, and that when used in combination with psychotherapy, hypnotherapy is more effective than psychotherapy alone. But the question about GBH specifically is still under investigation because no randomized clinical trials have yet been published on the technique. "Currently, a trial is being conducted under the auspices of the National Health Service of Great Britain, and the results thus far are quite compelling," Kramer said.

Who is a candidate for GBH? Due to its risks, actual bariatric surgery generally is limited to people who are morbidly obese, with a body mass index (BMI) of 40 or higher…or to obese people with a BMI of 35 to 40 who also have a serious weight-related health problem, such as type 2 diabetes, high blood pressure or severe sleep apnea. But because gastric band hypnosis is virtual and completely safe, it is an option not only for obese people, but also for those who are merely overweight.

Finding a practitioner: Many hypnotists work with patients who want to lose weight, but you may have to hunt some to find one who's trained in GBH. One option is to visit the website of the program's British originator, Sheila Granger (*www.sheilagranger.com*), which lists practitioners who have trained directly with Granger. Or check with established professional organizations such as the National Guild of Hypnotists and the International Association of Counselors and Therapists to find hypnotherapists near you, then contact them to ask whether they practice GBH. Note that techniques similar to GBH are known by other names, including virtual gastric band (VGB) and various trademarked terms.

The cost: Actual weight-loss surgery typically costs $20,000 to $35,000. Though GBH is far less expensive than surgery, it's not cheap, typically running $1,000 for the first four sessions, plus about $200 for each of the six subsequent monthly sessions, for a total of about $2,200. Unfortunately, health insurance generally does not cover these costs. However, hypnosis for medical reasons is an allowable expense for health-care flexible spending accounts and health savings accounts—and if it allows you to get your weight down for good, it could be an excellent investment in your health and well-being.

A Health Coach: Your Key to Long-Lasting Wellness

Karen Lawson, MD, assistant professor of family medicine and community health, director, health-coaching program, University of Minnesota Center for Spirituality & Healing, Minneapolis. CSH.UMN.edu

Working with a health coach can provide the motivation, individualized attention and accountability you need to turn your good intentions into positive actions.

Why try this growing trend? Because if you're like many people, you know what you should do to improve your health, but you have trouble getting started or sticking with a more healthful lifestyle…so nothing ever changes for long.

A health coach offers one-on-one, step-by-step support—whether your goal is to lose weight, eat healthier, sleep better, have more energy, exercise more, quit smoking, lower your stress level, reduce your risk for chronic diseases and/or recover from an illness or injury—that increases your odds of succeeding at making permanent life-enhancing changes.

How it works: "A new behavior must be practiced for at least 100 days to become an entrenched part of who you are and how you live, rather than just something that you're doing for a while. Most doctors aren't trained in helping patients make such sustainable changes. But a health coach can help you overcome your natural inertia, build internal motivation and incorporate lasting changes into the fabric of your daily life," said Karen Lawson, MD, director of health coaching at the University of Minnesota Center for Spirituality & Healing.

Research confirms the benefits. For instance, in a Duke University study, health coaching helped people with diabetes take their medications on schedule, exercise regularly and control their blood sugar better. And a study of nearly 175,000 people published in *The New England Journal of Medicine* found that participants who were coached via telephone spent less money on medical care and drugs and were 10% less likely to be admitted to the hospital than those who were not coached.

Health coaching is particularly helpful for people who have or are at high risk for chronic conditions such as diabetes or heart disease. However, it can benefit just about anybody who wants to enhance his or her health and well-being.

WHAT TO EXPECT FROM COACHING

Health coaching is very much a client-driven relationship, Dr. Lawson said, so the content and style of sessions vary widely depending on clients' particular goals. Sessions can be done individually or in groups...can be conducted in person, over the phone or via the video-chat program Skype...and generally last 30 to 60 minutes. A total of five to eight sessions would be typical.

A health coach's role is to help you...

• **Create a personalized plan for meeting your health goals,** whether those goals have to do with your physical, mental, emotional and/or spiritual well-being.

• **Recognize and shift the behaviors,** beliefs and emotions that have been blocking your success or your readiness to change.

• **Break your goals into manageable steps and track measurable progress.**

• **Learn specific strategies (for instance,** how to interpret food labels, carve out time for exercise or establish a sleep-enhancing bedtime routine) aimed at achieving your goals.

• **Communicate more openly with your doctors and other health-care providers.**

FINDING THE RIGHT COACH

Health coaches often come to the field by way of other health-care professions—so you may find a coach who also is a physician, chiropractor, nurse, nutritionist, acupuncturist, pharmacist, chaplain or psychologist. Other people become health coaches after initially working in a wellness-related field such as personal training, yoga instruction or massage therapy.

Caution: Since health coaching is a relatively new field, there is no national credentialing system yet in place to ensure high-quality training and professional competence—in fact, anyone can call himself or herself a health coach. (To learn more about national credentialing efforts, visit *www.ncchwc.org*.) So it is important to investigate any coach you're considering working with before you sign on.

To get started, ask your physician, therapist and/or friends for referrals to health coaches in your area...also check with your insurance company and local hospital. Then schedule a face-to-face or phone consultation with several candidates (generally this introductory session is free). *During the initial interview, ask the coach about his or her...*

• **Training.** You want at least 80 hours of education in health coaching from established and reputable training programs, such as University of Minnesota, Duke University, California Institute of Integral Studies, Wellcoaches School of Coaching (in Wellesley, Massachusetts) and Tai Sophia Institute at Maryland University of Integrative Health, Dr. Lawson said. Ask how people were trained—have they had supervision in actually doing coaching, or did they learn through online tutorials? Also consider how well the coach's background matches your needs—for instance, a nurse with a cardiac-care background might be an optimal choice if you are a heart patient but less ideal if your goal is to reduce stress or improve sleep.

• **Number of clients.** Choose someone who has coached a minimum of 30 clients, Dr. Lawson advised.

Best: Also ask for the names of three clients whom you can contact for references.

• **Fees.** These depend on your location and the coach's level of training, but typically range anywhere from about $70 to $250 per session. Some coaches do packages at a discount rate. Some employers and some health insurance plans cover at least part of the cost.

• **Coaching philosophy and particular interests.** This is inherently a holistic field, so coaches should have some working knowledge of a broad array of health topics, including nutrition, fitness, conventional medicine, complementary therapies, psychology and spiritual practices. Coaches who identify themselves as integrative in their training and practice generally have more familiarity with complementary or nonconventional therapeutic approaches. Weigh how well your personal goals mesh with a coach's particular area of expertise. For instance, if you want to make over your diet and lose weight, you might opt for a coach who is also an organic gardener or accomplished chef...if you want to relieve stress and enhance your creative life, you might prefer a coach experienced in meditation and art therapy.

Also remember: Pay attention to how you feel with each coach you interview. Like psychotherapy, coaching is a relationship-centered practice, Dr. Lawson said—so success depends in part on choosing a health coach you trust and respect and are comfortable with.

Still skeptical about trying a health coach? Think of it this way: You use professionals in many areas of your life—from cutting your hair to selling or buying a home. What area is more important than your health?

5 Tricks to Make Yourself Exercise

Robert Hopper, PhD, a Santa Barbara–based exercise physiologist and author of *Stick with Exercise for a Lifetime: How to Enjoy Every Minute of It!*

If you're like most people, those exercise resolutions you made at New Year's are just a distant memory. In fact, seven out of 10 Americans can't make exercise a habit, despite their best intentions. That's because the most common reasons for starting an exercise program—to lose weight in time for a reunion, for example—are weak long-term motivators.

But you can learn to motivate yourself to make exercise a regular part of your life. Elite athletes as well as everyday people who have made a successful commitment to life-long fitness use these insider tips. *Here are their secrets...*

●**Make your first experience positive.** The more fun and satisfaction you have while exercising, the more you'll want to pursue it and work even harder to develop your skills. Even if your first experience was negative, it's never too late to start fresh. Choose a sport you enjoy, and work to improve your skill level.

The key is finding a strong beginner-level coach who enjoys working with novices. For instance, the YMCA offers beginner swim lessons, and instructors are armed with strategies for teaching in a fun, nonintimidating way.

If your friends have a favorite dance class, play racquetball or practice karate, ask them for a referral to an approachable teacher. City recreation departments also often host beginner-level classes for a variety of indoor and outdoor activities. You might also try a private lesson. The confidence you gain will motivate you to try it out in a group setting next.

●**Focus on fun, not fitness.** Forcing yourself to hit the gym four times a week sounds like a chore, and you'll likely stop going before you have the chance to begin building your fitness level. But lawn bowling, dancing, Frisbee throwing, hiking, even table tennis—those all sound fun, and you'll still be getting physical activity that helps promote weight control...reduced risk for heart disease, diabetes and cancer...stronger bones...and improved mood. As you start to have more fun, you'll want to become more involved and your fitness level will improve over time.

No strategy is more crucial than this: Get hooked on the fun, and you'll get hooked on the activity for life.

●**Find your competitive streak.** We all have one, and you can tap into it, no matter what activity you choose. Jogging outside? Make it a game by spotting landmarks in the near distance, like trees or homes, and push yourself to pass them in a certain number of seconds. Swimming laps? Try to match the pace of the slightly faster swimmer in the next lane. Or keep track of the time it takes to swim 10 laps, and try to beat your time. Even riding the recumbent bicycle at the gym can be turned into a competition by moving your workout to the spin studio, where you can privately compete against other class members for pace or intensity.

• **Practice the art of the con.** If you've ever overheard a pair of weight lifters in the gym, you'll recognize this tip: The spotter encourages the lifter, "One more, just one more!" and then after the lifter completes one more lift, the spotter again urges, "Now one more!" Make this tip work for you by learning how to self-con. Let's say you're too tired to work out. Tell yourself, I'll just drive to the gym and park. If I'm still tired, I can leave. This is often enough to kick-start your workout. And while swimming laps, tell yourself you'll just do five, then two more, then just three more.

• **Cultivate a mind-set of continuous improvement.** Tennis great Jimmy Connors once shared what keeps athletes motivated—"Getting better." Lifelong exercisers have a yearning to improve that acts as both a motivator and a goal.

• **Help yourself get better by educating yourself about your sport.** To do this, read books by or about professional athletes...read articles about them in magazines, newspapers and online...and even book a private lesson to have your running gait/golf swing/basketball shot analyzed.

Also, offer yourself rewards for hitting certain benchmarks. Treat yourself to a massage after your first three months of walking your dog nightly for 30 minutes...or book a trip to a luxury ski lodge to celebrate your first year of skiing. You earned it!

Test (and Fix!) Your Fitness for a Long, Healthy Life

Marilyn Moffat, PhD, PT, a professor of physical therapy at New York University in New York City and a former president of the American Physical Therapy Association. She is coauthor of *Age-Defying Fitness*.

We all know that exercise is good for us, but some ways of exercising are particularly effective...and they don't require time-consuming maneuvers or expensive equipment.

Are you out of breath after walking up a flight of stairs? Do you feel discomfort or pain when looking over your shoulder as you back up a car? Is it becoming difficult to reach the top shelves of closets? Or after having sat through a movie, do you feel pain or stiffness when you stand up? Any "yes" answer means that exercise would be especially beneficial for you.

TO INCREASE FLEXIBILITY

Test: Put one arm over your shoulder, and reach behind your back. Then bring your other arm up behind your back, and try to touch the fingers of the hand that went over your shoulder.

Goal: To increase the flexibility of your arms, especially your shoulders.

Exercise: The "test" is also an exercise. Perform it several times a day, holding the stretch 30 seconds, then reversing your arms. Soon your fingers will easily touch. At that point, it's OK to reduce the frequency until you reach a level where you can consistently touch fingers.

Exercise for lower back and hamstring muscles: Sit toward the front of a chair with one leg stretched out straight with toes pulled toward you, and the other leg bent to a right angle at the hip and knee. With one hand on top of the other, reach your hands toward the toes of the straight leg.

Important: If you have osteoporosis or have had an upper-back fracture, do not do this exercise.

FOR BETTER POSTURE

Test: Stand with your back as flush as possible against a wall and both heels touching it. When you're in that position, does your head easily touch the wall? If it doesn't, you could use some work on posture, which can be vital to overall physical health.

Goal: To improve posture as quickly as possible.

Exercise: Once or twice daily, sit in a supportive chair, chin tucked in toward your chest. Breathe in as you bend your elbows at your sides and close your fingers in a relaxed fist. Gently press your elbows back into the chair. Stay in that position for 10 seconds as you continue to breathe deeply. Do not move. Breathe in again as you release the position slowly. Begin with three repetitions and build to 10 or 20.

Once your head effortlessly touches a wall when you stand against it, you'll know that your posture has improved. At that point, reduce the number of times you perform the exercise.

By experimenting with the frequency of the exercise, you can determine how many times you need to do it in order to maintain good posture. Keep in mind, however, that as you age, the number of times required will nearly always increase slightly from year to year.

FOR MORE STRENGTH

Test: In 30 seconds, how many times can you stand up from and sit down in a chair with your arms crossed on your chest?

Goal: Women between the ages of 60 and 64 should be able to stand and sit 12 to 17 times in 30 seconds. Men of that age should be able to perform the task 15 to 20 times. The benchmark drops slightly as your age increases.

Exercise: Perform the test two or three times a day until you can easily stand and sit within the benchmark range. Then do the exercise once every other day to keep in shape.

Also helpful: Unless you have problems with your hips and knees, walk up and down a flight of stairs two or three more times a day than you normally would.

To strengthen the arms, weighted dumbbells may be used. You should seek the guidance of a physical therapist before you start any weight training so that you perform the motions correctly and also use the correct amount of weight. An alternative to using weights is using elastic bands that can be cut into appropriate lengths for both arm and leg exercises. (See my book *Age-Defying Fitness* for many exercises with weights and elastic bands.)

Advantages of elastic bands: Unlike weights, there's no danger in dropping an elastic band when you exercise. Also, you can easily take an elastic strip with you when you travel.

TheraBand strips are available from many retailers that sell exercise equipment and from distributors (800-321-2135, *www.performance-health.com*).

Price: About $15 for 6 yards.

How to do it: Run the elastic band under the seat of an armless chair from side to side. Sit in the chair, and hold one end of the band in each hand. Then raise your arms high over your head, stretching the band as you do so and also breathing out. Cut the TheraBand strip to a length that lets you perform a set of eight to 12 stretches before tiring. Perform one or two sets of these exercises three times a week.

FOR BETTER BALANCE

Test: Cross your arms on your chest, then see how long you can stand on one leg. Then test the other leg.

Goal: To remain standing for at least 30 seconds. If you can't, your balance needs improving.

Exercise: Hold on to the counter with one hand and stand on your toes. Then, bend one knee back so that you're standing on your toes with one leg. After doing it only a few times, you may not need to hold on to the counter with your hand. Also try to rise up and down on your toes five to 10 times while standing on one leg.

TO INCREASE ENDURANCE

Test: Assuming that you do not have any heart or lung problems, try to march in place for two minutes, bringing your knees about halfway up to the level of your hips. Count only the number of times you bring your right knee up.

Goal: In two minutes, women ages 60 to 64 should be able to bring up the right knee between 75 and 107 times. For men of that age, the benchmark is between 87 and 115 times.

Exercise: March in place several times a week, slowly increasing the number of steps you take in each two-minute period. Traditional exercises, such as walking, running and bicycling, are also effective in building up endurance. Or use a treadmill or stationary bike. Whatever your choice of endurance exercise, you should gradually build up to 30 to 45 minutes each session anywhere from three to seven days a week.

GETTING STARTED

Note: If you're new to exercise, consult a physical therapist who will guide you through an appropriate exercise program. If you have heart, blood pressure or lung problems, also consult your physician before starting the program. To find a physical therapist, contact the American Physical Therapy Association (800-999-2782, *www.apta.org*) or contact your state's physical therapy association.

Weak Feet Wreak Havoc

Katy Bowman, MS, founder, Nutritious Movement, Carlsborg, Washington. NutritiousMovement.com

Our poor feet just don't get what they need to be healthy and happy—and you know who pays the price, don't you? According to Katy Bowman, MS, founder of Nutritious Movement in Carlsborg, Washington, modern life is hard on our feet. An astonishing 25% of the body's bones are in the feet, says Bowman, noting "every one of them has a job to do." We actually weaken our feet by wearing shoes—encasing them this way diminishes their natural strength and abilities. Walking on artificially flat surfaces does further damage, since the foot is deprived of the natural workout it is supposed to get from varying natural terrain. The result of all this is that we're no longer really using our feet, says Bowman. By midlife, most of us have lost not only muscle strength but also the fine motor skills that our feet need to properly support us. We end up using the ankle muscles instead and, in a vicious cycle, this further weakens foot muscles.

TEST YOUR FEET

Here is an easy way to test your foot muscle strength: Try to raise your big toe, by itself, and then the second toe with it. It sounds easier than it is—few are able to do more than lift the big toe slightly off the floor. When the foot is being used properly, however, all toes should retain their ability to move independently from the other four.

WALK THIS WAY

Foot problems start in your feet—your posture and style of walking play a role, too. You may never have noticed it but, if you are like many folks, you're likely walking with your feet slightly turned out, duck-fashion. This interferes with how the muscles and ligaments in the feet, knees and hips are supposed to work. Your feet should point straight ahead in the direction you are walking.

Try this: Find straight lines on the floor (a tile joint or wood slat works well), and line up the outside edges of both feet. Keeping that alignment, walk forward. As you try to adapt to this new gait, you may initially feel like you've become pigeon-toed and knock-kneed, but if you stay with it you'll soon notice how your hips are engaged and rotating smoothly —it all feels quite facile and natural.

STRAIGHTEN UP

When standing and walking, many people tuck their pelvises under, creating weak abdominal muscles—wearing elevated heels (men's shoes, too) further amplifies this effect. Coupled with the turned-out duck-walking style, this posture puts too much weight on the front of the feet, which is what creates bunions. Instead, the weight should be back over the heels and spread among four contact points.

Try this: Picture your foot as a rectangle with four corners. Now consciously distribute your weight equally to the inside of the heel... the outside of the heel...the ball of the foot... and just below the pinkie toe. And here's an exercise that can help you identify a forward-thrusting pelvis and poor weight placement: Stand barefoot and move your hips back until they are over your ankles—when you do this correctly, you should be able to lift all 10 toes off the floor. Do this near a chair or wall in case you need support. Once you learn what this centered position feels like, try to achieve it regularly.

WHAT TO WEAR?

Bowman advises walking shoeless often, and when footwear is required urges selection of heels that are as flat as possible. She said that an elevation of even an inch or so puts too much weight on the ball of the foot—it's like walking downhill. In fact, she recommends shoes that draw your weight back, onto the heels, such as those made by Earth, Inc. (*www.earthfootwear.com*). Arch supports may be helpful for people with very high or very low arches, but Bowman cautions that regular use weakens foot muscles.

Bowman is ardently against flip-flops—she says they force the wearer to scrunch the toes, which can cause hammer toes and also makes proper weight distribution (those four proper contact points) impossible. Neither does she favor the new types of workout shoes that rock the foot and purposely throw off the body's balance to make leg muscles work harder—including "FitFlops" and MBTs. She says the shape of the sole creates an unnatural gait pattern that can harm the feet, knees, hips and spine.

You can probably imagine how she feels about high heels. For dress-up occasions, she suggests women bring heels to put on at the last minute. If you wear them regularly, she advises visiting the chiropractor or a naturopathic physician to get some special attention for your feet and sacroiliac joints, which will help to minimize the damage.

EASY STEPS TO FEEL-GOOD FEET

The real path to pain-free feet, however, involves giving them tender, loving care in the form of regular exercises that stretch, balance and strengthen their muscles, tendons and ligaments. Start by simply spreading and lifting your toes as often as possible. *Other easy exercises…*

●**Toe lifts.** While standing, lift your big toe alone, followed in succession by each of the remaining toes... repeat in the opposite direction, big toe last.

●**Toe tucks.** Stand with one foot flat on the floor and the other pointed slightly behind you, toes tucked under so that the tops of your toes are resting on the floor. This stretches your upper foot. (This won't be easy or comfortable at first.)

●**Arch support.** Stand erect, shift your weight to the outside of one of your soles, and lift that foot's ball and toes... slowly lower the ball of the foot without letting your arch collapse, and then relax your toes back to the ground.

●**Toe spacers.** Available at nail-care salons, online and in many stores, they fit between your toes and spread them. They may feel odd at first, but then are soothing. If you use them fairly often, such as while reading or watching TV, your toes will eventually relearn their normal spreading motion.

●**Barefoot walking.** Do this as often as you can.

And here are some fast fixes for feet that hurt…

●**For instant relief of aching feet, run your foot repeatedly over a tennis ball—** start while you are in a seated position and then slowly stand, increasing the weight on your foot.

●**Elevating tired, sore feet feels great,** as does wrapping them in a warm, wet towel.

●**A gentle foot massage** or a session with a well-trained reflexologist does wonders for the heart and sole.

If You're Starting to Exercise, Expect to be Miserable…

Tyler C. Cooper, MD, MPH, a preventive medicine specialist at the Dallas–based Cooper Aerobics Center (*CooperAerobics.com*) and founder of Cooper Ventures, which helps people incorporate healthy living into every aspect of their lives. He is coauthor, with his father, Kenneth H. Cooper, MD, MPH, founder and chairman of Cooper Aerobics Center, of *Start Strong, Finish Strong.*

We all know that exercise is perhaps the single most beneficial action we can take to protect our health. So why are two of every three American adults still "sedentary"—meaning they get little or no exercise?

LIVE THREE YEARS LONGER!

Most people who want to start exercising do so because it's "good" for them. But to stay motivated, you should know exactly why you want to start exercising.

For example, compared with people who exercise regularly, sedentary people are three times more likely to develop metabolic syndrome—a constellation of risk factors including high blood pressure (hypertension), elevated "bad" cholesterol, high blood sugar and obesity. Regular physical activity also has been found to reduce risk for cognitive decline.

And if that doesn't keep you motivated, consider this: People who regularly exercise briskly live an average of three years longer than those who are sedentary. "Briskly" means exercising at an intensity that makes you perspire and breathe a little heavily while still being able to carry on a conversation. This is known as the "talk test."

HOW MUCH EXERCISE?

It's a common misconception that you must exercise daily to achieve significant health benefits.

In a study of 10,000 men and 3,000 women conducted at the Cooper Aerobics Center's clinic, we found that walking just two miles in less than 30 minutes three days a week is all that's needed to achieve a "moderate" level of fitness, which lowers risk for all causes of death and disease.

For a less demanding workout that confers the same benefits, you could walk two miles in 35 minutes four days a week...or walk two miles in 40 minutes five days a week. If you prefer other forms of exercise, such as biking or swimming, use these frequency guidelines, plus the talk test (described above) to achieve a moderate fitness level. By increasing the frequency and/or intensity, you'll achieve even greater health benefits.

HIT THE SIX-WEEK MARK

If you have not exercised regularly in the last six months and/or are overweight (for women, having a waist size of 35 inches or more...for men, 40 inches or more), the basic exercise requirement described above may be too much. You may want to start by walking only to the end of the block for a few days, then gradually increase the distance. Aim for an increase of up to 10% weekly—for example, from 10 minutes per week to 11 minutes the next week and so on.

Helpful: Expect the first few weeks to be miserable—you'll feel some muscle soreness for a while. Accept it—but make the commitment to keep going.

Important: If your muscle pain doesn't go away within several weeks, see your doctor to rule out an underlying condition, such as arthritis.

We've found at the Cooper Aerobics Center that few people quit after they've performed a program of physical activity for six weeks. Once people reach the four- to six-month mark, adherence to an exercise program approaches 100% for the long term.

DETERMINE YOUR BASELINE

If you've been sedentary, be sure to get a comprehensive medical checkup before starting an exercise program. This is particularly important for men age 40 and older and women age 50 and older—cardiovascular disease risk rises at these ages.

People of any age with underlying health problems or a family history of diabetes, hypertension, high cholesterol or heart disease also should get a checkup before starting to exercise.

Ask your doctor—or a fitness trainer—to give you baseline measurements for strength, flexibility and aerobic capacity, which will enable you to track future changes.

Checking these measurements (along with such markers as blood pressure, cholesterol and blood sugar) again in about three months will give you tangible evidence of your progress and can motivate you to keep exercising.

You Can Exercise Less and Be Just as Healthy

Barry A. Franklin, PhD, director of cardiac rehabilitation at William Beaumont Hospital in Royal Oak, Michigan. He is also coauthor, with Joseph C. Piscatella, of *109 Things You Can Do to Prevent, Halt & Reverse Heart Disease.*

Do you struggle to fit the recommended amount of exercise into your busy schedule? Well, what if we told you that the amount of exercise needed to reap health benefits might be less than you think? Maybe you could free up some of your workout time for other activities that are important to you and beneficial to your health—like playing with your kids or grandkids, volunteering for a favorite charity or cooking healthful meals.

THE LATEST IN EXERCISE RESEARCH

A recent study published in the *Journal of the American College of Cardiology* found that people lived longest when they ran, on average, for 30 minutes or more, five days a week. Surprisingly, that research also showed that people who jogged at an easy pace for as little as five to 10 minutes a day had virtually the same survival benefits as those who pushed themselves harder or longer.

Also surprising: A study recently done at Oregon State University found that one- and two-minute bouts of activity that add up to 30 minutes or more per day, such as pacing while talking on the telephone, doing housework or doing sit-ups during TV commercials, may reduce blood pressure and cholesterol and improve health as effectively as a structured exercise program.

HOW TO EXERCISE SMARTER, NOT HARDER

Here are four strategies to help you exercise more efficiently…

•**Recognize that some exercise is always better than none.** Even though exercise guidelines from the Centers for Disease Control and Prevention (CDC) call for at least 150 minutes of moderate exercise each week, you'll do well even at lower levels.

A *Lancet* study found that people who walked for just 15 minutes a day had a 14%

reduction in death over an average of eight years. Good daily exercises include not only walking but working in the yard, swimming, riding a bike, etc.

If you're among the multitudes of Americans who have been sedentary in recent years, you'll actually gain the most. Simply making the transition from horrible fitness to below average can reduce your overall risk for premature death by 20% to 40%.

•**Go for a run instead of a walk.** The intensity, or associated energy cost, of running is greater than walking. Therefore, running (or walking up a grade or incline) is better for the heart than walking—and it's easier to work into a busy day because you can get equal benefits in less time.

For cardiovascular health, a five-minute run (5.5 mph to 8 mph) is equal to a 15-minute walk (2 mph to 3.5 mph)…and a 25-minute run equals a 105-minute walk.

A 2014 study of runners found that their risk of dying from heart disease was 45% lower than nonrunners over a 15-year follow-up. In fact, running can add, on average, three extra years to your life.

Caution: If you take running seriously, you still should limit your daily workouts to 60 minutes or less, no more than five days a week. (See the next page for the dangers of overdoing it.) People with heart symptoms or severely compromised heart function should avoid running. If you have joint problems, check with your doctor.

•**Ease into running.** Don't launch into a running program until you're used to exercise. Make it progressive. Start by walking slowly— say, at about 2 mph. Gradually increase it to 3 mph…then to 3.5 mph, etc. After two or three months, if you are symptom-free during fast walking, you can start to run (slowly at first).

•**Aim for the "upper-middle."** I do not recommend high-intensity workouts for most adults. Strive to exercise at a level you would rate between "fairly light" and "somewhat hard."

How to tell: Check your breathing. It will be slightly labored when you're at a good level of exertion. Nevertheless, you should still be able to carry on a conversation.

Important: Get your doctor's OK before starting vigorous exercise—and don't ignore potential warning symptoms. It's normal to be somewhat winded or to have a little leg discomfort. However, you should never feel dizzy, experience chest pain or have extreme shortness of breath. If you have any of these symptoms, stop exercise immediately, and see your doctor before resuming activity.

TOO MUCH OF A GOOD THING?

Most people who run for more than an hour a day, five days a week, are in very good shape. Would they be healthier if they doubled the distance—or pushed themselves even harder? Not necessarily. *Risks linked to distance running include…*

• **Acute right-heart overload.** Researchers at William Beaumont Hospital who looked at distance runners before and immediately after marathon running found that they often had transient decreases in the pumping ability of the right ventricle and elevations of the same enzymes (such as troponin) that increase during a heart attack.

• **Atrial fibrillation.** People who exercise intensely for more than five hours a week may be more likely to develop atrial fibrillation, a heart-rhythm disturbance that can trigger a stroke.

• **Coronary plaque.** Despite their favorable coronary risk factor profiles, distance runners can have increased amounts of coronary artery calcium and plaque as compared with their less active counterparts.

Watch out: Many hard-core runners love marathons, triathlons and other competitive events. Be careful. The emotional rush from competition increases levels of epinephrine and other "stress" hormones. These hormones, combined with hard exertion, can transiently increase heart risks.

Of course, all this doesn't mean that you shouldn't enjoy a daily run…or a few long ones—just don't overdo it!

Strength Training for Beginners—No Gym Needed

Cedric X. Bryant, PhD, the chief science officer for the American Council on Exercise. He has written more than 250 articles and columns in fitness magazines and exercise science journals and is author or coauthor of more than 30 books, including *Strength Training for Women. AceFitness.org, twitter.com/DrCedricBryant*

Strength training not only builds muscles, it also improves bone density, speeds up metabolism, promotes balance and even boosts brain power. You'll also gain mobility, said Cedric X. Bryant, PhD, chief science officer at the American Council on Exercise, who designed the workout below.

Translation: This routine will help make everyday movements—such as getting in and out of a car, reaching overhead, bending and climbing stairs—much easier for you.

And not to worry…you won't be straining under heavy barbells. All the exercises below use just your own body weight or a simple elastic tube for resistance.

Recommended: Opt for a light-resistance tube with handles, available at sporting goods stores and online for about $15 (I like the durable SPRI brand, *http://bit.ly/aoG5fK*).

What to do: Get your doctor's OK first, as you should before beginning any new exercise routine. Perform eight to 15 reps of each of the following moves two to three times per week on nonconsecutive days—muscles need a day between workouts to repair and strengthen, Dr. Bryant noted. Always move in a slow, controlled fashion, without jerking or using momentum. When you can easily do 15 reps of a particular exercise, advance to the "To progress" variation.

No-equipment-needed exercises…

• **Wall Squat—for legs and buttocks.**

Start: Stand with head and back against a wall, arms at sides, legs straight, feet hip-width apart and about 18 inches from wall.

Move: Keeping head and torso upright and your back firmly pressed against the wall, bend knees and slide down the wall about four to eight inches. Knees should be aligned above ankles—do not allow knees to extend past toes. Hold for several seconds. Then, using thigh and buttock muscles, straighten legs and slide back up wall to the start position. Repeat.

To progress: Bend knees more, ideally to a 90° angle so thighs are parallel to floor, as if sitting in a chair. *http://bit.ly/19uRM9.*

• **Wall Pushup—for chest, shoulders and triceps.**

Start: Stand facing a wall, feet hip-width apart and about 18 inches from wall. Place hands on wall at shoulder height, slightly wider than shoulder-width apart.

Move: Tighten abdominal muscles to brace your midsection, keeping spine and legs straight throughout. Slowly bend elbows, bringing face as close to wall as you can. Hold for one second, then straighten arms and return to the start position. Repeat.

To progress: Start with feet farther from wall...and bring face closer to wall during pushup. *http://bit.ly/11hnyM.*

• **Supine Reverse March—for abdominals, lower back and hips.**

Start: Lie face up, knees bent, feet flat on floor, arms out to sides in a T position, palms up, abs contracted.

Move: Slowly lift left foot off floor, keeping leg bent...bring knee up and somewhat closer to torso...when left thigh is vertical to floor, stop moving and hold for five to 10 seconds. Then slowly lower leg and return foot to floor. Repeat. Switch legs.

To progress: As knee moves upward, raise both arms toward ceiling...lower arms as leg lowers. *www.acefitness.org/exerciselibrary/supine-reverse-marches.*

Moves with tubes...

• **Seated Row—for back, abs and biceps.**

Start: Sit on floor, torso upright, legs out in front of you, knees slightly bent, feet together. Place center of elastic resistance tube across soles of feet and hold tube handles in hands, arms extended in front of you, elbows straight.

Move: Bending elbows, slowly pull handles of tube toward chest (do not lean backward, arch back, shrug shoulders or bend wrists). Hold for several seconds, then slowly straighten arms and return to the start position. Repeat.

To progress: To increase resistance, rather than placing center of tube across soles of feet, anchor it firmly around an immovable object one to three feet in front of you. *http://bit.ly/9ORodb.*

• **Lateral Raise—for shoulders.**

Start: Stand with feet hip-width apart, anchoring center of elastic resistance tube under both feet. Hold tube handles in hands, arms down at sides.

Move: Keeping elbows very slightly bent and wrists straight, slowly lift arms out to sides so palms face floor and hands reach shoulder height (or as high as you can get them). Lower arms to the start position. Repeat.

To progress: To increase resistance, widen your stance on the tubing. *http://bit.ly/PdpDLw.*

Get a Full-Body Workout Wherever You Are

Nicole Glor, a New York City–based personal trainer. A group fitness instructor at Crunch NYC and a yoga instructor, she is also author of *The Slimnastics Workout* and the host of several fitness DVDs, including the "Fit Travel Workout." *www.NikkiFitness.com*

Perhaps you are staying at a small hotel or visiting a friend and have no access to exercise equipment. Or maybe you don't like to use exercise equipment at all. What's the solution?

By using nothing more than your own body, you can get all the benefits of a well-rounded exercise program—stronger muscles, a boost in energy levels, better balance and improved mood...as well as reduced risk for chronic diseases such as heart disease, diabetes, dementia, cancer and osteoporosis.

How it started: The following workout was created for travelers who stay at hotels without gyms, but it also works well for people who don't have much space in their homes for expensive, bulky exercise equipment. This workout is very simple, requires no equipment and works all your key muscles in less than 30 minutes. For best results, do the workout three times a week.

To add a cardio component to this routine: Do 30-second intervals of jumping jacks between each move.

If you have been sedentary or have not exercised for a long time: Start with fewer repetitions and smaller movements. You also can slow down the moves to half speed. And check first with your doctor before starting a new exercise program.

THE DO-IT-ANYWHERE WORKOUT

For comfort and safety, wear exercise clothing and sneakers. A proper warm-up is also crucial to help prevent injuries.

The warm-up: Begin by rolling your shoulders back and forth while marching in place for 30 seconds. Then do the following exercises for 30 seconds each—light jumping jacks… hamstring curls (with your weight on your right foot, bend your left knee and kick your left heel up behind you, repeat on the other side and continue hopping side to side)…and shallow squats. Finally, lift and lower your arms for 30 seconds, bringing your fingertips over your head. *Now for the workout…*

CLOCK SQUATS

Purpose: Works the fronts of your thighs, quadriceps, or "quads"…calves…and gluteus maximus muscles, or "glutes."

What to do: Stand with your hands on your hips and your feet together.  Lunge forward with your right leg until your knee bends at a nearly 90-degree angle in front of you at the 12-o'clock position. Keep your knee over your foot. The back leg should be slightly bent with the knee close to the floor but not touching the floor. The back heel should be off the floor. Next, step back to the starting position and drop to a squat—imagine you are sitting in a chair with your knees bent at 90-degree angles. Stand tall, then lunge behind you, so that your foot is in the six-o'clock position. Return to the starting position and squat. Repeat five times on the right side, then on the left side.

Note: If you have knee problems, do calf raises (rise up on the balls of your feet, then lower your heels to the floor) instead of lunges and do a more shallow squat.

TRICEP DIPS

Purpose: Strengthens and tones the backs of your arms, or triceps.

What to do: While sitting on the floor with your knees bent and back against the side of an ottoman or chair, grasp the edge of it  so that your fingertips are facing forward and down. While supporting yourself with your arms, carefully lift your upper body off the floor so that your arms are straight. Next, lower yourself slowly about eight inches (bend elbows at a 90-degree angle to avoid stressing the joints), then come back up. Do 20 repetitions.

Note: People with shoulder, elbow or wrist issues should avoid this exercise and do tricep push-ups against a wall—put your hands on the wall in front of your shoulders with your arms straight. Lower your body into the wall, bending your elbows but keeping them close to your rib cage. Straighten your arms to push away from the wall.

THE TALL SQUAT

Purpose: Works your quads, plus the glutes and calves.

What to do: Stand with your legs about hip-width apart. Squat down as if you're sitting in a chair, then curl your arms as you stand back up. When you reach a standing position, extend your arms straight up into the air and rise up onto the balls of your feet at the same time. Start with 10 squats and work up to 30.

DIP AND RISE

Purpose: Strengthens your glutes and your abdominal and back muscles, or "core."

What to do: Start with your feet hip-width apart with knees slightly bent and hands on your hips. Bend forward from your hips. Keep your back flat, and touch your knees with your hands. Squeeze your glutes as you bend and then rise. Perform 15 to 20 repetitions.

STANDING CRUNCHES

Purpose: Works the muscles (obliques) on the sides of your abdomen.

What to do: Start by balancing yourself on your left leg. Step your right foot out toward the right about 12 inches away from your left, then place the big toe on the floor. Raise both arms diagonally overhead to the left so that they are straight. Next, drop your arms down toward the center of the body with elbows bent as you lift your right knee toward your arms. Keep your shoulders and hips facing forward. Do 20 repetitions, then switch sides.

SPINAL EXTENSIONS

Purpose: Works your lower and upper back, core, chest, shoulders and triceps.

What to do: Get down on your hands and knees with your back straight. Put a mat under your knees if needed. Lift and extend your right arm in front of you. Hold for four seconds, then lower. Next, lift your left leg straight out behind you parallel to the floor. Hold, then lower. Repeat 10

times. Then do these movements with the opposite arm and leg. Inhale as you reach and extend. Exhale as you return to the resting position.

Once you can master this, try lifting the opposite arm/leg simultaneously.

Fast, Fun Core Workout

Gina Lombardi, RDH, NSCA-CPT, author of *Deadline Fitness*, and host of "Fit Nation" on Discovery Fit & Health. She is based in Tarzana, California, and is former chairperson of the Personal Training Committee, as well as 2003 Personal Trainer of the Year for the National Strength and Conditioning Association. GinaLombardi.com

Have you ever tried working out with kettlebell weights? They're cute, brightly colored, oddly shaped hand weights that can give you a fun and effective workout—an easy way to get intense exercise in a brief amount of time. If these shorter days and colder temperatures are motivating you to take your workout indoors, kettlebells may turn out to be just your cup of tea!

Kettlebells are chunky round weights that look like cannonballs with handles attached. Trendy as they are today, they're actually an import from 18th-century Russia, where the "girya" (as they were called) was used to build strength and endurance.

Kettlebells come in weights ranging from five to 106 pounds, and they're sold in a rainbow of colors, but looks are beside the point. What's great about kettlebells is that they build muscle, burn fat and boost endurance. Because the center of gravity is located six to eight inches from the handle, swinging kettlebells strengthens core muscles instead of muscles in your extremities. They are great at building you up for real-life physical challenges, such as carrying luggage or moving furniture.

Hollywood trainer and kettlebell instructor Gina Lombardi, NSCA-CPT, author of the book *Deadline Fitness*, gave us a sequence of exercises that delivers both cardiovascular and strength benefits. This workout is efficient and effective, provided you follow correct kettlebell form (as outlined below). Called Peripheral Heart Action (PHA), these moves (performed in this order) force blood to circulate from the small muscles around your heart to your extremities continuously throughout your routine.

SET YOURSELF UP FOR SUCCESS

Let's start with a note about safety. Swinging a kettlebell generates significant momentum. You can do some serious damage to yourself, bystanders or walls, furniture or windows if you aren't careful, so choose a spot where you won't bump anything when your arms are fully extended.

The workout is more intense than you might guess, so start with a weight that you can comfortably swing long enough to complete the exercises—women should begin with five to 15 pounds…men, 15 to 30 pounds. You can add weight as your strength and endurance increases, but always use the same weight throughout each workout.

Kettlebell workouts are based on time, not repetitions, so you will need to have a timer on hand or do your routine where you can see a clock. Beginners should do each exercise for one minute, taking time to catch a breath before going on to the next one. At the intermediate level, you'll be aiming for two minutes per exercise, while advanced kettlebellers clock three minutes with each move. You can add difficulty by abbreviating how long you rest in between moves as well.

GETTING INTO THE SWING OF IT

Since it's mostly the powerful thrust from your hips, butt and thighs that propels the swinging kettlebell, not the motion of your arms or shoulders, it's important to stand or squat correctly. Keep your back straight and shoulders back as you balance your weight on your heels. For most exercises, toes should be pointed straight ahead. When you squat, your thighs should be parallel to the floor… your knees should never extend beyond your toes… and you should sit back into your hips to get the full effect.

Two-Arm Swing: Place a kettlebell on the floor in front of you, then stand up straight, setting your feet a bit wider than shoulder-width apart. Bend your knees slightly and reach down with both hands to grab the sides of the handle (called the "horns"). Now stand, letting your arms hang down in front of the body, keeping your knees slightly bent. Slowly swing the bell back between your legs. Then thrust your hips forward, squeezing your glutes and straightening out your legs, using the momentum to swing your arms up until the bell is at chest level. Without breaking the rhythm, lower the bell smoothly back down between your legs, bending your knees slightly as before. Repeat the motion, again and again, without breaking the rhythm.

Upright Rows: Again, start with the kettlebell on the floor, feet shoulder-width apart, knees slightly bent. This time, however, grasp the top part of the handle with two hands, keeping your arms straight down in front. Lift the kettlebell, keeping it close to your body, straight up toward your chin by bending your elbows so that they wing out and upward—your elbows should be higher than your wrists. Lift the kettlebell nearly to your chest and then lower to starting position and repeat.

Single-Arm Deadlift: Stand in front of the bell with your feet shoulder-width apart, knees slightly bent. Squat down, keeping your back straight, and grab the bell with one hand and stand back up, keeping your arm between your legs and slightly in front of you. Your arm should not bend during this exercise. Slowly squat to lower the kettlebell back down to the floor, leaving it there. Use your other hand to pick it back up and once again stand. Repeat, alternating arms.

Be sure to end your training session with five to 10 minutes of stretching to cool down and prevent muscle soreness. Lombardi predicts that you'll find your first kettlebell workout to be tough—but exhilarating!

Most gyms have sets of kettlebells, and they're also easy to find at Walmart, in sporting-goods stores and online. Prices range from $13 for a single starter kettlebell to several hundred dollars for a graduated set.

The Quick, Powerful Workout You're Probably Not Getting

Wayne L. Westcott, PhD, a professor of exercise science at Quincy College in Quincy, Massachusetts, and a strength-training consultant for the American Council on Exercise and the American Senior Fitness Association. He is also coauthor of several books, including *Strength Training Past 50*.

Until recently, fitness gurus have advised people to "take the stairs" mainly as a substitute for do-nothing elevator rides.

Now: Stair-climbing is becoming increasingly popular as a workout that's readily accessible (stairs are everywhere)...often climate-controlled (indoor stairs)...and free.

It burns more calories than walking...strengthens every muscle in the legs...and is good for your bones as well as your cardiovascular system. It may even extend your life span.

Compelling research: A study found that participants who averaged eight flights of stairs a day had a death rate over a 16-year period that was about one-third lower than those who didn't exercise—and more than 20% lower than that of people who merely walked.

A CONCENTRATED CLIMB

Walking is mainly a horizontal movement, with an assist from forward momentum. Stair-climbing is a vertical exercise. Your body weight is lifted straight up, against gravity. Climbing stairs also involves more muscles—in the calves, buttocks and the fronts and backs of the thighs—than walking. Even the arms get a workout. Canadian researchers found that it required double the exertion of walking on level ground—and 50% more than walking up an incline.

As a weight-loss tool, stair-climbing is hard to beat. An hour of climbing (for a 160-pound person) will burn about 650 calories. That compares with 400 calories an hour for a 15-minute-mile "power walk"...and 204 calories for a leisurely stroll.

IT'S EASY TO START

Inconvenience is one of the biggest barriers to exercise. It sometimes feels like a hassle to change into workout clothes and drive to a health club...or even exercise at home. But you can always find a set of stairs—in your neighborhood, at work, at the mall or at home.

You don't need fancy workout gear to climb stairs (uncarpeted stairs are preferred). Because it doesn't involve side-to-side movements, you don't necessarily need to invest in specialized shoes. You can do it in any pair of athletic shoes or even work shoes, as long as they don't have high heels.

HOW TO CLIMB

When getting started, begin with a single flight of stairs. When that feels easy, take additional flights or increase the intensity by going a little faster. Work up to five minutes, then slowly increase that to 10, 15 and 20 minutes, if possible, three times a week. *Other tips...*

• **Keep your upper body straight.** There's a natural tendency to lean forward when you climb stairs, particularly because a forward-leaning position feels easier. Remind yourself to stand straight when you're climbing and descending. It will give your legs a better workout...strengthen your abdominal and other core muscles...and help improve your balance.

• **Swing your arms.** You don't need an exaggerated swing, but keep your arms moving—it helps with balance and provides exercise for your arms and shoulders. You'll often see stair-climbers with their hands or arms on the rails. It's OK to use the rails if you need the support, but it reduces the intensity of the exercise. It also causes the stooped posture that you want to avoid.

• **One step at a time.** Unless you're a competitive stair-climber, you'll probably do best by taking just one step at a time. Ascending stairs is a concentric exercise that increases muscle power...it's also the part of the workout that gives most of the cardiovascular benefit.

Coming down the stairs is an eccentric (also called "negative") movement that puts more stress on the muscles and increases strength.

Important: Descend the stairs slowly, and keep "jolts" to a minimum. It sounds counter-intuitive, but the descents cause more muscle soreness than the climbs.

You can take two steps at a time on the ascent—if your balance is good and you're bored with single-step plodding. The faster pace will increase the intensity of your workout, particularly when you give your arms a more exaggerated swing. To minimize jolts and maximize safety, however, stick to single steps on the descent.

TO END YOUR WORKOUT

The "Figure 4" stretch is a great way to conclude a stair-climbing workout. It stretches the calves, hamstrings, gluteals, low back and upper back.

What to do: While sitting on the floor with your right leg straight, bend your left leg so that your left foot touches your right thigh. Slowly reach your right hand toward your right foot. Then grasp your foot, ankle or lower leg, and hold for 20 seconds. Repeat on the other side.

Caution: Stair-climbing should be avoided if you have serious arthritis or other joint problems. It's less jarring than jogging, but it's still a weight-bearing exercise that can stress the joints. People with joint issues might do better with supported exercises, such as cycling, rowing or swimming.

Before taking up stair-climbing as a form of exercise, check with your doctor if you're middle-aged or older, have arthritis, a history of heart or lung disease or if you've been mainly sedentary and aren't confident of your muscle strength—or your sense of balance.

STAIR-STEPPING WITHOUT A STAIRCASE

If you want to climb stairs without using a staircase, consider buying a commercial "stepper," such as those from StairMaster. Some have components that work the arms as well as the legs. Stair-steppers, however, don't provide the benefit of actual stair-climbing, which uses more muscles because of the descents.

These machines can be costly (at least $1,500 for a new one but much less for a used one on Craigslist or eBay). They typically hold up for years of hard use.

Caution: I don't recommend "mini-steppers" that sell for as little as $50. They have hydraulics, bands or other systems that cause the steps to go up and down, but the equipment usually breaks quickly.

Walking? Leave the Weights at Home

Lewis G. Maharam, MD, a fellow of the American College of Sports Medicine and author of five books, including *Running Doc's Guide to Healthy Running: How to Fix Injuries, Stay Active, and Run Pain-Free.*

Is it a good idea to walk with hand weights or ankle weights?

No, it is not. Adding weight while walking will not burn significantly more calories or build extra muscle—instead, it may land you in the doctor's office. Why is that? If you have ever used a pedometer to track your footsteps, you know that people typically take thousands of steps each and every day. When you add extra weight to a natural repetitive movement such as walking, you overload your muscles and joints and create imbalances that can quickly lead to inflammation, pain and decreased range of motion in your neck, shoulders, back, knees and/or ankles.

Fortunately, there are safe and simple ways to boost the challenge of your walking routine without using hand weights or ankle weights. *To build up your muscle strength and cardiovascular stamina...*

• **Tackle some hills during your walk.**

• **Try to increase your walking speed.**

• **Include intervals in your workout by walking for four minutes,** then jogging for 30 to 60 seconds. Over time, as your fitness level improves, gradually increase the ratio of the time you spend jogging versus walking.

7 Mistakes That Can Sabotage Your Walking Workout

Robert Sweetgall, president of Creative Walking, a McCall, Idaho, company that designs walking and fitness programs for schools, corporations and other clients. He walked through all 50 states in 365 days, and he has walked/run across the US seven times. Sweetgall is coauthor, with Barry Franklin, PhD, of *One Heart, Two Feet: Enhancing Heart Health One Step at a Time.* CreativeWalking.com

We all know that walking is very good for us. Studies have shown that walking promotes heart health, strengthens bones, spurs weight loss, boosts mood and even cuts risk for diabetes, cancer and Alzheimer's.

But what most people don't realize is that they could significantly improve the health benefits of their walks by tweaking their walking techniques and using the right equipment.

Here are common walking mistakes—and what you should be doing instead…

Mistake #1: **Tilting forward.** Some walkers tilt their upper bodies forward, as though they're walking into the wind. They think that this position increases speed. It does not—and it greatly increases pressure on the lower back while straining the shins.

Better: Walk with your head high and still, shoulders relaxed and chest slightly out. In this position, you can rotate your eyes downward to survey the path and look ahead to view the scenery around you.

Mistake #2: **Swinging the arms inefficiently.** Many walkers waste energy by swinging their arms side to side or pumping their arms up and down. These exaggerated movements add little to cardiovascular fitness and make walking less efficient because arm energy is directed upward or sideways rather than straight ahead.

Better: For maximum efficiency, pump your arms straight ahead on a horizontal plane, like you're reeling in a string through your mid-

section. This motion improves balance, posture and walking speed.

Mistake #3: **Using hand and/or ankle weights.** While some people like to walk with weights to boost the intensity of a walking workout, the risk for injury far outweighs the benefits of using weights. The repetitive stress of swinging weights can cause microtears in the soft tissues of the arms and legs.

Better: To increase exertion, walk uphill or on an inclined treadmill.

Another good option: Try Nordic walking for a total-body workout. With this type of walking, you use specially designed walking poles (one in each hand) to help propel your body forward.

Compared with regular walking, Nordic walking can increase your energy expenditure by 20%, according to a study from The Cooper Institute. It works the abdominal, arm and back muscles and reduces stress on the feet, ankles, knees and hips while improving endurance.

Mistake #4: **Not doing a warm-up.** You're inviting muscle soreness and potential injury if you hit your top speed at the start.

Better: Be sure to warm up. Start slowly, accelerating over the first five to 10 minutes… and end slowly, decelerating over the last five minutes. A slow start allows your muscles to warm up and become flexible, while enabling your cardiorespiratory system to get used to higher workloads. A proper cooldown helps eliminate the buildup of lactic acid, which can lead to muscle soreness.

Mistake #5: **Doing the same walk every day.** It's best to alter your routine for maximum health benefits and to maintain motivation.

Better: Do shorter, faster-paced walks some days (cardiovascular conditioning) and longer, moderate-paced walks on other days (calorie burning). Also try walks on steeper terrains and walks that alternate faster intervals with slower intervals.

Mistake #6: **Not keeping a walking log or journal.** Every day, indicate how far and fast you walked and any other observations you wish to record in a notebook or on your computer. Keeping a journal helps foster a sense

337

of accomplishment and self-esteem and is the single most effective method for ensuring that you'll stick to a walking program.

Mistake #7: Choosing cushy shoes. A study in *The American Journal of Sports Medicine* found that, on average, expensive, high-tech footwear caused twice the injuries as shoes costing half as much.

Some high-priced, cushiony shoes can make you feel as if you're walking on a foam mattress, but they have an inherent "wobble" that can cause your foot to move side to side, leading to potential foot, ankle, knee and hip injuries.

Better: Thin-soled shoes with minimal support. They force the muscles in the legs and feet to work harder, which improves strength and balance and helps prevent injuries.

When transitioning to thinner-soled shoes, make the switch gradually, breaking them in on shorter walks. They can feel awkward at first, so give your feet time to adjust.

Of course the right shoe is a very individual choice, but I like Karhu shoes, which promote forward momentum.

Cost: About $55 to $140, depending on the model. Other people like the so-called "barefoot" shoes, such as Vibram FiveFingers.

Helpful: Avoid cotton socks, which can lose their support and shape after a few washings. Try socks made from blends that include acrylic fibers, Coolmax and/or spandex/elastic. Soft wool socks also can work.

Tip: Powder your feet with cornstarch before a long walk to reduce friction, heat build-up and blisters.

TAKE THE LONGEVITY TEST

The more steps it takes you to walk the same distance each year, the weaker your core muscles are becoming.

Self-test: Each year on your birthday, go to a track and walk one lap, recording the number of steps on your pedometer. Aim to complete the lap in about the same number of steps each year. If it takes you more steps each year, you are regressing toward the "senior shuffle" and compromising your core-muscle strength and overall vitality.

What to do: In addition to walking regularly, start a core-muscle strengthening regimen and a stretching program to tone your hip and leg muscles.

How Limber Are You? Take Our Quiz!

Diana Zotos, physical therapist and advanced clinician, rehabilitation department, Hospital for Special Surgery, New York City.

Marla Altberg, certified personal trainer and Pilates mat instructor, New York City.

Here's a fun fitness challenge for you.... Become more flexible this year—literally!

For anyone who wants to have a fit, healthy body, building more endurance and strength are common goals, but you rarely hear someone say, "By the end of the year, I want to be able to touch my toes with the palms of my hands while standing—and do it smiling!"

But improving and/or maintaining flexibility is key to your health, because being loose and limber makes it easier to build strength and endurance…it makes everyday activities, such as tying your shoes or reaching behind the driver's seat in a car, less painful…and it makes you less prone to injury.

And it just feels great.

So, how flexible are you?

Take our quick quiz to find out…and then, if you discover that you're not exactly like Gumby, don't worry—I'll provide you with some easy tips from an expert that'll make you flexible in no time.

YOUR QUICK FLEXIBILITY TEST

To get an idea of how limber you are (or aren't), take this simple test created by Diana Zotos, a physical therapist and yoga instructor at the Hospital for Special Surgery in New York City.

•**Shoulder Stretch.** Standing, place your right forearm behind your waist and then raise your hand as far up as you comfortably can. Repeat this move with your left forearm. *Can you…*

a. Reach your shoulder blades with your fingertips?

b. Reach your middle back?

c. Reach your lower back?

• **Trunk Rotation.** Sit up straight in a chair with your arms crossed lightly across your chest, hands touching opposite shoulders. Stare straight ahead. *When you gently twist your upper body and head from side to side, can you…*

a. Turn your torso to about the 3:00 position on your right side and 9:00 on your left?

b. Turn not quite as far—only to 2:00 and 10:00?

c. Turn only to 1:00 and 11:00, or not much further than your starting position?

• **Leg Reach.** Stand up straight with feet hip-distance apart. When you bend forward and simultaneously slide both of your hands as far as you can down your legs (with your right hand on your right leg and your left hand on your left leg), *can you…*

a. Reach below the knee?

b. Reach the knee?

c. Reach mid-thigh?

• **Toe Touch.** Sit on the floor with your back straight and your legs extended straight in front of you. *When you bend over, can you…*

a. Touch your toes?

b. Reach your ankles but no further?

c. Get only as far as your shins?

If you answered mostly As, good job—you're lithe and limber. Just keep stretching a couple of times a week. If you fall into the B range, you're getting a bit stiff and could benefit from stretching more often, three to five times a week. If you answered primarily Cs, watch out! You may not be moving around as much as you should, and as a result, you're losing a lot of flexibility—but it's never too late to reclaim it! Doing the following stretches can help you open up your muscles and start to see improvement in your flexibility in as little as one to two weeks.

LIMBER UP!

Marla Altberg, a certified personal trainer and Pilates mat instructor in New York City, assures that even if you have spent the holidays (or longer) on the couch, you can easily loosen up again by performing this 10- to 15-minute stretching routine…

On your back: To perform the following stretches, lie on your back with your knees bent, feet slightly apart and flat on the floor and arms by your sides with palms facing downward.

• **Triangle Stretch** (For hamstrings, quads, inner thighs and hips)…

1. Make a triangle by crossing your left foot over your right knee.

2. Grasp your right leg behind your thigh, and inhale as you bring it in toward your chest.

3. Take your left elbow and press it gently against your left knee.

4. Breathe naturally as you hold the stretch for 20 seconds.

5. Return to your starting position and repeat on the other side.

• **Leg Raise** (For hamstrings, quads and back)…

1. Leaving your left leg where it is, bring your right knee to your chest as you inhale, and then slowly raise your right foot straight up to the ceiling as you exhale.

2. Using both hands, grab hold of your right leg behind your thigh, and climb up your leg, hand over hand, as far as you can toward your foot.

3. Keeping your hands as close as possible to your right foot, pull your right leg toward you, keeping it as straight as possible while your knee moves toward your face, gently but carefully—never to the point of pain. At the same time, push the leg against your hands in the opposite direction. Hold this pose for a count of 10, if possible.

4. Walk your hands back down, and repeat on the other side.

• **"T" Stretch** (For back and side abdominals)…

1. Join your knees together and tilt them both over to the left side until they touch the floor (or come as close to the floor as possible).

2. Spread your arms out to your sides, so your body forms the letter "T," and turn your head and torso to the right.

3. Hold for 20 seconds, breathing naturally and deeply into the stretch. Repeat on the opposite side.

On your tummy: To perform the next set of stretches, roll over onto your stomach.

• **Ab Contraction** (For abs and back)…

1. Make a pillow with your hands, rest your forehead on it and position your feet hip-width apart.

2. Inhale deeply, and then exhale as you draw your abdominal muscles in and up. Hold for 5 to 10 seconds and release. Pause for just a few seconds and then repeat twice.

3. Next, make the same muscle contraction but, as you do so, slightly raise your head (keeping your forehead glued to your hands) and chest off the floor. Hold for five seconds and release. Pause for just a few seconds and then repeat twice.

• **Fly Like Superman** (For back, abs, butt and shoulders)…

1. Still lying on your stomach, extend your arms above your head, shoulder-width apart, with the palms of your hands facing downward.

2. Inhale deeply. Exhaling, contract your abs and raise your right arm and left leg slightly off the floor simultaneously.

3. Hold for a count of 3 to 5 and then release. Repeat on the other side, and then do one more set.

• **Cat Stretch** (For back and abs)…

1. Get on your hands and knees.

2. Inhaling, pull your stomach in, tip your pelvis forward and arch your back like a cat. Hold for 3 to 5 seconds.

3. Exhaling, gradually relax back into your original position. Pause for just a few seconds and then repeat twice.

Note: If you have a health issue such as a bad back, joint problems or heart disease, consult your primary care provider before beginning any new exercise program.

Walk This Way to Stay Happy and Fit Without Breaking a Sweat

Hirofumi Tanaka, PhD, professor and director, Cardiovascular Aging Research Laboratory, University of Texas at Austin. His study was published in *The Journal of Alternative and Complementary Medicine*.

When you are feeling blue, do you ever take a stroll to walk it off? If you do, you may be practicing something called walking meditation. Not only does this walking technique have the power to beat depression that is deep enough to send you to a psychiatrist, it is actually more heart-healthy, more stress-busting and a lot less strenuous than traditional aerobic fitness walking. No special equipment or exercise clothing is required either. *Just put on a pair of comfortable shoes, and go…*

BETTER THAN POWER WALKING

First, take a tip from a study from Thailand in which walking meditation, which was given a slightly aerobic twist, provided more cardiovascular and psychological benefit than regular aerobic power walking. Before you go for a walk, warm up (and cool down after your walk) with a few basic stretching exercises (see previous article). *Then…*

Stand tall with your arms at your sides.

Let your gaze be softly directed at the ground six feet in front of you, and begin to walk. Walk slowly…as if you're stopping to smell the roses. And really let yourself do that. Forget about the cares of the day. In fact, focus instead on the sole of each foot as it makes contact with the ground.

While you slowly walk, let your arms gently swing in unison forward and back—yes, that means both arms forward at the same time and both arms back at the same time, which is different from the way we normally walk but not difficult to do…and as you walk this way, repeatedly say or think, in rhythm with your movements, a word or short phrase that is personal and inspiring to you.

In the Thai study, participants repeated a term that, as Thais, was meaningful to them— "Budd" with each upward swing of the arms and "Dha" (Buddha) with each downward swing. For you, if you happen to be a spiritual type, you might want to choose a word or term from your own tradition. If not, choose any word or phrase that is uplifting for you, such as "Peace and serenity," "Easy breezy," "It's all good," "Sunshine and rainbows"— even the name of a pet or someone dear who gives you joy.

If your mind wanders to worries and concerns, that's OK. Catch yourself at it...take a relaxing breath...and return to focusing on your walk and your inspiring phrase.

Walk this way for 20 minutes at a time when you first begin, and aim to lengthen the time up to a maximum of an hour.

In the Thai study, a group of women between the ages of 60 and 90 who had mild-to-moderate depression were taught this walking technique. *After 12 weeks, there were some really fantastic benefits...*

• **Fitness.** Compared with prestudy timed walking scores, the walking meditation group improved by 84%. Amazing!

• **Weight loss.** Members of the walking meditation group had a 5% decrease in body fat.

• **Blood and cardiovascular health.** The degree of ease of blood flow improved by 88% in the walking meditation group. Blood pressure, total cholesterol, "good" (HDL) cholesterol, triglyceride levels and a blood measure of inflammation called C-reactive protein improved, but significant reductions in the "stress hormone" cortisol, "bad" (LDL) cholesterol and interleukin 6, a protein associated with inflammation, were seen.

• **Happiness.** A significant drop in depression occurred, with the average score dropping below that signifying a depression diagnosis.

The researchers commented that the findings from their study were similar to those reported in other studies of mind-body exercise regimens, such as tai chi and yoga.

So, if you need to lighten and brighten your day and want to stay fit without breaking a sweat, here's a kind of light and relaxing walk you can take with a happy song in your heart.

Tai Chi: A Great Workout for Your Body and Brain

Peter M. Wayne, PhD, assistant professor of medicine at Harvard Medical School and research director of the Osher Center for Integrative Medicine, jointly based at Harvard Medical School and Brigham and Women's Hospital, both in Boston. He has trained in tai chi for more than 35 years and is author, with Mark L. Fuerst, of *The Harvard Medical School Guide to Tai Chi.*

Perhaps you've seen people performing the graceful, seemingly slow-motion movements of tai chi in a nearby park. If you've never tried it before, you may think that this form of exercise is easy to do and provides little more than a mild workout.

The truth: Even though tai chi consists of slow, gentle movements, this exercise is no pushover. Long known for its stress-reducing benefits, it also gives you an aerobic workout that's as intense as walking at a moderate pace...increases muscle strength and flexibility...improves breathing...improves posture and balance (to help prevent falls)...and focuses the mind.

What's new: Tai chi, which was developed centuries ago in China as a means of self-defense, is now linked to a number of new health benefits, including improved cardiovascular health and bone density...and reduced back and neck pain.

Even better: Tai chi is safer than many forms of exercise because of its 70% rule: You never move your joints or exert yourself beyond 70% of your maximum potential.

Recently discovered benefits...

BETTER BREATHING

Many Eastern-based practices, including yoga, meditation and tai chi, emphasize diaphragmatic breathing, in which the muscles of the diaphragm (rather than the chest) are used to take in more oxygen. This style of breathing not only helps the lungs to move with less effort but also allows more oxygen to pass into the bloodstream.

Efficient breathing is more important than you might think. Multiple studies indicate that healthy breathing—as measured by "forced expiratory volume," the amount of air that you can exhale in one second—may help you live longer.

LOWER BLOOD PRESSURE

The stress relief that can come from tai chi, along with improved breathing and other factors, make it an ideal exercise for lowering blood pressure. In fact, research suggests that tai chi is at least as effective for lowering blood pressure as lifestyle changes that are usually recommended, such as losing weight and cutting back on sodium.

A Johns Hopkins study found that light-intensity tai chi improved blood pressure almost as much as moderate-intensity aerobic exercise.

PERIPHERAL NEUROPATHY

Millions of people with diabetes and other conditions have peripheral neuropathy, nerve damage in the hands and/or feet that causes numbness, tingling or pain. The condition is particularly troublesome because reduced sensations in the feet can impair balance and increase the risk of falling.

Research has found that people with peripheral neuropathy who practiced tai chi had improved sensitivity in the soles of the feet. They also had better balance and walking speed.

STRONGER BONES

You don't need to lift weights to increase bone strength and reduce risk for osteoporosis. Researchers in Hong Kong found that women who did tai chi three times per week had increased bone density within 12 months.

IT'S EASY TO GET STARTED

Tai chi classes are commonly offered at health clubs, YMCAs and even some hospitals. Classes are particularly useful because of the feedback given by the instructor and the group support, which helps keep you motivated.

342

Good goal: Two one-hour tai chi classes a week—plus at-home practice for at least 30 minutes, three times a week.

You can find a tai chi expert in your area at *www.americantaichi.net*.

ChiWalking

Danny Dreyer, a walking and running coach and nationally ranked ultra marathon runner based in Asheville, North Carolina. He conducts workshops and lectures at races and other events nationwide. ChiWalking.com

Chi (also spelled "qi" and pronounced chee) is the Chinese concept of a life force that animates all things. It is a type of energy that flows through your body and unites your body, mind and spirit. We all know that walking is good for us physically. But in ChiWalking, you apply the principles of chi to the simple act of walking to achieve more than just a workout for your body—you also gain balance and alignment in your life.

ChiWalking is a way to get stronger and healthier without stress or strain and with very little chance of injury. Unlike power walking or race walking, it doesn't involve walking in an unnatural or competitive way. Anyone at any age or level of fitness can learn ChiWalking.

MOVEMENT IS THE KEY

ChiWalking uses good walking form to help you walk more efficiently with less wear and tear on the body. The beauty of ChiWalking is that you can feel the benefits quickly. Many people with knee and hip problems can still enjoy ChiWalking, because when your body is in alignment and moving correctly, there's far less impact on your joints. I've even taught ChiWalking to people who use canes or walkers.

The basic principle of chi is that it must flow freely through your body. If your body is misaligned or your joints and muscles are tight, the flow of chi will be blocked, just as a crimp in a hose blocks the flow of water. When the principle of chi is applied to walking, it teaches us to align our spines, engage our core muscles and relax everything else. The energy flows and walking becomes fluid and easy.

A fit mind in a fit body—isn't that what we all want as we grow older? By following five mindful steps as you walk, your whole being gets an enjoyable workout every time. You can also suit the type of walk you do to harmonize with your current mood and energy level. *Here are the five mindful steps to successful ChiWalking…*

MINDFUL STEP 1: GET ALIGNED

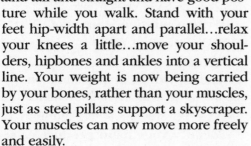

Body connection: Align your spine so that you stand tall and straight and have good posture while you walk. Stand with your feet hip-width apart and parallel…relax your knees a little…move your shoulders, hipbones and ankles into a vertical line. Your weight is now being carried by your bones, rather than your muscles, just as steel pillars support a skyscraper. Your muscles can now move more freely and easily.

Mind connection: The chi concept of "needle in cotton" applies here. Imagine a needle poked down through the middle of a ball of cotton. The needle is the thin, strong, straight line running through the center of the cotton. Think of your spine as the needle and your arms and legs as being as light as cotton. Gather energy in toward your spine and let your arms and legs relax. Get mentally aligned with your intentions for your walk.

MINDFUL STEP 2: ENGAGE YOUR CORE

Body connection: Your core muscles are the lower abdominal muscles that stabilize your pelvis when you stand, walk or run. They also hold your spine erect and help lift your legs. When your core muscles are strong, your body is stable. You can stand up straight easily and move your arms and legs easily. To engage your core muscles, level your pelvis—stand up straight in alignment, as described above, and then lift up on your pubic bone by using your lower abdominal

muscles. This may take a little practice, but you'll soon learn to feel those muscles and get them to work.

Once you've got your posture aligned and your pelvis level, stand tall and tilt your upper body forward just a quarter of an inch. This will keep your upper body aligned and moving forward—which allows gravity to do most of the work as you walk.

Mind connection: Your inner core is your internal sense of self. When you engage your inner core, you feel grounded and centered. You have willpower when you need it.

MINDFUL STEP 3: CREATE BALANCE

Body connection: Imagine your body in the shape of a letter C—your spine is straight, your chin is down slightly, and your pelvis is rising slightly in front because you're lifting it slightly, as explained in Step 2. Your upper and lower body are in balance and ready to move forward.

Mind connection: Take a balanced approach to your walks, spreading them evenly across the week and never going beyond what your body tells you is right. As you get fitter, feel how your mind and body become more in balance with each other.

MINDFUL STEP 4: MAKE A CHOICE

Body connection: Choose to walk regularly, even on days when you don't really feel like it. Try to walk for at least 30 minutes on most days but if you can't squeeze it in, even 15 minutes will improve your cardiovascular fitness and improve your outlook on life.

Mind connection: Overall, choose to create health. On a daily basis, choose the kind of walk you want. If you're feeling scattered or stressed, a slower, more meditative walk might be better than a fast cardiovascular workout.

MINDFUL STEP 5: MOVE FORWARD

Body connection: To walk, push your core ahead with each step, letting gravity move the rest of your body forward. Work with gravity—don't fight it. Listen to your body and

move only as fast as is comfortable for you. Good form is more important than speed.

Mind connection: Now is the time for action and resolve. As you walk, focus your mind on maintaining good form. Bear in mind that each step is part of going forward with your quest for lifelong energy and health.

THE PRACTICE OF WALKING

By "practice" I mean walking as a regular, mindful activity that works to enhance your quality of life. When you make walking a regular practice, you raise it beyond just healthful physical exercise. It becomes a way to focus your energy and to channel your thoughts because your chi is flowing freely.

Illustrations by Shawn Banner

Win the Inner Game of Stress

John Horton, MD, a physician specializing in preventive medicine and stress, Westlake Village, California. He is coauthor, with sports psychologist W. Timothy Gallwey and stress expert Edd Hanzelik, MD, of *The Inner Game of Stress: Outsmart Life's Challenges and Fulfill Your Potential.*

Stress creates unproductive panic, inhibits creative thought, contributes to chronic illness and is just plain exhausting. But no matter what's going on in our lives, we can tap into our inner resources to keep stress from doing its damage.

Different strategies work for different people. Below are some of the most effective ones...

THE INNER GAME

We all are playing an inner game whether we recognize it or not. That means that while we are all involved in outer games (overcoming obstacles in the outside world to reach our goals), we are at the same time faced with inner obstacles, such as fear, self-doubt, frustration, pain and distractions. These inner obstacles prevent us from expressing our full range of capabilities and enjoying our time to the utmost.

The secret lies in knowing that you have choices about how you look at external events, how you define them, how you attribute meaning to them and how you react to them mentally and emotionally. The key is to recognize that every person has the internal wisdom to bypass the frustrations and fears that pull them into the negative cycle of stress.

BECOME YOUR OWN CEO

Feeling powerless and victimized is among the most common sources of stress. You're likely to feel more in control if you consider yourself the CEO of your life. *To do so...*

•**Write a mission statement.** What is the primary mission of your life?

Examples: To create prosperity for myself and my family...to pay attention to my inner life as well as my achievements...to help others in my work or personal life.

•**Identify your main product or service.** What do you provide to others? These could be specific to a particular business or profession.

Example: As a doctor, my services would include being up-to-date in my knowledge... knowing the best specialists to refer a patient to...seeing patients quickly.

•**List your company's resources.** Include both internal resources—positive personal traits, such as your compassion, intelligence and humor—and external resources—your financial assets, friends and possessions. Ask yourself whether you are getting as much from each of these resources as you could.

LOST CONTROL?

Consider whether you have given up too much control of your corporation. What would it cost to buy back some of your shares?

Example: Did you sell too many shares of yourself for your big home? If massive mortgage payments fill you with stress—or force you to remain in a job that fills you with stress—perhaps you should move into a smaller home and take back those shares.

This CEO thought process serves as a reminder that we are not helpless. Your life is yours, and you get to decide everything. It is always your choice, even if you decide to comply with the wishes of someone else. Once you become aware of the limits that you place on your choices, your freedom will evolve and your stress will ease.

REGAINING CONTROL

Trying to control things that are outside our control is enormously stressful—yet many of us unwittingly do this. *When you feel stressed, consider…*

What don't I control here?

What am I trying to control here?

What could I control here that I'm not currently controlling?

Confronting these questions can help us focus on things that we can accomplish and reduce our stress over things that we cannot.

Example: When a man who is stressed over his wife's poor health asks himself these questions, he realizes that her health is not something that he can control, so he should stop trying to. What he can control is his attitude toward life. By remaining upbeat, he can help his wife remain upbeat.

THE MAGIC PEN

Select a stress-causing situation in your life, then write down your usual inner dialog on this subject. Once you have written everything that comes to mind, take out a new piece of paper and imagine that your pen has been magically endowed with one of your positive inner resources. This resource might be your clarity, compassion, candor, serenity or patience—any trait that you consider a personal strength. Try to empty your mind of all thought, then let your magic pen write a message to you about this stressful subject. Don't censor the pen—let it write everything.

Example: A man feels guilty about his grown son, who can't find direction in life. If he endowed his pen with his compassion, the pen might write that he did his best to raise his son and that his son is doing his best to live his life.

Yoga Can Change Your Life!

Mary Louise Stefanic, a certified yoga and qigong instructor with a focus on therapeutic yoga. Ms. Stefanic is a staff member at the Loyola Center for Fitness and Loyola University Health System, both in Maywood, Illinois. She has been teaching yoga since 1969.

Not that long ago, yoga was viewed primarily as an activity for "youngish" health nuts who wanted to round out their exercise regimens.

Now: Older adults—meaning people in their 60s, 70s, 80s and beyond—are among the most enthusiastic practitioners of this ancient healing system of exercise and controlled breathing.

YOGA GOES MAINSTREAM

Virtually everyone can benefit from yoga. Unfortunately, many people are reluctant to try it because they assume that it's too unconventional and requires extreme flexibility. Neither belief is true.

What's more, its varied health benefits are largely what's making the practice so popular now with older adults. More than 1,000 scientific studies have shown that yoga can improve conditions ranging from arthritis, asthma, insomnia and depression to heart disease, diabetes and cancer.

You look better, too: Yoga is quite useful in helping to prevent rounding (or hunching) of the back, which occurs so often in older adults. This condition can lead to back pain and breathing problems as the rib cage presses against the lungs.

My experience: After teaching yoga to thousands of students, I'm continually amazed at how many tell me that it has literally changed their lives by helping them feel so much better physically and mentally.

GETTING STARTED

If you want to see whether you could benefit from yoga, ask your doctor about trying the following poses, which address common physical complaints. These poses are a good first step before taking a yoga class.* Yoga is

*To find a yoga class near you, check your local community center and/or consult the International Association of Yoga Therapists (*www.iayt.org*).

best performed in loose, comfortable clothing and in your bare feet, so your feet won't slip. *Poses to try…*

•**Knees to chest pose.** For low back pain and painful, tight hips.

What to do: Lie on your back (on carpet or a yoga mat, available at sports-equipment stores for about $20). With your arms, hug both knees in to your chest. Keep your knees together and your elbows pointing out to each side of your body. Slowly rock from elbow to elbow to massage your back and shoulders. Take deep, abdominal breaths while holding your thighs close to your chest and hold for six complete inhales and exhales.

•**Mecca pose.** This pose also relieves back pain.

What to do: Begin by kneeling on the floor with your knees together. For added comfort, place a small towel behind your knees. Sit back on your feet, and lean forward from your waist so that your chest and stomach rest atop your thighs. Reach your arms out in front of you, resting your forehead to the floor while stretching your tailbone to your heels. Hold for six complete inhales and exhales.

•**Leg rotation.** For sciatica, a cause of back, pelvic and leg pain.

What to do: Lie on your back with both legs extended. Slowly bring your right knee to your chest and inhale. Rest your right ankle on the front of your left thigh, and exhale as you slowly slide it down along your left knee, shin and ankle to toes. This helps "screw" the top of your right thighbone into the hip socket, easing lower back and leg pain. Repeat on other side. Do three times on each side.

To conclude your session: While in a sitting position, press your palms together. Bring your thumbs into your breastbone. Tuck your elbows in and down, press your breastbone to your thumbs, lifting and opening your chest. Hold for six breaths.

Important: Even when you're not doing yoga, don't forget your breath. Slow, thoughtful, deep breathing is most effective, but don't perform it too quickly. I find the technique to be most effective when you hold the inhala-tion and exhalation for a certain number of counts.

What to do: Lie on your back, resting your hands on your belly so that your middle fingers touch across your navel. Inhale through your nose for a count of six, pushing your navel out so that your fingertips separate. Pause, then exhale for a count of nine, pulling your navel back in. Perform these steps two more times (more may make you dizzy). Do this in the morning and at night (deep breathing improves mental focus and can be energizing in the morning and calming at night).

To Get to Sleep Fast, Do These 6 Easy Yoga Moves

Loren Fishman, MD, assistant clinical professor of rehabilitation and regenerative medicine, Columbia Medical School, New York City, medical director, Manhattan Physical Medicine and Rehabilitation, and author of several books on yoga for health, including *Healing Yoga: Proven Postures to Treat Twenty Common Ailments—from Backache to Bone Loss, Shoulder Pain to Bunions, and More.*

Losing a good night's sleep is a bummer, isn't it? You walk around in a groggy fog the next day and run the risk of getting snippy with coworkers, friends and loved ones because sleep deprivation has made you grumpy. So many factors in modern daily life can make it tough for us to fall asleep, stay asleep and rest peacefully.

Yoga is a powerful tool to relieve stress and help your body relax and prepare for sleep. By stretching muscles, yoga poses trigger mechanisms in the body that send powerful relaxing signals to the brain. When performed daily, yoga can make us into better sleepers.

Do the following yoga routine nightly at bedtime. Poses can even be done while in bed. Otherwise, do them on a cushioned surface on the floor. A plush blanket or towel will do if you don't have carpeting or a yoga mat.

•**Seated forward bend.** This will give a great stretch to your legs and back muscles. To prepare for the forward bend, sit with your legs straight in front of you. First, stretch one leg and then the other by extending from the hip through the heel to elongate the leg. Then relax your legs and stretch your arms straight upward to feel your torso and back extend long and lean.

Now you are ready to bend forward from the hips and reach out with your hands to  grasp your ankles or feet (or as far down your legs as you comfortably can—you should be stretching, but not straining). Let gentle, deep breaths help you relax into the stretch. Hold this pose for one to three minutes.

• **Revolved abdomen pose.** This pose massages the abdominal organs, gives a nice stretch to the lower back and muscles across the rib cage and opens the chest so you can breathe more deeply. To do it, lie on your back, bend your knees to your chest and stretch your arms out to your sides. With bent knees pressed together, inhale. Then, while exhaling, twist from your hips to lower your legs to  the right while turning your face to the left. Again, give yourself a nice stretch, but do not strain or force yourself to go deeper into the pose than you comfortably can. Hold the pose for five breaths, then bring your knees and head back to center. Repeat the pose on the opposite side by dropping your knees to the left while turning your head to the right. Hold the pose for five breaths.

• **Reclining big toe pose.** This is a leg lift that gives a good stretch to the muscles all down the back of the leg. Unless you are very limber, you will need a prop to help you get the most stretch. The prop can be a long belt, scarf, cord or necktie that you can brace against the arch or ball of your foot and use as a lever to stretch your leg until  your foot faces the ceiling. To do this posture, lie on your back, take a deep breath, and, while gently exhaling, bend your right knee to your chest and loop the prop around the arch or ball of the right foot, holding the ends of the prop in both hands. Inhale while straightening your knee so that your right heel is turned toward the ceiling. Guide the prop to comfortably increase the stretch. Hold this pose for a minute or two and then repeat with the other leg.

• **Child's pose.** This restorative yoga pose helps get more blood flowing in the head and can be so deeply relaxing that when you roll out of it, you may just nod off to sleep like a baby. Begin by kneeling so that you are sitting on your heels, and take a nice, deep, relaxing breath. Bend forward while exhaling and place  your forehead on the floor (or on your bed if that's where you are doing the exercise). Place your arms at your sides so that the hands, palms turned up, are near your feet. As you breathe, especially focus on relaxing your back and shoulders. Hold this pose for five to seven long, slow deep breaths.

• **"Stop-action" breathing.** This is an easy and deeply relaxing breathing technique that strengthens the respiratory system. While lying down on your back in bed, exhale completely through the nose. Then inhale a little bit of air—just enough for a count of two or three seconds. Hold that little bit of breath for two or three seconds and, without exhaling, take another two or three seconds of breath, hold, and keep on taking those little sips of air, inhaling and pausing, until your lungs are full as if you've just taken only one big breath instead of a series of small ones. Hold for a second or two. Then slowly exhale in the same manner, exhaling a little bit for two or three seconds, pausing with breath held for two or three seconds and continuing like this until you've completely exhaled air from the lungs. Do four or five rounds of this breathing technique, taking a normal breath between each round of the stop-action breaths.

• **Corpse pose.** If you're not in your bed yet, it's time to crawl into it and get into this pose—you're going to be asleep soon! Lie on your back with your legs stretched out and your arms comfortably at your sides, palms turned up. Slowly inhale and exhale through the nose, feeling your abdomen expand and contract. While you do so, start mentally scanning your body, beginning at your toes and working your way up to the top of your head, assessing whether you are holding tension anywhere. Mentally release muscular tension as you go, allowing your body, inch by inch, to comfortably sink into the surface it is lying on. You may fall asleep in the process or you might simply hold the pose for five breaths and then slowly transition into your favorite sleeping posture to fall asleep.

Acupuncture Cure for Better Sleep

Pina LoGiudice, ND, LAc, is clinical director of Inner Source Natural Health, a center for integrative naturopathic care in New York City. She also is a member of the adjunct faculty of the Natural Gourmet Institute for Food and Health in New York City, and has appeared on various TV shows, including *The Dr. Oz Show*. InnerSourceHealth.com

Getting stuck all over with needles may seem the stuff of voodoo nightmares—but in fact, if you suffer from insomnia, it may be just the fix for your sleepless nights. We're not really suggesting that you volunteer to be a voodoo doll, though it may seem that way to you if you've never tried acupuncture. You just might have to set aside your squeamishness and give it some consideration.

There's a growing amount of real science behind my recommendation. For instance, a meta-analysis of 46 randomized trials found that acupuncture does ease insomnia. And a study published in a recent issue of *Asian Journal of Psychiatry* found that acupuncture may be as effective as the sedative drug *zolpidem* (Ambien) in alleviating sleeplessness, particularly for women and older patients.

Big advantage: Acupuncture has no serious adverse effects—unlike sleeping pills, which can lead to breathing problems, pounding heartbeat, chest pain, blurred vision and addiction.

Studies aside, you might still wonder how well acupuncture works for real insomniacs in the real world. New York City naturopathic physician and licensed acupuncturist Pina LoGiudice, ND, LAc, said, "I can confirm that acupuncture has helped many of my patients sleep. I use it on its own for mild insomnia… for chronic cases, I use it in combination with other natural modalities to address underlying conditions that can interfere with sleep."

How it works: From the perspective of Western medicine, acupuncture helps regulate various hormones and neurotransmitters—including melatonin, serotonin, endorphins and many others—that play major roles in sleep regulation, according to a recent study from Emory University School of Medicine. In traditional Chinese medicine, the theory is that various symptoms develop when a patient's qi (vital energy) gets blocked…and acupuncture removes these blockages by stimulating specific acupoints that correspond to different parts of the body. As Dr. LoGiudice explained, "Acupuncture strengthens the body's ability to heal itself. When tension and pain are removed, you eliminate much of what is causing the insomnia."

What to expect: While the course of treatment is tailored to an individual's needs, typically a patient receives 10 to 20 hypoallergenic needles at a time in a treatment session that lasts about 30 to 45 minutes. Placement of the needles depends on where the qi is blocked and on any underlying health problems that may be contributing to poor sleep. Discomfort is minimal—the needles are extremely thin and only go through the first layer of skin.

Insomnia patients typically go for treatment once per week for six to 12 weeks, then follow up once or twice a year for maintenance, Dr. LoGiudice said. When asked how soon patients can expect results, she said, "Some feel a difference as soon as the third treatment, while others may take up to 12 sessions. If we are not seeing results by the eighth session, I start thinking about adding nutrients or herbs to the treatment plan."

To find a qualified acupuncturist: Visit the website of the National Certification Commission for Acupuncture and Oriental

348

Medicine at *www.nccaom.org* and click on "Find a Practitioner." Dr. LoGiudice noted that acupuncture generally is safe for everyone...there are no side effects except for rare cases of slight bruising...and some health insurance policies now cover acupuncture—all facts that may help you sleep better as you consider this treatment option.

The Sleep Cure for Blood Sugar Balance

Michelle M. Perfect, PhD, associate professor, school psychology, University of Arizona, Tucson.

If you (or someone in your family) has diabetes and you do your best to manage your blood sugar levels throughout the day, yet your levels often are still curiously high, a recent study has shed light on why that might be the case.

Getting poor-quality sleep at night may be secretly sabotaging your blood sugar—even when you're doing everything right!

And this is a recipe for diaster. Study author Michelle Perfect, PhD, an associate professor of psychology, disability and psychoeducational studies at The University of Arizona in Tucson, explains...

A CHICKEN-AND-EGG CONUNDRUM

This study was done on kids with type 1 diabetes, but as you'll see later, this news about sleeping applies to all types of diabetics of all ages.

The study: Fifty children ages 10 to 16 with type 1 diabetes were compared with a matching number of similarly aged kids without the condition. Participants underwent a home-based sleep study for five nights, wearing equipment that measured their blood sugar, sleep stage (one of four stages ranging from light to heavy), speed of breathing and heart rate. Parents and children also answered questions about topics such as mood level and amount of daytime sleepiness. School records were obtained to analyze grades. And the kids and their parents were told to administer insulin as they normally would.

The findings, which appeared in the January 2012 issue of *Sleep*, were intriguing. Children in the control group (no diabetes) spent 19% of their sleep time in deep sleep, while children with diabetes spent only 15% of their sleep time in deep sleep. Sleep apnea—a serious condition that causes dangerous pauses in breathing during sleep and awakenings during the night and that heightens risk for heart attack and stroke—was experienced by about one-third of the children with diabetes. Compared with the control group, the diabetics were more likely to have high blood sugar, which was expected, said Dr. Perfect, since very few kids achieve perfect glucose control. But interestingly, the diabetic kids with sleep apnea had much higher blood sugar levels compared with diabetic kids who did not have sleep apnea.

So that raises the question—does poor-quality sleep cause blood sugar irregularities, or do these sugar fluctuations lead to troubled sleep? It could be either or both, said Dr. Perfect, who didn't set out to answer that question and said that more research needs to be done to figure out the answer. There are theories supporting both angles. For example, prior studies from other research teams established that not getting enough deep sleep causes the brain to release less of a chemical that helps stabilize blood glucose levels. But on the other hand, Dr. Perfect said that if you have diabetes, you may sometimes need to get up in the middle of the night to check your blood sugar, so having diabetes may also cause more sleep disturbances, though that wasn't specifically analyzed in this study. It's also possible that poor blood glucose control—such as not administering enough insulin at the proper times—could lead to sleep problems.

TIPS FOR SOLID SHUT-EYE

Dr. Perfect said that her findings support what other studies on type 2 diabetics and sleep have found—the better your sleep, the better your blood sugar control. So people of any age with diabetes should pay close attention to how well they're sleeping and should ask their family members to keep an ear out for lots of snoring or gasping while sleeping—a sign of sleep apnea, which is dangerous and would require immediate attention from a doctor.

Dr. Perfect advises diabetics of all ages to ask themselves the following questions…

Most of the time, do I feel refreshed when I wake up?

Am I easily awoken during the night?

If the answer to these questions is "no" and then "yes," then Dr. Perfect advises that you talk to your doctor, because it may mean that you're not getting enough deep sleep. There isn't any quick trick that can make you sleep deeply throughout the night, but you can be more diligent about ensuring good sleep habits—including minimizing light and noise in the bedroom…abstaining from caffeine and stimulating activities such as exercising or web surfing near bedtime…and keeping your bedroom a little cooler than the rest of the house. Quality sleep is important for everyone—and, it seems, even more so if you have diabetes.

Pill-Free Cure for Insomnia

YAWN! Not getting enough sleep is exhausting. Most people have trouble sleeping every once in awhile. If you just can't catch those Zs and you hate the groggy morning-after feeling you get from sleeping pills, try this acupressure trick. Just before you go to bed, press the center of the bottoms of your heels with your thumbs. The easiest way to do this is to lie on your back (on a carpeted floor is best) and bend your knees, using your right hand on your left foot and left hand on your right. Press as hard as you can without cramping your hands. Keep pressing for at least two minutes—up to four minutes is even better. You should feel yourself starting to really relax, with tension leaving your body. Ease into bed for blissful zzzzzzzs.

Lydia Wilen and Joan Wilen are sisters who are folk-remedy experts based in New York City. The sisters are coauthors of many books, including *Bottom Line's Household Magic* and *Secret Food Cures*.

Foods That Sabotage Sleep

Bonnie Taub-Dix, RDN, CDN, a registered dietitian and director and owner of BTD Nutrition Consultants, LLC, on Long Island and in New York City. She is author of *Read It Before You Eat It*. BonnieTaubDix.com

You know that an evening coffee can leave you tossing and turning into the wee hours. *But other foods hurt sleep, too…*

• **Premium ice cream.** Brace yourself for a restless night if you indulge in Häagen-Dazs or Ben & Jerry's late at night. The richness of these wonderful treats comes mainly from fat—16 to 17 grams of fat in half a cup of vanilla, and who eats just half a cup?

Your body digests fat more slowly than it digests proteins or carbohydrates. When you eat a high-fat food within an hour or two of bedtime, your digestion will still be "active" when you lie down—and that can disturb sleep.

Also, the combination of stomach acid, stomach contractions and a horizontal position increases the risk for reflux, the upsurge of digestive juices into the esophagus that causes heartburn—which can disturb sleep.

• **Chocolate.** Some types of chocolate can jolt you awake almost as much as a cup of coffee. Dark chocolate, in particular, has shocking amounts of caffeine.

Example: Half a bar of Dagoba Eclipse Extra Dark has 41 milligrams of caffeine, close to what you'd get in a shot of mild espresso.

Chocolate also contains theobromine, another stimulant, which is never a good choice near bedtime.

• **Beans.** Beans are one of the healthiest foods. But a helping or two of beans—or broccoli, cauliflower, cabbage or other gas-producing foods—close to bedtime can make your night, well, a little noisier than usual. No one sleeps well when suffering from gas pains. You can reduce the "backtalk" by drinking a mug of chamomile or peppermint tea at bedtime. They're carminative herbs that aid digestion and help prevent gas.

•**Spicy foods.** Spicy foods temporarily speed up your metabolism. They are associated with taking longer to fall asleep and with more time spent awake at night. This may be caused by the capsaicin found in chili peppers, which affects body temperature and disrupts sleep. Also, in some people, spicy foods can lead to sleep-disturbing gas, stomach cramps and heartburn.

FOODS THAT HELP YOU SLEEP

Carbohydrate-based meals increase blood levels of tryptophan, used by the body to manufacture serotonin, a "calming" neurotransmitter. *Also helpful…*

•**Warm milk.** It's not a myth—warm milk at bedtime really will help you get to sleep. It settles the stomach, and the ritual of drinking it can help you calm down and fall asleep more easily.

•**Cherry juice.** A study published in *Journal of Medicinal Food* found that people who drank eight ounces of tart cherry juice in the morning and eight at night for two weeks had about 17 minutes less awake time during the night than when they drank a non-cherry juice. Tart cherries are high in melatonin, a hormone that regulates the body's sleep-wake cycles. The brand used in the study was Cheribundi.

Helpful: Tart cherry juice has 140 calories in eight ounces, so you may want to cut back on calories elsewhere.

Dangers of Sleep Apnea

Ralph Downey III, PhD, D, ABSM, physician, Sleep Disorders Center, Cleveland Clinic. He is former adjunct associate clinical professor of medicine and past chief, sleep medicine, Loma Linda University Medical Center, Loma Linda University Children's Hospital.

Doctors have long known that obstructive sleep apnea (repeated interruptions in breathing during sleep) can harm the overall health of men and women who suffer from the condition.

Now: Recent research shows that sleep apnea is even more dangerous than experts had previously realized, increasing the sufferer's risk for heart attack, stroke, diabetes and fatal car crashes.

What you need to know…

NO ROOM TO BREATHE

Sleep apnea occurs about twice as often in men as in women, but it is overlooked more often in women. An estimated 70% of people with sleep apnea are overweight. Fat deposited around the neck (men with sleep apnea often wear a size 17 or larger collar, while women with the disorder often have a neck circumference of 16 inches or more) compresses the upper airway, reducing air flow and causing the passage to narrow or close. Your brain senses this inability to breathe and briefly awakens you so that you can reopen the airway.

The exact cause of obstructive sleep apnea in people of normal weight is unknown, but it may involve various anatomical characteristics, such as having a narrow throat and upper airway.

Red flag 1: **About half of all people who snore loudly have sleep apnea.** One telling sign is a gasping, choking kind of snore, during which the sleeper seems to stop breathing. (If you live alone and don't know whether you snore, ask your doctor about recording yourself while you are sleeping to check for snoring and other signs of sleep apnea.)

Red flag 2: **Daytime sleepiness is the other most common symptom.** Less common symptoms include headache, sore throat and/or dry mouth in the morning, sexual dysfunction and memory problems.

DANGERS OF SLEEP APNEA

New scientific evidence shows that sleep apnea increases risk for…

•**Cardiovascular disease.** Sleep apnea's repeated episodes of interrupted breathing—and the accompanying drop in oxygen levels—takes a toll on the heart and arteries.

Recent finding: Heart attack risk in sleep apnea sufferers is 30% higher than normal over a four- to five-year period, and stroke risk is twice as high in people with sleep apnea.

•**Diabetes.** Sleep apnea (regardless of the sufferer's weight) is linked to increased insulin resistance—a potentially dangerous condition in which the body is resistant to the effects of insulin.

Recent finding: A Yale study of 593 patients found that over a six-year period, people diagnosed with sleep apnea were more than two-and-a-half times more likely to develop diabetes than those without the sleep disorder.

•**Accidents.** Sleep apnea dramatically increases the risk for a deadly mishap due to sleepiness and impaired alertness.

Recent finding: A study of 1,600 people, presented at an American Thoracic Society meeting, found that the 800 sleep apnea sufferers were twice as likely to have a car crash over a three-year period. Surprisingly, those who were unaware of being sleepy were just as likely to crash as those who were aware of being sleepy.

DO YOU HAVE SLEEP APNEA?

If you think you may have sleep apnea, see a specialist at an accredited sleep center, where a thorough medical history will be taken and you may be asked to undergo a sleep study. This involves spending the night in a sleep laboratory where your breathing, oxygen level, movements and brain wave activity are measured while you sleep.

BEST TREATMENT OPTIONS

The treatment typically prescribed first for sleep apnea is continuous positive airway pressure (CPAP). A stream of air is pumped onto the back of the throat during sleep to keep the airway open. The air is supplied through a mask, most often worn over the nose, which is connected by tubing to a small box that contains a fan.

In recent years, a larger variety of masks have become available, and fan units have become smaller and nearly silent. A number of adjustments may be needed, which may require trying several different devices and more than one visit to a sleep lab.

Other treatments for sleep apnea are usually prescribed to make CPAP more effective, or for people with milder degrees of the disorder who have tried CPAP but were unable or unwilling to use it.

These treatments include…

•**Mouthpieces.** Generally fitted by a dentist and worn at night, these oral appliances adjust the lower jaw and tongue to help keep the airway open.

•**Surgery.** This may be recommended for people who have an anatomical abnormality that narrows the airway and for whom CPAP doesn't work. The most common operation for sleep apnea is uvulopalatopharyngoplasty (UPPP), in which excess tissue is removed from the back of the throat. It works about 50% of the time.

HELPING YOURSELF

Several measures can make sleep apnea treatment more effective and, in some cases, eliminate the condition altogether. *What to do…*

•**Lose weight, if you are overweight.** For every 10% of body weight lost, the number of apnea episodes drops by 25%.

•**Change your sleep position.** Sleeping on your side—rather than on your back—typically means fewer apnea episodes. Sleeping on your stomach is even better. Some obese people who have sleep apnea do best if they sleep while sitting up.

•**Avoid alcohol.** It relaxes the muscles around the airway, aggravating sleep apnea.

•**Use medication carefully.** Sleep medications can worsen sleep apnea by making it harder for your body to rouse itself when breathing stops. If you have sleep apnea, make sure a doctor oversees your use of sleep medications (including over-the-counter drugs).

Sleep Device Bonus

Recent research: When a person with sleep apnea begins treatment with a continuous positive airway pressure (CPAP) device, which forces air into the lungs during sleep, the person's resistance to insulin (a hallmark of diabetes) improves dramatically.

If you have sleep apnea: Treatment with a CPAP device may not only improve your sleep but also help lower diabetes risk.

Imran H. Iftikhar, MD, assistant professor of internal medicine, University of South Carolina, Columbia.

Sleep Soundly: Safe, Natural Insomnia Solutions

Rubin Naiman, PhD, psychologist specializing in sleep and dream medicine and clinical assistant professor of medicine at the University of Arizona's Center for Integrative Medicine. He is author of the book *Healing Night* and coauthor with Dr. Andrew Weil, of the audiobook *Healthy Sleep*.

A good night's sleep...there's nothing more restorative—or elusive...for the 64% of Americans who report regularly having trouble sleeping. A disconcertingly high percentage of the sleepless (nearly 20%) solve the problem by taking sleeping pills. But sleeping pills can be dangerous addictive, physically and/or emotionally—and swallowing a pill when you want to go to sleep doesn't address the root cause of the problem. What, exactly, is keeping you up at night?

SLOW DOWN

According to Rubin Naiman, PhD, a psychologist and clinical assistant professor of medicine at the University of Arizona's Center for Integrative Medicine, most of our sleep problems have to do not with our bodies, per se, but with our habits. The modern American lifestyle—replete with highly refined foods and caffeine-laden beverages, excessive exposure to artificial light in the evening, and "adrenaline-producing" nighttime activities, such as working until bedtime, watching TV or surfing the Web—leaves us overstimulated in the evening just when our bodies are designed to slow down...and, importantly, to literally cool down as well.

Studies show that a cooler core body temperature—and warmer hands and feet—make you sleepy. "Cooling the body allows the mind and the heart to get quiet," says Dr. Naiman. He believes that this cooling process contributes to the release of melatonin, the hormone that helps to regulate the body's circadian rhythm of sleeping and waking.

DEEP GREEN SLEEP

Dr. Naiman has developed an integrative approach to sleep that defines healthy sleep as an interaction between a person and his/her sleep environment. He calls this approach Deep Green Sleep. "My goal was to explore all of the subtleties in a person's life that may be disrupting sleep. This takes into account your physiology, emotions, personal experiences, sleeping and waking patterns and your attitudes about sleep and the sleeping environment." This approach is unique because it values "the subjective and personal experience of sleep," he says—in contrast with conventional sleep treatment, which tends to rely on "computer printouts of sleep studies—otherwise known as 'treating the chart.'"

It's important to realize that lifestyle habits and attitudes are hard to change, so Dr. Naiman cautioned that it often can take weeks, even months, to achieve his Deep Green Sleep. The good news is that the results are lasting and may even enhance your waking life.

Here are his suggestions on how you can ease into the night...

• **Live a healthful waking life.** "The secret of a good night's sleep is a good day's waking," said Dr. Naiman. This includes getting regular exercise (but not within three hours of bedtime) and eating a balanced, nutritious diet.

• **Cool down in the evening.** It's important to help your mind and body cool down, starting several hours before bedtime, by doing the following...

• **Avoid foods and drinks that sharply spike energy,** such as highly refined carbohydrates and anything with caffeine, at least eight hours before bedtime.

• **Limit alcohol in the evening**—it interferes with sleep by suppressing melatonin. It also interferes with dreaming and disrupts circadian rhythms.

•**Avoid nighttime screen-based activities within an hour of bedtime.** You may think that watching TV or surfing the Web are relaxing things to do, but in reality these activities are highly stimulating. They engage your brain and expose you to relatively bright light with a strong blue wavelength that "mimics daylight and suppresses melatonin," said Dr. Naiman.

•**Create a sound sleeping environment.** It is also important that where you sleep be stimulation-free and conducive to rest.

In your bedroom…

•**Be sure that you have a comfortable mattress, pillow and bedding.** It's amazing how many people fail to address this basic need—often because their mattress has become worn out slowly, over time, and they haven't noticed.

•**Remove anything unessential from your bedside table that may tempt you to stay awake,** such as the TV remove control or stimulating books.

•**When you are ready to call it a night, turn everything off**—radio, TV and, of course, the light.

•**Keep the room cool (68°F or lower).**

•**Let go of waking.** Each day, allow your mind and body to surrender to sleep by engaging in quieting and relaxing activities starting about an hour before bedtime, such as…

- Gentle yoga
- Meditation
- Rhythmic breathing
- Reading poetry or other nonstimulating material
- Journaling
- Taking a hot bath.

Sex seems to help most people relax and can facilitate sleep, in part because climaxing triggers a powerful relaxation response, Dr. Naiman said.

•**Consider supplementing with melatonin.** If sleep is still elusive after trying these Deep Green Sleep tips, Dr. Naiman often suggests a melatonin supplement. Dr. Naiman believes that this is better than sleeping pills since melatonin is "the body's own natural chemical messenger of night." "Melatonin does not directly cause sleep, but triggers a cascade of events that result in natural sleep and dreams," he said, adding that it is nonaddictive, inexpensive and generally safe. Not all doctors agree however, so it is important to check with your doctor first.

If you're interested in learning more about Dr. Naiman's Deep Green Sleep program, you can visit his website (*www.drnaiman.com*) and take a free quiz that helps identify your particular sleep challenges. But, since it is computer-based, make sure you do it several hours before bedtime!

Good Oral Health Lowers Risk for Diabetes and More

Robert J. Genco, DDS, PhD, distinguished professor in the department of oral biology, School of Dental Medicine, and in the department of microbiology, School of Medicine and Biomedical Sciences at the State University of New York at Buffalo.

Until recently, most people who took good care of their teeth and gums did so to ensure appealing smiles and to perhaps avoid dentures. Now, a significant body of research shows that oral health may play a key role in preventing a wide range of serious health conditions, including heart disease, diabetes, some types of cancer and perhaps even dementia.

Healthy teeth and gums also may improve longevity. Swedish scientists recently tracked 3,273 adults for 16 years and found that those with chronic gum infections were significantly more likely to die before age 50, on average, than were people without gum disease.

What's the connection? Periodontal disease (called gingivitis in mild stages…and periodontitis when it becomes more severe) is caused mainly by bacteria that accumulate on the teeth and gums. As the body attempts to battle the bacteria, inflammatory molecules are released (as demonstrated by redness and swelling of the gums). Over time, this complex biological response affects the entire body, causing systemic inflammation that promotes the development of many serious diseases. Scientific evidence links poor oral health to...

•**Diabetes.** State University of New York at Buffalo studies and other research show that people with diabetes have an associated risk for periodontitis that is two to three times greater than that of people without diabetes. Conversely, diabetics with periodontal disease generally have poorer control of their blood sugar than diabetics without periodontal disease—a factor that contributes to their having twice the risk of dying of a heart attack and three times the risk of dying of kidney failure.

•**Heart disease.** At least 20 scientific studies have shown links between chronic periodontal disease and an increased risk for heart disease. Most recently, Boston University researchers found that periodontal disease in men younger than age 60 was associated with a twofold increase in angina (chest pain), or nonfatal or fatal heart attack, when compared with men whose teeth and gums are healthy.

•**Cancer.** Chronic gum disease may raise your risk for tongue cancer. State University of New York at Buffalo researchers recently compared men with and without tongue cancer and found that those with cancer had a 65% greater loss of alveolar bone (which supports the teeth)—a common measure of periodontitis. Meanwhile, a Harvard School of Public Health study shows that periodontal disease is associated with a 63% higher risk for pancreatic cancer.

•**Rheumatoid arthritis.** In people with rheumatoid arthritis, the condition is linked to an 82% increased risk for periodontal disease, compared with people who do not have rheumatoid arthritis.

Good news: Treating the periodontitis appears to ease rheumatoid arthritis symptoms. In a recent study, nearly 59% of patients with rheumatoid arthritis and chronic periodontal disease who had their gums treated experienced less severe arthritis symptoms—possibly because eliminating the periodontitis reduced their systemic inflammation.

•**Dementia.** When Swedish researchers recently reviewed dental and cognitive records for 638 women, they found that tooth loss (a sign of severe gum disease) was linked to a 30% to 40% increased risk for dementia over a 32-year period, with the highest dementia rates suffered by women who had the fewest teeth at middle age. More research is needed to confirm and explain this link.

STEPS TO IMPROVE YOUR ORAL HEALTH

Even though the rate of gum disease significantly increases with age, it's not inevitable. To promote oral health, brush (twice daily with a soft-bristled brush, using gentle, short strokes starting at a 45-degree angle to the gums) and floss (once daily, using gentle rubbing motions—do not snap against the gums). *In addition...*

•**See your dentist at least twice yearly.** Ask at every exam, "Do I have gum disease?" This will serve as a gentle reminder to dentists that you want to be carefully screened for the condition. Most mild-to-moderate infections can be treated with a nonsurgical procedure that removes plaque and tartar from tooth pockets and smooths the root surfaces. For more severe periodontal disease, your dentist may refer you to a periodontist (a dentist who specializes in the treatment of gum disease).

Note: Patients with gum disease often need to see a dentist three to four times a year to prevent recurrence of gum disease after the initial treatment.

Good news: Modern techniques to regenerate bone and soft tissue can reverse much of the damage and halt progression of periodontitis, particularly in patients who have lost no more than 30% of the bone to which the teeth are attached.

•**Boost your calcium intake.** Research conducted at the State University of New York at Buffalo has shown that postmenopausal women with osteoporosis typically have more alveolar bone loss and weaker attachments between their teeth and bone, putting them at substantially higher risk for periodontal disease. Other studies have linked low dietary calcium with heightened periodontal risk in both men and women.

Self-defense: Postmenopausal women, and men over age 65, should consume 1,000 mg to 1,200 mg of calcium daily to preserve teeth and bones. Aim for two to three daily servings of dairy products (providing a total of 600 mg of calcium), plus a 600-mg calcium supplement with added vitamin D for maximum absorption.

Helpful: Yogurt may offer an edge over other calcium sources. In a recent Japanese study involving 942 adults, ages 40 to 79, those who ate at least 55 grams (about two ounces) of yogurt daily were 40% less likely to suffer from severe periodontal disease—perhaps because the "friendly" bacteria and calcium in yogurt make a powerful combination against the infection-causing bacteria of dental disease.

• **Control your weight.** Obesity is also associated with periodontitis, probably because fat cells release chemicals that may contribute to inflammatory conditions anywhere in the body, including the gums.

• **Don't ignore dry mouth.** Aging and many medications, including some antidepressants, antihistamines, high blood pressure drugs and steroids, can decrease saliva flow, allowing plaque to build up on teeth and gums. If you're taking a drug that leaves your mouth dry, talk to your doctor about possible alternatives. Prescription artificial saliva products— for example, Caphosol or Numoisyn—also can provide some temporary moistening, as can chewing sugarless gum.

• **Relax.** Recent studies reveal a strong link between periodontal disease and stress, depression, anxiety and loneliness. Researchers are focusing on the stress hormone cortisol as a possible culprit—high levels of cortisol may exacerbate the gum and jawbone destruction caused by oral infections.

• **Sleep.** Japanese researchers recently studied 219 factory workers for four years and found that those who slept seven to eight hours nightly suffered significantly less periodontal disease progression than those who slept six hours or less. The scientists speculated that lack of sleep lowers the body's ability to fend off infections. However, more research

356

is needed to confirm the results of this small study.

Don't Make These Common Mistakes When Brushing and Flossing

Tom McGuire, DDS, a holistic dentist consultant in Sebastopol, California. He is author of several books, including *Healthy Teeth–Healthy Body: How to Improve Your Oral and Overall Health*. DentalWellness4U.com

If you're like most Americans, you brush your teeth every day—and may even use floss. But as surprising as it may seem, most people don't do either of these daily rituals correctly—and fail to take other small, but highly effective, steps to protect their oral health.

Doing everything you can to care for your teeth and gums is important because, as you probably know, poor oral health has been linked to heart disease and other chronic diseases, such as diabetes and respiratory infections.

Common mistakes to avoid…

Mistake 1: Assuming that electric toothbrushes are better than manual ones. It's true that electric and ultrasonic toothbrushes produce more strokes per minute than manual toothbrushes. However, the shape and size of the handle of the typical electric or ultrasonic toothbrush can make it more difficult to access all the teeth, particularly the backs of the last teeth.

My advice: Use both types of toothbrushes. Each time you brush, begin with an electric brush to maximize the strokes per minute… and finish up with a manual one for 30 seconds or so to access teeth you may not have fully reached. Be sure to use a soft-bristle manual brush.

Mistake 2: Not brushing long enough. Most dentists recommend brushing for two minutes in the morning and again in the evening. However, if you have tiny spaces between your teeth or an advanced gum condition, such as periodontitis, you may need to brush for four or even six minutes to adequately clean your teeth.

And don't forget to brush your gums. Regular, gentle brushing can help toughen the gums and keeps the gum tissue more tightly attached to the tooth.

My advice: Brush a minute or so longer than usual (most people don't brush long enough). Then ask your dental hygienist during your next visit if you need to adjust the amount of time you brush.

Mistake 3: Not flossing correctly. Most dentists recommend flossing once daily. But people who have areas in their mouths in which food routinely gets trapped should floss after each meal, as well as after they brush. Flossing after brushing allows you to remove food particles that may have been pushed into any spaces between your teeth with your toothbrush.

My advice: For convenience, keep containers of floss everywhere—in your coat pocket, glove compartment, bag, desk and near your seat when you watch TV. Also important: Opt for white floss (waxed or unwaxed is fine). Colored floss makes it hard to see bleeding from the gums, a sign of gum disease.

Mistake 4: Not considering a dental irrigator. Dental irrigators, such as those by Waterpik, Oral-B and Philips, rinse away leftover food particles that brushing and flossing leave behind. Not everyone needs a dental irrigator, but those who have pockets (spaces between the gum and the teeth) of more than 4 mm (as measured by your hygienist) should use one.

My advice: Make irrigating the third step of your daily oral-care routine. As with brushing and flossing, it's important to be gentle. Start with a low setting on the machine, and gradually work up to harder pulsations over a period of days. Ask your hygienist how long you should irrigate each day.

Mistake 5: Thinking mouthwash can replace flossing. Mouthwash is easier to use than floss but does not heal gum disease—it should be used only as a supplement to brushing, flossing and irrigating.

Mouthwash is generally thought of as a breath freshener and bacteria fighter, but some brands that contain added minerals claim to also build enamel. Enamel is composed of minerals, but the mouthwash's "re-mineralization" occurs only at the surface level.

My advice: If you don't have gum disease, mouthwash is optional. If you do, use mouthwash (either with alcohol or alcohol-free) with an irrigator after each brushing.

Mistake 6: Forgetting to scrape your tongue. Bacteria become trapped and breed on the tongue's rough surface, which can lead to bad breath and cavities.

My advice: Scrape your tongue whenever you see a grayish or whitish coating. A healthy tongue is pinkish. Many commercial tongue-scraping tools are available, but you can use a dry toothbrush or even the edge of a spoon.

Important: Each person's specific oral care needs are different, but most people can complete these steps in about three to five minutes each time they brush. If you feel you don't have that much time, ask your hygienist for advice on what areas of your mouth need the most attention and which tools he/she recommends you use most often.

Recipe Index

Index

and whey protein, 79
Insulin resistance, 9, 15, 18, 30, 39, 60, 148, 245, 313, 316
Insulin sensitivity, 152, 309
Integrative physicians, 219
Interleukin-6, 15
Intestinal inflammation, 303
Intestinal permeability, 46
Inulin, 74
Iodine, 295
Irritability, 58
Iron, 3, 25, 307, 310
Isoflavones, 88, 101, 276–77
Isothiocyanates, 300

J

Jelly beans, 83
Jerusalem artichokes, 73–74
Jicama, 91
Joint, artificial, 207–8
Joint pain, 144, 165
Journal or diary, 29, 337, 345
Juice, 83, 94
Junk food, 319

K

Kale, 31, 46, 148, 308
Keratin, 213
Kettlebell weights, 333–34
Kidney disease, 14, 62, 100, 168, 228–31
   risk factors, 230
Kidney function test, 171
Kidney testing, 161
Kiwi, 146, 239, 240
Konjac flour, 150, 152
Kudzu, 101–2

L

Lactase, 88
Lactate, 183
Lactic acidosis, 180
Lactose, 309
Lamb, 240
L-arginine, 78
Latent autoimmune diabetes in adults (LADA), 60
Laughter, 269
L-carnitine, 209, 210, 219, 263
LDL-P (LDL particle number), 66–67
Leaky gut syndrome, 45–46, 314
Lecithin, 218
Legs:
   amputation, 205
   claudication, 260, 262, 263
   compression stockings, 223, 224
   edema (swelling), 144, 223–24
   elevation of, 223
   exercises for, 330–31, 339
   and neuropathy, 263
   peripheral artery disease, 260–63

Legumes, 16, 71–72, 89, 93, 150, 219, 259
Lemon, 315, 316
Lentils, 31, 71, 259, 305
Leptin, 197, 294, 309
Levodopa, 80
Life expectancy, 193
Lifestyle:
   modification, 6–7, 24, 27, 191, 274, 283
   sedentary, 328
Lignans, 41, 300
Lipid peroxide, 203
Lipoprotein-associated phospholipase A-2 (Lp-PLA2), 251–52
Lipoproteins, 3, 153, 266
Liquor, see Alcohol
Liraglutide (Saxenda), 196
Liver (food), 285–86
Liver damage, 214
Liver disease, 14, 61
Loop diuretics, 217
Lovastatin (Mevacor), 26–27, 267
Loving kindness, 257
L-taurine, 220
L-theanine, 287
Lunch:
   coffee for, 41
   food choices, 292–93, 296
Lung cancer, 99
Lunula, 60
Lutein, 167, 239
Lycopene, 218

M

Maca, 154–56
Macadamia nuts, 149
Mackerel, 70, 149, 166
Macular degeneration, 104
Magic pen (for stress relief), 345
Magnesium, 15–17
   depletion of, 16
   and fatigue, 166–67
   and hearing loss, 218
   and potassium, 65
   roles of, 41
   sources of, 16, 78, 93, 275, 298, 310
   supplements, 16, 54, 167, 246, 307, 308
Mango, 146
Mannitol, 96
Marathon running, 330
Massage, 48–49, 223
   foot, 327
Mathematical models, in research, 272
Meals:
   appetizer, 22
   eating too quickly, 21–22

   exercise after, 139
   food choices, 292–93
   four or five a day, 306
   frequent, 234
   "grazing," 294
   meal plans, 108
   never skipping, 160
   not eating before bedtime, 306
   portion size, 22, 46, 54, 81, 160, 291
   restaurant, 48
   small, 8, 160, 234
   three a day, 54, 294, 295, 296
   timing, 306
   2-1-1 formula for, 5
   two large meals, 179–80
   see also Eating
Meats:
   buying from butcher, 36
   free-range, 319
   lean, 299
   pasture-raised, 319
   red, 285–86, 296
   searing, 291
Medic Alert, 173
Medical ID jewelry, 172–73
Medications, 2
   Beers Criteria for, 15
   diabetes risk from, 14–15
   and dry mouth, 356
   eliminating, 142–43
   magnesium-draining, 16
   and memory, 63–64
   and nutrient deficiency, 308
   optimal dose of, 17
   over-the-counter, 161
   overtreatment with, 175–77
   side effects of, 80, 168, 176
   and sleep, 352
   staying up to date on, 161, 168
   supercharging, 151–52
   timing of doses, 164, 179
   and weight gain, 168
Meditation, 210, 257, 284, 295, 296
   walking, 340–41
Mediterranean diet, 138, 287, 305, 319
Melatonin, 351, 353
Melons, 278, 313
Memory, 28, 63–64, 155
Menopause symptoms, 144, 156
Mercury, 218
Metabolic acidosis, 23
Metabolic health, 84
Metabolic swings, 189
Metabolic syndrome, 78, 101–3, 303, 317
   and obesity, 152, 179, 219, 297, 306
   risk factors, 219, 255, 314

Don't miss these other titles from Bottom Line books and newsletters

MEGA CURES

1,137 SECRETS FOR LIVING WELL WITH DIABETES

SAY NO TO NURSING HOMES

BOTTOM LINE NEWSLETTERS

SPEED HEALING

SHOP NOW FOR THE LATEST BREAKTHROUGHS

BOTTOMLINESTORE.COM